WAR IN WORLD HISTORY

VOLUME **1** TO 1500

WAR IN WORLD HISTORY

Society, Technology, and War
from Ancient Times to the Present

Stephen Morillo
Wabash College

Jeremy Black
University of Exeter

Paul Lococo
Leeward Community College, Hawaii

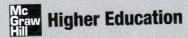
Higher Education

Boston   Burr Ridge, IL   Dubuque, IA   New York   San Francisco   St. Louis
Bangkok   Bogotá   Caracas   Kuala Lumpur   Lisbon   London   Madrid   Mexico City
Milan   Montreal   New Delhi   Santiago   Seoul   Singapore   Sydney   Taipei   Toronto

Higher Education

Published by McGraw-Hill, an imprint of The McGraw-Hill Companies, Inc., 1221 Avenue of the Americas, New York, NY 10020. Copyright © 2009. All rights reserved. No part of this publication may be reproduced or distributed in any form or by any means, or stored in a database or retrieval system, without the prior written consent of The McGraw-Hill Companies, Inc., including, but not limited to, in any network or other electronic storage or transmission, or broadcast for distance learning.

This book is printed on acid-free paper.

1 2 3 4 5 6 7 8 9 0 QPD/QPD 0 9 8

ISBN: 978-0-07-052584-9
MHID: 0-07-052584-6

Editor in Chief: *Michael Ryan*
Publisher: *Frank Mortimer*
Sponsoring Editor: *Jon-David Hague*
Editorial Coordinator: *Sora Kim*
Marketing Manager: *Pamela Cooper*
Production Editor: *Holly Paulsen*
Manuscript Editor: *Thomas L. Briggs*
Design Manager: *Margarite Reynolds*
Text Designer: *Linda Robertson*
Cover Designer: *Margarite Reynolds, Asylum Studios, and Stephen Morillo*
Art Editors: *Sonia Brown and Robin Mouat*
Illustrators: *Mapping Specialists, Dartmouth Publishing, and Stephen Morillo*
Photo Research Coordinator: *Alexandra Ambrose*
Photo Research: *Emily Tietz, Editorial Image, LLC*
Production Supervisor: *Louis Swaim*
Composition: *10/12 Galliard by ICC Macmillan Inc.*
Printing: *45# New Era Matte Recycled, Quebecor World*

Cover: Heads of Two Warriors. Painting on a Chalcidian vase, 6th-century BCE. H. 39 cm. Inv. V.I.3153. Photo: Juergen Liepe. Antikensammlung, Staatliche Museen zu Berlin, Berlin, Germany. © Bildarchiv Preussischer Kulturbesitz/Art Resource, NY.

Credits: The credits section for this book begins on page C-1 and is considered an extension of the copyright page.

Library of Congress Cataloging-in-Publication Data
Morillo, Stephen.
   War in world history : society, technology, and war from ancient times to the present. Volume 1, to 1500 / Stephen Morillo, Jeremy Black, Paul Lococo.
      p.   cm.
   Includes index.
   ISBN-13: 978-0-07-052584-9 (v. 1 : alk. paper)
   ISBN-10: 0-07-052584-6 (v. 1 : alk. paper)
   ISBN-13: 978-0-07-052585-6 (v. 2 : alk. paper)
   ISBN-10: 0-07-052585-4 (v. 2 : alk. paper)   1. Military art and science—History.
2. Military history.   3. War.   I. Black, Jeremy.   II. Lococo, Paul.   III. Title.
   U27.M63 2008
   355.02—dc22
                                                                        2008027488

From SRM to Lynne, who has never known me without this project!

Contents

Preface

This book is a history of the world as viewed through the lens of war. It is designed for use at the college level as a textbook for military history courses or as a textbook or supplemental reading for world history courses. As a general introduction to and synthesis of this topic, we believe it will also interest general readers, especially those interested in military history. But while military history is undoubtedly a popular topic, popularity alone cannot justify a new textbook in intellectual terms. What can a world history textbook focused on warfare offer to students and teachers, in college or outside the curriculum?

WHY WAR?

Warfare has been one of humankind's most prevalent activities throughout history. Military preparations and organization have been central to the internal structures of many human communities. War itself is one of the major ways in which those human communities have interacted with each other, and it has often been intimately connected to other significant forms of contact and influence, whether as a vector for spreading disease, an accompaniment to or form of trade and economic exchange, or a partner of religious expansion.

Because making war has been such a central activity of so many human communities, it makes a good lens through which to view the rest of history, providing a thematic connection among many facets of human experience, as well as being a topic important in its own right. The stresses of war sometimes cast a particularly revealing light on social structures, exposing the strengths and weaknesses of institutions and testing the cultural cohesion of communities in ways that few other activities do.

Despite this, warfare has been largely unexplored up to now as a theme in world history. True world history textbooks are far more common now than they were even ten years ago. Many of the most recent, in attempting to organize the mountain of material world historians face, have begun structuring their narratives around themes such as technology or cultural contact. Some have even taken an almost entirely thematic approach, exploring various cross-cultural topics, such as the family, religion and the state, or frontiers, from a global perspective. War almost never shows up in these lists of themes except perhaps as an aspect of the conflicts of the twentieth century.

This neglect of military history is doubly odd given that the last twenty-five years has seen an explosion of specialist studies in the field, works that have fundamentally redefined military history as an arena of academic investigation. The nineteenth- and early-twentieth-century traditions of military historiography, dominated by ex-military men writing about decisive battles and the "Art of War" for other ex-military men and amateur war buffs, nearly killed the field for serious historians. But since the mid-1970s, the "new military history" has revitalized military studies. European medieval historians, examining a society organized for war, played a leading role in creating the new military history; more recently, fierce and productive controversies over the early modern period's Military Revolution and the modern age's "revolution in military affairs" have extended the new approaches to histories of war to many times and places.

Central to the new military history has been the process of placing warfare in context or, more accurately, in its many contexts—socioeconomic, institutional, and cultural. One of the aims of this book, therefore, is to synthesize and integrate the new military history from a global perspective. As a military history text, then, we attempt always to examine war and warriors as parts of functioning societies. The mutual relationships between war and its contexts—both the effects of war on society and the effects of society on war (including the development of new technologies as part of both)—are fundamental to understanding why wars have been fought in the many ways history has witnessed. Unlike many histories of warfare, we integrate naval warfare and maritime activity (as well as air war in the twentieth century) into this big picture of the development of armed force through the millennia. In general, the aims and methods of the new military history have shaped the focus of our text.

Focus

Thus, what we write about is war and its contexts. Students of military operations will find some campaign history here. The vast scope of chronology and geography entailed by a global history necessarily limits the amount of detailed narrative possible. The emphasis is on analysis rather than storytelling. Nevertheless, each chapter highlights battles and campaigns that demonstrate classic and sometimes unchanging aspects of the "Art of War," as well as illustrating changes in tactics and practices in response to new challenges, weapons, and environments.

But the larger emphasis, as noted above, is on contexts. Three broad areas stand out in this respect.

First, **political and institutional contexts:** The institutional organization of warfare in all societies has always had important connections to the powers of elites and states and to methods of rulership and government. The structures of power place important constraints on military organization and activity—for example, in influencing who can be recruited and how. The exercise of force has also been a consistent and often paramount factor in the distribution of political power within polities; politics and political institutions in turn affect the use of warfare as a tool of state policy. War not only is affected by but also affects its institutional context.

Second, **social and economic contexts:** This area includes the effects of class structure (closely related to political contexts) and the issue of economic support for military activity. Economic productivity and the technologies of transportation shape logistics in decisive ways, and logistics—the art of keeping military forces in being—has been perhaps the dominant constraint on methods and patterns of waging war throughout history. The economic sphere also includes

technology generally. Changing weaponry springs to mind naturally when technology is mentioned in relation to warfare, but technologies that were either nonmilitary, such as the printing press, or only military tangentially or partially, such as the steam engine, have consistently played a major role in shaping how war has been waged. Finally, armed conflict has always had significant effects on societies and economies ("the effect of war on society" was an early rallying cry of the new military history), most often wreaking havoc and destruction, but in a significant minority of cases stimulating economic growth and inventiveness.

Third, **cultural contexts:** From the point of view of world history, war is not just an activity, it is a nexus of cultural production. Given the elite status of many warrior classes in world history, warrior values have shaped many cultures. War and religion have frequently been in alliance (holy or unholy depending on one's perspective). Many cultures have placed various ritual constraints on the practice of war, while reactions to warfare ranging from glorification to condemnation are probably rivaled only by love as a dominant theme in world literature, with war far outdistancing romance in popularity in many cultures.

War literature as a source for military history brings us to another aspect of the focus of this volume. The sources available from the world's many societies and the amount of secondary historical investigation published for different areas vary tremendously. A work of synthesis such as this one is dependent on the specialist work of many previous scholars and is inevitably shaped by these questions of availability. In our case, the result is an emphasis on the major Eurasian civilizations and, up to 1700, the central Asian nomads with whom those civilizations coexisted. Within that ecumene, the literature tends to place somewhat more emphasis on western Europe than some other areas of historical inquiry. This focus is almost inevitable for the last two centuries of European military dominance (with a few important exceptions). Before that time, the merits of such emphasis are more debatable but were for us less a matter of debate than of necessity. While we have tried always to keep our perspective global, we must await further research for a more even balance of details from across Eurasia.

We have undoubtedly shorted the military histories of sub-Saharan Africa, the pre-Columbian Americas, Australia, and Oceania. Partly, this is again a matter of the available secondary literature. But it is a matter partly of defining war and looking only at what rises over our own arbitrarily chosen "military horizon," one of two preliminary questions we must examine before proceeding.

Two Preliminary Questions

These two questions, to which there are no clear answers, are these: What counts as *war,* and what are the origins of war in human history?

With regard to the first question, there is clearly a vast range of human violence. But the boundaries separating one sort of violence from another—in particular, organized warfare from more individual and perhaps random acts of violence—are fuzzy in the extreme. Limiting a definition of warfare to "organized state activity" not only eliminates many violent tribal conflicts that probably should count as some form of warfare but also is too restrictive even if we don't consider tribes. Much of the armed conflict in early medieval Europe and most of the aggressive activity of nomadic peoples from the Asian steppes have been unproblematically treated as warfare despite the fact that "states" among some of those peoples existed only tenuously at best and had no monopoly on war making even where they did exist. Mere numbers cannot serve to distinguish true warfare from something less, for the violent application of armed force by states has often been carried out by remarkably small forces. Attempts to distinguish "real" warfare from more ritualized forms of violence in terms of seriousness of intent or casualty rates fail both for vagueness and because almost all forms of warfare have had a significant ritualistic element, which simply removes the question one step without resolving it. In short, there are no clear criteria for the ranking of human violent activity on a continuum from murder to melee to missile strike.

The very attempt to make such divisions, however, points up the near universality of warfare, at least under broader definitions, as a feature of human culture. This brings us to the question of the origins of war.

There is a vast and complex literature on this subject, and one that is changing rapidly. The investigations span the fields of evolutionary biology and evolutionary psychology, neuroscience and brain studies, anthropology, sociology, and history. As yet, however, no clear consensus has emerged. This is in part because any explanation for the origins of war depends on how war is defined: Organized warfare as a cultural invention of complex, hierarchical cultures clearly differs in origin, at least to some extent, from the sorts of conflicts hunter-gatherer tribes may have engaged in. The lack of consensus also derives from the politically charged nature of the topic. Explanations for the origins of war are taken, rightly or wrongly, to have implications for the issue of the inevitability of war versus possibilities for modern peace movements.

The topic is also politically charged, at least potentially, in terms of gender, because war has been and continues to be largely a male activity, even when recent gender integration of armed forces is taken into account. In the past, of course, females have had close connections to warfare as victims of rape, abduction, and killing; as producers in the economies that supported war; as camp followers, wives, and a key part of "home fronts"; as cementers of alliances through marriage; and as pretexts for going to war, even if there were never a Helen who saw a Troy. But females have participated in war only occasionally as leaders and even more rarely as fighters, a fact that complicates both the explanations for and the politics of explaining the origins of war.

In this text, we will answer the first question, of what counts as war, only by implication, and our answer is probably arbitrary at that. We will attempt to answer the second question, about the origins of war, briefly in Chapter 1. This introduction will lead us quickly to the established presence of war in the earliest civilizations of southwest Asia—ancient city walls speak eloquently to the necessities of communal defense even at that early stage of settled cultures— and simply trace its evolution since then. Does the near universal presence of war in history mean that war is an inevitable part of the human condition? Perhaps, but until very recently, slavery was a near universal feature of human societies. It is now much less common. Conditions change, and the organized responses of communities evolve accordingly. Our job as historians is to help understand the past. Predicting the future is far trickier.

Organization: Chronological Sections

In tracing the evolution of warfare through the ages and around the globe, we have divided this study into six chronological parts of five chapters each. In the first five parts, four of the chapters cover warfare on land, divided along geographic and cultural lines. The fifth chapter examines naval warfare and maritime activity from a global and comparative perspective. By the sixth part, land, sea, and, increasingly, air warfare are woven together in chapters that are all global. The parts are as follows.

Part 1: The Ancient World, 2000 BCE–400 CE. This section moves from the rise of the earliest armies, built first around infantry and then the war chariot, perhaps the world's first complex weapons system, to the armies of the classical worlds of Greece, Persia, Rome, India, and China. The section examines the creation of the cultures of war among early civilizations, the rise and perfection of massed infantry armies, and the invention of galley warfare in the Mediterranean.

Part 2: The Age of Migration and Invasion, 400–1100. This section begins with an examination of nomadic life and warfare on the central Asian steppes, and the threat that nomadic peoples posed through several millennia to settled societies. From the Chinese frontiers to the Western Roman Empire, this was an age shaped by the forces of migration and nomadic invasion, including at sea, where nomadic peoples carried out one of the two major types of maritime activity.

Part 3: The Age of Traditions in Conflict, 1100–1500. Major nomadic conquests, culminating in the Mongol Empire, continued in this period as well, joined by religious crusades and merchant activity as forces of increasing cultural interchange. Growing merchant activity and improved technology began to transform the potentials of naval power, while interaction both spread ideas and techniques of warfare farther afield and threw the particular characteristics of separate military traditions into sharper relief.

Part 4: The Dawn of Global Warfare, 1500–1750. Gunpowder weaponry dominated this period. In Europe, an ongoing transformation reached revolutionary proportions, while cannon and musketry were implicated in military transformations in much of Asia and in the taming of the nomadic threat to settled societies. Above all, guns and ships launched the new age of global integration, beginning with the conquest of the Americas, and created a new age of naval power that was no longer simply an adjunct to land warfare.

Part 5: The Age of Revolutions and Imperialism, 1750–1914. Eighteenth-century linear tactics and the first attempts at raising mass armies in revolutionary and Napoleonic France initiated a period of rapid social, technological, and economic change, with direct and revolutionary implications for the practices of warfare. Industrialization, mass armies, and the beginnings of a firepower transformation launched

European nations on the path to global dominance. At sea, the perfection of the age of sail gave way to ironclads and naval arms races.

Part 6: The Age of Global Conflict, 1914–Present. Rapid technological change continued to transform warfare as first firepower and then transportation and maneuver saw revolutionary advances. The results were played out on the battlefields of two world wars, as military doctrine struggled to keep up with the pace of change both before and after 1945. War in the air joined war on land and sea, and by the late twentieth century, the use of combined-armed forces in terrains and theaters around the world, often against unconventional opponents in unconventional wars, posed new problems for the planning and execution of military operations.

ORGANIZATION: VOLUME DIVISIONS

The standard edition of this text is available in a two-volume format split at roughly 1500: Volume 1 includes Parts 1–3 and Volume 2 includes Parts 4–6. This format follows the usual division of western and world civilization courses, for which this book can be used as a supplementary (or even main) text, and allows a standard semester split of military history survey courses.

But teachers using this text should note that a number of other options are readily and easily available through McGraw-Hill's Primus system for custom-published texts. Simply go to Primus on the McGraw-Hill Higher Education website at www.mhhe.com/primis, choose Social Sciences/Humanities and then History, and choose *War in World History* from the available texts. Then create your own splits. You can order single parts by themselves. Those on a quarter system can create three volumes: up to 1100 (Parts 1 and 2), from 1100 to 1750 (Parts 3 and 4), and since 1750 (Parts 5 and 6).

There is no limit to what Primus will let you do. Interested in teaching a naval history survey? Put together Chapters 5, 10, 15, 20, and 25, and you've got naval history from the dawn of boats to the beginning of the twentieth century. Focused on European land warfare? Chapters 7, 12, 16, 21, 22, and 23 cover the topic from 400 to 1900; add Chapters 3 and 4 for Greece and Rome and Part 6 for war since 1900. *War in World History* gives you comprehensive coverage. Primus gives you customizable flexibility. The combination lets you build the course you want to teach.

FEATURES

Within the chronological sections, *War in World History* offers a number of features designed to enhance the usefulness of the text. Each chapter includes, in addition to the main text, material set off in boxes that deals in more detail with some aspect of military history. We have included three types of boxed material, each aimed at illuminating a different aspect of the topic.

Sources boxes provide selections from primary source material, giving students a window into the past, a look at the writings professional historians use to draw their conclusions, and the opportunity to draw their own.

Highlights boxes focus on particular battles, sieges, or campaigns, providing the opportunity to examine operational details and aspects of specific strategies and tactics not possible in the course of the main text.

Issues boxes raise and explore historiographical controversies—how historians are currently arguing about important issues in military history—and examine historical topics of general or long-term relevance in a comparative perspective and in the framework of the content of the chapter.

In addition to the boxed material, each chapter concludes with a short list of **Suggested Readings** on the chapter's topics. **Maps and illustrations** act as visual guides to the geography of politics, campaigns, and battles, and show the appearance of warriors and warfare, including arms, weapons, and fortifications, in ways that words cannot convey. Finally, each five-chapter part concludes with a **Commentary** section that sums up the key themes of the five chapters and examines global and comparative developments outside the geographic framework of the chapters. We hope that these features help make this text a useful and engaging introduction to the world of military history.

ACKNOWLEDGEMENTS

The authors would like to acknowledge the helpful comments of many readers of the manuscript at various stages; their feedback, both formal and informal, helped improve the book significantly. They include:

Richard Abels, *US Naval Academy*

William Thomas Allison, *Weber State University*

David Bachrach, *University of New Hampshire*

Jonathan M. Beagle, Western *New England College*

Porter Blakemore, *Mary Washington College*

Theodore F Cook, *William Paterson University*

Phyllis Culham, *US Naval Academy*

Hugh Dubrulle, *Saint Anselm College*

William Hamblin, *Brigham Young University*

Steven Isaac, *Longwood University*

Wayne Lee, *The University of North Carolina at Chapel Hill*

Michael V. Leggiere, *LSU-Shreveport*

Timothy G. Lynch, *California Maritime Academy, CSU*

John Lynn, *University of Illinois*

Alex Roland, *Duke University*

Jonathan Roth, *San Jose State University*

Frederick Schneid, *High Point University*

Spencer Tucker, *VMI*

Everett L. Wheeler, *Duke University*

Our editor at McGraw-Hill, Jon-David Hague, helped immeasurably in moving the project forward. Special thanks go to Michael Pavkovic, United States Naval War College, who originally conceived the project but who was unable to be a part of its completion for personal reasons.

PART 1

THE ANCIENT WORLD, 2000 BCE–400 CE

CHAPTER 1

Bronze and Chariots: Eurasia, 10,000–600 BCE

War has seemingly always been a part of human history. In many cultures, the invention of writing, and the keeping of those written records that are the basis of most historical research today, is heralded by accounts of the wars of kings and heroic tales of mighty warriors. But the early history of warfare is actually shrouded in mystery. For millennia before the invention of writing, there were humans living as hunter-gatherers around the globe. Did they engage in warfare? Even after warfare became a known part of the human repertoire of activities, the scarcity and haphazard availability of source material means that we can know the course of particular wars or the forms of military organization that lay behind the campaigns in only fragmentary and uncertain ways.

Of course, problems of source material—the incompleteness of the record of evidence, the often biased or problematic nature of the sources we do have, and the different perspectives from which the surviving evidence can be interpreted—are common to all historical investigations. Throughout this book, we highlight some of the instances of these problems in sections set off from the main text.

In this chapter, we move from a brief examination of what can be known about the origins of warfare; to a survey of the major themes of ancient warfare, themes that will recur and form the framework of analysis of the rest of this book; and, finally, to a closer look at the ancient wars and military organizations about which we know enough to say something substantial.

THE ORIGINS OF WAR

A Biological Component

The starting point for assessing the evidence about the origins of war is understanding the positions regarding the biological component of war making.

The two poles of this argument are, on one side, that aggression and war are human instincts, with the implication that war is and always has been an inevitable part of human existence, and, on the other, that war is a purely cultural construction with no biological component, implying that war can be eliminated from human affairs. It is the politics of the implications on both sides that matter and that cause this argument to be so heated at times. On purely biological grounds, the issue is unanswerable, based as it is on a false dichotomy between nature and culture. Humans are such complex biological mechanisms, genetically programmed to form complex, linguistically based cultures, that separating the influence of biology from culture in the makeup of different societies is as impossible as separating the influence of nature from nurture in the makeup of individuals. It is, inevitably, both, which gets us no closer to an answer as to the potential biological origins of war. Nor does looking at our closest relatives, the great apes, help, for the social biology of primate groups varies widely and includes cultural components. Just among chimpanzees, our closest relatives among the apes, levels of interpersonal and intergroup conflict vary widely, though tending to the nonviolent, and so offer no clear lessons about human nature. We must turn to the evidence from early human history.

Such evidence is, of course, quite sparse, and written evidence does not show us a time when war did not exist. Therefore, many historians and anthropologists have turned to studies of those hunter-gatherer groups that survived into the twentieth century to try to gain insight into our primitive past, on the assumption that such peoples live as our ancestors did millennia ago. One much cited case involves the Yanamamo of the Amazon basin, who exhibit high levels of interpersonal (especially intergender) and intertribal violence. This has often been cited as evidence in support of the proposition that the inclination to warfare is part of human nature. But the assumption that such peoples live as our early ancestors did is questionable. Anthropologists have reinterpreted the original field studies of the Yanamamo, taking into account the broader colonial history of South America. They point out that, far from being isolated, the Yanamamo have been in direct and indirect contact with neighboring (and often more complex) societies for centuries—societies that themselves practiced organized warfare, exported weapons, and in general tainted the supposedly pristine evidence provided by the Yanamamo or, indeed, by any other hunter-gatherer society that managed to survive into the twentieth century. Furthermore, every example of a violent group is matched in the anthropological literature by a counterexample of a group living peacefully. The anthropological record, at least as it pertains to studies of living peoples, is therefore problematic for answering questions about the origins of war.

That brings us to the archaeological record of early human existence. The archaeological record is also problematic because it is far from complete. It does, however, provide the tentative outlines of an answer, although there is intense debate among specialists about this issue. Archaeologists and paleo-anthropologists have studied skeletal remains of *Homo erectus,* the widespread ancestor of modern humans, as well as tools from the limited tool kit *Homo erectus* used (basically, stone hand axes) associated with the skeletal remains; these come from sites across Eurasia, dating to between 2 million and 100,000 years ago. Added to this evidence are the prehistoric skeletons they have found of *Homo sapiens,* the modern human species, dating to between 150,000 and 10,000 years ago and scattered across a far wider range than *Homo erectus* achieved, along with modern humans' much more varied toolkit. Of these several thousand skeletons of both species, few bear any unambiguous signs of human-inflicted violence, and those that do are isolated cases. None of the exceptions are *Homo erectus;* it seems that, at the least, organized violence is the product of the modern human species among hominids, dating to no earlier than about 150,000 years ago. But even among the modern human remains, evidence of organized, weapons-assisted aggression between groups (as opposed to individual murder) is nonexistent prior to perhaps 10,000 years ago.

Therefore, if we define war as organized human violence against other humans, as opposed to the odd murder, there is almost no evidence for it prior to about 8000 BCE. Aside from one isolated case in Egypt, a mass burial of several hundred skeletons showing clear signs of the impact of human weaponry at a site in northern Iraq from around that date is the earliest of a type that becomes increasingly common from that point on. At roughly the same time, fortifications began to appear in the same part of the world—as, for instance, at Jericho in northern Palestine (though the earliest forms of these walls were probably for flood control rather than defense against human enemies). Evidence of this sort spreads rapidly from this point of origin through Europe and the Near East and also appears independently later in places such as northern China and Central America.

This suggests that warfare was an invention, a cultural phenomenon that, though it inevitably contains some biological component simply because humans are biological creatures, was not a product of biological determinism. (Whether the dynamics of the interaction of human societies since then makes war inevitable *as a social and cultural phenomenon* is a separate question.) What we must then ask about are the conditions that characterized the places where and times when warfare sprang into existence after millennia of peace.

Inventing Warfare: Causes

The places and times involved suggest that the conditions are associated with (though not dependent on) the emergence of agriculture. Put another way, the same conditions that gave rise in various places to agriculture also contributed to the invention of warfare. Rising population is the crucial variable. In especially fertile areas and rich hunting grounds, greater numbers of people began to put pressure on even those food resources. At the same time, because resources were at least initially plentiful, populations in such areas, even before agriculture, became less nomadic. They would thus have increasingly staked claims to territorially defined settlements. This trend was simply reinforced by agriculture where and when it arose. Fixed settlements could accumulate resources that provided both a tempting target for plunder and a possession worth defending.

Rising population not only put pressure on resources but also changed social structures. More people in an area, both in absolute numbers and in terms of the density of settlements, led inevitably to the rise of defined social hierarchies and mechanisms of community governance. Such mechanisms, perhaps in the form of tribal leadership functions increasingly held in one family line until a hereditary chiefdom emerged, as well as in the solidifying of a socially elite and powerful group of families around the ruling family, probably first arose to deal with questions of intracommunity dispute resolution and economic redistribution. After all, the larger a group is, the harder it is to settle quarrels informally through the mediation of family members or friends, because increasing numbers of people won't be closely connected this way. It is also harder for people to simply trade and share their resources directly within the group for the same reason. Thus, a chief or equivalent emerged to handle what in modern terms we would recognize as a version of policing and justice on one hand, and taxation and spending "for the communal good" on the other. But a recognized chief and his supporters (those who might help enforce the decisions of the chief within the community) not only met these internal needs but potentially provided the means for a more organized, centralized, and effective communal response to outside threats. The rise of such social and political hierarchies and structures did not *necessitate* the invention and use of war, but they *facilitated* such a move—that is, made it more possible, even if not making it inevitable. They were the preconditions for war.

The rise of political hierarchies, even in limited form, was accompanied by increasing trade in prestige goods, whose display showcased and legitimized the power and status of elites. Both the trade itself and the limited sources of supply that characterized prestige items (which are by their nature rare) formed another potential nexus for conflict to arise. That political decision makers and their status were implicated in this nexus of conflict made for an even more powerful inducement to war.

Many societies, in different places and times, independently reached this stage of economic and sociopolitical development. The final factor that seems to have pushed some of them over the edge into the use of organized violence against neighboring groups was environmental. First in northern Iraq, and then in several later cases where war making arose apparently independently, there seems to have been a severe environmental crisis—widespread drought brought on by a slowly warming and drying climate, for example. Sudden and widespread shortages would have placed an especially great strain on established resource levels, triggering the move to military action. Thus, formerly peaceful neighboring peoples resorted to organized violence against each other to protect their place in the world. It should be noted that both warfare and agriculture, according to this interpretation of the evidence, arose after the end of the last Ice Age. Since that period of global warming was not always conducive to sustaining food supplies, both warfare and agriculture can be seen in part as adaptive responses to significant environmental change.

The Origins of Warfare: Consequences

Furthermore, the consequences of warfare and agriculture often reinforced each other, contributing to the spread of each. Once warfare had been invented in an area, a number of dynamics contributed to the tendency for warfare to spread rapidly beyond its points of origin, and indeed beyond places where the initial conditions held. First and most obviously, it was a successful technique, at least from the perspective of the initially victorious societies. They were, of course, the ones best placed to exploit the new way of life, because success in one war would have generated additional resources for survival, support for further war efforts, and vital experience in how to conduct war. Faced with a society that could threaten war, neighbors had no choice but to respond in kind or submit, and their conversion to a war footing forced their neighbors, in turn, to confront the same choices. In short, once there were war-making powers on the sociopolitical map, any society in contact with them had to adopt the new mode of organization or risk conquest and extermination. The spread of the idea of war by this dynamic could have been very rapid—in fact, the archaeological evidence suggests that it was.

Perhaps even more important, then and thereafter, for the perpetuation of warfare as one of the tools a society could deploy was the interaction of warfare with social class and political leadership. War became widespread, as we noted, even in areas where the initial conditions that gave rise to it did not apply—areas, therefore, presumably, lacking the necessity of war for survival, at least in some cases. The basic dynamic at work was that in the sorts of hierarchical societies that could have resorted to war successfully, the interests of social elites naturally diverged from the interests of the masses. Since elites were more likely to use their social and economic positions of privilege to specialize in the bearing of arms, thereby becoming warrior elites, they also thus stood to garner the most in terms of glory and riches from waging war. In short, warfare was potentially more beneficial to the elites than to the farmers. In fact, in many circumstances, war must have been a burden for farmers, increasing the demands of their own elites for resources and exposing them to destructive raids by the enemy. Elite support for war may have worked against the economic interests of their own farmers, contributed to political tensions within communities, and encouraged elites to tighten their control of their people. At its extreme, this process could have reduced free farmers to peasant or even slave status. Since the meager surplus wealth produced by an agricultural economy encouraged the political domination of farmers by elites, so that the elites could guarantee their (disproportionate) share of the surplus, war simply reinforced the tendency of agricultural economies to create elite-dominated, hierarchical social structures.

Furthermore, as the most intense form of crisis that societies now faced, warfare made strong leadership at the very top all the more crucial. Tribal leaders, chiefs, or kings recognized this and so favored war as policy more than their society as a whole would have. Thus, leaders made war because war reinforced their authority and status, not because it necessarily benefited their societies. In this way, too, warfare reinforced and intensified the pressures for unified leadership that all agricultural societies, operating in conditions of scarcity and limited means of communication, faced. Thus, warfare contributed to the prevalence of monarchy as the predominant form of political organization for much of human history since the end of the last Ice Age.

Between the external threat posed by warrior societies and the internal dynamics of hierarchical political organization, avoiding warfare was no longer an option. War gradually became the global constant in human history—complete with fortifications, arms races, and wide-ranging social and cultural effects—that the rest of this book will explore.

THE ELEMENTS OF MILITARY DEVELOPMENT TO 3500 BCE

The dynamics of the origins of war outlined in the previous section had implications for the further development of warfare and military organization. While the shortage of evidence for specific wars and military systems (such as they may have been) in the period between the invention of warfare and the second millennium BCE prevents detailed surveys of cases, some general trends can be discerned. These trends fit into the major categories of thematic analysis that this book is organized around, so they are worth surveying as the foundations of military practice and history. While most of our scattered evidence comes from Egypt and the Near East, where records of the earliest civilizations are most plentiful, what we know of early China, India, Mesoamerica, and other areas fits the same patterns.

War and Social Organization

The first trend involves the external and internal consequences of the invention of warfare for social organization. Understanding the reciprocal impact of war and social organization on each other requires a quick typology of social complexity. Roughly, sociopolitical organizations can be divided into *simple* societies and *complex* societies. Simple societies lack hierarchical organization—all members of the group have roughly the same status, and differences tend to arise from individual characteristics and to not be heritable. This description clearly applies to hunter-gatherer *bands*, small groups usually consisting of a single extended family group. Although *tribes*, combinations of several bands, do sometimes have recognized leaders, especially when the tribe is large, they too count as simple societies. But, if a tribal leader and the families who support him attain hereditary chief status and develop permanent or semipermanent mechanisms of governance, the society crosses the ill-defined border into complexity and becomes a *chiefdom*. At the highest level of complexity, with permanent bureaucracies, formal offices, and, usually, urban political organization and some form of permanent record keeping (writing, in most cases), is the *state*. (It is important to note that the hierarchy of organization sketched here moves from less to more complex, but this does not imply a move from "worse" to "better" or from "barbaric" to "civilized.")

The evidence for the invention of war traces back far enough that it predates any society that would fit the usual definition of a state-level polity. Whether the earliest war-making groups were large tribes or proto-chiefdoms is impossible to know. What is more certain is that making war stimulated advances in social complexity. Organizing groups of men (and women?) for war was not easy and entailed the deployment of mechanisms that could coerce labor, resources, and even military service out of a community or, even better, that could convince community members to contribute such things more or less voluntarily. Warfare was therefore one significant factor contributing to the development of both organizational and ideological bonds tying human communities more tightly together. Specific technologies that facilitated such structural and cultural advances—above all, writing—are (not surprisingly) closely though not exclusively associated with the spread of warfare. Of course, this process of political consolidation associated with war was by no means inevitable or unproblematic. War could just as easily destroy a community, and not just the losing side. Even a successful war could create political tensions within a society, overextend its resources, or make it too large to govern effectively, any and all of which could trigger the collapse of political unity and social cohesion.

The influence of war on social organization can be seen in the external relations as well as the internal dynamics of ancient polities, especially state-level societies. Ancient states had a tendency to expansionism, since new land and peoples were the main way governments could add to their resource base. The peoples on their margins thus were often forced to respond not just in terms of creating their own war-making capabilities but in terms of adapting to the ideologies of their powerful neighbors. The result was more organized chiefdoms and states politically. Culturally, the process is known as *ethnogenesis,* or the creation among border groups of a separate cultural, ethnic, identity, which, in turn, complicated expansion and the assimilation of such groups for the dominant state. The importance of the connection between war and sociopolitical organization is reflected in the fact that many of the earliest historical figures about whom we know any details are royal military leaders such as Sargon of Akkad (in ancient Babylonia) and Menes of Egypt.

War and Technology

The indirect connection between war and mechanisms of social and cultural control have just been noted. More directly, warfare from very early on has been associated with the development and spread of different forms of technology. However, we must be careful not to fall into the trap of asserting *technological determinism,* a view of the past that simplistically ascribes

all significant change in military history (and, at times, in history as a whole) to changes in technology. The impact of specific technologies varies widely depending on the economic, political, and cultural contexts into which they are introduced, a theme to which we will return repeatedly in this book. Still, certain technologies undeniably had a significant impact on the waging of war, even if that impact was varied.

In early warfare, the key developments were in metallurgy, fortification, and animal domestication. The invention or discovery of metals—first bronze and later iron—that could hold an edge (and, conversely, could be shaped into body armor) raised the effectiveness of armies from metallurgically advanced societies, while fortification of fixed sites was one of the sure signs of the spread of warfare to an area. The key domesticate, of course, was the horse: Use of the horse first to draw war chariots and later to carry warriors, as well as the more general use of horses and other beasts of burden to transport supplies, brought major transformations to warfare that will be discussed later in the chapter (pages 10–11).

The main form of technology in war is, of course, weaponry. Ancient warfare saw the same basic division of weapons that persists in some form even today between weapons of hand-to-hand combat, such as clubs, daggers, and spears, and missile weapons, such as javelins, slings, and bows. The weapons of early warfare undoubtedly evolved out of the tools of big-game hunting but rapidly acquired specialized forms designed specifically for mass use in killing other armed and armored humans. The sword has never been a hunting weapon, for example. (The bow, on the other hand, easily crosses over from hunting to war.) Weaponry is closely associated with tactics, but we know so little about ancient battles that no firm conclusions can be drawn about how armies actually fought until well into the second millennium BCE, as we will detail further.

War and Culture

The sociopolitical implications of waging war inevitably carried over into cultural expressions. We noted above the role of royal propaganda in bonding communities together for war efforts. Accounts of royal military triumphs, accurate or not, burnished the reputation of the leader, showed him performing a central function of kingship in protecting the community, and thus helped legitimize monarchical rule. Based at least loosely on actual contemporary events, such accounts are among our first historical sources for military history.

But at least as significant were the variations on warrior culture that arose among military aristocracies and elites wherever they appeared. The warrior ethos—often constructed around bravery, loyalty, and other values common to effective military groups—had the chance, because it represented the views and interests of a significant social group rather than those of formal royal power, to pervade a society's cultural outlook more thoroughly than royal propaganda often could. War tales—the literary expressions of a warrior ethos, often in poetic form (and in many places extant as oral epic poetry long before being written down)—stand at the source of many traditions of literature. Homer's *Iliad* is probably best known to Western readers, but the genre includes many of the stories that became the basis of the Hindu religious tradition, and the earliest literary epic we have in written form, the *Epic of Gilgamesh,* tells the story of a mighty warrior-king. A common element of all warrior cultures is that they are highly gendered. From the earliest cases for which we have evidence, war, martial feats, and the exercise of armed force (and, by extension, the legitimate exercise of authority) have all been constructed as intimately if not exclusively associated with masculinity. We do not know much for certain about gender roles and identities in the long age of human development before the rise of organized warfare, but it is likely that the gendering of power and the masculinizing of public life that characterizes, to one degree or another, almost all societies before modern times have their roots in the cultural consequences of the use of violent force in hierarchical societies. Women throughout history have participated in warfare as leaders, fighters, and close supporters of armies, though not in large numbers, but the image of warfare as a masculine preserve has remained unaffected by such counterexamples. When Artemesia, queen of Halicarnassus, distinguished herself as a war leader on the Persian side at the naval battle of Salamis (see Chapter 5), her overlord Xerxes, looking down on the otherwise disastrous battle from a high hill, is said to have exclaimed, "My men have become women and my women, men." The implications for women's rights of this gendering of armed force have, for most of history, been fairly grim.

ORGANIZED WARFARE, 3500–600 BCE

Archaeological evidence for warfare after 8000 BCE, including mass burials, weapons caches, and razed villages, covers a broad swathe of Eurasia, from modern Belgium to north China, and similar evidence appears, though significantly later, in the Americas. Interestingly, most of it is associated with evidence suggesting levels of political organization that rise to no more than chiefdoms. The areas where urban, state-level societies first arose, in Mesopotamia, Egypt, the Indus valley, and, a little later, north China, seem not to have been the areas of most intense warfare. Thus, though warfare enhanced the power of leadership in chiefdoms, intense warfare in prestate societies seems not to have been a sufficient stimulus to even higher levels of political organization. Indeed, the destructiveness of warfare may have hindered the accumulation of resources and the concentration of population necessary for the rise of the first states. (Once states existed widely, the ascent from chiefdom to state was easier because models to copy and resources to exploit existed already.)

The result was that the appearance of warfare in history predates the appearance of true state-level societies by about 5000 years, and, for almost another 1000 years after the rise of urban states, warfare was not the focus of states' political organization or activity. Early city-states in Mesopotamia engaged in warfare regularly but at low levels of intensity (at least as far as we can tell), and the self-image of rulers was far more often connected to their religious roles than to their leadership in war. Egypt, unified into a kingdom early on after what looks like a brief and low-intensity period of armed competition, and isolated by the deserts surrounding the Nile valley, lived through nearly a millennium of civilization virtually without war or armies. The archaeological record of the Harappan civilization of the Indus valley in Pakistan is ambiguous enough to prevent firm conclusions about the role warfare played there, but it does not seem to have been prominent. The early states of the Yellow River valley in north China may have fought more often, but the warfare appears to have been limited in scope and intensity. Indeed, the energies of early city-states outside of Egypt were mainly devoted to the struggle to harness nature's fickle rivers through irrigation. It was probably the internal organizational imperative connected with irrigation that combined

The Standard of Ur
The Standard of Ur is a wooden box inlaid with shell and lapis lazuli. The "War" panel, shown here, depicts an army that includes spearmen, swordsmen, and heavy four-wheeled chariots drawn by asses or onagers. The "Peace" side shows what may be a postvictory feast.

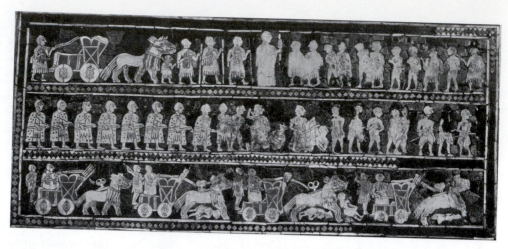

with war leadership to push chiefdoms in Mesopotamia to state level between 3500 and 3000 BCE. Mesopotamian developments almost certainly influenced the rise of states in Egypt and the Indus valley. Chinese states emerged, probably independently, by about 1000 years later. Still, even if early states were not focused on war making, war constituted an important part of their history, and urban political organization had important consequences for the patterns of warfare.

City-States at War, 3500–1700 BCE

Cities and War The emergence of state-level societies was marked above all by the appearance of cities (except perhaps in Egypt, where various urban centers were rapidly subordinated to a precociously centralized kingdom). As massive centers of gravity in political, administrative, economic, and social terms, it was inevitable that cities would also become the focus of the warfare conducted by city-states. The centrality of cities to early warfare is reflected in the archaeological evidence: Even the earliest Mesopotamian cities are surrounded by major walls clearly designed for defense against hostile armies. Massive walls had surrounded even earlier settlements, the best-known example being the famous walls at Jericho, dating to around 7000 BCE. But those walls were not as obviously designed for defense against human enemies, and the most recent interpretations see them arising initially as mechanisms of flood control. At cities such as Uruk, on the other hand, the presence of towers placed at intervals along the walls and jutting out from them so as to provide angles for flanking

archery fire leaves no doubt as to the purpose of the structures.

The fortifications that extended in many cases around a perimeter of several miles, often to a height of more than 30 feet with bases up to 60 feet wide (the walls of Mesopotamian cities were basically earthen, faced in baked brick, and so had to taper upward from a broad foundation; the walls around the early cities of the Yellow River valley were similarly constructed of rammed earth), suggest the use of conscript peasant labor. This same pool undoubtedly provided most of the soldiers for urban armies. Given the limited populations and resources early cities could have harnessed to war efforts, it is probable that such armies were essentially part-time militias with little training and only a small core of elite warriors connected to the monarch. In addition, the pictorial evidence for early foot soldiers, as in the Standard of Ur, shows very light or nonexistent armor and few weapons other than simple bows and spears. Warfare in such a physical and social context was thus dominated by sieges, not just because defeating an enemy meant breaking into his city, but because armies were not yet instruments capable of fighting decisive battles. Battles undoubtedly occurred but were also undoubtedly minimally led affairs. Furthermore, the lack of cavalry meant that such armies had little capacity to exploit a victory in pursuit, and so defeated armies could usually retreat within their city walls where they had to be besieged. Sieges were difficult, however, for if a surprise assault did not break a city's defenses immediately (and the height of city walls made scaling difficult whether by surprise or during a siege), an earthen ramp had to be built up to the top of the wall to make

SOURCES

Gilgamesh and Images of Kingship

Being a war leader was one element of the image of kingship projected in both literary and pictorial sources. Here we present a carving of Hammurabi receiving authority from the sun god Shamash and the opening of the Epic of Gilgamesh, *each depicting aspects of a war leader in the world's first civilization.*

■ ■ ■

Surpassing all kings, powerful and tall
beyond all others, violent, splendid,
a wild bull of a man, unvanquished leader,
hero in the front lines, beloved by his soldiers—
fortress they called him, *protector of the people,*
raging flood that destroys all defenses—
two-thirds divine and one-third human,
son of King Lugalbanda, who became
a god, and of the goddess Ninsun,
he opened the mountain passes, dug wells
on the slopes, crossed vast oceans, sailed
to the rising sun, journeyed to the edge
of the world, . . .
renewing the statues and sacraments
for the welfare of the people and the sacred land.
Who is like Gilgamesh? What other king
has inspired such awe? Who else can say,
"I alone rule, supreme among mankind"?
The goddess Aruru, mother of creation,
had designed his body, had made him the strongest
of men—huge, handsome, radiant, perfect.

The city is his possession, he struts
through it, arrogant, his head raised high,
trampling its citizens like a wild bull.
He is king, he does whatever he wants,
takes the son from his father and crushes him,
takes the girl from her mother and uses her,
the warrior's daughter, the young man's bride,
he uses her, no one dares oppose him.

Hammurabi

SOURCE: Stephen Mitchell, *Gilgamesh: A New English Version* (New York: Free Press, 2004), pp. 71–72.

an attack possible. Failing that, cities had to be starved into submission, and the besieging army was as or more likely to run out of food first.

Small and unprofessional armies, massive walls, and limited logistical capabilities meant that the defense had a significant advantage, and successful attacks depended on putting together coalitions of several states, coalitions that proved hard to sustain. Thus, for almost a millennium after the appearance of the first cities between 3500 and 3000 BCE, Mesopotamia remained divided into numerous independent states waging indecisive, low-intensity warfare under royal war leaders such as Gilgamesh (see the Sources box "Gilgamesh and Images of Kingship"). The early history of China looks similar, and the same must have been true of the Indus valley if those cities even engaged in warfare. Egypt was a united kingdom, but one lacking in warfare during this period.

Akkad and the Origins of Empire

Around 2400 BCE, some rulers seem to have begun to find ways to transcend the limitations of city-state warfare. The process appeared decisively with Sargon, the king of Akkad, who sometime between 2400 and 2250 (the dates are uncertain, though normally accepted as 2371–2316 BCE) created an empire that may have stretched from the Mediterranean to the southern Iranian plateau, encompassing most of Mesopotamia. Although the empire barely outlasted its creator, and we know almost nothing about how Sargon constructed or ruled it, Sargon's success pointed the way toward later developments.

The basis of Sargon's success seems to have been his ability to maintain a small standing army: Inscriptions from his reign claim that "5400 soldiers ate daily in his palace." A permanent force would have given him a significant advantage in siege warfare: Not only could he have maintained sieges over greater durations, but several innovations in siege techniques appear, probably as a result of accumulated expertise made possible by a permanent force. *Mining*, or digging through or under the walls at chosen spots, is referred to in the sources, and pictorial evidence shows siege machines that look essentially like large battering picks, sometimes covered to protect them from missiles lobbed from the walls. To counter defensive missile fire, Sargon's engineers deployed mobile siege engines that acted as platforms for firing back from a height at least equal to the defenders'. They also worked out ramp building with precision and could therefore rapidly force a city to negotiate a surrender to avoid an inevitable sack. At the same time, personal infantry weapons saw gradual improvement. More powerful composite bows supplemented simple bows, increasing the range and penetrating power of arrows significantly, and bronze swords began to appear in greater numbers as slashing weapons.

Crisis and Recovery

The Akkadian Empire was probably never more than a loosely ruled confederation, and it collapsed completely around 2200 BCE. But its demise coincided with the end of the Old Kingdom in Egypt and the beginning of the collapse of civilization in the Indus valley, and probably with a period of crisis that preceded the emergence of the first historical dynasty, the Shang, in China. This pan-Eurasian crisis of early Bronze Age societies suggests some deeper causes than simply political weakness. Many historians point to environmental factors, including climate change combined with local ecological degradation resulting from intensive farming, and the limits of early states' material and cultural capacities for organizing their societies, as crucial in explaining this crisis.

Yet in all cases save India, where the Harappan culture disappeared and state-level societies did not emerge again until after 600 BCE in the Ganges valley (see Chapter 2), recovery followed the period of crisis. The Egyptian Middle Kingdom and the Babylonian Empire of Hammurabi rebuilt and extended the states of their predecessors, using military techniques essentially unchanged from earlier times. It was only after the collapse of Babylon and the Middle Kingdom around 1700 BCE and a period of disorder and invasions from beyond the margins of civilization that middle Bronze Age states achieved more intense political organization. New kingdoms emerged beginning in the middle of the seventeenth century BCE. New forms of sociopolitical organization intimately tied to new military technologies, combined in the person of the chariot warrior elite, led the way.

Chariots and Kingdoms, 1700–1200 BCE

Chariots and Elites

Horses were domesticated, probably first in the steppes north of the Black Sea, as early as 4000 BCE by nomadic pastoralists who would later constitute a source of significant military power in Eurasia (see Chapter 6). But, as yet, the combination of riding and shooting had not been mastered, at least as a military skill, and horses spread southward into southwest Asia and eastward into China initially as draft animals for ceremonial carts. A suite of new technologies that seems to have come together by 1700 BCE then combined with the horse to create a major new weapons system, the war chariot, with major implications for the social and political structures of the kingdoms it affected.

The technology suite consisted of two horses pulling a light chariot with two spoked wheels, a vast improvement over solid wooden disks. Reins connected to bits, another invention, allowed a driver to control the horses while an expert archer wielding an improved composite bow fired at the enemy. (Later,

Assyrian War Chariot This carving shows a chariot with the classic pairing of driver and archer.

especially in the Hittite tradition, a third man was added as a shield bearer.) This innovation, in turn, stimulated the development of the first significant body armor, bronze scales sewn onto leather, which protected the archer and sometimes the horses. The result was a fast, mobile missile platform, squadrons of which could now dominate battlefields—indeed, their ability to maneuver in units probably made battles in the sense known to military history truly possible for the first time. Furthermore, the warriors who rode on the chariots now possessed specialized skills in combination with expensive technology. Possession of both virtually ensured (or resulted from) their position as not just a military but a sociopolitical elite, and the kingdoms of the age of chariots were dominated by an aristocracy of chariot warriors attached to kings in central palace-cities.

The armies of the so-called chariot kingdoms continued to include large numbers of infantry, but they play almost no role in the battles narrated in enough detail by the sources that we can at least attempt to reconstruct them (see the Highlights box "Kadesh," for example). It may be that this simply represents the elite bias of those sources, but it is more likely that it represents reality. That is, chariot-age infantry remained minimally trained peasant conscripts, useful as labor in siege warfare and as camp or city guards but having little worth on the battlefield. Battles thus consisted of mass confrontations of hundreds of chariots on each side. The lightly built chariots, designed for speed and maneuverability, probably did not charge each other directly, but rather engaged in mass drive-by shootings, something like a mass battle of light tanks. Feats of individual prowess, possible in

such loose and mobile action, clearly figured into the culture of chariot warfare.

The relatively untrained and lightly armed conscript infantry would not have been much use against mobile chariots. Therefore, even if they remained on the battlefield, they would have played an immobile and passive role. But there is evidence for more professional light infantry skirmishers or runners who supported chariots in battle, assisting their own fallen chariot warriors and finishing off fallen enemy warriors.

The origins of chariots and chariot warfare are obscure, but linguistic evidence suggests that their inventors were the Aryans of central Asia, speakers of the language ancestral to an entire branch of the Indo-European language family. Certainly, Aryan terms for chariots and chariot warriors and the technologies and tactics of chariot warfare were common throughout southwest Asia even in areas where Aryan was not spoken or had died out in general use, and chariot-using elites were associated with the Aryan pantheon (most familiar still as the main gods of Hinduism) even in the midst of other religious traditions. The *Bhagavad Gītā*, the tale of the chariot warrior Arjuna and his driver Krishna (the god Vishnu in disguise), became a central ethical text of Hinduism, which speaks to the centrality of chariot warrior elites to Aryan (or Vedic, in its Indian context) society.

Chariots and Kingdoms The Aryans and their chariot culture seem to have spread from the area south of the Caucasus Mountains. Evidence for the new style of warfare appears at Troy in Asia Minor shortly after 1700 BCE, and it made its way to Egypt with the Hyksos, Amorite and Hurrian invaders from Asia Minor and Syria, around 1650. The Hittites, also based in Asia Minor, adopted the new style, and in 1595, a Hittite army campaigned all the way down into Mesopotamia, sacking Babylon and demonstrating decisively the range and power of chariot warfare.

The power of chariot warfare contributed to a shared culture of chariot warriors led by kings whose role as leaders of chariot armies became much more important, as attested by a major shift in the style of royal propaganda away from religious legitimation and toward military heroism. (This is not to say that religion became unimportant: It legitimated and even motivated warfare in many places, and provided the ritual elements that held armies together politically, culturally, and in terms of morale on campaign.) The political organization that resulted was based in

Kadesh

Disputes over territory in Syria erupted into open warfare between New Kingdom Egypt under Ramses II and the Kingdom of Hatti (the Hittite realm) under Mutawallis II in 1275 BCE. Mutawallis gathered the Hittite army and a large number (according to Egyptian sources) of subordinate allies and established a base outside the fortified city of Kadesh in north Syria, at the borders of the kingdom. Meanwhile, in little over a month, Ramses II marched the Egyptian army from Egypt to the vicinity of Kadesh. This rate of progress, approaching fifteen miles a day, compares favorably with rates of march by other infantry or mixed armies throughout history before mechanization. It also speaks to the organization of the Egyptian army and the care taken over supplies, which were probably mostly provided along the route of march by allies and subordinate provinces, who would have been apprised in advance of the coming of the king's army; carts and pack animals must have carried some supplies and equipment, including stores of arrows. The army was divided into four divisions, named for Egyptian gods. Each contained chariots and infantry; the sources put the total number of Egyptian chariots at 1000. The Hittites are said to have had 2500 of their own chariots plus 1000 from allies, as well as a large force of infantry (Figure 1.1).

The last day of marching brought Ramses' lead division to a camp northwest of Kadesh, near the Hittite camp northeast of the city, across the river Orontes. Whether from poor scouting, misleading intelligence, or simple overconfidence, Ramses seems not to have anticipated that the Hittites might hit his following divisions as they marched from the previous day's camp north past Kadesh to join the pharaoh's force the next day. Mutawallis sent the Hittite chariots across the Orontes south of Kadesh to strike the second Egyptian division on the march. This surprise attack—portrayed in the Egyptian sources as a cowardly ruse—scattered the second division completely, and the Hittites then turned north to attack Ramses' division in its camp. Ramses managed to get enough of his chariot force deployed west of the camp to counter the Hittite force. Mutawallis, observing from the heights of his camp, sent in his allies as reinforcements. But the timely arrival from the north of a force of Syrians allied with Ramses, and probably of the third Egyptian division from the south, pressured the Hittite force on both flanks. Tired already from long fighting, the Hittites fell back across the river, and fighting ended for the day. The Hittite infantry seems to have taken no part in the battle. The Egyptian second division's infantry was scattered with their chariots, while that of Ramses' division was confined to his camp. The battle had been between the chariots on each side.

Fighting resumed the next day, probably on more conventional terms, with neither side having the advantage of surprise. It proved indecisive: The Hittites could not drive the Egyptians off, but Ramses could not drive the Hittites away or into Kadesh and beseige the city. A truce let the Egyptians claim victory, but the true result was reflected in the peace treaty signed fifteen years later, in which each side recognized the other's possessions and as a result of which Ramses married a Hittite princess.

opulent palaces. That shared culture and the range of chariot armies brought the major kingdoms of Egypt, Mesopotamia, and the eastern Mediterranean into regular and direct military and diplomatic contact for the first time. The kingdoms that could afford large chariot forces recognized each other as great powers and disputed control of the lands that separated their respective cores. Syria, in particular, became a prominent battleground, disputed and dominated at times by the Hittites of Asia Minor, the

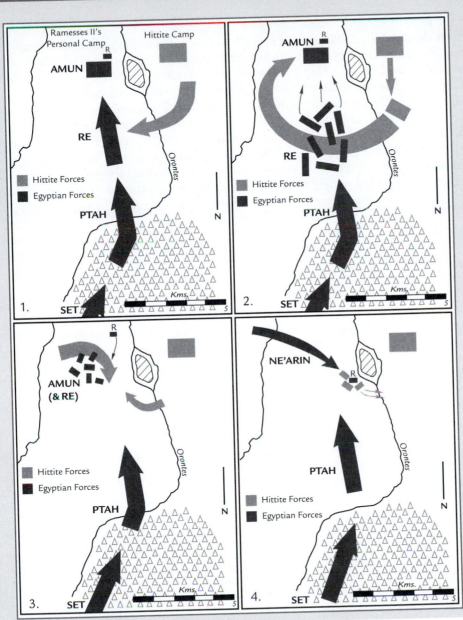

Figure 1.1 Battle Plan of Kadesh

Mitanni based in northern Mesopotamia, and a newly aggressive and imperialistic Egypt—the three mutually recognized Great Kingdoms.

Warfare became one of a number of tools of statecraft in this context. Marriage alliances, economic exchanges and treaties governing trade, and the fortification of frontiers were combined according to circumstances to provide defensive security and pursue imperial expansion where possible. The cultural need for kings to establish their ruling credentials by

ISSUES

Catastrophism and "Military Revolutions"

The causes of the end of the Bronze Age have long been the subject of scholarly debate. Military technology and tactics entered into this debate in full force with the publication of Robert Drews' *The End of the Bronze Age: Changes in Warfare and the Catastrophe ca. 1200 B.C.* in 1993. Drews placed increased infantry effectiveness, based on better armor and weaponry and heightened social cohesiveness that translated into battlefield cohesion, at the causal center of that debate. Specifically, Drews claimed that it was infantry weapons and tactics that brought down chariot elites, destroyed their palaces and thus their states, and disrupted beyond repair the general system that those states drew on and contributed to.

Drews' thesis was controversial almost from the moment it was published. While some found it persuasive, many specialists, particularly archaeologists but also ancient historians, criticized his conclusions even as they acknowledged the depth and breadth of his scholarship. In fact, almost every reviewer appreciated Drews' account of the various events that marked the end of the Bronze Age kingdoms, even those who contested the rhetoric of lumping them all together under the rubric of "The Catastrophe." Indeed, it was the very complexity of those events and the length of time over which they occurred that led many to doubt what looked like an overly monocausal explanatory scheme. In addition, the precise mechanisms by which the new military capacities of barbarian infantry spread so rapidly and destructively seemed unclear to many, especially given that many of the external raiders appeared as "Sea Peoples," not infantry armies, in contemporary records. In fact, Drews conceded the importance of piracy and saw military change not as the sole engine of change but as the central mechanism uniting systems collapse, raiding, and other causes. Further, that military change is associated with the transformation from Bronze Age to Iron Age polities is generally accepted, partly because Drews' revisionist account of chariot warfare is generally accepted. But his causal emphasis on military change has not won wide acceptance.

demonstrating military process prompted a number of campaigns early in reigns by Great Kingdom forces against carefully selected minor targets. However, relations with other Great Kingdoms remained kings' foremost concern. In those relations, legalistic attention to justifying military action, including formal declarations of war framed in terms of legal disputes, reflects the common culture of chariot elites across southwest Asia and Egypt, despite differences in languages and local cultures within different kingdoms. This common culture included a tradition of battle in which the two sides seem to have agreed ahead of time on a place of battle as a means of settling disputes. Material and logistical considerations contributed to this tendency as well: chariot battles required large, open plains, and the presence of fortifications and fortified cities further constrained where armies could meet. Strategic surprise was therefore difficult to achieve, though tactical surprise based on chariot mobility was possible (see the Highlights box).

A common culture of chariot elites also emerged across the many provinces or small states of Shang China. However, the general cultural framework of Yellow River states was more homogenous than that in southwest Asia, which was more open geographically to migrations, nomadic invasions, and cross-cultural influences.

Infantry and Empires, 1200–600 BCE

The End of the Bronze Age   In the half-century around 1200 BCE, that openness to migrations, invasions, and external influences played a significant role in bringing the Bronze Age and the age of chariot warfare to an end. Between about 1225 and 1175, the centers of virtually every major civilization in the eastern Mediterranean and southwest Asia suffered

The military changes Drew described might well be characterized as a "military revolution." This concept has gained tremendous traction in military history circles since the late 1980s because of the "Military Revolution" debate among early modern European historians (see the Issues box in Chapter 16) and the "Revolution in Military Affairs" debate among modern military theorists and historians (see Chapter 30). Drews' thesis demonstrates some of the consistent patterns and problems of Military Revolution historiography that we will revisit periodically throughout this book. The central features of claims for a Military Revolution include emphasis on sudden, broad, catastrophic, or revolutionary change; changes in military practices as the central cause of revolution; and, usually, technological change as the central cause of military change. The simplicity and directness of such theories account in large part for their power and popularity, for the countervailing position is messier, more complicated, and less easy to convey. But the elements of the response are fairly consistent as well. For example,

change is slower (and continuity more important) than revolution theories allow, with the impression of revolution as often being a result of historical time compression; military change is almost always a product rather than a cause of broad changes, as military organization reflects underlying social, economic, and political contexts and cultural assumptions; and technological change is not deterministic, because the uses made of technology are so dependent on those same contexts and cultural perceptions.

This text holds firmly to the latter view, as readers will see. That is, military revolutions play only a small role in our account of military history: The two biggest revolutions in military practice that we describe are simply aspects of the two major transformations in human history— the agricultural and industrial revolutions. The former is covered in this chapter, and the latter from Chapter 23 forward. Military Revolution theories are neat and therefore attractive, but reality is messy, and so we prefer more complex explanations of it.

destruction. From Egypt, Crete, Troy, and Mycenaean Greece to the realm of the Hittites, dynasties fell and entire kingdoms dissolved, many never to return. The Kingdom of Assyria, successor to the Mitanni in northern Mesopotamia, survived the initial crisis but by a century later had shrunk to a small heartland.

The causes and even the nature of the transition marked by these events are complex and controversial (see the Issues box "Catastrophism and 'Military Revolutions'"). Military changes may well have played a part and certainly constitute one of the features that marked the end of the Bronze Age and the beginning of the Iron Age. In fact, these traditional names for the two historical periods reflect an older notion of causation rooted in changing technology, including military technology. But modern accounts stress a number of contributing factors that are both interrelated and hard to distinguish from one another in the limited evidence available through archaeological and written sources.

Unlike the crisis of 2200 BCE, when the Akkadian Empire collapsed, no general ecological change is evident, though some major earthquakes may have coincided with the crisis in some areas. Nor is there clear evidence of massive migrations. But increased raiding by barbarians from around the fringes of the civilized worlds does seem to have played a role, though whether as cause or effect is debatable. And those barbarians, at least in some cases, were armed with better shields, personal armor, and short slashing swords (first bronze and later iron), which increased their effectiveness as infantry fighters and challenged the supremacy of chariot warriors. Increased raids may have contributed to the disruption of trade networks that supported the wealth of the central palace-based authority in settled states. Such disruptions, in turn, may have contributed to internal changes in the economy and social structure that tended to spread effective power to a broader ruling class, leading to a general systems collapse. Whatever the exact sequence and relationship of causes that contributed to the transformation, the foundations of palace-based chariot warrior states crumbled.

Infantry Effectiveness and the End of Chariot Warfare

Whatever the precise causal role changes in warfare played in the demise of the Bronze Age kingdom system, that warfare changed during that time is undeniable. Heavy infantry played a newly prominent role, assuming the central place in warfare that it has never relinquished since, although effective cavalry, which emerged by the eighth century BCE, joined infantry as the other major component of most military systems until well into the nineteenth century CE. We therefore need to pause and consider the bases of infantry effectiveness.

The key to effective infantry is cohesion: An infantry unit must be able to hold together while marching, defending, attacking, or facing the threat of attack. Keeping individuals from running away, and thereby reducing their unit to a crowd or a scattering of individuals, is the toughest task facing military leaders. And doing so with masses of men on foot, men who may come from various, mostly nonmilitary backgrounds, is usually harder than getting socially elite warriors—men raised to fight (at least in part in defense of their social privileges)—to stick together whether they fight on foot or, as they more often did, on horseback. Cohesion may be encouraged by the use of deep, dense formations, and better armor and weaponry can help. However, the main sources of military cohesion in infantry are either preexisting social cohesion—the men of a unit are already neighbors, friends, and communal coparticipants—or training directed by a central authority capable of gathering and forging an infantry unit into an artificial community through drill. These sources are not mutually exclusive. And, in either case, experience on campaign and in battle vastly increases the effect of communal or training-based cohesion: In effect, experience anneals the forging accomplished by community or training. (Cavalry, of course, benefits from cohesion as well, but its mobility both complicates and complements cohesion as a source of effectiveness, making cohesion less central to cavalry than to infantry.)

It appears to be a reasonable hypothesis that, up until the end of the Bronze Age, these two sources of infantry cohesion were weak. Early states, though they had the resources to gather fairly large numbers of conscript infantry, did not have the resources, material

or administrative, to train them rigorously. At the same time, the agricultural and hierarchical organization of society militated against the development of social cohesion among an infantry class. The societies outside early states, though sometimes warlike, did not have the combination of large enough numbers and social cohesion to produce effective infantry, especially since community size and social cohesion would have varied inversely.

The success of the Bronze Age kingdoms, however, probably contributed to new contexts that made better infantry possible and simultaneously undermined the bases of the palace-based chariot warrior elite. The economic prosperity they were built on and that they fostered and spread across trade networks inevitably enriched both broader sections of their populations and of the societies around their margins. Richer, somewhat larger communities, instantiated as small kingdoms such as the Aramaeans, Israelites, and city-states in Greece, began to emerge in the centuries after 1200 BCE as new sources of military power, and each relied on community-based infantry. Richer communities could also afford better armor and weapons. Some of their early activities may have disrupted the same trade systems that helped spawn their power. However, such systems tended not to end catastrophically, but to diffuse, and where connections were eventually broken, they inevitably reappeared later in a less centrally monopolized form.

In Greece and Rome, this communal infantry model would have a longer and more notable history than elsewhere in the Mediterranean and southwest Asia. We will examine these cases in Chapters 3 and 4. Two further developments, however, limited the impact of the small powers outside of Greece and Rome built around communal infantry. One was the emergence by 800 BCE of effective true cavalry. The other was that a large state, Assyria, learned to harness both cavalry and drilled infantry together into a system backed by large state resources, enabling the creation of a new form of empire. The Romans eventually converted to the Assyrian training model for maintaining their infantry armies. It was also on the basis of training and large state resources that effective infantry and centralized imperial government emerged in China, completely separately, several centuries after Assyria's rise, led by Qin, the state that created the first Chinese Empire (see Chapter 2).

Cavalry, Assyria, and the "Modern" Military-Political Package

Although horses had been domesticated on the central Asian steppes as early as 4000 BCE,

Assyrian Spearmen In Formation These armored, disciplined warriors formed the core of the Assyrian army.

as noted above, and riding as a skill emerged well before 1000 BCE, wild horses and their early domesticated kin were too small to carry men far or in battle, accounting in part for their military use as chariot drawers. But selective breeding for size or at least toughness (steppe ponies remained relatively small down through the time of the Mongols and beyond) eventually produced horses capable of acting as battle platforms themselves, and by 750 BCE, cavalry had replaced chariots as the mobile element in Assyrian armies. The skills of mounted archery and shock combat then spread rapidly.

But the core of the Assyrian army was its heavy infantry—armored, armed with spears, and operating in dense, disciplined formations that could attack and defend equally well. Cavalry support led to the creation of the first true combined arms tactics. Assyrian siege capabilities were equally impressive, and the Assyrians pioneered the use of deliberate mass terror in siege warfare: Having captured a city, they would not just sack but destroy it, piling the skulls of their victims up as monuments to their ferocity, in a display designed to encourage the rapid surrender of subsequent targets.

After an initial expansion in the tenth century BCE that operated on the loose, hegemonic pattern of

Bronze Age kingdoms had collapsed, connected reforms of political and military administration created the basis for the Assyrian Empire of 750–600 that employed the combined arms and terror tactics just described. New conquests were divided into provinces just as the Assyrian heartland was, each ruled by an Assyrian governor and providing standardized units of the standing Assyrian army, which therefore included an increasing number of non-Assyrian auxiliaries. The Assyrians also engineered mass deportations of conquered populations in order to break up local opposition to their rule, divide conquered elites from their peoples, and repopulate devastated areas of the empire. Such techniques aroused intense opposition, and the empire collapsed suddenly around 600, overthrown from within by the Babylonians and Medes and succeeded by the Persians. But the utility and effectiveness of Assyrian techniques is attested by the fact that their successors borrowed most of their administration and military organization. The parallels with Qin China and its replacement by the Han, who adopted Qin administration but gave it a more humane face, is striking. Variations on the Assyrian-Qin theme would dominate the warfare of sedentary states until the Industrial Revolution.

CONCLUSION

The broad set of transformations in human settlement, economic subsistence, and social and political organization that often go under the title "The Agricultural Revolution" inevitably had a major impact on warfare as an aspect of human history. Indeed, as this chapter argued, warfare only arose in conjunction with the changes associated with (though not always caused by) agriculture, including sedentarism and territoriality, as well as hierarchy and socioeconomic specialization. Even then, the development of warfare was slow and halting. The wars of chiefdoms seem rarely to have exceeded a certain organizational level, which is not to say that they were not destructive—their very destructiveness may have inhibited the further development of political hierarchy in warring chiefdoms. The development of warfare in state-level societies, or civilizations, lagged behind political and cultural innovations (especially from our modern perspective of military technology as cutting edge and global in its potential impact) for millennia.

It was only with the Assyrians and Qin that all the major elements of warfare as it would be practiced by most major state-level societies came together in a single military system: At the tactical level, with heavy, disciplined infantry, true cavalry, and (siege) artillery; at the organizational level, with standing military units and logistical support systems run by a central administration; and at the strategic and political level, with the use of this military system in the service of a centralizing, transformative imperialism, directed by a culture of the inseparability of war and state. The following four chapters will trace the working out of the implications and variations of this sort of military society in Persia, Greece, Rome, China, and elsewhere, on land and sea. The rest of the book simply extends that story.

SUGGESTED READINGS

Dawson, Doyne. *The First Armies.* London: Cassell, 2001. A well-organized and up-to-date survey of early military history—indebted to Drews (below) in its explanatory scheme, and generally persuasive, though with a narrow focus on military causation.

Drews, Robert. *The End of the Bronze Age: Changes in Warfare and the Catastrophe ca. 1200 B.C.* Princeton: Princeton University Press, 1993. An important and controversial reconsideration of the end of the Bronze Age, placing the explanatory emphasis on military change, especially the effectiveness of heavily armed, disciplined infantry.

Ferguson, Brian. "The Birth of War." *Natural History* (cover story), July/August, 2003, 28–35. An accessible version of Ferguson's conclusions; they are available in scholarly form in his "Archaeology, Cultural Anthropology, and the Origins and Intensifications of War," in E. Arkush and M. Allen, eds., *Violent Transformations: The Archaeology of Warfare and Long-Term Social Change* (Gainesville: University of Florida Press, 2005); see also his "Violence and War in Prehistory," in Debra L. Martin and David W. Frayer, *Troubled Times: Violence and Warfare in the Past* (Langhorne: Gordon and Breach, 1997). Ferguson supports the theory of a cultural invention of war with a detailed and global survey of the archaeological evidence; his is currently the essential body of work in this field.

Ferrill, Arthur. *The Origins of War: From the Stone Age to Alexander the Great.* New York: Thames and Hudson, 1985. A useful historical survey of the evidence as it stood in the mid-1980s. Ferrill was an early proponent of the cultural invention position on early warfare.

Keeley, Lawrence. *War Before Civilization: The Myth of the Peaceful Savage.* Oxford: Oxford University Press, 1996. The most cited text in support of the theory that warfare has been a constant part of human activity since the earliest days of the species. While valuable, the book is overly polemical, and all of Keeley's hard evidence in fact dates from very late in the archaeological record, when no one disputes the existence of warfare.

Otterbein, Keith. *How War Began.* College Station: Texas A&M, 2004. A useful account in which Otterbein agrees with Ferguson on the late origins of war while disagreeing about the exact mechanisms, putting more emphasis on the transition from big-game hunting to warfare.

Partridge, Robert. *Fighting Pharaohs: Weapons and Warfare in Ancient Egypt.* Manchester: Peartree, 2002. A clear introduction to the military role of pharaohs and the organization of Egyptian armies in the chariot age.

Saggs, H. W. F. *The Might That Was Assyria.* London: Sidgewick and Jackson, 1984. A general history that includes some details of military organization and operations.

CHAPTER 2

Empires, Elephants, and Ideologies: Asia, 800 BCE–200 CE

As we saw in Chapter 1, once chariot warriors appeared on the stage, they dominated the early history of warfare, forming military and social elites in many of the societies of Eurasia before 1200 BCE. Although they would disappear from Greek history when the socioeconomic arrangements that supported them collapsed in the wake of the Trojan War (see Chapter 3), and were never a force in the Italian peninsula before the rise of Rome (see Chapter 4), they remained a significant force in Egypt, and southwest, south, and east Asia. After about 800 BCE, an age that witnessed greater interactions between civilizations, greater social and cultural complexity within civilizations, and technological innovations including the spreading use of iron technology for both agriculture and war, those elites mostly adapted, becoming cavalry elites who, if not dominating warfare the way chariot warriors had in the Bronze Age, still played an important role on the battlefield and in politics.

The new cultural and political systems societies developed between 800 BCE and 200 CE in response to the challenges of this new age were significant enough that some historians call the early centuries of this period an Axial Age, a time when the development of civilizations turned on an axis and pointed in new directions. Crucial to this conception was the rise of new philosophies and religions: This was the age not just of Socrates, Plato, and Aristotle in Greece but of Confucius, Buddha, Zarathustra, and other thinkers whose influence is felt to this day. But the rise of many of these systems of thought was intimately connected with the military transformations that formed part of the political response to the new challenges the world posed. Indeed, the combination of sociomilitary transformation and emerging ideology proved a key tool in the formation of a set of empires that characterize the latter centuries of this period, often called the Age of Empires.

The relationship of the old chariot elites (and their successors, the cavalry elites) to the new forces of centralization and empire building was a crucial element in the history of this period militarily, socially, and politically. The ideological arrangements that emerged often reflected the role (or lack thereof) that such elites assumed in the new order of things. The symbolic displays imperial rulers deployed to promote and legitimize these arrangements—including the use of elephants, the creation of parade armies, and the staging of grand imperial hunts—were, as a result of their origins in the chariot or cavalry elites, almost always military in form. Thus, in this chapter, we focus on the military history of much of Asia in this period as the story of empires, elephants, and ideologies.

IRAN: THE PERSIAN EMPIRE

During the latter part of the eighth century and early decades of the seventh century BCE, the Iranians made their appearance in the history of the ancient Near East. During that time, the Iranian tribes known as the Medes and the Persians showed up in the records of the Assyrian kings. Apparently, those tribes had been steadily replacing some of the existing non-Iranian states on the fringes of the Assyrian Empire. At certain times, they held tributary status to the Assyrians, but at others, they were arrayed against them, usually in alliance with other peoples. By the late seventh century, the Medes seem to have established a confederacy of sorts and become the dominant Iranian kingdom, ruling over the Persians and controlling a small empire.

During the reign of the king Cyaxares, the Medes are said to have made military reforms including the division of soldiers according to their function—cavalry, infantry archers, and infantry spearmen—

and then brigading these types together into units. Cyaxares used his new-model army to expand the Median kingdom, fighting a war against the Lydians that ended in a marriage alliance between the two states. In about 615 BCE, he and his forces, in alliance with the Babylonians, fought against Assyria and in 612 BCE sacked their capital at Nineveh. Further Median expansion seems to have been halted by an invasion by the Scythians, nomadic horse archers from the steppes of central Asia (see Chapter 6 for the steppe nomads).

The Rise of the Achaemenids

The dominance of the Medes would, however, last less than a century. In the mid-sixth century BCE, the Medes would be replaced by another Iranian tribe, the Persians. The rise of the Persian dynasty known as the Achaemenids occurred under Cyrus the Great. Herodotus tells the story of Cyrus's rise to power via a successful revolt against the Medes after being marked for death as a child by his grandfather, the Median king Astyages. The story seems to stem from a Near Eastern tradition of kingship, paralleling such leaders as Sargon of Akkad and Moses. It seems more likely that Cyrus was, in fact, a client king of the Medes in the mid-sixth century and exploited that position to lead his revolt; however, some elements in Herodotus's story seem to have a basis in fact. For example, we are told that Astyages sent an army against the upstart Persian and that the general of that force, who had been wronged by the king, defected along with a large portion of his troops. Indeed, Cyrus does seem to have been joined by disaffected troops from the Median army. With a large force of Persians whom he had mustered at Pasargadai ("camp of the Persians," the eventual site of a palace complex and his tomb) and his new Median allies, Cyrus marched against Astyages and defeated him in 550 BCE. Cyrus then assumed the kingship of the former Median Empire.

Shortly thereafter, Cyrus began the first in a series of campaigns to expand the Achaemenid Empire. The first realm to be defeated was Lydia, the rich kingdom that occupied Anatolia west of the Halys River. Lydia was, due to its position and trade interests, a strong and wealthy state, with an army that included an excellent cavalry force and a number of mercenaries. In 547 BCE, the Lydian king Croesus marched against Cyrus, and an indecisive battle was fought. Croesus then retired to his capital at Sardis, planning to raise additional troops and renew the war the following year. But Cyrus daringly continued the campaign against the Lydians, even though the campaigning season was coming to an end. In the next battle, Cyrus showed his tactical flexibility by neutralizing the powerful Lydian horsemen with a screen of camels (horses will not advance on camels due to the latter's odd odor) and won the victory. In subsequent campaigns, Babylon and areas of eastern Iran were added to the empire. In fact, Cyrus spent nearly all of his reign in the field, in 530 BCE perishing in battle with the Massagetai along his northwestern frontier.

An able administrator, Cyrus set the pattern for what would become the Persian method of ruling a large, multiethnic empire. While borrowing many structural elements of Assyrian political and military organization, Cyrus avoided their harshness. He showed a willingness to be extremely tolerant in dealing with his subjects—in particular, embracing the priesthoods of conquered peoples. In Babylon, for instance, he identified his success with the approval of the deity Marduk, and he provided the Jews with the resources to rebuild the Temple in Jerusalem. Cyrus also allowed non-Persians to hold important positions in both the civil administration and the army.

Cyrus was succeeded by his son Cambyses, whose reign was not as successful as his father's. Cambyses did not show the same tolerance toward his subjects, nor was he as skillful at managing the Persian elite for royal ends. He did, however, add Egypt to the empire, in a campaign in 525 BCE that foreshadowed the sophisticated nature of subsequent Persian operations. He arranged for a supply train of camels carrying the water and food necessary to support his army, and he augmented this by mounting a joint operation using a Phoenician fleet, both to provide logistical support and to deal with the Egyptian fleet. But after his conquest of Egypt, Cambyses faced rebellion at home. His brother (or an imposter pretending to be his brother, as Cambyses may have murdered his brother) organized a revolt back in Iran. Before he could suppress the rebellion, Cambyses died of infection after being accidentally stabbed by his own dagger while hurriedly mounting his horse. In the wake of his death, a group of nobles called the Seven defeated the rebels in a civil war and chose one of their number, Darius, to be king.

Under Darius I (the Great) the Persian Empire would reach its largest territorial extent, with the borders reaching Thrace in the west and the Indus River valley in the east (Figure 2.1). Darius also

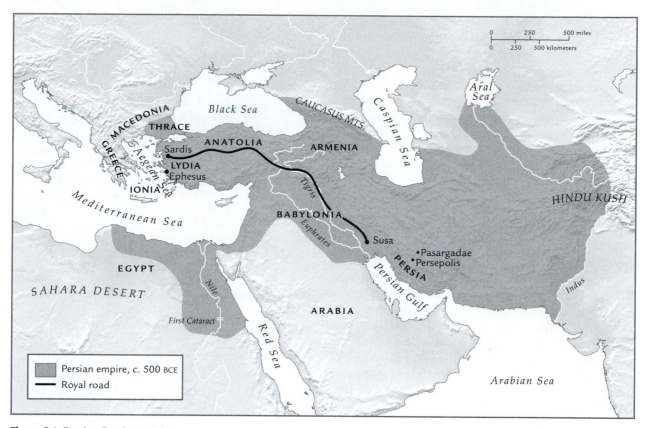

Figure 2.1 Persian Empire, c. 500 BCE

undertook to organize the empire both administratively and militarily. Although he continued to extend the frontiers, the frenetic pace of expansion that characterized the reigns of his predecessors slowed, giving Darius the opportunity to formalize the organization of the state.

Achaemenid Provincial and Military Organization

Darius organized the Persian Empire into twenty large administrative units called satrapies, governed by officials known as satraps. The satrapies were made up of several peoples, usually centered on one particular group, who supplied the empire with tribute and troops in time of war. The satraps from the time of Darius onward were, with few exceptions, members of the Persian nobility—powerful individuals with financial and military resources. In order to keep the satraps' political ambitions in check, the Great King maintained an official known as the King's Eye who, in turn, maintained a number of listeners (the King's

Ears) who were sent out to the provinces to observe the satraps. In this way, the Persian elite were both co-opted and controlled.

The Royal Army The incessant campaigns of Cyrus the Great required the creation of a standing army. This army initially seems to have consisted of 10,000 Persian infantry and 10,000 Persian cavalry, as well as a force of Medes. This was an important development in the history of Persian rule since it made the army an instrument of royal authority and lessened the king's dependence on the Persian nobility and their retinues.

The Persian army has often been portrayed as an ineffectual force, driven into battle under the lash of its officers. This view emerged from a generally hostile Greek tradition dating to the Persian Wars: The Greeks of the fifth and fourth centuries held the Persian army in low esteem since they had defeated them. But the reality was surely different—the Persians acquired the largest empire in world history to that time, and that empire was won by force of arms.

Careful reading of Greek texts also reveals a grudging admiration for the martial ability of the Persian troops, as well as their bravery and tenacity in battle. This fits with what we know of virtues that were held dear by the Persian nobility. In both the Greek texts and Persian royal inscriptions, the Persians place paramount importance on the role of skill in warfare. Persian inscriptions emphasize the king's ability to use both bow and spear, whether on horseback or on foot, and young Persians were taught "to ride, use the bow, and to speak the truth."

The emphasis on speaking the truth is a clue to the ideological development of Persian civilization, for it was during this period that Zoroastrianism developed as the religion of the Persian elite. The prophet Zarathustra may, in fact, have lived several centuries earlier (firm historical evidence of his life is mostly lacking), but the religion based on his teachings seems to have developed in conjunction with the growth of Persian power. It served to legitimate and reinforce royal authority, helping the royal house subordinate the Persian aristocratic elite to the wider purposes of ruling subject peoples. This, in turn, helped shape the development of the military system and, more broadly, provided the underpinnings of a Persian ethnic identity capable of resisting assimilation by the older cultures absorbed into the Persian Empire (see the Issues box "War and Ideologies").

In order to inculcate military skills and religious tenets into Persian youths and so provide the forces necessary to rule the empire, the government put selected Persian boys through an education system designed to prepare them as soldiers. From age 5 until age 20, they were trained in the use of weapons (spear, javelin, and bow), riding, and running long distances; they were also expected to get at least some of their supplies through theft. The similarities to the Spartan *agogē* (see Chapter 3) are remarkable. The period of military service, however, seems to have lasted only until age 24.

Units and Equipment   The Persians were organized on the Assyrian model into units of 1000 men called *hazarabam*, commanded by a *hazarapatiš*. The *hazarabam* were, in turn, divided into subunits of 100 men, and those into squads of 10 men. These troops, clad in light scaled armor, used the traditional Persian weapons of bow and spear. There is some question as to how these arms were coordinated in battle, but it seems as if the Persians employed a variation on the archer-and-shield pair used by the

Persian Immortals   These crack regiments formed the King's Guard.

Assyrians. Most likely, each squad was deployed into a single file. The soldier in the front rank was armed with a spear and a large wicker shield known as a *spara*. This soldier would set up his large shield in conjunction with others like him and create a barrier to the enemy. If the enemy drew near, he would defend his file with his spear. The other nine members of the file would be equipped with bows and perhaps spears as well. Their role in battle was to launch volleys of arrows against the enemy. Persian cavalry seem to have been similarly equipped but would have carried only the spear, or javelin, and bow, not the unwieldy *spara*.

The most important of the standing Persian regiments were the ten *hazarabam* known as the Immortals, who formed the King's Guard. The most elite unit of these crack regiments, in turn, was the *hazarabam* known as the Applebearers, from the golden apples that served as counterweights on their spears. This unit seems to have served as the personal bodyguard to the Great King himself. There were also at least 1000 cavalry who formed part of the Royal Guard, as

ISSUES

War and Ideologies

Zoroastrianism was a religion with universal claims (Ahura-Mazda is said to have created the entire universe), whose practice was restricted to a Chosen People, the Persians, who stood in a special relationship to the deity. Much like the developed form of Judaism that emerged at the same time (and probably in mutual influence with Zoroastrianism), the Persian religion served in part to bind together and give a stable identity to a minority people in a large, multiethnic, multicultural empire—although the Persians, unlike the Hebrews, were the ruling minority. Thus, Persian religious development was at least in part a product of warfare, and in particular of the Persians' success at creating through conquest a vast empire of which they formed only one element. The tenets of Zoroastrianism that stressed truth telling and personal ethics based in individual choice between good and evil may well, in turn, have influenced Persian efforts at creating a government benevolent to all peoples of the empire. Warfare did not determine the specific features of Zoroastrian theology and cosmology. But warfare, conquest, and a religion with origins in a chariot-riding warrior elite (it emerged from an earlier Indo-European religious complex in which a war god played a central role and that was to develop in different ways in India) were intimately linked in the rise of a religion that had deep influence on subsequent religious developments in southwest Asia.

This link between warfare, warrior elites, and new systems of thought constitutes one of the defining characteristics of this age in Eurasia, though the resulting philosophies and religions differed widely, as did the social and political structures that emerged in tandem with them. In India, the Aryan warrior elite that shared common Indo-European origins with the Persians (and, in fact, with the Greeks) dominated early Indian society, as did Persian chariot warriors. Unlike Zoroastrianism, which helped co-opt the warrior elite into a stronger central state, the Vedic religion that evolved into Hinduism cemented the social and political dominance of warriors in the system of class and caste that structured Indian life, often to the detriment of the development of lasting strong central government, as we will see. But through the *Bhagavad Gitā* story of the great warrior Arjuna and the ethical dilemma he faces on the battlefield, a dilemma his charioteer Krishna (really the god Vishnu in disguise) helps him solve, the warrior ethos became the metaphorical foundation for ethical thought about social duty throughout Hindu society. Thus, in Persia and India, religious transformation and development was tied closely to warfare and to warrior elites.

Unlike in Persia and India, where warfare raised questions of the divine role in history or society and only indirectly touched on questions of government, in China, the warfare of the Warring States era formed the focal point of a much more secular examination of how to govern states and societies efficiently and humanely. This gave rise to a range of philosophies that included Confucianism, Daoism, and Legalism, as well as a vast literature directly concerned with warfare itself as a tool of state (see the Sources box "Sun Zi" later in the chapter). China's culture of war and violence originated, as elsewhere, in the idea of a chariot-riding warrior elite. However, the emphasis on autocratic state power that became central to Chinese political and secular philosophies during the Warring States era was accompanied, not by a co-opting of the elite into government as in Persia, nor by the continued dominance of warriors as in India, but by the elimination of warrior elites as a separate class in Chinese society.

Finally, as we will see in Chapter 3, *poleis* (city-states), phalanx warfare, and Greek philosophy developed in mutual influence with each other, producing another major tradition of secular philosophy. It is significant and not coincidental that the great intellectual traditions of this age had their origins in how people thought about, conceived, and justified the use of violence.

well as regiments formed from other Iranians including Medes, Cissians, and Hyrcanians. Some *hazarabam* may have been formed from mercenaries and others drawn from the more martial peoples of the empire, including Scythians. These seem to have served in military colonies where they may have been subjected to Iranian forms of training, equipment, and tactics.

Parade Armies   The Iranian regiments formed the heart of the Persian forces that fought in the great wars of the fifth century BCE. But Herodotus and others describe great gatherings of troops drawn from virtually every nationality throughout the empire, reinforcing the image of an unwieldy, poorly integrated Persian military. In all likelihood, only small contingents of these satrapal levies were actually taken on campaign. The Great King used large "parade armies" and reviews of provincial troops, not to actually fight, but to demonstrate the vastness of his empire and his power to his enemies abroad and to his own people, including his elites.

The End of the Achaemenid Empire

After the wars against the Greeks (see Chapter 3), the Persian Empire was beset by military troubles in the form of sporadic rebellions carried out by rebel Persian satraps as well as more ethnically motivated uprisings in satrapies such as Egypt. Moreover, the defeats suffered in Greece must have taken a toll on the manpower of those Iranian groups who had formed the mainstay of the Royal Army and on the prestige of the Royal Army. Over the course of the next century and a half, the Persian Empire was forced to make changes to its military establishment.

The king was able to maintain an Iranian Royal Guard—there are mentions of Applebearers and Kinsmen who fought beside the king in the fourth century—but their numbers may not have been as large as in the fifth century. In addition to the Royal Army, there is evidence for the increasing use of troops maintained by the satraps and other members of the Persian nobility. These forces could number in the hundreds and be very well equipped. The most famous example was the 600 heavily armored cavalry who formed the bodyguard of Cyrus the Younger in his failed effort to assume the throne. Ultimately, the Persians were forced to make more extensive use of foreign mercenaries, especially Greeks. The most famous example involved the 10,000 Greek mercenaries hired

by Cyrus the Younger in 401 BCE. This trend continued until the very end of the dynasty in the 330s. The last Persian king, Darius III, hired tens of thousands of Greek mercenaries in his war with Alexander and used Greek officers as high-ranking commanders (see Chapter 3).

The Persians did, however, try to create a homegrown force, called *Kadakes,* to replace the lost Iranian regiments. The idea was to draw on the extensive manpower of the empire but to train the recruits in the Iranian military system. This was achieved by allowing non-Iranians to enter the Persian military training system (which has already been described). The effort seems to have been fairly successful, since *Kadakes* apparently formed the majority of at least one major Persian army during the fourth century. Moreover, after conquering the empire, Alexander appears to have modified the Persian education system to train young Persians to fight like Macedonians.

With the Alexandrian conquest, the Persian Empire went into eclipse for several centuries. But the cultural and ideological infrastructure created by the Achaemenids would survive among the Persians, to be drawn on (in modified form, certainly) first by nomadic Parthians who wrested control of the area from its Hellenistic rulers in the second century BCE, and then decisively after 226 CE by the Sassanians, a native dynasty that consciously revived the symbolism of and connections to Zoroastrianism that underlay much Persian success under the Achaemenids (see Chapter 8).

CHINA: THE QIN AND HAN EMPIRES

The loose and hegemonic political unity of China during the Shang and early Zhou eras had been completely destroyed by the beginning of what the Chinese called the Warring States era (480–221 BCE). This name is a fairly accurate representation of the primary concern of Chinese statesmen of that time. Given the larger scale and intensity of warfare, a whole class of thinkers arose to provide military advice to the rulers of the various states. As warfare became an almost constant feature of life, its practitioners became more professional, and Chinese society itself came to be dominated by full-time warriors and their concerns. Unification of China under the Qin (221–206 BCE) and Han (202 BCE–220 CE) dynasties saw the addition of systems designed to maintain central control over the vast armies that were used to ensure domestic peace and expand the borders of the Chinese empire. These borders were not peaceful. As China became unified, the steppe nomads to the north formed their own loose union and posed a significant military threat to the settled peoples to their south. Both the Qin and Han dynasties found it necessary to devote a significant amount of energy and resources to countering the threats from the north.

The Warring States Era, 480–221 BCE

After a particularly brutal raid by northern steppe armies in 771 BCE, the unity of China shattered. The result was literally hundreds of independent states, all nominally owing allegiance to the Zhou king. In spite of various conferences, treaties, and the like, these states engaged in a series of wars, both large- and small-scale, as small states became absorbed into larger states, and large states broke up into smaller states. And the warfare of this era was not as gentlemanly as portrayed in much of the literature of later times. In fact, by the fifth century BCE, battles had become increasingly deadly, with mass slaughter of defeated opponents becoming almost regular affairs.

Wars of Unification   Deadly warfare led to a need for larger and larger armies. By the third century BCE, some armies had reached sizes of several hundred thousand men. Military campaigns became intricately planned and executed operations, in which battles might last several days, rather than one or two as was usual in the past. The Warring States era also saw the construction of vast numbers of castles, walls, and other defensive fortifications, with new building materials and techniques developed to combat sieges. Besiegers countered defensive works with innovative tools and techniques of their own, including the use of besieging armies that reached enormous sizes. Interestingly, the tremendous efforts required in this era to overcome the sometimes elaborate defensive fortifications led to a general reluctance of commanders throughout Chinese history to engage in sieges.

States were forced to innovate in government and to actively promote the economic development of their lands. In agriculture, freeholding became the norm, replacing the serfdom that had characterized earlier periods. It was found to be more efficient to tax the production, and resources that had been used to supervise manorial estates could be put to other uses. The states also encouraged trade and other commerce

through massive irrigation works and road-, canal-, and bridge-building projects. Professional bureaucracies were instituted to ensure efficient collection of taxes and management of the public works projects.

Military and economic reforms that proved successful were quickly adopted by other states. Really, they had little choice, as those states with advantages would soon use them to destroy their weaker neighbors. By the third century BCE, the seven major states contending for domination were engaged in an almost endless round of warfare (Figure 2.2). One of the first to institute such reforms was Qin. Qin's location and early adoption of reforms such as a policy of accepting in its employ men of talent wherever they hailed from provided it with advantages, but its main advantage was the weakness of its enemies. For example, in 260 BCE, the state of Zhao, one of Qin's most formidable foes, suffered a serious defeat in which it reportedly lost over 400,000 men. While remaining politically intact, Zhao was unable to regain its earlier strength, succumbing a few years later to another determined attack by Qin. The same situation later befell the state of Chu, for most of the period considered the most powerful of the contending states. In 221 BCE, Qin armies succeeded in uniting China with the defeat of Qi.

A Shift to Infantry-Based Militaries   Early in the Warring States era, most battles began, as in the past (and as in Bronze Age southwest Asia), with a core of chariots backed up by several thousand infantrymen of dubious quality. The main job of the infantry was to mop up the scattered remnants of a defeated enemy. As the armies became larger, the role of chariots decreased. Also, the increasing use of the deadly crossbow—introduced sometime in the fifth century BCE—greatly reduced the effectiveness of mobile chariots.

The growing need for large numbers of soldiers for campaigns led to several military-related reforms, the most significant being the use of various forms of conscription to fill the ranks. As freeholding became the dominant form of agriculture, the male farmers of a certain age were registered by government agents. Villages were organized into militia units for defense, with the members equipped by the government and trained at set times of the year. Upon mobilization for large-scale operations, the militia units were integrated into the regular army. Thus, states created fairly large reserves while minimizing the costs to their treasuries.

Figure 2.2 Warring States China, c. 350 BCE

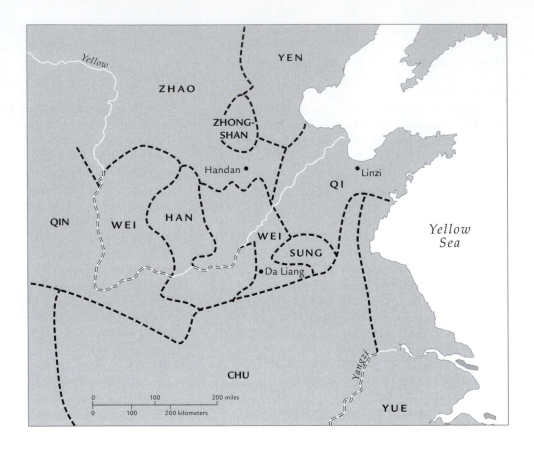

Increasing Military Professionalism As the fighting of the Warring States era became deadlier, statesmen found it necessary to hire professionals for their armies. Aristocratic ancestry as a prerequisite for a military commission faded into unimportance at a time when defeat in battle often meant slaughter for the defeated. Those with military skills, knowledge, and especially experience were in high demand in all the states, and success in battle was the quickest route up the social scale.

This period also saw the proliferation of military manuals and treatises on warfare, the most famous of which was Sun Zi's *The Art of Warfare* (see the Sources box "Sun Zi"). In this way, military practices, often described in detail in these manuals, set precedents for many of China's later warfare traditions. These traditions included an emphasis on a professional army, with command positions being predominantly gained through merit; a preference for massed formations, rather than small-unit combat; patience in building up large forces prior to a campaign, including supply preparations; use of

diplomacy as an integral part of military strategy; and a desire to gain a military advantage—through numbers, use of topography, surprise, diplomacy, trickery, and so on—so as to cause the opponent to surrender or retreat without having to engage in combat. If fighting was necessary, a strategy of both lenience and ruthlessness was used to ensure victory. This might require some explanation. In the Warring States era, military theory and practice stressed the basically moral nature of war. Simply, a ruler should go to war for moral causes—in particular, to maintain or restore justice. In such a righteous war, the opponent was seen as an enemy of heaven, of the natural order of the universe. If he could be made aware of the seriousness of his transgressions, then he should be treated leniently. However, if he persisted in his opposition, the ruler was morally justified in using any and all means to crush him. Hence, we see extraordinary tolerance for those who surrendered or defected along with extraordinary cruelty for those who were defeated in battle.

SOURCES

Sun Zi

The earliest Chinese treatise on warfare is The Art of Warfare, *traditionally said to have been written by Sun Wu (more commonly referred to as "Sun Zi," or "Master Sun"), but including at least a few additions and modifications from later centuries. The exact date of its compilation is not clear, though it was widely read by the late Warring States era. It is impossible to exaggerate the influence of this work on later Chinese military history. There are a vast number of commentaries still extant, by later Chinese military thinkers and commanders, and from the early Ming dynasty (1368–1644), knowledge of Sun Zi's* The Art of Warfare *was required of all prospective officers in the military.*

■ ■ ■

In this excerpt, Sun Zi notes the importance of diplomacy as an aspect of military affairs.

It takes a person of civil virtue to bring peace to the empire; it takes a person of martial virtue to quell disorder in the land. The expert in using the military has three basic strategies that he applies: The best strategy is to attack the enemy at the level of wisdom and experience; the second is to expose the injustice of the enemy's claims; and the last is to attack the enemy's battle position.

And when it has been decided to resort to force, Sun Zi's advice is unequivocal.

Thus in war, I have heard tell of a foolish haste, but I have yet to see a case of cleverly dragging on the hostilities. There has never been a state that has benefited from an extended war. . . . Hence, in war prize the quick victory, not the protracted engagement. Thus, the commander who understands war is the final arbiter of people's lives, and lord over the security of the state.

In the next exerpt, Sun Zi discusses the role the commander plays in preparing his men for battle—the importance of obtaining and maintaining their loyalty and obedience. We can also note the personal nature of the relationship between a commander and his men, a common feature of Chinese military thinking.

In war it is not numbers that give the advantage. If you do not advance recklessly, and are able to consolidate your own strength, get a clear picture of the enemy's situation, and secure the full support of your men, it is enough. . . . If you punish troops who are not yet devoted to you, they will not obey, and if they do not obey, they are difficult to use. But once you have their devotion, if discipline is not enforced, you cannot use them either. Therefore, bring them together by treating them humanely and keep them in line with strict military discipline. This will assure their allegiance.

SOURCE: Sun-Tzu, *The Art of Warfare,* trans. Roger Ames (New York: Ballantine Books, 1993).

Most of the military writings of the age have been lost. Nevertheless, it is clear that, during the late Warring States era, military commanders were expected to be familiar with the basic principles of military organization, training, strategy, and tactics, as explicated in those works. Many of the battles of the era were consciously fought along lines set forth in *The Art of Warfare* and other texts. By the end of the Warring States era, the Chinese had come to increasingly agree that the political division of the land was unnatural and that harmony and justice required that China be unified, by force of arms if necessary.

The Qin and Han Eras, 221 BCE–220 CE

The unification of China did not lead to the end of warfare in China. The first Qin emperor worked to create a unified military system subject to his control, and his armies were kept busy quelling internal resistance to Qin rule and expanding the borders of the empire in all directions. After the chaos of the collapse of the Qin, the early Han emperors employed their military forces primarily to ensure internal order and to defend against the aggressive raids of the

Xiongnu to the north. Expansion on a large scale resumed under the emperor Han Wudi, but Han armies found it difficult to control the Xiongnu, who were often able to avoid battle merely by running away into the vast depths of the steppes.

In the Qin era, military matters were dominant in public life. Military men held a large proportion of influential and prestigious positions, and the military was seen by many as a means of social mobility. The succeeding Han dynasty also came to power through military means, and, in the early years, military men continued to play important roles. Efforts were undertaken even under the first Han emperor to place the military under some measure of civilian control. By the second century CE, this included placing trusted eunuchs in command of armies. However, stresses both internal and external forced such reliance on the military that by the end of the dynasty most of China was under the control of military men, who eventually abolished the Han imperial rulers.

Centralized Control Under the Qin

Final battles began with the ascension of Prince Zheng of Qin in 246 BCE. The westernmost of the warring states, Qin benefited from centuries of warfare against the nomadic tribes along its western borders. Once these tribes had been subdued, Qin was prepared to expand eastward. Geography assisted Qin in its task, protected as it was by chains of mountains whose passes were relatively easy to defend. By taking control of Ba and Shu (modern-day regions of Sichuan Province), Qin also gained access to abundant agricultural products, as well as further protecting its rear.

It is remarkable that the warfare of the various states that had lasted centuries ended with a few years of fighting, the result being the unification of China under the Qin dynasty. The guiding philosophy of the state of Qin was Legalism, which emphasized strong central rule of most aspects of society and most especially exalted military prowess. Legalism also stressed the use of capable professional officials, and, as noted earlier, Qin had already earned a reputation as being open to the hiring of competent civil and military men from other states.

The period of Qin rule of China was marked by the imposition of centralized and systematized control of the whole empire, in accord with Legalist philosophy. The role of the army was critical to this process. At the head of each command was a general, responsible not only for maintaining domestic peace but also for crushing resistance to Qin reforms. While

Qin Tomb Soldiers   The fearsome First Emperor of the Qin dynasty had over 6000 full-size terra cotta soldiers buried with him, symbolizing the terror and militarism that both centralized China and made the First Emperor an object of fear and hatred.

strictly speaking not responsible for civil administration, in practice these generals and their armies often became dominant in nonmilitary-related affairs. It is no exaggeration to say that Qin China was in essence a military state.

Almost immediately after subjugating the remaining states of China, Qin armies engaged in expeditions to expand the territory of the empire. In the north, armies under the general Meng Tian pushed Qin territory far beyond the Ordos region, inflicting several defeats on the Xiongnu. Unfortunately, the records are not clear regarding almost anything involved in this undertaking, so we know little about the numbers or the course of the campaign. Somewhat clearer are the records of campaigns to the south, where large Qin infantry armies wrested control of much of the present-day provinces of Fujian and Guangdong from the tribal peoples who lived there. A naval fleet was also constructed to take advantage of the rivers that criss-crossed much of southern China. Qin military innovation was required as the local peoples hindered and harassed Chinese armies through guerrilla warfare. However, most of these territories reverted to local control after the collapse of the Qin and had to be reconquered by the succeeding Han dynasty.

The disruption of peoples' lives caused by the centralization policies of the Qin, such as almost confiscatory tax rates, led to a great deal of discontent. Within two years of the death of Qin Shihuangdi (the First Emperor) in 210 BCE, fighting broke out in several areas. The new leaders of the dynasty lacked the dynamism and ability of Shihuangdi, and Qin armies were unable to contain the spreading rebellion. Most of the old aristocracy had been destroyed either during the warfare of the Warring States era or by the Qin, and so rebel armies were most often led by men of commoner status, and even some of peasant stock. A key figure in the rebellion and later civil wars was Liu Bang, who was serving as a minor local official at the beginning of the Qin collapse. Courage in battle and proven leadership ability led Liu Bang to command one of the main rebel armies. He gained many adherents and much local support through policies that stressed incorporating defeated enemies into his army and drastically restricting the looting and pillaging of his soldiers. In 202 BCE, after defeating his main rival for power, Liu Bang proclaimed the Han dynasty and himself as its first emperor, called Gaodi.

Center–Periphery Conflict Under the Han

From its founding in 202 BCE to roughly 130 BCE, most of the military efforts of the Han dynasty concerned internal conflict rather than external expansion or defense. Han China was certainly threatened by outsiders during this period, subjected to often destructive raids by the Xiongnu, who were emboldened by the civil wars engulfing China. A few military expeditions were launched against the Xiongnu by the early Han emperors, but these proved almost universally to be failures. In fact, in one campaign led by Gaodi himself, the Chinese army was destroyed, and the emperor barely escaped capture.

Actually, the Xiongnu were interested not so much in conquest as in the goods that could be acquired through plunder. With almost two-thirds of the Han realm in the hands of semi-independent kings, many of whom felt they were entitled to rule even more of the land, the imperial court decided to essentially pay off the Xiongnu while concentrating their military efforts on subduing the recalcitrant kings. The Xiongnu probably were aware of their advantageous position, and their demands increased as time went by. When Han courts refused to meet the added demands for silk, jewelry, and other products, the Xiongnu resumed raiding—in one instance, over 30,000 of their mounted archers penetrated deep into China and left a wide swath of devastation.

In subduing the kingdoms, Gaodi took advantage of the facts that his territory was larger than that of any single king and that he could usually count on the loyalty and support of at least a few of the other kings. His initial moves were cautious. Under various pretexts, he was able to defeat one king after the other, replacing them with Liu family members. Several of these campaigns were major military endeavors that required the mobilization and dispatch of tens of thousands of infantry and even at times included the use of allied Xiongnu cavalry. Gaodi was mortally wounded in 195 BCE in a battle against one of the more aggressive kings. By this time, Gaodi had succeeded in placing family members on the thrones of nearly all the remaining kingdoms and in further circumscribing their independent power. However, his successors, determined to further assert central control, found that family ties were no guarantee of obedience. The Han court's taxation policies and civil and military administration increased their reach and efficiency, such that a rebellion in 122 BCE by the remaining kings was relatively easily overwhelmed by imperial armies.

The Campaigns of Han Wudi

The reign of Han Wudi (141–87 BCE) represented not only the triumph of imperial centralism but also the high point of Han expansionism. Tremendous economic growth during the early decades of the Han dynasty meant greatly increased resources for the imperial government, even with tax rates far below those that had been imposed in the late Warring States and especially Qin eras. A professional bureaucracy based on the Confucian ideal of appointment according to merit (and Warring States and Qin era experiences) was able to efficiently collect the taxes and utilize them to raise and maintain a large, professional military force and to fund vast military campaigns in China's frontier regions.

There were several stimuli for these campaigns, including increased threats from the Xiongnu to the north, the need to secure trade along the Silk Road, a desire to spread the reach of Chinese civilization, and the will of the emperor Wudi. Indeed, the Silk Road did not exist before the Chinese military campaigns secured the trade routes of Inner Asia. The emperor spent large sums constructing this gateway to Central Asia from the east and to China from the west, and he established garrisons to protect the way stations along the route. Wudi also responded to increased Xiongnu raiding activity by adopting an aggressive policy of conquest and subjugation. A desire to expand direct and indirect Chinese control, cultural as well as political, and a curiosity about other lands also animated Wudi to dispatch Chinese armies far from the Central Plain. The will of this emperor, then, was the crucial factor in the initiation of the major military campaigns of the Han dynasty. Still, it was economic growth and an efficient bureaucracy that made these campaigns possible. These gave Chinese armies the resources needed, as well as in most cases superior weapons. Han opponents, with the possible exception of Korea, did not have the technological skills—especially in metallurgy—to compete in the manufacture of mass quantities of high-quality weapons.

Early in Han Wudi's reign, Chinese armies were dispatched to reconquer the Min region (present-day Fujian Province). The lands there were fairly quickly subdued, but many of the native peoples were able to continue fighting, using several small islands along the coast as bases. Hit-and-run attacks apparently were very bothersome. In order to deprive the attackers of potential targets, the coastal population was removed to the interior. Although scholars doubt the evacuation was fully carried out, the Min region remained directly administered by the Han court.

In 112 BCE, Wudi dispatched his first expedition against the south (roughly, present-day provinces of Guangdong and Guangxi), as well as the small southern kingdom of Nanyüe (present-day northern Vietnam). This region had been briefly occupied by Qin armies but had reverted to independence during the chaos attending the fall of the Qin dynasty. Peoples in the Nanyüe region, including many Chinese who had fled there, had established a kingdom organized roughly on Chinese lines and accepted nominal Han sovereignty. Wudi decided to impose direct Chinese control over the region, and hundreds of small watercraft were constructed to transport the Han armies. The local peoples were no match for the Chinese, who reportedly arrived with armies of over 100,000 men. The sophisticated Han supply train

kept its forces for the most part well fed and well supplied with technologically advanced weapons. Nanyüe, like the Min region, was incorporated as a directly administered region of the Han realm.

During the Warring States era, many Chinese refugees had fled to Korea, bringing their skills and culture along with them. The Qin period saw an even larger infusion of Chinese into Korea, including one Wei Man (Wiman in Korean), who had been made military commander of Korea by the king. In 190 BCE, Wei Man had used his army to take control of Korea and begin a new dynasty, which maintained amicable relations with Han China. On various pretexts, Wudi in 109 BCE sent military forces to invade Korea. A force of 60,000 traveled overland along with a force of about 7000 by sea. However, there was no coordination between the two groups, and the Korean army was able to force a withdrawal. Later in the year, a second expedition attacked Korea with more coordination, and this one proved successful. Northern Korea was incorporated into the Han realm, although this did not last more than a few years.

The largest, most complex, and most significant of Wudi's campaigns were those directed against the Xiongnu. Beginning in 129 BCE, Wudi dispatched several expeditions against the Xiongnu, with armies that numbered in the tens of thousands. As in most military campaigns of the early and mid-Han era, the armies usually consisted of a core of regular or "military colony" troops, with most of the men being conscripts drawn from throughout the empire. Campaign armies also normally contained several units of cavalry. It is not clear how all the cavalry forces were raised, though we know that most came from allied nomadic tribes, including subjugated Xiongnu. Wudi's military commanders were aware that without cavalry they were unlikely to catch their Xiongnu opponents, who could evade the more plodding Chinese infantry simply by withdrawing farther into the steppes. (See Chapter 6 for more on steppe armies.)

Wudi's expeditions were meticulously planned, with logistics (carts, oxen, laborers, food, weapons, and so on) carefully considered before the army left its camps. As northern territories suitable for agriculture were acquired, colonists—often convicts and their families—were settled to further solidify Chinese control (see below). These colonies also provided men and supplies for later expeditions. In Turkestan, the Han established fortified garrisons, especially in or near major cities along the Silk Road. The increased trade, and taxes obtained from such, was expected to defray much of the cost of the military campaigns.

At great expense, Wudi and his armies succeeded in extending Han control over much of the north and west. Chinese armies were not always victorious, especially in the last decades of Han Wudi's reign. One of the worst defeats came in 99 BCE, when the Xiongnu defeated a major Han force under the illustrious general Li Guangli, resulting in the deaths of tens of thousands of Chinese soldiers. In 90 BCE, Li blundered into a Xiongnu ambush, losing many thousands more of his men and being captured himself. Defeat in battle was deadly for both sides, as Chinese victories also often led to the slaughter of thousands of Xiongnu. Control of the captured regions remained tenuous throughout the Han dynasty, and the enormous expenses of the campaigns led to an almost empty treasury on the death of Han Wudi.

Later Han Developments   One major aspect of Han control of the northern and western frontier regions was the establishment of *tun-tian,* or "military colonies." In the first century BCE, garrisons were established along the frontier and in newly acquired territories, especially along the Silk Road. These were augmented agricultural colonies populated sometimes by tens of thousands of colonists, who were expected to make garrisons as self-sufficient as possible, provide men for regular and militia forces, and contribute toward sinicizing the regions. As new territories were acquired in Xiongnu lands, additional colonies were established and older ones greatly expanded. In some cases, the geography of the land was modified to suit agricultural settlement: Irrigation works and canals were constructed, and in one case a major river was redirected.

While only a few of the colonies were ever really self-supporting, the colonization was so effective that dismantling of the colonies was a perennial bone of contention in diplomatic contacts between the Xiongnu and Han China. A large colony at Turfan—a main station along the Silk Road—was subject to almost yearly Xiongnu raids and changed hands several times over the last two centuries of the Han dynasty. For defense of the colonies, the Han relied on large numbers of crossbowmen mounted along palisades and other walled fortifications.

Han domination of the Silk Road and its northern regions (including Xiongnu territories) depended on the ability of its armies to match the mobility of the Inner-Asian nomadic tribes. Thus, acquisition of a steady supply of horses was essential to the dynasty's continued control. The need for horses for offensive operations also limited the Han's ability to defend its territories. Several expeditions, including the famous Heavenly Horses campaign, were launched for the express purpose of acquiring horses for imperial armies. This need was an important reason for another Han policy—that of utilizing some border peoples as allies against Han enemies. Several Qiang tribes (a Tibetan people) were settled within Chinese territory, where, in return for Chinese goods, they assisted in maintaining order. Some of these Qiang tribes were successfully sinicized and, under Han supervision, were often deployed in campaigns against the Xiongnu. However, by the second century CE, Qiang raids rivaled those of the Xiongnu in terms of the damage inflicted on Han China. Now cut off from a steady supply of horses, and facing increased threats, the Han began a steady retreat from the northern and western territories. Although several major battles were fought late in the century as the Han attempted to recover territory, in fact, much of north China was coming increasingly under the control of barbarian regimes, a pattern that would continue for over 300 years following the fall of the Han dynasty.

In contrast, the southern and southwestern territories acquired during the Han era remained under Chinese control even after the fall of the Han dynasty, in the main due to large-scale Chinese migration and successful sinicization of the region. Korea also remained within the Chinese cultural sphere even if not directly ruled by China. In the north and northwest, an aggressive military policy had for many decades protected the trade flow along the Silk Road but provided only temporary—and expensive—respite from Xiongnu attacks. Often, a policy of payment of tribute proved more effective—or at least cheaper—in maintaining the peace along the borderlands of Xiongnu territory.

Military Regionalism and the Fall of the Han
Most of the last two centuries of the Han dynasty (23–220, sometimes referred to as the Later Han dynasty) saw large areas of northern and particularly western China come under the control of the Xiongnu and other nomadic peoples. In an expansion of its policy regarding some of the Qiang tribes, the Han court for a while allowed several Xiongnu tribes to reside within Chinese territory, providing a buffer to the more aggressive tribes and serving as the Han's cavalry arm.

By the mid-second century CE, nomadic raids combined with local Chinese rebellions to seriously weaken the Han. Socially and economically, this period also witnessed the rise of great Chinese families who, in effect, ruled territories from great estates and maintained their own private militaries. Eunuch influence increased at court, and, by the 170s, eunuchs were being put in command of armies; at one point, a eunuch was even appointed as overall commander in chief of the army. Nomad raids, internal rebellions, private armies, and increasingly powerful regional military governors were all signs that the dynasty was in trouble.

The 180s saw the most serious internal rebellion, by a group calling themselves "Yellow Turbans," which required a major expansion of military force. After successful suppression of the rebellion, the eunuchs at court attempted to reduce the power of the victorious generals and demobilize their armies. Instead, one of the generals marched on the capital, deposed the emperor, and placed another on the throne, while his troops engaged in wholesale slaughter of eunuchs. A coalition of other generals stepped in to "restore" the Han dynasty, but, in reality, China was now divided into almost independent territories under regional military commanders. In 220, the Han dynasty was formally abolished, and several of the regional lords proclaimed new dynasties. For over 350 years, China remained divided and often at war—with itself and outside invaders.

Weapons and Equipment By the Warring States era, the main weapon of the Chinese soldier was the crossbow, mainly for the infantry, but also for many of the cavalry. Making its appearance sometime in the fifth century BCE, the crossbow became the main weapon of the infantry by the late Warring States era. Development of the crossbow reached a high point in the early Han era. Han armies marched to battle with their front and flanking units equipped normally with various spears, long axes, or halberd-type weapons, while the main body of troops were armed with crossbows.

Most infantrymen during this whole period were also equipped with some sort of armor, depending on their function and need—and also a shield, though, by the early Han dynasty, fewer troops were routinely equipped with shields. Camps were sometimes protected by mounting connected shields to the sides and tops of carts, which would then encircle the camp. Records suggest that sometimes these "deer horn carts" were also used on a smaller scale as mobile platforms.

The Chinese had learned cast-iron technology by the fifth century BCE, long before its invention in the West, and produced some weapons, although until the Han iron was mainly used for agricultural implements. In the Warring States era, rulers needed large quantities of foodstuffs in order to maintain their large armies, and iron implements contributed greatly to the increased efficiency of agricultural productivity. During the Warring States and even the Qin eras, Chinese weapons were made predominantly of bronze, and by the third century BCE, the technology of bronze-working was so advanced that the strength and durability of Chinese weapons was unrivaled in the world. The use of iron increased significantly in the third century BCE; by the Han period, a large proportion of blade weapons were made of cast iron.

Assessing Ancient Chinese Warfare

The Warring States era in Chinese history saw a dramatic increase in the level and intensity of warfare. The various states developed an enormous capacity to make war, made possible by an economic and administrative transformation of China that influenced greatly the historical development of Chinese society.

With the resources made available from the tremendous economic growth, the various states raised enormous armies. Professional bureaucracies were also instituted to manage the recruitment, training, and maintenance of these armies. The soldiers and their officers became professional warriors, and men of talent and experience often offered up their services to the highest bidder. Battles became less frequent but increasingly intense, sometimes lasting several days, with the losers subject to horrific slaughter.

Centralization under the Qin and Han dynasties essentially ratified or sometimes modified the changes that had occurred earlier. The professional bureaucracies were able to ensure that the large military expeditions of the Qin and the Han under Wudi were adequately supplied with men and materiel. The manuals of the Warring States era became standard reading for commanders in the subsequent imperial period, as were certain principles that guided actions during and after war. Both the Qin and Han imperial courts strove to maintain a delicate balance between military effectiveness and civil control of the armies. Military men came to dominate society by the late

HIGHLIGHTS

The Battle of the Hydaspes

Alexander entered India at the invitation of the king of Taxala, a kingdom in the northwest of India, who saw in Alexander a potentially useful ally against his rival Porus, the most powerful king in the region. (Centuries later, Islamic raiders would also gain entry into India in part by invitation of Hindu kings to whom assistance in local rivalries outweighed the potential threat of invasion that appears foreign only if one falsely assumes Indian unity.) Happy to extend his conquests even farther, Alexander marched east into the Punjab until his army, by now numbering roughly 20,000, was halted by the flooded Hydaspes River. On the far bank sat King Porus with an army of perhaps 35,000, including as many as 100 war elephants.

Unless Alexander could cross the river, his plans for further conquest would be thwarted. But crossing the high waters in the teeth of enemy opposition was impossible. Alexander therefore made camp, as if to wait for the river to subside, and began what may be interpreted as a test of the comparative discipline and stamina of the two armies. Over the course of several weeks, he sent portions of his army both up and down the river in a series of feigned attempts at surprise crossings. Porus responded each time, but his troops began to meet the feints with less vigor—Alexander's constant, apparently pointless, activity lulled them into complacency—and they grew restless at the lack of real action. Meanwhile, Macedonian scouts discovered a ford some distance upstream from their camp. Noting the decreased vigilance of the Indian troops,

Alexander chose a dark, rainy night and marched half his army to the ford and across the river while the rest remained in the camp, ostentatiously making another feint downstream.

Alexander now had about 6000 cavalry, including the elite Companions, and 5000 infantry, including a portion of the phalanx and some *hypaspists* (shield bearers; see Chapter 3 for more on Alexander's army) and light-missile troops, on Porus's side of the river. Porus drew up his army with the elephants in front, knowing that the horses of Alexander's cavalry would not face them. Alexander responded by sending half his cavalry on a wide flanking maneuver around the Indian right wing. Anchoring his own right flank on the river and refusing his left to prevent encirclement by Porus's larger force, he then had his missile troops harass the elephants until they went out of control, disrupting their own lines. At that point, Alexander's flanking cavalry caught the advancing Indian right wing in the rear and continued down the line while Alexander charged with both the Companion cavalry and the phalanx. After vigorous fighting, Porus's army fled and Porus was taken captive. Macedonian discipline and combined arms tactics had proven their worth again, with far-reaching consequences for Indian warfare. The symbolic might and elusive military potential of elephants were not destroyed at the Hydaspes, however: They continued in use in India for centuries and were adopted at least in small numbers by Alexander's successors, who divided his empire between them after his death.

Han, when China was effectively divided into semi-independent, military-ruled territories.

INDIA: THE MAURYAN EMPIRE

Fourth-century BCE India had seen some consolidation, mostly by force of arms, of numerous small territories into a few larger kingdoms. But when

Alexander the Great invaded India in 326 BCE, he met armies that in equipment, organization, and tactics still closely resembled Indian armies of the earlier Vedic Age (see the Highlights box "The Battle of the Hydaspes"; see also Chapter 1). War elephants and an elite chariot corps formed both the practical and the symbolic core of such armies, intended as much as a display of the nobility and grandeur of the ruler and the warrior elites who supported him as an optimally efficient military force. This elite core was backed up by a mass of poorly trained and equipped infantry. Thus, in contrast to China in the Warring States era, continuity in arms, tactics, and, above all, the social composition of armies prevailed even as the size of military forces grew significantly and the strategic use of these armies in offensive warfare increased. This oddly static military situation owed much to the rigidly hierarchical nature of Indian society—in particular, the privileged position of warrior elites in the emerging caste system. This system seems to have become entrenched enough that centralizing efforts by ambitious Hindu monarchs could not bring about the sort of social transformation that characterized the Chinese experience. In effect, ideological barriers proved strong enough to prevent either the co-opting or the crushing of the Indian warrior elite along either Persian or Chinese lines.

Alexander's victories and the model of his army, however, stimulated the rise of a new group of young, dynamic, and innovative military leaders. The most successful of these leaders, Chandragupta Maurya, applied the lessons of the Greek wars to construct a new military system with which he, his son, and his grandson carved out an enormous empire. But, despite its success, the Mauryan Empire would prove short-lived by Roman or Chinese standards, breaking up within 140 years of its founding. This suggests that even the powerful military machine of Mauryan expansion had a less transformative impact on Indian society than did the military systems of the other great empires.

Mauryan Expansion, 322–250 BCE

Alexander's victories in 326 BCE had disrupted the political landscape of northwestern India. The kingdom he established before he left became a major player in north Indian politics, but it was soon to be eclipsed by a rising power farther east, one that eventually created an empire that covered most of the Indian subcontinent. Our knowledge of Chandragupta Maurya and the Mauryan Empire is limited and comes overwhelmingly from a few Indian literary sources, such as the *Arthashastra,* and Greek writings, such as that of Megasthenes. Apparently, Chandragupta came from a noble house in the kingdom of Magadha and had distinguished himself but was limited in how high he could rise in the army of the kingdom. He observed Alexander's victories, and at some point, though without success, he sought Alexander's assistance in overthrowing the king of Magadha. After this rebuff, he worked to create a

new army, incorporating the lessons learned from the defeats suffered at the hands of Alexander. In 322 BCE, Chandragupta marched his new army into Magadha and, after a series of very bloody battles, including a siege of the capital city of Pataliputra, the king was deposed and killed.

Once having ascended the throne of Magadha, Chandragupta embarked on nearly continual campaigns of conquest. The Greeks in Sind and Punjab he considered to be his most formidable opponents, but he was prepared, and his army was for the most part better equipped and led than the earlier Indian armies that had opposed the Greeks. Also, in a major innovation, Chandragupta relied on an expanded cavalry arm, much like Alexander, with the horses being armored to an extent not seen before in India. Finally, Chandragupta greatly expanded the size of his army by supporting local militia forces and promoting guerilla warfare.

Victory over Greek forces in India led Seleucus, the Greek ruler of former eastern portions of Alexander's empire, to dispatch a major military force in 305 to recover the lost territories and defeat the new power in north India. Once more breaking with India's military tradition, on learning of the approaching Greek force, Chandragupta decided to meet the Greeks in battle before they had traveled far into his territory. With the Indus River to their rear, the Greeks were surprised at the sudden appearance of their adversary. Chandragupta's victory was in large part due to the numbers he could bring into the battle (600,000 soldiers if the sources can be believed), including 20,000 well-trained cavalry.

Chandragupta and his successors devoted much of their energy toward expanding the empire and organizing the territory under their rule. The third Mauryan monarch, Ashoka (268–233 BCE) engaged in a long, bloody war to subdue the small kingdom of Kalinga (in modern Orissa), after which, tradition states, he became a devotee of Buddhism and ended the expansionist wars. Whatever the reason, after the conquest of Kalinga, his government's focus shifted from conquest to administration of the realm. By this time, Ashoka's empire included almost all of present-day south Asia (Figure 2.3).

The Mauryan Military System

The military conquests of the Mauryans were extraordinary, made possible not only by military reforms instituted by Chandragupta but also by an efficient

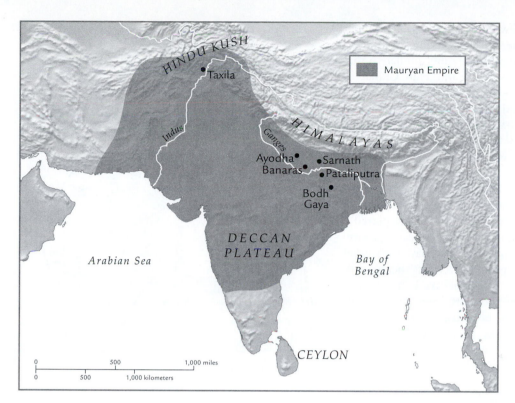

Figure 2.3 The Mauryan Empire, c. 250 BCE

government administration of the empire. Much like contemporary Warring States China, most of the political and economic focus of the Mauryan government was on military affairs. Centralized control and administrative efficiency were crucial to maintaining the large military forces of the empire, which was in an almost constant state of war. The Mauryan tax system was rationalized, and a professional bureaucracy administered it. This bureaucracy also was tasked to oversee vast public works projects, improve agricultural production, promote trade, and provide transportation and communications links for the military. This bureaucracy even directed military logistics, apparently managing to supply the armies in the field, even in the treacherous terrain of southern India. Consequently, Mauryan India during the reign of Ashoka was an economically prosperous, socially progressive land that was at the same time capable of supporting enormous armies on a nearly continuous war footing.

Organization and Strategy   The Mauryan army was on the surface organized in a traditional Indian manner, in four sections—infantry, cavalry, elephants, and chariots—with each section being supervised by a government board in the capital. The military forces

of the Mauryas also included a naval arm, of which we know little. The standing army of the Mauryans reportedly consisted of roughly 600,000 infantry, 30,000 cavalry, 9000 elephants, and 8000 chariots. However, it is probable that by this time chariots served more as status symbols for the elite than as vehicles in actual combat operations.

The Mauryans relied on a standing army, in which the soldiers were expected to serve for life. Recruitment into the army was not limited to those of the warrior caste, something that would often serve as a hindrance in Indian armies of later ages, when the caste system became much more rigid. Pay was reportedly quite good, and armies on campaign were accompanied by large numbers of servants and cooks, as well as artisans who built siege machines and made weapons. Generals served both as commanders in the field and as civil governors of districts. Being so critical to the prosperity and security of the empire, either trusted and proven comrades or royal family members were assigned to these posts.

Campaigns were usually carefully planned in advance, both to ensure the greatest chance of success and to keep disruption along the line of march to a minimum. Armies were not expected to live off the land, and so imperial agents went out ahead to gather such things as water, firewood, and fodder. Most other supply items were either brought along or supplied from the rear, in a system remarkably similar to that found in Warring States, Qin, and Han China. In addition, an extensive corps of spies would travel to the lands of the intended target to gather intelligence that would be relayed back to the army. At the same time, these spies worked to spread dissension and disinformation among the enemy.

Mauryan armies took full advantage of their size to overwhelm enemies. The Mauryans also broke with Indian military tradition in their willingness to engage in night fighting. The cavalry arm played a much more significant role than it had in earlier Indian armies, while chariots and elephants played a smaller role. Yet most battles were decided by the mass of infantrymen, who were almost always better trained and equipped than their opponents. Interestingly, while Chandragupta reformed his cavalry arm to more resemble that of the Greeks, he did not do the same with the infantry even though he had himself witnessed the efficacy of the Greek phalanx.

Weapons and Equipment   All weapons and equipment were provided by the imperial administration. As noted above, Mauryan soldiers were considered well paid and, when in garrison, were supplied with myriad servants, as men in garrison were expected to spend most of their time in training. A vast corps of artisans was organized in the camps to make the weapons and other equipment of war. As with the army itself, recruitment into this artisan corps was not limited by caste, and a major inducement was an exemption from certain taxes. And, much as in the Achaemenid Persian system, imperial supervisors circulated through the garrisons, ensuring that training was being carried out and that officers were not abusing their positions.

Weaponry was standardized, at least officially. Each infantryman was equipped with a longbow, which when used in combat was lodged between the ground and the man's left foot while the string was drawn back. Each infantrymen was also furnished with a small sword, and some used a long javelin rather than a bow. Many, though not all, infantrymen were also furnished a breastplate. The cavalry was equipped with lances, with the introduction of horse archery coming much

Mauryan War Elephant   Missile troops occupied the castle on the elephant's back, while its *mahout*, or driver, carried a spiked club to drive into the animal's brain in case it panicked and rampaged.

later in Indian history. Finally, each elephant normally carried three archers, and sometimes additional sword and javelin-bearing riders.

Assessing Ancient Indian Warfare

Much like the Achaemenid Persians and Alexander the Great, the Mauryan rulers sought to create a world empire. At its height, the Mauryan Empire constituted nearly the whole of the Indian subcontinent, as well as a portion of Central Asia. Except for the role of chariots, the military that was used to create this empire did not so much break from prior Indian military traditions as make them more efficient. Just as important were the administrative measures taken to efficiently govern the large empire. Without this, the large and effective Mauryan armies would not have been possible.

CONCLUSION

The syntheses of military and political systems, ideologies, and social structures that emerged during this age, syntheses profoundly influenced by warfare and the varying role of warrior elites, proved to have lasting influence on the course of societies in different parts of Eurasia. The major civilizations moved from this age into a period of increasing divergence of traditions built on the foundations laid during this time.

Two factors tended, however, to mitigate, at least to some extent, the trend toward divergence. The first was the growing importance of seaborne trade contacts and the increasing cross-cultural contact and exchange of goods and ideas. This carried with it the potential for increasing levels of naval warfare, the early history of which is the topic of Chapter 5. The other factor that increased cross-cultural contact was a period of renewed movement of peoples through migration, often resulting in invasions of settled societies. These migrations, which are the topic of Chapter 6 and link all the chapters in Part 2, were often the result, directly or indirectly, of the growth of imperial power that characterized the age covered in this chapter.

SUGGESTED READINGS

Briant, P. *From Cyrus to Alexander: A History of the Persian Empire.* Peter T. Daniels, trans. Winona Lake, IN: Eisenbrauns, 2002. A history of the empire including excellent coverage of administrative and military matters. Briant further develops some of these themes in his chapter, "The Achaemenid Empire," in K. Raaflaub and N. Rosenstein, *War and Society in the Ancient and Medieval Worlds* (Cambridge: Cambridge University Press, 1999).

The Cambridge History of Ancient China; From the Origins of Civilization to 221 BCE. Michael Loewe and Edward L. Shaughnessy, eds. Cambridge: Cambridge University Press, 1999.

The Cambridge History of China: Volume 1: The Ch'in and Han Empires, 221 B.C.–A.D. 220. Denis Twitchett and Michael Loewe, eds. Cambridge: Cambridge University Press, 1986. A valuable discussion in several chapters from both books of not only the political, social, and economic background of the military forces of ancient China but also the makeup of the armies of China.

Cook, J. M. *The Persian Empire.* New York: Barnes and Noble, 1983. A very detailed history of the Persians from the time of Cyrus until the destruction by Alexander. Cook assumes a previous knowledge of ancient Near Eastern history.

Frye, R. N. *The History of Ancient Iran.* Munich: C. H. Beck, 1983. A general history of Iran from earliest times through the fall of the Sassanians; includes sections on military and political organization. Particularly useful are Frye's discussions on sources and literature.

Kar, H. C. *Military History of India.* Calcutta: Firma KLM, 1980. Includes solid sections on the history, structure, and organization of the Mauryan military.

Lewis, Mark Edward. *Sanctioned Violence in Early China.* Albany: SUNY Press, 1992. A sophisticated analysis of the cultural causes and consequences of military transformation in Warring States China, showing the mutual development of ideology and organization. See also Lewis's "The Han Abolition of Universal Military Service," in *Warfare in Chinese History,* Hans Van deVen, ed. (Brill: Leiden, 2000), for a discussion of the basic structure of the Han armies, as well as evolving military strategy of the Han dynasty.

Loewe, Michael. "The Campaigns of Han Wu-ti." In *Chinese Ways in Warfare,* Frank A. Kierman Jr, ed. (Cambridge: Harvard University Press, 1974). A useful account of the Han military.

Mielczarek, M. *Cataphacti and Clibanarii. Studies on the Heavy Armoured Cavalry of the Ancient World.* Lodz: Oficyna Naukowa MS, 1993. A discussion of the evolution of the heavy cavalry that formed the basis of later Iranian armies, including the sources and their impact on the West.

Nath, Rajendra. *Military Leadership in India: Vedic Period to Indo-Pak Wars.* New Delhi: Lancers Books, 1990. Contains good, comprehensive sections on the influences on Mauryan military leadership

Thapar, Romila. *Early India, from the Origins to 1300.* Berkeley: University of California Press, 2002. A thorough survey of early Indian history, placing military and political developments in their social and cultural contexts.

CHAPTER 3

Polis and Phalanx:
Greece and Macedon, 800–200 BCE

The age of disruptions in southwest Asia and the eastern Mediterranean that began around 1200 BCE saw the eventual reemergence of imperial states in most of that area, a pattern mirrored in developments in China and, in different ways, in India. But developments in Greece would follow a different course, with significant implications for military history. Instead of following the large-state path of military-political development, the Greeks developed small-scale political organizations that generated an effective style of infantry shock combat. The Macedonians then perfected this style and fit it into a combined arms force unmatched in ancient times for its tactical flexibility and effectiveness. It was a style that would carry Macedonian arms and Greek culture to vast areas of southwest Asia. This chapter traces those developments.

GREECE: THE RISE OF COMMUNAL INFANTRY

The general crisis noted above befell the Mycenaean states in Greece. With their destruction came the end of many of the attributes of civilization and, perhaps for a time, even sedentary agriculture, initiating the Dark Ages, a period of more than three centuries of development culminating in the creation of the civilization of classical Greece. The beginning of the Dark Ages saw a precipitous decline in the number of inhabited sites and a wave of migration throughout Greece. Some of these migrants left the peninsula and made their way to the coast of Asia Minor. Others came together and began to reestablish communities in Greece and return to a more sedentary lifestyle.

The Homeric World

Given the nature of the disruption at the end of the Bronze Age, little is known for certain about warfare during the majority of the Dark Ages. There are,

however, glimpses in the works of Homer, the *Iliad* and the *Odyssey*. Although Homer's epics are set in the world of the Bronze Age Mycenaeans, much of the descriptions of warfare and social organization more likely refer to conditions in the eighth century BCE, when the Homeric tradition assumed written form.

The warfare described in the *Iliad* is best characterized as aristocratic. Battles centered on individual combats between the leaders of various contingents. These heroic warriors were carried into battle on chariots but then dismounted to engage in hand-to-hand combat. Such combat cannot be representative of the Mycenaean period, whose elite fought from chariots as their Near Eastern counterparts did (see Chapter 1), rather than using the so-called battle taxi (chariot) tactics of the *Iliad*. But the basic nature of warfare in this period can be inferred from Homer's description. Homer undoubtedly knew that, like the horse in his time, the chariot of the Mycenaeans was a status symbol as well as a mode of battlefield transportation. It might be assumed that Homer merely linked the chariot rather than the horse to the heroes of the *Iliad,* knowing that his own aristocratic warriors rode into battle on horses and then dismounted to fight on foot. Moreover, the manner of combat was to fight at close quarters with spear, sword, and battle-axe, with body armor and shield for defense. Only infrequently, and with a certain amount of disdain, did the bow, the weapon par excellence of the chariot warrior, appear.

The Homeric epics also provide evidence for the value system of the Mycenaean warriors of the eighth century BCE. These aristocrats were clearly *status warriors,* men motivated to fight in pursuit of individual glory and honor. This type of warfare was generally rather small in scale and was dominated by raiding in search of booty, which was awarded to individual warriors by their leaders as a sign of status. The most famous Homeric example involved Achilles'

Figure 3.1 The Mediterranean and the Greek World

disagreement with Agamemnon, who claimed for himself the woman Achilles took as a prize after sacking her town and killing her husband and brothers. This affront to Achilles' honor led Achilles and his men, the Myrmidons, to withdraw from the fighting.

Achilles' men showed that, although the aristocratic warriors were the dominant force on the battlefield, they were not the only ones present. Commoners participated in warfare as aristocrats' retinues, overshadowed by the nobility but constantly present. Large-scale combat was part of the warfare described in the epics, showing eighth-century warfare in a state of transition in which the common man began to emerge as a factor on the battlefield. Within a century, the transformation of Greek warfare was complete as the community of the Dark Ages became the *polis* (pl., *poleis*) of Classical Greece.

The Rise of the Polis

The eighth century BCE witnessed a rebirth of Greek civilization. By the end of that century, the number and size of urban centers had grown, colonies were being founded throughout the Mediterranean, and Greeks were once again writing, having adopted and improved on the alphabet they borrowed from the Phoenicians. But the key development during this period was the transformation of Greek communities into poleis, or city-states (Figure 3.1).

The Nature of the Polis   During the Archaic period (c. 800–500 BCE), many of the Greek communities grew from villages to full-fledged towns. The Greek term for such an urban center is *asty* (pl., *astē*). Most *astē* had two major components: The first was a gathering place, or *agora,* where public meetings were held and where market activities could take place. The second was a place of refuge, often located on an easily defended position such as a hilltop. The term for such a hilltop fortification is *acropolis;* the Acropolis at Athens is the most famous of many such places. Because it was the safest place within the *asty,* those buildings that were important to the entire community, such as temples and, later, treasuries, often were located there. Not every village became an *asty;* some were absorbed within the community of a nearby *asty,* becoming part of the agrarian hinterland that supported the urban center. These villages and agricultural land were known as the *chora.* In some regions, such as Laconia, an urban center never developed.

There also emerged a sense of community that tied together the members of the *asty* and the *chora* into a new institution, the polis. What made the polis distinct from the *asty* was that it was not just a tangible collection of buildings but a collection of ideas. It was an urban center, true, but it also included its hinterland and people, and it was recognized as a political entity with an independent foreign policy—hence our reference to the polis as a city-state. Moreover, although we generally refer to poleis by place names such as Athens, Corinth, or Sparta, the ancient Greeks thought of the polis as the community of people. Thus, inscriptions refer not to a place but to a people: "the council and assembly of the Athenians decree . . . " or the "constitution of the Spartans says . . . " are the ways in which the activities, laws, and decisions of a polis are stated. In fact, the idea of the polis was so important to the Greeks that it became part and parcel of what it meant *to be* Greek, along with speaking the Greek language. This is illustrated by Aristotle's famous statement that "man is by nature an animal intended to live in a polis."

Along with the development of the polis, there was a definite growth in the population of Greece. Although most poleis were initially ruled by elites of a sort, descendants of the earlier Dark Age aristocrats, there was clearly an increase in the number of ordinary farmers who occupied substantial portions of the polis's land. This social change would extend and complete the transformation in warfare already visible in the epics.

Armies and Warfare

The armies that defended the poleis of classical Greece were markedly different from those described by Homer. Gone were the heroes who sought out battle with their peers in the opposing camp, rode to combat in battle taxis (chariots), and cut bloody lanes through the ranks of the common troops of their opponent's retinue. They were replaced by an army of heavily armed foot soldiers called *hoplites,* who fought in closely packed, disciplined formations called *phalanxes.*

Hoplite Warriors in Phalanx Formation Note the overhand thrusting mode of spear wielding and the piper, to whose playing the phalanx would march in time.

A Hoplite Revolution? How did this transformation come about? Did it follow or cause political change in the polis? One school of thought holds that sometime in the eighth century BCE, new types of equipment were introduced, including a large round shield known as the *hoplon,* the enclosed Corinthian helmet, and a bronze cuirass that protected the upper body. This panoply was not well suited to the type of heroic warfare described earlier—the shield was too large and heavy to move about quickly, the enclosed helmet was detrimental to the vision required in individual combat, and so on. The new equipment was much more suited to fighting in cohesive groups whose effectiveness would, moreover, be enhanced by greater numbers. Thus, by about 650 BCE, the farmers who made up an increasingly important portion of the population and who could provide the necessary arms, *hopla,* were allowed to join the new phalanxes. Having become crucial to the defense of the community, these men then demanded a greater say in the community's decision making, breaking the aristocratic monopoly on politics.

This model is problematic, however, for both military and political reasons. First, the introduction of new military equipment without a preexisting doctrine on how to use it, especially in a premodern economy where doing so would be a risky economic venture, seems highly unlikely. What seems more reasonable is that a form of fighting involving closely formed ranks, and probably substantial numbers of men, was already in the process of replacing the earlier form of heroic combat, as we have already seen emerging in Homer's descriptions of war. The arms in use then evolved to be more effective in the new style of fighting. Moreover, as men from non-elite families became more important to the state economically as well as militarily, we can assume that they asserted claims to an ever-increasing role in the political life of the community over time. The enfranchisement of these individuals during the sixth and fifth centuries BCE should not then be seen as something new based on their new role in defending the state, but rather as the culmination and formalization of an interlocked socioeconomic, political, and military process that had been taking place for nearly 300 years. In other words, development of a coherent community led to effective infantry tactics as much as infantry warfare built communities. The social reorganization of some poleis into economically defined groups systematized and made more efficient the link between politics and military manpower.

The Cause of Wars   As the individual poleis consolidated their territories and their populations expanded, most of the arable land in Greece was claimed. This led to small-scale border clashes over disputed land. But notions of polis honor and the micro-imperialism of the tyrants who ruled many city-states in the sixth century also triggered wars. And even in this period when most wars involved individual poleis fighting each other, larger alliance systems could develop, as in the Lelantine War, which some historians see as the first Greek world war. In short, the sophistication of states and their external policies probably developed, not surprisingly, more quickly than the tactical forms of warfare and military organization.

Strategy and Tactics   One of the aggrieved states would begin to muster its force of hoplites. These men were not professional soldiers—they were farmers or merchants, rich and middling. They supplied all of their own equipment, which likely varied within certain basic parameters. They were thus limited in the type of campaign they could mount. The campaign could not be fought during critical periods of the agricultural year, nor could it last too long. Campaigns therefore occurred in the few months after planting and before the harvest. As there was no formal command or logistical structure, hoplites were expected to bring along all they would need for the campaign, limiting actual campaigning to a matter of

weeks at most. The hoplites would muster at a prearranged place, often in the company of family and clan members. They might be accompanied by slaves to help them with their panoply (armor and weapons) and supplies. This force would then march off to meet the enemy phalanx. If the enemy were obliging, the two phalanxes would meet on level ground—perhaps agreed on in advance. If the enemy were not ready to meet in open battle, deciding instead to remain behind their walls, the hoplite force would begin to ravage the territory of the enemy, though how much actual damage such ravaging caused is a matter of debate. But physical damage is probably a moot point, as the effect was psychological: It was simply not acceptable to the members of a polis for the land belonging to their fellow citizens, members of their community, to be trampled by the feet of an invader—in effect, the individual honor of Homeric heroes had become the collective honor of the community. Only a strong personality such as Pericles, Athens' leader during the Peloponnesian War, could restrain hoplite forces from giving battle after such an insult.

Once the two forces had arrived at the level plain that was to be their battlefield, the hoplites would begin to order themselves within their respective phalanxes. There was no formal organization for the armies of most poleis. Instead, hoplites would form up in ranks with their kinsmen and, perhaps, fellows from their neighborhood or village. It was these ranks that likely provided the context for the training hoplites received, which would not have been large-unit drill but rather small-unit and individual practice, often formalized in competitions at festivals. In general, a formation of eight or so ranks was most common. The formation would include men of various ages, ranging from very young to very old. Each might contribute in his own way: Young men could be deployed as skirmishers while the presence of older, experienced men tended to steady the ranks.

Forming up took time, and while waiting for the order to advance, many hoplites would take the opportunity to lay down their shields and remove their helmets—some men would even indulge in a prebattle cup of wine. Once both sides were fully deployed, the order would be given to advance. Overseeing deployment and putting the phalanx in motion was the only real role for officers in the world of phalanx warfare; generals led either by virtue of their social and political position or, in democracies, were elected.

There was little need to do more once the phalanx was in motion, as maneuvering tended to be minimal: The phalanx simply moved forward toward the enemy. The hoplites were drawn up in tight formation with each man's shield overlapping that of the man to his left. This led the phalanx to drift to the right as it advanced, as each man tried to stay as close to his neighbor's shield as he could. The men on the extreme right wing, with no one to protect their unshielded side, ended up willingly overlapping the enemy left.

As the two phalanxes drew close to one another, they surged forward into combat. At this point, reconstruction of hoplite combat is controversial. Some historians stress tight formations and shock: In this view, as the two lines came together, there was a tremendous tumult as spears struck shields—and sometimes snapped—and shields clashed together. After the initial hand-to-hand combat of the charge, the *othismos*—a pushing—would occur as men supported their comrades in the front ranks or stepped up to replace the fallen. Other historians think looser formations prevailed, with spears wielded in a variety of ways and the fighting resembling a mass of individual duels. In either case, the battle continued until one side began to give way. At that point, panic tended to spread through the losing side, and it would break ranks and run. Casualties were often highest in the brief pursuit that followed, as men abandoned shields and turned their backs to their enemies.

Battle in ancient Greece was thus a struggle between the hoplite forces of contending poleis. The great majority of the men involved fought in the ranks of the phalanx. In the early period of hoplite warfare, there is little mention of other forces. Occasionally, light infantry forces are mentioned, usually consisting of men who were not able to provide the equipment required of a hoplite. Cavalry is rarely mentioned until later in Greek warfare.

Historians have sometimes called hoplite battle ritualistic, and it is easy to see why. All of the forces fought according to the same set of rules and even at agreed-on sites. Ritual, especially in the form of religious ceremonies before battle, formed an element of the cultural context within which battle took place. After the battle, truces were declared, allowing the defeated to claim their dead and the victors to erect a trophy, dedicated to Zeus, displaying arms taken from the enemy casualties. While this is certainly a formalized, ritualized style of warfare, it was not *ritualistic,* a term usually used to refer to warfare

in which the spilling of blood is minimized—combat often ending with the first wounds inflicted. Such was not the case in Greek warfare. Battles were quite bloody, although limited pursuit and immediate post-battle truces kept forces from being annihilated. Such battles did, however, settle disputes, at least for a time, and have led some historians to credit the Greeks with inventing the idea of *decisive battle,* which is allegedly central to Western warfare (see the Issues box "A 'Western' Way of War?"). But long-term solutions were, in fact, rare, and war usually broke out again in the near future.

The Spartan Anomaly

The Spartan Anomaly   Sparta was the one city-state in Greece that deviated from the pattern of warfare described above. By the sixth century BCE, the Spartans had established the only real standing army in Greece, training hoplites who can be classified as professionals. Sparta's deviation from the norm stemmed from a war fought in the eighth century in which Sparta had defeated neighboring Messenia. Sparta had then reduced many of the citizens of that region to the status of serfs, called *helots.* The helots, who lived quite a distance from Sparta, had to turn over half of their produce to their Spartan masters. In the middle of the seventh century, the helots, emboldened by a Spartan defeat at the hands of rival Argos, rebelled against Spartan control. The uprising by the Messenians nearly ended in defeat for the Spartans, but they were able to put down the rebellion. Afterward, Spartan attitudes hardened, and the Spartan system of the classical period developed.

The Spartans reduced the helots to the status of slaves of the state and allotted land and helots to work it to each Spartan. As a result, rather than serving part-time as citizen-farmers, the Spartans could spend their time training for war, preempting the threat of another war with Messenia or Argos. The Spartans also made use of terror to control the helot population and make them more docile servants of the state. For example, the Spartans annually declared war on the helots so that Spartans could kill helots with impunity. Even more frightening was the work of the *Krypteia,* the Spartan secret police. All men under age 30 served for two years in the *Krypteia.* Under certain circumstances, most likely when a helot revolt threatened, these young men were sent out armed only with a dagger and a supply of rations. They were to kill every helot they met, and they sometimes sought out particularly strong helots to slay.

A "Western" Way of War?

There is, without doubt, a "Western" tradition of philosophy (reading "Western" as short for western European and later American) dating back to Socrates, Plato, and Aristotle. There are also associated intellectual traditions in mathematics, art, and natural philosophy or science, dating back to cultural traditions established largely in fifth-century Athens and the wider Greek world of which it was a part. Is there also a "Western" way of war whose roots reach back to the classical Greek poleis and their warfare? Yes, at least according to historian Victor Davis Hanson, who sees two elements of Greek warfare as foundational to so-called Western warfare. First, there is the *civic militarism* of warfare conducted by a population of citizen-soldiers whose participation in politics and the military is intimately linked; and second, there is the tradition of face-to-face combat aiming at *decisive battle* that made Western warfare more brutal but also more effective than non-Western warfare, which tended to be more indirect in its strategic and tactical approaches. Hanson claims that these two characteristics in combination, embodied not just in military practice but in a military intellectual tradition, produced a style of military organization and warfare that has had unmatched success in world history and has dominated the globe from the nineteenth century on.

Hanson's thesis has received widespread attention. It is also, in the opinion of this book's authors and an increasing number of other historians, fundamentally wrong. It can be criticized on a number of counts. Perhaps most important, unlike the intellectual traditions mentioned above (and despite Hanson's claims for a military intellectual tradition), historical continuity between classical Greek warfare and modern Western warfare is impossible to demonstrate. Any tradition of civic militarism was already dying in Greece after the Peloponnesian War (see below), and despite a revival in different forms in Macedon and the early Roman Republic, it was definitively dead in imperial Rome. Medieval and early modern European warfare cannot possibly be characterized by civic militarism. Only with the American and French revolutions does a relationship between military service and citizenship reappear in Western history, and that revival was hardly inspired by Greek models.

Hanson is also wrong about the effectiveness of Western warfare, even ignoring the civic militarism argument. Western armies, putative heirs to the Greeks, lost battles and wars throughout history to foes of all sorts—only through a highly selective use of examples can Hanson maintain an illusion of unbroken military success for Western arms. Hanson's selectivity extends to who counts as Western. Carthage, geographically west of Rome, does not, since Rome eventually won the Punic Wars (despite losing most of the decisive battles to Hannibal). In addition, Byzantium, direct institutional and cultural heir to Rome, replete with a continuous tradition of military literature, does not, presumably because civic militarism could only be applied to Byzantium laughably, and Byzantine strategic and tactical traditions stressed avoiding battle. (Of course, the most famous Roman military writer in the West, Vegetius, also advised avoiding battle, in which advice he is indistinguishable from the Chinese writer Sun Tzu.) Also, Byzantium eventually disappeared. Who counts as Western exposes the unexamined philosophical assumptions underpinning the Western label, assumptions that prove, on closer inspection, to be both untenable and often Eurocentric. If civic militarism (that is, an intimate connection between political and military participation) and brutal military effectiveness are the essential components of a Western way of war, then the nomads of the Eurasian steppes are the supreme exemplars of that tradition (see Chapter 6 for more on nomadic warfare).

Finally, modern doctrine in the U.S. army—presumably, a Western force—stresses not face-to-face mass charges, as in Greek phalanx warfare, but indirection, weak spots, and mobility, the very strategies and tactics that for Hanson characterize inferior, non-Western ways of war. It is hard to see what, other than a politically motivated polemic, can be salvaged from Hanson's thesis—certainly, nothing of value for serious military history.

Spartan Hoplites   The effectiveness of all Greek phalanxes was built on the intimate social ties that bound the men of the phalanx together; the Spartans added rigorous training to that social solidarity.

In order to create the army necessary to enforce this system, the Spartans began preparing young men for war virtually at birth. All male Spartan newborns were inspected by the elders of their tribes; those deemed unfit were thrown into the gorge of Mount Taygetus. Those deemed fit lived at home until age 7 and then entered the *agogē*, the Spartan way of life. They were taught to live on modest rations and to endure being left alone, and they learned dances that involved the weapons of a hoplite to accustom them to moving to the sound of the flute (phalanxes marched in time to flute playing). At age 12, training became more intense—boys were deprived of food and encouraged to steal rations, since this would prepare them to live off the land (stealing was fine—but those who were discovered were whipped for having been caught). To prepare for the rigors of campaigning, the boys received but a single thin cloak to be used year-round and slept on a bed of reeds. At age 18 or 20, the young men joined a mess of about fifteen men. They would live in the barracks with their messmates until age 30, at which time they could start their own households (they could marry at 20 but still lived in the barracks).

This harsh system allowed the Spartans to create a superlative hoplite force. The Spartans organized their phalanx into companies and regiments unknown to other phalanxes and had a more formal command structure than anything seen elsewhere in Greece. They drilled in special maneuvers that made the Spartan phalanx much more effective and flexible on the battlefield. And the harsh training gave the Spartans a fearsome reputation as doughty soldiers capable of enduring hardship in silence.

There was, however, a price for this system: a perennial shortage of manpower. Some of this was made up for by the inclusion in the Spartan army of *perioikoi* (literally, "those who dwell around"), members of nearby towns who had surrendered control of their foreign policy to the Spartans in return for protection. They governed themselves but followed Sparta's lead in foreign affairs. Sparta also had allies organized into a confederation known as the Peloponnesian League, although Spartan control of the league varied greatly. The nature and extent of Sparta's manpower problems have been debated—there was probably no shortage of actual Spartans, just of ones well off enough to contribute to the mess and thus serve in the phalanx—but it was severe enough that at times the Spartans promised helots freedom and rights in exchange for military service, often far from home.

Greek Warfare in Transition: The Persian Wars

The essential nature of Greek warfare remained relatively static until the early fifth century BCE. At that point, the rise of Persia (see Chapter 2) forced the Greeks to reconsider their way of war. The Persians first made contact with Greeks living in Ionia in Asia Minor in the middle of the sixth century when the Persians conquered the Lydian kingdom. This then brought the Persians into conflict with mainland Greeks. The Persians' ability to wage war on a massive scale on land and at sea presented a threat of a type no Greek state had ever faced before. By the early fifth century, the Persians' more sophisticated form of warfare forced the poleis of the Greek peninsula to adapt or face conquest. Greeks had to cooperate on a more extensive level than they usually had before and to think in terms of strategic, operational, and tactical options that their method of warfare did not often require.

The Persian conquest of Ionia in the 540s BCE seems not to have had an immediate negative effect on relations between the Greeks of the region and the Persians. Indeed, when Darius I launched a disastrous campaign against the Scythians in 514, it was Ionian Greeks who secured his bridgehead over the Danube, allowing the remnants of his army to cross back to safety. But in 499, the Ionians rose up against the Great King, undoubtedly because the autocratic nature of Persian kings led them to interfere in the internal affairs of the Ionian poleis, something that was antithetical to the Greeks' concept of autonomy. Political intrigues at Miletus triggered the revolt; Aristogoras, its ruler, sought aid from mainland Greece when things went badly. He looked first to the Spartans, but they declined. He then approached Athens, whose close ties to the Ionians led them to send twenty warships. The rebels and their allies did well initially, even taking and burning the local Persian capital of Sardis. But shortly thereafter, the Athenians withdrew; the revolt came to an end in 493 BCE.

The Battle of Marathon

In order to avenge the burning of Sardis and prevent further Greek interference in Persian affairs, Darius I ordered an expedition against those Greeks who had come to the aid of the Ionian rebels. After securing his control over Ionia through symbolic concessions while waging a diplomatic and psychological offensive throughout Greece, in 490 BCE, he dispatched a force of some 600 ships (one-third warships and two-thirds transports) and about 25,000 troops. The Persian fleet sacked coastal cities and established a base at Marathon, where there was a secure place to beach their ships and an open strip of land that would allow the Persian cavalry to maneuver.

Apprised of the landing, Athenians debated their course of action. With requested Spartan aid delayed and uncertain, ostensibly for religious reasons, some argued in favor of staying within the city walls and preparing for a siege, but a pro-Persian faction in the city made waiting potentially treacherous. Others, led by Miltiades, a general who had fought in the Ionian Revolt and knew the Persians, successfully urged marching out to meet "the barbarian." The Athenians took up a position blocking the main route to Athens. What happened next is disputed, but it seems that after several days of waiting in sight of each other—the Athenians for Spartan reinforcements, and the Persians for a signal from the pro-Persian faction in the city—the Persians sent perhaps 10,000 men, including most of their cavalry, in the fleet to Athens. Learning from Ionian deserters of the fleet's departure, Miltiades decided to attack the remaining 15,000 Persians the next day, risking all on a quick victory and a forced march back to Athens.

To counter the broader frontage of the Persian line, Miltiades thinned his ranks in the center, opposite the best Persian troops; the center would fight a holding action while the wings crushed the weaker Persian levies. The Athenian army advanced at first light, breaking into a run at about 150 yards when the first volleys of Persian arrows fell amid their ranks. The fighting was fierce, but the heavier armor and weapons and the tight formation of the Greeks proved decisive on the flanks. The center was on the verge of breaking when the victorious wings wheeled in, inflicting heavy casualties among the Persian troops. After a valiant fight, they broke and fled to their ships. The Persians lost 6400 killed, an unknown number of prisoners, and seven ships; the remainder of the fleet and army sailed home on hearing the news. The Athenians lost a mere 192 hoplites.

The Great Invasion, 480–479 BCE

The victory at Marathon left the "men of Marathon" convinced of the superiority of the hoplite phalanx defending its polis and of the ability of Greece to resist another Persian invasion using traditional methods of warfare. The heavy armor and weapons of the citizen-soldiers had given them an advantage over the lighter armor, wicker shields, and light spears and bows of the Persians—at least when the hoplites were able to choose their ground and negate the threat of the Persian cavalry.

Back in Persia, however, Darius set the powerful administrative machinery of his empire in motion, not for a small expedition, but for a major invasion of mainland Greece. For a decade, the Persians mustered their near-limitless resources, provoking rebellions with their demands for manpower, ships, money, and supplies. Darius died in 486, but his son Xerxes completed the preparations, suppressing the revolts, constructing more than 1300 warships, and calling for nearly 200,000 troops. He established numerous supply depots in friendly territories and sent envoys to Greece demanding submission and spreading the word of the size of his forces. In Greece, reactions to this threat were mixed. Some Greek states considered submitting or collaborating, at times for reasons of internal politics. Other states, notably Athens and Sparta, made clear their intention to resist by executing Persian envoys. For most of the decade, few concrete preparations took place, but by 481, Athens was cooperating with the Peloponnesian League; they met at Corinth to discuss matters. Poleis from all over Greece sent representatives to discuss the pan-Hellenic security problem and to determine a common strategy. Though the Greeks did not have any structure to discuss strategy—there was no alliance high command—they managed to cobble a plan together with Sparta taking overall command, although the lines of authority were informal and there was no way to coordinate logistical support. The league also sent representatives to the powerful Greek tyrant of Syracuse in Sicily. He promised to send massive aid: 20,000 hoplites, 200 triremes, and 8000 cavalry and light troops. But they never appeared because of an attack in 480 by Carthage.

Only in Athens did more substantial planning take place, and it was the work of one man—Themistocles. Themistocles was a politician who saw that the Greeks could win only if they could effectively counter the sophisticated Persian war machine on land *and* at sea. To do this, the Greeks needed a substantial fleet. In the years after Marathon, Themistocles worked tirelessly to isolate those who opposed his plans and to change the government at Athens, putting more power in the hands of the board of generals on which Themistocles frequently served. When Athenian silver mines hit a massive new vein of ore in 483, Themistocles got the money appropriated to building a fleet of nearly 200 triremes.

Xerxes mustered his army at Susa in 481 and began the long march to the Greek mainland. In 480, he crossed over from Asia Minor into Europe at the Hellespont on a pair of pontoon bridges built on the hulls of 600 of his warships. His army was huge, but what does that mean? It may have numbered as many as 180,000–200,000, made up of a core of Persian troops, including the 10,000 Immortals who formed the imperial guard, and supported by provincial levies designed to advertise the size and strength of the empire. A fleet of perhaps 700 warships and numerous supply vessels supported the army. Xerxes demonstrated his religious tolerance by providing gifts to various Greek religious sanctuaries along the way. All of these activities were part of the Persians' systematic propaganda campaign.

The Peloponnesian League met again to try to firm up their strategy. The dubious loyalty of many Greek poleis rendered several northern lines of defense politically and strategically untenable. A force of several thousand, led by 300 Spartans under King Leonidas and with their seaward flank supported by Themistocles' fleet, defended the pass at Thermoplyae for three days before Xerxes turned their inland flank using a little-used path. The fleet was compelled to withdraw.

The Greeks now had another strategic decision to make. The league decided to defend the Isthmus of Corinth, but this left Athens open to attack. Themistocles, however, convinced many of the fleet commanders to meet at Salamis rather than retreat to the Isthmus. He planned to evacuate Athens and stake everything on a naval engagement, which, if successful, would also keep the Isthmus line from being outflanked. Many Athenians agreed to evacuate to islands including Salamis and Aegina. Themistocles was able to entice the Persian fleet into a general engagement in the narrow straits at Salamis and win a decisive victory, which tipped the balance of naval forces in favor of the Greeks (see Chapter 5 for details of naval warfare).

The victory at Salamis had major consequences for the outcome of the war. The Persian fleet, having lost perhaps 200 ships to 40 Greek triremes, withdrew to protect the pontoon bridges over the Hellespont. The Persians still had a formidable army, but the loss of the fleet forced some of the army to return home for lack of logistical support. As Xerxes had ravaged Attica and sacked Athens just before Salamis, he withdrew claiming victory and leaving the subjugation of Greece to his lieutenant Mardonius.

Mardonius had some of the best Persian troops, including many of the Persian regulars and the Immortals. But the size of his army was greatly reduced, and in 479, the Greek allies risked battle near Plataea, on terrain that allowed the Greek phalanx relatively secure flanks. The Persian cavalry caused serious problems for the Greeks until their commander was killed and his coordinated attacks came to a halt. After a hard fight, the allies prevailed. At almost the same time, the Greek fleet landed troops in Ionia and defeated Persian forces there. The Persian threat was ended.

Comparison of the Greek and Persian Systems

Two very different military systems based on two very different societies fought the Persian Wars. The Greek victory at Plataea once again showed that hoplites on carefully chosen ground had an advantage over more lightly equipped Persian infantry, lending weight to a modern perception of the Persians as militarily ineffective Orientals—a view that is based heavily on anti-Persian rhetoric by later Greeks writers and politicians. On closer examination, however, the Persians were, in fact, a more capable military, at least on the strategic and operational levels, and they influenced the Greeks in these areas. On the strategic level, the Persian Wars, especially the campaign in 480 BCE, showed that the Greeks were virtually incapable of any sort of concerted action. In the wake of the war, the Greeks created more formal leagues with voting structures and war chests. On the operational level, the superiority of the Persians in planning and executing joint operations between land and naval forces influenced the Greeks greatly—even the Spartans recognized the need for a navy by the end of the century. Lastly, on the tactical level, though the hoplite phalanx would remain the force of choice on Greek battlefields, Persian archery and cavalry had exposed the tactical limitations of armies built exclusively on heavy infantry, however effective, and Greeks made increasing use of cavalry and light troops in the fifth century BCE.

The Peloponnesian War, 431–404 BCE

In the remainder of the fifth century BCE, Greek politics in mainland Greece and in the Aegean polarized around two great leagues—the Peloponnesian League, headed by Sparta, and the Delian League, headed by Athens. The Peloponnesian League had existed for some time. The Delian League formed at first to carry on the war against Persia and to form a bulwark against Persian aggression. Initially, all its states contributed men, ships, and money to a war chest; but, over time, Athens monopolized the league's military force, converting allied contributions of men and ships to money and making it clear that membership in the league was no longer voluntary. The Athenians then reinterpreted allied monetary contributions as tribute, and the league became their empire.

The empire was crucial to the further development of Athenian democracy. The money the Delian League generated for Athens allowed it to pay the lower-class rowers of the Athenian navy that held together the empire, whose members were largely on Aegean islands and in Ionia. Money and military participation for the naval class, too poor for hoplite service, were closely linked to full and continuing political enfranchisement. Imperially based democracy and the cultural self-confidence Athens had gained from fifty years of military success since the time of Marathon were a crucial part of the context for the developments in philosophy, history, drama, and art for which Athens is best known. In short, the arts of war and the arts of peace went hand in hand.

The Causes of the War   The growth of Athenian power troubled the Spartans. Sparta was the status quo power in Greece. It had led, at least in name, the allies in the war against Persia in 480–79 BCE, and it was the dominant power for at least twenty years thereafter. But as Athens' power grew, the Spartans' position was jeopardized. Tensions were heightened by the obvious political difference between democratic Athens and monarchical Sparta, a difference central to the internal politics of many of both cities' allies. Thucydides explicitly states that Sparta was motivated by fear when it began the great Peloponnesian War in 431. When Corcyra, an Athenian ally, and Corinth, a member of the Peloponnesian League, went to war in 431, mediation failed, both leagues lined up behind their allies, and the war began. Some still opposed war: The astute Spartan king Archidamus noted that Sparta might need to go to war with Athens, but not at this time—if it did, it would be a war Spartans would leave to their children. He was proved right, as the changes in Greek warfare latent since the end of the Persian Wars transformed the limited engagements of the sixth century into a long and bitter conflict in which the customs of earlier Greek combat went by the boards.

Strategy   The Peloponnesian War saw numerous actions both on land and at sea, and in these actions, the impact of the Persian Wars can be seen. Strategically, the Greeks had learned much from the war with Persia, and both alliances planned and executed complex strategies. The war's complicated alliances dictated operations on several fronts at once. The Athenian strategy formulated by Pericles at the beginning of the war would have been impossible sixty years earlier: He succeeded in convincing the Athenians to abandon Attica and remain within the walls of Athens, her fortified naval arsenal at Piraeus, and the famous Long Walls that connected them, relying on the fleet for supplies. He hoped that after two or three years the Spartans would give up when they could not draw the Athenians into a hoplite battle. Unfortunately, Spartan resolve lasted longer than Pericles anticipated, and something of a strategic stalemate developed between Spartan land power and Athenian naval power.

Subversion of allies and conversion of neutrals became important tools in the conflict; the correspondingly increased need to securely hold allies in place led both sides, especially Athens, into increasingly brutal measures against revolts and resistance. Both sides also looked farther afield for ways to break the stalemate. This proved disastrous for Athens when its expedition against Syracuse in 415–13 resulted in a major defeat for both its fleet and its army. Still, Athenian forces recovered in the years after Syracuse and remained more than a match for Peloponnesian forces at sea. But Sparta brought Persian naval forces and money into its war effort in 408, and a series of naval victories combined with a near-constant land siege of Athens brought the war to an end in 404.

Operations and Tactics

On the operational level, joint operations of land and naval forces became commonplace during the war. An Athenian expedition to Pylos culminated in the defeat and capture of a Spartan regiment, for example. Some of these expeditions were massive in scale: The Athenian expedition to Sicily involved hundreds of ships and thousands of troops. Ultimately, it was the Spartan ability to build and maintain a fleet—with financial aid from Persia—that allowed her to defeat Athens, as noted above.

Tactically, the effects of the Persian wars showed in the increased use of both light infantry, often mercenaries, and cavalry. The importance of these troops in scouting and carrying out the more complicated operations that were becoming common played a role in their increasing employment. On more than one occasion, light infantry or cavalry had a part in defeating more traditional hoplite forces. One of the best examples comes again from the operation at Pylos, where Athenian light infantry whittled down the Spartans, who were unable to respond. The Spartans later used young hoplites called *ekdromoi* to run out of the phalanx and drive off the enemy skirmishers.

Armies and Society

The prolonged nature of the war increasingly forced states to maintain standing forces that they retained even when the war ended. Argos may have led the way by raising a force of 1000 hoplites maintained at state expense. Sparta's Peloponnesian allies followed suit, copying Sparta's uniformity by adopting standardized shield blazons. Such state troops were called *epilektoi*. In Athens, the *ephebes*, young men performing compulsory service, manned Athenian defenses on the borders of Attica. The most famous of the new professional units was the Sacred Band of Thebes, formed from 150 pairs of men, one older and one younger, bound by training and relations best seen, on today's terms, as bisexual (the older men were often married). This elite unit spearheaded Thebes' rise to military dominance in the 370s BCE.

Professional forces allowed greater experimentation with troop types and tactics. Iphicrates in Athens regularized the use of light supporting troops around the phalanx. Most famously, Epaminondas of Thebes invented the use of an oblique line of battle for the Theban phalanx, advancing and heavily weighting one wing, led by the Sacred Band, and withdrawing the other, creating a crushing preponderance of force on one flank that allowed him to roll up the opposition. He died in the victory over the Spartans that cemented Theban dominance, however, and his lessons passed to Philip of Macedon and his son Alexander. In general, it was the fourth century BCE that saw the consolidation and maturation of the lessons of the Persian and Peloponnesian wars.

Such sweeping changes in the nature of war—long conflicts involving numerous states, the creation of standing military forces, and the use of mercenaries—had social and political implications for a polis system built around citizen militias that were profound and often corrosive. It was no longer possible for poleis to rely exclusively on citizen-soldiers. Consequently, there was a fundamental change in who was fighting: Mercenary soldiers begin to replace citizen hoplites, and their numbers increased greatly. Of course, when they could not find employment at home, many sought a living abroad. The Persians, who were happy to hire Greek mercenaries to augment their forces, employed many Greeks, sometimes whole armies. In the fourth century BCE, the Persians paid tens of thousands of Greeks to serve in their forces (see the Sources box "Xenophon").

The social and economic effects of extended war could also appear in more immediate and deadly form: The crowded conditions in the city of Athens attendant on Pericles' strategy contributed to an outbreak of plague in 430 that killed the great war leader himself.

To many Greeks, such changes undermined the foundations of the polis. A school of philosophy developed, pan-Hellenism, that advocated finding a leader who could direct the attentions of the Greeks toward their real enemy, Persia. This would allow for the liberation of the Ionians and perhaps the founding of new poleis to transform the mercenaries into citizen hoplites once more. No Greek was able to achieve the vision of pan-Hellenism. But on the periphery of the Greek world a leader was about to come to power who would.

SOURCES

Xenophon

The following passages from Xenophon's Anabasis *show the professional nature of Greek mercenary forces after the Peloponnesian War. It is also useful to note the Persian reaction to Greek troops. We can assume that the descriptions are relatively accurate since Xenophon was both a participant and skilled soldier.*

■ ■ ■

He (Cyrus the Younger) held a review in the plain of both his Greek and native troops. He ordered the Greeks to fall in and stand in their normal battle order; each officer should see to the order of his own men. So they stood on parade in fours, with Menon and his men on the right wing, Clearchus and his on the left, and the other generals in the center. Cyrus first of all inspected the native troops, who marched past in bands and also formation; then he inspected the Greeks, driving in a chariot along their front with the Queen of Cilicia in a covered carriage. They were all wearing bronze helmets, red tunics and greaves, and had their shields uncovered. He rode along the whole parade and then stopped his chariot in front of the center of the phalanx and sent Pigres, his interpreter, to the Greek generals with the order to make their troops bring their spears to the ready and for the whole phalanx to advance. The generals passed on the order to the soldiers, the trumpet sounded and, with their spears at the ready, they moved forward. Then as the soldiers quickened their pace and shouted, they found that they were actually running towards their tents. All the natives were terrified; the Queen of Cilicia fled in her covered carriage, and the people in the market ran away leaving their stalls behind them, while the Greeks went laughing to their tents. The Queen of Cilicia was amazed when she saw the brilliant show the army made and its discipline, and Cyrus was delighted when he observed the panic which the Greeks caused among the natives.

The following passage is a description of the Battle of Cunaxa where Cyrus the Younger, although his Greek mercenaries were victorious, was killed.

By now the two armies were not more than between six and eight hundred yards apart, and now the Greeks sang the *paean* and began to move forward against the enemy. As they advanced, part of the phalanx surged forward in front of the rest and the part that was left behind began to advance at the double. At the same time they all raised a shout like the shout "Eleleu" which people make to the War God, and then they were all running forward. Some say that to scare the horses they clashed their shields and spears together. But the Persians, even before they were in range of the arrows, wavered and ran away. Then certainly the Greeks pressed on the pursuit vigorously, but they shouted out to each other not to run, but to follow up the enemy without breaking ranks. The chariots rushed about, some going through the enemy's own ranks, though some, abandoned by their drivers, did go through the Greeks. When they saw them coming the Greeks opened out, though one man stood rooted to the spot, as though he was at a race course, and got run down. However, even he, they said, came to no harm, nor were there any other casualties among the Greeks in this battle, except for one man on the left wing who was said to have been shot with an arrow.

SOURCE: Xenophon, *Anabasis, Book 1,* ch. ii and vii, trans. Michael F. Pavkovic.

MACEDON: KINGS AND COMBINED ARMS

Throughout most of the classical period, Macedon was a backwater to the Greeks. The people there spoke a dialect of Greek that was unintelligible to their southern neighbors. They lived not in poleis but in a decentralized kingdom dominated by a powerful landed aristocracy supported by peasants. Their kings were generally weak, although occasionally a strong leader would emerge. During the Peloponnesian War, Macedon could field only 400 noble cavalry and several thousand ill-armed foot soldiers, although at the end of the war the industrious King Archelaus made some improvements. Nevertheless, based on the general state of the Macedonians, the Greeks numbered them among the barbarians. Yet it was these barbarians who perfected phalanx warfare, integrating it into a flexible combined-arms tactical system and using it in campaigns of conquest that carried Greek civilization far beyond its fifth-century boundaries.

Philip II and the Macedonian Army

At no time in Macedonian history did things look more dismal than in 360 BCE, when Balkan tribes killed the king and overran much of Macedon. But the king's younger brother Philip immediately took control of the kingdom and initiated the reforms that would turn the Macedonian army into a well-organized war machine. The first step was raising the effectiveness of the peasant foot soldiers. Drawing on funds from silver mines, Philip introduced standardized weapons and the discipline of the phalanx formation. Within two years, he increased the size of the Macedonian army to over 10,000 and drove out the invaders. Not only did his victory strengthen the power of the monarchy, but the newly effective infantry balanced the political influence of the nobility.

Using his new strength, Philip introduced over the next twenty years further reforms in both organization and weaponry. He forged the Macedonian nobles into a drilled and disciplined heavy cavalry force organized by territorial squadrons. He gave them the title Companions (*hetairoi*) to emphasize their social and political relationship to the king, winning their loyalty to a more centralized military system and reducing their independent influence in the kingdom. They wore armor and carried a shorter version of the infantry *sarissa*, or pike, more suited to fighting on horseback. The Companions formed a mobile offensive strike force the equal in quality if not numbers to the best Persian cavalry and unmatched in any Greek army.

Philip also expanded the heavy infantry further, recruiting men from parts of Macedon that traditionally had been outside the direct control of the king, such as the rugged cantons of western Macedon, and tying them to the king with grants of land. Philip's intention was to create an army of citizen-soldiers who derived their status from military service to the king, in effect fusing two sources of infantry cohesion: communal ties as developed in the Greek poleis, and centrally imposed drill and discipline. The result was the creation of a large Macedonian infantry force organized into territorial battalions. These units formed a phalanx of some 18,000 men, much larger than any Greek state could raise. Philip armed these troops with a *sarissa* roughly 15–18 feet long. The *sarissa* allowed Philip to lighten the armor of his infantry, providing them with a small shield strapped to the left arm and only light body armor. The *sarissa* and lighter armor increased both the mobility and the offensive striking power of the Macedonian phalanx, as multiple spear points now preceded the front line of soldiers into combat. To emphasize the royal nature of the infantry in the political structure of the realm, Philip called them his Foot Companions (*pezhetairoi*). Though their privileges did not match those of the noble Companion cavalry, the infantry received regular pay, which allowed them to maintain their farms by buying slaves or hiring labor, giving the Macedonian kings the best qualities of citizen militia and professional soldiers in one force.

The tactical combination of phalanx and heavy cavalry could be formidable, with the infantry acting as an anvil, holding the enemy for the hammer blow of the Companions. But these two heavy elements alone lacked flexibility and maintained connection with each other only with difficulty. The crucial third unit of the Macedonian army was, therefore, an infantry force of 3000 men who formed the Royal Guard—the hypaspists, or shield bearers. These men differed from the regular infantry in that they were not organized territorially, but were recruited from throughout the kingdom. Their equipment is a matter of much debate but seems to have included a larger shield than the men of the phalanx carried, a short sword, and a shorter, lighter spear. They were thus more lightly armed than the heavy infantry; their equipment, even more intensive drill, and their smaller units of organization made them more mobile than the phalanx. Thus, one role of the hypaspists was to act as a link or hinge between the phalanx and the heavy cavalry in set-piece battles. But their skill and tactical flexibility made the hypaspists useful for a variety of tasks, and under Philip's son Alexander, they became the "special forces" unit of the army.

Philip also included light infantry and skirmishers in the regular army organization, and he added specialized troops from allies or mercenaries, including Thessalian heavy cavalry, Cretan archers, and Agrianian mountaineers. Such troops added both firepower and skirmishing and scouting capabilities to the army, giving Philip and later Alexander a set of tactical and operational tools that could meet almost any

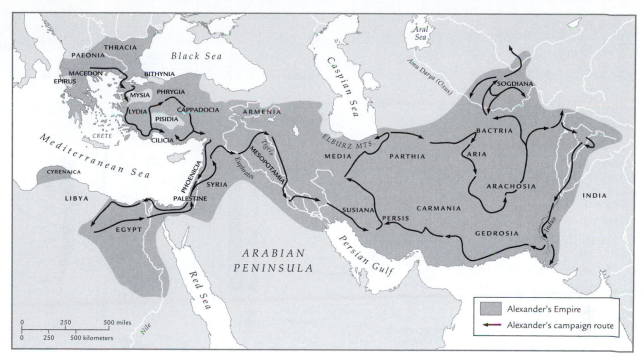

Figure 3.2 Alexander's Campaigns

challenge. And, in fact, one important hallmark of Philip's use of his new army was his ability to coordinate the various types of infantry and cavalry in a coherent battle plan.

Operationally and strategically, Philip emphasized mobility. He had his troops carry their own supplies and limited the number of pack animals. Unlike the forces of the Greeks, his army could campaign all year long. Philip also understood the importance of siege warfare and organized a mobile siege train that included engineers and war engines, some of which were light enough to be used as field artillery in battle. Philip had created a complete war machine.

Philip was now ready to take up the challenge of the pan-Hellenists and lead a great war against the barbarian Persians. Unfortunately, the Greeks considered him a barbarian, too. Therefore, he brought his army into Greece, and in 338 BCE at Chaeronea, he defeated an army of Athenians and Thebans, destroying the Sacred Band. During the battle, his son Alexander won distinction at the head of the Companion cavalry. By 336, Philip, now *hegemon* of the Greek League as well as king of Macedon and leader of Thessaly, was ready to invade Persia. He sent an advance guard to Asia Minor, but before he could join them, he was assassinated.

Alexander the Great

While he rebuilt the army and royal power, Philip also used the Macedonian tradition of polygamy as a diplomatic tool. One of his wives, Olympias of Epirus, gave birth to his second son, Alexander, in 356 BCE. Philip and Alexander had a tumultuous relationship, in part due to Olympias's claim that Zeus rather than Philip was Alexander's father. But Alexander was groomed for the throne because his elder bother was clearly less capable. At age 16, he was left in charge of the kingdom and put down a rebellion, perhaps overstepping his charge by renaming the capital of the rebels as Alexandropolis. He received the best Greek education (Aristotle was his tutor for a time), participated in Greek-style athletic festivals, and soaked in Greek culture (the playwright Euripides had been resident at the Macedonian court before Alexander's birth). His favorite book seems to have been Homer's *Iliad*. When Philip was assassinated, Alexander assumed the throne and immediately proved his effectiveness as a leader, ruthlessly suppressing rebellions in the Balkans and at Thebes, where he razed the city, sparing only the house of the poet Pindar. King of Macedon and hegemon of the Greek world, he then turned his attention eastward (Figure 3.2).

The Battle of Gaugamela

At the end of September 331 BCE, Alexander entered the open plains near ancient Nineveh with an army of about 40,000 infantry and 7000 cavalry. He stopped to rest his army overnight, refusing in the meantime a peace offering from Darius that would have given him half of Darius's kingdom. Arrayed against him was a Persian army whose numbers are impossible to determine with any accuracy—some sources claim up to 200,000, but such a figure is at the outer limits of logistical believability

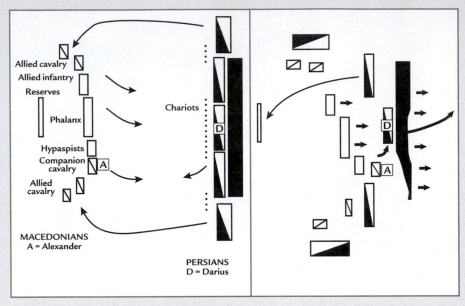

Figure 3.3 The Battle of Gaugamela

and is probably an exaggeration. In addition, Persian losses at the Granicus and at Issus had reduced the numbers of elite Persian infantry and Greek mercenaries available to the Great King, who probably had to rely more on provincial levies and the still effective and numerous Persian cavalry, as well as a corps of chariots and a small group of war elephants. In other words, it is certain that the Persians outnumbered Alexander's army significantly, but by how much and with what quality is open to

question. Darius drew up his army to maximize his advantages, with the chariots and elephants backed by the Royal Guard cavalry and his remaining Greek mercenaries anchoring the center, and masses of cavalry on the wings whose job was to envelop the smaller Macedonian force (Figure 3.3).

Alexander disposed his army to counter the Persian deployment. He could not possibly match the length of the Persian line, so, as at Issus, he

Alexander's Campaigns In 334 BCE, Alexander launched his great war against the Persians—a new Trojan War, as he may have seen it, with himself in the role of a new and greater Achilles—crossing the Hellespont with an army of about 30,000 infantry and 5,000 cavalry. His first major action was at the Granicus River, which was defended by 20,000 Persian cavalry and an equal number of infantry including a large number of Greek mercenaries. Alexander used his infantry to pin down part of the Persian forces while concentrating his cavalry for the decisive

blow. The Persian horse fled, leaving their infantry, including the Greeks, to be slaughtered.

Alexander recognized that, although he had won a significant victory over a Persian army, the Persian fleet could still threaten his communications with Macedon and cause trouble in Greece. He therefore captured Persian naval bases at Miletus and Halicarnassus, the first steps in a larger strategy of neutralizing the Persian fleet by capturing the entire eastern Mediterranean coast before turning inland to finish off the heart of the empire. He secured western Asia

refused his left wing, leading on the right with his Companion cavalry and the hypaspists, with the phalanx in the center. Thessalian cavalry covered the left flank. In addition, he posted mixed units of light infantry and cavalry behind each wing, ready to wheel outward and counter Persian attempts at envelopment, and posted a unit of Thessalian infantry in the rear to guard the Macedonian camp. The formation provided capacity both for all-around defense and for a tactical reserve.

The Persian army had been up all night expecting a night attack by Alexander's inferior force, but Alexander did not move until the next morning, October 1. As his army approached the Persian line, it drifted to the right, perhaps intentionally. Persian attempts to shift their own more cumbersome line resulted in a gap opening in the left-center. Alexander seized the opportunity this presented him, leading the Companions and hypaspists in wedge formation in a charge into the gap and straight for Darius and his personal bodyguard. Darius panicked and fled, and the entire left and center of the Persian host began rapidly to give way.

Alexander could not pursue Darius immediately, however, because both Persian wings had charged when Alexander attacked the Persian center, and the cavalry on the Persian right wing had driven back the Thessalians and was pressing the Macedonian reserves, threatening to get behind the phalanx and envelope the whole Macedonian army. In what was perhaps the most remarkable feat of the day, Alexander managed to comprehend, from the midst of combat in the middle of a vast battlefield, the danger to his left and center (a testimony to the messenger system that connected Alexander to his subordinates) and then to wheel the Companions and hypaspists around from the fighting they were already engaged in and charge into the flank and rear of the Persian horsemen. The Persians broke, and the entire engagement now became a massive pursuit, breaking the Persian army decisively. About 500 Macedonians died; perhaps another 5000 were wounded. Persian losses are even harder to determine than their total army size but may well have exceeded 50,000.

It is too easy in retrospect to see the outcome at Gaugamela as a foregone conclusion, based on the superior fighting qualities of the Macedonian army. But the Persians had plenty of elite troops, a significant superiority in cavalry, and ideal geography in which to deploy their advantages. The same Macedonian army under less decisive leadership could easily have been surrounded, worn down, and slaughtered. But not only did Alexander unhesitatingly seize the right moment and place to attack, in the rush of a triumphant charge, he also never lost sight of the larger dynamics of the battle. His tactics in the battle at the Hydaspes (see Chapter 2) may, in fact, have been even better, but Gaugamela was a masterpiece of Alexander's generalship—one that won him an empire.

Minor, dividing his forces on the overland marches to ease his supply problems—close attention to logistics, including advance scouting and arrangement of markets, would characterize Alexander's entire career.

Next, Alexander moved into Cilicia, preparing to proceed down the coast of Syria. But the Great King, Darius III, and his army managed to get behind him and cut the Macedonian lines of communication. Alexander turned back and attacked Darius on a narrow plain between the sea and hills at the Battle of Issus. Significantly outnumbered by an army composed of some of the best Persian troops including the Applebearers (descendants of the Immortals), Greek mercenaries, and a large cavalry force, Alexander advanced obliquely, refusing his left flank while leading the Companions and hypaspists against the Persian left, which he drove off. He then turned and rolled up the Persian center, hotly engaged with the phalanx; Darius fled, and the Persian army broke.

After this victory, Alexander returned to securing the coast. He besieged and captured the Phoenician island city of Tyre using a combination of land assaults over an artificially constructed causeway and attacks by ship; the causeway eventually silted up and turned the island into an isthmus, making Alexander one of the few generals to permanently alter geography. By 331, having secured Syria and Egypt and captured most of the Persian fleet and all their bases, Alexander controlled the sea. He was now ready to move east. He advanced unmolested to the Euphrates, crossed over, and marched south along the Tigris, where fodder was plentiful for his animals and grain was easily obtainable in undefended villages. Seeking out the gathering Persian army, Alexander defeated the forces of Darius on the plains of Gaugamela in the final battle for control of the Persian Empire (see the Highlights box "The Battle of Gaugamela").

With the defeat of Darius at Gaugamela, the heartland of the Persian Empire was open to Alexander. Alexander captured Persepolis, the ceremonial capital and treasury, which was then burnt, allegedly by accident. Alexander pursued Darius, who was hoping to fall back and rally the forces from the eastern provinces; but, along the way, Darius was slain by some of his own nobles. Alexander eventually killed the regicides; he had defeated the Achaemenids and conquered the heart of their empire.

Alexander would continue to move east through Afghanistan and into the Indus River valley. These later campaigns are characterized by flexibility, both tactically and logistically. Alexander successfully altered his tactics to suit his enemies, dividing his army to ease logistical problems and concentrating it for battles or sieges, whether against fortified mountain strongholds, Scythian nomads, or Indian armies with chariots and elephants—his battle at the Hydaspes River against King Porus was perhaps the hardest of his career (see Chapter 2). Alexander continued east, intent on bringing the entire world under his command, until his homesick, weary army mutinied at the Hyphasis River and demanded to return home. After a week-long Achilles-like sulk in his tent, Alexander turned south along the Indus River for the trip home.

Alexander's Impact   Alexander returned to Babylon and began organizing the resources of his empire. He initiated some interesting army reforms, including the integration of Persians and other Asians, especially horse archers, into the Companion cavalry and foot archers and Persian spearmen into the Macedonian infantry. In doing so, he may have taken advantage of extant Persian institutions for military training (see Chapter 2). Historians debate Alexander's

motives—was he trying to integrate Macedonians and Persians in the rule of his empire, or did manpower shortages in Macedon force his hand? The question is in one sense irresolvable, because Alexander's premature death in 323 BCE prevented his plans from being fully implemented. But, in a larger sense, Alexander had already set in motion a fusion of Greek and Persian civilizations that would shape the military, political, and cultural history of southwest Asia and the eastern Mediterranean for centuries.

Alexander founded new cities wherever he went, many named Alexandria (including the most famous in Egypt) and one named after his horse Bucephalus. Modeled on Greek poleis and often populated in part by retired Macedonian soldiers, these cities carried the Greek culture Alexander loved to all corners of his empire. They became the model for military colonies founded by Alexander's leading generals, who became the Diadochi, the successor kings of a divided empire; these colonies supported the scarce Macedonian manpower that was the key component of successor kingdom armies. This style of army went unchallenged until the Roman legions entered eastern Mediterranean politics a century later (see Chapter 4).

The colonists often married Persian or other non-Greek women, a policy encouraged and practiced by Alexander himself, furthering the cultural syncretism these urban foundations inspired. Perhaps even more important, Alexander fused these cities into a larger conception of imperial rule, using them as the administrative connection between localities and his kingship. For that kingship, he drew on Persian (as well as Egyptian) notions of divinely supported rule and a sense of his own divinity, inherited from his mother, to create a political structure neither fully Macedonian and Greek nor fully Persian, but successful enough—and enhanced by the tremendous prestige of his seemingly superhuman conquests—to inspire imitation and flattery by later Roman emperors, whose empire also featured divine kingship laid over an urban network of local rule. His model certainly formed the ideal of the Hellenistic world he created and reflected at the grandest political level the fusion of polis communalism with the resources of centralized kingship.

If Alexander had a weakness, it was his reckless courage. He led from the front and was wounded several times, most seriously in a siege of an Indian city when he took an arrow in the lung, a wound that probably contributed to his death from fever a year later. But such conspicuous bravery was integral to his generalship and his ability to inspire his men to feats few armies have matched. Few individuals change the course of history in a significant way. Harnessing his father's army to his own genius for generalship in all its phases, Alexander certainly did so.

CONCLUSION

The nature of warfare in the Greek world was dramatically transformed over the period of two centuries. At the beginning of the fifth century BCE, Greek warfare matched the needs of Greek society. It tended to be localized and fought on a relatively small scale. The Persian invasion served as the catalyst of transformation, forcing the Greeks to think about war on a larger scale and to make strategic, operational, and tactical adjustments. The incessant conflict of the late fifth and much of the fourth centuries led to more standing and diverse military forces. The culmination of these developments appears in the army reforms of Philip of Macedon and their strategic and tactical employment by Alexander. The key to their success was building a complete, combined-arms force around effective heavy infantry.

Such was the prestige of Alexander's army and empire that his successors in the Hellenistic kingdoms would see their style of warfare as the pinnacle of the art of war. It would remain so in this part of the world until a new twist on the citizen-soldier, the legions of Rome, surpassed it. Yet, from another perspective, both Alexander and his successors, and later the Romans, ended up where the great Asian empires had already arrived: as autocratic, imperial political structures supported by professional military organizations, which depended more on training than on communal sources of cohesion for their effectiveness, and with subject populations whose "citizenship," even where the concept existed, had become both attenuated and separated from military duty. The history of Rome as a military power, the topic of the next chapter, demonstrates that evolution most clearly.

SUGGESTED READINGS

Anderson, J. K. *Military Theory and Practice in the Age of Xenophon*. Berkeley: University of California Press, 1970. A solid general survey focused on the fourth century BCE.

Engels, D. *Alexander the Great and the Logistics of the Macedonian Army*. Berkeley: University of California Press, 1978. A groundbreaking logistical analysis of Alexander's campaigns, influential far beyond classical military history.

Hammond, N. G. L. *Alexander the Great: King, Commander, and Statesman*. Park Ridge: William Andrew, 1980. An authoritative examination of the life of one of history's great commanders. See also his *The Macedonian State: Origins, Institutions, and History* (Oxford: Oxford University Press, 1989), which ranges more broadly.

Hanson, V. D. *The Western Way of War: Infantry Battle in Classical Greece*. New York: Knopf, 1989. A widely noted but controversial "face of battle" study of Greek phalanx conflicts. See also his edited collection *Hoplites: The Classical Greek Battle Experience* (London: Routledge, 1991) and his more general *The Wars of the Ancient Greeks* (London: Cassell, 1999).

Lazenby, J. F. *The Spartan Army*. Warminster: Bolchazy-Carducci, 1985. The standard investigation of Spartan military and social organization.

Parke, H. W. *Greek Mercenary Soldiers: From the Earliest Times to the Battle of Ipsus*. Oxford: Oxford University Press, 1933. An old but still useful examination of a topic that has not received its share of recent attention.

Pritchett, W. K. *The Greek State at War*, 5 vols. Berkeley: University of California Press, 1971–1991). A magisterial overview examining many aspects of Greek warfare in great detail.

Rich, J., and G. Shipley, eds. *War and Society in the Greek World*. London: Routledge, 1993. An essential collection of articles covering a range of topics and setting Greek warfare in its social context.

Sidebottom, H. *Ancient Warfare: A Very Short Introduction*. Oxford: Oxford University Press, 2004. A short, thematically organized overview that effectively disputes Hanson's "western way of war" thesis.

Spence, I. G. *The Cavalry of Classical Greece*. Oxford: Oxford University Press, 1994). An important analysis of a neglected arm of Greek armies and the continuing influence of the social class from which the cavalry emerged.

Van Wees, H. *Greek Warfare: Myths and Realities*. London: Routledge, 2004. The essential starting point for further investigation of Greek warfare. See also his *War and Violence in Ancient Greece* (London: Classical Press of Wales, 2000).

CHAPTER 4

Legion and Empire: Rome, 500 BCE–400 CE

The rise of Rome from small city-state to world empire is probably one of the best-known stories of military history, at least in broad outline, and Rome remains an archetype of both military efficiency and imperialism in the modern world. At that archetypal level, Rome's rise can seem both inexorable and inevitable. But it was neither, nor was it an unproblematically triumphal march. Rome's growth as a state and empire entailed significant internal changes both socially and politically, changes that, in turn, had implications for its patterns of military organization and activity. Unlike the Greeks, whose communal infantry was eventually swallowed and appropriated by large states external to Greece, Rome assumed the role of swallower, if not appropriator. But the communal infantry of the early Roman Republic disappeared with the state and society that spawned it, replaced from within by a professional army serving an autocratic empire. Thus, though it took a different route, Rome ended up at roughly the same destination: the sort of large-state military-political formation pioneered by the Assyrians and Qin. The latter's successor, the Han, joined with Rome to bookend Eurasia in the Age of Empires.

Yet the different route still mattered. Ideologically and culturally, Rome as an empire bore the stamp of its Republican origins, and if Rome, Han China, and Mauryan India shared deep structural similarities, they differed significantly in ideology and culture, as well as the relationship of their military elites to the state. Part of that difference goes to the very origins of Rome, for—unlike China, India, southwest Asia, and even Greece—Rome had no native chariot warrior elite in its past, and its collective mythic history, based in reality, begins with the expulsion of kings, not their ascent to power.

THE EXPANSIONIST REPUBLIC TO 167 BCE

Roman tradition held that they threw out their Etruscan royal rulers in 510–9 BCE, though evidence suggests that the Etruscans retained influence in Rome into the 480s. The rest of the fifth century BCE saw the city-state, located on a group of hills on the Tiber River in the north end of the plain of Latium, engaged in constant but small-scale warfare against its neighbors for control of agricultural land. The growing population of central Italy and the aggressive role of peoples from the hills around the plain stimulated this warfare, but, for nearly a century, Rome gained no real advantage from it. Indeed, in 390, Gauls from the Po valley sacked Rome itself.

The sack seems to have prompted a reorganization of Rome's army, for shortly thereafter, Rome began winning its wars regularly and expanding its sphere of influence in central Italy. After the defeat of the Latin League, a coalition of allies who rebelled against Rome's increasing dominance in 338, the process of expansion accelerated, and by 280, almost all of Italy south of the Po was ruled by Rome (Figure 4.1). This led to conflict with non-Italian powers, first with Pyrrhus, king of Epirus, in south Italy, and then in Sicily with Carthage. The first two Punic Wars, extending from 264 to 202, effectively brought this first phase of Roman history to an end.

State, Politics, Society, and War

During this period of almost yearly campaigning and constant expansion, there was a very tight relationship between Roman social, political, and military organization and activity: Citizenship meant service in the army, and expansion was both the focus of

Figure 4.1 Early Roman Expansion

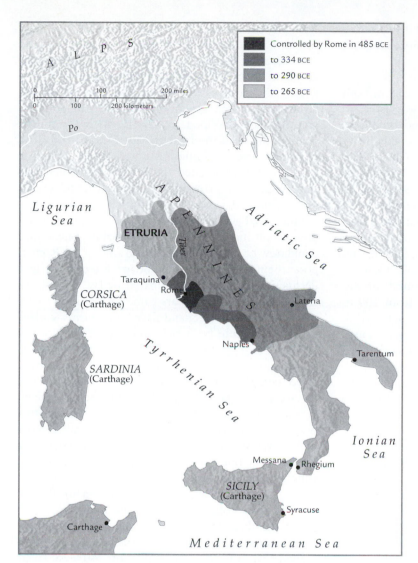

politics and the lubricant smoothing out Roman social conflict.

State and Society   Though lacking kings and the sort of elites found in large, rich states, there was still a large gap separating the rich landowners who dominated Roman social and political life in the early Republic and the small farmers, the poorest of whom were often at the edge of debt bondage, who formed the bulk of the population. The state was run by the Senate, a body drawn from the rich who had served as magistrates—the primarily military leaders elected annually at a gathering of all Roman citizens at the *campus Martius,* or Field of Mars, the god of war,

outside the city. Military leadership and personal glory therefore drove Roman elite politics. Recognition of the vital role of the plebs, or common people, in the manpower of the legions into which Roman forces were organized led to the creation of the office of tribune to represent their interests in the state.

The Roman state around 400 BCE faced two major challenges: increasingly aggressive neighbors, especially the city of Veii, which challenged Rome for dominance in the Tiber valley; and increasing social tension between rich and poor, landowners and debtors. Central to this tension was access to the *ager publicus,* the public land controlled by the state. For poor farmers, use of a piece of the *ager publicus* could be the difference between prosperity and debt; for the rich, public land promised even larger, more efficient, and more profitable farms.

Manpower   Warfare was the central activity of both state and society: Every Roman citizen was liable for military service, though the landless or indebted were prohibited from serving in the legions, the heavy infantry core of the army. Citizens with land were divided into six classes by wealth that determined what sort of equipment they owed; the richest served as cavalry, and most of the rest as heavy infantry of one sort or another (see below). Perhaps into the fourth century BCE, service was unpaid and voluntary; but, no later than the defeat of the Latin League in 338, and perhaps earlier, the state began to pay regular wages to the army, funded by a special tax instituted for this purpose. Over the course of the period from 400 to 202, probably between 10 and 15 percent of the adult male population served each year in the legions, usually for a term of several years. In times of crisis, such as at the climax of the Samnite Wars or during Hannibal's invasion of Italy, upward of 25 percent of the adult male population was under arms. The casualties from military service must at times have constituted a stunning proportion of the population as a whole.

Even at these levels of commitment, Roman manpower was inadequate to meet all its military needs. Two mechanisms increased the base of manpower Rome could draw on. First, from early in its expansion, Rome planted colonies of its citizens at strategic locations throughout central (and later all of) Italy. The number of Roman citizens could therefore continue to increase, despite war losses. Second, Rome fought in alliance with other cities from its earliest wars. Although initially voluntary on both sides, Rome came to dominate the relationship with its allies in the sixty years after 400. Military service, indeed, was the key and sometimes only obligation allies owed to Rome.

The Structures and Dynamics of Expansion   In the two decades after 400, the various factors outlined above, in the context both of increasingly successful warfare starting with the final defeat of the rival city of Veii in 396 and of the threat of disaster represented by the Gallic sack of the city in 390, became more tightly tied together into a set of structures that encouraged continual expansion of the Roman state within Italy.

From this point, when Rome won a war, it took land, slaves, and booty from the peoples it defeated.

Each element proved important. The land went into the *ager publicus,* allowing both the poor and the rich increased access to public land. Of course, more farmland enabled further population growth, maintaining the pressure to acquire still more land, but levels of indebtedness among the Roman poor do seem to have dropped steadily through the fourth century. Some of the land provided the basis for the planting of new colonies, as noted above. Strategic considerations governed the siting of colonies, but the colonies also provided a further outlet for excess population and a source of land for the poor.

Increased access to public land for the rich, however, simply increased their need for labor, a need that could now be met less readily from among the Roman poor themselves, as debt bondage for citizens first declined and then was eliminated by law. The slaves captured in successful wars came increasingly to fill this need. Land hunger and slave hunger thus worked together to unite both rich and poor in support of expansion.

Conquests also added to the circle of Roman allied cities, both through voluntary alliances and among cities that became allies after being initially defeated. Roman statesmanship proved vital in this process. Unlike Greek city-states, which maintained a highly exclusive notion of citizenship even when, like Athens, they built an empire of conquest, Rome was willing to extend citizenship (though, in the case of allies, citizenship without voting rights in Rome) beyond natives of the city itself. The identity of interest this mechanism created between Rome and many of its former enemies was not perfect—some revolted individually, and the Latin War of 340–338 faced Rome with a major coordinated rebellion of allies and colonists. But lenient treatment of the rebels after their defeat seemed to cement their loyalty thereafter, which proved crucial in the Second Punic War. Still, the need to call on allied manpower simply to enforce the terms of alliance, as well as to keep that manpower occupied so it could not be turned against Rome, constituted a further structural incentive to constant expansion.

The politics of glory among the Roman elite contributed a crucial cultural framework for these material causes. Competition for offices and personal glory was the coin of political influence, expressed above all in the institution of the triumph, the public celebration of a general's military success. Monuments to Roman victories also rose throughout the city, funded by the plunder gained in successful wars. Thus, the dynamics of land

and slave hunger, alliance management, and cultural politics all contributed to the pattern of annual campaigning and continual expansion that carried Rome to domination of all of Italy south of the Po by the 270s, and thence to the conflicts with Carthage that would carry expansion beyond the Italian mainland.

The Army of the Expansionist Republic

We have little direct evidence for the organization and tactics of the early Roman army. Before the Gallic sack of Rome in 390 BCE, the Romans seem to have fought in the Greek way, as a spear-bearing phalanx. It was probably clashes with the loose-ordered, sword-wielding Gauls (or perhaps the Samnites) that prompted a reorganization and continuing evolution that resulted, at some point in the fourth or early third century, in the *manipular* legion, or legion built around the unit of the *maniple*. This style of legion remained the basic tactical unit of the Roman army into the early first century BCE.

Troop Types and Formations   The legion formally comprised four types of troops. The youngest and least experienced served as *velites*, light-armed skirmishers. Next in age and experience were the *hastati*, the front line of heavy infantry organized in ten maniples of two centuries each; each century contained 60–80 men. The best veterans formed the *principes*, the second line of heavy infantry, also in ten maniples of two centuries each. The oldest, most experienced, troops were the *triarii*, the third line of heavy infantry, whose ten maniples contained only one century each. Thus, a full legion consisted of 3000–4000 heavy infantry, another 600 or so light infantry, and 300 cavalry. Each Roman legion was accompanied by an allied legion, identically organized except for having 300 more cavalry. Two Roman and two allied legions made up a full consular army, capable of fully independent field operations.

The key to the tactical flexibility of the manipular legion was the arrangement and relationship of the three lines of heavy infantry. Each maniple deployed in a block about twenty men across and six ranks deep, with somewhat more space between each rank and file than in a Greek or Macedonian phalanx. The space between maniples equaled the frontage of a maniple, and the second and third lines deployed behind the gaps in the line in front of them, creating a checkerboard pattern. The lines could thus advance or retreat into each other, reinforcing or relieving their tired comrades as needed. The legion's more open order compared to a phalanx made it easier to maneuver and keep order over rough terrain and more capable of meeting threats to its flanks and rear.

Weapons and Tactics   Changes in weapons accompanied changes in formation. The *hastati* and *principes* carried a *pilum*, a javelin rather than a thrusting spear. It is unclear, however, when the *pilum* assumed its classic form, with the iron head attached to the wooden shaft by a soft iron sheath or a breakable pin, so that it would bend or crack when it stuck in an enemy shield, simultaneously rendering the shield unwieldy and the *pilum* useless for throwing back at the Roman line. They also carried a short stabbing sword whose classic form, the *gladius*, may be of Iberian design, entering Roman use during the Punic Wars. The *triarii*, the last line of reserve and defense, continued for a time to carry a spear as their main weapon, as well as the *gladius*. The skirmishers carried javelins, and allied or mercenary missile troops, including slingers and archers, sometimes added to the skirmishing firepower of the legion. The cavalry carried a short spear and a sword, while the heavy infantry wore helmets and body armor. Roman tactics were geared to the attack. Even when receiving an attack, the front lines of a legion would tend to charge as the enemy approached, hurling their javelins from 30 to 50 meters away, then drawing swords for a final rush to hand-to-hand combat.

The legions of the expansionist Republic, though still technically a militia-style force, developed high levels of skill through training (which became increasingly necessary as the Republic grew and men from all over Italy found themselves fighting side by side), extensive experience, and firm discipline, in effect self-imposed as the consuls who led Roman armies were elected. They proved consistently successful against both the looser-ordered, less disciplined forces of Gauls and Italian hill tribes and the denser but less flexible phalanxes of Pyrrhus and later the Macedonians, and were perfectly suited to the varied and often hilly terrain of Italy and the western Mediterranean world. They were the tool first of the Roman conquest of Italy, then of the conquest of Rome's first imperial provinces.

Consular armies were, it should be noted, far from perfect military machines tactically. Consular leadership, ever-changing and sometimes divided,

Cannae and Zama

The strengths and weaknesses of the manipular legionary armies are highlighted by the two most famous battles of the Second Punic War—Cannae and Zama (Figure 4.2).

At Cannae in August 216 BCE, a large (over 60,000) but relatively inexperienced army under the alternating command of the consuls Lucius Aemilius Paullus and Gaius Terentius Varro camped in the vicinity of the camp of Hannibal's army of perhaps 35,000. On August 2, when Hannibal knew Varro would be in command, he moved out to offer battle. With his flanks secured by terrain, he advanced the center of his thin line of Iberian swordsmen toward the Romans. Varro massed his men in a deep, dense block, compensating for their inexperience and hoping to crush Hannibal's center by force of numbers. By design, Hannibal's center gradually gave ground, drawing the Romans on.

Meanwhile, his heavy Spanish and Gallic cavalry on his left crushed the Roman cavalry opposite them and rode around the Roman rear to drive away the allied cavalry engaged with the Numidian cavalry on his right. As they did, the heavy phalanxes of African infantry that anchored each end of Hannibal's line of swordsmen turned inward against the flanks of the Roman column, while the cavalry closed the ring from the rear. What had been a triumphant advance turned to panic, and over 50,000 men squeezed together too tightly to wield their weapons effectively were systematically slaughtered, though 10,000 fought free. Hannibal lost around 6000 men. His double envelopment of the Roman army, the high point of his military career, has remained a classic in studies of the "art of war" ever since.

The tables were turned in March 202, however. This time, Hannibal had the larger (48,000 man) but more inexperienced army, facing Scipio Africanus's 34,000 seasoned veterans and 9000 allied and Numidian cavalry. Hannibal counted on a number of war elephants to create an advantage for him, but Scipio made use of the flexibility of the manipular formation to line his maniples up with the gaps aligned, creating lanes through which the elephants were driven with minimal disruption of the Roman infantry. The Roman cavalry forces then drove off the Carthaginian horse while Scipio's *hastati* and *principes* cut down Hannibal's first two lines of inexperienced infantry. Hannibal's veteran third line (the three-line formation reflecting Roman influence on Hannibal's tactics) resisted the Romans, now joined by the *triarii*, until the Roman cavalry returned from the pursuit and charged the rear of their formation. Hannibal escaped, but 20,000 of his troops died and another 15,000 were captured, compared to losses of 1500 Roman dead and several thousand wounded.

Both battles illustrate some common features of ancient (and most premodern) battles. For one thing, the surest way to defeat foes was to panic them. Aside from killing or driving off their leader (as Alexander had done at Gaugamela), this was most easily accomplished by getting to the flanks and rear of their formation. This gave cavalry an important role even in infantry-dominated battles. And most casualties happened in the pursuit (or, as at Cannae, slaughter) phase of the battle, as it was much easier to kill a man who was no longer actively resisting. Finally, although numbers often mattered, experience could count even more: A steady, veteran formation could maintain its cohesion under pressure much more readily than even well-trained new recruits, and so could carry the day in the face of superior numbers.

was usually but not always competent and tended to be unimaginative—apart from exceptional individuals such as Scipio Africanus, victor over Hannibal at Zama (see the Highlights box "Cannae and Zama"). (Of course, on the whole, this makes the record of Roman generalship no worse than any other institutionalized military's leadership, and the Romans always seemed to find the general they needed in a crisis.) Roman

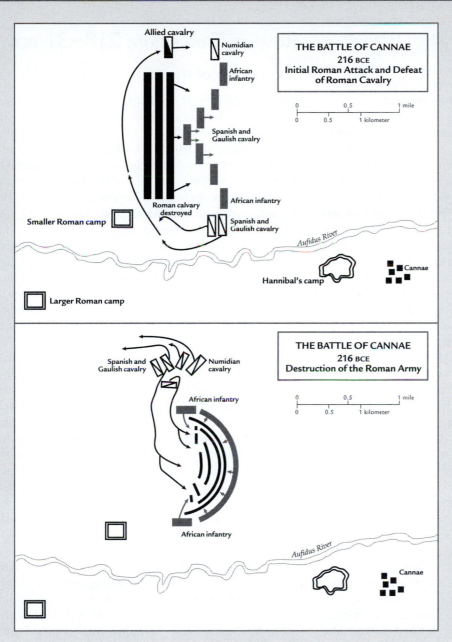

Figure 4.2 The Battle of Cannae

siege craft in this era was deficient compared to that of the Macedonians and Persians. Above all, Roman cavalry was barely adequate—Hannibal's cavalry exposed it a number of times, crucially at Cannae (see the Highlights box)—and Republican Rome never had to fight on the terrain of or against forces built around truly effective heavy cavalry: Even the cavalry of the Macedonian and Seleucid armies they defeated had declined since Alexander's day. Still, they eventually triumphed against every challenge they faced.

Strategy and Grand Strategy   That Roman wars almost always ended in victory was only partly due to the adaptability and tactical efficiency of the legions, however. Their most remarkable triumphs came as much despite massive tactical defeats (especially against Hannibal) as because of battlefield victories. To explain this, we need to examine Roman strategy and grand strategy under the expansionist Republic.

Roman strategy is probably best characterized as the direct approach. Roman leaders at war tended to lead their armies straight at the crucial positions, whether cities or armies, of the enemy, aiming to defeat their main force directly. Such an approach could lead to disaster—Hannibal exploited the tendency in destroying three Roman armies in a row in the first two years of his invasion of Italy, turning Roman aggression against itself. But it just as often served to draw Rome's enemies into a direct and sometimes attritional struggle in which Rome's usually superior manpower and grand strategic will could carry the day. Therefore, the direct approach was probably one benefit of the rotating consular system of generalship, as each consul, elected only for a limited term, wished to earn glory (and a triumph) as quickly as possible. It took a dictator (a temporarily appointed emergency military commander), Quintus Fabius Maximus, appointed in the aftermath of defeats at Hannibal's hands at Trebbia and Lake Trasimene, to follow a more cautious strategy. In the process, he earned the nickname *Cunctator,* or "The Delayer," reflecting the ambivalence with which even a successful indirect approach was met in Republican Roman military culture.

The direct approach in strategy was matched by a grand strategic approach that is best characterized as relentless. Expansionism, as we have seen, was built into the social and political structures of the early Republic, which is why we are calling it the expansionist Republic here, and thus constitutes an implicit grand strategy. But it was in the face of real threats to Roman survival that the true character of Roman grand strategy emerged: They refused to consider surrender and inevitably simply outlasted the political and military will of their opponents. The fanatical determination of the Roman Senate casts the half-heartedness and in-fighting of the Carthaginian Senate in a particularly harsh light. Relentless, ferocious aggression thus lay at the heart of Roman military

practices from the grand strategic to the tactical and individual levels. They were true heirs of the Assyrians, and comparable to their contemporaries the Qin, in this regard.

ROME IN TRANSITION, 218–31 BCE

The Legacy of the Punic Wars

The First Punic War (264–241) brought Rome into conflict over territory outside mainland Italy for the first time (entailing Rome's first serious foray into naval warfare, for which see Chapter 5). The result was Roman rule in Sicily, the first Roman conquest governed, not directly as part of the Roman state or as an ally, but as an imperial province. Aside from the Roman seizure of Sardinia in 238, the war did not immediately draw Rome into a broader conception of its role in the Mediterranean world, nor had it entailed a significant change in the pattern of yearly campaigning by consular armies raised for limited terms of service. It represented, in short, a logical extension of the expansion that had been going on since 400 BCE.

The Second Punic War (218–202), however, was a different matter, one that initiated changes in the Roman state, society, and military organization that would have significant consequences. Republican institutions, patterns of war, and culture persisted but were gradually transformed, so that by 31 BCE the Roman Republic had ended and the Roman Empire had begun. From 218 to 31 is thus an era of transition from expansionist Republic to early Empire. There is not room to narrate in detail the struggle against Carthage and its great general Hannibal Barca, but a number of the effects of fighting a war that took place simultaneously over much of central and southern Italy, southern Gaul, Iberia, and Africa may be outlined.

Conquests and Provinces   The war drew Roman armies farther afield than ever before, especially with a long-term campaign in Spain as the major second front while Hannibal was contained in Italy. Hannibal's diplomacy drew Macedon into conflict with Rome; three wars resulted by 167 in Roman rule over Macedon and hegemony over Greece, though conquest had not initially been the Roman aim. War with Macedon drew Rome increasingly into the diplomatic tangle of the Successor States in Asia Minor, Syria, and Egypt. Meanwhile, the continued Gallic threat led to the conquest of the Po valley shortly after the Second Punic War ended. By the mid-second century, Roman provinces extended the length of the Mediterranean, though not comprehensively.

The campaigning necessary to prosecute wars in these more distant regions, as well as the garrison troops needed to hold areas that differed significantly from Roman (and even broader Italian) culture, meant that legionary recruits now tended to serve longer terms of service—six to ten years versus the one to three of early Republican times. This had implications for recruitment (see below), and the Romans also had to work out mechanisms for governing their new possessions, which involved questions about economic exploitation of the provinces and the political advantage to be gained from overseas appointments.

The shift to overseas conquest also had a significant impact on the pattern of Roman warfare. Campaigning, conquest, and expansion ceased being such regular activities. The number of foreign wars Rome fought decreased steadily after 202 (and dramatically after 146); conversely, the number of years of peace increased, causing some politicians to worry about the military virtues of the Roman population being lost. In fact, the proportion of the Italian population who served in the army probably did begin to fall as wars became less frequent and as more distant theaters encouraged long-term service by a more select set of recruits.

Conquests therefore now tended to be larger—entire kingdoms or regions at a time—but much more sporadic. Partly, this was a simple practical matter: It took longer to pacify larger, more distant regions, and the troops occupied by garrison and police duties were then not available immediately for another campaign of conquest. Diplomatic opportunities for justifying aggression and conquest probably also became more complicated on the larger stage of the Mediterranean world. But, partly, the decline in the number of wars of conquest Rome fought after 202 reflects the dynamics of elite politics and the raised stakes of glory involved in overseas wars. The reward for bigger conquests was more glory and greater political advantages for the consuls who led the successful campaigns. Ironically, this led to fewer such campaigns, because every potential conquering consul had many rivals in the Senate who were happy to derail the would be conqueror's ambitions. The stakes of individual wars, in other words, had become

high enough that balancing the benefits and spreading the glory had become problematic.

In fact, this pattern of sporadic expansion resembles that of the Empire more than that of the expansionist Republic. What disguises that similarity and makes the *Pax Romana (Roman Peace)* stand out as an attribute of the Empire is that the level of internal warfare went up steadily in the late Republic. Understanding that requires examining the changing relationship of Roman warfare to social change and elite politics.

War, Society, and Politics

Social Change   Perhaps the most important long-term consequence of the shift from Italian expansion to overseas provincial expansion was that conquests stopped adding to the *ager publicus,* the stock of public land that served the interests of both large estate owners and poorer farmers. Roman colonies within Italy could no longer be established, and in the developing competition for a now-limited resource, the poor inevitably found themselves at a disadvantage against the rich, whose supply of slaves capable of working ever-larger estates did not dry up—in fact, it skyrocketed—with the shift to overseas conquests. Debt rose again, and though debt bondage no longer existed, defaults and sales of small farms to the rich increased the number of landless in the Roman state. Many of these former farmers found their way to Rome itself, where they formed a newly volatile element in popular politics.

These social changes thus intruded into politics. By the middle of the second century BCE, land reform had become a major political issue. This issue was raised most forcefully by Tiberius and Gaius Gracchus, each elected tribune, in 133 and 123, respectively, on a platform of land redistribution—and both ended up dead at the hands of elite opponents, directly or indirectly. Land use in the form of large estates worked by slaves provoked another sort of opposition: The years 135–132 saw the first of a series of large slave revolts, this one on Sicily; slaves on Sicily rose up again in 104–99, and Spartacus led a third revolt that controlled much of southern Italy in 73–71. Each was suppressed, but at great cost and after initial failures by Roman armies in battles with the rebels. Additionally, as the economic benefits of overseas conquests flowed back disproportionately to Roman citizens, the scope and benefits of Roman citizenship also became a source of conflict that erupted in the Social War of

91–88, in which almost all of Rome's Italian allies revolted at Rome's refusal to grant them citizenship. Rome won the war by conceding the point, and citizenship was extended throughout Italy. Gaius Marius, often credited with significant reforms in army organization (see below), emerged as a major leader during these wars.

Elite Politics and Military Dynasts   Even as these social and servile wars wound down, civil wars between rival individuals and factions within the Roman elite heated up. The senatorial dynamic, outlined above, that tended to limit the ability of consuls to pursue further conquests operated less effectively in times of social and political strife, and internal social conflicts also provided the opportunity for ambitious politicians to gain glory as "saviors of the Republic." A series of civil wars and power-sharing arrangements extended over three generations, from 88 to 31, until Octavian emerged as the first emperor.

Octavian was the adopted nephew of Julius Caesar, who along with Crassus, victor over Spartacus, and Pompey had formed the first triumvirate. Pompey had risen to prominence under Sulla, victor in the first civil war. All three were thus part of the concentration of military command in the provinces and political leadership in Rome in an increasingly small set of families. The narrowing of military leadership was partly a result of the reduced opportunities for active command in the provinces, noted above, and partly the result of the fact that the riches available through agriculture and trade in an expanding empire led the ambitions of many elites away from military leadership (though no Roman noble would admit openly to investing in mercantile activity). It was not just larger numbers of commoners who were becoming more distanced from war, in other words. This demilitarization of segments of the senatorial class effectively heightened the competition among the remainder. This competition was further intensified and polarized by the class antagonisms that tended, in the last years of the Republic, to divide politics and military conflict between proponents of conservative elites and populists, with both sides purporting to fight for the preservation of the Republic as they understood it.

In hindsight, it is easy to say that the Empire had become too large, complex, and lucrative an enterprise to be run successfully by a collective, especially one such as the Republic, whose culture stressed competition and for whom military leadership (and thus the potential for coercive power that successful

command conveyed) remained a central ideal—even if honored less often in practice. Instability was bound to result and could be ended only by the establishment of unified rule or the collapse of the Roman state and dissolution of the empire. Yet the culture and ideals of the Republic were deeply ingrained, and so collective government not only died hard but left its imprint on the form of imperial rule that followed.

The Changing Roman Army

The stresses of new sorts of campaigning, both in foreign realms and in civil wars, set against changes in Italian society, affected the Roman army, which underwent its own transformation during this period of transition from Republic to Empire.

Social changes affected recruiting, as noted above. Landownership continued to be a prerequisite for service in the legions into the first century BCE—Marius's famous call-up allowing landless men to join the legions is now seen not as a major and permanent policy change but as a temporary expedient that was not institutionalized fully until Octavian's reorganization of the army (see below). Still, poorer men tended to serve disproportionately, as successful service in the army remained a route, albeit a limited and dangerous one, to upward social mobility. Terms of service continued to lengthen gradually, and soldiers began to demand rewards at the termination of their service, demands promoted by their commanders, who thereby enhanced the loyalty of their legions to themselves.

Given this more socially limited base of recruitment, not surprisingly, the old formal distinctions based in age and wealth that had been used to assign troops to different lines and troop types in the manipular legions broke down. Now, all legionary infantry tended to conform to a single type, armed with *gladius* and *pilum,* wearing a bronze helmet and corselet, and carrying a large, curved rectangular shield. This homogenization of the heavy infantry was reflected organizationally. The cohort, an administrative unit of the manipular legion consisting of a maniple each of *hastati, principes,* and *triarii* plus cavalry, now, without the cavalry, became the basic tactical unit of the legion. Ten cohorts of 450–500 men (plus cavalry) thus still made up a legion, which still tended to be arranged in three lines deployed in a version of the old checkerboard formation. But larger cohorts with smaller gaps between them gave the legion a

A Roman Soldier   This depiction of a Roman soldier shows not only the standard equipment of a legionnaire—the *pilum,* or throwing spear, the *gladius,* or short stabbing sword, and the *scutum,* or shield—but also idealizes the soldier as representative and defender of civic virtue.

more continuous front without sacrificing much in the way of tactical flexibility.

Thus, aside from the tendency to a more phalanx-like frontage, the tactics of what is sometimes called the Marian legion (as Marius initiated some of the reforms that furthered the evolution of the Republican legion toward the form it assumed institutionally under Augustus) were not vastly different from its predecessor. Standards of discipline, training, and experience varied and were liable to diminish in times of civil strife and crisis. But these legions achieved some of the most impressive victories in Roman history because of the increasing professionalization of the army and especially of its officer class—above all, the centurions whose bravery and initiative are so praised by Caesar in his accounts of his generalship (see, for example, the Sources box "Caesar on Pharsalus").

It was probably in the relationship of legions to their overall commanders and thus, indirectly, to the state that the most significant changes occurred in this period. By the first century BCE, armies were becoming more often the creation (in terms of training, loyalty, and expectations of future reward) of the great commanders who led them. For example, Pompey got his start at age 23 by being able to bring to Sulla three veteran legions that had essentially "belonged" to his rich father; and Caesar's armies were *his* armies, advancing the cause of the Roman state when he led them in Gaul, but advancing his political cause when he led them across the Rubicon and into Italy. Such commanders had longer careers and played much more to the nonmilitary populace in Rome than had the constantly rotating consuls of the early Republic. They also commanded troops who served for longer periods away from home, which now included the whole of Italy. Thus, the tight relationship between citizenship, military service, and Roman civic identity that had launched the city on the road to conquest had been considerably loosened: Roman soldiers and civilians were diverging in identity and interests. This, too, was a legacy of Republican political competition that Augustus had to deal with in constructing an effective imperial government.

EMPIRE, 31 BCE–400 CE

Caesar Augustus

Conquests   Octavian, assuming the name Caesar Augustus when he emerged as the ultimate victor of the civil wars of the late Republic, launched a series of campaigns in northwestern Spain, Egypt, the Alps, much of the Balkan peninsula, and Austria south of the Danube. The resulting conquests, following immediately on the heels of nearly a century of civil wars and social conflict, contribute to the impression that the bellicosity and expansionism of the early Republic continued unbroken into Augustus's reign. But, examined further, this burst of expansionism resembles more closely the sporadic wars of expansion of the transitional period (218–231 BCE). Those campaigns mostly rounded off already extant provinces such as Spain to their natural geographic limits or, as in Egypt, formalized Roman control of areas already dominated by Roman power.

Caesar on Pharsalus

In this extract from his Bellum Civile, *or* The Civil War, *Caesar (who refers to himself in the third person) describes the decisive battle between his forces and those of his rival Pompey at Pharsalus in 48* BCE.

■ ■ ■

[3.90] [Caesar exhorted] his army to battle, according to the military custom, and spoke to them of the favors that they had constantly received from him, . . . After delivering this speech, he gave by a trumpet the signal to his soldiers, who were eagerly demanding it, and were very impatient for the onset.

[3.93] . . . our men, when the signal was given, rushed forward with their javelins ready to be launched, but perceiving that Pompey's men did not run to meet their charge, having acquired experience by custom, and being practiced in former battles, they of their own accord repressed their speed, and halted almost midway, that they might not come up with the enemy when their strength was exhausted, and after a short respite they again renewed their course, and threw their javelins, and instantly drew their swords, as Caesar had ordered them. Nor did Pompey's men fail in this crisis, for they received our javelins, stood our charge, and maintained their ranks; and having launched their javelins, had recourse to their swords. At the same time Pompey's horse, according to their orders, rushed out at once from his left wing, and his whole host of archers poured after them. Our cavalry did not withstand their charge, but gave ground a little, upon which Pompey's horse pressed them more vigorously, and began to file off in troops, and flank our army. When Caesar perceived this, he gave the signal to his fourth line, which he had formed of the six cohorts. They instantly rushed forward and charged Pompey's horse with such fury, that not a man of them stood; but all wheeling about, not only quitted their post, but galloped forward to seek a refuge in the highest mountains. By their retreat the archers and slingers, being left destitute and defenseless, were all cut to pieces. The cohorts, pursuing their success, wheeled about upon Pompey's left wing, while his infantry still continued to make battle, and attacked them in the rear.

[3.94] At the same time Caesar ordered his third line to advance, which till then had not been engaged, but had kept their post. Thus, new and fresh troops having come to the assistance of the fatigued, and others having made an attack on their rear, Pompey's men were not able to maintain their ground, but all fled, nor was Caesar deceived in his opinion, that the victory, as he had declared in his speech to his soldiers, must have its beginning from those six cohorts, which he had placed as a fourth line to oppose the horse. For by them the cavalry were routed; by them the archers and slingers were cut to pieces; by them the left wing of Pompey's army was surrounded, and obliged to be the first to flee. But when Pompey saw his cavalry routed, and that part of his army on which he reposed his greatest hopes thrown into confusion, despairing of the rest, he quitted the field, and retreated straightway on horseback to his camp, . . .

[3.97] Caesar having possessed himself of Pompey's camp, urged his soldiers not to be too intent on plunder, and lose the opportunity of completing their conquest.

[3.99] In that battle, no more than two hundred privates were missing, but Caesar lost about thirty centurions, valiant officers. . . . Of Pompey's army, there fell about fifteen thousand; but upwards of twenty-four thousand were made prisoners. . . .

SOURCE: Julius Caesar, *Bellum Civile*. Retrieved from http://ancienthistory.about.com/library/bl/bl_text_caesar_bellumciv_3.htm.

Caesar Augustus   Caesar Augustus established not only most of the borders of the Roman Empire but the main elements of imperial style for nearly two centuries—an odd mixture of traditional Republican forms and deification of the emperor.

These campaigns also seem to have been similar in motivation also. Although Augustus had defeated his immediate opponents, he probably felt the need to cement his political prestige and position with military triumphs against foreign foes, in the manner of earlier consuls and budding military dynasts including his uncle Julius Caesar in Gaul. Furthermore, he needed to cement the loyalty of the army, clearly the most important institution of imperial political control, through successful campaigning and the distribution of rewards and plunder. This also had the virtue of keeping the army occupied on the frontiers, with only the most loyal guard troops left in Rome with Augustus when he wasn't with the army on campaign.

This round of conquest and legitimation ended in 9 CE when Germanic tribes ambushed and wiped out three legions in the Teutoburgerwald between the Rhine and the Elbe rivers. Augustus seems to have planned the conquest of Germany at least up to the Elbe; after this disaster, he withdrew his legions behind the Rhine and the Danube and advised his successors not to expand the frontiers further. His advice was largely followed, but as much for practical reasons (the danger of losses loomed as large as the potential gains of victory for an emperor's prestige) as out of respect for his wishes. Indeed, when emperors came to the throne in need of bolstering their legiti-

macy, they pursued further conquests, as did Claudius (a fairly unmilitary man) in Britain after 43 and Trajan (the first non-Italian emperor) first in Dacia from 101–107 and then in Mesopotamia.

Institutionalization of the Professional Army

Augustus's conquests went hand in hand with institutional arrangements designed to stabilize and pacify the Empire internally. Above all, this meant dealing with the army. The number of troops in the various armies left at the end of the civil wars was over 500,000 in sixtysome legions, not all at full strength. Through consolidations and the practice of paying off veterans with both cash and land grants in colonies throughout the empire, Augustus reduced the number of legions to twenty-eight and troop strength, counting auxiliaries and the newly established Praetorian Guard, Augustus's personal bodyguard, to under 300,000.

The terms of service in the reorganized army regularized and institutionalized practices that had emerged haphazardly but broadly since the time of Marius around 100 BCE. The prerequisite of land ownership for joining the legions was officially eliminated. The army became a definite profession, as the length of a term of enlistment rose from 6 to 20 years (16 of which were on active service with another 4 on reserve duties). The practice of rewarding soldiers with land on the termination of their service, first instituted by Marius, became part of the standard terms of service. Pay rates were such that service in the army was not lucrative, but finding recruits seems not to have been a problem for most of the Pax Romana. Most of the army was stationed near the major frontiers, especially on the Rhine and Danube rivers and in the east facing the Parthian Empire (see below). Military colonies, based on the land grants that retired soldiers received, tended to grow up near the major permanent encampments of active units.

The Army and Political Culture

Augustus's formalization of a professional, long-service army that constituted the major permanent organ of the state naturally put that army into a special relationship with the emperor, a relationship that was closest between the Praetorian Guard and the emperor, and inevitably inserted the army into the politics of the Empire. As early as 41 CE, the Praetorian Guard intervened to assassinate the emperor Caligula, who had gone mad, elevating his uncle Claudius to the throne, and Vespasian emerged from the brief civil war of 69 that broke out when troops in different provinces, as well as the Praetorian Guard, advanced the claims of different commanders to the throne. Although the army then stayed out of emperor making (formally) until the third century, it remained the center of gravity of Roman politics.

This should be seen not merely as a result of institutional arrangements but as one of the cultural imprints on the Empire of the prestige of military command and battlefield success that developed under the Republic. The instructive contrast is with China. There, the consolidation of imperial state power under the Qin involved the delegitimation of warfare and the submergence of the remnants of the old chariot warrior elite under civilian state mechanisms in favor of a monopoly of legitimacy on the part of the central ruler. The Romans, having no chariot elite to depose and having built a state on an antimonarchical basis around a militarized aristocracy, population, and ethos, arrived at similar structures of centralized state power, although animated by a different culture of the relationship of warfare and the state.

This divide in political culture also shows up at the level of the individual soldier in the Chinese and Roman armies. Both institutions stressed discipline and training, but the officer corps and soldiers of the Roman army retained a notion of competition and of individual glory, within the structures of hierarchical command, that translated into individual initiative on the battlefield. Thus, Roman generals could give broad orders and trust their subordinates down to the centurion level to make the most of the opportunities they encountered. The centralizing Qin political ideology, on the other hand, as played out in military manuals such as Sun Zi's, vested all decision-making authority in the general, reducing subordinates and soldiers alike to military automata. It is hard to say whether one system was militarily superior to the other (though the modern, Western, prejudice is to see the virtues of the Roman system more clearly); both were quite successful. But they were certainly poles apart culturally despite sharing deep structural similarities.

The Pax Romana to 180

The Augustan settlement of the military and political structure of the Empire established the foundations for a period known then and since as the Pax Romana, or Roman Peace. While subjugated peoples could

(and did) argue about how peaceful the Pax Romana really was, given that it was established and maintained by force of arms, the Empire largely maintained internal stability and external security throughout the period from Augustus's reign down to the end of the second century. Stability and security rested on a number of structures that had the army at their core.

The Geostrategic Map   The distribution of legions from Augustus' time forward, though not absolutely fixed, remained relatively stable, and reflected Roman perceptions of the major threats facing the Empire (Figure 4.3). Some legions, as in Spain, remained in the interior in garrison and policing duty, but the largest concentrations were posted close to the frontiers along the Rhine and the Danube and facing the Parthian Empire in the east, the one major power that Rome engaged directly. The disaster that had befallen Crassus's army at Carrhae in 53 BCE had given the Romans a healthy respect for Parthian military capabilities on their own ground, and diplomacy was more often the tool of choice than war on the eastern frontier during this period.

It is important to realize that the nature of the frontiers was not a sharp divide between "civilized" and "barbarian," nor even a clear demarcation of the limits of Roman control and influence, as any map will tend (misleadingly) to imply. The frontiers were porous zones of interaction that extended far beyond any notional border on both sides. More or less Romanized tribes engaged in trade and adopted Roman ways, especially in Germany—one reason they felt justified in entering the Empire later when pressured by influxes from the east by the migrations of less acculturated tribes. Such an understanding of the frontiers, as well as awareness of the often personal nature of Roman diplomacy and political decision making, complicates any attempt to define a Roman grand strategy. In the sense that emperors tried to match resources to commitments and threats, there certainly was one. In the modern sense of a clearly conceptualized system of defensive arrangements, there was not. Indeed, the construction of Roman legionary camps made them much less defensive strongholds than bases for offensive operations, and although conquests after Augustus were rare for practical reasons, the ethos of the Empire remained expansionist.

The Army as an Institution   The imperial Roman army ranks as one of the great institutions of the premodern world. Named and numbered legions

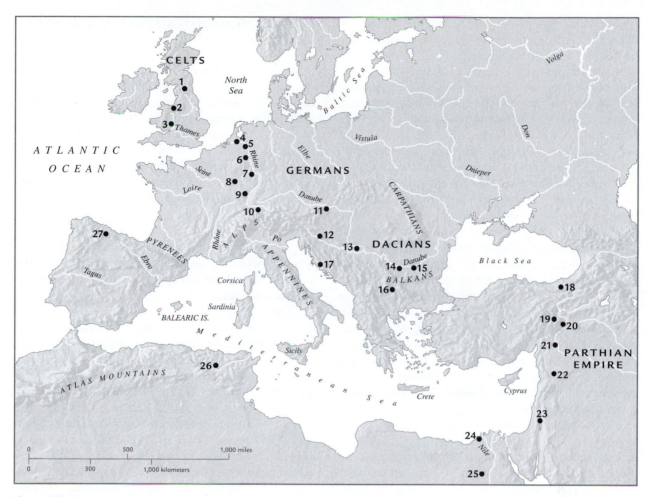

Figure 4.3 Deployment of Roman Legions

maintained institutional and cultural continuity over several centuries and provided the essential framework of recruiting, training, and retirement that kept the army going. The network of fortified camps that housed the army and the roads the legions marched on long outlasted the Empire itself. Expenditures on the army and its infrastructure dominated the Empire's budget. Given the close association of the army with internal imperial politics, it is not much of an exaggeration to say that the army was the (central) Roman state.

The military state existed on the foundation of a Roman socioeconomic world structured around cities and trade networks. Perhaps the key problem for Roman rulers (as for many similar large empires) was maintaining the relationship between state and society as a symbiotic one—with the state and army providing security for the economic structure and

prosperity that made a large military possible—and not as a parasitic one in which the cost of security ate its own support. Augustus's reduction of the size of the army clearly worked in this regard, but the total size of the military establishment crept up over time, and when the number of threats it had to deal with also rose after 180, that balance proved harder to maintain.

The Army and Society The Augustan settlement had other implications for the relationship between army and society that played themselves out more ambiguously over the course of the next two centuries. The chief change, and probably one that was unavoidable given both the size of the Empire and the resulting need for a professional army, was the social marginalization of soldiers. If being a Roman citizen under the early Republic meant also being a soldier, being a citizen under the Empire (a category that expanded significantly when all free men in the Empire were granted citizenship in 212) meant, for most, benefiting from the protection of soldiers. Longer terms of service for individuals and the reduced size of the military establishment after Augustus's reforms meant that an even smaller proportion of the population of the Empire served in the army than in the transitional Republic, and the cultural divide between civilian and soldier grew wider.

One curious result of this was that, while military glory remained a central aspect of Roman culture, its expression and the prestige that glory generated were increasingly vested in the institution of the army and in its overall commander, the emperor, rather than in individual soldiers. (Within the culture of the army, glory remained both a generalized value and something achieved by individuals through bravery in action, which translated into benefits both tangible—promotions and bonuses—and intangible. But neither the glory nor the social prestige soldiers gained within the army translated automatically beyond that institution into society at large, whereas in earlier centuries the two had been inseparable.) The concentration of military glory in the person of the emperor to the exclusion of other individuals and the marginalization of military values also operated at the level of elite culture. Political courtiers and cultural elites dominated at the capital, while local urban elites focused on civil service and civic and religious building projects; both, especially the former, showed little understanding of or sympathy for military values and the life of soldiers. The identity between Roman society and its army had been transformed into a near-polar opposition.

Points of contact did remain. Soldiers who settled long term in permanent camps naturally developed ties, both economic and social, to the local population. Soldiers were supposed to remain unmarried for the duration of their active service, but informal ties inevitably developed, and the settlement of retired soldiers with their families in the vicinity of permanent camps further connected local society to the military. But such ties remained limited and localized, and economic interactions with localities could just as often prove burdensome as profitable, depending on the state of local economic development. For most of the Pax Romana, the estrangement of army and society was not terribly problematic, because it operated under the umbrella of the successful symbiosis of state and economy noted above. But it had potentially negative implications should that large-scale relationship break down.

The Army at War   Institutional continuity and the development of a written culture of military handbooks contributed to the efficiency of the Roman army at war. Roman armies followed a standard order of march and a marching routine that included establishing a fortified camp at the end of each day's movement. Camps were laid out on a standard grid that reflected the unit organization of the army, and camp discipline was generally strictly enforced. Equipment was also relatively standardized; many weapons and armor were produced in large state workshops, and the army's demand for food, clothing, and shelter was significant. As noted, although in some areas that demand stimulated economic activity, in others it proved a burden.

The Roman army remained a reliable and generally efficient battle-fighting machine. Tactics did not change much in the transition from late Republic to Empire, although the scope of the Empire and the range of subject peoples it could call on to provide auxiliaries gave it even greater tactical flexibility. The cavalry in particular, long a weakness of Roman armies, improved with the regular recruitment of auxiliaries from Spain and North Africa. While the highest levels of tactical command varied in quality, now according to the vagaries of political appointment rather than election, the professionalism of the lower-level officers down to centurion rank was such that many Roman armies could fight well with minimal direction from above. And while expansionism and conquest at the strategic level became rare, the aggressive, offensively oriented culture of Roman battle, resulting from the creative tension between competition for individual glory and group cohesion and discipline, continued to operate throughout this period.

Where the armies of the Empire clearly outshone their predecessors from the early Republic was in military engineering, an aspect of the general Roman talent for engineering and construction that produced not just roads and fortifications but cement, aqueducts, amphitheaters, and so forth. The entrenching that characterized Roman encampments could also be turned directly against enemy forts. Roman siege craft advanced significantly under Caesar in Gaul (and Sulla had used field entrenchments in battle to protect his flanks at Chaeronea in 86 BCE). Imperial armies had siege trains that could deploy significant numbers of siege engines of a variety of types, ranging from giant steel bows that served essentially as antipersonnel weapons and could be deployed on battlefields, to antifortification stone throwers that operated on both torsion and tension principles. They also developed formations such as the *testudo* (or "tortoise," in which legionnaires held their shields over their heads) designed for assaults on walls, employed sappers to mine walls, and in 70 CE, at the siege of Jerusalem during the Jewish Revolt, revived the old technique of building a massive earthen ramp up the walls.

The Jewish Revolt illustrates one of the sorts of tasks the army carried out. Suppression of rebellions and insurrections—in effect, internal policing on a large scale—was vital and shows that not all the Empire's subject peoples appreciated the supposed benefits of Roman rule unambiguously. It also illustrates Roman values at work in battle: Josephus, the great historian of the war, records (or plausibly invents) a Roman commander's speech before a battle with the rebels in which he reminds his soldiers that the Jews fight merely for their god and their country, while the Romans fight for glory, the far-greater motive.

Purely defensive campaigns against external invasions were rare, for even temporary defensive activity was likely to be followed by punitive offensives that aimed at delivering a message while at the same time gathering plunder. Such offensives were also launched to reinforce diplomatic pressure or to respond to diplomatic slights or threats. Though rare, campaigns of conquest did still occur, most famously under Trajan in the early second century, in Dacia and Parthia.

Crisis and Transformation, 180–280

Beginning in the late second century CE, Rome was faced with an increased level of military threat on its borders. Tribes beyond the borders, some more acculturated to Roman influence than others, began to migrate over the borders. Some asked permission to enter and were allowed in by Roman authorities, often on terms that included military service; others, either refused permission or not asking for it, moved more or less forcibly and met Roman resistance. This pressure was especially intense along the Danube frontier of the Empire in the Balkan peninsula, but it also erupted at times along the Rhine. The reasons for this rise in external pressure are complex but certainly involve the migrations of peoples from farther east, including steppe nomads, moving west under pressure, in turn, from their eastern neighbors. Some of the origins of

this chain reaction trace back to the expansion of the Han Empire in the first century BCE.

Another source of increased threat arose on the Empire's eastern borders, where a revived Persian Empire under the Sassanians replaced the declining Parthians in 226 CE (see Chapter 2). Their revival of Zoroastrianism combined with increased Roman bellicosity in Armenia and northern Mesopotamia to turn what had been a diplomatically managed frontier into a source of military problems that would persist, in greater or lesser degrees of intensity, until the sudden eruption of the Arabs and Islam in the seventh century transformed the entire region (see Chapter 8).

Complicating matters further was a significant rise in the third century of internal instability and civil wars. Since provincial armies formed the crucial support base for contestants for the throne, dynastic conflict often resulted in frontier regions denuded of their troops, who were busy marching on Rome. Civil wars had two further effects on the army. First, standards of discipline and training declined; and second, prior to 180, detachments from legions and auxiliary units often had been sent to reinforce areas of major conflict, but such *vexillations*, as they were called, had always returned to their parent units when the crisis had been dealt with. In the continual crises, internal and external, that characterized the middle of the third century, detachments and the mixing of units tended to become permanent, diluting the traditions and unit cohesion of the old legions. Emperors gradually increased the size of the army, in part to compensate for its declining quality and in part simply because it was the only way to meet more widely dispersed threats. But this both increased the tax burden on an economy that was already stressed by conflicts within the Empire's borders and complicated the task of maintaining discipline. Recruiting depended ever more heavily on barbarians, though the meaning of this term must be examined critically (see the Issues box "The 'Barbarization' of the Roman Army"). In short, the Augustan military system was breaking down.

The Late Empire, 280–400

By the middle of the third century, the survival of the Empire was in question. But a series of reforms instituted by the emperor Diocletian (284–305) and cemented by Constantine (314–337) reorganized

The "Barbarization" of the Roman Army

The nature of the transformation of the late Roman army has been a subject of historiographical controversy for almost as long as there have been historians writing about Rome. Indeed, in some ways, the question goes back as far as Vegetius, not a historian but the fifth-century CE writer of a late-Roman manual of military affairs that emphasized a decline in discipline and training as the root of the army's troubles, and even further back to Tacitus, the early imperial Roman historian.

But the modern form of the controversy in many ways dates to the late eighteenth century and Edward Gibbon's monumental *Decline and Fall of the Roman Empire*, which some historians consider the first modern, scholarly work of history. Gibbon, influenced by Enlightenment rationality, saw two linked causes for the disintegration of Roman power: barbarians, not just as invaders but as military recruits by Rome, and the rise of Christianity. While few historians today would give much weight to changing religion as a cause of military decline, the role of barbarians—Germanic tribes moving into the Empire either as enemies or as federated soldiers—has had a more influential role in the historiography.

Until the past thirty years, this role was cast in terms of the conflict and eventual fusion of *Romanitas* and *Germanitas*—that is, of separate and opposed sociocultural worlds, one Roman and one German, the former representing sophisticated "civilization," the latter primitive "barbarism." For Gibbon, the moral terms of this conflict were clear, and the "good guys" (civilization) lost. But the picture was complicated by nineteenth-century nationalist historians, many working in Germany and England, who saw in the Germanic tribes the forebears of their own peoples and attributed to them the virtues of vitality and egalitarianism, in contrast to the decadence and autocracy of Rome. English historians, in particular, were prone to see the roots of democracy in the warbands of the Germanic chiefs, in which the chiefs' followers, all the free men of the tribe, had considerable influence over a sort of collective decision making. This view of Germanic warbands ultimately traces back to Tacitus's picture of the *comitatus*, or warband, and his ethnography of German tribes, dating to the first century CE. In this view, the fall of Rome was not necessarily a bad thing, as it opened up space for the birth of modern nations.

both the administration of the Empire, civil and military, and the field army. These reforms proved effective enough that the Empire survived another century and a half in the west and another millennium in the east. But they also transformed the nature of the Empire and its military forces.

State and Society   Recognizing that the administrative and military burden on a single ruler had become unmanageable, Diocletian divided the Empire into halves, each ruled by a coequal Augustus aided by a Caesar, or junior emperor. Significantly, Diocletian ruled the eastern half of the Empire, which was richer, more urban, and in some ways more defensible than the western half, from a capital at Nicomedia in Asia

Minor; Constantine later founded a new capital at the Bosporus, which he named Constantinople (ancient Byzantium, and present-day Istanbul). Rome, though symbolically still significant, ceased to be the center of the Roman Empire—a deliberate move on the part of Diocletian and Constantine, who aimed to reduce the influence of both the Senate and the Praetorian Guard, the latter of which Constantine abolished.

The system of divided rule did not prevent civil wars after Diocletian stepped down in 305. Multiple ruling courts increased further the tax burden on a Roman society that was at best demographically stagnant by this time, despite migration into the Empire by Romanized barbarians (always smaller in number than popular imagination would have them) and an

But recent work on both Tacitus and late Roman institutional history has destroyed this romantic picture. Tacitus's picture of the *comitatus* has been shown to be largely invented, owing more to his own critique of Roman society than to accurate knowledge of the Germanic peoples. More important, frontier archaeology and institutional studies have shown that Germanic-speaking peoples outside the empire were far more Romanized than the nationalist view could admit. Further, even when so-called barbarian tribes were incorporated into the Roman army, they adopted Roman military (and political) organization (as well as they could) and, in some sense, thought of themselves as Romans. Institutional evolution under pressures of military necessity, socioeconomic transformation, and political competition and fragmentation worked from Roman roots, and the institutional contribution of *Germanitas* has disappeared from modern accounts. In this view, the barbarization of the army was a fiction.

But the various tribes still exist in the sources, and this more recent account still implicitly accepted a basic ethnic division between the populations of the empire and those outside it, and assumed the organic unity of the peoples who became Romanized. Most recently, this aspect of the problem has come under scrutiny by historians working from the perspective of cultural studies. For them, the whole notion of ethnicity is a product of cultural constructions. In other words, "barbarian" (including any particular tribal identification) was an identity adopted by various peoples for various reasons, with the tribes themselves as political rather than ethnic constructions. And in terms of military recruiting, the reason for any individual to adopt a barbarian identity was that barbarians were the ones hired by the state to fight, and thus often exempted from certain taxes. In short, "barbarian" came to mean "warrior," while "Roman" meant, basically, "taxpayer," and the boundaries between the two categories were porous and fluid. Thus, in this most recent formulation, while the picture of institutional evolution within Roman frameworks remains intact, the Roman army really was barbarized. But this simply doesn't mean what historians once thought it meant. It has everything to do with ethnogenesis, or the cultural construction of group identities, and little or nothing to do with the corruption (or invigoration) of Roman civilization by barbaric (but democratic!) Germans.

economy already stressed by war and taxes. Social changes were accompanied by religious transformation following Constantine's legalization and then promotion of Christianity, which by the mid-fourth century had become the official religion of the Empire—a shift with consequences for foreign policy, especially on the Persian frontier, where Christianity and Zoroastrianism came to add a new element of ideological conflict to warfare between the two empires (see Chapter 8).

The problems of ruling a more socially divided, less secure empire were reflected in the increasingly autocratic nature of the Roman state, symbolized by the decline in importance of the Senate. It was thus in this period that the Republican imprint on the political culture of the Empire, maintained by the fictions of the Augustan settlement, definitively faded, a process mirrored by changes in the army.

The Army   Diocletian and Constantine reorganized the army significantly. The total military establishment had by now grown from the roughly 300,000 troops under Augustus to somewhere between 400,000 and 500,000 men. Reform divided the troops into two forces: those stationed on the frontiers, called *limitanei*, and a group of mobile field armies, the *comitatenses*, which were stationed as reserves. Although theoretically of similar status and drawn from the same recruiting bases, the field armies were paid more and had lighter equipment (among the infantry); they also included the bulk of the much more prominent and numerous cavalry forces Rome was now raising. Lower pay meant that many frontier troops worked at least part-time in the civilian economy, reducing their practical mobility. The legions of the frontier forces were reduced in size to around 1000, reflecting the realities of the earlier creation of vexillations of about this size. But the theoretical flexibility this measure provided tended to be undermined by the tendency for frontier units to become even more attached to their localities. Thus, service in the field armies became more prestigious, causing morale problems for the frontier units, whose military effectiveness and political influence gradually decayed.

The increased organizational importance of the cavalry arm was evident in the creation of two new offices of military command immediately subordinate to the emperor—the Master of the Foot and the Master of the Horse, who replaced a Master of the Troops, an office that had proven dangerously powerful. Stronger cavalry forces also reflected the rising importance of auxiliaries—non-Romans serving in their own units and sometimes with their own weapons and tactical traditions—in the army (see the Issues box). The relationship of the late Roman army to the society that it protected became, in these circumstances, even more attenuated than the relationship between the professional but still citizen legions of the Augustan system and their society and was a far cry from the identity of army and society obtaining under the Republic.

Warfare: Training, Cavalry, and Mobility

Tactical and operational considerations contributed to the rising importance of cavalry in Roman forces in the mid-third century. Obviously, mounted troops could move more quickly from one theater of operations (or a central reserve station) to another than could foot soldiers. The number of separate threats the Empire faced and the mobile nature of the invaders put a premium on rapid responses. "Mounted troops" in this case included what could be called mounted infantry: troops who rode horses for strategic mobility but tended to enter combat on foot. But cavalry units—troops who remained mounted both on campaign and in battle—assumed a greater tactical role as well. This was partly in response to the cavalry deployed by groups such as the Visigoths, who employed heavily armed and armored horsemen who charged into close combat, and later the Huns, who employed the swift mounted archers typical of steppe peoples (see Chapter 6). That such groups were not just enemies but also

recruits in the Roman army further highlights the greater role for cavalry in late Roman warfare.

But declining standards of training and discipline in the Roman army also contributed to the rising importance of cavalry, because large-unit training was more important to the cohesion of infantry forces than of cavalry, which could effectively operate in smaller units and tended to be bound together by elite social ties more than were infantry. Thus, the apparent rise of cavalry actually in large part reflects a relative decline in infantry quality, which, in turn, reflects the declining effectiveness of Roman central authority over its military forces. On the other hand, this trend should not be exaggerated. Infantry units remained numerically predominant in Roman forces and continued to play vital roles on the battlefield, particularly as the solid defensive base around which cavalry could maneuver, and even more so in the less glamorous but equally important work of siege warfare and defense of fortified positions.

Landlords, Warlords, and Division

The generally declining effectiveness of Roman central government, especially in the western half of the Empire, where urban-based economic and social resources for maintaining order were scarcer than in the east, naturally had repercussions beyond the composition and effectiveness of the army. Social changes occurring in conditions of instability and declining and fragmenting central authority had important implications for the nature of military service.

The key development, again predominantly in the less urbanized western half of the Empire, was the growing privatization and localization of political, social, and military power. Two social groups led this trend from opposite but converging directions. One was the owners of great rural estates, whose social and economic power allowed them to hire private soldiers to act as bodyguards and defenders of their employers' landed interests. The other was the leaders of Roman military units, especially federated units organized around loyalty to their leader (and marked increasingly by barbarian cultural tribal identities, as noted in the Issues box). These groups' control of coercive force allowed them to appropriate landholdings in order to secure the economic base of their power in a time when tax collection and central disbursement of pay was becoming more problematic.

The result was a growing class of leaders with Roman pedigrees, either social or military, but whose private interests and power were becoming increasingly separated, in reality, from the exercise of public authority on behalf of the state—although they maintained the appearance of state appointment and state-conferred office, and they deployed the mechanisms of state-sanctioned enforcement as much as possible because of the prestige and legitimacy state titles still carried. Ironically, this brought about the beginnings of a reconnection of military force and society very different from the separation that had characterized the Empire at its height. But this reconnection was beyond the reach of the Roman state, a state that had emerged originally as the framework for the unity of society and army in the Republic, and had been, of course, the overarching institutional unifier of

separate civilian and military spheres under the Empire. The result was thus not the re-creation of the early Republic, whose antimonarchical ethos had by now been totally effaced, as Augustine's writings attest. Rather, the result was the emergence of the foundations for the barbarian kingdoms that would succeed the Empire in the west when the old edifice finally broke apart in the fifth century (see Chapter 7).

The restriction of this result to the west, however, highlights the fact that the "fall of Rome" was a partial and largely evolutionary phenomenon, for the Empire survived in the east, where institutional continuity and a central role for the state remained much more evident through periods of subsequent transformation (see Chapter 8).

CONCLUSION

The Roman Empire, originating in the expansionist Republic, outlasted its contemporaries in India and China in history's Age of Empires. Its afterlife, especially in the west, resembled the Mauryans' more than that of the Han, in that its lasting influence would be as a lost ideal of unity carried forward in cultural memory rather than as an institutional foundation on which rebuilding could take place. Even in the east, transformation and restriction more than balanced continuity in the later history of what would become known as the Byzantine Empire. Despite successors such as the Holy Roman Empire (which some histo-

rians have said was neither holy, Roman, nor an empire), the Roman empire never returned.

This should not obscure the remarkable achievements of the Roman state over the course of the more than eight centuries covered by this chapter. The Roman army was at the heart of that achievement and represents one of the two high points, alongside the armies of Qin and Han China, of military organization in the ancient world. There is a reason that the "grandeur that was Rome" continues to hold a prominent place in modern Western images of military history.

SUGGESTED READINGS

Campbell, Brian. "The Roman Empire." In K. Raaflaub and N. Rosenstein, *War and Society in the Ancient and Medieval Worlds*. Cambridge: Cambridge University Press, 1999. A short, readable synthesis of imperial Roman military development by a leading expert in the field. See also his *The Roman Army, 31 BC–AD 337: A Sourcebook* (London: Routledge, 1994), a valuable collection of primary sources.

Cornell, Timothy. *The Beginnings of Rome: Italy and Rome from the Bronze Age to the Punic Wars (c. 1000–264 B.C.)*. London: Routledge, 1995. An important reassessment of the early stages of Roman expansionism.

Goldsworthy, Adrian. *The Roman Army at War, 100 BC–AD 200*. Oxford: Oxford University Press, 1996. A thorough and insightful examination of Roman military practices, from organization to logistics to battle, with an emphasis on actual performance. See also his excellent *The Punic Wars* (London:

Cassell, 2001), a detailed history of these pivotal conflicts, and his other books on Caesar, Cannae, and Roman warfare generally.

Harris, William. *War and Imperialism in Republican Rome, 327–70 B.C.* Oxford: Oxford University Press, 1979. A foundational study of the interrelationship of society and military in early Roman expansion.

Kagan, Kimberly. "Redefining Roman Grand Strategy." *Journal of Military History 70* (2006): 333–62. An effective summary of the main ideas in Edward Luttwak's *The Grand Strategy of the Roman Empire* (Baltimore: Johns Hopkins University Press, 1976), the critical responses that work drew from classicists, and a reasonable middle ground defining Roman grand strategy in Roman terms.

Lendon, J. E. *Soldiers and Ghosts: A History of Battle in Classical Antiquity*. New Haven: Yale University Press, 2005. An intriguing analysis of Greek and Roman battle that stresses the creative tension between discipline and individual heroism in Roman combat.

Rich, John, and Graham Shipley, eds. *War and Society in the Roman World*. London: Routledge, 1995. An essential collection of articles on various aspects of Roman warfare; especially strong on the changing relationship of army and society in Roman history.

Rosenstein, Nathan. "Republican Rome." In Raaflaub and Rosenstein, *War and Society in the Ancient and Medieval Worlds*. A clear, concise overview of republican Roman military development.

Speidel, Michael. *Riding for Caesar. The Roman Emperors' Horse Guards*. Cambridge: Harvard University Press, 1994. A useful examination of the elite cavalry units of the imperial army.

Webster, Graham. *The Roman Imperial Army of the First and Second Centuries A.D.* Norman: University of Oklahoma Press, 1985. A standard survey, now a bit dated and traditional in its interpretations, but still useful.

CHAPTER 5

Oars and Rams: Ancient Naval Warfare to 400 CE

The history of naval warfare has often been over-looked within military history. Partly, this may reflect a general neglect of maritime history as part of history as a whole, a problem only recently drawing attention with the growing recognition of the importance of maritime connections in the patterns of global development. But partly, it reflects some truths about naval warfare. Naval warfare developed later than land warfare and long remained something of an adjunct to land warfare, acquiring semi-independent freedom of action only after 1500 CE. Indeed, most popular naval history focuses on the past two centuries and traces rapid technological development and the great naval battles of World War II. And yet, the close links between land and naval warfare, rather than justifying neglect of naval history, in fact point out the importance of considering it alongside the land warfare with which it often worked in tandem. Although we tell the story of naval warfare before the twentieth century in separate chapters, roughly one for each chronological part of this book, this is designed to highlight naval developments, not marginalize them. Given the key role of maritime activity in global developments noted above, separate naval chapters will also allow us to examine naval history in comparative and global perspective more readily.

EARLY MARITIME ACTIVITY

Maritime activity of some sort dates to fairly early in the spread of the modern human species. For example, the populating of Australia around 40,000 years ago required people to cross open waters on some sort of raft or simple boat such as a dugout canoe. The small-scale use of such craft arose in many places where human habitation bordered on or encompassed rivers, lakes, and seashores. Especially for carrying goods for trade, boats have a natural advantage

over land transport: They can carry heavier loads more easily, and so farther at lower cost, than can humans, animals, or even carts on land. But the scope of maritime activity remained restricted for a long period, even after the rise of hierarchical states and land-based warfare, due to limitations of technology, geography, and climate. Regions that combined relatively calm and enclosed seas, friendly coasts (shoal-free and with suitable natural harbors or beaches), favorable wind patterns, and access to land areas with substantial populations and economic activity were not that common for the ships of 4000 years ago. Thus, maritime trade and exploration spread only gradually in the wake of technological developments and the accumulation of navigational and geographic knowledge.

Naval warfare as distinct from maritime trade or troop transport arose even more slowly, because creating ships capable of acting as weapons or even weapons platforms required even more specialized technology (and, usually, more manpower) than did merchant marine activity. Further, naval warfare required not just concentrations of people and economic activity near shores, concentrations that generated the sailing traditions and infrastructures of maritime activity on which navies had to be built; it also required states capable of organizing military forces, states for which sea-lanes linked (but not too distantly) strategically important and contested locations. A brief survey of early maritime activity shows just how restrictive this set of conditions was.

As noted previously, low-intensity exploitation of rivers, lakes, and even narrow seas using dugout or bark canoes, sometimes with outriggers, coracles (skins stretched over a light wooden frame), or rafts, any of which could be powered by paddles or simple sails, was ubiquitous around the ancient world (Figure 5.1). Despite a lack of state-level societies, relatively large-scale exploration, commerce, and even transport of warriors in such contexts eventually

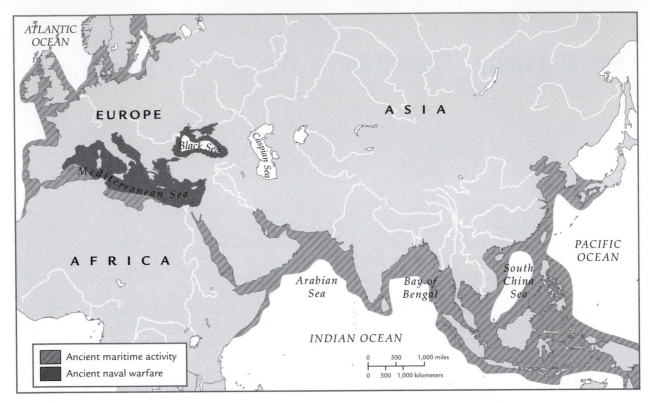

Figure 5.1 Ancient Areas of Maritime Activity

reached significant levels in the Caribbean and, especially, across the Pacific, climaxing there with large fleets of war canoes deployed by the warring chiefdoms of the Hawaiian archipelago. However, the political context, as well as rough and stormy seas, limited developments in the narrow waters of the North Sea and Baltic and the Yellow and China seas. For example, the potential maritime influence of China was hindered by its inland center of gravity and the difficulty of navigating its major rivers. The Indian Ocean saw the fairly early rise of long-distance maritime trade between hierarchical societies, based on the regularity of the monsoon wind pattern: The winds blew in one direction for six months and the opposite direction the other six months, making for predictable round-trips. But long distances and open seas militated against such trade becoming the basis for seaborne political competition, and no specialized warships (nor even much in the way of troop transport) developed there.

Only in the Mediterranean, and at first only at its eastern end, did conditions lead to the rise of naval warfare in the ancient world. It is on developments in this world that the rest of this chapter will focus.

THE EMERGENCE OF NAVAL WARFARE

Geography and Technology

The eastern Mediterranean is a relatively calm sea, especially in summer, with fairly limited tides and prevailing winds from the northwest. Except for parts of North Africa, its shores have an abundance of natural harbors and beaches, without much in the way of shoals, including on the many islands, some substantial, that break up the open sea-lanes. It is, in short, amenable to navigation even in ships of limited technological sophistication. In ancient times, the lands bordering the Mediterranean to the north and east possessed abundant forests—notably, the cedar forests of Lebanon—that produced good wood for ship building. Egypt, while short of wood, grew reeds that could be dried and bundled into material suitable for building small craft, at least, while its flax could be turned into linen for sails. Though the earliest boats in any area were paddled, both rowing and sailing were more efficient, especially for ships of any size. The calmn waters of the eastern Mediterranean meant that oared propulsion was an option, and it could be combined with sails to overcome the problem of winds that tended to blow from the same direction the boats travelled.

The economic stimulus for taking advantage of this potential highway came from the rise of two substantial areas of civilization—or state-level, hierarchical societies with specialized economic activity—on or near its shores, in Egypt and Mesopotamia. The growth of these centers, in turn, stimulated the rise of numerous small states around the edges and on the islands of the Mediterranean. Of these, Egypt initially led the way in the development of maritime technology and activity. This is probably because, unlike the unpredictable and often rocky Tigris and Euphrates in southwest Asia, the Nile offers a broad, flat run of navigable water uninterrupted by rapids or falls for nearly 500 miles from its mouth to the First Cataract. The Nile also flows north, into the prevailing winds, so boats could drift or row downstream with the current and then sail back upstream, making round-trips easy. Early on, the Nile became the central highway of the Egyptian kingdom, and by the late third millennium BCE, the ships developed to exploit it ventured out into the Mediterranean to carry Egyptian trade up the coast of Palestine.

Meanwhile, small states along the coasts of Syria and Asia Minor, on Crete, and in Mycenaean Greece also ventured across the waters seeking commerce and wealth. Trade contacts meant political contacts, and Egyptian oared ships soon carried armies and their supplies as well as trade goods into Palestine. In this way, the basic conditions for naval warfare were already in place, for, at this early stage, a warship was simply a ship full of soldiers. Actual fighting was, as far as we know, still confined to land, not only for Egyptian armies but for the Mycenaeans whose warriors sailed their own ships to Asia Minor to besiege and sack the city of Troy. But that war, immortalized in Homer's *Iliad*, reminds us of the close connection that had arisen by 1500 BCE in ancient maritime activity between trading and raiding—a connection that would persist and was often determined by the preparedness of a coastal settlement to resist violence. It also presaged a time of troubles for eastern Mediterranean societies that led to the emergence of true naval warfare. Unidentified Sea Peoples raided widely throughout the area in the decades around 1200 BCE, and a substantial contingent even entered the mouth of the Nile around 1190. A fleet of ships sent by Pharaoh Ramses III seems to have surprised them there, however, and, in ship-to-ship fighting, the invaders were

slaughtered, a feat Ramses immortalized in a temple relief, the first known depiction in history of a naval battle. The age of naval warfare had arrived.

The Invention of Specialized Warships

Tactics By the time the disruptions begun around 1200 had settled down around 900, two new peoples and a crucial new technology had entered the picture. The peoples were the Greek heirs of the Mycenaeans (see also Chapter 3) and the Phoenicians of coastal Syria. Both lived in city-states, and their close maritime trade connections are indicated by the Greek adoption of a form of that then-unique Phoenician invention—the alphabet. Both made a living partly from trade, and both, when faced with population pressures in their home cities, turned to sea-borne colonization as a means of relieving that pressure and extending their mercantile connections. Greek settlements appeared all around the Aegean and into the Black Sea, as well as in southern Italy and France; Phoenician settlements spread along the coast of North Africa, most famously at Carthage, and into Iberia. The technology was the ram.

The galley, a long, narrow ship powered primarily by oars, had emerged as the main vessel of Mediterranean trade and warfare by the mid-second millennium BCE. Two types had already developed. Broader, heavier, and slower versions carried bulkier goods or large groups of people. Lighter, narrower, and thus faster versions tended to be used by raiders (whose warriors manned their own oars) and navies (who loaded a contingent of marines on ships with separate rowers). The lighter galleys were favored for military purposes because their speed enabled them to run down slower ships, whether merchant vessels or other warships, thus giving birth to both piracy and the possibility of blockading ports. But naval combat on such ships consisted exclusively of coming close enough to enemy craft to fire missiles at the opposing crews and, ultimately, to grapple and board the enemy ships. This was because such ships could not carry missile weapons large or accurate enough to do damage to the enemy ships themselves. (The only other way to sink an enemy ship would have been to burn it, and no safe and reliable system of projecting combustible material onto enemy decks yet existed.) In short, naval combat was land warfare aboard ships.

Rams, first used in the mid-ninth century BCE, introduced a radical new option. Now, the ship itself had become a weapon that could disable or even sink an opposing vessel. But delivering the right sort of blow introduced new tactical imperatives. Rowing crews needed to be more highly trained, so as to be able to change speed and direction more rapidly, including being able to backwater and extricate the ship from its victim after ramming it. And they needed to be directed by experienced captains who could judge the speed and direction of their own and enemy ships accurately. This created the potential for some navies to gain a skill advantage, which, in turn, meant that divergent tactical traditions could develop, as less skilled navies had some incentive to continue to rely on the brute-force method of boarding. In addition to skill, the rams now put an even greater premium on speed and maneuverability, which led to further technological developments in the galleys themselves.

Technology The obvious solution to the need for greater speed under oars, given that galley hulls were already narrow and streamlined, with length-to-beam ratios of as much as ten to one, was to add more rowers. Simply lengthening the hull and adding more rows of seats rapidly reached a practical limit, however. Longer light and narrow hulls became structurally weaker and thus more vulnerable to the effects of ramming, and beyond a certain length (about twenty-five rows of rowing benches) tended to hog, or sag at the ends and threaten to break in the middle, especially in any sort of rough seas. Adding more men per oar was certainly an option, and one that would be pursued later, but it seems to have been a secondary option at first because doing so necessitated widening the hull, thereby impairing its performance. (Putting more than two men on an oar also necessitates a completely different style of rowing, one that requires the oarsmen to stand at the start of each stroke and then fall back onto the bench, rather than remaining seated the whole time.) The solution that emerged in the eastern Mediterranean in the eighth century BCE was to add a second tier or bank of rowers above the first. Galleys had relatively low freeboard (the amount of exposed hull between the waterline and the gunwale, or top of the hull); building up the sides enough to add a second bank of rowers proved relatively easy. The top row, after a period of experimentation, rowed over the raised gunwale, and the bottom row through portholes cut in the side.

Given more power behind them, rams evolved as well. At first fairly pointy, so as to maximize the chance of puncturing the target hull, rams became blunter and heavier. Not only did this sort of battering ram design allow for a crushing and perhaps extended blow that would spring more seams and do wider damage, it lessened the chance that the ramming ship would drive so deeply into its target as to impale it on the ram and be unable to withdraw, leaving it easy prey to other enemy ships. The bow end of ramming galleys was also now massively reinforced to withstand the impact of the collision.

The end result was a one- or two-tiered war galley carrying around fifty rowers (Greek, *pentekonters*, or "fiftyers"), a small crew, and a variable number of marines. No longer could just any galley serve as a warship with the addition of a contingent of soldiers. Instead, naval warfare was now the province of specialized warships that were both weapon and fighting platform. Variations on the oared ramming galley would dominate the Mediterranean until the 1580s and the advent of full-rigged sailing ships with masses of inexpensive cannon capable of firing massive broadsides.

Strategic and Economic Implications The emergence of this sort of specialized warship had a number of strategic and economic implications for the prosecution of naval warfare. First, building and manning them required at least some concentration of economic and administrative resources. *Pentekonters*, the main fighting ship between about 800 and 500 BCE, were still small and cheap enough to be affordable by almost any city-state with trade connections and a maritime infrastructure. However, developments that further raised the cost of individual ships (see below) ensured that naval power in the Mediterranean would become and remain closely tied to the demographic, fiscal-economic, and political strength of states. This is in contrast with some areas, such as the North Sea and south India, where significant naval activity arose in the context of weak or barely emergent states (see Chapter 10).

Second, oared-galley warships directly shaped the strategies of naval warfare. A large part of this stemmed from the logistics of galleys. Long, narrow, and stuffed with rowers and crew, they had limited cargo capacity even for necessities such as food and, above all for rowers in hot Mediterranean summers, water. Thus, galley fleets had extremely limited cruising ranges and had to put into shore almost every night when on campaign so the crewmen could find food and water. Galleys were light enough to be simply drawn up on a beach, but they were then vulnerable to attack by an enemy fleet or land force. Therefore, regularly projecting naval power to any distance from a fleet's home required a series of safe ports within easy reach of one another. In other words, unlike the sailing ships of the seventeenth century and later, which could stay at sea for weeks at a time, galley fleets could not cruise open waters.

This meant that control of the sea in any modern sense was simply not possible. Ships could not be blockaded in port by an enemy fleet sitting offshore and occupying the sea-lanes. Even when galley fleets took part in the close siege of a port city, they had to be based on a nearby beach or port, which meant that fast enemy galleys stood a fair chance of running the blockade into or out of the besieged port. Even merchant sailing ships could sometimes evade the besiegers. In a larger sense beyond close sieges, naval dominance meant having a navy capable of successfully challenging the appearances of rival fleets, but not of effectively preventing them. Nor could galley fleets shut down merchant activity as effectively as later sailing ships could.

Indeed, naval operations throughout the age of galleys were essentially amphibious, combined-arms affairs entailing close cooperation between fleets and armies. Strategy focused of necessity on establishing and defending bases, especially major ports and key islands that dominated heavily traveled trade routes, and on attacking the bases of an enemy. Such bases allowed a state to use the sea-lanes to project military force and to defend its economic interests. Ultimately, the only way to control the seas was to control the lands surrounding them, thus depriving potential enemy fleets of any possible base of operations. We will see this strategy pursued several times with great success by states initially at a significant disadvantage in naval power.

The search for speed and power did not stop with two-tiered *pentekonters*. The next development in the naval architecture of specialized warships ushered in the first great age of naval warfare in history.

CITY-STATES AND TRIREMES: THE AGE OF ATHENS

Triremes

The seventh century BCE witnessed an upsurge in the mercantile activity and general prosperity of the Greek world. Corinth led the way in both maritime connections and the development of the naval power that accompanied it. Probably by the middle of the century, Corinthian shipbuilders had worked out the main features of a galley that the sources call a *trieres*, or "three-fitted," and that historians today refer to as

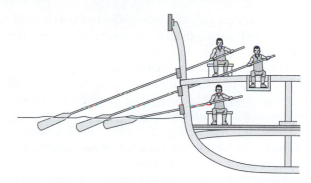

Arrangement of Rowers in a Trireme This drawing illustrates the tiered and staggered arrangement of rowers in a trireme. The top tier rowed through an outrigger, and the bottom two tiers through ports in the hull itself. Making such an arrangement work required group training and individual skill.

a *trireme*. Though not widely adopted by Greek (and other) navies until around 500 BCE, it then dominated naval warfare for 200 years.

The arrangement of oars and rowers in a trireme was for a long time a matter of much controversy among historians, some of which continues with regard to the larger ratings—four- and five- and even larger fitteds—that superceded the trireme in the Hellenistic period. But careful reexamination of all the evidence, the development of new evidence from naval archaeology, and, above all, the modern reconstruction of a trireme (see the Issues box on p. 86 for more on the controversy and new forms of evidence) have largely settled the issue of how a trireme was designed. The "three" in a three-fitted refers to a group of three rowers, each with his own oar, arranged in three tiers. What kept the ship from having to be built up too high was that the second tier was fully over the lowest tier (Aristophanes jokes about them farting in the faces of the first tier), but the third tier was only about half again higher than the second; all three tiers were staggered, and the third tier also sat somewhat outboard of the second and rowed through an outrigger overhanging the hull. The second tier rowed through the gunwale, and the first through portholes in the hull close enough to the waterline that they were sealed with leather bags wrapped around the oars.

This arrangement allowed 170 rowers to be fit into a hull barely longer than that of a single-tiered *pentekonter*—Athenian triremes measured about 120 feet long and 19 feet wide—but with much more rowing power. The reconstructed trireme could sprint at eight knots and cruise for hours at four knots, with half the rowers taking turns, and it could turn fully around in the equivalent of two-and-a-half boat lengths. With a small crew, officers, and fourteen marines, the standard contingent of an Athenian trireme was 200 men. A central gangway connected decks on each side; the gap between the gangway and the decks could be covered with hides to fully enclose and protect the rowers, making a *cataphract* (covered, or armored) *trireme,* though most Athenian triremes were left open, or *aphract.* The trireme was thus fast, maneuverable, and far more powerful than anything afloat at the time.

Given that manpower was the most expensive element in maintaining a war fleet, however, nearly quadrupling the number of men aboard the standard warship raised the economic and administrative stakes of naval power considerably. Many smaller city-states slipped out of the ranks of naval powers, leaving the field to the biggest and richest (or to alliances) of Greek city-states and to the Phoenician and Greek cities of Asia Minor that fell under the rule of the Persian Empire, which had come to dominate the eastern Mediterranean world by 500 (see Chapter 2). It was in this context that Athens rose to naval prominence.

The Rise of Athens

Athens had had a war fleet in the sixth century, mostly made up of *pentekonters;* from midcentury, it had also included some triremes. But Athens was not a major naval power; despite its size, it looked to land domination of Attica and relied on its hoplite phalanx (see Chapter 3) as its main weapon of war. But Themistocles persuaded his fellow citizens in around 493 to expand and fortify the Piraeus, Athens' port, and build up its navy, initially against Aegina, a Greek rival with whom Athens was at war. In the next decade, the long walls that connected Athens to the port were built, and, in 483, the state launched a major trireme-building program, funded by income from new silver mines. Themistocles proved far-sighted, for the fleet of nearly 200 triremes Athens took to war with Persia under Themistocles' leadership in 480 saved the city and Greece from Persian domination.

The Persian War Naval power was crucial to Xerxes' invasion of Greece in 480. His army crossed the Hellespont on a bridge of triremes and *pentekonters* tied together, and the navy escorted the supply ships vital to sustaining his army in Greece. The confederation of Greek states opposing him assembled a combined fleet nominally under Spartan leadership but in which the Athenian contingent and the strategic and

tactical advice of Themistocles dominated. The Greek forces checked the Persians at Artemesium but retreated to the island of Salamis off the Attic mainland when they learned that the land defense at Thermopylae had been defeated.

At Salamis, the fleet first evacuated the population of Athens to the island, save for a few who interpreted literally an oracle that said Athens would be saved by its "wooden walls". They barricaded themselves in the Acropolis behind a wooden wall, only to perish when the Persians sacked the city and stormed the citadel. Meanwhile, Themistocles worked to persuade the allied contingents of the fleet to make a stand in the Salamis straits and not to retreat to the isthmus at Corinth, where the Spartan-led land forces prepared to defend the Peloponnesus. As the Persian fleet approached and it appeared he would lose the argument, he sent a secret message to the Persian commanders advising that the Athenian fleet was prepared to come over to the Persian side but that the remaining Greeks were threatening to flee to Corinth. An Egyptian squadron then moved to block the western end of the strait, forcing the Greeks into battle the next morning. The date of the battle is uncertain, falling sometime in September.

The Persian fleet (made up of Persian subjects and allies—the Persians were not sailors) heavily outnumbered the Greeks, but the narrow straits restricted their ability to bring their numbers to bear (Figure 5.2). The stiff breeze that blew up early in the battle hindered their ships more than it did the Athenians, whose ships were somewhat heavier and perhaps lower in profile. Though the Persian ships carried more marines, mostly Persians who would try to turn the fight into a land battle, as well as assuring the loyalty of suspect allied crews, the roll of the sea threw off the aim of the Persian bowmen, giving the advantage in hand-to-hand fighting to the Greek hoplite marines.

Yet it was Athenian ability to maneuver and ram that proved decisive. While much of the fighting must have been an opportunistic melee, Athenian units on the more open Greek left wing probably tried variations of the standard tactics used to gain an advantage when two lines of galleys faced each other bow to bow in line abreast. These included the *periplus,* or "sailing around," by which one line would flank the other and so attack from the side and rear; and the more difficult but even more effective *diekplus,* or "breaking through," in which one line would row through the gaps in the enemy line to suddenly turn and attack from behind. Artemesia, the queen of Halicarnassus in Asia Minor, was one of the few Persian commanders to

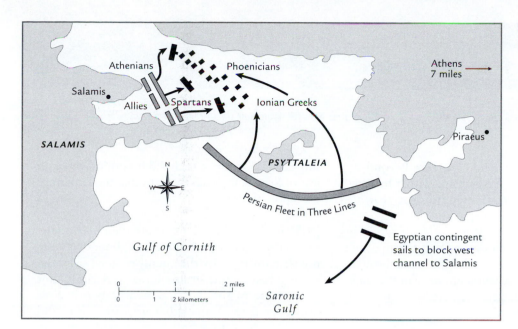

Figure 5.2 The Battle of Salamis

perform well on that day of naval dogfighting, ramming nine Athenian ships, as well as ramming and sinking another Persian ship to escape from an Athenian pursuer, who thus mistook her for a Greek. Xerxes, looking down at the battle from heights on the mainland, mistook her victim for a Greek and is said to have exclaimed, "My men have become women, my women, men!" By the end of the day, with over 200 Persian ships sunk and the rest in flight, the logistics of the Persian invasion were wrecked; Xerxes withdrew with much of his army shortly afterward, and the Greek land forces defeated the remainder the next year (see the Sources box "Herodotus on Salamis").

Salamis is commonly rated one of the decisive battles of world history for its role in saving western civilization, at its origins, from oriental despotism. While this considerably overstates and oversimplifies the case—and, indeed, a recent historian of the battle reckons that Greek civilization might not have developed too differently even had the Greeks lost—Salamis was decisive in its own context, proving the wisdom of Themistocles and the importance naval power had assumed in warfare. Its impact on the subsequent development of Athenian naval power was even more dramatic and important.

The Athenian Navy and the Delian League
In 477, three years after Salamis, the Athenians put together a naval alliance, the Delian League, with a number of other city-states in Greece and around the

Aegean, designed not just to defend Greece against further Persian invasions but to carry the struggle to that empire by freeing Ionian Greek cities from Persian rule in Asia Minor. Each league member contributed ships and men or money, with the treasury based on the island of Delos giving the league its name. Given both the preponderance of Athenian resources in the alliance and the ambitions Athens nurtured in the wake of its triumph in 480, not surprisingly, within twenty years, the Delian League had become, not an alliance of free states, but the mechanism of Athenian imperialism.

The contributions in ships and men from other states were gradually commuted to cash payments, with Athens monopolizing the building and manning of the warships of the league. Athens increasingly deployed this naval power against reluctant or renegade members to keep them in line, and their contributions came to be viewed as tribute. The treasury was moved from Delos to the rebuilt temple to Athena in Athens, where it joined the growing naval administration whose main office and functions had been created by Themistocles when he founded the navy. (Ironically, Themistocles was exiled in a power struggle in the 470s, and, by 464, he found himself working for the Persians as a regional administrator.)

The fleet remained ultimately under the control of the democratic Athenian assembly, which had final say on when and where the fleet was deployed, often on the advice of the Council of 500 that ran day-to-day government. In addition, a naval board supervised the

SOURCES

Herodotus on Salamis

In the following passages, the Greek historian Herodotus gives a vivid account of the historic sea battle.

■   ■   ■

[8.44] From the mainland of Greece beyond the Peloponnese, came the Athenians with a hundred and eighty ships, a greater number than that furnished by any other people; . . .

[8.48] Most of the allies came with triremes; but the Melians, Siphnians, and Seriphians, brought penteconters. . . . The whole number of the ships, without counting the penteconters, was three hundred and seventy-eight.

[8.84] The fleet had scarce left the land when they were attacked by the barbarians. At once most of the Greeks began to back water, and were about touching the shore, when Ameinias of Palline, one of the Athenian captains, darted forth in front of the line, and charged a ship of the enemy. The two vessels became entangled, and could not separate, whereupon the rest of the fleet came up to help Ameinias, and engaged with the Persians. Such is the account which the Athenians give of the way in which the battle began; but the Eginetans maintain that the vessel which had been to Egina for the Aeacidae, was the one that brought on the fight. It is also reported, that a phantom in the form of a woman appeared to the Greeks, and, in a voice that was heard from end to end of the fleet, cheered them on to the fight; first, however, rebuking them, and saying "Strange men, how long are you going to back water?"

[8.86] Far the greater number of the Persian ships engaged in this battle were disabled, either by the Athenians or by the Eginetans. For as the Greeks fought in order and kept their line, while the barbarians were in confusion and had no plan in anything that they did, the issue of the battle could scarce be other than it was. Yet the Persians fought far more bravely here than at Euboea, and indeed surpassed themselves; each did his utmost through fear of Xerxes, for each thought that the king's eye was upon himself.

[8.89] . . . Of the Greeks there died only a few; for, as they were able to swim, all those that were not slain outright by the enemy escaped from the sinking vessels and swam across to Salamis. But on the side of the barbarians more perished by drowning than in any other way, since they did not know how to swim. The great destruction took place when the ships which had been first engaged began to fly; for they who were stationed in the rear, anxious to display their valour before the eyes of the king, made every effort to force their way to the front, and thus became entangled with such of their own vessels as were retreating.

[8.91] When the rout of the barbarians began, and they sought to make their escape to Phalerum, the Eginetans, awaiting them in the channel, performed exploits worthy to be recorded. Through the whole of the confused struggle the Athenians employed themselves in destroying such ships as either made resistance or fled to shore, while the Eginetans dealt with those which endeavoured to escape down the strait; so that the Persian vessels were no sooner clear of the Athenians than forthwith they fell into the hands of the Eginetan squadron.

[8.93] The Greeks who gained the greatest glory of all in the sea-fight off Salamis were the Eginetans, and after them the Athenians.

SOURCE: Herodotus, *History*. Retrieved from http://www.herodotuswebsite.co.uk/Text/book8b.htm.

operations of the shipyards at Piraeus, oversaw the courts of justice connected to service in the navy, and administered the funds disbursed for building, maintenance, and recruiting. The dock installations at Piraeus kept stocks of necessary equipment, specified in great detail in documents that archaeologists recently discovered. The state shifted part of the administrative burden from itself by requiring rich citizens to sponsor the building and maintenance of a trireme for a year; in return, the citizens received formal command of the ship, though they rarely exercised it in person, leaving effective captaincy to professionals.

Above all, the rowers for the fleet were drawn from the poorer, often landless, but free citizen classes of the city, hired at competitive wages. The importance of the fleet for Athenian defense translated into political importance for its rowers: Athenian democracy both sustained and was sustained by the state's large-scale employment of landless men in the fleet. But as the fleet was also integral to Athenian imperialism, it embodied the contradiction at the heart of post-Salamis Athenian politics and the creative tension that arose from it. The ideal of democracy fit uncomfortably at the theoretical level with the oppressive practices of empire, and if most Athenian citizens seem to have been content to ignore the failure of their city to live up to its ideals in its foreign policy, some of its best minds, including playwrights, philosophers, and historians such as Herodotus and Thucydides, were not. Their Socratic gadflying on the topic produced some of the greatest masterpieces of Athenian literature in the fifth century and represent the most lasting legacy of Salamis.

Disaster and Recovery   The rise of Athens to imperial dominance in the Delian League excited not just suspicion from Persia but deep mistrust from Sparta, the erstwhile leader of united Greek military ventures, and led in 431 to the outbreak of the Peloponnesian War. We traced that conflict in some detail in Chapter 3; here we will focus on the naval aspects of the war.

Athenian strategy in the war, as formulated by Pericles, rested on two bases: its walls, which were effective because of the primitive nature of Greek siege warfare, and the navy. Athens could afford to withdraw behind the walls that surrounded the city and connected it to its port, abandoning mainland Attica to Spartan depredations, because its fleet protected its maritime trade connections to colonies as far afield as the coast of the Black Sea that supplied the city with grain. As its subject allies were almost all on islands around the Aegean, the fleet guaranteed the safety of the empire and allowed Athens to keep those same allies in line by force.

Yet the limitation of the Athenian navy was that it could not project force inland and so could not threaten Spartan power in its homeland, since Sparta was not dependent on overseas trade for its economic survival. Thus, a strategic stalemate between Spartan land power and Athenian naval power characterized the war. Ironically, it was the naval power, even with its external contacts, that was unable to establish alliances with the land forces that might have brought Sparta to terms. Instead, Spartan diplomacy brought Persia into the picture, with Persian resources funding the construction of a fleet to rival Athens'. And part of the opportunity to challenge Athenian naval power resulted from Athens' own disaster in Sicily in 415–413, the strategic overreach the expedition represented having been made possible by the freedom of action Athens' fleet gave it. The difficulty of conducting joint land-sea operations, especially the siege of a major city such as Syracuse, showed up even for a fleet as experienced as Athens'. Eventually, the fleet found itself blockaded in the Syracusan harbor, lacking the room to maneuver and ram that were its strengths. The loss of 9000 hoplites and about 200 triremes was serious but, especially in the case of the ships, not insurmountable. The disaster was the loss of 25,000 trained rowers: The decline in quality of the fleet, which had to be manned by new recruits and even freed slaves, opened the door to the combined Spartan-Persian effort that brought the war to an end in 404.

This defeat was hardly the end of Athenian naval power, however. Within twenty years of the end of the war, the Athenian fleet had been completely rebuilt by a naval administration that survived in all its essentials. A new generation of trained rowers—perhaps 60,000 of them manning over 400 triremes and even some larger vessels at the height of Athens' fourth-century power—took their places at the oars and in the democratic assembly of the city. It took the rise of Macedon to end Athenian naval power and introduce a fundamental shift in naval warfare generally.

KINGDOMS AND COLOSSI: HELLENISTIC ARMS RACES

Alexander and Naval Power

Philip's Macedon was not a naval power. We noted in Chapter 3 that Alexander's strategic approach to neutralizing superior Persian sea power, securing his lines

Rowing Arrangements and Naval Archaeology

The arrangement of rowers in a trireme was a matter of considerable controversy until the middle of the twentieth century. There were basically three possibilities. The word *trieres* in the literary sources could mean three men to an oar (the sort of arrangement adopted by medieval and early modern galley fleets in the Mediterranean); it could mean three men on a single angled bench, each with his own oar of a specific length; or it could mean three levels of rowers arranged vertically one above another. Various arrangements along each line were proposed, but none found universal scholarly acceptance.

At midcentury, classicist John Morrison began a thorough reexamination of all the literary evidence,

The Reconstructed Athenian Trireme *Olympias* Under Oars   The process of reconstructing a trireme and then operating it clarified many aspects of ancient sources, written and pictorial, and showed just how skilled ancient shipbuilders were.

but he crucially correlated it with all the available pictorial and archaeological evidence, much of which was recently found. Both excavations of the

of communication back to Greece, and blocking the Persian ability to foment trouble in Greece itself was to capture the fleet's bases, first at Halicarnassus and Miletus in Asia Minor, then especially Tyre in Phoenicia, and Egypt. In the process, he captured much of the fleet itself, which was added to the naval contingents of his Greek allies.

Given the chance, as at the siege of Tyre, Alexander made creative use of naval resources. Captured contingents and new naval allies from Cyprus gave him over 200 triremes to use to blockade the city from the sea while his army built a mole (a massive pier or breakwater) out from the shore to the island city. But the difficulty of attacking the city walls from the mole convinced Alexander to make more aggressive use of

his ships. He used some of them to carry catapults and other siege engines to harass the defenders on the walls, and he mounted battering rams on other ships and barges to attack the walls from the sea, the only known instance of this tactic in naval history. He also used crane ships to remove large stone blocks that hindered the ram ships' access to the walls, anchoring them with chains when Tyrian divers cut their anchor ropes. Eventually, the battering ram ships opened a breach in the city walls, and other ships ferried the assault forces to the breach and into the city.

The conquest of all the Persian coastal bases left only the potentially troublesome Athenian navy to threaten Alexander's control of the sea. In a battle off

Piraeus, Athens' harbor, and new developments in underwater archaeology that brought many ancient shipwrecks to light, added to historians' knowledge of how ancient ships were built. Morrison was able to show persuasively that the three-level arrangement was the correct one, though the upper level was not as high over the middle as the middle was over the lower.

But doubts remained about the workability of his proposed arrangement until what might be called experimental archaeology entered the scene. Working with naval architect John Coates, and with funding from the Greek government and private sources, Morrison and Coates directed the reconstruction of a full-sized Athenian trireme in the late 1980s. The *Olympias*, commissioned as an official vessel of the modern Greek navy, underwent extensive sea trials with a crew of volunteer rowers, some of whom had been championship oarsman in racing shells. Despite oars that were probably too heavy and limited training time, the ship achieved speeds and maneuverability comparable to those claimed in the literary sources. Not only did the process of reconstruction confirm the practicality of Morrison's proposed arrangement, but other problems that the naval architects solved during the building process shed considerable light on other source passages that had heretofore been somewhat obscure.

But the amount and clarity of the literary and pictorial evidence for larger galleys is less than that for the trireme, and the arrangement of rowers in those ratings remains somewhat speculative. The extreme positions in the debate, derived from the old trireme debate—that each number represented either an additional tier or the number of men on one oar—are clearly ruled out by the existence of ratings over eight, as the maximum number of men who can practically wield a single oar is eight while the practical limit of tiers is probably three. Thus, some combination of tiers and multiple rowers per oar must account for ratings above three. But whether a five (for example, a Roman quinquereme) had a single tier with five men to an oar, two tiers with three and two men per oar, or three tiers with two tiers of two and one tier of one oarsman (and indeed whether different fives were arranged differently) remains unclear based on the sources available at present. Perhaps marine archaeology will discover a wrecked classical warship that will clarify things.

the island of Amorgos in 322, Alexander's fleet defeated the Athenian fleet, bringing an end to Athens' role as a naval power. In that battle, both sides' fleets already included a substantial number of ships larger than the trireme, and it is to the development of these that we now turn.

The Successor Kingdoms

Beyond the Trireme   In the wake of the disastrous Athenian invasion noted above, Dionysus of Syracuse had seized power and built up the influence of Syracuse over eastern Sicily, working mainly against the increasing influence of Carthage, originally a Phoenician colony in North Africa, over the island.

It was probably the maritime power of that opponent, rather than the experience of the war with Athens, that prompted him to use the increased resources of the city and its expanding possessions to build up his navy. Crucially, he did not simply build large numbers of triremes but began experimenting with tetreres and penteres—four-fitteds and five-fitteds—purportedly inventing the latter. What the arrangement of rowers in these larger ratings was is still a matter of some debate (see the Issues box "Rowing Arrangements and Naval Archaeology"), but they were clearly larger, more powerful, ships than triremes, and they upped the ante still further in naval competition. By the time of the Battle of Amorgos, in 322 BCE, both the Athenian and Macedonian fleets had substantial numbers of fours and fives (50 fours and 7 fives for Athens) alongside their triremes, while Dionysus II, son of the inventor of fives, had introduced sixes into the Syracusan navy by the 340s.

The Successors and Naval Competition   After Alexander died, the competition among his generals resolved itself after two decades into a three-way competition between the Seleucid dynasty in Asia, the Antigonids in Macedon, and the Ptolemies in Egypt. The first remained exclusively a land power, but the latter two engaged in a fierce naval competition that stimulated further developments in the architecture of warships. Antigonus and his son Demetrius initially led the way, with Ptolemy and his successors playing catch-up, although eventually the largest ships were Ptolemaic.

Fours, fives, and sixes could have been created simply by adding an extra rower to the oars on one, two, or all three tiers—that is, by slight modifications to the trireme. But putting more than two men on an oar entails a significant change in the style of rowing. More than two men cannot row from a seated position but must, due to the length of the oar, stand to get the oar into the water at the start of the stroke and then fall back onto the bench. It seems to have been Demetrius who initially designed the new kind of ship that could accommodate this style of rowing when he introduced sevens into his navy.

The broader hulls required to accommodate extra rowers on the oars would have reduced maneuverability somewhat at the expense of raw power and size, but such ships had corresponding advantages. Putting multiple men on an oar provided extra power without demanding extra numbers of skilled rowers, for only the man at the head of the oar needed to be trained; the others simply supplied muscle. For the large kingdoms with abundant untrained manpower, such ships thus allowed expansion of naval manpower without the training—or indeed, political—issues raised by the skilled crews of triremes. Furthermore, while reduced maneuverability corresponded with a decrease in ramming tactics (though all warships retained rams for opportunistic use), broader hulls meant more deck area on which to carry marines for boarding tactics and catapults or other large missile weapons as antipersonnal or possibly even ship-killing weaponry. Here, too, such navies favored large, autocratic states with abundant manpower.

The obvious advantages of size and numbers of marines for naval combat in this environment pushed designers to build ever-larger ratings. Tens and elevens became common, and from twelves to twenties not uncommon, and by the mid-200s, Ptolemy II was building thirties that performed well and saw action. But there is no arrangement of three tiers of oars with up to eight men to an oar that can produce a thirty, never mind the forty constructed by Ptolemy IV around 205. These two, the top ratings ever built, were clearly double-hulled ships—oared catamarans made of yoked-together fifteens or twenties, connected by a broad deck that could have carried hundreds of marines.

The sight of these monsters, almost like oared aircraft carriers, clearly impressed contemporaries who wrote about them. And they were meant to. Ptolemy IV's forty never saw action and was probably designed from the start as a ceremonial ship meant to show off the monarch's wealth, power, and grandeur. In this respect, the Hellenistic naval competition was psychological as well as military and paralleled cultural and political developments in other areas of the Hellenistic world, which had moved a long way from the small, sometimes democratic city-states that had launched trireme fleets. But the naval arms race between the Successor Kingdoms of the eastern Mediterranean had reached a sort of stalemate by the beginning of the second century BCE and would be brought to a conclusion not by any of the powers engaged in it, but by the winner of another naval competition going on at the same time in the western Mediterranean.

THE RISE OF ROME

The First Punic War

Originally, Rome's imperial military power was land-based, and most of its subsequent fame in military history rests on the achievements of its armies (see Chapter 4). Although it is sometimes overlooked, the Romans took to naval warfare with the same determination, organization, and success that they brought to land warfare, an achievement all the more impressive for having begun against one of the great naval powers of the time, Carthage. The First Punic War (265–241 BCE), the greatest naval war of ancient history (and one of the largest and most extended ever), launched Rome on its way to complete domination of the Mediterranean.

Both powers were oligarchies, whose states had been built up from a single city-state to a significant regional force through a combination of conquest and subsequent alliance with those subjugated. Rome's advantage in recruitable manpower was offset by Carthage's advantage in trade-generated wealth, which also gave Carthage the edge in terms of trained sailors and rowers for manning fleets—Rome probably had a small fleet of twenty triremes for much of the fourth century, but little experience or history of success with them. Both sides proved capable of mobilizing vast resources fairly rapidly in building fleets: Rome once built a fleet of over 200 quinqueremes in three months. Carthage just about matched that on one occasion, but Rome repeated the feat several times in the course of the war, proving far more capable of absorbing losses of both ships and men. Ribs and other parts recovered from a wreck from the war are marked with letters indicating what pieces went where, indicating a level of organized mass production with predesigned parts that would not become common until the Industrial Revolution.

Technology   The standard ship on each side was the quinquereme, or five-fitted, though what the arrangement of rowers on these ships was remains uncertain. Some historians think that the Roman fives were single-banked with five-man oars, accounting both for their lesser performance compared to Carthaginian ships and for their ability to carry large numbers of marines (120 per ship became standard during the war) on the broader decks a single-tiered five would have had. In contrast, the Carthaginian fives, renowned for their skill at ramming, were probably three-tiered descendants of triremes. But since Polybius, our main source for the war, states that the Romans copied the design of a Carthaginian five captured when it ran aground near Syracuse, it may be more likely that the relative experience of shipwrights and crews can account for most of the difference in performance, and 120 marines could fit on a three-tiered five. Indeed, later in the war, the Romans copied a particularly fast five they captured during the siege of the Carthaginian base at Lilybaeum, trained their oarsmen more intensively, and by the end of the war performed at least as skillfully in battle as their foes.

Still, the Romans entered the war at a serious disadvantage in seamanship skills. Therefore, they sought consciously to turn naval combat into boarding contests in which the Roman legionnaires serving as marines could deploy their skills, rather than trying to beat the Carthaginians at maneuvering and ramming. One of the great naval secret weapons of all time gave them success in this goal. The *corvus*, or "raven," was a 36-foot gangway whose lower third was slotted around

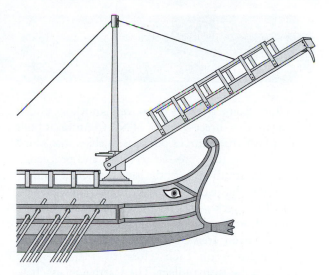

A Corvus The corvus allowed the Roman fleet to maximize its advantage in the quality and quantity of its fighting men and to minimize its disadvantages in seamanship. But it exacted a toll on the seaworthiness of Roman ships.

a 24-foot pole with a pulley at the top, allowing the gangway to be drawn up next to the pole, swiveled around, and dropped onto the decks of enemy ships. A large iron spike that stuck out of the bottom side of the gangway, looking like a bird's beak and probably giving the device its name, speared the deck, holding the enemy ship fast and allowing the marines to rush across the corvus and overwhelm the enemy. The Romans deployed it with tremendous success against an enemy unprepared for its first appearance in 260 at the Battle of Mylae and continued to use it with success—they did not lose a battle while using it—until 253. In that year, the Romans lost nearly their entire fleet in a storm off the south coast of Sicily, the second time in three years storms had destroyed their navy. The corvus, whose height and weight at the bow of the ship may have contributed to these disasters by affecting the seaworthiness of Roman vessels, disappears from the sources after this date. The only Roman loss in battle, at Drepana in 249, occurred after the corvus was abandoned.

Tactics   As the technology reflected, the Romans and Carthaginians took different approaches to the tactics of naval combat. The Carthaginians looked to create and exploit gaps in the Roman line, so as to use their superior maneuverability to execute the *periplus* and the *diekplus*, which would allow them to ram Roman ships from the rear or far enough back from the side so as to avoid the corvus. Conversely, the Romans tried to

Ecnomus

In 256, Rome decided to go for a knockout punch and launch a direct invasion of North Africa. It built up a fleet that sources put at 330 ships that sailed south along Italy, crossed to Sicily, and proceeded along the south coast of the island, where it rendezvoused with the consular army in Sicily and took on board the pick of the infantry and a cavalry force whose horses were carried in over 30 horse transports. Given crews of about 300 per ship, plus 120 marines on each, close to 140,000 men sailed in the Roman fleet. The Carthaginians, having decided at the same time on a major effort to seize control of the waters around Sicily, had assembled a fleet of 350 ships. With similar-sized crews and quite possibly similar numbers of marines, this meant close to 150,000 men on the Carthaginian side. With 290,000 men involved, this was probably the largest naval battle ever, and possibly the largest ancient battle of any kind.

The two fleets met off Ecnomus, a hilly cape with a roadstead (an open harbor) where the Roman marines had boarded the fleet (Figure 5.3). The Romans adopted an interesting formation designed, it seems, to protect their flanks and rear from Carthaginian encirclement. The two lead squadrons, each under the command of a consul in a six,

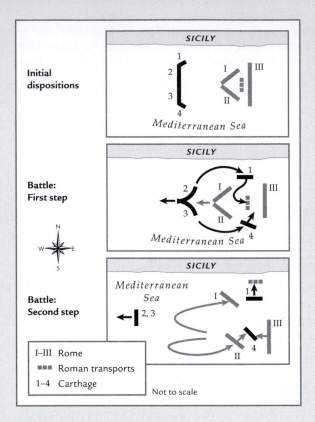

Figure 5.3 The Battle of Ecnomus

maintain relatively tight formations that would provide mutual support and reduce Carthaginian maneuvering room, so as to let the battle be decided by boarding fights. Despite their relative lack of experience, Roman crews proved capable, seemingly, of turning quickly enough to keep their corvuses in play, so that even when a Carthaginian line broke through and threatened a successful *diekplus,* as seems to have happened at Tyndaris in 257, it resulted in only a few Roman ships being sunk, while Carthaginian losses to capture and sinking were high. Even when Carthaginian plans to split the Roman fleet into separate squadrons worked, as at Ecnomus (see the Highlights box "Ecnomus"), they could not turn that advantage to victory.

It may be that the size of the fleets normally involved in major battles during the war—usually over

200 on each side, and probably well over 300 each at Ecnomus—hindered the usual Carthaginian approach. Larger fleets were harder to keep under any effective command control, which, given the primitive state of signaling and how low in the water even the highest ships sat, was hard to exercise anyway. Given that galleys' masts and sails were stowed away (or even left on shore) in preparation for battle, lookouts did not even have a high point to climb to. The only Carthaginian naval success of the war, at Drepana, involved relatively small fleets of about 130 ships on each side. It also developed unusually: A Roman fleet sailed north along the Sicilian coast to try to catch the Carthaginian fleet in harbor, but the latter got word from lookouts in time to escape the harbor, sailing west around an island that guarded the harbor entrance and

lined up in echelon, each ship behind and to the outside of the one before it. These squadrons thus formed the apex of a triangle closed by the third squadron, which followed in line abreast, towing the horse transports. The fourth squadron, larger than the third, followed it, also in line abreast. The Carthaginians approached in the traditional line abreast, with their left, landward wing advancing at an angle.

As the fleets drew near, the Carthaginian center began to withdraw in an attempt to draw the first two Roman squadrons away from the third and fourth and so to break the fight up into three or four separate and more open actions. The Carthaginian left swooped around onto the Roman third squadron, which cast off the horse transports and retreated toward the shore. Their retreat was covered by the fourth squadron, which turned seaward to face the flank attack of the Carthaginian right.

Despite the success of the Carthaginians' grand tactical scheme, they could not turn it into a tactical advantage. The weight of the first two Roman squadrons began to tell as they engaged with the Carthaginian center, which eventually broke and fled. What then won the battle was the fact that both Roman consuls managed to detail a few ships to pursue the beaten center and then to rally most of their ships to turn about and come to the aid of the hard-pressed third and fourth squadrons. The first squadron fell on the rear of the Carthaginian left, which had pinned the Roman third squadron against the shore but had been reluctant to move in for the kill against a defensive formation whose corvuses could not be flanked. The Carthaginian left now found itself trapped, and many vessels were sunk or captured. Similarly, the second squadron came on the rear of the Carthaginian right, which broke and fled, losing many ships. The day had been won by a remarkable feat of Roman command control and discipline.

Although more than half of the Carthaginian fleet escaped, its morale was shattered by losing a battle fought largely on its terms, and Carthage never again attempted an offensive campaign. If Ecnomus was thus something less than a decisive tactical victory for Rome, it was a huge strategic victory, opening the way for the Roman invasion of North Africa and demonstrating the different strategic outlooks and levels of resolve on each side, differences that would eventually lead to Roman victory.

trapping the Roman fleet against the shore. With sea room behind them to maneuver in and no corvuses to deal with, the Carthaginians were able to sink three-quarters of the Roman fleet.

Given the large crews, often large number of marines, and large number of ships sunk in the course of the war, the naval side of the First Punic War was enormously expensive in terms of men and resources. It is estimated that the Romans lost over 800 ships (perhaps 500 of which succumbed to storms), while the Carthaginians lost 500 ships, almost all to Roman action. This represented a loss in lives of as many as 160,000 on the Roman side and perhaps 100,000 on the Carthaginian. Census figures cited by the Roman historian Livy indicate a significant drop in the number of Roman citizens between 260 and 240.

Strategy   Such costs affected strategy on both sides. In the wake of the loss of two fleets to storms and a third at Drepana, the Romans essentially abandoned the naval war between 248 and 242. Rome raised its last fleet of the war through private subscriptions from rich Roman citizens, the state having exhausted its fiscal resources. Yet the Romans did continue the war effort and proved willing to make the sacrifices necessary for final victory. In contrast, the potential costs of battles, on land and sea, seem to have induced hesitancy and caution in Carthaginian leadership. Given the opportunity to press their advantage after Drepana, the Carthaginians instead effectively disbanded their fleet. Their response to the final Roman effort in 241 had little of the popular or elite support demonstrated by the Roman aristocrats who bought ships for the state. Further, by then, the Carthaginians had trouble finding enough experienced rowers for their fleet.

In more specific terms, the fleets of the First Punic War were part of amphibious operations designed to secure control of the Sicilian coast and its ports and harbors, as the land forces of either side, if cut off from support from their homeland, stood little chance of survival. At this level, too, the Romans showed a more aggressive strategic approach, identifying the key Carthaginian bases and actively going after them, whereas the Carthaginians seemed content mostly to play defense. This difference is even more apparent in the campaigns that extended beyond Sicily. The Roman invasion of North Africa, threatening Carthage itself and raising rebellion among the city's African subjects, indicated a clear conception of what victory meant and how it could be achieved: The Romans were fighting to knock out Carthage, whereas Carthage was fighting not to be knocked out. The raids Hannibal conducted into Italy after the Romans abandoned the sea were minor inconveniences for the Romans, in contrast.

As noted previously, the First Punic War was the largest, longest, and most significant naval war in ancient history. In terms of the number of men involved in particular battles, it was also one of the largest ever. It created the first provinces of what would become the Roman Empire, led directly to the Second Punic War, and so launched Roman expansionism beyond Italy. That expansion would take Rome from being the dominant naval power in the western Mediterranean to conquering the eastern Mediterranean and eliminating all rival navies.

The End of Hellenistic Navies

Naval power played a lesser role in the Second Punic War than in the First. Despite having a fleet large enough to match the Romans' (who had let their fleet decline after 241), the Carthaginians showed no inclination to challenge the Romans at sea, even in 202 when the consul Scipio invaded Africa with a fleet of 400 transports escorted by only 40 warships while a Carthaginian fleet of 130 sat idly by. Thus, for most of the war, the Romans were able to move armies and supplies freely about the western Mediterranean, especially into Iberia, while Hannibal's army in Italy was mostly cut off from reinforcement from Africa or Spain.

After the war, naval forces continued to play a role in further Roman expansion in the west, into Spain

and Gaul, and eastward, though Rome initially showed no inclination to challenge the Hellenistic naval powers directly. The social changes in Italy attendant on the Second Punic War, however, which rendered the peninsula and especially the capital city itself increasingly reliant on grain imports from Sicily, Africa, and Egypt, ensured that Roman interest in naval power would flare up at least sporadically. Roman naval advances were assisted by the fragmentation of states and navies in the eastern Mediterranean after 200. This meant that Rome could find ready allies, including at times Rhodes and Pergamum, which had done serious damage to the Macedonian fleet at Chios in 201. Roman and allied fleets played important roles in Roman wars against Macedon and Seleucid Syria, allowing them to seize the strategic initiative and stretch their enemies' defenses. Having eliminated any real naval opposition by 170, land conquests followed. By 136, with the final destruction of Carthage, Roman fleets had assisted in adding substantially to the empire around the Mediterranean.

But the elimination of state-level navies, except in Ptolemaic Egypt, which because of the importance of its grain trade was of necessity largely friendly to Rome, led to complacency. As maritime trade increased rapidly with Roman domination, so too did piracy, partly with the connivance of the Roman landowning elite, who needed the slave trade generated by the pirates. But when pirate activity began to threaten grain shipments from Egypt and even Sicily, and the pirates gained the support of Mithradates of Pontus, a major naval effort under the direction of Pompey was authorized by the Senate in 67. With a newly assembled fleet of over 200 warships and a large army, Pompey swept the seas of pirates and in the process gained a significant weapon for himself in his civil war with Julius Caesar. He mishandled his naval advantage in that war, however, allowing Caesar to win the conflict on land.

The Pompeian fleet then fell partly to Marc Antony in the east and partly to Pompey's son Sextus Pompey in the west. The latter launched a major piracy campaign based on Sicily, which necessitated a major amphibious operation by Octavian and his able commander, Marcus Agrippa, to suppress. That left Octavian and Marc Antony, supported by Cleopatra of Egypt, facing each other in the final civil war, which ended in 31 BCE with the naval battle at Actium, which put an end to both naval competition in the Mediterranean and to the Roman Republic.

Though an experienced soldier, Marc Antony was unfamiliar with naval warfare and managed to get his land and naval forces blockaded at Actium in the Gulf of Ambracia by Octavian's navy under the command of Marcus Agrippa. Unable to entice Octavian's army into a land battle, Antony and Cleopatra's fleets, totaling around 220 ships, attempted to fight their way out of the blockade. The fleet was dominated by quinqueremes but was undermanned, as malaria had taken a heavy toll on the fleet's rowers before Octavian's forces had even arrived. Agrippa's ships were mostly smaller but faster and more maneuverable, and they had full and fresher crews. They managed to avoid grappling with Antony's biggest ships, gradually wearing down the attackers with ramming attacks. Cleopatra and her sixty ships fled, followed by Marc Antony, who escaped on a small, fast galley. The rest of the fleet was sunk or captured, and Antony's army largely deserted him in the wake of this defeat. In the next year, 30 BCE, both Antony and Cleopatra committed suicide, Egypt became a Roman province, and large-scale naval warfare in the Mediterranean ceased for the time being.

Imperial Naval Power

Octavian became the *princeps* Caesar Augustus and rapidly disbanded the bulk of the Roman navy. The fleet he retained was designed to transport troops rapidly from one theater to another and to suppress pirates. For these jobs, speed was far more valuable than size, and so large galleys mostly disappeared from the Roman naval establishment. Significant numbers of large ships had continued to be the backbone of fleets of the first century BCE. The giant fifteens, twenties, and even thirties found at the height of the arms race had largely disappeared by the second century BCE, but ratings between seven and ten were still common right down to Actium. That battle revived reliance on skill and ramming, and Augustus's fleet had few ships bigger than triremes. Roman rowers, who signed up for twenty-eight-year terms of service and consisted mostly of men from the Hellenistic lands of the eastern Mediterranean, received intensive training, which contributed to this emphasis on speed, skill, and smaller ships.

The main naval bases were near Naples and Ravenna, whose squadrons had a six and a five as flagships, respectively. But most of the fleet consisted of triremes and smaller, swifter, two-tiered galleys. Smaller naval bases with squadrons exclusively made up of such ships were scattered around the Mediterranean. Under efficient administration, these fleets carried out their tasks effectively, extending the benefits of the Pax Romana to the sea-lanes of the Empire.

The only other frontiers that required a naval presence were in the northwest, where the addition of Britain as a province of the Empire led to a need for protection of communications across the English Channel. Meanwhile, the establishment of the Rhine as the frontier with Saxony after 9 CE led to the creation of a riverine fleet to patrol that river. A riverine fleet protected the Danube as well.

But service in the navy always remained a distinctly inferior option socially and politically to service in the army. Thus, both naval administration and the fleets themselves fell on hard times during the upheavals of the late second and early third centuries CE and never really recovered. In the early fourth century, Constantine reorganized the riverine and coastal defenses of the northwest under the command of an official known as the Count of the Saxon Shore, but this proved only temporarily effective against the increasing seaborne activities of Saxon raiders. Likewise, what little was left of the Mediterranean fleet could do little to stop Goth piracy in the Aegean and Vandal depredations in North Africa. Maritime and naval activity would reemerge on a large scale in the North Sea on very different social and political bases than had generated Mediterranean oared navies. Even the revival of Roman naval power in the eastern Mediterranean under Constantine and continuing into what became known as the Byzantine Empire owed little to direct inheritance from Rome, except in terms of general administrative traditions. Even triremes went out of fashion after Constantine's navy won a major battle in 325 using *pentekonters*.

CONCLUSION

The first great age of naval warfare had drawn to a close. When significant levels of maritime activity resumed after 400 CE, based on a wider network of global trade connections and the slow spread of improved ship technology, the naval establishments and warfare that activity spawned would have a more varied and geographically dispersed character than the galley warfare of the Mediterranean world covered in this chapter. Those developments are covered in Chapter 10.

The navies of the classical age of galley battles had a significant impact on warfare and contributed to broader historical developments. From the invention of the alphabet by the sea-going Phoenicians, to the triremes at Salamis launching the great age of Athenian culture and conquest, to the quinqueremes of the First Punic War laying the foundations of Roman imperial expansion, to the end of the Roman Republic at Actium, naval warfare played a central role in the military history of the ancient Mediterranean world. Its further development would extend that role to wider realms of global history.

SUGGESTED READINGS

Casson, Lionel. *Ships and Seafaring in Ancient Times.* Austin: University of Texas Press, 1994. An update and popularization of his important *Ships and Seamanship in the Ancient World* (Princeton: Princeton University Press, 1971), a fundamental work.

Goldsworthy, Adrian. *The Punic Wars.* London: Cassell, 2000. Contains accessible sections on the naval aspects of the wars.

Jordan, Boromir. *The Athenian Navy in the Classical Period.* Berkeley: University of California Classical Studies 13, 1972. A detailed study of the administration of the Athenian fleet and its connection to political structures of the Athenian state.

Lazenby, J. F. *The First Punic War.* Stanford: Stanford University Press, 1996. An authoritative study of this conflict, based on careful evaluation of the sources and cautious judgments about controversial points.

Meijer, Fik. *A History of Seafaring in the Ancient World.* New York: St. Martin's Press, 1986. A thorough narrative of naval warfare from earliest times through the height of Roman imperial power.

Morrison, J. S., and J. F. Coates. *The Athenian Trireme. History and Reconstruction of an Ancient Greek Warship.* Cambridge: Cambridge University Press, 1986. A fascinating and well-illustrated account of the building of the *Olympias*.

Strauss, Barry. *The Battle of Salamis: The Naval Encounter That Saved Greece—and Western Civilization.* New York: Simon and Schuster, 2004. A lively and readable but also reliable account of the campaign and battle. Despite the subtitle, Strauss in fact downplays the historical impact of the battle in the terms in which that impact is usually stated.

Commentary: Part 1, to 400 CE

The precise origins of warfare must remain a problem that cannot be solved definitively, given the paucity of evidence available to answer the questions we have. It seems likely, however, as we argued in Chapter 1, that warfare as we conceive of it today—the mass use, by one group of humans against another, of violence organized along social lines, with that organization often rising to the level of a chiefdom or state in political terms—arose late in human history. The evidence for warfare relates exclusively to the modern human species, and within the 200,000-year existence of that species, exclusively to the past 12,000 or so years, in association with the conditions that also led to the invention of agriculture and the rise and spread of complex forms of political organization. Even then, it took many more millennia before warfare had evolved to a level of maturity comparable to what we are familiar with in most history in the past 2000 years. It was in Assyria and then in Qin China that the full tool kit of warfare—a tool kit with social, political, technological, and cultural components—first appeared. From that point on, we can trace the set of themes that will carry forward throughout the rest of this book.

War, State, and Society

One of these is the intimate connection between warfare and state power in world history. Cooperation was always necessary to the functioning of human social groups, but coercive force became more necessary as the size of polities grew and as different states came into more constant and competitive contact with each other. Warfare thus became a major component of both external relations and the keeping of internal order. The growth of empires during the period covered by this part of the book shows the increasing effectiveness of military force, in conjunction with more sophisticated administrative mechanisms of rule and more persuasive ideologies of social control, in allowing states to govern larger and more diverse territories. Yet the relationship between warfare and state power proved complicated as early as it arose. Successful conquests could strengthen a state by providing it with increased resources, especially in the form of agricultural land and the labor that worked it, as well as control over important trade routes and elimination of dangerous enemies. But it could equally prove disastrous: For every big winner, there was at least one big loser. And the costs even of victorious warfare were high for states built on fragile agricultural economies characterized by low productivity. Over-expansion, unsustainable tax rates, and rebellion could threaten imperial powers, especially pioneering conquerors such as the Assyrians or the Qin.

Successful warfare also complicated the relationship between the state and its elites, particularly when, as was commonly the case, the elite class was composed of warriors. While conquests could provide new lands with which monarchs could reward warrior elites for their service and loyalty, such rewards eventually had to end, raising the prospect of internal strife, and could in the meantime enrich provincial leaders enough so as to threaten central control. At times, as in the history of Rome, elites took themselves out of military roles to enjoy the fruits of political dominance, while their military values became institutionalized in a professional army. At other times, similar results were achieved by central effort: The Qin systematically suppressed the Chinese warrior aristocracy using both material and ideological methods. Yet the dominance of warfare in state policy, the necessity for the establishment of a competent military leadership class, and the almost inevitable congruence in preindustrial societies between social status and political power meant that the problem of warrior elites was bound to recur regularly. It was states such as the Han and Roman empires, states that achieved relatively stable (or, more important, adaptive) institutional solutions to this problem that showed the greatest staying power in a complex world of warring states.

The relationship of war to the state also arose at the lower end of the social structure, above all in terms of the bases of unit cohesion and military effectiveness in infantry. Two roads to effective infantry emerged as early as the end of the Bronze Age. The first was social and communal: Infantry units' cohesion reflected the social ties of the community from which the military unit came—indeed, the social community and the military force were, in terms of the adult male members of the community, often essentially identical. The second was state-centered: A state with enough financial and administrative resources could afford to raise and train effective infantry, essentially creating through drill, education, and experience units that became communities. The communal model probably came first and provided the model for what effective infantry forces should look like (at least in the Near East and the Mediterranean worlds; the Chinese case is less clear). However, the state-centered model proved more stable—communal infantry was subject to decline with every transformation of the society itself, transformation often brought about by military success—and capable of providing far-larger forces. Thus, where sufficiently strong states existed (an important and restrictive condition), their infantry was a force to contend with. But the separation of army and society implied by this model could also prove problematic. At times, the creation of naval power, though still limited, added to the social roles and state functions associated with military force.

The pinnacle of state-dominated military organization was achieved first, as noted above, in Assyria and Qin China. Though the details varied, the major components of a centralized fiscal-administrative state supporting a permanent professional army—with society and the economy organized and tapped in service to the militarized state, and with culture and ideology used to legitimize and glorify the entire structure—appeared in both. And they were reproduced in their major imperial successors, whether Persian, Han, Alexandrian, Mauryan, or Roman. But the very success of these giants of the Age of Empires complicated the job of their successors in reproducing such organization. They spread the tools of militarized state rule, raising new potential enemies both within and beyond their borders, and connected the Eurasian world in ways that further complicated states' struggle to survive. Connections and new enemies met most clearly and threateningly among the horse nomads of the Central Asian steppes. Their armies would dominate the age of migrations and invasions dealt with in the next part of this book, often reducing the centralized (sedentary) military state to a historical but unrealizable ideal looked back on by more decentralized and warrior-dominated kingdoms.

WAR AND TECHNOLOGY

The early history of warfare also saw the establishment of the major technological components of warfare. Fundamentally, these consisted of the abilities (social and political as much as technological) to build walls, to harness stored energy (whether through muscle, torsion, tension, counterweight, or, later, explosion) to hurl missiles at men and walls, to shape hard metals into weapons and armor, to domesticate horses, and to build seagoing ships. None of these abilities was necessarily military in nature; that they were put to military use says as much about the cultural contexts into which they were introduced as it does about the impact of technology on war.

These technological components would remain essentially stable at least into the seventeenth century, when improved ships and firearms began to alter some of the balance of these components in some places. And more fundamentally, the limitations of nature and technology faced by ancient armies lasted until the Industrial Revolution and in some cases beyond—armies still marched on foot or rode on horseback beyond their own railheads well into the twentieth century.

That none of the technological abilities fundamental to military activity were necessarily or purely military in themselves and that they remained stable illustrates what will be a consistent theme of this book: Technology in war is largely a dependent variable. That is, technologies' effects vary according to the social and cultural contexts into which they are introduced. Further, once the essential suite of technologies—walls, missiles, metal weapons and armor, domesticated horses, and seaworthy ships—had been incorporated into warfare, no particular invention or technology would alter the fundamental patterns of warfare until the steam engine, which was itself not, of course, a necessarily military technology.

WAR AND CULTURE

Organized warfare from earliest times had major implications for culture, and different cultures affected warfare in different ways. From the beginning, war as a major activity of kings and elites generated myths: in epics such as the *Epic of Gilgamesh,* one of the oldest pieces of literature in the world, and the Homeric epics with their glorification of a warrior elite; and in court histories designed to glorify and legitimize the kings and elites. Military affairs are thus closely associated with the very process of writing history right from their origins. This connection accounts both for the existence of much of the source material we have for military history and for some of the problems with that material in terms of biases and reliability. Major sorts of military literature, epic and historical, reflect and helped to construct the different cultural emphases and interests of warrior elites and dynastic states.

The impact of culture on military organization and patterns of warfare can be seen most clearly in comparisons of the major fiscal-military states of the Age of Empires. Structurally, they all appear similar. But their reasons for going to war; the methods they thought of as acceptable, glorious, treacherous, and so on; the value they placed on warfare in terms of its ability to generate personal glory and domestic political capital; and the ethical perspectives conquerors brought to ruling those they conquered—all were products of cultural outlooks that could vary considerably despite the structural similarity of these states and the military challenges they faced, both internally and externally. Cultural variation and the mutual impact of war and culture will show up consistently as one of the themes of this book.

Culture also marks one of the general areas of transition from the classical age into the age of migrations and invasions considered in the next part of this book. Consideration of these changes highlights the general characteristics of war and culture in ancient times. First, many of the great traditions emerged in the Age of Empires out of separate (though not entirely isolated) cultural spheres. In other words, though structural similarities emerged based on fundamental economic and technological limits on the organization of hierarchical human societies, cultural divergence dominated. But the broader horizons of communication and trade that empires made possible, at least in part, contributed to an age when cultural borrowing, interaction, and conflict would become more prominent. Second, many of the cultural and ideological constructions that emerged in this period were, not surprisingly given the context in which they arose, focused on the needs and values of states and elites. The rise and spread of salvation religions would often introduce ideas friendlier to common people but would, in turn, further complicate the ideology and culture of warfare. These developments are taken up in Part 2.

THE AGE OF MIGRATION AND INVASION, 400–1100

CHAPTER 6

The Nomadic World: Central Asia to 1100

Over the past 2500 years, the Eurasian steppes have spawned a series of pastoral peoples who have lived on and wandered through that great landmass. These peoples have lived on the fringes of the world's great civilizations—in Europe, the Middle East, south Asia, and China—and their relationship with the sedentary peoples who lived on the periphery of their world has been complex and often characterized by raiding and warfare. On more than one occasion, these pastoral warriors parlayed the skills they learned on the steppes into an overwhelming military dominance that led to the conquest of their more civilized neighbors. In almost every case, however, these nomads found it easier to conquer than to rule. These peoples came from a variety of ethnic and linguistic groups including various Indo-European Iranian tribes and Turkish peoples. Regardless of their ethnic origins or language, all of these groups were tied together by a common cultural tradition and lifestyle.

THE RISE OF NOMADIC CULTURE

Geography: The Steppes

The world of the nomads was the central Asian steppes, a vast grassland sea extending from the northern and western reaches of China across Asia to the southern plains of Russia north of the Black Sea, with a small extension into the Hungarian plain even farther west (Figure 6.1). This is a midcontinental region of often harsh climates: hot and dry in the summer, bitterly cold in the winter. It is also, crucially, too dry over most of its extent to support agriculture, and it was therefore not an area where settled, sedentary states could establish themselves, relying as they did on peasant farmers as the foundation of their wealth. Instead, the steppes were the home of pastoralists: peoples who lived by the management of herds of domesticated animals but who made little use of domesticated plants. The organization and dynamics of nomadic society flowed from this fundamental economic fact.

Nomad Economics: Horses, Herds, and Wagons

The culture of the pastoralists who lived on the Eurasian steppes was based on the relationship of three key components: equestrian expertise, herds of grazing animals (in particular, cattle or sheep), and wagons usually pulled by oxen. These three components combined to make the peoples of the steppes exceptionally mobile: They could move en masse from one pasture to another as the seasons dictated. They did not generally wander aimlessly but, rather, moved between a few pasturelands that would allow yearlong grazing; indeed, they even practiced limited agriculture while there. But mobility also allowed these nomads simply to pick up and move when political, economic, or climatic exigencies dictated.

Horses and Warfare From a purely military perspective, the most important component of steppe culture was the development of horseback riding skills. The horse had always been an important animal for the peoples who lived on the grasslands of Eurasia. In early times, the horse was simply a game animal, hunted for its meat like almost any other prey. At some point in the distant past, horses were domesticated. They were not yet ridden, but they were kept and raised for their meat, hides, and milk. It was then discovered that the horse could also be ridden. Traditionally, it has been argued that the use of the horse as a mount dates to around the middle of the second millennium BCE. However, recent

100

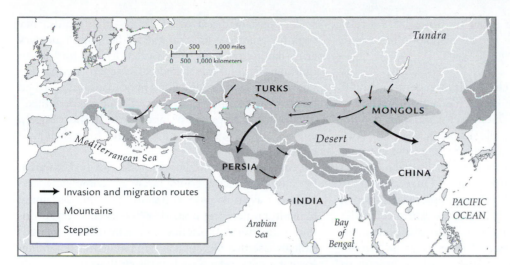

Figure 6.1 The Central Asian Steppes

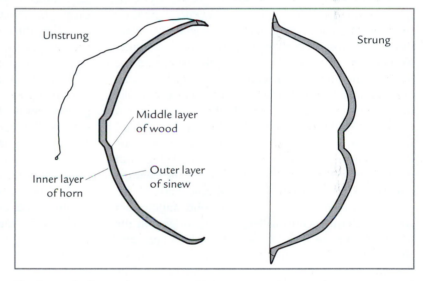

The Composite Bow   Short yet powerful, the composite bow was the main weapon of the mounted steppe warrior.

archaeological evidence has pushed the date back nearly 2500 years to approximately 4000 BCE. In any case, the taming of the horse as a riding animal had a profound impact on nomadic culture. It allowed the steppe peoples to range over a much wider distance than had been possible before. Individual tribal groups now had access to additional resources and markets, and they came into contact and conflict with other tribes and peoples.

In warfare, the ridden horse gave the warrior several important advantages over the man fighting on foot. Strategically, the horse provided access to a larger sphere of operations. A mounted man can cover two to three times the distance of a man on foot in a comparable time. This allowed mounted warriors to strike an enemy without horses with near impunity. Moreover, once on the battlefield, the horseman had tactical advantages as well. He had, of course, greater mobility, which allowed him to move quickly and to concentrate his efforts at a particular point. But, for the early mounted nomad, perhaps more important than the offensive potential was the security provided by the horse. The horse made it possible for the warrior to flee without fear of serious pursuit. It is no doubt from this tradition of evading ineffective

pursuers that the later nomadic tactic of *feigned flight* originated.

The full potential of the horse as part of a devastating tactical system was realized when it was combined with another steppe innovation, the composite bow, bringing together both mobility and firepower. The composite bow appeared during the second millennium BCE. Made of three different materials—wood, horn, and sinew—the bow was constructed by laminating, gluing, and drying the components so that the bow curved back on itself. This meant that the composite bow was short yet powerful. Its relatively small size made it the ideal weapon for a man on horseback.

Oxen and Wagons   The herds of grazing and draft animals and the vehicles of the pastoralists might not at first glance seem pertinent to a discussion of warfare as it developed on the Eurasian steppes. They did, however, play an important role in the conduct of war for the nomadic tribes, especially when in conflict with more sedentary peoples. Once again, the herds and wagons used by these peoples made them a mobile society. Not only could the warriors of the steppe peoples range widely on their horses, but so, too, could their families and their logistical base—their herd animals. This mobility made it difficult to bring the nomadic tribes to battle. Such was the case in 512 BCE when a large Persian army under Darius I crossed the Danube into the territory of the Scythians (see below). These nomads par excellence sent their herds and families out of harm's way while the main force of warriors—which included some of the younger women, who also fought in the ranks—harassed the Persians and employed a scorched-earth policy, denying supplies to the Persians. Darius was eventually forced to withdraw with heavy losses.

The carts and wagons of the nomads may have had yet another impact on warfare. A growing body of archaeological evidence points to the vehicles of the pastoralists being the prototypes of the chariots that dominated warfare in the Middle East, India, and China during much of the second millennium BCE. The chariot seems to have had its origins in the wheeled vehicles of the steppe folk, which appeared about 2000 BCE (see Chapter 1). This, however, raises the question as to why chariots would be used by warriors who had already mastered the art of riding horses. We cannot be certain of the answer. Perhaps the composite bow had not yet been perfected in its small, handy form for use on horseback. It has recently been argued that chariots were, at least among the steppe nomads, symbols of status used in rituals and races rather than in warfare, where horses were indeed superior. (See the Issues box "Stirrups and the Effectiveness of Cavalry" for another key cavalry technology.)

Life on the steppes gave nomadic military forces one further advantage over their sedentary enemies: They were used to constant campaigning. Life on horseback following herds meant that entire nomadic societies lived in tents and camps, with a limited diet,

under constant threat of attack. In other words, they took for granted a life that the soldiers of a sedentary army had to get used to and often looked forward to quitting. The endurance and barbaric ferocity that settled peoples saw and disdained in nomads was matched by nomadic disdain for the "soft, effeminate, perfumed" inhabitants of cities, towns, and farms. In short, a deep cultural gulf separated pastoral nomads from their agricultural neighbors.

And, yet, the two worlds could not be separated, because pastoralism could rarely be completely self-sufficient as an economic system. Though disdaining agricultural peoples, nomads often needed the products of agricultural societies, especially those made possible by a settled life, such as large-scale metalworking. Even if some products such as silk cloth were not strictly necessary, they had value to nomads both in practical terms and as status symbols. As a result, the settled and nomadic worlds were in constant contact with each other. Sometimes, this relationship took place peacefully through trade, for nomads could offer some products—wool, skins, hides, even horses—in demand in settled areas. But nomads quickly found that they could parlay their military superiority into possession of settled goods in several ways: They could raid and pillage; they could (especially if they had already raided successfully) agree not to raid on condition of receiving tribute; or they could invade, conquer, and put the settled area's administration to work for them collecting taxes. Which route any particular nomadic group chose depended on a number of factors, and the entire pattern of trade/raid/tribute is closely related to the question of the political organization of nomadic societies.

Political Structures and Patterns on the Steppes

Limited Political Hierarchy   The geography of Inner Asia was mostly inimical to the development of strong centralized military or political systems. Pastoral nomadism allowed disgruntled or dissatisfied tribes to leave larger groups without serious disruption to the social or economic life of the tribes' members. Tribes required only pasturelands and/or access to trade routes or raiding opportunities. Unlike settled peoples, the nomads were rarely tied to particular land or even a particular region. A supratribal leader, then, was limited in his ability to control or direct the tribes in his domain, let alone punish errant

ISSUES

Stirrups and the Effectiveness of Cavalry

The impact of certain technologies on the military effectiveness of steppe nomad armies is clear. Domestication of the horse was undoubtedly a technological breakthrough of the first magnitude (construing "technology" broadly), rivaled only by metallurgy, widespread use of gunpowder, and the technologies of the Industrial Revolution in military significance. The composite bow, by adding firepower to the mobility the horse provided, turned horse-archery into an enduringly successful weapons system. There is much less agreement, however, about the impact of the stirrup on the effectiveness of cavalry. The stirrup was a latecomer in the arsenal of cavalry technolgy, and one difficulty in assessing the impact of the stirrup is that it is not easy to pinpoint when or where it originated. Scattered pictorial and archaeological evidence points uncertainly to an origin in the eastern part of the steppes or the western part of China late in the first millennium BCE. Stirrups seem to have been in use throughout East Asia by the second or third century CE, and to have spread westward across the steppes in the same period. They likely reached Persia in the fifth or sixth century, Byzantium shortly after, and western Europe probably in the eighth century.

What was their impact? The stirrup makes it easier for a horseman to stay on his horse, replacing a precarious balance and knee grip with a firm foothold. The most common argument for the impact of the stirrup, therefore, has been that it made mounted shock combat possible by anchoring the horseman to his horse, allowing him to hold a heavy lance underarm and to bring the full weight of horse and rider to bear with the lance, a tactic that would result in his being thrown off the back of his horse without stirrups. In this view, mounted shock combat, in turn, accounts for shifts from infantry- to cavalry-based military systems—the change from Roman legionnaires to medieval knights, for example.

But such arguments do not, in fact, account very well for patterns of cavalry use, and they misunderstand the mechanics of mounted combat. Heavy cavalry, including the armored cataphracts of some steppe tribes, predate the use of stirrups in many places. It is clear that, in the days before the introduction of the stirrup, cavalry made use of saddles that essentially locked the horseman in place. One of the best-attested examples is the Celtic-style saddle used by the Celts and the Romans. Recent tests have shown that using horns to support the rider's lower back and wrap over his thighs creates a steady platform for fighting from horseback. But the real effectiveness of a heavy cavalry charge, especially against infantry, rests in its psychological impact— the terror it inspires—rather than on the actual force of its impact. For horses can rarely be made to impale themselves, and since infantry weapons almost always outrange related cavalry weapons—pikes are longer than lances, for example—the cavalry must open holes in an infantry formation before it comes to blows, or the charge will fail (see also the Sources box, p. 111).

This is not to say that the stirrup was not an advance. It made the horseman's job easier, and, once invented, it spread steadily. In particular, the stirrup gave an advantage to those peoples who were not by nature horsemen. It was perhaps most advantageous in battles between horsemen, which may account for its more rapid spread through the steppes than beyond them. However, it was not decisive in any sense, and it created no new capabilities for cavalry, but rather only enhanced capabilities already long established.

subordinates, who could simply depart with their people and flocks to other pastures.

Whatever centralized authority did exist was normally in the form of a confederation of tribes, in which the confederation leader could not rely solely on the stick of military force to keep his subordinates in line. Instead, unity and obedience to the leader were maintained primarily through that leader's ability to successfully lead the confederation on raids for plunder. In other words, control over the acquisition and distribution of the spoils of war was the primary carrot by which confederation leaders ensured their continued rule. An influx of tribute could substitute for plunder economically. But first, the leader had to prove his worth as a warrior by leading a successful raid, and it took the distribution of truly large amounts of tribute to quell even temporarily the factionalism of subordinate tribes.

Leadership   The formation of tribal confederations took place only after a sometimes long series of battles, as the various tribal chiefs demonstrated their ability to lead, especially in battle. Tribes not directly involved in the fighting for leadership watched carefully before committing themselves, as the successful chief was expected to lead the confederation on raids against neighboring settled populations. Such large-scale raids were almost without exception far more profitable than if individual tribes raided on their own. Also under consideration was the ability of the leader to direct the defense when the confederation came under attack from the armies of settled peoples or other Inner Asian tribes.

The leadership of the confederation was personal and seldom hereditary until after the process of testing in battle had been completed. The confederation leader was also expected to lead his forces personally in battle, both in the raids of settled lands and on campaigns to punish wayward tribes. War was a constant feature of the life of tribal confederations; in fact, periods of peace were likely to lead to a collapse of the confederation unless the influx of tribute were substantial enough to allow the leader to buy the loyalty of subordinates instead of enforcing it. Xiongnu, Seljuk, and other tribal confederation leaders spent almost as much time directing their military forces against tribal dissenters as they did in raiding civilized peoples. Once the leader died or suffered a serious defeat, the confederation usually collapsed, to begin the cycle anew.

Leadership and Culture   In terms of nomadic relationships with their sedentary neighbors, several seemingly paradoxical results flowed from the dynamics of steppe leadership. The first was that nomadic confederations were often strongest when they interacted with a strong (or at least prosperous) settled civilization, for prosperity generated the wealth of tribute and booty necessary for the creation of political hierarchy among the nomadic tribes. Even better for nomadic political stability was a long-term rivalry between two settled areas, each of which could pay

for nomadic allies—the Byzantine and Persian rivalry of the sixth century is an example (see Chapter 8).

The second was that the strongest nomadic confederations were often the ones most influenced by the culture of their settled neighbors, despite their disdain for sedentary peoples. This is because the goods that flowed to the steppes from civilizations were not value neutral. Rather, they often came with ideas and cultural values embedded in them, especially ideas about the organization and display of political power. Certain types and colors of Chinese silk implied certain levels of diplomatic recognition, for instance. Goods also came, at times, with people attached: either diplomats or, more often, daughters of settled rulers (as wives for nomadic leaders). All of this meant that nomads nearer to a settled civilization tended to acculturate to the values of that civilization, at least in certain ways. This could make military alliances between the settled and nomadic powers easier, but it could also heighten the interest of the nomadic tribes in conquering settled areas that had become familiar through raiding and tribute.

Nomadic and Settled Worlds: A Trend   Nomadic conquerors, familiar with but unbound by the traditions of the settled states they conquered, had the opportunity to invigorate the leadership of those states. But nomadic conquerors also faced a difficult problem: It was impossible to remain a nomad and rule a settled state effectively. Conquest therefore often introduced a tension between those nomads who wished to become the settled elites of the area they conquered and those who wished to remain true to their roots. Thus, after a period during which nomadic rule united pieces of the steppe and agricultural worlds, the two parts would split again as the fundamental incompatibility of nomadic and settled life reasserted itself.

The trend, over the several millennia of settled–nomadic interaction, was for settled areas to gain at the expense of nomadic areas in splits. The trend was slow and was neither uniform nor locally irreversible. But it was clear, and it resulted primarily from demographics: Agriculture could simply support far more people than pastoralism could. Thus, despite the military advantage nomads deployed, they could never dominate settled states for long.

We now turn to a survey of the most important nomadic peoples and confederations over the period from roughly 2000 BCE to 1100 CE, including those who made up the two waves of nomadic activity that peaked around 400 CE and 1000 CE and that bound and in many ways define the period of world military history covered in this section.

THE SCYTHIANS: THE ARCHETYPAL STEPPE WARRIORS

The Scythians and the Civilizations of the Middle East

The Scythians are the earliest of the pastoral peoples about whom we have solid information. These Iranian-speaking Indo-Europeans made their appearance on the stage of world history in the seventh century BCE. They seem to have migrated from the steppes, settling in the area north of the Black Sea that they had wrested from another nomadic people, the Cimmerians. For much of the seventh century, the Scythians raided and ravaged the prosperous kingdoms of the Middle East. One of their most successful raids took place in 612 BCE when, in conjunction with the Medes, also originally steppe nomads, they sacked the Assyrian capital of Nineveh. Shortly thereafter, the Medes and Scythians seem to have had a falling-out, and, according to the Greek historian Herodotus, the Medes treacherously killed the Scythian leaders at a feast.

For the next century or so, the Scythians remained on the steppes north of the Black Sea. But in 512 BCE, they seem to have drawn the attention of the rising power of the Middle East, the Persians, who also had nomadic origins. The great Persian king and conqueror, Darius I, mustered a large expedition that easily handled the Thracian tribes across the Hellespont and then proceeded into the land of the Scythians north of the Danube. The Scythians seem to have been caught unawares by the Persian invasion. They realized that without time to consolidate their forces they would stand little chance against Darius's massive, well-equipped invasion force. Rather than face Darius's army in open battle, they sent their families to the north, while the main body of warriors drew the Persians away. Darius followed, leaving a substantial rearguard at his bridge across the Danube. For some twenty days, Darius pursued the Scythian warriors. While the nomads grew stronger as reinforcements swelled their ranks, the Persian army dwindled in the face of the scorched-earth policy of the Scythians. The Persians followed the nomads along the northern coast of the Sea of Azov. But, because he was not able to bring the Scythians to battle, Darius was forced to withdraw to the Danube. At this point, the Scythians became more aggressive and attacked Darius's foraging and flanking parties. Darius withdrew across the bridge under cover of his rearguard, whom the Scythians had tried to convince to abandon their Persian overlords. Darius learned the painful answer to a question Herodotus would later ask: "How can such a people [the Scythians] fail to defeat the attempt of an invader not only to subdue them, but even to make contact with them?" This tactic used by the Scythians may be the strategic version of feigned flight, designed to draw the enemy in and then turn on him after he has lost his cohesion and discipline.

Scythian Society and Warfare

Social Organization Like most nomads, the Scythian tribes were loosely organized and, fortunately for their neighbors, tended not to cooperate very often. At the time of the Persian invasion in 512, there were three main Scythian leaders, who cooperated only in this time of great need. This was, in the eyes of the Greek historian Thucydides, indeed fortunate; he commented that no nation could stand against the warlike Scythians should they cooperate.

The Scythians had a reputation as a savage and warlike people. Herodotus recorded that their customs included head-hunting—the skull of an enemy would be used by the warrior who killed him as a drinking cup—and taking scalps, which were used to adorn the bridle of the Scythian's horse. Indeed, young men were not permitted to cut their hair until they had killed their first enemy in battle. The warlike nature of the Scythians was not restricted to the men of the tribe—Scythian women were probably expected to fight as well. Certainly, a number of burials of Sarmatian women (see below) have been found that include a bow, arrows, *gorytos* (bow case), knife, javelin, and other warrior gear. These finds support literary evidence that women could and did engage in combat. It is, therefore, no coincidence that when the Greeks portrayed Amazons in art, they are in Scythian garb.

Scythian Warfare Most, but not all, Scythian warriors fought on horseback, with the majority of these horsemen lightly armed commoners. When going off to battle, every Scythian carried a bow. When not in use, the bow was carried in a *gorytos,* which also served as a quiver for the arrows. Based on Scythian burials,

A Scythian Horse-Archer   In addition to a bow, the mounted warrior might also have been armed with a javelin or spear, an axe, and a sword, as well as a shield.

most of the warriors seem to have also carried a javelin or spear. Likewise, axes and swords seem to have been reasonably common. For protection, most warriors also carried a wicker or wooden shield, perhaps covered in metallic scales.

In addition to these commoners, every Scythian army fielded an elite force of more heavily armed horsemen drawn from the tribal princes and nobles and their retainers. In addition to the weaponry carried by all the warriors, the lance seems to have been favored by these nobles. They were well protected by shields, like those carried by the common warriors, and by metal armor. This armor was usually iron or bronze scales sewn on a leather corselet; there is even evidence for leather leggings, similar to western chaps, reinforced with metal scales. Some of the wealthiest warriors even had such reinforced leather breastplates for their horses.

THE XIONGNU AND CHINESE CIVILIZATION

The Rise of the Xiongnu Confederation

The archetypal nomadic peoples of the eastern end of the steppe world, the east Asian equivalent of the Scythians, are the Xiongnu. Our knowledge of the Xiongnu comes mostly from Chinese sources. The very name "Xiongnu" comes from the name given by the Chinese of the Zhou (1050–256 BCE) and Han (206 BCE–220 CE) periods to all the nomadic peoples

who inhabited the Mongolian region. The term literally means "Savage (or Violent) Slaves," and according to the Chinese, the Xiongnu traced their ancestry to a king of the mythical Xia period of Chinese history. Populating the mostly arid lands of the northern Ordos region near the loop of the Yellow River, Xiongnu customs and religious practices were typical of the steppe nomadic peoples of the day. They practiced Shamanism and the ritual sacrifice of horses on special religious occasions—but in the distinctive Xiongnu version, the sacrificial horses had to be white. The Xiongnu allegedly first made their appearance as opponents of the settled Chinese civilization in the early eighth century BCE. However, only in the third century BCE do the Xiongnu show up in the records as horse-riding archers who regularly plundered the lands of the Chinese.

There was a traditional story told about Maodun, unifier of the Xiongnu tribes: According to the Han dynasty Chinese historian Sima Qian, the Xiongnu were in a state of constant training when not in the field. Maodun supposedly had his personal command trained so well that they would, at a word, immediately shoot arrows at whatever target Maodun chose. One day in 209 BCE, he decided to impress his father, the Shanyu (great leader) of the tribe, and, in rapid succession, he had his men shoot at his horse, his favorite wife, and his father's horse. He executed those who were too slow. Maodun then suddenly pointed his bow at his father, who was immediately pierced by several arrows. Thus had Maodun secured for himself the rulership of the Xiongnu. We also see once again the precariousness of rulership in Inner Asia.

Maodun's control of the Xiongnu confederation adheres closely to the model of Inner Asian leadership. After eliminating his father, he killed a brother who was a rival, as well as his brother's supporters, and then spent the next few years cementing his authority in a series of battles against Xiongnu and other nomadic tribes. Following victory, he divided any captured flocks with his supporters, proving to them his ability both to lead in battle and to provide loot, and not coincidentally firming up their loyalty to him. He then immediately turned his attention to raiding into China. The Han dynasty, after several embarrassing defeats at the hands of Maodun (see Chapter 2), agreed to provide large quantities of tribute in return for a pledge to refrain from raiding. Maodun, then, was able to obtain the fruits of raiding without actually having to raid. This enabled him to focus on subjugating nomadic tribes and strengthening his

HIGHLIGHTS

Xiongnu Raiding

The nomadic empires—such as those of the Scythians, Xiongnu, and Turks—were in reality confederations, with centralized control being either very loose or reliant on the personality and talents of a charismatic leader. Even then, successful continuance of the confederation depended on acquiring material goods and peoples of the sedentary lands. This usually took the form of raids for plunder, with the nomads sweeping into settled lands on their horses and ponies and departing with loot and slaves. Xiongnu raids were an integral aspect of the confederation's political and social unity in its early years, and an examination of the raiding strategy and tactics of Maodun gives us a somewhat closer glimpse into the importance attached to this activity and its multiple goals.

Nomadic raids into China, of course, had the primary aim of acquiring quantities of loot. However, the large-scale raids, such as those organized and led by Maodun, served broader political and strategic goals as well. One of the largest of these raids took place soon after Maodun had militarily unified the steppe lands. Maodun expended considerable effort to subdue neighboring nomadic tribes, especially the powerful Yuezhi to his west. Once the Yuezhi had been pounded into submission (many fled westward, eventually terrorizing Persia and northern India), Maodun confiscated their flocks as a means of asserting control and providing rewards to those who had fought with him. Yet this was merely a temporary state of affairs, as there were few spoils to distribute among the loyalist tribes.

Within months, the remaining Yuezhi were made a part of Maodun's nomadic confederation and included in a pillaging expedition into China. This expedition saw several tens of thousands of Xiongnu destroy numerous settled communities in north China. Jewelry, textiles, supplies of grain and wine, and implements and weapons made of iron were taken. In addition, slaves were acquired, often artisans and young women, but also some farmers who were to be used to till the small agricultural plots of the Xiongnu. All were packed up into confiscated carts and transported back to the Xiongnu lands to the north. Small Chinese military outposts or militia forces were destroyed, but, for the most part, the major military centers were avoided. When larger Chinese military units attempted to confront the Xiongnu, the nomads retreated—and lacking large cavalry forces, the Chinese could not pursue.

The degree of coordination involved in Xiongnu raids such as this should not be exaggerated. The purpose of these raids was not confrontation with the major military forces of China, and central command became involved only at the beginning and end of a raid. Division of the areas of attack was decided by Maodun and the tribal leaders, and the tribes then took off under their own direction. Unified action might have become necessary when determined resistance was encountered, in which case the role of Maodun and his successors as Xiongnu leader was quite important. When fleeing China with their loot, the relatively slow-moving Xiongnu became more vulnerable to attack, and here central direction of defense became necessary. In part to hinder pursuing Chinese forces, Maodun ordered destruction of croplands, requiring the Chinese to transport even more of their foodstuffs.

The destruction of crops—like that of the people and their settlements—served another interest as well. Maodun and his successors used raiding not only to acquire plunder but also to terrorize the Chinese into the payment of tribute. This tribute, unlike the spoils of raids, was indeed significantly under the control of the central Xiongnu leadership, enhancing and strengthening the personal authority of the ruler.

personal control of the Xiongnu confederation. Maodun died in 174 BCE. His successors reestablished similar relations with Han China, but not before leading raids of plunder as Maodun had, proving their fitness to lead in combat (see the Highlights box "Xiongnu Raiding").

As long as the Xiongnu had a military advantage over the Chinese, they could count on the receipt each year of vast quantities of silk, iron, and other goods. The distribution of these goods ensured the loyalty of the subordinate tribes, but the Shanyus (roughly translated as "undisputed leaders") also kept their warriors busy fighting with neighboring nomadic tribes. The large cavalry armies the Xiongnu could put into the field made them without rival on the steppes. Only when the Chinese succeeded in outflanking Xiongnu territory by cutting off their major source of foodstuffs did the confederation's unity become fragile. A series of defeats at the hands of the Chinese in the 80s and 70s BCE also led to a loss of prestige by not only the Shanyu but the Xiongnu in general. The Xiongnu then became engaged in quelling a chain of rebellions by subjugated tribes, further weakening the confederation leader's ability to supply his subordinates with loot. In 60 BCE, the Xiongnu confederation was ripped apart by civil war, though some form of Xiongnu military alliance would remain in place through the first century CE.

Xiongnu Society and Warfare

As with all the nomadic societies discussed in this chapter, the Xiongnu saw all able-bodied males as liable to military service. In fact, martial duties were for the most part the sole occupation of Xiongnu males. When not on campaign, a good portion of their time was taken up with training and perfecting their skills. In preparation for an adult life of combat and combat training, Xiongnu boys as young as 3 were taught to ride sheep and handle a bow, shooting at birds and rats; later, they would learn to ride ponies and shoot at larger game. Group effort was also emphasized, so that the Xiongnu warrior who faced settled opponents had already undergone years of training and discipline.

The main business of the Xiongnu was warfare, normally directed in major annual campaigns of pillage against China. Following the typical pattern of leadership of Inner Asia, the Shanyu had full control of the tribes only during periods of warfare. When not on campaign, the various tribes and Xiongnu groups reverted to the control of their traditional leadership. Once the call to battle had been transmitted, the tribesmen normally gathered at Hehehot, a fairly fertile land where the men could find grazing land for their horses while awaiting the arrival of others.

Like most Inner Asian nomadic warriors, the Xiongnu were mounted archers. All warriors were armed with the composite bow. Other standard equipment included small swords and shields and various types of fighting knives. Many were also armed with lances and, during the centuries of warfare with China, many of the tribal leaders wore a kind of body armor. A great deal of the weaponry of the Xiongnu was produced by Chinese prisoners of war or other captured Chinese craftsmen, who were settled in small villages deep within Xiongnu territories.

The Xiongnu also acquired many of their weapons in battle with the Chinese. This was necessary since the Xiongnu lands were deficient in iron, and there were too few craftsmen who could produce iron weapons in the quantities needed by the Xiongnu warriors. After a victorious confrontation with the Chinese, it was not unusual for the Xiongnu to scavenge the field of battle for weapons. Large quantities of weapons were also often purchased by the Xiongnu from Chinese border guards, the persistence of which practice led to numerous Han dynasty edicts threatening harsh punishment for such actions.

THE KUSHANS: STRATEGIC EMPIRE BETWEEN PARTHIA AND CHINA

During the first two centuries CE, the Kushans created a powerful and expansionary empire between the Parthians and the Chinese. The Kushan Empire lay along a strategic portion of the Silk Road and played an important role in the promotion of both trade and Buddhism. Throughout this period, the Kushans took territory from the Parthians and, at times, fought with the Chinese against common enemies, such as the Sogdians, and, at times, fought against the Chinese. Mostly, they maintained uneasy trade relations with China.

Although there is still some dispute over this, the Chinese sources, coinage, and other artifacts from the region indicate that the Yuezhi were the Kushans. Or, rather, the Kushans were one tribe of Yuezhi who migrated from Central Asia and created an empire sometime in the first century CE.

The height of Kushan power and influence came with the reign of Kanishka, who ruled during most of the first half of the second century CE. He took the empire to its greatest extent, ruling most or all of present-day Uzbekistan, Tajikistan, Afghanistan, Pakistan, and northern India, including the lands of Magadha. He located his capital at Kashgar, thus

A Sarmatian Cataphract This somewhat fanciful drawing shows the scale armor and conical helmet (but not the heavy lance) that made such cavalry a formidable weapon of shock combat. It also shows (though in an impossible way) that the horse, too, was fully armored.

indicating that the Kushans' Central Asian domains remained the most important to them. Stories about Kanishka include one about the destruction of a Parthian army of 900,000, after which he suffered a great deal of remorse for the death he had inflicted—a retelling of the Ashoka story (see Chapter 2). Kanishka's actions in the promotion of Buddhism led to his being considered by Buddhists to be the greatest friend of the religion since Ashoka.

Kanishka and the Kushan rulers before and immediately after him benefited from the weakness of their two main neighbors, the Parthians to the west and the Chinese to the east. There is also some evidence of a sort of informal alliance with the Roman Empire against Parthia.

The earliest accounts of the Yuezhi/Kushans show their military forces to be essentially typical Inner Asian mounted bowmen, with weapons, tactics, and formations much like those of the Xiongnu. However, as the Kushans conquered the lands of northern India, their armies became much larger, incorporating many new elements. Elephant units and Indian infantry forces became part of the mix, and much of the nobility went into battle much more heavily armored, including—according to some depictions—riding armored horses. Thus, the armies of Kanishka were not only much larger than but also more capable of more varied types of combat than those of his predecessors.

THE SARMATIANS: STEPPE WARRIORS ON THE ROMAN FRONTIER

By the second century BCE, the Scythians had been replaced along the north shore of the Black Sea by a related group of people, the Sarmatians. Like their Scythian cousins, the Sarmatians were an Iranian-speaking people; they were organized into a number of tribes including the Alans, the Roxolani, and the Iazyges. During the first and second centuries CE, the Sarmatian tribes would come into repeated conflict with Rome. In these struggles with the Romans, the Sarmatians employed another form of warfare that had developed on the steppes as well—cataphract warfare.

Sarmatians and Cataphracts By the third century BCE, a new form of warfare had developed on the steppes, that of the *cataphract,* or fully armored horseman. This form of warfare emphasized different principles from those of the Scythians. Whereas the Scythians brought together mobility and firepower, the Sarmatian cataphracts combined the mobility of the horse with the shock effect of charging with the lance.

The Sarmatian cataphract was the descendant of the Scythian noble horseman. But, by the third century BCE, advances in horse breeding allowed him to wear much more armor than had the Scythians. The major advance was the introduction of larger, stronger horses that could carry much more weight than the steppe ponies ridden by the Scythians. (The term *steppe pony* should not be taken too literally. It simply refers to a hardy horse no more than fourteen hands high, not to be confused with genuine dwarf breeds such as the Icelandic.) The Sarmatian horseman went to war armored literally from head to toe, equipped with a helmet of bronze or iron and protected by a corselet of horn or metal that reached at least as far as his knees. Depictions of Roxolani horsemen on the Column of Trajan in Rome show cataphracts with scale leggings that extend down to the toes, though such armor may be Roman artistic fancy in that it would have made it nearly impossible for the horseman to move when dismounted. In addition, the horse of the cataphract was fully armored, with scale armor covering not only the breast but, at least in some cases, the flanks as well.

For his offensive weapon, the cataphract relied on a heavy lance called the *contus,* which was often wielded with two hands. There has been considerable discussion about how effective these Sarmatian lancers could have been without stirrups. But as we have seen, the Romans more than compensated by developing an effective saddle, which allowed for the use of all types of weapons by mounted soldiers (see Chapter 4). Undoubtedly, a steppe folk such as the Sarmatians would also have developed such a saddle.

The charge of a body of cataphract cavalry was very dangerous, especially for infantry, as the sight of a mass of armored horsemen must have caused all but the best-disciplined foot soldiers to break and run. We are fortunate to have the orders issued by the Roman general Arrian to his troops when facing the Alans in 135 CE. These orders give us unique and valuable insights into the concerns of a commander facing a dangerous charge of cataphracts.

Arrian clearly had two concerns as he issued his orders. His first was that he halt the charge of the cataphracts with firepower so that they did not draw near enough to cause a panic among his troops. Thus, his heavy infantry was formed in close order and armed with a mixture of missiles, both the traditional Roman *pilum* and lighter throwing spears. Moreover, the main battle line was supported by archers drawn up with the legionnaires and artillery. It was his hope that the soldiers in the battle line would never be subjected to the psychological impact of the charge since, as he said, "because of the indescribable number of missiles . . . the Scythians . . . not even once come charging the infantry line."

His second concern was that, after the Alan charge had been halted, his men did not break their formation and pursue the Alans. Arrian was obviously aware of the possibility of a feigned flight and was concerned enough to guard against it by taking great pains to ensure that there was no willy-nilly pursuit of the Alans. Instead, Arrian ordered that only half of his horsemen were to pursue, with the remainder to follow in formation so that, should the Alans' flight be a ruse, they would not be able to wheel on only disordered troops. Moreover, he advised that his infantry "advance more swiftly than at a walk, so that if something stronger should be encountered from the enemy, once again the infantry formation . . . be placed as a bulwark in front of the cavalrymen." Arrian clearly understood the danger of feigned flight.

It has been argued that the nomadic tactic of feigned flight was transmitted to Europe by the Alans when they settled there. Certainly, western European horsemen used the tactic regularly through the Middle Ages, including most famously at the Battle of Hastings in 1066 (see the Highlights box in Chapter 7).

THE HUNS

The Hunnic Way of War

In general, the Huns fought in much the same way as the Scythians had since the seventh century BCE. Most of the Hunnic warriors, at least until the fifth century, were lightly armed horsemen whose main weapon was the composite bow; like the Scythians, the Huns were reputed to be expert archers. In addition to the bow, the Hun warrior was well suited to hand-to-hand combat. Although the typical warrior did not usually have much in the way of armor, most seem to have been supplied with weapons for melee such as the sword and the lasso, which was used to drag their opponents to the ground (see the Sources box "Ammianus Marcellinus on the Huns").

Like the earlier nomadic peoples, the Huns also fielded a body of noble cavalry who were better armed and equipped. This must have been particularly true of the Hunnic armies of the fifth century CE, when we know the Huns defeated a number of Roman armies and made use of arms and armor taken from slain and captured Romans. The Hunnic nobles undoubtedly wore metallic armor and, in addition to bow, sword, and lasso, carried a lance.

SOURCES

Ammianus Marcellinus on the Huns

Ammianus Marcellinus, the fourth-century Roman soldier and historian, gives us a glimpse into the customs of the Huns in a lengthy digression. He provides us with the sedentary Romans' perception of these nomadic warriors from the steppes. Ammianus views the Huns as almost subhuman savages, yet he also betrays the Romans' grudging admiration of their endurance and martial skills.

■   ■   ■

1. However, the seed and origin of all the ruin and various disasters that the wrath of Mars aroused, putting in turmoil all places with unwonted fires, we have found to be this. The people of the Huns, but little known from ancient records, dwelling beyond the Maeotic Sea near the ice-bound ocean, exceed every degree of savagery. **2.** Since there the cheeks of the children are so deeply furrowed with the steel from their very birth, in order that the growth of hair, when it appears at the proper time, may be checked by the wrinkled scars, they grow old without beards and without any beauty, like eunuchs. They all have compact, strong limbs and thick necks, and are so monstrously ugly and misshapen, that one might take them for two-legged beasts or for the stumps, rough-hewn into images, that are used in putting sides to bridges. **3.** But although they have the form of men, however ugly, they are so hardy in their mode of life that they have no need of fire nor of savory food, but eat the roots of wild plants and the half-raw flesh of any kind of animal whatever, which they put between their thighs and the backs of their horses, and thus warm it a little . . . **6.** They cover their heads with round caps and protect their hairy legs with goatskins; their shoes are formed upon no lasts, and so prevent their walking with free step. For this reason they are not at all adapted to battles on foot, but they are almost glued to their horses, which are hardy, it is true, but ugly, and sometimes they sit them women-fashion and thus perform their ordinary tasks. From their horses by night or day every one of that nation buys and sells, eats and drinks, and bowed over the narrow neck of the animal relaxes into a sleep so deep as to be accompanied by many dreams. **7.** And when deliberation is called for about weighty matters, they all consult as a common body in that fashion. They are subject to no royal restraint, but they are content with the disorderly government of their important men, and led by them they force their way through every obstacle. **8.** They also sometimes fight when provoked, and then they enter the battle drawn up in wedge-shaped masses, while their medley of voices makes a savage noise. And as they are lightly equipped for swift motion, and unexpected in action, they purposely divide suddenly into scattered bands and attack, rushing about in disorder here and there, dealing terrific slaughter; and because of their extraordinary rapidity of movement they are never seen to attack a rampart or pillage an enemy's camp. **9.** And on this account you would not hesitate to call them the most terrible of all warriors, because they fight from a distance with missiles having sharp bone, instead of their usual points, joined to the shafts with wonderful skill; then they gallop over the intervening spaces and fight hand to hand with swords, regardless of their own lives; and while the enemy are guarding against wounds from the sabre-thrusts, they throw strips of cloth plaited into nooses over their opponents and so entangle them that they fetter their limbs and take from them the power of riding or walking.

SOURCE: Ammianus Marcellinus, *Res Gestaea Fine Corneli Taciti*, Book 31, ch. 2, trans. M. Pavkovic and S. Morillo.

One characteristic of Hunnic warfare was the ability of their armies to move quickly. This was a result of more than the simple fact that all the Huns were mounted and traveled with all their possessions in carts. Many of their contemporaries had cavalry troops, but none could keep pace with the Huns. The reason for this was that the Hun warrior had not a single horse, but a string of horses that could be

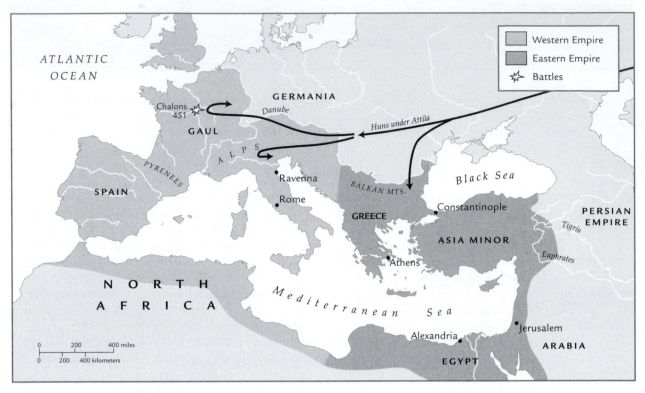

Figure 6.2 The Huns Under Attila

ridden in turn during a campaign. This allowed the Huns to cover much greater distances without wearing out their mounts, a tremendous advantage over the Roman cavalryman with his single mount.

By the middle of the fifth century, however, there are indications that the Huns had fragmented into several groups, not all of whom were mounted. It has been suggested that when the Huns settled in Hungary, which possessed the only great plain in Europe that could support a significant number of horses, some of the Huns were, out of necessity, unhorsed. After all, the Hungarian plain was not the steppes; it has been suggested that it could support no more than 150,000 horses, enough for only 15,000 warriors. The rest of the Huns mimicked some of their Germanic subjects, taking up farming and fighting on foot. It has been suggested that in their last great open battle against the Romans in 451 CE, the majority of the Huns fought on foot.

The Huns in the Age of Attila

By the 440s CE, there had been a great transformation in the role the Huns played in western Europe.

Prior to that period, the Huns had primarily been seen as raiders and brigands. Their incursions were often serious but not devastating. All of that changed with the rise of a new leader among the Huns—Attila. By the end of the 440s, Attila had transformed the Huns; there were no longer a number of savage kings of the Huns, but only one king who exerted control, albeit less than absolute, over the various Hunnic groups. During the final decades of the western empire, Attila was the Hun with whom the Romans dealt.

On several occasions, Attila, who was apparently aggrieved because the Romans were behind in their tribute, raided imperial territory. But his great campaign was launched in 451 (Figure 6.2). Attila invaded Gaul where he fought and lost a battle at Chalons in July. He then turned toward Italy in 452, but the Romans under their general Aetius countered the Huns' speed with a new strategy. The western Romans, awaiting aid from the eastern empire, withdrew from northern Italy. Attila sacked several cities, but Roman civilians and soldiers withdrew before the Huns who, laden with booty, were unable to pursue them effectively. Attila spent the summer of 452 in

Milan where his army was afflicted by the plague. At the same time, he found himself facing not only a reinforced western army under Aetius but a second eastern Roman army as well.

This was too much for the Huns, and Attila was forced to withdraw in strategic defeat. Not only was his ability to exact tribute from Rome totally undermined, but he had lost more warriors than he could afford to. This proved to be the undoing of the empire of the Huns and, perhaps, of Attila, who died in early 453.

THE TURKS

The name "Turk" has come under considerable scholarly inspection, with the only consensus being that the Turks as a people did not arise spontaneously on the steppes. The name refers to a broad group of peoples speaking a Turkic language. It is sometimes said that "Turk" was the name of a mountain considered to be the ancestral homeland of the Turks. Its shape was said to be that of a helmet, called "Turk" in the local language. The local people then called themselves by this name.

The land of the Turks, "Turkestan," accordingly, was a vast, almost indeterminate, region that ranges from the Aral Sea to the Gansu corridor in China and gradually merges into Mongolia. It was a land of deserts, oases, and dry and wet steppes. Turkestan was thought of historically as two lands, one western and one eastern. The people of Western Turkestan traditionally were oriented toward Persia and even Europe, while those of Eastern Turkestan were oriented primarily toward China.

The two Turkestans were linked by caravan routes and a roughly common language group and pastoral nomadic existence, but little else. Western Turkestan is also often referred to as Transoxiana, or the drainage area of the Amu and Syr Darya rivers (also called the Oxus and Jaxartes rivers). This was a region not subject to severe climate variations and even possessing some lands suitable for agriculture as well as grazing. This region also was home to several major cities, such as Bukhara and Samarkand.

In contrast, Eastern Turkestan (later also called Chinese Turkestan) was a mostly empty land of deserts and dry steppes, with vast ranges in climate. The population lived primarily in a series of oases situated around the Tarim Basin, in Mongolia, where the first major Turkish confederation appeared.

The First Turk Confederation

The Turks do not appear in Chinese records until sometime in the sixth century CE, when they were said to have been slaves of other tribal groups in Eastern Turkestan, renowned for their ability as ironsmiths. As the craftsmen who produced the majority of weapons for their masters, the role of the Turks was very important and possibly carried a great deal of social prestige. At some point, the various Turkish clans came under the charismatic leadership of a chieftain named Tumen, who led successful raids on neighboring tribes. The defeat of these neighbors and the parceling out of the spoils solidified Tumen's position, and, in 551, he formed a trading and even marriage alliance with the Western Wei dynasty in north China. This alliance bore fruit the following year, with Tumen's Turkish tribesmen defeating their major rivals for dominance on the steppes, and the Western Wei slaughtering the refugees who streamed into their territory. Also in 552, Tumen had himself proclaimed Qaghan, a title similar to the Xiongnu title of Shanyu, meaning "undisputed leader of the confederation."

The usual Inner Asian nomadic tradition continued, in which success in battle (and consequent ability to provide spoils) led other tribes, clans, and groups to join the confederation. Within a few short years, Tumen's Turkish confederation had built an empire that spread from the Mongolian plateau through most of Central Asia. The Turks maintained trade relations not only with China but also with Persia and even the Byzantine Empire. Control of the caravan routes linking China and the western lands was extremely lucrative and reduced the Qaghan's need to lead his forces on campaigns of plunder. The control of north China was no longer in the hands of the Western Wei but of two successor dynasties. Both were openly fearful of raids or invasion by the enormous Turkish Empire and so provided lavish gifts to Tumen, including tens of thousands of rolls of silk.

Relations with Sassanid Persia and the Byzantines also contributed to Turkish wealth and confederation stability. The Turks formed a military alliance with Persia, and this alliance succeeded in destroying several hostile nomadic tribes living between the two powers. Once informed of the powerful Turkish state to the east of their Persian enemy, the Byzantines also worked for an alliance. While no Turkish-Byzantine military alliance ever materialized, the threat of such a powerful grouping led the Persians to offer many concessions to their Turkish neighbors.

The Turkish confederation was dependent on a strong, charismatic leader. This, of course, was a necessary component for all steppe nomadic confederations, and the passing of such a leader normally led to civil war until a new leader emerged. On the death of Tumen in 553, his powerful brothers did not contest the succession but allowed Tumen's son to inherit the title. For nearly thirty years, the succession continued smoothly laterally through all of Tumen's surviving sons. In 581, however, when it became necessary to choose an heir from the next generation, the Turkish confederation was plagued by civil wars, as the various descendants of Tumen fought for the right to the title of Qaghan.

The Second Turk Confederation

Struggles for power led for a time to the creation of two distinct Turkish confederations, antagonistic to each other. This period corresponded with the unification of China and the establishment of two strong dynasties, the Sui and Tang. The histories of both dynasties were intimately tied to that of the Turks (see Chapter 9), and, during the period of struggle, the Chinese worked hard either to disrupt the Turks or to keep them as allies in their campaigns against others. Often, Chinese rulers would support one Turkish confederation at the expense of the other or would support particular contenders for power. One thing remained constant for potential Turkish leaders: their need to acquire goods for distribution to their member tribes. This could be accomplished by raiding in China or by concluding agreements with the various Chinese dynasties providing for the provision of tribute. Sometimes both methods were used at the same time, confusing the Chinese strategists, who did not always understand the dynamics of the Turkish succession struggles.

The early rulers of both Sui and Tang China were very familiar with Turkish culture and politics, especially the second emperor of the Tang dynasty, Li Shimin (later known as Tang Taizong). Using a deft combination of diplomacy, bribery, and military force, by 630, Tang Taizong had succeeded so well that nearly all of the Turkish lands were under his control, and he had proclaimed himself Qaghan, in addition to being emperor of China. For roughly five decades, the Turks were a part of the military system of the Tang dynasty (see Chapter 9).

Many Turkish tribal leaders were not pleased at this subservience to a settled people and sought to restore the confederation. Chinese control of the Turks therefore required a tremendous degree of vigilance; but, as the years passed, attention was directed more and more to internal matters. Taking advantage of this distraction was Khutlugh, a descendant of one of the last Qaghans, who, following the familiar pattern, engaged in military actions to expand the territory under his control. By all accounts, Khutlugh was adept at personal combat, skilled at battlefield strategy, perceptive in politics, and stirring in oratory. His success reached its height in 690, by which time he controlled a large part of Eastern Turkestan and had forced the Chinese to pay large amounts of tribute. When he died two years later, the succession went smoothly to his surviving brother, Khapaghan. Apparently possessing many of his brother's personal, political, and military skills, Khapaghan pursued a two-pronged strategy of warfare to expand his control of the steppe lands and frequent (and sometimes extraordinarily destructive) raids into China for the booty needed to secure his hold over his subordinates. For a time, Khapaghan even toyed with the idea of conquering all or part of China itself, but, instead, he settled for large amounts of tribute to be presented by the Chinese.

Although Khutlugh and Khapaghan succeeded in re-creating the extent of the first Turkish empire, this appearance of unity was misleading. Battle with subordinate tribes was constant, and instability was encouraged by the nature of Turkish rule of their confederation, which contributed to both stability and fragmentation, as contradictory as that may seem. Much like the Seljuks of a later century, but unlike the Xiongnu, the Turkish confederacy or empire was fairly decentralized. The Qaghan was more than simply a first-among-equals, but he had limited direct control over subordinate Turkish tribes and even over subject nomadic tribes. A bureaucracy supported the Qaghan, primarily designed to collect and distribute tribute and spoils of battle and to provide some mediation of disputes. Under the Qaghan were up to four subordinates who also took the title of Qaghan. During the reign of Tumen and his immediate successors, his brother Ishtemi (sometimes, Istami) was given charge of the western half of the Turkish domains, which were autonomous in most respects. In addition, the Qaghan appointed governors to oversee the subordinate tribes and ensure that they joined in campaigns. Other officers of the Qaghan were appointed to pay particular attention to the non-Turkish components of the confederation. However, tribal leaders maintained a good deal of control and autonomy regarding the oversight of their tribes, and succession struggles within tribes were often allowed to run their course without significant central interference.

When Khapaghan died in 716 (in an ambush set by an enemy tribe), civil war broke out once again. The sons of Khutlugh restored a semblance of unity and kept the rulership in the family. When the last of these sons died in 741, however, the fragility of the Turkish confederation became clear, as the vast empire completely disintegrated.

Successors to the Turkish Empire

The Eastern Steppes   The immediate successors to the Turkish Qaghanate in the eastern steppes were the Uighurs. They formed a close alliance with Tang China, which was wracked by civil war, and helped prop up the regime. But as Chinese power faded, so did the coherence of their nomadic allies' polity, and a power vacuum developed in the eastern steppes. As a result, the center of gravity of nomadic power shifted north and east, into Mongolia and even Manchuria. The Mongolic Qitans and the part-Manchurian Jurchens established northern Chinese states at the expense of the new Song dynasty. (These developments are taken up in more detail in Chapter 9.)

The Western Steppes   The second Turk confederation had never exercised very effective control over the western steppes, which since the end of the first Turk confederation in 581 had witnessed struggles between several related groups for dominance. The most important of these were the Bulghars and the Khazars. The latter eventually drove the former into the Balkans, where they established a kingdom on the borders of the Byzantine Empire. The Khazars became staunch Byzantine allies in the empire's struggles with the Persians and later the Arabs—with the Khazars halting Arab expansion northward through the Caucasus around 740, at about the same time that Arab armies met defeat before Constantinople (718) and in France at the hands of Charles Martel (732). The Khazars, in turn, were succeeded as the dominant western steppe power in the late tenth century by the Pechenegs. Other nomadic groups, mainly Turkic and based farther east, developed complex relationships in the eighth to eleventh centuries with the Muslim states of southwest Asia.

Cultural Influences on the Steppes   With no dominant power controlling the entire steppe world, and with successor states drawn into intense and ongoing diplomatic and military dealings with various adjacent realms, the period from the end of the second Turk confederation in 741 to the mid-eleventh century saw a significant incursion of sedentary cultural and religious traditions into the steppe world, traditions that both competed and blended with nomadic traditions. The major salvation religions—Buddhism, Christianity, and Islam—were especially important in this process. Some examples illustrate the sorts of cultural exchange explained in general terms earlier in the chapter.

The Qitans, for instance, had already adopted a writing system based on Chinese characters before they established the Liao dynasty in north China, and Buddhism became a significant part of their religious beliefs. The Bulghars, despite consistent hostility toward Byzantium, eventually converted to Orthodox Christianity (and were substantially "Slavicized" after they settled in the Balkans). The Uighurs established the world's only Manichaean state in the centuries after 744. Perhaps most interestingly, the Khazars converted to Judaism, reportedly after inviting representatives of that religion, Christianity, and Islam to a great debate presided over by the Khazar Qaghan. Why Judaism? Though Byzantine allies more often than not, the Khazars valued their position as potential power brokers between Byzantium and the Muslim Abassid Caliphate (see Chapter 8), so that a choice of either of the major religious traditions of those rivals would have reduced their freedom of action. But a connection to one of the broader religious traditions of the settled world was important in facilitating diplomacy, trade, and alliances. Judaism therefore seems to have appeared to the Khazars as a convenient, neutral choice from among the monotheisms on offer.

In the long run, however, the most important influence to enter the steppes during this period was Islam. In the complex diplomatic and military maneuvering along the northern borders of the Islamic world, various Turkish groups converted. Conversion was often a strategy in intertribal conflict—a bid for allies, or a way of distinguishing one tribe from another—and Islam was by no means the dominant religion of the central steppes even by the mid-eleventh century. But at least part of the nomadic world gradually became tied more closely to Islam. The consequences were important in both directions. Islamic trade and diplomacy reached farther into the steppes; conversely, Turks became the most important source of the slave soldiers who rapidly assumed a central place in Islamic military organization after 850 (see Chapter 8). And newly converted Turkish tribes often became the most active *ghazi,* or frontier, warriors for the faith, in Islam. Finally, Islamicized Turks moved directly into the politics of the Islamic world as conquerors. One Turkish tribe, the Seljuks, would be particularly important in leading this new wave of nomadic conquests.

The Seljuk Turks

In the eleventh century, the Seljuk Turks had been Muslim for only a short period. Yet, from their beginnings as typical nomadic *ghazi* warriors, within a century, the Seljuks would claim rule of the vast lands of Persia, Mesopotamia, and Syria, in the process transforming from raiders to invaders. They created the first unity this region had seen since the heyday of the Abbasid Caliphate, but it was a fragile unity, as even the most able of the Seljuk rulers could never fully secure their control over their subordinates.

Seljuk Conquest of Settled Lands   The Seljuks first arrived as major actors in Central Asia in the late tenth century, when the tribesmen enlisted in the service of the Samanids and Ghaznavids as *ghazi* warriors, primarily attacking non-Muslim Turkish tribes. In return for their successes, the Seljuks were awarded grazing lands for their flocks and horses (the Seljuks were also famous for their expert use of camels), and within a few decades, many other *ghazi* Turks joined the Seljuks.

The first wave of Seljuk conquests of the settled lands came with the ascension to power of Toghril-beg in the mid-eleventh century. He was a brilliant and charismatic leader, who first directed his tribal armies in coordinated campaigns against the various Islamic principalities and kingdoms of Central Asia. At the very time Toghril-beg succeeded in uniting the Turkish tribes under the Seljuk banner, the Islamic world was suffering through a great deal of disunity, with Persia the scene of near-constant warfare among competing factions.

After securing his Central Asian base, Toghril-beg swung his armies into Korasan in eastern Persia,

where he continued to meet with success. However, the Seljuk forces were not under strict centralized direction, and Toghril-beg's control depended on his continued success in leading his forces on raids of pillage. As much as possible, Toghril-beg placed family members in positions of command, but even their loyalty could not always be counted on. This need to satisfy his subordinates meant that in the early years of the Seljuk attacks on Persia the goal was rarely permanent conquest, and the Seljuks found it extremely difficult to assault cities. Not until the victorious conclusion of the siege of Isfahan revealed the wealth to be obtained from looting cities was Toghril-beg able to convince his men to endure the frustration involved in besieging major population and wealth centers.

Like the earlier Turkish conquerors of China, Toghril-beg learned that utilizing the administrative, tax, and other systems of the settled peoples he ruled was a more secure method of obtaining wealth, as well as serving to enhance his authority as ruler. From 1055, Toghril-beg devoted most of his time to subduing his subordinates and imposing a Persian bureaucratic system on what became known as the Great Seljuk Empire, relying on Persians to run the administrative machinery (Figure 6.3).

The Seljuks of the eleventh century were attested by their enemies to be the best horse-archers of the time. The Persians, Byzantines, and Crusaders remarked in fear at the ability of Seljuk armies to coordinate the loosing of arrow storms while at a gallop (see Chapter 11). To be sure, the Seljuks trained constantly while not in combat, but it is not clear that their battlefield strategy and tactics were notably superior to those of other nomadic warriors, such as the Mongols of a later century (see Chapter 13). While expert in the use of the compound bow, as were nearly all of the Inner Asian nomadic warriors, the Seljuks distinguished themselves from the others in their use of a relatively small, light spear, used much like a lance. After an arrow storm, the Seljuk mounted spearmen wreaked havoc in enemy lines. Most soldiers also carried either a sword or axe, with which they often fought dismounted. As a result of their effectiveness, Turks came to dominate the military forces of the Islamic states of southwest Asia, both as slave soldiers and as provincial levies (see Chapter 8).

The revival of Islamic fortunes the Turks led came at a steep price, however. To deal with the usual problem facing nomadic conquerors—how to remain nomads while ruling a settled, agricultural society—and to maintain the strength of their forces as they moved

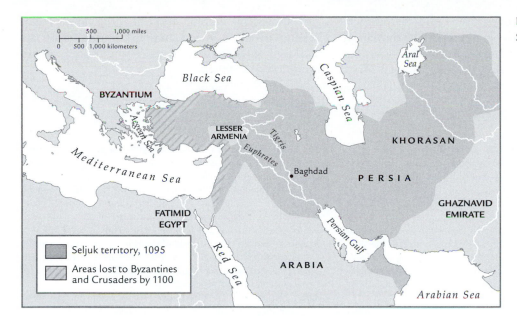

Figure 6.3 The Great Seljuk Empire in 1095

farther into the Islamic (and, later, Byzantine) world, the Seljuks encouraged the displacement of farming populations and the reversion of agricultural areas to pasture in significant areas, especially in Korasan and Anatolia. The cost in economic vitality is hard to measure but was certainly significant.

The Decline of Seljuk Power Like the earlier Turkish confederations, the Great Seljuk Empire contained tendencies to decentralization from the start. In the Seljuk conception, sovereignty was vested, not in a supreme office or even in one person and his direct descendants, but in the entire family of the ruler. This notion of collective sovereignty meant that Toghril-beg and his immediate successors felt compelled to grant rule over provinces of the empire to various relatives, who then tended to divide their possessions among their sons. Though technically subordinate to the Seljuk sultan, these regional rulers rapidly came to see themselves as independent and even began fighting among themselves rather than continuing the expansion of the empire. Thus, the unity that Seljuk conquests had temporarily imposed on the Islamic world proved ephemeral. As a result, though the Seljuks inflicted a disastrous defeat on the Byzantines at Manzikert in 1071 and subsequently overran much of Asia Minor (see Chapter 8), Alexius Comnenus was able to take advantage of Turkish disunity to revive the fortunes of the Byzantine Empire after 1081. Even more significantly, the fragmentation of Islamic southwest Asia by 1095 made possible the success of the First Crusade (see Chapter 11).

CONCLUSION

Even in decline, the Turks remained formidable fighters—their problem was internal politics, not military ineffectiveness, a combination that echoes Herodotus's assessment of the Scythians. This similarity is no accident, as it reflects the continuity of factors shaping the historical experience of steppe nomads from their earliest appearance in written records down to the eleventh century. Nomadic influence waxed and waned—peaks of nomadic conquering activity characterized both the beginning and the end of the period 400–1100, and there had been many earlier periods of nomadic incursion, as this chapter has shown—but the threat of nomadic military action was a constant for rulers of sedentary civilizations that bordered the steppes. As a result, the nomadic role in ongoing cultural exchanges throughout

Eurasia can hardly be overstated. And the pinnacle of nomadic conquest was yet to come: The thirteenth century campaigns of Chingiz Khan's Mongols are detailed in Chapter 13. But, as the Mongol leader's title shows, his empire stood in direct line of succession to the nomadic imperial traditions of the Turkish confederations: *Khan* is simply an alternate rendition of *Qaghan*.

SUGGESTED READINGS

Adshead, S. A. M. *Central Asia in World History.* New York: St. Martin's Press, 1993. A readable overview with special emphasis on the important connections between the nomadic and nonnomadic worlds.

Barfield, T. J. *The Perilous Frontier: Nomadic Empires and China.* Oxford: Basil Blackwell, 1989. An important conceptualization of the character of nomadic "frontiers" and the role of nomadic empires on the political development of China.

Christian, David. *Inner Eurasia from Prehistory to the Mongol Empire.* Oxford: Blackwell, 1998. A broad survey that emphasizes the symbiotic relationship between nomadic and sedentary societies.

Golden, Peter B. *Nomads and Sedentary Societies in Medieval Eurasia.* Essays on Global and Comparative History. Washington, DC: American Historical Association, 1998. A good introduction to the outlines of nomadic history, if a bit heavy on narrative; contains a good bibliography.

Kafesoglu, Ibrahim. *A History of the Seljuks.* Ed., trans., and intro. by Gary Leiser. Carbondale: Southern Illinois University Press, 1988. A classic Turkish account of the rise of the Seljuks, with emphasis on the creation of the Great Seljuk Empire.

Maenchen-Helfen, Otto. *World of the Huns.* Berkeley: University of California Press, 1973. An excellent survey of Hunnic culture as well as a narrative of Hunnic history; draws on archaeological and literary evidence.

Sinor, Dennis, ed. *The Cambridge History of Early Inner Asia.* Cambridge: Cambridge University Press, 1990. An excellent comprehensive introduction to steppe history.

CHAPTER 7

Chiefs and Warbands: Western Europe, 400–1100

INTRODUCTION

Migrations and invasions of peoples from the Asian steppes began to affect the Roman world as early as the reign of Marcus Aurelius (161–180). By the reign of Diocletian (284–305), these stresses had transformed the social, economic, and military structures of the Roman Empire. Diocletian's administrative division of the Empire recognized a growing differentiation of the eastern and western halves of the Roman world. Another influx of invaders brought an end to the Western Empire in the fifth century. Two centuries later, Islamic Arab conquests divided the old Roman world again, this time between north and south.

By the mid-600s, the Roman world had split into three: Latin Europe, the Eastern Roman Empire (Byzantium), and the Islamic world, all of which were heir to some aspects of Roman civilization and military tradition. Roman infrastructure shaped warfare for another millenium as Roman walled cities continued to be the focus of campaigns, especially in Mediterranean lands, and Roman roads continued to serve as military highways. Successor states continued to use and imitate Roman military (and civil) administration, with varying degrees of success. And Christianity—the religion that had triumphed in Rome following Constantine's conversion—not only provided an administrative and cultural link to the past but also increasingly infused warfare with a new ideological significance. Conquest and conversion were married; paganism, different brands of Christianity, Christian heresies, and Christianity's new cousin, Islam, entered a long battle waged with words and swords.

Each of the heirs of Rome developed its own distinctive identity. Chapter 8 will examine Islam and the Byzantine Empire. This chapter looks at Latin Europe from 350 to 1050, a world of strong connections to the later empire and the transformed Roman world after Diocletian, but also a world of significant change.

The Successor Kingdoms, 350–700

The military forces of the Germanic successor kingdoms reflected the fusion of Roman and barbarian elements that characterized the whole society (Figure 7.1). Frankish, Burgundian, and Gothic kings and their rivals consciously attempted to maintain Roman systems of recruitment and organization. But the socioeconomic conditions of the time and the invaders' own traditions made complete continuity impossible.

Social and Economic Conditions

The population dwindled for several centuries, due to plagues and the disruptions of the Germanic migrations themselves, and the demographic pattern became more rural. Cities shrank within their walls, reflecting not just population loss but a decline in trade and commerce. This less monetized economy, operating closer to subsistence levels in many areas, had clear implications for the ability of rulers to employ paid professional soldiers or mercenaries.

The problem of reduced economic resources was compounded by reduced administrative resources. A general decline in lay literacy made bureaucracies harder to maintain, a trend offset only marginally by the survival of the Christian Church as a literate institution. The legal reach of governments contracted as customary laws displaced written codes. Authority tended to fragment and become privatized: Governing, especially at the local level, tended toward a form of estate management. Again, in such a context, the ability of rulers to maintain professional, centrally administered armies clearly waned.

119

Figure 7.1 Germanic Invasions and Successor Kingdoms

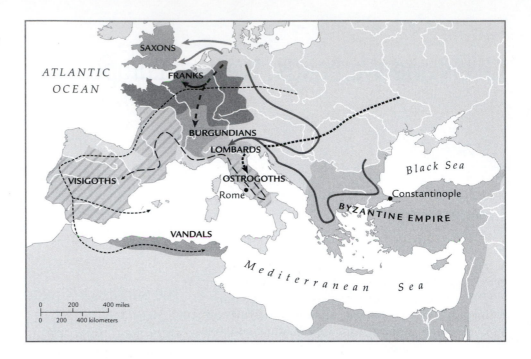

Social changes were also significant. Late Roman society had seen the rise of powerful rural magnates, replacing urban elites as the backbone of local society. Powerful men were powerful by virtue of the number of their followers, armed and otherwise. The intrusion of barbarian military commanders and their followers fit neatly into this pattern, though their presence increased the insecurity of the civilian population. Such insecurity made powerful patrons with armed followers even more important for protection and stimulated the formation of self-help groups, especially in cities and towns. This volatile social mixture was further stirred by the connection of constructed barbarian ethnicities with military service and exemption from taxes and by religious ferment. The alliance of the Franks and the papacy as defenders of orthodoxy against Arianism demonstrates the potential for an ideological dimension to warfare in this period.

Armies and Warfare

In many ways, the arrival of the Germans simply harmonized with or accelerated changes ongoing in the Empire since at least Diocletian's time. The reforms of Constantine and Diocletian had divided the Roman army into *limitanei,* border units guarding against small raids, and a mobile field army designed, with increasingly fortified urban centers, to allow a "defense in depth" against major incursions. Over

the fourth century, the *limitanei* tended to merge into the local population, while the field army and palace guard units came to be dominated by barbarians, a category that reflects ethnogenesis (cultural constructions of identity) more than actual ethnic descent (see the Issues box "'Barbarization' of the Roman Army," page 72). Whether barbarians are seen as Romanized Germans, Germanicized Romans, or both, they served under terms that maintained the structure of the Roman military system, at least in theory. But the "barbarization" of the army, including the use of federate troops who were not subjected to Roman organization, had significant results for military organization and warfare. These results can be seen in the aims of war, the constitution of forces, and the patterns of war.

Grand Strategy   At the broadest level, the successor kingdoms were the heirs of Rome's defensive posture. Under regular external threat, this civilization struggled merely to maintain its boundaries; in fact, it suffered losses to Justinian's eastern Roman forces in the mid-500s and to Islam with the conquest of Iberia in the early 700s (see Chapter 8). Further Germanic pagan invasions, such as the Saxon conquest of Britain, were countered, slowly, only by conversion of the invaders. But there was no coherent grand strategy of defense or cooperation, simply an inability to do much else than hang on. Most of the conflict in the period consisted of small wars over dynastic claims and of local power grabbing. Domination of towns and the countryside as sources of wealth tapped either through rudimentary taxation or by pillage was the goal of ambitious magnates and warband leaders. Even kings, though important as symbols and foci of an often artificially constructed tribal unity (see below), and adopting as far as possible the symbols of Roman and Christian legitimacy, were ultimately measured by their ability to distribute gifts to their followers, gifts usually gained in pillaging raids. In short, warfare was transformed from a state into a personal and dynastic enterprise.

Armies and Society   The makeup of the armed forces of the successor kingdoms is an obscure and much debated topic. But several broad trends are visible. Perhaps most important, like wars, forces got smaller. Armies in the tens of thousands were rare; most would have numbered under 10,000, and many under a 1000. In part, this reflected the fragmentation of political authority: Each kingdom could raise only a fraction of the forces Rome had deployed over the region as a whole. But the demographic, economic, and administrative constraints outlined above undoubtedly affected the total numbers that could be raised. And forces got smaller despite two trends that probably tended to mitigate the weakness of states in raising armies and to increase the proportion of the population under arms.

First, armed forces, like politics, became increasingly privatized. The key components of armies were the followers of great men—armed forces maintained, not at state expense out of tax revenues, but out of the private wealth of the magnates (which could be built on theoretically public sources of income). In effect, there was a devolution of responsibility for supporting armies from the center to the localities. Therefore, kings had available to them warriors whom they did not have to support themselves—but only if they could maintain the loyalty of the magnates who followed them, by no means an easy task. (Nor were magnates always sure of the loyalty of their followers.)

Second, the militarization of society, represented among the elite by private warbands, extended to lower levels as well. We should probably not think of armed peasants—farming and soldiering have always been difficult jobs for the same set of people to engage in consistently, and the slaves and semifree tenants who made up much of the rural population were poor candidates for fighting effectively. But townsmen certainly were armed and organized for self-defense. Urban forces could also join royal expeditions, and they outnumbered magnate warbands in some armies. Further, it is unclear how low on the social ladder the reach of warbands went, as the followers of followers were undoubtedly often men of little substance. The militarization of society is neatly summarized in the common definition of freedom: "Free men" had the right to bear arms along with the widely recognized obligation to come to the defense of the kingdom when summoned by the king. Early in this period, freedom and the right to bear arms was also associated with Germanic or barbarian ethnic identity: barbarians fought, while Romans paid taxes. This led to widespread adoption of barbarian identity among soldiers and the powerful: The "Germanness" of many Germans was a choice. (This helps account for a Frankish kingdom that claimed a Germanic ethnicity but that ended up speaking a vulgar form of Latin.) When barbarian ethnic identity had become widespread enough to lose its usefulness in distinguishing warriors from commoners, military-aristocratic pedigree emerged to replace it, becoming one of the key social distinctions of medieval Europe thenceforward.

Patterns of Campaigning   The social and economic context of the successor kingdoms also affected the patterns of warfare. There was a marked tendency toward localism, as poor communications made coordination of large-scale enterprises more difficult, though not impossible. Above all, logistical constraints—where armies could find food for themselves and fodder for horses, always a major concern for any preindustrial army—probably tightened even more, keeping forces small.

Pillaging was the most common activity of war. Pillaging provided supplies and booty, reduced the enemy's resources (if carried out in enemy territory), and sent a message to rivals, hostile populations, and rebellious subjects. It could intimidate a fortified town into surrender, and it could also serve as revenge for earlier plundering—and could easily descend into pointless cruelty. And distribution of the loot gained in pillaging further underpinned royal authority.

Fortified towns were centers of supply as well as centers of control of the surrounding countryside, and thus were the focus of some campaigns. Especially where conquest or control of a polity was at issue, military leaders sought to capture enemy strongholds and defend their own. Thus, sieges and siege defense remained part of the prosecution of war. The outcome of sieges often turned on whether the fort or the besiegers ran out of supplies first. A relief army could lift a siege merely by harassing the besieger's foragers and causing a supply crisis. Battles were sometimes the result of a determined besieger facing off with a determined relief force.

Two contradictory impulses influenced leaders' attitudes toward battle. On one hand, battles were risky—above all for commanders who led from the front to prove their prowess—and advanced the territorial aims of a campaign only indirectly even if successful. (A battle that destroyed all enemy field forces allowed the victor to pursue sieges without threat of a relief force showing up, but it did not guarantee success.) So, from this perspective, battles were to be avoided except as a last resort, as Vegetius, the late Roman writer on military affairs, advised. On the other hand, a leader's need to maintain his honor and the loyalty of his followers impelled him to meet invasions head-on and prevent the ravaging of his and his followers' lands. The widespread view that, in fighting a battle, combatants submitted the outcome of the dispute to the judgment of God (whichever god(s) it happened to be) reinforced this incentive to fight and added an almost ritual element to the face-to-face confrontation of rival armies (see the Sources box "Gregory, Bishop of Tours"). Thus, battles were fought regularly. There is little to say about tactical developments in this period: Barbarian attacks in wedge formation may have been new, but, for the most part, declining professionalism and insecure command control enforced simplicity in battlefield dispositions.

Infantry and Cavalry   One final effect of the changing social and administrative context on patterns of war had to do with the tactical and operational balance between infantry and cavalry. As we saw in Chapters 1–4, there are two main bases of infantry effectiveness. In the Greek model, massed infantry derived from its communal origins the cohesion and morale necessary for it to face a cavalry charge and maneuver on the battlefield. Neighbor fought shoulder to shoulder with neighbor, and the communal identity of the polis held the whole together. Such units, to be most effective, also had to fight frequently, because experience in the field was the only serious training they got. They were, in other words, part-timers, for the ability of a small community to support a full-time, professional, and drilled body of soldiers was very limited—only the Spartans among the Greek poleis managed it. On the

other hand, in the imperial Roman (and Chinese) model, infantry gained its cohesion from training and drill imposed by a central authority on full-time troops. Such a model required a much larger polity and population base, and much higher levels of governmental income, administrative expertise, and central control. In the late Roman world and its successors in the west, both bases of effective infantry suffered serious erosion.

The Roman model virtually disappeared—not surprisingly, given the economic and administrative conditions outlined above. One of Vegetius's most frequent complaints involved the decline in standards of infantry training that he saw in his day. This left the Greek model. We have seen that urban militias continued to constitute an important part of the armed forces of the successor states. But even here, some decline was evident. For one thing, economic contraction reduced the material resources and the morale of many urban communities. Even more important, urban militias in the successor states operated most frequently in a strictly defensive capacity, guarding their own walls. They did not campaign enough to gain a critical level of experience in the field, and even those that did fought battles infrequently, unlike the phalanxes of the poleis, whose reason for campaigning was to fight a battle. As a result, their usefulness in combat, outside of standing in a defensive block, remained limited. Finally, the economic and military elites of this society were often based outside the towns, unlike those of the Greek poleis, so that as military communities the towns were deprived of their heads, so to speak. In fact, urban infantry was at its best on the battlefield when the better-equipped and more experienced warriors of magnate warbands fought as their front rank.

With the decline in the quality of infantry, cavalry forces assumed greater prominence in the warfare of this age compared to Greek and Roman times. This phenomenon has often been attributed to a significant increase in the quality of cavalry. The Roman defeat at Adrianople in 378 at the hands of Ostrogothic horsemen used to be taken as the beginning of an age of cavalry, for example. Alternately, the introduction of the stirrup is supposed to have lifted the horseman to dominance, in either the 300s or perhaps the 700s. But the coming of an age of cavalry was neither sudden nor overwhelming. The evidence for the development of the stirrup is disputed, as the wide range for the dating of its introduction indicates. By making the rider more secure on his horse, the stirrup did make some

Gregory, Bishop of Tours

Gregorius Florentius, the sixth-century Frankish prelate and bishop, describes the battlefield religious experiences of one monarch of the day, as well as battle and seige tactics.

■ ■ ■

[The Conversion of Clovis, King of the Franks]
It happened that many were killed as the two armies were fighting fiercely, and Clovis's army began to fall apart in the slaughter. Seeing this, raising his eyes to heaven, with remorse in his heart, and bursting into tears, he cried: "Jesus Christ, whom Chlotilda [Clovis's wife] claims to be the son of the living God, who is said to give aid to those who are struggling and to give victory to those who place hope in you, I beg the glory of your help, such that if you grant me victory. . . . I will believe in you and be baptized in your name." . . . And when he said this, the Allamanni turned their backs, and began to give way in flight. And when they perceived that their king had fallen, they put themselves under Clovis' rule. . . .

[Battle Tactics] Afterward Theodoric [king of the Franks], not forgetting the perjury of Hermenfred, king of the Thuringi, called his brother Chlotar to his aid and prepared to go against him, promising king Chlotar a part of the plunder if the gift of victory be conferred on them by God. . . . The Thuringi prepared traps against the coming of the Franks. For in the plain where the fight was to happen they dug ditches, which by covering the openings with thick turf they disguised as a level plain. Thus many of the horsemen of the Franks fell into these snares when they began to fight and it was a great obstacle to them; but after learning of this trap they began to watch out for it. And then when the Thuringi saw themselves being fiercely slaughtered, and with the flight of their king Hermenfred, they turned their backs. . . . Having achieved victory [the Franks] seized that country and brought it under their control.

[Siege Tactics] Fifteen days passed in this siege, and Leudeghisel prepared new engines to destroy the city [Comminges]: carts with battering rams, woven branches and planks under which the army was to move forward to demolish the walls. But when they approached they were so battered down by stones that all who got near the wall died. They tossed out pots with burning pitch and fat over them, and pushed others full of stones down on them. But when night stopped the battle the army returned to the camp. . . . As morning came the army again rose for battle, and they made bundles of sticks as if to fill the deep trench which was on the eastern side; but here the engine could do no harm. And Sagittarius the bishop circled the walls frequently in arms and often threw stones from the wall with his own hand against the enemy.

SOURCE: Gregorio di Tours, *La Storia dei Franchi*, ed. Massimo Oldoni (Fondazione Lorenzo Valla, 1981): II.30 (v. 1, p. 168); III.7 (v. 1, pp. 220–22); VII.37 (v. 2, pp. 212–14), trans. S. Morillo.

difference in cavalry-versus-cavalry combat, and it was in universal use in western Europe probably by the ninth century. But morale and cohesion were the key to infantry's ability to face cavalry. If a wall of foot soldiers stood fast in the face of an intimidating charge, the horses would refuse (pull up short in the face of an obstacle they could neither jump nor go around), and the charge would devolve into hand-to-hand combat.

The stirrup made no difference to the psychological effect of a charge. Cavalry became more important on the battlefield, not because it got better, but because infantry got worse.

In military terms, this is a limited claim, for as we have seen, battles were only part of warfare. Infantry forces remained crucial to armies of the age because of their role in siege warfare, and they often constituted the bulk of forces numerically. Western Europe was unsuited, geographically and climatically, to supporting mounted armies such as arose on the steppes, and it was far enough from the centers of nomadic lands and power to be less affected than many areas by nomadic cavalry tactics. We should qualify the claim in two other ways. First, soldiers of this age were not fixed in their tactical roles, as our terms *infantry* and *cavalry* may misleadingly imply. Mounted soldiers could and often did dismount to fight on foot, becoming, for that battle, infantry. Second, and related to the first point, there was a significant difference between the use of horses as a battlefield weapon system and the use of horses for strategic mobility. The small size of many armies meant that they could be mounted for purposes of campaigning and pillaging, without that having much bearing on whether such forces usually fought battles on foot or on horseback. Thus, even if a decline in infantry quality (rather than improved cavalry technology) did create the beginnings of an age of cavalry, we must be careful about the parameters of this claim.

Nevertheless, it is a significant claim because of its social ramifications. In many places and times, dominant social elites have ridden horses as a way of displaying their superiority and wealth (horses being large and expensive items). The great rural men who increasingly dominated this society took up the horse for the same reason. They were a warrior class, and their ability to control resources made them the elite warriors of the age in terms of equipment and experience. They dominated armies, courts, and countryside from horseback, but in a sense were cavalry only incidentally and could fight equally well as infantry. Thus, an age of men on horseback gradually dawned in western Europe as a social as much as a tactical development.

THE CAROLINGIANS, 700–830

From the time of the reign of Clovis (481–511, the legend of whose conversion is recounted above), the kingdom of the Franks had been the dominant power among the successor states of Latin Europe. By the mid-500s, the Franks ruled nearly everywhere from the Rhine valley west and south to the Alps and Pyrenees. They had been the most successful of the barbarians to harness their military vigor to the influence and skills of the old Gallo-Roman elites. But the Frankish custom of dividing an inheritance among all surviving sons splintered the kingdom and led to

frequent internecine conflict. By the late 600s, the kingdom was fragmented.

Charles Martel, mayor of the palace (a sort of prime minister, and by this time the real power behind the throne) of the Merovingian king from 714 to 741, began reuniting the Franks, as well as repulsing a major Muslim invasion at the Battle of Poitiers in 732. His son Pepin III, crowned king in his own right in 751, and his grandson Charles the Great (Charlemagne—the Latin *Carolus,* for "Charles," is the basis of the family designation, Carolingian) completed the unification and extended Frankish rule considerably. There was no major change from the Merovingian to the Carolingian period in economic, social, or administrative developments or in military systems. However, the successes of the early Carolingians demonstrated the potential of the system when it was well led and its strengths were systematically exploited. But the fragmentation of Charlemagne's empire in the century after his death in 814 also demonstrated again the weaknesses of military and political force in this period. Nevertheless, the conquests of Charlemagne had lasting consequences.

The Carolingian Military System

The foundation of Carolingian military success was the class of great magnates who were the kings' immediate vassals (sworn followers). United by the leadership of the Carolingian kings, they extended the reach of royal power to the many regions of the kingdom. When called on by the king, they, in turn, called on their followers and mobilized the soldiers in the regions they controlled. Estimates of numbers in medieval armies are problematic—the surviving evidence does not allow for accurate assessment, and the total pool of manpower would never have been called out at one time. But the kings clearly could call on vast manpower resources, which were crucial to the Carolingian conquests.

Frankish armies almost always had a numerical advantage over their enemies. But the Carolingians also used their manpower advantage to advance into enemy territory in multiple columns, each strong enough to campaign independently. This allowed them to outflank border defenses and to launch converging columns on enemy positions. It also permitted operations on multiple fronts against different foes when necessary. Further, by using rotating or selected callouts the Franks could keep forces in the field longer than their enemies could: In 798, Frankish forces even campaigned in winter, breaking a final Saxon rebellion.

The same group of magnates who made possible raising and maintaining such numbers were also crucial to this pattern of flexible deployment. For they provided the loyal and competent subordinate commanders who could lead independent operations; the king did not have to be everywhere at once. How were the early Carolingians able to draw on their resources of leadership and manpower so successfully?

One key was that almost all the early Carolingian wars were offensive. Offensive campaigns produced plunder and made warfare attractive and profitable for the king's followers. In a self-reinforcing spiral, success made recruiting men and retaining their loyalty easier, which made further success more likely. The other key was that the early Carolingians made administrative arrangements that were remarkably effective, at least for a time, despite limited resources. A large part of this had to do with a close and mutually beneficial partnership with the church, which provided an administrative and territorial structure descended directly from the late Roman Empire. Bishops had significant military responsibilities, including leading their personal retinues to muster, and reforms directed from Charlemagne's court revitalized this structure. On the secular side, the empire was divided into counties, each headed by a count who served at the king's pleasure and could be transferred or removed. Counts were the highest public officers of the realm and in border areas oversaw local defense arrangements.

Through this administrative system, the Carolingians issued a comprehensive set of military regulations. These set out the obligations of royal vassals in providing forces; the obligations of individual soldiers, based on their landed wealth, to appear in specified circumstances with specified levels of equipment; and the sorts of equipment (siege machinery, carts for supply, and the like) that larger units should bring to campaign. Exporting of arms and armor was prohibited, and regulations governed logistics and discipline. By tying service and equipment obligations to landed wealth, a vast but economically underdeveloped empire harnessed its resources as efficiently as possible, and military leadership and rank conformed to social status. Grouping smaller estates, so that, for example, four landholders in a group of five would contribute to the equipping and campaign expenses of the fifth, helped spread the burdens of service at lower social levels. Similar arrangements made

service in distant theaters of operations possible: The farther off a campaign, the lesser the proportion of a district's soldiers had to serve. Though it is doubtful that reality throughout the empire conformed to the ideal of the regulations, their ambition and scope is impressive.

The methods the early Carolingians, especially Charlemagne, used in employing their forces on campaign were equally well developed. Raiding and pillaging became less ends in themselves than part of the arsenal used in systematic conquests. Several years of raiding were often preparatory to large-scale invasion, softening up the target. And methods of conquest were fitted to the foe. Against areas such as the Lombard kingdom in Italy or in northern Spain, the Frankish siege train focused on key fortified cities. The unified Lombard kingdom was conquered in one campaign. In northwest Germany, Saxony, with no real cities and a decentralized political structure, posed a tougher problem. But engineering proved crucial here, too, as Saxon forts fell easily to Frankish siege techniques. The Franks then built lines of border forts connected by roads to provide a launching pad for operations, and the network of forts would be steadily advanced into enemy lands. Permanent garrisons held the forts and responded to local uprisings. It was a slow method—operations in Saxony lasted thirty-three years, and Charlemagne eventually resorted to warfare against the Saxon population, including massacres and mass deportations, to seal the conquest. But the method was relentless and produced lasting results. The conquest of Saxony was the jewel in Charlemagne's imperial crown.

The elite forces of the Carolingian army, the followers of magnates both lay and ecclesiastical, were mounted for campaigns. The size of the empire and the range of its offensive operations put strategic mobility at a premium. This (and social prestige) dictated a substantial mounted contingent. Tactical factors did not. An influential school of thought long held that the adoption of the stirrup by the Frankish cavalry led to their tactical dominance on the battlefield and formed the basis of their success (and created the basis for feudalism—see the Issues box "Feudalism"). However, more recent scholarship has cast doubt on this thesis. The best evidence is that the stirrup was not widely adopted until the end of the eighth century, after the bulk of Frankish expansion. There is no evidence for a change in cavalry tactics; the charge with couched lance—the supposedly irresistible stirrup-based tactic—was not widely used for

Feudalism

The political fragmentation and military arrangements of ninth-century Europe have often been described as contributing to the birth of feudalism. But what is "feudalism"? Most medieval historians these days consider it a misleading term that does more to obscure our view of the past than to illuminate it. For the term *feudalism* is paradoxically both too vague and too precise.

Though based on the medieval word *feudum,* Latin for "fief" (discussed below), the word *feudalism* was coined by reformers in the eighteenth century to describe (unfavorably) the system of rights and privileges enjoyed by the French aristocracy, especially with regard to landholding and peasant tenancy. This broad socioeconomic meaning was taken up and extended by Marxist historians, for whom the "feudal mode of production" succeeded the classical mode and preceded the capitalist mode. For military historians, this has always been far too broad a definition. Indeed, if a privileged landholding class and a subject peasantry constitutes feudalism, then most civilization before the Industrial Revolution was feudal, and the term loses any real analytic usefulness.

Military historians have usually taken a more restricted view of feudalism. For them, it referred to the system of raising troops in which a lord granted a fief—typically, a piece of land—to a vassal (Latin, *vassus*). In return, the vassal gave the lord a defined and limited term of military service, usually forty days a year and usually as a fully armed and armored horseman—a knight. Sometimes the lord provided armor and weapons, but often the vassal provided his own. The fief was the payment for service and was also known as "the knight's fee."

Feudalism in this sense has also often been taken as a sign of weak central authority with limited cash resources, limited and somewhat ritualized warfare (knights fought not to kill but to capture and ransom other knights), lack of discipline, individualistic tactics, and incompetent leadership. While there is some truth in the assumptions about central authority, the rest is simply wrong. And the mistakes stem from problems in the definition of feudalism, problems arising from spurious precision.

Recent research has traced modern conceptions of feudal service to the terms and definitions of the *Libri Feudorum,* an Italian legal handbook written in the twelfth and thirteenth centuries. Its academic view of fiefs and vassals became the basis for interpreting feudal institutions in the sixteenth century and have held sway since. But this view does not, in fact, fit the medieval evidence. *Feudum* and *vassus* were vague and mutable terms, and military systems from the ninth to the fourteenth centuries were far more varied, flexible, and rational than conventional interpretations have allowed.

several more centuries, was never the exclusive method of effective cavalry, and, as noted above, made little difference against infantry. But most important, battles were inconsequential to Carolingian success. Charlemagne fought only two battles in his career, and all his subordinates only a few others.

Instead, engineering—building forts and bridges, and besieging strong points—cemented Charlemagne's conquests. And engineering was the province of men on foot (whether they rode on campaign or not). Careful logistics opened the road for the engineers. Supporting the large Frankish armies on

campaign required well-planned supply arrangements. Expeditions usually followed a spring meeting of the great men of the realm, called when the season had advanced enough to make fodder for the horses abundant. Foraging, which always had the potential of degenerating into ill-disciplined plundering in which armies were vulnerable to counterattack, was kept organized and was carefully supplemented by the use of cartage of supplies where possible. Naval transport was harder to arrange, but supply boats on the Danube accompanied an invasion of the Avar kingdom in 791. Herds of cattle accompanied armies, providing

Restricted service in return for granted land was inherently limited as a basis for military force and has been vastly overrated as the basis of medieval armies. Soldiers did serve for land. But often they were *household knights*—young men who lived with their lord and served him in military and non-military capacities—who were rewarded for long service with land of their own and who served in expectation of this reward. And even service for land already granted was far less defined and restricted than the traditional "forty days a year" formula implies. *Feudal service*—unpaid service by the vassals of a lord—worked best on the "let's go, boys" model: A lord in need of armed support in his local disputes and in serving his lord (if he had one) said to the young men who were his friends, relatives, hunting and drinking companions, and social dependents, "Let's go, boys," and they went. Social cohesion in the lord's military household (Latin, *familia*) translated into military cohesion, and constant hunting and fighting together imparted small-unit skills.

Should we then define feudalism more generally as a landed support system for unpaid military service? There are several problems with this. First, individuals and groups also served for pay from an early date, wherever economic conditions made it possible and even when they owed feudal service. And paid service became increasingly common in the period after 1050. Second, in a global context, there have been many forms of "soldiers' lands" in different times and places, in combination with paid service and not. To call all these feudal is again to arrive at a uselessly broad definition. To try to distinguish some as feudal has inevitably involved the privileging of the European model, for no other reason than that it was studied first. For military historians, the term is probably best avoided, to be replaced by functional descriptions of the world's (and Europe's) varied military systems of landed support and militia service, and the social hierarchies that accompanied them.

Legal historians of Europe will rightly come to a different conclusion. In the more settled European conditions of the twelfth century and later, the informal arrangements of an earlier age tended to crystallize into formal legal arrangements with defined terms of service and defined inheritance rights on the part of the vassal. This process marked the decline of feudalism as a viable military system but the rise of feudalism as a fundamental legal system. Indeed, the lord–vassal tie of landholding became crucial as one of two key bonds (with marriage, which it resembled) among the European aristocracy. The twelfth-century English system of fief law became the basis of most later English estate law and thence of modern American property law. Feudal property law has a definite history. The mistake is to read the legal history back into the military sphere.

self-transporting supplies. And engineering worked hand in hand with logistics: The Carolingians did not build roads like the Romans, but they did build bridges to improve their communications, and their forts served as supply depots.

Weaknesses and Influences of the System

In short, Charlemagne's armies wore down their enemies with superior numbers and logistics, and then engineered them into submission. The Carolingian expansion thus bears a marked similarity to the creation of the early Roman Empire under the Republic. It would not, however, prove as lasting. For the Carolingian army was still a product of its time, with the same social and economic limitations the successor states had faced. As a result, every Carolingian strength had a corresponding weakness.

The empire's expansion slowed to a halt after 800, and campaigns became less frequent. Around 810, Charlemagne faced the first Viking raids on the empire. They were repelled easily, but defensive warfare already showed signs of making recruiting harder, as it offered little prospect of plunder or profit. For a system whose armies were not paid, defense thus threatened to undermine the basis of reliable manpower and the loyalty of subordinates. But continued expansion was difficult because, in an age of slow communications, the very size of the empire posed a threat to the personal ties that were the key to holding the administrative system together. Like the army, the officials of the empire were not paid cash salaries out of central tax receipts—neither the economy nor the government were that monetized. Instead, they received land grants and shares of the income of the districts they governed. Such a system had a tendency to decentralization, with regional officials becoming the focus of local loyalties in preference to a distant central authority. This tendency was exacerbated by the fact that land was a poor substitute for money as compensation to officials. Local officials could more easily become possessive about a district than a salary. They would build up local support networks and entrench themselves and their families in office. Eventually, transferring or removing officials became a royal prerogative in theory more than fact. In short, offices tended to become heritable, reducing central control.

None of these problems were necessarily fatal. But they were all made more acute by the central flaw in the political structure of the empire: Frankish custom still dictated division of the realm among the king's surviving sons. Under Charlemagne's grandsons, internal conflict exploded. Civil war and renewed external invasions (see below), piled on top of the inherent weaknesses of the system, brought low the structures of Carolingian imperial and military power in less than a century after Charlemagne's death in 814.

Nonetheless, the Carolingian Empire had a lasting influence in some areas despite its short period of glory. Perhaps most important was the conquest of Saxony. Along with the conquest of Muslim-held lands in southern France and northern Spain and the extension of Carolingian rule or influence into Bavaria and the upper Danube, it permanently reversed the contraction of this civilization. By adding significant territory east of the Rhine to the Latin Christian world, it also shifted the civilization's center of gravity north, away from the Mediterranean, and brought more land that had never been part of the Roman Empire into the cultural mix of Latin Europe. Carolingian successes against the pagan Saxons, who were forcibly converted, and against the Muslims strengthened the relationship in this civilization between warfare, Christianity, and conversion. The participation of Frankish bishops in the organization and leading of military forces added to the link, which was given a sort of papal seal of approval by the crowning of Charlemagne as emperor of the west in 800. The link was mutually beneficial, at least in theory: The church gained powerful defenders and a spearhead for conversion, while wielders of military force gained in legitimacy and prestige.

The coronation and the connection of the church to military organization also reinforced the influence of surviving Roman ideals and institutions. Perhaps the most significant and lasting of these were the counties that were the backbone of Carolingian regional organization. Underneath the level of the counties, social and military relationships continued to be influenced by the forms of Carolingian vassalage, formalized and tied to military obligation by Charlemagne's military regulations.

Yet these survivals would work their influence in a changing world. Internal conflict and renewed invasions in the end significantly altered the social structures of this world. Carolingian Europe survived a siege, but not intact.

THE SIEGE OF EUROPE, 800–950

Charlemagne's only surviving son, Louis the Pious, inherited the empire intact in 814, but conflict broke out among Louis' three sons even before his death in 840, when full-scale war erupted. The Treaty of Verdun in 843 formalized division of the empire into East Frankia (German lands) under Louis the German, West Frankia (the future kingdom of France) under Charles the Bald, and a middle kingdom extending from the Low Countries through Burgundy and into Italy, called Lotharingia after Lothair, who took the imperial title. But the treaty failed to stop the warfare among the brothers and their descendants. Over the next fifty years, treachery, shifting alliances, and the movement of the imperial title undermined central authority throughout Carolingian lands. Regional officials and powerful magnates increasingly pursued their own interests, building local power bases virtually independent of royal control. But they, too, had to contend

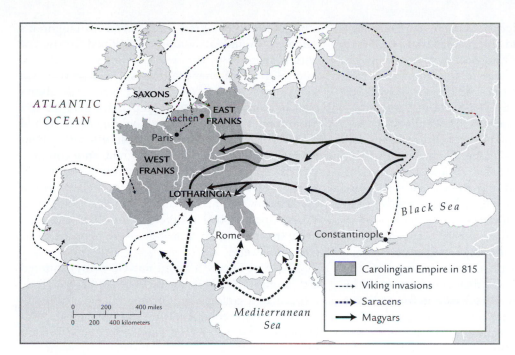

Figure 7.2 The Siege of Europe

Map legend:
- Carolingian Empire in 815
- Viking invasions
- Saracens
- Magyars

with the unruliness of their subordinates in troubled times.

Invaders: Vikings, Saracens, Magyars

Carolingian internal strife opened the door to external threats, which exacerbated the decline of royal authority and added to the insecurity of the age. Three main threats emerged (Figure 7.2). The Vikings were pagan seaborne raiders whose origins and methods are described more fully in Chapter 10. Their raids began around 800 and lasted more than a century, peaking in the 860s–880s. Initially, they launched small-scale raids, but larger Viking forces began establishing fortified camps and wintering in their target areas, and some even turned from pillage to permanent conquest.

Saracen pirates established bases in the Balearic Islands and along the coast of southern France, whence they preyed on shipping and raided into Italy and south France. Their operations, too, began early in the ninth century, reaching their worst in the last third of that century but continuing longer than those of the Vikings, well into the eleventh century. They were part of a larger pattern of Mediterranean amphibious warfare also described more fully in Chapter 10.

The Magyars were a pagan people, another among the Central Asian nomads whose interactions with the civilized world so influenced this age throughout Eurasia. Typically of such peoples, their military forces consisted of light cavalry armed with bows. Driven west by pressure from other nomads, they moved in the 890s into the plains of the middle Danube. Once settled, they launched widespread destructive expeditions throughout the first half of the tenth century into neighboring Slavic lands, and into much of Germany, northern Italy, and eastern France.

Mobile Raiders The military challenge presented by all three invaders was their mobility. The Vikings and Saracens used the sea and rivers as highways for rapid movement and withdrawal, striking where defenses were weak or nonexistent. The Magyar light horsemen were capable of rapid overland marches that could bypass or outrun local defenses. Monasteries, unguarded storehouses of wealth, were the favorite targets of all three. This habit and their non-Christian religions make them loom as especially terrible threats in the chronicles of the time, which were written mostly by monks. But we should not overrate their military abilities. The level of their threat reflected the weakness of the defenders as much as the strength of the invaders.

None were much good at siege warfare—their very mobility precluded the regular transporting of siege engines with their forces. In any case, sieges were difficult, and the aim of their raids was easy plunder. Some Viking armies did besiege strongholds (see the Highlights box "The Siege of Paris, 885," page 188), but rarely successfully. The lack of siege capability limited the invaders' opportunities for permanent conquest. Where Vikings did make permanent conquests, the areas generally lacked sophisticated fortifications, as in Ireland and Russia, and had loose political structures into which Viking bands could insert themselves as local rulers.

Nor were any of the invaders especially well armed and armored or tactically sophisticated. If they could be brought to battle, they could sometimes be defeated—the problem was they could not easily be pinned down for a battle. By the time defensive forces could gather in response to a raid, the raiders were long gone. The weakness and division of Carolingian central authority made this problem acute when the invaders first appeared.

Political Impacts   The invasions thus stimulated a process of political fragmentation and localization that internal strife had set in motion. In the absence of strong central leadership, localities were often left to devise their own defenses against the raiders. But central authorities did play some role in devising defenses, and, therefore, regional responses varied, as did the effects of the invasions.

The West Frankish kingdom (France) suffered the worst breakdown under the pressure of the invasions. Viking bands used islands off the coast and in rivers as semipermanent bases for raiding. Charles the Bald (843–877), preoccupied with wars against his brothers and rebellious nobles, at first could do little against Viking raiders. When he could turn his attention to them, he followed a strategy of building fortified bridges designed to block the fleets' passage up or down rivers, with some success. But he often simply purchased peace with tribute, and dynastic chaos after his death reopened the door to massive sustained ravaging. Royal authority virtually collapsed, to be rebuilt only very slowly from a restricted base around Paris.

Vikings in England pursued a strategy of conquest, and out of a number of Anglo-Saxon kingdoms in the early 800s, only Wessex, the kingdom of the West Saxons under Alfred the Great, remained independent of Viking rule by 870. In the course of a bitter struggle, Alfred reorganized his kingdom's defenses around a system of fortified towns, or burghs, manned by the *fyrd,* the forces of the Saxon landholders and their followers. *Fyrd* service was reorganized so that part of the force was always available for garrison duty and part for field service. Mounted for mobility (though fighting on foot) and based in the burghs, the *fyrd* could effectively limit the ability of Viking forces to raid and conquer. Wessex not only survived but, in the century after Alfred's death in 899, went on to reconquer most of the Danelaw, the half of England under Viking rule. Viking invasion had resulted in a unified and relatively strong English monarchy—the opposite of its effect in France.

The East Frankish kingdom (Germany) suffered little from the Vikings but by 900 had become little more than a collection of ethnic duchies, suffering much the same fragmentation as West Frankia. But Henry of Saxony, elected king in 919, and his son Otto (936–973) prevented further fragmentation and even rebuilt royal prestige in the fight against the Magyars. Like Alfred, Henry contained his foe with a combination of fortifications and a reorganized and strengthened field army. Infantry played their role in the army, but the spearhead was a force of heavily armed cavalry, drawn from the nobility and mobile enough to keep up with the Magyars while possessing a decisive advantage over them in armor and weapons for close fighting. Under Otto, German forces not only defeated the Magyars at the Lechfeld in 955, effectively ending their raiding days, but also pushed into Slavic territory and conquered north Italy. The Italian expeditions added prestige and a renewed imperial title to the German king's portfolio. However, although its prestige was high and the territories it ruled were vast, the German kingship lacked well-developed mechanisms of power within Germany itself. Italian cities retained significant freedom of action even under imperial rule, and it was their independent initiative at sea that turned the tide against the Saracen pirates (see Chapter 10).

Responses to the Invasions

Despite different styles and very different results for the central authorities of the affected areas, some common themes clearly emerge in the responses to the invasions. Fortified strongpoints were the lynchpin of each defense strategy. The invaders, as noted, had little ability to overrun a fortified position, provided its defenses were in good repair and it was adequately manned. Forts could thus act as places of refuge when a raiding force swept through. But they allowed more than passive defense: Forts restricted the scope of raiders' possible targets, and the forces manning them could harass and ambush enemy forces on the march. Raiders were particularly vulnerable on their return march, when they were loaded with booty and so were slower and perhaps less vigilant. As Alfred's system of burghs shows, forts could also act as the bases for strategic offensives, gradually hemming in raiders and winning back control of territory they had occupied.

Fortified strongpoints went hand in hand with some sort of system for maintaining a substantial force of well-armed men for both garrison duty and field operations. The measures adopted here varied widely, with some having a more public character than others. But in all areas, wealthy landholders were the backbone of any system of maintaining military forces, given the continuing financial and administrative limitations of governments of the age. The invasions, therefore, further highlighted the importance of a warrior elite in Latin European civilization. (Whether the members of this elite were always, or even primarily, the benevolent protectors of the weaker members of the culture is another question, which we will explore more in Chapter 12.)

In every case, nonmilitary measures complemented armed defense. Especially early on, the most effective local defense measure was simply to buy off the invaders. Paying tribute was clearly only a temporary solution and tended simply to shift the assaults elsewhere, but it could buy valuable time. The paying of tribute again reminds us not to overrate the military effectiveness of the defense measures. So, too, does the fact that, in the cases of the Vikings and to a lesser extent the Magyars, the invasions ended as much for reasons internal to those two societies as to military defeat: Both societies seemed to settle down and become "normal" after years of plundering expeditions. Conversion to Christianity contributed to this process and was often linked to military measures. Alfred baptized the Viking leader Guthrum after defeating him at Edington, for example. Once again, the ideological and cultural dimension of armed conflict was of central importance to the warfare of this age. Conversion was less of an option against Muslim foes. But against pagans, the sword and the Word were two sides of a broad process of taming dangerous enemies and bringing their peoples into the Christian community of nations, a process that would turn increasingly outward after the invasions ended.

TOWARD RECONSTRUCTION, 950–1050

The period from roughly 950 to 1050 was a fundamentally important age of transition for Latin European civilization. It saw a broad set of linked changes in economic activity and social structure that would have immeasurable consequences for government, military organization, and culture. These changes established patterns that would remain central to western European civilization down to the Industrial Revolution.

The end of the siege of Europe unleashed a vast potential for growth as conditions became somewhat more secure. New peasant settlements began to spread out from the old population centers, eating into the tracts of wilderness within Latin Christendom and pushing this world's frontiers steadily outward (see Chapter 12 on this external expansion). The population began to rise. A land of more people, less wilderness, and fewer invasions made for easier communications. New towns sprang up, and the pace of economic activity and trade quickened. Rising agricultural and mercantile wealth were resources that beckoned to rulers who could put them to effective use. But it would be locally powerful men, lay and ecclesiastic, who would make first use of the new conditions—would, in fact, decisively shape them—leaving kings and princes to harness the achievements of the strongmen later. For the reconstruction of authority began with the reconstruction of the European aristocracy.

Castles and the Aristocratic Reconstruction

The starting point of this reconstruction was a new technology that had spread rapidly in the disorder of the time of invasions: the private castle. Private castles differed from earlier fortifications in several crucial ways. First, they were much smaller. The area enclosed by the walls and tower of a castle was tiny compared to an Anglo-Saxon burgh or the typical town or city walls. The castle was designed to protect a lord and his household, not the population at large. This is part

The Motte-and-Bailey Castle   Their small size and earth-and-wood construction meant that these castles could be built quickly and cheaply.

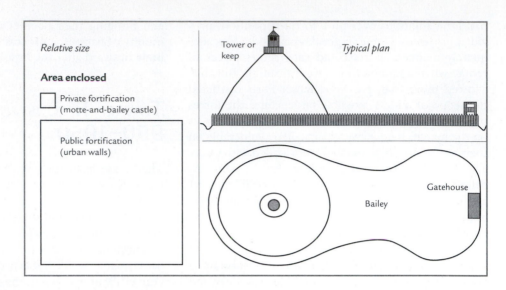

of what made it private: It was not a communal defense. Even the castles of kings and counts were private in this sense. The small size of castles meant that they could be effectively defended by small forces—well under 100 men. The typical form of early private castles was the motte-and-bailey design, in which a wooden walled enclosure, the bailey, projected from a motte, a steep mound of earth, either natural or more often man-made, topped by a wooden tower. Small size and earth-and-wood construction meant that a motte-and-bailey castle could be built quickly and cheaply, so that even local lords could fortify themselves. Stone construction was slower and more expensive but more secure. Stone construction thus spread more slowly but was widespread in some areas by the mid-eleventh century as new sites were built in stone and old motte-and-bailey castles were rebuilt. (A man-made motte had to settle for several decades before a stone tower could be built on it.)

Castles were often private in another way, aside from not being communal, as local lords built them without (or against) the public authority of kings and counts. Charles the Bald was already issuing edicts against the building of unlicensed castles in the 860s, but the problem simply got worse. A lord with a castle and a group of vassals could with some impunity defy his superior. The spread of castles therefore both accompanied and contributed to the fragmentation of political authority characteristic of this period. The private castle spread as the technology of local lordship, while castles, in turn, stimulated a reconstruction of the social structure of the European aristocracy and transformed the foundations of local and regional governance.

Up to this time, the kinship structure of the European aristocracy had been rather loose. Collateral connections to both maternal and paternal families had been important, and inheritance patterns had been varied and tended toward the division and reshuffling of land within the extended kin group—the Frankish custom of dividing lands among sons has already been noted for its political consequences. But the introduction of the castle as the focus of lordly power began to change this pattern. Local lords who had built up a compact landed estate around their castle in order to supply it with men and provisions became more loath to see their estate divided after their death. Inheritance patterns thus began to evolve toward a more strictly patrilineal system and toward primogeniture—the passing of most if not all of an estate intact to the eldest surviving son, with younger sons left to make their own way. Family names began to appear in the form "of *x*", where *x* was the name of the castle that was the family seat. Lineage and primogeniture have been the structure of European aristocratic families ever since.

In addition to estates, these new "castle lords" gathered to themselves the mechanisms of local governance. Powers of taxation and justice—supposedly public powers—passed widely into the private possession of local strongmen. In the absence of a strong central authority that could dispense wealth and prestige to its adherents, local lords found it necessary to develop their own resources more fully. The close connection between lordship and society as a whole that this fostered turned European governance at the local level even more into a form of estate management and tied political authority firmly to fixed localities.

Elements of a New Sociomilitary System

The structure of aristocratic families was the backbone of the entire social structure, and the transformations of this structure after 950, stimulated at least in part by the spread of the private castle, had enormous consequences for European social, governmental, and military organization. A new system emerged, what we might call a sociomilitary system, that would be a fundamental part of European development for the next 800 years and more. The key elements of this system were castles, knights, and urban or non-knightly soldiers, with each being far more than just a military component.

Castles   The military function of the castle was simple. It provided a place of refuge for the lord and his military followers who controlled it, as well as a secure base of operations for forays into the countryside. A contingent of mounted men based in a castle could control the countryside for up to ten miles around the castle (half a day's ride out and half a day's ride back). Such domination gained political expression in the functions gathered in the castle. It was the site of the lord's court and so of the dispensing of local justice, it could act as a jail, and it could house the lord's storehouse of provisions and his treasury. The connection between governance and the running of the domestic household of a castle is visible in the domestic origins of the titles of medieval government officials from the local to the royal level: chamberlains, chancellors, marshals, and constables. All ran some aspect of the lord's house and, by extension, of the polity the lord controlled.

Individual castles were important, but they could control only a limited area and were vulnerable to being isolated. Castles became the foundation of larger political units when a regional ruler could tie a set of castles, newly built or taken over, into a network. This required the regional lord to bind the individual local lords to him in some way that ensured their loyalty, a tricky task given the ease with which a castle holder could resist punishment. Where regional lords failed to tame castle holders, such as in much of southern France, central authority developed slowly. But a regional ruler who could secure a network of castles, each a day's march from the next for mutual support and domination of all the intervening countryside, created a military foundation for extended rule. Such a network did not seal off borders, but instead created something that combined the characteristics of a defense in depth and a garrison state, guarding against both external threat and internal uprising.

Knights   The second element of the emergent sociomilitary system were knights, a term that requires careful definition. "Knight" is usually used to translate the Latin *miles* (pl., *milites*). The classical meaning of this term was simply "soldier," and it was the word used for the legionnaries of the imperial Roman army—in other words, for heavy infantry. It referred especially to elite soldiers into the eleventh century, but by that time, as we have seen, the elite soldiers of this society rode horses. Ownership of a horse was an essential aspect of being well armed and conveyed elite status socially as well as militarily. Thus, we find that *milites* began to acquire a second meaning roughly equivalent to *equites,* or "cavalry," in distinction to *pedites,* or "infantry." Armies are described in the sources as composed of *milites peditesque,* or cavalry and infantry. Yet it is important to remember that the equivalence was only rough, because *milites* always retained the connotation of elite status, which was social as much as military. Thus, *equites* remained in use to describe horsemen who might not be knights or when the cavalry function of a group of soldiers was primary for the author. Similarly, a phrase such as *milites gregarii,* or "common knights," could be used to describe soldiers with the arms and equipment of horse soldiers but who were otherwise poor, landless, or of low origin—that is non-elite socially. Further, *milites* who dismounted became *pedites*—that is, knights became infantry. There was no medieval equivalent for "dismounted cavalry," nor for "mounted infantry," as those terms imply a rigid classification of soldiers into set types that did not exist in medieval armies. We should beware of imposing such rigidities through anachronistic terminology.

Knights, then, were well-armed, mounted warriors. Well armed in this period meant a mail shirt, conical helmet, sword, lance, and shield. Horses gave them the mobility to patrol from castles, to act as armed escorts, and to meet threats rapidly. In the continental tradition, knights were trained to fight from horseback. Anglo-Saxon *thegns,* the equivalent of continental knights, rode on campaign but always fought on foot. But even continental knights did not have to fight as cavalry; knights often dismounted to fight as infantry, depending on the situation. Knights would usually have more than one horse, riding one on campaign and keeping the best charger for action in battle.

In addition, knights were usually the retainers of aristocratic lords. The aristocracy themselves were knights in the military sense: They were armed in the same way and led their knights in war. But it is important to keep in mind the socially based distinctions among knights. Knights in this period ranged from the sons of great lords to landless adventurers who won a place for themselves through their skill in war—prior to 1050, knights were a functional group, not a closed social class, and talented newcomers could make their fortune with some luck. As a rule, however, since the bond of vassalage was essentially a contract freely entered into by free men with obligations on both parties, unfree men could not become knights. (A peculiar class of unfree knights did arise in Germany, though.)

Terms of service, as we noted above (see the Issues box, p. 126), were correspondingly undefined as yet. Men served for their daily bread at the lord's table, in the hope of future land grants, and in exchange for land already given. Vassals became "the man of" a lord for a variety of reasons; military service was only one aspect of the bonds that tied vassals to lords. Kinship connections remained a powerful bond among the knightly and aristocratic segments of society, for instance. And in many areas, men held land from multiple lords, and lords granted land to each other. But military power still lay at the heart of the network of bonds in this period, because lords needed armed followers, and lesser men needed protectors and patrons. So we can imagine that many vassals served their lord far more than forty days a year, with the level depending on a combination of necessity and bargaining. After 1050, the terms and obligations of knighthood became gradually more defined, and, in the process, knights came to be a defined social class (see Chapter 12). But the situation prior to 1050 was more fluid.

As the warriors with the best equipment, training, and connections that this society could provide, knights were the backbone of armed force at the local level and the spearhead of larger armies. Knights also furnished leadership to nonknightly contingents of armies, cavalry and infantry. Knights were not professional soldiers in the sense that Roman legionnaires were—knighthood was not a salaried job with mass training imposed from above by a strong central authority. Large armies of knights and infantry never held regular peacetime maneuvers and drill, and their battlefield capabilities were correspondingly more limited than a professional army could achieve. But knights were as professional as the age could make them. Knights were trained in the skills of horsemanship and weaponry from a young age, and small groups such as a lord's *familia* gained experience and cohesion by hunting, fighting, and living together. Warfare was not a knight's profession so much as his lifestyle. As a result, knightly armies were capable of remarkable feats of bravery, endurance, and skill, and they often exhibited far more discipline than historians have given them credit for.

Urban and Nonknightly Soldiers   The third element of the emergent sociomilitary system was the nonknightly soldiers drawn primarily from urban populations, but also at times from the margins of civilization, such as Wales. Whereas social connections among the ruling class bound knights together, nonknightly soldiers were held together by a variety of forces, including communal solidarity, paid service, and ethnic identity.

Urban soldiers and other outsiders were, first and foremost, nonknights socially. Just as knights could fight on foot as infantry or on horseback as cavalry, urban soldiers were flexible tactically. They normally fought, of economic necessity, on foot, including with missile weapons such as the crossbow, but they did not do so exclusively. Spanish urban militias would come to include substantial mounted elements, and other urban and nonknightly soldiery often included horsed soldiers, especially, as in Italy, where economic development gave a segment of a city's population the resources to arm themselves to knightly levels. There is no automatic equation of townsmen or other outsiders with the infantry. But, in general, this group was the source of infantry forces in western European armies.

Thus, outside of the Anglo-Scandinavian world, where the elite warriors traditionally fought on foot, most infantry in this period and for centuries to come were urban based (at least in origin—bands of infantry were widely available for hire far from their home bases). The Greek model for infantry effectiveness was still the only one extant, given the rudimentary powers of central governments in this period. But the slow revival of trade and growth of urban life began to revitalize this basis for good infantry, and indeed, one crucial part of the development of European armies over the next eight centuries was to be the steady improvement of infantry skills, first on the Greek model and later on the Roman model. For now, the most effective infantry usually came from the two most urbanized areas of Europe—northern Italy and Flanders.

Given the importance of castles, and thus of siege warfare, infantry had an important role in the system, despite the social dominance of the knights. The connection between infantry and sieges is indicated by the rapid spread in this period of the crossbow. Crossbows of a sort had been around since late Roman times, but only now became a prominent infantry weapon. The crossbow had greater range and penetrating power than the traditional short bow, but it took longer to load. It was thus ideally suited for the defense of castle and town walls, whence crossbowmen could reload in safety and fire at the besiegers. Crossbowmen, in turn, provided covering fire for besieging armies. But heavy infantrymen, mostly spearmen, were regularly used as well. Spearmen were less skilled than crossbowmen and so cheaper, and they could provide a stronger defensive mass against enemy cavalry on a battlefield. Many armies included both types of infantry, as a combination of defensive strength and firepower was valuable in siege work and in battle. But infantry forces were less important to small raiding expeditions in which mounted troops would ravage the countryside.

While nonknightly soldiers were an important part of this military system, we should not think of the system as either designed from the top down or completely harmonious. There was often tension between the towns, with their increasing legal liberties and wealth, and the more rurally based knights. Urban infantry forces existed as much for self-defense against lordly demands as to support knightly forces in a larger system. Where a castle existed as part of a town's defenses, it acted both to thwart besiegers and to overawe the town itself, standing as a symbol of the dominance of the town's lord. The combination of castles, knights, and urban forces that began to emerge in the period 950–1050 was a dynamic, tension-filled balance of cooperating and competing interests, with as yet little direction or control from above.

Such a sociomilitary system would prove turbulent but capable of dramatic conquests—as, for example, William of Normandy's conquest of Anglo-Saxon England in 1066 (see the Highlights box "The Campaign and Battle of Hastings")—as well as significant change and adaptation through time, and would become the foundation of a steady expansion of the frontiers of this civilization, of renewed state building, and of a particular European culture of war. These topics are taken up in Chapter 12.

Conclusion

Like many other areas of the world, western Europe underwent significant changes in the wake of the migrations and invasions that characterized this period of world history. The collapse of Roman political and military structures left Latin Christendom pieces of a tradition to work with. But the changed social and economic context of warfare meant that the fragments of Roman tradition would be merged with many new elements and that Latin Christendom ultimately would have to reinvent itself politically and militarily. In the century extending roughly from 950 to 1050, the various elements that had developed over the preceding 600 years came together into a new sociomilitary system based on castles, knights, and urban soldiery.

The system reflected a world of underdeveloped government and insecure control of society by a somewhat crude and violent aristocracy. It fostered a political structure that connected lordship to economic development, both agricultural and mercantile, and to an unusually mutual, contractual notion of political rights, liberties, and privileges. Underdeveloped government and insecure aristocratic control extended such notions not only to towns, where merchants began to carve out a world of their own, but even to peasants, who benefited in favorable tenure terms from the competition among lords for laborers on their estates.

In short, the period 350–1050 in western Europe produced a civilization whose elites were never fully

The Campaign and Battle of Hastings

Edward the Confessor, king of Anglo-Saxon England, died at Christmas 1065. Harold Godwinson, greatest earl of the realm, took the throne but faced rival claims by William, duke of Normandy, and Harald Hardraada, king of Norway and a veteran of wars in Russia and the Byzantine Empire.

To launch an invasion, William first had to gain the support of his own nobles. Aggressive diplomacy obtained papal approval for the expedition. By midsummer, he was camped at the mouth of the Dives, attracting adventurers and merce-

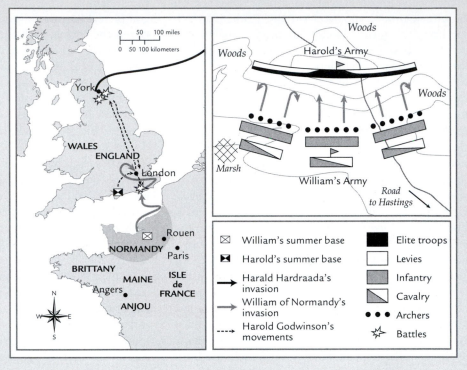

Figure 7.3 The Campaign and Battle of Hastings

naries from all over northern France with the promise of plunder, and gathering and building a fleet. Meanwhile, Harold Godwinson had mobilized the *fyrd* in May along the south coast of England, responding to a raid by his rebel brother Tostig, and stationed himself with his fleet on the Isle of Wight, ready to fall on William's force when it landed. But the mobilization proved premature. Harold kept the fleet and army on guard through the summer, rotating two shifts of the *fyrd*. But despite remarkably effective supply arrangements, provisions ultimately ran out, and on September 8, the *fyrd* dispersed and the fleet returned to London.

William's invasion force was ready to sail in early August but did not. Whether the delay was deliberate, in expectation of Harold's supply problems, or a result of contrary winds is a matter of much dispute. In any case, by September, it was growing dangerously late in the sailing season, and on the 12th of that month, perhaps in response to Harold's demobilization, William attempted to invade. A

squall blew his fleet to St. Valery at the mouth of the Somme, where contrary winds held him up for another two weeks. In the meantime, Harald Hardraada appeared off north England with an invasion fleet of at least 300 ships, landing near York on September 18. He defeated the northern *fyrd* under the earls Edwin and Morcar at Gate Fulford on 20 September, took York, and camped nearby at Stamford Bridge. Harold moved with astonishing speed on hearing of the invasion, covering the 190 miles from London in under a week. On September 25, he surprised the Danes in their camp and won a decisive victory in which Hardraada and the rebel Tostig perished.

But two days later, the wind having finally shifted, William landed at Pevensey and shortly moved to Hastings, building motte-and-bailey castles at both sites. He then began to ravage the countryside, hoping to draw Harold into a battle that was his only real chance for conquest. It was the only time in his career that William adopted a battle-seeking strategy. Harold complied. He hurried south with his battered army, pausing only a week in London to gather more troops. He may have hoped to repeat his success at Stamford Bridge with a sudden attack, or he may have meant to blockade William on the Hastings peninsula and let the Normans exhaust their supplies. But William, a master of reconnaissance, learned of his approach on October 13. The next morning, William seized the tactical initiative, advancing on the Saxon army at dawn. Harold occupied a strong position at the top of a ridge, but was forced initially to fight a defensive battle (Figure 7.3).

The Bayeux Tapestry   Norman cavalry charging Anglo-Saxon infantry. Note the similarity of arms and armor on the two sides, and the overarm use of the lance by the Normans.

The size of the armies cannot be determined with any accuracy, but probably neither side had more than 6000 men. Harold's housecarls (his elite household troops) fronted a shieldwall of *thegns* and local *fyrd*. He was short of archers, and none of his troops fought as cavalry. William commanded a mixed force of heavy infantry, archers, and heavy cavalry. The mix of arms distinguished the two armies, but their levels of training, discipline, and armor were nearly identical, and the fight would be very even.

William attacked first around 9:00 AM, and immediately ran into difficulties. The Bretons of his left wing retreated in confusion, and the panic spread to his whole army with rumors of William's death. Harold may have ordered a general counterattack at this point, but if he did, for unknown reasons (the deaths of his brothers leading the advance?), it failed to materialize. William, baring his head, rallied his troops and cut down the scattered pursuit that did leave the shieldwall.

Most medieval battles would have ended by now, but this one lasted the rest of the day. Harold now had little chance to win, but he could still avoid losing. "A strange sort of battle" ensued, according to one chronicler, in which the Normans launched attacks and drew more defenders from the hill with feigned retreats, while the Saxons stood fixed like rocks. The Saxons were worn down but not broken, and had William's last assault of the day not succeeded, his strategic position would have been dire. But he ordered high-angle fire from his archers; Harold may have been struck in the eye by an arrow from this barrage. A final attack by William's infantry and cavalry at last broke through the shieldwall, and Harold was cut down under his dragon standard. The king's death made the victory decisive.

Campaign and battle proved both leaders to be fine commanders. William outgeneraled Harold slightly but mostly was much luckier. After the battle, he made a cautious approach to London, ravaging as he went. With the death of the king and his brothers, no effective resistance could be organized, and in mid-December, the main Anglo-Saxon leaders submitted to William. He was crowned on Christmas Day, 1066. William the Bastard had become William the Conqueror.

able to unify and monopolize power, prestige, and privilege—were never able, in other words, to cement a truly traditional civilization. Instead, a culture emerged that would prove unusually prone to political and social flux and conflict and, so, to innovation and change. The military development of this civilization since 1050 is one ongoing symptom of this result.

SUGGESTED READINGS

Abels, Richard. *Lordship and Military Obligation in Anglo-Saxon England*. Berkeley: University of California Press, 1988. A close examination of the institutional and social arrangements that supplied military manpower in Saxon England. See also his *Alfred the Great: War, Kingship and Culture in Anglo-Saxon England* (London: Routledge, 1998), a readable study of the great English king.

Bachrach, Bernard. *Merovingian Military Organization*. Minneapolis: University of Minnesota Press, 1972. An important work by a leading military historian of early medieval Europe, who stresses (in an extreme way) the element of Roman continuity in the period; his views have not found wide acceptance. See also his *Early Carolingian Warfare: Prelude to Empire* (Philadelphia: University of Pennsylvania Press, 2001) and *Fulk Nerra, Neo-Roman Consul* (Berkeley: University of California Press, 1993), as well as other books and numerous articles.

Contamine, Philipe. *War in the Middle Ages*, trans. M. Jones. Oxford: Oxford University Press, 1984. Dense, but the most comprehensive single-volume introduction to medieval warfare.

Halsall, Guy. *Warfare and Society in the Barbarian West, 450–900*. London: Routledge, 2003. The essential work on this period. Brilliantly traces the coevolution of military force and social structure, with theoretically sophisticated attention to questions of barbarian identity and valuable use of archaeological evidence.

Hooper, Nicholas, and M. Bennett. *The Cambridge Illustrated Atlas of Warfare. The Middle Ages, 768–1487*. Cambridge: Cambridge University Press, 1996. An extremely well-illustrated overview of medieval warfare—a touch Anglo-centric but with good maps and sound judgments. An excellent introduction.

Keen, Maurice, ed. *Medieval Warfare: A History*. Oxford: Oxford University Press, 1999. A solid edited collection.

Leyser, Karl. "The Battle at the Lech, 955: A Study in Tenth-Century Warfare." With other useful articles in Leyser's *Medieval Germany and Its Neighbors 950–1200* (London: Routledge, 1982), a scholarly analysis of war and politics under the Ottonians.

Morillo, Stephen. *The Battle of Hastings: Sources and Interpretations*. Woodbridge: Boydell and Brewer, 1996. A collection of primary sources and secondary articles on one of the decisive battles of the early middle ages.

Reynolds, Susan. *Fiefs and Vassals: The Medieval Evidence Reinterpreted*. Oxford: Oxford University Press, 1994. The leading revisionist view of feudalism in medieval history.

Sawyer, Peter. *Kings and Vikings. Scandinavia and Europe*. London, Routledge, 1982. A solid overview of the Vikings' impact on European society.

Scragg, Donald, ed. *The Battle of Maldon, AD 991*. Oxford: Oxford University Press, 1991. A collection of studies that uses Maldon as a window onto tenth-century warfare.

CHAPTER 8

Caliphs and Cataphracts: Islam and Byzantium, 400–1100

INTRODUCTION

As we saw in Chapter 7, continuity from Roman imperial times was attenuated in the western half of the empire by economic decline, political division under barbarian kings, and social dislocation. Initially, in contrast, the eastern half of the empire retained a more vital economy and urban social organization and, above, all maintained political unity centered on Roman imperial ideology and mechanisms of rule. The military organization of the state historians often refer to as the Eastern Roman Empire therefore also showed greater continuity with late Roman military institutions. Indeed, many units of the Roman army could trace their history back several centuries in 350 and would continue to be able to until the 1070s.

But transformation came to this part of the Roman world just as it did in the west. Long-term economic and demographic developments played their part as they did in the Germanic kingdoms, but the crucial period of transformation was the first half of the seventh century. First, East Rome entered into a protracted life-or-death struggle with the Persian Empire, revived under the native Persian Sassanid dynasty, over control of the provinces of Syria and Egypt. Then, just as those wars had been settled in Constantinople's favor, Arabs united under a new religion burst out of Arabia. Persia was swallowed whole, and the richest Roman provinces again fell to conquest, this time for good. The truncated and reorganized empire that survived to face another century and a half of life-or-death struggle against the Caliphate is what historians usually call Byzantium. Though still an heir to Rome, its connections to the past were more distant, and its original features more prominent.

The Islamic world that emerged from the Arab conquests was also an heir of Rome and an element of transformation. Like the west and Byzantium, much Islamic territory saw patterns of warfare shaped by surviving Roman infrastructure—roads, city walls, and even administrative structures—while Islamic culture absorbed a large measure of Roman and Hellenistic science. On the other hand, outside of the organization of its naval forces (see Chapter 10), Islam was in some ways the farthest from Rome politically and militarily. In this chapter, we examine these developments in detail.

THE EASTERN ROMAN EMPIRE AND PERSIA TO 630

The Eastern Roman Empire

The continued survival of the Eastern Roman Empire during the period 400–600, in contrast to the dissolution of the empire in the west traced in Chapter 7, depended on the continued viability of a strong central administration capable of extracting taxes from an economy that remained more urban, trade-connected, and vital than that of the west. Imperial territory included Egypt and, at times, at least parts of Mesopotamia, the richest provinces of the southwest Asian–Mediterranean world. That administration, in turn, supported a paid professional army and the construction of significant fortifications that protected vital towns, cities, and communications routes and provided bases for offensive action by the army. The heart of a system that was increasingly centralized lay in the imperial city of Constantinople, protected from the late fourth century onward by massive walls built by the emperor Theodosius (379–395).

The organization of the army itself reflected the reforms of Diocletian and Constantine in the decades around 300. The army consisted of two major types of

The Walls of Constantinople The Silvergate, a reconstructed section of the Theodosian land defenses of Constantinople, shows the multiple walls and towers that guarded the city for a thousand years.

units: the *limitanei,* or soldiers settled near the borders of provinces for local defense, whose connections with local society were strong; and a mobile central army designed for offensive action. The latter contained an increasing proportion of cavalry, reflecting both the need for mobility and offense and the fact that Rome's major foe in the east, the Sassanid Persian Empire, depended heavily on cavalry forces. A significant Roman navy completed the military system of the empire and enhanced the strategic mobility of the field army.

The combination of financial resources, strong central control, professional forces, and a virtually impregnable capital allowed the Eastern Empire to weather invasions by Goths, Huns, and others (though often by bribing them to head west to the more vulnerable western provinces) and even, under Justinian (527–565), to go on the offensive against the Vandals in North Africa, the Visigoths in Spain, and the Lombards in Italy (Figure 8.1). But Justinian's most important wars, and the training ground for his brilliant general Belisarius, were always against Persia, where simply maintaining the frontiers rather than expanding them was the realistic goal. And the cost of his expansionism was high in both economic and political terms. The financial and manpower resources of the empire were strained by constant warfare combined with massive building programs. In addition,

Justinian had barely survived a massive revolt early in his reign and dealt autocratically with potential opposition thereafter. He was suspicious of rivals, which accounts in part, along with parsimony, for his forcing Belisarius to conduct his wars with minimal forces and even imprisoning him for a time for treason. His reign coincided with outbreaks of plague and probably some population decline that reduced the empire's resources by the last quarter of the sixth century. By 600, Justinian's legacy included a mounting crisis in renewed war with Persia, discussed further below.

Further, the continuity of Roman institutions was affected by two somewhat contradictory forces of change. First, the army tended increasingly in the east, as in the west, to recruit troops from among its barbarian foes, often incorporating them in large groups. This created an increasing gulf between the central mobile army and the society it protected. The consequences for the ideology of the army and its loyalty to Roman principles of politics tended to promote instability and alienation of social support for the state. But, second, the increasingly important ties between imperial government and the Christian Church, which had become by Theodosius's time effectively a branch of government, especially in the east where imperial rule remained strong and undivided, tended to produce a more complicated set of effects. Christianity,

Figure 8.1 Justinian's Conquests

as in the west, began to develop a set of ideologies condoning and even supporting war against heretics and unbelievers; in the Eastern Empire, this ideology became focused in the role of the emperor. Governance in general and military campaigns in particular gained in legitimation and potential popular support as a result. The church also constructed a second avenue, outside of official administrative channels and probably more tapped into popular culture, of organizing and administering the population. On the other hand, the dominance of Constantinople and a creed defined there in increasingly legalistic terms gave alternate (heretical) forms of Christianity political potential. The provinces of Syria and Egypt, whose patriarchs resented the claimed primacy of Constantinople, were by the late sixth century largely adherents of the Monophysite heresy (Monophysites denied the human part of Christ's nature). The doctrinal details need not concern us, but the political effect was divisive, though its effect on the basic loyalty of the provinces to the empire is a matter of debate among historians and has probably been exaggerated. In the crisis after 600, the effects of Christianity would come decisively to outweigh those of a socially separated army.

Sassanid Persia

That crisis involved increasingly bitter warfare with East Rome's only superpower foe, the Sassanid Persian Empire. Persia, along with large but varying parts of Mesopotamia and regions to the east and north bordering India and the Central Asian steppes, respectively, had come gradually under Parthian control in the first century BCE, highlighted by the Parthian victory over Roman forces at Carrhae in 53 BCE (see Chapter 4). The Parthians, originally steppe nomads, continued to dominate the area into the third century, though their political control was more in the way of a loose confederation than a unitary empire, and they generally acknowledged the superiority of Rome in upper Mesopotamia. Around 200, a series of civil wars seriously weakened Parthian power. Ardashir, governor of the central Persian region of Persis, consolidated his control of the heartland of Persian power in the decade after 200 and then challenged his Parthian overlords. By 226, he had defeated the Parthian ruler and proclaimed his dynasty, the Sassanids, as the successors of the Achaemenids of Cyrus the Great and Darius (see Chapter 2).

Ardashir thus reestablished a consciously Persian identity for the imperial power of southwest Asia, an identity intimately tied up with Zoroastrianism. Under the Achaemenids, this had been a predominantly elite religion that ruled tolerantly over a multitude of local religious traditions. But the Sassanids promoted Zoroastrianism in ways that, while retaining its vital ties to the Persian aristocracy and its legitimization of royal power and the Persian state, made it a more popular religion. Rulers encouraged conformity of practice and perhaps belief, developing an equation of Zoroastrianism not just with "Persianness" but with loyalty to the monarchy. This coincided with a rebuilding of Persian military power around a traditional core, the heavy cavalry forces of the Persian aristocracy, backed by infantry and archers drawn from the broader population and inspired by wider adherence to Zoroastrianism.

Sassanid Persia and East Rome went to war chronically between 230 and 600, usually struggling for control of the rich provinces of Mesopotamia, with the Persians dominating in the south and the Romans more successful in the north, nearer their bases in Asia Minor. Roman organization and military engineering, especially the strength of their fortifications, tended to be balanced fairly evenly against Persian advantages in mobility and cavalry skill and in theaters of conflict that lay closer to Persian centers of power than to Roman ones. The wars tended toward indecisiveness and often ended in a truce by mutual agreement to avoid fiscal crisis. Both empires also faced enemies on other fronts—East Rome in the Balkans and Persia in the borderlands to the Asian steppes to the north—that forced their attention elsewhere.

These wars in the last half of the sixth century became more intense, partly militarily but partly ideologically, as the clash of Christian and Zoroastrian universalisms fueled a rivalry that was already fierce simply on political and economic grounds. The Sassanids, in particular, learned lessons in organization and statecraft from their Roman neighbors. As a result, the political structure of the Sassanid Empire became, like East Rome's, progressively more centralized over the course of the sixth century while, again like East Rome, its religious culture became more militant externally and more intolerant internally (though a host of smaller religious traditions continued to exist in the spaces between the great powers, especially in culturally heterogeneous and fragmented southern Mesopotamia).

Rome Versus Persia

The wars between Persia and Rome came to a climax between 603 and 628, with significant consequences for each empire and for subsequent world history. Sparked by mutual interference in each other's dynastic disputes, Chosroes II of Persia opened the wars against the emperor Phocas, who murdered his own predecessor, Maurice, who had helped Chosroes gain the Sassanid throne. But with initial success against an East Rome both politically divided—Heraclius overthrew Phocas in 610, assuming command of Roman forces—and threatened by a major Avar invasion in the Balkans, Chosroes's ambitions grew. By 615, he had conquered Syria and Armenia, the latter a major Roman recruiting area; then, between 616 and 619, he conquered Egypt, cutting off Constantinople's

main grain source. With forces established across the Bosporus from Constantinople in 616, Chosroes allied with the Avars; the new allies approached the mighty city in 619. East Rome was on the verge of extinction, and the empire of Darius on the verge of being reestablished.

Heraclius nearly fled to Africa, but a religious revival led by the patriarch Sergius convinced him to stay, and the church then provided resources for rebuilding the Roman position. Heraclius bought off the Avars and used his naval superiority to renew the war in Syria, drawing the Persians away from his capital. Then, in a daring and brilliant series of campaigns between 623 and 627—during which Constantinople was besieged in 626—he bypassed the reconquest of the provinces completely, striking directly into the heart of Persia. At the decisive battle of Nineveh in 627, he routed the Persian army and pursued the survivors to the gates of the Persian capital of Ctesiphon. The Persians killed Chosroes, installed his son Kavadh II as king, and accepted terms that returned all of Chosroes's conquests to Roman rule.

It was an amazing recovery, but one that was to be undone rapidly from an unforeseen quarter, in part by the consequences of the sort of warfare each side waged, for both the religious and political impact of the wars spread beyond the confines of the two empires. Some historians have come to call Heraclius's campaigns against the Persians the first "crusade" because of the importance that Christianity assumed for the morale and fighting spirit of the troops under his command. They marched with crosses on their banners, and the notion of being surrounded by enemies but backed by God contributed to a growing sense in Constantinople that the eastern Christians were a Chosen People. But, of course, similar sentiments opposed the Romans on the other side: These wars could be considered both the first and the last Zoroastrian crusades. At the same time, both sides, given the desperation of the struggle, looked for any allies they could find. The Avars played this role for a time for the Persians, but for the most part, both sides looked to Arab client kingdoms to the south for manpower and diversionary attacks. The result was a flow into Arabia of wealth in the form of bribes to enemies and subsidies to allies, linked to intense ideological pressure in the form of monotheistic religions. This inflow prepared the ground for surprising state formation and religious creativity by one Arab leader in particular, the Prophet Muhammad. What the resulting Arab religious state would meet were two exhausted empires and provinces in Syria and Egypt only recently reintegrated into the structures of Roman rule.

THE ARABIC EXPLOSION, 630–680

The results of the meeting of an expansionist Arab state and the old civilizations of southwest Asia became clear by around 700: Large parts of southwest Asia and North Africa were permanently under Arab political control, and Islam was the region's religion. But how those results were achieved in the fifty or so years between the death of Muhammad and the accession of the caliph (successor to the Prophet) Marwan in 684 is not at all clear. The sources for early Islamic history are somewhat problematic: Almost all of the Islamic sources date from after 685 and reflect political positions relevant to that later period. Non-Islamic sources are scarce and short. Specific events, including the key battles that led to the Arab conquests, are either not narrated or are narrated in multiple, conflicting, versions. Even the specific tenets of Islam during this period are hard to recover. We can see the general shape of what happened, but not all the details.

Background

The nature of the Arab conquests is grounded in pre-Islamic Arabia, which can best be compared to the steppes of Central Asia (see Chapter 6). A fringe of settled, agricultural land and trade-oriented cities along the western and southern edges of the peninsula bordered a vast desert, too poor to support horse herding as in Central Asia and so dominated by camel-herding Bedouins (nomads). The poverty of the land had two consequences. First, unlike the steppe nomads, the Arabs could not generate the resources for building hierarchical chiefdoms and states themselves—in fact, they could barely do so with outside infusions of wealth. Such infusions were, in turn, less likely because the Arabs were neither as numerous nor, usually, as threatening as the steppe nomads. And the Arab border with civilization was at the opposite end of the peninsula from the economic center of gravity of the Arab world, further complicating potential state building. Second, the lack of competition for poor land meant that, again unlike the steppes and its constant churning of peoples and ethnic identities, Arab tribal culture and identities were extremely stable and deeply rooted, and so potentially more resistant to assimilation by the cultures of surrounding civilizations. Deep tribal divisions also contributed to the difficulties faced by would-be state builders, however.

But the half-century of intense East Roman–Sassanid Persian rivalry up to 630 created some new potential, politically and culturally. Economic resources came in, religious rivalries heated up, and Muhammad turned out to be the right leader at the right time to harness that potential. Whatever the details of his new faith and his role in it, he clearly managed to create a state centered at Medina. In competition with other Arab political groups, Muhammad's Medina benefited from the ideological lure of a religion that drew on Arab notions of ethnic identity through their claimed descent from Abraham via Ishmael, that therefore incorporated the Christian and (even more important) Jewish traditions already in the area, that also managed to absorb the Arab pagan tradition, and that justified Arab unity and external conquest in the name of a universal god. Muhammad died in 632 having built Arab unity and (probably—the sources are unclear) initiated attacks into Roman Syria. His successors built rapidly on his foundation.

Arab Armies

The Arab armies that accomplished the early conquests were efficient but unremarkable in many ways. They drew first on a selection of the adult males of the Arab population of Arabia and later on recruits from conquered areas, especially among Arab populations already in Syria and Mesopotamia but also among some non-Arabs. They served for a share of the booty to be gathered from conquered lands, which rapidly took the form of a share of the taxes the conquerors began to collect using local administrative mechanisms soon after their conquests began. Thus, the army of the conquests was not exactly a militia. And it was paid but not exactly professional, as the right to a share of tax income was taken by many in the army to be their heritable right in return for service already rendered, rather than pay in expectation of continued service as the caliphs (mostly) wished to see it. The total number of soldiers theoretically available to the Caliphate grew to perhaps 200,000 by 700, but individual field armies were normally around 20,000–30,000 and rarely much over 50,000–60,000 due to logistical constraints.

Figure 8.2 Arab Conquests

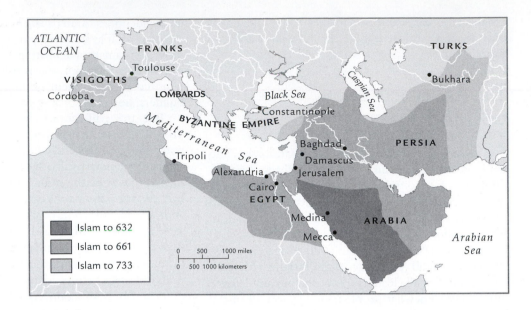

If recruiting and pay arrangements were slightly odd, equipment and tactics were not. Probably only a minority of soldiers had body armor of some sort, either scale armor or mail; iron helmets were more widespread. The vast majority served as infantry, most of whom carried spears that they used in defensive formations against cavalry charges and attacks by other infantry, with the first rank often kneeling to ground their spears more firmly. They also carried swords, which were their primary offensive weapon. Some were archers. The cavalry, limited in numbers by the expense of horses, also carried swords and often dismounted in battle, especially on the defensive. They shared a high level of religiously inspired morale with their chief opponents, but probably gained at the small-unit level from the cohesion of tribal groupings that fought under their own banners. The degree of discipline and determination demonstrated by early Arab armies, as well as perhaps the Roman legacy of the Syrian population they conquered, shows up in their frequent use of the *khandaq,* or field fortification, which could range from an improvised battlefield ditch to a full, Roman-style fortified camp constructed at the end of each day's march. These same qualities and engineering skills gave them success in siege warfare: Improvising, and often using siege equipment captured from enemies or acquired from defectors, they consistently ground down defenders, especially those isolated by Arab battlefield successes.

Tactical tenacity and defensive prowess combined their other great strength at the strategic level: a sig-nificant level of strategic mobility. Horses and especially camels often transported troops to battle, though they played no role tactically; and even pure Arab infantry marched light and fast, partly a result of being paid in coin and thus being expected to buy their own provisions at markets along the march rather than relying on baggage trains. Arab commanders could therefore seize the strategic initiative and choose their place of battle while being able to opt for the advantages of the tactical defensive. This combination probably accounts for a good deal of the success of armies that had no real advantage in equipment or even morale over their main foes, though both East Rome and Persia may have suffered from war weariness and harder-than-normal recruiting in their early encounters with the Arabs. In addition, it took some time for the Arabs to appreciate the importance of sea power (see Chapter 10).

Settlement and Internal Conflict

Syria, Mesopotamia, Persia, and Egypt fell to the Arab armies between 632 and 642, with the decisive battles occurring at Yarmuk in Syria in 636 against the Romans and at Qadisiya in 637 against the Persians. Consolidating the conquests took longer—Egypt had fallen by 642 but a Byzantine fleet nearly retook Alexandria in 645, and the highlands of Persia were not secure until 650 or so. Further expansion came more slowly (Figure 8.2), partly because of the distances involved and partly because the success of the conquests created tensions among the conquerors that involved not just practical problems of administration but ideological questions about the succession to the Caliphate, Arab identity, and the very nature of Islam. Three civil wars and significant transformations of the Islamic state between 650 and 750 resulted without solving some of the deepest problems.

Wishing neither to lose their Arab identity in the cultures they conquered nor necessarily to share their religion at first, the Arab armies of conquest settled in garrison cities largely isolated from the surrounding populations. Within the garrisons of Mesopotamia, Egypt, and Persia, settlement reproduced the tribal divisions and rivalries of the homeland. Syria became the effective core of the Caliphate, with Medina retaining symbolic primacy. The separation of military from society that this created was initially a separation between Muslims and non-Muslims, but subject peoples began to convert. Whether converts had rights to military tax income became one point of dispute in the Muslim community; the division between Muslims who had done military service and those who had not became another, especially as the garrisons of Mesopotamia in particular lost their military effectiveness in the later 600s. Finally, the ideological attachment to tribal Arabia that motivated isolated garrison settlement implied hostility to the monarchical, bureaucratic rule of the Romans and Persians. Yet effective administration of the empire demanded something approximating monarchy and bureaucracy, producing another source of tension.

Conversion and settlement inevitably also weakened tribal affiliations as an alternate source of organization. As the garrisons lost their military significance, they became home to a class of urban scholars with strong mercantile connections. This development, which bypassed local aristocracies, not only separated the leadership of Muslim Arab society from landholding as a source of prestige but also separated landholding from service to the state—a strange development by traditional standards. Meanwhile, the rural peasantry escaped to the cities when they could, converting to Islam and becoming clients of the Arabs to escape taxation, as the local aristocracies could no longer protect them. This had the triple effect of undermining the old aristocracies and the imperial traditions they might have supported, spreading the values of the Arabs who controlled their clients throughout society, and thus steadily diluting the exclusively Arab tribal ties of Muslim society.

The first civil war, in 657–661, over succession to the Caliphate, resulted in the split between Shi'a and Sunni Islam and established the aristocratic Umayyad family in the Caliphate. The second, in 680–684, established the primacy of Syria, whose professional army took over garrisoning the entire Caliphate after what amounted to a new round of conquests (see the Highlights box "The Battle of Ra's al-Ayn, 685"). Both results, in fact, damaged the legitimacy of caliphal government in the eyes of many Muslims, though both the caliphs, on the one hand, and the emerging *ulema*, the scholars who interpreted Islamic law, on the other, contributed to the defining of Islam in the process of arguing with each other. Those arguments, combined with the problems of maintaining military forces that developed from the professionalization of the Syrian army, had deep consequences for Islamic political structure and resulted in a third civil war, in 747–750, discussed further below.

ISLAM, 680–1050

The Umayyads

Control of Egypt and Iraq made the Umayyad Caliphate the sole southwest Asian superpower; steppe nomads to the north of the Caucasus were the only military force capable of meeting the Caliphate on equal terms. The conquerors inherited a strong fiscal organization, and over 80 percent of government revenues went to support of the army. However, much of that revenue was collected and disbursed locally, severely reducing the power and flexibility of the central authority. Meanwhile, the legitimacy of caliphal rule was eroded by the succession dispute that created the party of Ali, on the one hand, and by the anti-imperialist ideology of the tribal traditionalists in the ulema, on the other. The party of Ali disputed the Umayyad claim to the Caliphate, while the tribal traditionalists objected to the urban, royal style of the governing house.

The professional Syrian army was the bedrock of Umayyad power, but it carried its own problems. It was tied together by personal allegiance to the military leaders who had access to the fiscal resources of the state through their control of the governorships of the provinces. In one way, apparent tribal divisions continued to be important; however, old tribal names provided the rationale for division of the army into factions competing for control of those same governorships, which were appointed by the caliph. The governors, in turn, worked to control the caliph, who

The Battle of Ra's al-Ayn, 685

A last flare-up of resistance to the Umayyad victory in the second civil war resulted in a battle that is well documented and illustrates some of the key features of early Islamic warfare. A small (perhaps 5000 men) army of rebels from southern Mesopotamia (Iraq) moved up the Euphrates valley toward the routes into northern Syria. They paused at the old Roman fortified city of Qarqisiya (Circesium) to buy supplies at a market outside the city. Sulayman bin Surad, leader of the rebel force, was advised by the governor of the city to make the most of the small size of his army and their many horses to beat the approaching Umayyad force, larger (perhaps 20,000) and mostly on foot, to Ra's al-Ayn. He could then place the town and its water supplies (as well as a potential escape route) at his back. He was also advised to deploy his army in small units and a flexible order so that units could dismount or mount at need to support each other and to avoid a set-piece battle with the more numerous enemy, as he risked being surrounded by doing so.

Sulayman managed to occupy the appropriate ground first but disregarded the rest of the advice. He drew his army up in the standard formation of a line divided into a center and two wings and prepared for a set-piece battle, dismounting all his troops. When the Syrian army arrived, divisions in their command seem to have delayed decisive action for a time. But two days of skirmishing escalated by the third day into a full-scale attack in which the numbers of the Syrians began to tell. Sulayman had his men break their sheaths and advance in a final desperate attack, but the Syrians formed a spear line, sent in reinforcements that included a number of archers, which the rebel force lacked, and indeed surrounded the rebels. Sulayman died, and the banner of command of his forces passed down a predetermined chain until the last designated leader led a successful breakout that night and fled with the remnants of the rebel army back home.

While of little significance in any larger strategic picture, the battle does illustrate a number of features common to Arab battles, including infantry dominance, stalwart defensive tactics, and combined arms ability. It also stands as another example of the professionalism of the Syrian army that buttressed Umayyad rule.

was not usually a military leader. The Umayyad Caliphate was therefore characterized by continual factional infighting in the provinces that nevertheless kept the state unified because it was directed at control of the center. The professional army, in effect, played politics to guarantee its continued access to the tax income that was, in the absence of a landed aristocracy, its only support. This also caused most subjects of the Caliphate outside Syria to view the army as a semiforeign occupying elite. When factionalism spread to the capital, the Caliphate imploded in the third civil war of 747–750.

The Abbasid Revolution, 750–850

The Abbasid State   Victory in the civil war by the Abbasids, based in Khurasan in northern Persia, resulted in the movement of the capital to Baghdad in

Iraq and the replacement of the army of Syria by the army of Khurasan as occupiers of the provinces. The Abbasids elaborated the machinery of state: The bureaucracy grew, and a spy system kept an eye on provincial leaders. The Abbasids should have been stronger than the Umayyads, but their regime still lacked legitimacy in many Muslim eyes and still had a professional army that played politics to guarantee its access to money, outside of any effective civilian control. The Umayyads had at least been able to claim leadership of Arab tribal society with spiritual ties to Arabia. However, the Abbasids could satisfy neither the Shi'ites with their hereditary claims (they were of the Prophet's Hashimite clan but descended from Muhammad's uncle al-Abbas, not through Ali) nor the ulema traditionalists with their claims to have saved Islam from Umayyad oppression, as their state apparatus was even more developed. Unable to base their

Arab Armies   Though this manuscript illustration of the civil war between Muhammad's cousin Ali and his adversaries—the origin of the Sunni–Shi'a division—dates to the thirteenth century, it accurately shows the dominance of sword-armed infantry and cavalry in early Arab armies.

fomented trouble, Abbasid leaders turned increasingly to their personal dependents to run the state. And to ensure their reliability, such dependents were increasingly foreign and sometimes servile.

The Rise of Foreign and Slave Soldiers

The same process that affected the civil service also affected the army, combined with a growing tendency to recruit outside the empire. Starting in Spain and North Africa in about 800 and in Baghdad by 830, when Persian aristocrats had failed in ruling the capital, the leaders of the Abbasid state turned to foreign soldiers for their military forces.

The key characteristics of these armies were a powerful separation of the soldiers from society and an equally powerful dependence on the ruler for their livelihood. Separation and dependence came from foreign origins and, increasingly in the century after 850, from servile status. (Servile status was comparatively rare among the initial Abbasid recruits.) In the hand of a strong ruler, such armies could be effective instruments of control. And when drawn from steppe nomads, especially the Turks on the northeastern borders of the empire, they could be efficient military forces—it was with the rise of these armies that horse-archery began to supplement the infantry tactics of the early Arab armies as the dominant Muslim military style east of Egypt. (In Africa, and later in Muslim-controlled areas of the Balkans, *mamluks,* or slave soldiers, usually served as heavy infantry.) But their dependence on the ruler and separation from society and thus from meaningful politics meant that they were not a military-social elite, but instead were elite military automata. Their usual connection to politics was through palace coups designed to ensure their access to monetary support. Many mamluks were manumitted (freed), and many rose to positions of wealth and importance; in extreme cases, as later in Mamluk Egypt, mamluks took over the state. But their separation from civilian Muslim society remained profound.

Mamluk armies—armies of slave soldiers—were therefore the ultimate expression of Muslim states' problematic relationship to Muslim society and the failure of Muslim civilian administrations to effectively control their armies. The institution spread rapidly throughout the Muslim world and no farther: Virtually no one else adopted this military model (see the Issues box "Slave Soldiers"), nor could most Muslim states do without it. It seems an odd result for a religion that makes religious law so central to all

rule on minority Shi'ite support, the Abbasids were forced into the arms of the ulema. But the latter's hostility to any mechanisms of power that impinged on society—for example, Muslim law has injunctions against enslaving or keeping in servile status fellow Muslims, which made conscription problematic from early in Islamic history—especially its powerful classes, resulted in the failure of the Abbasids to create viable service aristocracies, either civil or military. Unable to draw on the resources of their society and faced with a politically unreliable professional army whose factions

Slave Soldiers

Even the most powerful figures in history have at times been frustrated by limitations on the *legitimate* use of their power and so have turned to personal dependents outside the system to enact their will. Witness the eunuchs of Chinese emperors, used to circumvent the rules of the Confucian bureaucracy, or President Ronald Reagan's similar use of Colonel Oliver North to circumvent congressional restrictions on aid to Nicaraguan contras. Such figures tended in the traditional world to be slaves, eunuchs, or women, because these groups stood outside the usual bounds of political legitimacy. Incapable of exercising authority on their own, they were utterly dependent on (and therefore in theory completely loyal to) the ruler who employed them. They also tended merely to supplement the operations of legitimate governments run by free males of the polity, however "free" was defined. Likewise, slaves have fought in wars throughout history, from Roman gladiators to African American slaves during the American Revolution. They appeared in large numbers, however, only in emergencies and were almost universally manumitted either before or after their service. Only in unusual circumstances did governments feel so restricted in their legitimate use of power that they depended exclusively on outsider groups to enforce their will through the creation of slave, or female, armies that excluded free men.

This condition was most pervasive in the Islamic heartland, where the conquests effaced pre-Islamic sources of political authority without providing an adequate substitute, as traced elsewhere in this chapter. Mamluk armies became a standard feature of this civilization, the only major civilization in which slave armies are known. But the effect of the conquest and the problem of maintaining a paid professional army without an established bureaucracy or service aristocracy—and not anything intrinsic to the Muslim religion—were vital in the emergence of the mamluk institution.

The institution was never directly copied but arose independently outside the Muslim world a number of times, especially in the slave-trading societies of west Africa. The Wolof kings of Senegal, for example, enslaved their own subjects (much as the Ottomans would do to sustain their Janissary Corps) and relied almost exclusively on slave soldiers. A state that sells its own subjects and collects protection money from those it doesn't sell clearly exercises little claim to legitimate use of power. In Islamic armies, foreignness complemented servile status in alienating soldiers from society. Gender served the same function in some other societies that used female slaves as palace guards—for example, Mauryan India, the kings of Dahomey, and a fourth-century ruler of Hunnic invaders of China. In all these cases, something that fundamentally alienated the ruler from the society, whether the foreign origins of imperial institutions or a crisis of ethnic identity, prevented an appeal to the usual sources of political legitimation, and insecure rulers turned to unorthodox sources of support.

Thus, no matter how effective particular slave armies were—and mamluk armies of nomadic Turks were often very effective—their mere presence signified a deep problem of political structure and legitimacy in the states where they appeared.

aspects of society. But then, Islam is a world religion that began as the exclusive tribal faith of the Arabs, so paradoxical results are not unknown to it.

Fragmentation and Decline   Unfortunately for the Abbasids, the beginnings of mamluk armies coincided with rulers who either were weak or had no field on which to prove their military prowess. The borders of the empire were distant, and the caliph was not preeminently a military leader. As a result, almost as soon as mamluk armies came to Baghdad, they started causing trouble. Political chaos ensued, and within a century, the Abbasid revolution resulted in the breakup of the unitary Islamic empire. An Umayyad restoration separated Spain; the great provinces—Egypt, Syria, Persia—became effectively independent; then even the provinces fragmented into smaller warring emirates. Fragmentation brought a decisive end to Islamic expansion and, in fact, even allowed Byzantium to resume the offensive in Palestine in the 900s (see below) by picking off frontier emirates one at a time. The Caliphate itself receded into feebleness and figurehead status, and an era of smaller Islamic states began.

Islamic States, 950–1050

Military Organization   These smaller Islamic states resembled the post-Roman states of western Europe in drawing on certain common elements of military organization throughout the Muslim world, though with significant regional variations on the theme. At the core of most states' armies were the personal slave soldiers of the emir, sultan, or other political leader. Indeed, at times (as in Mamluk Egypt), the slave army dispensed altogether with a nonslave leader and took over governance directly. Such armies were replenished each generation with new imports of slaves bought or captured along the frontiers; military service rarely descended within mamluk families.

These cores provided the standing army for each state but were usually relatively small. Local levies of free men and, above all, foreign mercenary groups filled out the ranks in times of emergency. The *iqta'* an institution imported first by Turkic slaves and later by Turkic conquerors, increasingly provided a decentralized way of paying for military manpower (as well as for nonmilitary administrators). An *iqta'* was a set of rights to revenue of particular lands; these rights were granted to mamluks and nomadic tribesmen in exchange for seasonal military service. While the system bears a superficial resemblance to the system of fief holding developing in Europe at the same time (see Chapter 7), the differences are crucial. The *iqta'* holder was a dependent with regard to central authority (not, as a fief holder was, a participant in that authority), and a mercenary with regard to the land (not, as a fief holder was, a steward and, effectively, owner). *Iqta'* holders were thus neither an aristocracy of service nor an aristocracy of local power, but rather represented mamluk military organization spread across the land. In short, *iqta'* did not remedy the lack of connection between settled Islamic society and the military

states that governed it. Only at the edges of the Islamic world, where *ghazis*, frontier raiders, carried a still-military *jihad* to the infidel, was there any such connection, and the usually tribal *ghazi* was a marginal figure to mainstream Islamic society.

The Military and Society   The institutional heritage of the Abbasid revolution thus gave Islamic states after 950 (including those after 1050 such as the Seljuk and Ottoman empires and Mamluk Egypt) the character of permanent conquest societies. That is, the settled, agricultural societies of the Islamic world were consistently ruled by states dominated by tribal or slave soldiers from the nomadic pastoral world. The lack of organic connection between Islamic societies and states meant that the states had little internal opposition when they were strong but also little internal support in times of crisis or weakness. They therefore oscillated between despotism and anarchic infighting.

One crucial result of this character of Islamic states was a serious decline in agriculture in the Islamic heartland of Iraq. Periodically plundered by out-of-control slave armies and ruled in the best of times by armies with little cultural interest in settled agriculture, peasants throughout the Islamic world escaped when they could, with pastoralism advancing at the expense of agriculture. In Iraq, where continued farming depended on maintenance of the complex irrigation system, the decline was particularly steep and hard to reverse. The decline of Iraq shifted power within the Islamic world to Egypt and increased the importance within the larger world of southwest Asia of the Turkic nomads to the north.

In fact, the widespread use of Turkic slaves as the core of Islamic armies opened a pipeline to the nomadic world that could not remain in the control of Islamic states. Periods of weakness or infighting created openings and effectively extended invitations for nomadic conquests. While such conquests often led to the revitalization of Islamic states and to temporary unification, they also reinforced the conquest nature of those states and maintained a distance between rulers and subjects that undermined political legitimacy, leading to the continuation of mamluk armies even after nomadic conquests.

Finally, the Abbasid heritage marginalized military power in Islamic society. Warriors were either geographically marginalized as frontier *ghazis* or socially marginalized as foreign slaves in the standing armies of Islamic states. The core of Islamic society was civilian, but unlike the civilian government and society of China, which kept close control over its armies, this was a civilian society with little control over or even connection to its wielders of military power.

THE BYZANTINE EMPIRE, 630–1081

Heraclius's recovery of Syria and Egypt from Persia in 626–628 was the last hurrah for the old Eastern Roman Empire. In addition to the provinces lost to the Arabs, Avars and Slavs wrested major areas of the Balkans and Thrace from imperial control. By 700, the empire had contracted to the capital and Asia Minor to the Taurus Mountains, plus small coastal territories in Greece and Italy: Half the population of the empire and perhaps two-thirds of its revenue were lost for good.

The grand strategy of the empire became strictly defensive—indeed, until the mid-eighth century, Byzantium fought for its very survival, repulsing sieges of Constantinople in the 670s and again in 717–718. The empire depended for its defense on its navy (see Chapter 10) and on a reorganized army. Losses of manpower and economic reserves and the limited opportunities for plunder imposed by a defensive posture meant that, while traditions of organization and of strategic and tactical thinking dating from Maurice's *Strategikon*—a sixth-century military manual that was based on older Roman military handbooks—continued to inform Byzantine military policy, severely restricted resources forced significant change in the implementation of that policy.

Social and Economic Contexts

Military change was part of a larger set of changes in the empire. The loss of great economic and cultural centers such as Antioch and Alexandria gave the capital at Constantinople dominance of Byzantine government, society, and culture. The patriarch of Constantinople gained in importance and prestige within the reduced world of eastern Christianity but became even more a part of the imperial system under the leadership of the emperor. Constantinople truly became "The City" in an empire whose cities generally were smaller and less important than they had been in the Roman period.

The prominence of Constantinople created an enduring characteristic of Byzantine life: a division between the center and the provinces that had a number of aspects and consequences. Economically, the provinces were overwhelmingly agrarian: Taxes on farmers, in cash and in kind, were the backbone of government revenues, the vast majority of which were used to support the army and navy. The capital was the center of the empire's trade, where the government regulated and taxed merchants and craftsmen. Control of trade, with its ability to generate cash and its connections to the often hostile outside world, became part of the government's defensive grand strategy. Socially, the provinces were increasingly the world of military aristocrats—men who were significant landholders and held positions of leadership in the provincial army. Such men were also important in the capital but were balanced and rivaled by the scholar-bureaucrats of the central government. A similar division existed between the government-dependent churchmen of the capital and the great landholding monasteries of the provinces, which were relatively independent.

Given the diminishing resources available for military use and the increasing importance of aristocratic landholders in society, Byzantium saw changes similar to those affecting western Europe in this period. But the restriction of resources was never as great, and so the rise of the aristocracy took place in the context of a central authority that retained its strength and dominance in this civilization. The wealth and security of the capital behind its walls contrasted with the poverty of the provinces and their continued openness to Arab invasions, at least through the 840s, reinforcing the fact that appointment to military command by the government, rather than independent dynasty building, remained the path to power and success in the empire. As the key to power, Constantinople held the remains of the empire together.

The conquests also affected the cultural tone of the empire. The Eastern Roman Empire had been Christian but had also retained significant elements of Roman secular culture. The loss of the great eastern Mediterranean centers of culture resulted in an empire whose culture was pervasively Christianized. The lost provinces had been religiously unorthodox, Monophysite, in their Christianity and Coptic or Syriac in language; their loss actually increased the homogeneity of the church, making it more Greek and more dependent on the leadership of the emperor. Finally, the pressures of defense, especially against a rival salvation religion, moved this Christianity toward greater

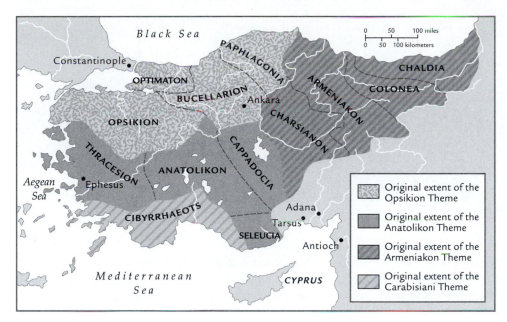

Figure 8.3 The Byzantine Theme System The original four themes were subdivided over time, and the system was extended to European provinces and to newly conquered areas in Asia.

militance and intolerance. This tendency had appeared even during Heraclius's Persian wars: His campaign to retake Jerusalem in 628 and to regain the fragments of the True Cross taken from the city by the Persians is sometimes called the first "crusade." And the tendency was magnified in the battle against Islam. Byzantine soldiers entered battle saying prayers to a conquering Jesus, and the central religious dispute in the empire, the Iconoclast controversy of the 700s (over the religious use of images) was influenced by the spiritual crisis prompted by Arab success and had implications for army morale and organization. The more sharply defined Greek Orthodox character of Byzantine Christianity affected not only warfare against the Arabs but Greek missionary work, which was tied more clearly to imperial authority than western missions were to any secular power. It also affected Byzantine relations with western Europe, which became increasingly strained as time went on.

The century from 630 to 730 was the crucial one for most of these changes. It was also the critical period for the emergence of a new military posture, one which allowed Byzantium to survive and eventually prosper.

Byzantium on the Defensive, 630–840

Evolution of the Theme System Heraclius withdrew the four Roman field armies in the east—the armies of Armenia, the East (Anatolian), and Illyricum (Thrace), and the central reserve army (Obsequium)—

into Asia Minor, eventually abandoning all the frontier areas beyond the Taurus Mountains and most of Thrace. Each field army (or *theme,* a word with origins in the steppe nomad world) was assigned part of Asia Minor as its home base, from which it was to draw support and recruits. In addition, a coastal area was later assigned to the rowers of a thematic navy. A fiscal crisis forced significant reductions in army pay, but in the impoverished empire, any cash salary was valuable, and recruits continued to be available, while taxes in kind provided various supplies.

The permanent basing of armies in regions of Asia Minor inevitably created an identification between the themes (armies) and their geographic areas (which also came to be called themes). This eventually had a major effect on provincial government. Roman government had maintained a clear division between civil and military authority. Increasingly, however, from the mid-eighth century, the *strategos,* the commander of the theme as a military unit, also became the military governor of the theme as a province. Civil authority thus was steadily subordinated to military officials. This streamlined provincial administration but had the potential to make the *strategoi* into powerful political figures who could threaten the emperor's control. The shift to military administration in the eighth century, however, was accompanied by the subdivision of the original themes to reduce their political weight, while themes added when the empire again expanded tended to be small (Figure 8.3).

Byzantine Soldiers
This manuscript illustration of a Byzantine army in action shows the coordination of cavalry (foreground) with spear-armed infantry (background).

The shift to smaller themes was also accompanied by a subtle shift in strategic outlook. The thematic armies of the seventh century were still field armies that tried to meet invasions at the frontiers and, at least in theory, maintained offensive capability for reconquest of the empire's lost provinces. But the realities—the dominance of the Caliphate as well as the creation of a central field army, the *tagmata* (see below)—pushed the themes toward being a more purely defensive militia.

The Thematic Armies in Operation   Some of the thematic forces were infantrymen armed with spears or bows. Defensive armor among the foot soldiers was often minimal—padded tunics, felt caps, and an oval wooden shield—as mail or other metal body armor seems to have been beyond the resources of most infantry. The cavalry were more likely to have iron helmets and some body armor, though not all did; cavalry weapons included lances, swords, maces, and bows. Though probably numerically inferior to the infantry, the cavalry were clearly the more prestigious and better-supported force, drawn from prosperous middle-level landowners. As in western Europe, cavalry's advantage over infantry was thus as much a matter of social factors as tactical ones, factors that tended to influence levels of armament and morale in the cavalry's favor as well. A support system in which soldiers provided their own arms exaggerated the disparity.

Thus, Byzantine infantry suffered some of the same decline, compared to the legions of the classical empire, that infantry in western Europe did, for the same reasons. Above all, the Byzantine thematic forces were not full-time professionals and did not drill regularly (if at all) in peacetime—only regular campaigning provided some experience and cohesion. Moreover,

the influence of nomadic horse armies on tactics and army composition was stronger than in western Europe, because Byzantine frontiers were so much closer to the grasslands of the nomadic invaders, and the climate was generally more suitable for horsed armies than that of western Europe. Also, the normal patterns of campaigning by thematic forces put a premium on the mobility that cavalry forces provided.

Nonetheless, the Byzantine system was built on carefully coordinated cooperation between infantry and cavalry forces, each of which had their roles to play. Solid masses of spear- and bow-armed infantry provided a secure defensive base for the cavalry during battles, defended and besieged fortifications, and defended tenaciously in restricted terrain such as mountain passes. A well-guarded pass could either block an enemy invasion or, more often, block the return of a raiding army to its home bases and allow other forces time to harass the raiders. In turn, the cavalry provided security and scouting for infantry columns on the march and could forage farther afield for supplies on campaign.

The defensive function of the thematic forces was dictated by the disparity in resources between the empire and its chief enemy, the Caliphate. The population of the Caliphate was many times larger than Byzantium's 10 million or so, and the Arab economy was more advanced. The result was that the Caliphate's cash income was perhaps twenty times that of the empire at the time of greatest disparity and probably seven times greater even in the mid-ninth century. The numbers of the Byzantine military establishment are much disputed because the sources are so scanty and unreliable, but it is likely that the entire Byzantine army at its height totaled little more than 40,000 soldiers—and probably less. But even if it were much larger, as some authors argue, only a fraction of the total could campaign at any one time: Byzantine armies in the seventh century never exceeded 20,000 and only rarely reached 40,000 in the eighth, while the largest Arab armies could regularly exceed 40,000. A significant thematic force could be as small as 3000 men.

In the face of such disparity in numbers and resources, there was at times little Byzantine forces could do against major Arab invasions. Byzantine diplomacy represented a constant search for ways to divert Arab forces and for allies drawn from the nomadic steppe world north of the Caucasus and Black Sea, the only military powers capable of meeting the Caliphate on equal terms. The Khazar Empire was long the bulwark of this approach; it was in the wake of the Khazar collapse that Byzantine connections with the Rus—the Scandinavian rulers of Kiev who gave their name to what became Russia—took shape. When allies could not divert Arab attention, the Byzantine army had to perform a holding action.

Thus, campaign doctrine, not surprisingly, stressed indirect action and counseled avoiding battle unless the enemy had already been worn down and demoralized by ambushes and supply problems. Spies would attempt to warn of impending invasions, and scouts would track approaching forces as the troops from threatened areas were alerted and gathered—a time-consuming process that made stopping invasions at the border fairly difficult. Smaller invasion forces moved too fast to be reliably intercepted, whereas larger but slower forces could prove too dangerous to confront directly with only a small local force. Campaigns thus became matters of guerrilla warfare. Byzantine forces would attempt to harass the enemy's foragers, restricting their supplies. Detachments would be ambushed, potential campsites occupied ahead of the enemy's arrival, and cities fortified to resist sudden assaults and restrict the enemy's freedom of movement. The aim was to wear down the invaders, try to restrict the damage they did, and then reoccupy the land after the invaders left. Such a strategy took advantage of logistics and often consisted of little more than a waiting game: Arab armies large and small campaigned when fodder was available for their horses and resisted staying in Anatolia during the cold winters. The thematic armies thus proved bad at preventing Arab pillaging—a tactical concession to Arab strength—but good at preventing permanent conquest.

The insecurity of the Byzantine situation affected more than just strategy. Byzantine armies maintained the Roman practice of making fortified camps while marching. Laid out in a square, the camps would be made defensible, especially when an enemy force was in the area, with a ditch. The earth from the ditch was used to make a wall reinforced by a shield palisade. On the march, the square formation of the camp translated into a square infantry formation guarding the baggage train and guarded, in turn, by cavalry units. If a battle threatened, the infantry square became the focus of the army's deployment, with the baggage sent to the rear and the cavalry now shielded inside the infantry.

The system did a remarkable job of preserving the empire against heavy odds, but it never stopped the pillaging and major invasions. The security of the empire was only really assured by the successful defense of Constantinople in 718 and the subsequent shift in Muslim priorities after the Abbasid revolution and the founding of Baghdad. The ninth-century political fragmentation of the Muslim world then leveled the playing field considerably along the Byzantine frontier.

Creation of the Tagmatic Forces

At the accession of Constantine V in 741, the leader of the Opsikion Theme led an uprising that took two years to crush. The fifth revolt by this theme alone since Heraclius's reign, it highlighted the danger of basing a large thematic army so close to the capital. Constantine responded by breaking up the Opsikion Theme into several smaller themes and by creating (partly from Opsikion soldiers) standing full-time units called *tagmata* based in and around the capital. Created from old units that had for centuries been ceremonial palace guards, the tagmata became the elite core of the Byzantine army. They received not only salary and lands but arms, equipment, rations, horses, and fodder from the government. Two units of infantry guarded the walls of the Imperial Palace and defended the City; a third took charge of the central baggage train and support services; and three elite cavalry units gave the emperor a personal army that counterbalanced the political weight of the themes. The tagmatic forces immediately proved their worth on campaign as well, re-creating an offensive capability for the Byzantine army. Constantine launched a successful raid of the Caliphate in 745, spearheaded by the tagmata. Tagmatic forces also contributed to Byzantine conquests in Greece and Macedonia, though a new enemy, the Bulgars, soon disputed the region.

Byzantine Military Culture

The continuity and unusual self-consciousness of Byzantine military culture was expressed partly in a series of military manuals that continued a late Roman tradition of theoretical and practical writing about military organization and war. Often written by emperors, the manuals explained unit structures and command hierarchies, gave advice on strategy and campaigning, and laid out tactical precepts. Attention was paid to the place of war among the various tools available to the empire in dealing with foreign foes, including diplomacy, bribery, and trickery. Particular attention was given to the unique characteristics of the different enemies the empire faced—something most premodern military writing did not do. The combination of antiquarian form and vocabulary ("Romans," for example, remained the Byzantine word for themselves) with adaptation to new foes and conditions that the manuals show symbolize the continuity and flexibility of the whole Byzantine military tradition.

■ ■ ■

[**Maurice**, *Strategy* (c. 600)] Warfare is like hunting. Wild animals are taken by scouting, by nets, by lying in wait, by stalking, by circling around, and by other such strategems rather than by sheer force. In waging war we should proceed in the same way, whether the enemy be many or few. To try simply to overpower the enemy in the open, hand to hand and face to face, even though you might appear to win, is an enterprise which is very risky and can result in serious harm. Apart from extreme emergency, it is ridiculous to try to gain a victory which is so costly and brings only empty glory. . . .

[**Leo VI**, *Tactics* (c. 900)] As regards the Turkish nation, it is very numerous, sets little store by objects of luxury and ease, and devotes itself only to war and to making itself redoubtable in combat. . . . They are much given to discharging arrows from horseback. They take with them a quantity of mares and cows, whose milk they drink. They do not camp, like the Romans, in redoubts; rather, up to the actual day of fighting, they are separated into tribes and families. They post their guards far away and so thickly that they cannot be easily taken by surprise. . . . In their order of battle, they do not divide their army into three parts, as the Romans do. . . . They like to fight from a distance, set ambushes, simulate flight, disperse, and suddenly come back to charge. . . . With regard to the Franks, they are brave

---

The tagmata differed from the thematic forces in being full-time professionals with higher standards of equipment and training. But they were organized similarly and fought side by side with thematic forces. They began to provide Byzantium with offensive capability and reduced the incidence of rebellion by thematic generals. However, the tagmata themselves became a political force: Constantine may have created them in part to enforce his Iconoclastic religious policies in the capital, and subsequent emperors had to take account of tagmatic interests in their policies. And Byzantium remained generally on the defensive for another century after the tagmata were created. Only in the mid-800s would a series of developments begin to alter the empire's grand strategy.

Byzantium on the Offensive, 840–1025

The founding of the tagmata coincided with the beginnings of a period of demographic and economic growth in the empire. Outbreaks of plague, which had struck periodically since Justinian's reign, ceased, and Arab raids decreased somewhat in frequency and destructiveness. The population began to grow, and the government found its income improving. Around 840, in the wake of a major Arab invasion and revolts among the thematic forces, the emperor Theophilus took advantage of the empire's resources to improve the army. He added to its numbers, partly by settling a large group of religious rebels from the Caliphate throughout the themes and enrolling them in the

and daring almost to the point of foolhardiness. . . . They do not form up for battle as the Romans do, by companies and battalions, but by tribes and families. Those bound by friendship, and by a sort of brotherhood, also join together. . . . [An] excellent tactic is to attack them at night with archers, because they camp separately and dispersed. . . . I now move on to the Saracens, ever our enemies. . . . They blaspheme against Christ, whom they do not regard as true God and Savior of the world. . . . We who follow a holy divine law detest their impiety and make war on them to support the faith. . . . Their order of battle is a long square, set back everywhere and very difficult to break into. They use this pattern in marches as in battles. In fact, they imitate the Romans in many of the usages of war and methods of attack, which they have learned from us.

[**Nicephoras Phocas,** *Military Precepts* (c. 965)]
As the enemy draws near, the entire contingent of the host, every last one of them, must say the invincible prayer proper to Christians, "Lord Jesus Christ, our God, have mercy on us, Amen," and in this way let them begin their advance against the enemy, calmly proceeding in forma-

tion at the prescribed pace without making the slightest commotion or sound. . . . It is necessary, before all else, to check and see in what place the enemy commander happens to be and aim the triangular formation of the cataphracts directly at him, with the two units on either side of it, the outflankers. . . . The cataphracts and the two units on either side of them must remain in formation while our units make their attack against them. Should the enemy remain in formation while our units make their attack against them, as soon as the enemy's arrows begin to be launched against the front of the triangular formation of the cataphracts, our archers must strike back at the enemy with their arrows. Then the front of the triangular formation must move in proper formation at a trotting pace and smash into the position of the enemy commander while the outflankers on the outside encircle the enemy as far as possible and the other two units proceed on both flanks with perfect precision and evenness with the rear ranks of the cataphracts without getting too far ahead or breaking rank in any way. With the aid of God and through the intercession of His immaculate Mother the enemy will be overcome and give way to flight.

---

thematic forces. He probably doubled the pay of the whole army, and he established small border districts at the key passes through the Taurus range, strengthening the forward-reaction capabilities of the army at the frontiers.

Theophilus's reforms seem to have immediately improved the morale and performance of the army. The interior of Asia Minor was largely secured against raiders, further encouraging demographic and economic recovery. Byzantine forces began consistently to go on the offensive against the Muslims to the east and southeast, against the Bulgars in the Balkans, and even in southern Italy and against Muslim naval forces based on Crete. The offensives were still limited in scope—several centuries of defensive mentality would not disappear overnight—and did not always

succeed. But the pace picked up steadily from the founding of the Macedonian dynasty by Basil I in 867 and peaked between 963 and 976 under the emperors Nicephoras Phocas and John Tzimisces. The move to an offensive posture had significant implications in a number of areas.

Offensives reemphasized the connection of religion and warfare, though in different ways on the empire's two fronts. Against Muslim forces, a form of holy war intensified from the Christian side, as the Byzantines generally proved resistant to allowing a Muslim population to remain in areas added to the empire. This often involved the expulsion of Muslims from areas not already depopulated by Byzantine raiding, though some groups converted to Christianity and joined the empire. In the Balkans, Byzantine military action became part of a more general cultural offensive, as first the Bulgars and then the Russians were converted to the Orthodox Church, though conversion by no means secured peace with these groups. Such conversions did expand the scope of a Byzantine commonwealth that reached well beyond the actual borders of the empire for the first time.

Offensives also offset the increased cost of the army to some extent. Offensive campaigns allowed Byzantine armies to live off the resources of their enemies and to reverse the flow of plunder to the empire's benefit. And the naval offensive in the Aegean (see Chapter 10) cleared Muslim pirates from the seas and made trade more secure and so profitable.

Offensive warfare also affected the organization of the army and the balance of the forces within it. The tagmatic forces, as full-time professionals, were more valuable for offensive campaigns than the thematic forces, and this period saw several new tagmata created. The tagmatic forces were divided into eastern and western units and were often now stationed in the provinces, closer to theaters of action. The thematic forces, on the other hand, tended to be called out less often than before, and more selectively: Tenth-century military manuals advise picking the best men from a muster of provincials and recognizing specialties among the forces available—Armenians provided the best heavy infantry, for example. (See the Sources box "Byzantine Military Culture" for more details.)

The ultimate tactical expression of the new Byzantine offensive capability came with Nicephoras Phocas's creation of a special unit of heavy cavalry, the *kataphraktoi,* or cataphracts. This unit, probably no more than about 500 strong, consisted of men who wore mail body armor from head to foot and rode horses covered with hardened hide armor that came down around the horses' knees. Armed with maces and swords, and supported by lancers and horse-archers, they were intended as an irresistible shock force on the battlefield. They formed up in a blunt wedge formation and aimed their charge, at the crucial point of a battle, at the enemy commander and the heavy infantry forces around him. The charge, executed at a trot, depended as much on its psychological effect in terrorizing the target as it did on heavy armor and weapons to smash resistance, and it required considerable discipline on the part of the cataphracts themselves. Launching the attack at the enemy commander reflected a recognition that battles were often won by the death or flight of the enemy

general. The cataphracts led conquests of Antioch, Syria, and northern Palestine under Nicephoras Phocas and John Tzimisces.

The increased importance of tagmatic forces and the trend toward selectivity in calling up the themes reinforced the effects of internal peace on interior themes, whose troops began to lose their military training and value. This provided further scope for economizing on costs and increasing revenues as the government began collecting payments from some thematic soldiers in lieu of their service in person, using the income to pay the tagmata. But the decay of the thematic forces held potential dangers and was connected to deeper social transformations stimulated by offensive warfare. The military aristocracy of the provinces, who held most of the positions of command in the increasingly numerous themes and the tagmata, and whose household retainers were often a major part of the tagmata, posed the biggest threat. As the population increased and the empire became more secure, land became more valuable, and the class interests of the aristocracy came into conflict with the interests of the central government. In addition, the extensive reconquest of the Near East that the military aristocrats seemingly envisioned threatened the dominance of Constantinople and its civil elite within the empire.

Basil II fought hard against this trend. He secured his throne only with the help of the Varangian Guard, a body of 6000 Scandinavian-Russian heavy infantry hired en masse, against the eastern tagmata, and dependence on bodies of foreign mercenaries increasingly characterized the Byzantine army thereafter. Save for completing the conquest of Bulgaria, which kept eastern forces busy away from their bases of power, he largely called a halt to expansion, especially eastward. The triumph of Constantinopolitan interests under Basil came at a cost, however.

The Road to Disaster: 1025–1081

By 1025, the Byzantine Empire was larger than it had been since the days of Heraclius, prosperous, and much more powerful militarily than any of its neighbors. Yet fifty years later, the empire and its army were irretrievably damaged. What happened?

The empire back into Roman times had always been dependent on strong leadership for military success. The worst foreign invasions and defeats almost always came in the wake of civil wars, succession crises, or rebellions that weakened and distracted the empire's armed forces. The fifty years after Basil II's death saw just such a period of disputed successions and weak, nonmilitary emperors and empresses, the effects of which compounded ongoing structural problems. Through 1042, the empire remained generally successful in its wars and even expanded its influence in Italy. But then a serious decline set in.

The army in 1042 was bloated, with far more men on the payroll than there were effectives. A successful military emperor, with the support of the active army, could probably have decommissioned the least useful units and cut back the pay of others. But the army as an institution resisted such measures from less proven leaders. Cuts therefore tended to come in the form of lighter coins or debased currency, which reduced the entire army's effective pay, and neglect of the armed forces as a whole. This led to revolts by generals and the aristocracy of the provinces. The emperors between 1042 and 1067, mistrustful of the aristocracy and army, relied increasingly on foreign mercenaries for their personal military support. Constantine X did decommission a large group of thematic forces around 1050, releasing them from service in exchange for a tax. But

because of his fear of revolt by active soldiers, he dismissed not the rusty interior themes but the most active ones, in the Armenian frontier provinces—precisely the region now facing a dangerous new threat, the Seljuk Turks.

A competent military leader, Romanus Diogenes, took the throne in 1067 and set about desperately trying to retrain the army. Attempting to stabilize the eastern frontier, he met the Turks at Manzikert in 1071 with a mixed force of mercenary, thematic, and tagmatic troops. However, treachery by relatives of the late Constantine X led to his defeat and capture. Civil war broke out, and over the next decade the Turks were allowed to overrun almost all of Asia Minor. The entire army, themes and tagmata, disintegrated. The last western tagmata fell fighting the Normans at Dyrrhachium in 1081 under Alexius I Comnenus.

Alexius would manage to rebuild the empire after 1081. But he could not rebuild the army. Units that could trace their history back 1000 years ceased to exist, and, with their end, the direct line of Roman military tradition also died out.

CONCLUSION

The complementary histories of the Islamic and Byzantine worlds down to 1050 demonstrate the importance of political organization to military success. Byzantium survived the attacks of a Caliphate that deployed vastly superior forces largely because of the cohesion of its political-military system with its focus on a Constantinople whose walls and naval defenses proved impregnable. But it could resume the offensive only when the political unity of Islam disintegrated, a result of internal forces, not of Byzantine pressure. The Caliphate and its successor states in the Islamic world, on the other hand, found efficient application of their resources to warfare hindered by the problematic relationship of state

and society that developed in the wake of the initial Arab conquests.

The central role the state assumed, whether positively or negatively, in the histories of Byzantium and Islam to 1050 contrasts interestingly with western Europe, where military force arose more out of the fabric of social relations and class structures. As a result, the state in western Europe was more a product of a sociomilitary system than the controlling feature of the military landscape that it was for the other heirs of the Roman state. Relations among all three civilizations and the nomadic world of the steppes would develop further in the age of the Crusades, a story taken up in Chapter 11.

SUGGESTED READINGS

Crone, Patricia. *Slaves on Horses. The Evolution of the Islamic Polity.* Cambridge: Cambridge University Press, 1980. A fundamental analysis in broad comparative perspective of the rise of slave soldiers in Islam and the shaping of Islamic states.

Donner, F. M. *The Early Islamic Conquests.* Princeton: Princeton University Press, 1981. The best narrative account of pre-Islamic

Arabia and the early campaigns, though perhaps too accepting at times of details in Arab sources.

Frye, R., ed. *The Cambridge History of Iran. Vol. 4: From the Arab Invasions to the Saljuqs.* Cambridge: Cambridge University Press, 1975. A standard, comprehensive account; useful, if dated in interpretive terms.

Gordon, M. *The Breaking of a Thousand Swords: A History of the Turkish Community of Samarra.* Albany: SUNY Press, 2001. The best general account of the rise of Turkish military influence in the Islamic world.

Haldon, J. F. *Warfare, State and Society in the Byzantine World, 565–1204.* London: Routledge, 1999. An excellent synthesis of the interrelationships of social formation, politics, and military power in Byzantium. Both Haldon and Whittow (below) stress the small size and limitations of Byzantine armies. See also his *Byzantine Praetorians* and *Byzantium in the Seventh Century.*

Hawting, G. R. *The First Dynasty of Islam: The Umayyad Caliphate,* AD *661–750,* 2nd ed. London: Routledge, 2000. A solid analysis of the dynamics of Umayyad rule and the political problems the dynasty faced.

Kaegi, Walter. *Byzantium and the Early Islamic Conquests.* (Cambridge: Cambridge University Press, 1992. A detailed examination of the early Byzantine–Arab wars, though more from the Byzantine perspective.

Kennedy, Hugh. *The Armies of the Caliphs. Military and Society in the Early Islamic State.* London: Routledge, 2001. A thorough and balanced survey of the armed forces of the Arab conquests and the Caliphate to the mid-tenth century. Especially strong on the fiscal relationship of state and army.

McGeer, Eric. *Sowing the Dragon's Teeth. Byzantine Warfare in the Tenth Century.* Washington, DC: Dumbarton Oaks, 1994. Both an edition and a critical study of Byzantine military manuals, with much detail on army composition and tactics in the tenth-century age of Byzantine expansion.

Treadgold, Warren. *Byzantium and Its Army 284–1081.* Stanford: Stanford University Press, 1999. A survey of the linked development of the Byzantine state and army, with emphasis on institutions and finances as a window on army size, which he sees, unconvincingly, as much larger than Haldon and Whittow do.

Whittow, Mark. *The Making of Byzantium, 600–1025.* Berkeley: University of California Press, 1996. An excellent reinterpretation of Byzantine history, with a revealing focus on political and military strategy in the broad context of Near Eastern geography, economics, and society.

CHAPTER 9

From Cavalry to Conscripts: China, 400–1100

The collapse of the Han dynasty in 220 CE had serious repercussions in China and Inner Asia. Most important, it left China divided into several independent states for the first time since the Eastern Zhou period (771–221 BCE). The northern Chinese states during this period of disunion (220–589), like much of Europe after the fall of the Western Roman Empire, came under the control and influence of various wandering, raiding peoples. The southern Chinese states, although much more securely preserving the cultural legacy of the Han dynasty, were eventually conquered by the north in the sixth century CE. The result was a tension between the two regions of China and between China and its nomadic neighbors that characterized the entire period from the fall of the Han into the 1100s.

The Tang dynasty (618–907) mostly succeeded in controlling the nomadic threat; throughout the Northern Song dynasty (960–1135), the nomadic peoples had the upper hand. Chinese society changed in connection with this armed conflict: At the beginning of this period, military matters and warriors played prominent roles in Chinese society. By the twelfth century, these roles had been reduced significantly, and Chinese society had been decisively civilianized.

THE PERIOD OF DISUNION, 220–589

The period of disunion in China saw north China ruled by a succession of nomadic dynasties from the north and west that relied on their mostly cavalry armies to maintain control of the region. Nearly all of these dynasties established dual administrations, in which the Chinese areas were ruled primarily by Chinese in civil matters, while the non-Chinese peoples and the military as a whole were ruled separately by the tribal rulers. They usually took care to maintain their tribal armies as the mainstay of their rule. The dynasties took care to keep their armies free from Chinese civilian control or even administration.

All of these conquest dynasties—indeed, every native Chinese dynasty throughout the history of China—had to pay special attention to threats from other tribal peoples in the north. Failure to do so led several times to changes in the groups that ruled all or part of northern China. (See Chapter 6 for more on the Central Asian nomads.) One of the most successful of these conquest dynasties was the Northern Wei (386–534), which eventually gained control of nearly all of northern China.

Military Systems

The Northern Wei dynasty was founded by a Turkish people called the Toba, who were, like all the steppe peoples, horse-riding nomads. The Toba rulers soon saw the advantages of Chinese-style rulership, with a theoretically all-powerful ruler, and began a process of selective sinicization. For example, in 398, the Northern Wei ruler ordered the construction of a Chinese-style capital city, complete with Confucian halls and a library. Yet the early Northern Wei rulers understood that to maintain their control of north China, they had to retain their military edge over their competitors on the steppe lands. This consisted primarily of their tribal cavalry forces, but the Northern Wei also recognized that their control of north China provided them with advantages not possessed by their competitors. The most striking advantage was the vast number of people in China compared with the steppe lands. While numbers are difficult to ascertain with certainty, the Northern Wei ruled over a land of at least 30 million people, and probably many more. The Northern Wei, then, utilized its main elite military force of Toba and other steppe cavalry to put constant pressure on the northern nomads. To protect its territories in China, the dynasty established a string of garrisons along the frontiers, commanded by Toba nobles and consisting of a mixed grouping of Chinese and other nomadic tribesmen. These garrisons defended the frontier from nomadic incursions and provided a ready force to assist in expeditions into the steppes.

Although the Northern Wei system had its unique features, much of the system resembled that of the Cao Wei dynasty of the Three Kingdoms period (222–265), in which vast numbers of people were resettled along the frontiers, provided with agricultural land, and utilized as a militia to defend the borders of the dynasty. The Northern Wei system initially relied more on an integration of settled Chinese and tribal peoples, but, gradually, these garrisons became quite large, and many of the officers in them came from Chinese aristocratic families allied with the Toba nobility. Eventually, a separate military class of Chinese was established by the Northern Wei in these garrisons, which were expected to be fully self-supporting. Soldiers and their families were registered as military households. Soldiers trained with their units and, when not training, were expected to engage in the agricultural activities that supplied food for the garrison. The rest of the military family was likewise tied to the land, working on communal plots, the production of which was turned over to the unit commanders.

Members of this military class could only marry from within it and were restricted to the area of the garrison; special permission was required to travel outside the garrison district. And these military families were expected to provide soldiers for generations. Although the soldiers themselves were apparently treated relatively well, for most of the members of this military class, their lives were not much better than that of slaves, and most hoped to get out of this situation. However, military households could not change their status (that is, become registered as civilian households) without going through a complicated process. Basically, only the Northern Wei emperor could change their status, and this was only rarely done.

Sinicization

Over time, the Northern Wei dynasty became more sinicized and neglected matters along its frontiers. The lot of the military households became worse,

and new military households were added by settling the garrisons with the families of criminals or those thought to be rebellious. There was enormous deterioration in the quality of these soldiers, though this process was not sudden. The tribal elements of the garrisons for the most part became indistinguishable from the Chinese, and by the early sixth century, their military effectiveness was highly questionable.

The Northern Wei dynasty moved its capital to Luoyang in 494, an area deep within the Chinese world, and the sinification of the Toba Turks was almost complete. Chinese-style walls were erected around the main Northern Wei cities, and sinicization went so far that the wearing of steppe-style clothing was prohibited. Neglect of the military garrisons on the frontier eventually led to a massive rebellion by many of the garrisons. Large numbers of the dynasty's officials in the region were slaughtered, but, instead of forcibly suppressing the rebellion, the court agreed to resettle most of the military families in the interior of China, which was more fertile than the lands on the frontiers. The basic system remained intact, and was even added to, but its genesis as a frontier defense system had been seemingly forgotten.

Eventually, the Northern Wei split into two new dynasties—a sinicized dynasty in the east and a nomadic dynasty in the west, more in the tradition of the conquest dynasties of the age. The more nomadic dynasty in the west, calling itself the Western Wei (505–556), attempted to reverse the sinicization process. In an attempt to turn Chinese into mounted archers, they required all soldiers to take a Turkish surname, to wear Turkish-style clothing, and to obey commands issued in Turkish.

THE SUI DYNASTY, 581–618

The attempt at reverse sinicization would probably not have been effective in any case, but it did not last long. Rebellions broke out throughout north China, many of these upheavals the backwash of the overthrow of the Northern Wei decades earlier. By 581, a new Chinese dynasty, the Sui, had unified north China, and in less than a decade, it went on to unify nearly all of China (Figure 9.1). The new Sui dynasty initiated a long period of centralized rule in China, instituting a ruling system more reminiscent of the Legalist Qin dynasty than the more Confucian Han dynasty, though most Sui offices had titles taken from the Han. It

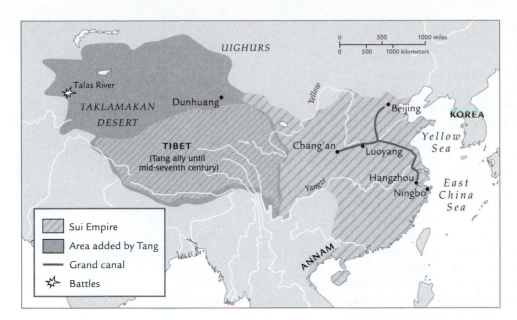

Figure 9.1 Territories of the Sui and Tang Dynasties, as Well as Korea's Silla Kingdom, Between 589 and 907

engaged in a massive program of military expansion, including allied nomadic tribesmen as well as vast numbers of Chinese recruits.

Sui Expansionism

In organizing his military, Sui Wendi, the first Sui emperor, made some significant changes to the previous systems established by the conquest dynasties. The military household class was abolished, and all families were registered as civilians. Although many families might be required to provide sons for the military, this resembled conscription rather than a separate hereditary military class. The military itself was reorganized into twelve military districts, with a trusted general in charge of each. For his mounted forces, Wendi relied primarily on steppe tribesmen, but these forces were kept on the frontiers, to be used more as a buffer than as an integral part of the Sui military.

One aspect of Wendi's Legalism was the need not only to unify the Chinese world but to expand beyond its borders as well. In particular, he took steps to subdue the Turks on China's northern and northwestern borders. He was able to accomplish this through diplomacy and the good fortune that, in the late sixth and early seventh centuries, the Turks were divided and quarrelsome among themselves. His policies toward the Turks were followed by his successor, who if anything was even better at playing steppe politics. But the early Sui had uneven success here and elsewhere.

In Vietnam, a successful invasion was undone by epidemics in the army; Vietnam remained a tributary state rather than coming under direct Chinese rule. Sui Wendi and his successor, Sui Yangdi, both planned to subjugate the Korean kingdom of Koguryo, and both were unsuccessful despite huge investments of men and materials. Korean delaying tactics led to logistical breakdowns, exacerbated by summer rains and severe winter weather. Turkish allied cavalry units failed to show up. In the end, the massive effort destabilized the Sui rather than accomplishing the conquest of Korea. By 617, the dynasty had fallen into chaos.

THE TANG, 618–907

The Early Tang: Challenges and Successes

Seizing on the Sui disasters, Li Yüan, a high-ranking Sui general, rose against the emperor and went on to establish the Tang dynasty (see Figure 9.1). The men under his command on the day of his revolt totaled roughly 30,000, both infantry and cavalry. Like many of the generals who hoped to replace the Sui, he was able to enlist the aid of several thousand Turkish cavalrymen. By the time Li Yüan had captured the city of Changan, which was proclaimed the Tang capital, he had picked up an additional 200,000 men. Many of these were men who had deserted the Sui army during and after the disastrous Korean campaigns. Li Yüan divided this force into twelve divisions, each led by a trusted general, for there was still much fighting to come before China was securely in Tang hands.

These were true divisions, expected to be able to operate on their own with a full complement of various types of weapons and soldiers, both infantry and cavalry. In addition, the soldiers were allotted lands on which their families were to be settled. The production of these lands was to make the divisions self-sufficient in supplies, an institutional continuation of the Northern Wei and Sui military systems. Like the Sui founder, Li Yüan and his son and successor, Li Shimin, understood the importance of pacifying both China and the lands to the north. This was why Li Yüan took such care to settle large numbers of his soldiers on lands near to the steppes. Li Shimin, better known by his reign title of Tang Taizong, was particularly successful at this, using both military and diplomatic strategies to become not only emperor of the Chinese but Qaghan (essentially, "Emperor") of the Turks as well.

Unlike members of the traditional ruling classes of southern China, but like Tang Taizong, many of the leading figures of the early decades of the Tang were very comfortable with steppe traditions such as hunting and the relative freedom of women—a result of the intermingling of Chinese and nomadic peoples during the period of disunion. Applying this knowledge, Taizong took advantage of disunion among the various steppe tribes to insinuate himself into their politics and feuds. The result was that many of the nomadic tribes became an arm of the Tang military system. Taizong thus solved—at least for a time—the main problem plaguing Chinese armies since the Zhou period: the lack of horses, needed to create a credible cavalry arm. The nomads made up the bulk of the Tang cavalry during the reign of Taizong, and they were called on at times to assist in his campaigns for the consolidation of Tang rule within China proper. Those few times steppe tribes refused to heed his orders, he sent Tang armies, aided by other steppe cavalry, to bring them to heel.

Taizong was accepted due to his adaptation to steppe traditions, especially his knowledge of steppe politics and military tactics. Frequently, he led his soldiers in person, often when outnumbered by enemy forces, reportedly having four horses shot out from under him during the course of his campaigns. He was also acquainted with the steppe military tactic of the feigned retreat, adapting this tactic successfully

Tang Taizong   Tang Taizong, second emperor and co-founder with his father of the Tang dynasty, demonstrated a combination of military and political skill that made him one of China's great emperors. His mastery of the nomadic threat is especially notable.

from its use with cavalry forces to use with primarily infantry forces (see the Sources box "Tang Taizong: 'Questions and Answers'").

Later Tang emperors were unable to maintain the sort of personal authority that was necessary to control the steppe nomads. But nomadic internal rivalries allowed the Tang dynasty to keep its northern frontier fairly secure for a few decades after Taizong's death. Even after Tang control on the frontiers weakened later in the eighth century, the dynasty could often call on nomadic armies for assistance. But Tibetan invasions and the An Lushan Rebellion in the mid-eighth century, coupled with ongoing transformations of the Chinese economy and society, would finally destroy the almost symbiotic system of nomadic cavalry alongside settled Chinese infantry.

The Tang Army

The Fubing System   The Tang dynasty, especially from the time of Tang Taizong, consciously worked

SOURCES

Tang Taizong: "Questions and Answers"

Tang Taizong, the second Tang dynasty emperor, was a skilled military leader as well as civil administrator. His military leadership came from practical experience and through study of the Chinese military classics. In the following selection, the emperor engages in discussion of his military experience with Li Ching, possibly the Tang dynasty's most successful military commander, who was also deeply knowledgeable regarding the military classics. The emperor wishes to place his military experience in the context of the ancient Chinese military classics.

■ ■ ■

The Taizong said: "At the battle in which I destroyed Song Lao-sheng, when the fronts clashed our rightward army retreated somewhat. I then personally led our elite cavalry to race down from the Southern plain, cutting across in a sudden attack on them. After Lao-sheng's troops were cut off to the rear, we severely crushed them, and subsequently captured him. Were these orthodox troops? Or unorthodox troops?"

Li Ching [one of Taizong's generals and strategists] replied: "Your majesty is a natural military genius, not one who learns by studying. I have examined the art of war as practiced from the Yellow Emperor on down. First be orthodox, and afterward unorthodox; first be benevolent and righteous, and afterward employ the balance of power and craftiness. Moreover, in the battle at Huo-I the army was mobilized out of righteousness, so it was orthodox. When Jian-cheng fell off his horse and the Army of the Right withdrew somewhat, it was unorthodox."

The Taizong said: "At that time our slight withdrawal almost defeated our great affair, so how can you refer to it as unorthodox?"

Li Ching replied: "In general, when troops advance to the front it is orthodox, when they [deliberately] retreat to the rear it is unorthodox. Moreover, if the Army of the Right had not withdrawn somewhat, how could you have gotten Lao-sheng to come forward? The *Art of War* states: 'Display profits to entice them, create disorder [in their forces] and take them.' Lao-sheng did not know how to employ his troops. He relied on courage and made a hasty advance. He did not anticipate his rear being severed nor being captured by your majesty. This is what is referred to as using the unorthodox as the orthodox."

The Taizong said: "As for Huo Qubing's tactics unintentionally cohering with those of Sunzi and Wuzi, was it really so? When our Army of the Right withdrew, Gaozu [Taizong's father and the emperor] turned pale. But then I attacked vigorously and, on the contrary, it became advantageous for us. This unknowingly cohered with Sunzi and Wuzi. My lord certainly knows their words."

The Taizong said: "Whenever an army withdraws can it be termed unorthodox?"

Li Ching said: "It is not so. Whenever the soldiers retreat with their flags confused and disordered, the sounds of the large and small drums not responding to each other, and their orders shouted out in a clamor, this is true defeat, not unorthodox strategy. If the flags are ordered, the drums respond to each other, and the commands and orders seem unified, then even though they may be retreating and running, it is not a defeat and must be a case of unorthodox strategy. The *Art of War* says: 'Do not pursue feigned retreats.' It also says: 'Although capable display incapability.' These all refer to the unorthodox."

SOURCE: Translated by Paul Lococo.

---

to create a system whereby the dynasty was primarily defended by citizen-soldiers. Like the Han dynasty, the Tang was suspicious of large professional armies, believing that skilled professionals were much harder to control or to keep loyal than an army composed of free citizens. The Tang also believed that some skilled professionals were necessary, especially for the expeditions the dynasty planned in both the north and south and as a mobile strike force. As we have seen, the cavalry arm was primarily made up of nomadic horsemen who could be both used as a buffer and called on to assist in military expeditions. In the next section, we will discuss the skilled professional force that was kept near the capital. In this section, we will focus on the large forces of citizen-soldiers called the Fubing Army.

The term *Fubing* has been translated in various ways, the most common being "militia." This is not satisfactory. Militia usually refers to men who are soldiers only part-time or part of the year; the rest of the time, they engage in their primary occupation. The members of the Fubing, however, were primarily professional soldiers, members of a standing army who spent all or nearly all of the year in military units, training or engaging in security duties.

The confusion in meaning comes from how the Fubing were recruited, and, sometimes, the Chinese sources from the Tang period are themselves unclear as to what the functions of the Fubing were. Nonetheless, in tracing the evolution of the Fubing, we learn that in the early Tang, at least up until the end of the eighth century, it was the most effective part of the Tang military, maintaining the security of the Tang frontier and assisting in several of the early Tang military expeditions. The Fubing commanders were some of the best in the whole Tang military.

Li Yüan established the capital of Tang China at Changan, located in the Guanzhong Province. As we saw earlier, by this time, he had over 200,000 men in his command. Although more fighting would be necessary to establish control over the rest of China, Li Yüan needed to ensure that the northern frontier was secure. To that end, many of these soldiers and their families were settled in agricultural communities. When additional soldiers were needed for his armies, Li Yüan had these families furnish them, along with their equipment and weapons. As these communities were expected to be self-supporting, the Tang court was spared a large expense. When this system—obviously extensively copied from the Sui military system—was expanded to include all ten of the provinces under Tang Taizong, the Tang had seemingly solved all three of the main Chinese military concerns. That is, there were military forces on the northern frontier to protect against nomadic threats; scattered military units were available for internal uses; and, because all these forces were self-supporting, there was little drain on imperial finances.

When the Fubing system was established, there were 623 communities, each with 800–1200 soldiers plus their families, making a total military force of well over 600,000. While the soldiers trained, their families were required to work their assigned lands, much as in the Sui and the Northern Wei earlier. But a key difference was that during the Tang dynasty, little private landownership was allowed in China, and all land was divided up according to a very complicated formula. This Equitable-Field system was implemented throughout the early Tang and was the basis for the Fubing military system. Those communities classified as military were allotted a certain amount of land, which in the early decades of the Fubing system was quite large. In return for providing soldiers and supplying military needs, these communities were exempted from many taxes. Officers from the Imperial Guards in the capital were dispatched to the Fubing communities to oversee the administration of the lands and to lead the soldiers when necessary. This was to prevent local commanders from bonding too tightly with their men and gaining too much independent power, though lower-ranking officers usually came from within the ranks.

Recruitment was not by universal conscription, nor was it a strictly hereditary duty as under previous systems such as the Sui. Instead, roughly once every three years, officers of the Imperial Guards would circuit the Fubing communities and recruit, choosing on the basis of wealth, physical fitness, and number of adult males in a military household. Though the age of recruitment varied over time, generally a man was enlisted from age 20, and he would serve until age 60, when he could retire. Membership in the early decades was considered an honor, and those families with wealth and influence were able to get a higher proportion of their sons accepted. It is not clear how rigidly the physical requirements were enforced, but recruits were supposed to be in good health and were tested on physical strength. Those from frontier communities were also tested on their horsemanship.

After being accepted as a Fubing soldier, the new recruit and his family were expected to provide all of his rations, armor, and weapons. Groups of families were required to provide horses, mules, or oxen for use by the Fubing. This was a relatively cost-free way for the Tang to maintain a standing army, its only expense being the allocated land.

The three main duties of the Fubing were, in order of importance, garrison troops on the frontier, guardsmen in the capital area of Changan, and combat troops on expeditions. Local commanders of the Fubing were expressly forbidden to move their troops out of their camps without authorization from the court. There were exceptions in emergencies, but a commander who did move his men without prior approval had to notify the court immediately. Punishment for failing to follow these rules was exile or even death for the offending commander. Throughout the seventh century, the Fubing acquitted itself well along the frontiers and also maintained the Tang hold over the newly unified southern territories.

Guard duty in the capital area was considered a particularly important function of the Fubing by the Tang court. A complicated rotation system was devised to determine which Fubing units had guard duty and when. At any given time, there were tens of thousands of Fubing soldiers in various defensive positions in Changan and the immediate area. They were not the only military forces in the capital, but they were considered a check on the Palace Army that was supposedly the personal military force of the emperor (see below).

Taking part in Tang military campaigns was the third duty of the Fubing. Rarely did the Fubing campaign on their own. Most often, they went into combat with large numbers of other Tang military units. The Korean campaigns, for example, were manned primarily by troops recruited from regions near Korea, but the Fubing were often the backbone of the expeditionary force. Also, an expeditionary force sent to subdue the kingdom of Nanchao (the present-day Chinese province of Yunnan) contained a large number of Fubing soldiers.

There is general agreement that through the 600s the Fubing were a competent, efficient military force that remained loyal to the Tang court. However, changes in Tang China's economy and society in the early- to mid-eighth century led to the decline of the Fubing. The Equitable-Field system was without doubt the foundation of the Fubing military system, but in the early 700s, aristocratic families, government officials, religious orders, and others with influence were gaining effective private ownership of land. Many of the Fubing lands passed into private hands, and many military households saw their share of land reduced drastically. Service in the Fubing became less prestigious, and families increasingly saw classification as a military household as a burden and attempted various means to have their status changed to civilian. Many families attached themselves to Buddhist temples or religious orders as a quick way to relieve themselves of the bur-

Tang Horseman   Horses, with and without riders, were a frequent subject of Tang ceramic makers, indicating their prestige in the culture. This rider wears Central-Asian-style headgear and clothing.

den of supplying the Fubing. Many others fled to newly reclaimed lands, becoming tenant-farmers or laborers on the lands of the wealthy in preference to service as a Fubing household, testament to how burdensome that service had become. Reports in the 740s told of massive desertions from the Fubing armies, at the same time that fierce Tibetan armies were raiding the northern and northwestern frontiers. The Fubing system was formally abolished in favor of a system of voluntary, recruited soldiers in 749.

The Palace Army   In addition to the Fubing units that were expected to be composed of citizen-soldiers, the Tang maintained a professional force at the capital of Changan, designed as the personal army of the emperor. This was the Palace Army, composed originally of those units used by Li Yüan in his revolt against the Sui dynasty. Often, this army is called the "Northern Army" because it was originally posted in a defensive position just north of Changan, as well as in the northern sector of the city. By Tang Taizong's time, nearly all of the soldiers in this army were from noble or wealthy families located in the capital region.

At its height of effectiveness in the late seventh century, there were probably no more than 60,000 men in the Palace Army. In this early period, it was the core of Tang military strength and even included a cavalry element. Members of this army trained constantly together, and those who were tall and strong and showed ability at horse-archery were admitted to the cavalry, commanded mostly by specially recruited Turkish officers.

Other than some of the cavalry officers, most officers in the Palace Army came from the Imperial Guards. Indeed, most of the top Fubing officers were also Imperial Guardsmen. The Imperial Guards were recruited exclusively from the families of nobles and former high-ranking officials, and some have seen this as a modified version of the "hostage system" that had been used by the Han dynasty to maintain some measure of control over powerful families. As long as membership in the Imperial Guards was esteemed, there was a constant flow of competent, energetic officers for both the Palace Army and the Fubing. But by the late seventh century, the Imperial Guards—and therefore the Palace Army—had become involved in imperial succession struggles, and their effectiveness had diminished considerably.

The empress Wu (690–705) greatly expanded the Palace Army, enlisting men from outside the traditional recruiting grounds. This could have been an invigorating move that revitalized the military efficiency of the Palace Army; but, instead, a major unit of the Palace Army was used in 705 to depose the empress, and various other units later were frequently called on to assist in court intrigues. During the outbreak of the An Lushan Rebellion in 755, the Palace Army simply melted away as the rebel forces approached. Only 1000 of the supposedly elite force were left to accompany the emperor as he fled the capital.

The Decline of Tang Military Efficiency

New Frontier Armies Constant and growing threats from a newly unified Tibetan kingdom in the late seventh century demonstrated the increasing feebleness of the Fubing military system. The Tang relied to a large degree on their Uighur and Turkish nomadic allies, who by this time could no longer be considered

even remotely under the control of Tang China. The Uighurs had been especially effective in assisting the Tang, but they did not come cheap. By the 670s, vast amounts of silk and other goods were necessary to buy Uighur assistance. When the payments slacked, the Uighurs would strike within China to exact payment and, since the Fubing garrisons were significantly weakened, their raids were often successful. To lessen reliance on the hired Uighur cavalry and protect the frontier, the Tang replaced the Fubing system with one of long-serving volunteer frontier armies, led by imperially appointed military governors possessing a good deal of civil as well as military authority.

For military encampments for these new troops, the Tang constructed massive fortresses across the three provinces that bordered the steppe frontier. The frontier fortresses were connected to and communicated with each other and the capital by post roads and beacon towers. In some cases, the fortresses were constructed on former Turkish territory. While the Turks were away in battle with tribes further west, the Tang army moved in swiftly to secure the area, constructing fortresses and denying the Turks some of their prime pasturelands. By the 720s, there were well over 65,000 soldiers with 15,000 horses stationed in Guanzhong alone, with comparable numbers in the adjoining two provinces.

This entailed an enormous expense, and, though the Tang was a fairly prosperous time in China's history, this level of outlay proved difficult to maintain. Unlike the Fubing forces, these frontier armies were not self-supporting, nor could they be, with many of the soldiers posted relatively far north in lands less suited to settled agriculture. The difficulty of paying these forces prompted dangerous political arrangements. Taxing authority was given over to the military governors, who increasingly ruled independently of the court.

Until 750, the system appeared to be working. Tang China faced a series of ups and downs in terms of security along their frontiers, but none of the problems they encountered was very serious. Trade through the Tang possessions in Central Asia continued fairly smoothly, and the nomadic peoples on all fronts were, if not fully pacified, at least not of serious concern. But the year 751 saw three major military disasters for the Tang. The first occurred at the Talas River on the western frontier, where a major Chinese force under the veteran Korean general Gao Xianzhi was decisively

HIGHLIGHTS

The Battle of Talas River, 751

The Battle of Talas River was fought in Central Asia in July 751, with possibly momentous historical consequences. The battle was fought between Muslim Arab armies with some Turkish allies against Chinese armies—led by the Korean general Gao Xianzhi (Kao Hsien-chih)—and their Turkish Qarluq allies. Tang dynasty China was at the height of its power and influence, while the Muslim Arabs were still in their expansionary phase.

In the mid-seventh century, Arab armies destroyed the Sassanid Empire in Persia and over the next decades continued to expand the Muslim area of influence and control. By the 740s, the Arabs were particularly active in Central Asia, forming alliances with various tribes and nomadic groups. The Tang court expended much military effort to blunt and even reverse what it saw as Arabian encroachment in its sphere of influence. Chinese armies in and near the region were large and commanded by experienced generals, most of whom, like Gao Xianzhi, were of non-Han Chinese ancestry. When in 747 negotiations between the Arabs and a Tibetan kingdom threatened to result in a dangerous alliance, Tang armies under the command of General Gao marched swiftly to defeat the Tibetans in several engagements. The following year, Gao once again took to war in Tashkent to prevent Turkish tribes there from allying with the Arabs.

The Tang court's ongoing efforts to maintain its position in the region have been seen by some as an untenable long-term proposition, as many of the tribal groups in the region greatly desired a counterweight to mighty—and domineering—China. Still, Tang armies in the 740s were quite successful in keeping their Central Asian opponents divided and militarily crushing those who resisted Chinese hegemony. These armies were able to impose order primarily through the use of swift-moving cavalry forces and the establishment of infantry garrisons to maintain the peace. Chinese diplomacy also helped provide Turkish allies to assist the armies.

General Gao's forces met the Arab armies (which included a fair number of Turkish allies) near the city of Talas (along the river of the same name) in late July 751. It is not clear what the exact numbers are, but both sides were roughly evenly matched with about 30,000 troops each, mostly cavalry. The fighting was reportedly fierce, with neither side gaining a clear advantage. On the second or third day of fighting, the Qarluqs, Turkish allies of the Chinese, changed sides, but Gao was able to retreat to the city in fairly good order. Darkness ended fighting for the day, and Gao gathered with his commanders to decide how to proceed. It was decided that risk of decisive defeat was too great, and so the Chinese armies began to withdraw. Arab forces attacked the retreating Chinese, whose escape route now became jammed by panicked men and animals. Gao's most disciplined units slaughtered those blocking their way and so evaded capture.

This decisive defeat effectively ended the expansion of Chinese influence westward and enabled the continued expansion of Muslim Arab influence farther eastward. It also disrupted Buddhist influence along the Silk Road. Tang China had been thought to be the most powerful land in the world, and people all along China's borders had been fearful of upsetting the Tang. But everything changed with this defeat. When many of the remaining Chinese armies withdrew from Central Asia due to the civil upheavals of the An Lushan Rebellion, Muslim armies were well positioned to take advantage.

defeated by a combined Arab-Turkish force (see the Highlights box "The Battle of Talas River, 751"). Another Chinese army, on the northeastern frontier, led by the Turkish-Soghdian general An Lushan, was decisively defeated by a predominantly Khitan nomadic force. Then, a major Chinese army was defeated and wiped out in an invasion of the Nanchao kingdom in the southwest, leaving the Sichuan area of China vulnerable to renewed Tibetan attacks. The combination of defeats seriously destabilized the dynasty.

Transformation and Decline   The Tang dynasty faced two big problems in trying to rebuild its military forces after the disasters of the mid-700s. First, although the large frontier armies did not fare well in combat against foreign forces, internally, their commanders continued to accrue tremendous independent power. The threat to central authority posed by military commanders and the great warrior aristocracy became acute in the 800s as commanders gained control of the civil government in their provinces and won the right to hereditary succession to their commands. In the end, independent warlords brought down the dynasty—a development that would significantly influence the military policy of the succeeding Song dynasty.

Second, the increasing demographic and economic influence of southern China in the empire as a whole had significant ramifications for the social and military structure. The south was even more unsuitable terrain for raising horses and maintaining cavalry traditions than the north of China. As a result, Chinese reliance on nomadic tribes for cavalry became even greater at the same time as the rulers of China became even more distanced from the culturally syncretic milieu that had produced the leaders of the early Tang. Thus, Chinese control over their nomadic allies waned, and cavalry warfare became more and more divergent from native Chinese military traditions. This, too, would fuel the Song reaction against great warrior aristocratic families, who most strongly embraced those traditions.

Events reached crisis proportions because of the independent power of military commanders. An Lushan, the most powerful Tang general and a court favorite, rebelled in 755. After seven years of chaotic fighting, the various rebel forces were finally defeated, but only with significant aid from nomadic Uighur horsemen, who became a problem in turn. A succession of emperors rebuilt a central army around the core of a loyal frontier army; this Shence Army was led by eunuchs, reflecting an effort to solve the problem of commander loyalty. Though temporarily successful—the Shence Army was instrumental in putting down another rebellion by military governors in 781—the institution had little success controlling the nomadic frontier because of its central location in the capital. Further, its power was steadily diluted by aristocratic influence, money shortages caused by the independence of the military governors, and involvement in court politics. Increasingly enfeebled, the Tang dynasty finally fell in 907, ushering in several decades of warfare that would accelerate the underlying changes in China's political, social, and military structure.

THE ERA OF THE FIVE DYNASTIES, 907–960

The Five Dynasties era in Chinese history (907–960) was a time a constant warfare, both internally and against foreign invaders and raiders. The major cities in north China were attacked and devastated several times in these decades. Eunuchs were slaughtered by the thousands, and those aristocratic and elite families without military support or ties who had been lucky enough to survive the destruction of the late Tang were almost completely wiped out. The label "Five Dynasties" is actually misleading, as in central and southern China there were at least fourteen dynasties established, each with its own emperor claiming universal rule over China. Traditionally, though, the southern dynasties have been called the "Ten Kingdoms." The Five Dynasties refers to those that were established in the north, each also boasting its own emperor and claiming universal rule. All of these dynasties, north and south, were established by generals leading their armies in wars of conquest or in military coups. Supporting these large mixed armies of Chinese and nomadic soldiers was very expensive, and, in addition to the threat of destruction of their lands, the peasants faced enormous taxes to pay for the armies. One innovative general during this era enhanced his financial status through the destruction or confiscation of thousands of Buddhist temples and monasteries.

The main reason for the short life of the many dynasties in this era was their inability to create a core of loyal officers and troops. Each general-ruler fought his neighbors, trying to take or defend territory. Successful subordinates in high commands rarely felt a strong sense of loyalty to their ruler, often initiating coups before the new dynasty could be firmly established. The last of the Five Dynasties, the Later Zhou, was seemingly on the verge of breaking this cycle, systematically reuniting Chinese territory while creating an elite, loyal palace guard army, when the ruler was killed in battle.

Ironically, the commander of the Later Zhou's palace guard army, Zhao Kuangyin, succeeded in founding a new dynasty, the Song, that went on to unify most of China and survive in some manner for

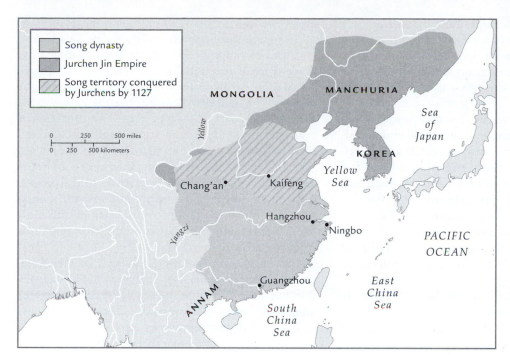

Figure 9.2 Song China and Its Northern Enemies

more than three centuries. Zhao, crowned as Song Taizu, used this palace guard as the cornerstone of a refashioned military system that was in most respects very unlike that of the Tang dynasty.

THE SONG, 960–1279

The Founding of the Northern Song Dynasty

Historians traditionally divide the Song dynasty into two parts. The Northern Song ruled from 960 to 1127, with its capital at Kaifeng in central China (Figure 9.2). The Southern Song ruled southern China from 1127 to 1279, after the Jurchen conquest of the north; this era is covered in Chapter 14.

Although the Song had control of most of northern China, Taizu faced tremendous obstacles to unifying the whole of China. South China was still divided into several territories, and there were two independent entities in the north with their own dynasties. In addition, there were two powerful nomadic kingdoms, one in the northwest established by the Tanguts (a Tibetan people), known as Xi Xia, and one in the northeast established by the Khitans, known as Liao. While Xi Xia territory was predominantly a

non-Chinese land, the Khitans controlled a large Chinese territory called the "Sixteen Prefectures" and launched numerous raids farther into China throughout the tenth century. At one point, the Khitans had penetrated as far as Kaifeng in central China, which city would later become the capital of the Northern Song.

Taizu turned first against the south. He had to leave behind some of his more gifted generals to keep the north secure, but the gamble paid off. The southerners could not resist the veteran northern armies of the Song, with their large complements of nomadic cavalrymen. In some cases, Taizu had propaganda spread that barbarian northern soldiers cooked and ate prisoners of war. Taizu was able to take control of most of south China with little actual fighting.

The growing economic difference between northern and southern China influenced these campaigns, as naval forces rather than cavalry became the crucial complement to infantry armies and fortifications: The vast river system of the south compelled the development of an inland navy. Most of the ships were obtained through capture as the army moved south, and the navy was used to transport men and material, protect against amphibious assaults on Song forces, and assist in sieges of fortifications along the waterways. The Song navy would eventually total thousands of ships, some large enough to carry over 1000 men. However, when Taizu's attention shifted back north, resources were siphoned from the navy. The Song navy would not again attain such size and importance until after the Jurchen invasions of the early twelfth century.

Once the south was secure, Taizu shifted his attention to the conquest of the Sichuan region in the west. This required sending his army up the Yangzi River, past a series of fortifications, some quite large and defended with huge catapults that sent large rocks and flaming substances onto approaching craft. These fortifications were not easy to overcome, and Taizu was often dependent on defectors to create dissension and inform him of weak spots. Taizu also used a policy of terror in the countryside around these fortifications, reducing their local support. These actions were successful, but the enraged local population engaged in rebellions for years afterward.

Having secured the rest of China, Taizu turned his attention back to the northern frontier, focusing his efforts against the Khitans of Liao, who controlled the Sixteen Prefectures. Decades of fighting under Taizu and his successors resulted in military stalemate, and a treaty finally ended the war. The Song in effect bought peace with Liao by paying annual tribute and recognizing the Liao ruler as an equal of their emperor, a provision far more grating than the tribute payments. There were additional smaller wars between the two antagonists, but neither was able to expand at the expense of the other.

Civilianization of the Military

From Taizu's reign through to the end of the dynasty, Song rulers and government officials were constantly and consciously concerned not to reenact what they saw as the failings of the Tang dynasty. Foremost among those failings, they believed, was the level of both power and prestige attained by military men. The founder of the dynasty had himself been a military man who attained his position through military means. The Song went to great lengths both to ensure imperial control over the Song military and to reduce the prestige of the military as a career. The first result was a centralized army, controlled personally by the emperor, that never threatened to break free of that control. The second, less positive, result was an army incapable of projecting imperial power beyond the limits of Song territory and eventually incapable even of defending the empire from large-scale invasions.

Taizu accomplished the coup that established the Song dynasty through his command of the palace guard army of the Later Zhou dynasty. Throughout his reign, he worked to ensure that the Palace Army was both loyal and the best of all the Song armies. For example, units from other armies that distinguished themselves in battle were transferred to the Palace Army. Units of the Palace Army that were considered substandard, in turn, were transferred to the provincial armies. Taizu's successors continued this policy, as well as often flooding provincial armies with civilian inspectors and spies and constantly rotating units from one army to another.

As Taizu took control of an area of China, he placed a trusted general in charge as military governor, but soon thereafter, he sent a civilian to oversee administration of the province. Once the area was secure, the military governors were replaced by civil officials directly answerable to the emperor. This not only was a check on the possibility of a military governor acting independently, as had happened in the Tang dynasty, but it also set the stage for the eventual replacement of the military governor with a civilian.

Taizu's successors took care to not allow regional military commanders to build up centers of power. Those officers, even of low rank, who distinguished themselves in combat or who impressed imperial representatives were transferred to the Palace Army, which remained posted primarily in the capital district. What the Song thereby succeeded in creating was a military in which there were no personal bonds—at least no permanent ones—between officers and men. A whole bureaucracy was created to evaluate, promote, reward, and punish the officer corps. All officers of a certain rank were placed in a pool from which the imperial court would draw in making assignments, whether for military expeditions or for garrison duties. In addition, rank was unconnected to command—high rank did not necessarily denote command of larger numbers of men. The approval of enlisted men was completely immaterial for officers' reward and advancement. For example, after a particular military campaign, the troops would return to their garrisons whereas the officers were administratively returned to the officer pool, awaiting their rewards, promotions, and next appointments. To emphasize personal loyalty to the emperor, all promotions had to be approved with his seal, promotions to high ranks were conferred in a special ceremony with the emperor, and the emperor personally attended periodic reviews of Palace Army units. When military expeditions were launched, the commanders were provided with detailed instructions on how the campaign was to be conducted. Failure to obey these instructions often led to severe punishment, sometimes execution.

The only exceptions to the principle of the temporary nature of command were officers assigned at the *ying* level. This was a unit of roughly 500 officers and men that formed the basic building block of the Song army. The imperial court knew that such a small force was no threat to the dynasty, and if any *ying* commander had antidynastic ideas, they could be quickly and easily squelched.

One of the most effective means of reducing the army's potential threat to the dynasty involved reducing the army's importance in society. Instead, prestige, position, and wealth were attained through success in the civil bureaucracy. It was in the Song that the civil examination system became the primary means of access to high-government appointment and all its attendant benefits, a process aided by the invention of block printing, which allowed wider diffusion of the Confucian classics on which the exams were based. The Neo-Confucian revival that characterized Song intellectual life grew out of this milieu, and the main lines of Neo-Confucian thought were civilian, not military, in orientation. As a result, military officers and military service were increasingly looked down on by elite society, and few wealthy or powerful families saw the military as a desirable career choice for their sons. This trend was also made possible in part by the tremendous growth of the Song economy, especially overseas trade. Commerce became a serious alternative to landownership as a source of wealth, undermining whatever remained of the dominance of the great landowning families with ties to old military traditions and cavalry practices.

The policies and cultural attitudes that diminished the threat posed by powerful generals carried a corresponding risk of military weakness. In the late eleventh century, however, the Song court was convinced that it could afford the military weakness its policies caused for two reasons. First, the Khitans and Tanguts were divided and in any case no longer posed a serious threat to China. The tribute sent each year kept these two peoples relatively pacified and represented an almost imperceptible drain on the Chinese economy. Second, the lack of a flexible, talented officer corps was balanced by an enormous army that, it was felt, could overwhelm an enemy through sheer numbers. And Song military production was a nice complement to the large numbers of troops, able to provide a vast array of weapons, uniforms, and other supplies for these large armies.

The Song army grew to immense size. By 1020, there were almost 900,000 men in the army, and within a couple decades, the number had grown to over 1.2 million. Again, the thriving Song economy made this expansion in numbers possible, as government revenues increased significantly. The army was composed not of citizen-soldiers, in the manner of the early Tang, or conscripts, but mostly of paid volunteers—but not well paid, individually. Recruitment of soldiers was from the ranks of criminals, the destitute, and vagabonds, further reinforcing the negative image of soldiering in the culture as a whole. The individual soldier was looked down on and treated very poorly. Most soldiers were tattooed or branded on the head and hands to reduce their chances of successfully deserting the ranks. Only in the Palace Army was discipline emphasized, but even there not too rigorously. In the early years of the dynasty, there was regular training in everything from physical fitness to siege warfare. By the late eleventh century, however, this had tapered off. It was during the Song dynasty that the famous Chinese expression of disdain for military men became current: "Good iron is not used to make nails, and good men are not used to make soldiers."

The metaphor held another message as well: The quality of the soldiers may often have been quite poor, but they were well supplied and equipped. Contributing to Song economic growth was significant technological development. China had a very large and sophisticated iron industry, with production dwarfing anything in the rest of the world until the advent of the Industrial Revolution in Europe in the eighteenth century. Uniforms, armor, weapons, and other equipment were mass-produced in government factories. Millions of crossbows, arrows, swords, shields, and such gunpowder weapons as small cannons, flamethrowers, and explosive grenades were produced for use by the army. It is hardly surprising that Song political leaders felt confident that their enormous, well-supplied and -organized forces were more than competent enough to carry out the tasks assigned to them by the court.

Unfortunately for the government, the growth of its army outstripped even the increased financial resources available to it. By the early 1070s, nearly 80 percent of government revenue was being used to fund the large army. The Song court was desperate for a way out of this predicament. It was primarily the enormous costs associated with maintaining the huge Song army that prompted the emperor in 1068 to call on Wang Anshi to serve as prime minister with a mandate to institute reforms. While Wang Anshi's tenure in office (1068–76, 1078–85) saw him initiate a range of reforms of the economy and bureaucracy, it was in the military field that he put forth the most radical policies. First, several hundred thousand men were released from the army; most were expected to form new agricultural communities. Second, roughly 130 small, permanent garrisons of no more than 3000 soldiers were established on the frontier. No longer would all the best soldiers be assigned strictly to the Palace Army. Many of these were now sent to the frontier garrisons, where they were expected to partially support themselves through farming—a system much like that of the Tang dynasty. Third, to engage the common people in the task of national defense and mutual security, Wang Anshi instituted a militia system called *bao-jia*. In return for reductions in taxes, families supplied men for militia duty. Recruitment was organized around groups of ten families supervised by a local official; higher officials oversaw groups of ten such family groups. Officials were sent from the imperial or regional capital to equip and train these militias and to supervise their patrol and mutual security duties.

The *bao-jia* system in particular greatly reduced the amount of the imperial budget allocated for military purposes. In its early years, the militias were often grouped in large units to train alongside regular army units. As Wang envisioned it, primary responsibility for defense was to be given to the *bao-jia* militia, along with the new, nearly self-supporting frontier garrisons. The regular army, then, was to be redesigned for offensive operations.

However, this vision was never to be realized. The most important result of Wang Anshi's military reforms was a serious decline in the morale of the regular army, which led, in turn, to a large diminution of its combat effectiveness. The large reductions in army size caused a great deal of apprehension among those who were left, and nobody wanted to be posted on the far frontiers. Morale also suffered as a result of the shift toward a militia as the mainstay of imperial defense. The military function of the *bao-jia* was difficult to organize, and it was gradually abolished after Wang was removed from office in 1085. The *bao-jia* system was retained for local law and order through the end of the imperial era in the twentieth century, but its militia function was never again seriously revived. The frontier garrisons also were not maintained or regularly supervised, and those that remained in the early twelfth century were mostly insignificant to Song defense. Instead, the regular army gradually increased in numbers until it reached roughly its earlier size, and the costs to maintain it rose as well. Morale, however, did not improve, and the Song army was in no shape to react to the major challenge posed by the rising Jurchen Empire in the north.

Jurchen Invasions and Destruction of the Northern Song

By the early twelfth century, a rough peace existed among Northern Song China and its neighbors the Liao in the northeast and the Xi Xia in the northwest. Although there were some skirmishes, major campaigns were resisted, with the Song seemingly reconciled to the loss of the Sixteen Prefectures. The Khitans had also relaxed their previously very sharp military guard. The cavalry wing of the Khitan army saw little major action over several decades, and suppression of the frequent uprisings in the Chinese areas of the empire did not require much sustained or large-scale military response. This relative serenity was shaken severely by the rise of a people on the far northern reaches of Liao territory, the Jurchens.

The Jurchens were a Tungusic people from northern Manchuria, the ancestors of the Manchu peoples who would conquer China in the seventeenth century. We know little about them prior to the early twelfth century—mainly that they subsisted primarily through hunting and that the Khitans considered them to be particularly fierce warriors. Never happy as subjects of the Liao, the Jurchens often rebelled. Jurchen tribal division and Khitan unity kept these uprisings from threatening Liao control, but this situation changed rapidly once the Jurchens became unified under a dynamic leader, Aguta. In 1115, after defeating a local Liao army, Aguta proclaimed himself emperor of a new dynasty, called "Jin" (Gold, the name of a river in the region).

The united Jurchen army—a cavalry force organized much like the Khitan army, with a heavily armored vanguard, two, more lightly armored, wings, and a reserve in the rear—quickly swept through the Liao domains in Manchuria. Within three years, nearly all of Manchuria was in the hands of the Jurchen Jin, though the main Liao armies were still located within the Sixteen Prefectures. The Song court saw an opportunity to recover their lands and concluded a treaty of alliance with the Jurchen. The allies organized a joint campaign of assault on the remaining Liao territories, with the Jin to attack from the north and the Song to attack from the south and west. The Song were to get the Sixteen Prefectures, and the Jin all the rest of Liao territory, an arrangement borrowed from Tang practice. Even more than the Tang, however, given the economic and social developments outlined above, what the Chinese Song dynasty lacked was a cavalry force. So, as the Tang did with the Uighurs, the Song bought a cavalry force in the Jurchens.

It turned out the Song were playing with fire. The joint attack took place in mid-1122, and within three years, the Liao dynasty was no more. The overconfident Song then snubbed their dangerous allies, and within another three years, all of north China including the Song capital at Kaifeng had fallen to the Jurchens. The remnants of the Song court and army fled south, with a son of the previous emperor taking the throne.

The rump Song court was faced with a dilemma: The only hope of survival was to raise new armies with generals given more flexibility in command and control than had been done since the early days of the dynasty. Commoners were conscripted as militia and given rudimentary training, but most recruitment efforts went toward volunteers for the regular army. Civil officials were called on to perform military duties as officers at all levels of the revived army. However, due to decades of denigration of the military and things martial, nearly all of them refused. This was almost certainly a good thing for the dynasty, for the result of civil officials leading the Song armies almost certainly would have been continued disaster. It was obvious to many Chinese that their very civilization depended on having an army that could defeat the rampaging Jurchens. It was not, however, obvious to all. Many others argued that strong, independent Chinese generals were more threat than protection; to them, the civilization could survive foreign conquest, but not a revival of Tang-style militarism.

Those who supported a strong defense won out at this time, and anyone who could raise an army to defend the dynasty and fight the Jurchens was welcomed. The result was that new-style armies were created, led by charismatic leaders who had complete control over command, administration, and deployment. Although there was some communication and coordination, for several years, these armies acted as independent entities, held together primarily by the personal bonds among commanders, officers, and men.

The Jurchens also found that fighting in the region south of the Yangzi River, with its extensive marshes, myriad rivers, and uneven terrain, was not ideal territory to deploy their primarily equestrian force, though they, like the Khitans, had recruited thousands of Chinese to form their infantry component. They caused much destruction all the way to Hangzhou, the new Song capital, but by 1130, the newly raised Chinese armies had been able to use the topography to their advantage to first stop and then push back the Jin forces. Competent Song generals came to the fore, utilizing the superiority in numbers and weaponry that Song China possessed.

Within a few short years, the Jurchens had been not only ejected from southern China but nearly expelled from the north as well. At this point, with south China secure for the dynasty, the Song court entered negotiations with the Jurchen, signing a treaty in 1142 that divided China between them. The border was set along the Huai River, and the Song was required to pay tribute roughly equal to what they had paid previously to the Liao. The Song armies were ordered to return south, and their commanders were removed, with most executed, to ensure continued civilian dominance of the military. (See the Issues box "The Military's Role in the Song Dynasty: The Case of Yue Fei" for an in-depth look at this curious turn of events.)

From 1142 to 1279, we usually speak of the Southern Song dynasty. The descendants of Zhao Kuangyin continued to rule and to claim sovereignty over all of China, but they would never again gain control of the north. Instead, more effort was put into new armies that were stationed along the frontier. Officers were career military men who gained promotion internally; civilian administration of the army's finances and equipment continued.

The Military's Role in the Song Dynasty: The Case of Yue Fei

There is no debate among scholars that one mark of the Song dynasty was an ongoing concern to bridle the military under civilian control, or at least to ensure that the military could not threaten the dynasty. The question has been to what lengths the Song court was willing to go to ensure its dominance of the military. Some believe that the dynasty was willing to give up nearly half the territory of China rather than risk a military overthrow of the dynasty or a situation like that of the late Tang, with powerful, virtually independent, military governors dictating to the court. This discussion of the extent of the dynasty's willingness to restrict the military concerns the fate of the great Song general Yue Fei.

His statues and temples are scattered throughout China and Taiwan to this day, and his story has been taught to Chinese children for centuries, an exemplar of Chinese nationalism. Beyond the myths and tales, however, it is difficult to get a clear picture of Yue Fei (1103–1141) since so many of the records are lost or were deliberately tampered with. What we do know is that in the Northern Song period he chose a military career at a time when the military and the military arts were in much disrepute. At age 19, he attached himself to a powerful local family, taking charge of their security needs. In this capacity, he primarily protected their lands from bandits and other criminal gangs and suppressed uprisings by the poor tenant workers.

Yue Fei later gained an appointment as a staff officer under a general assigned a major role in the 1122 campaign against the Khitan Liao, who occupied the Sixteen Prefectures in China proper. Yue was part of an army whose assignment was to retake the Liao capital of Beijing. Song forces were soundly repulsed, but Yue gained experience that would become invaluable later when Song China was invaded by the Jurchens. He formed his own independently recruited and led army that spent much of the years 1126–28 fighting other independent commands. All sources agree that Yue Fei was fiercely loyal to the Song dynasty, and it was only in later years that he questioned commands given him by the Song court.

For the next several years, Yue's army was one of several that forced the Jurchens to abandon their gains in south China, and in 1134, he was given the major role in the offensive campaign to recover north China from the Jurchens. In this he was tremendously successful, reaching the outskirts of Luoyang, the old Tang capital, in early 1140. He and his army seemed unstoppable as they pushed the Jurchens back toward their Manchurian homeland. At this point, on the verge of achieving the goals of the Song court, he and the other Song armies were ordered to withdraw below the Huai River. Behind the backs of the military commanders in the field, the Song court had been negotiating with the Jurchens and had agreed to terms. The two powers agreed to divide China between them, with the Huai River as the dividing line. In return for Jurchen promises to leave south China unmolested, the Song agreed to recognize the Jurchen's Jin dynasty as the rulers of north China. Yue Fei was publicly outraged by what he considered a treasonous act. He contemplated disobeying the court's orders, but the other Song armies obeyed the command, meaning that Yue's army was exposed far north near the Yellow River. He complied and returned to the Song court, where he was relieved of his command and later arrested and executed.

The question that has led to such debate is why the Song court capitulated to the Jurchens on the verge of complete victory. Nationalist Chinese since the time of the betrayal have most often seen this mainly as a naked power play by Yue Fei's main rival at the Song court, the civilian prime minister,

Qin Gui. Long an advocate of negotiating with the Jurchens, Qin Gui had the most to lose if Yue Fei succeeded in recovering the north. He also worked feverishly to complete his centralization of power soon after Yue Fei's death by publicly charging and executing most of the other major military commanders and purging most of Yue Fei's immediate subordinates. Over the next few years, the whole Song officer corps was subjected to periodic purges. Even Yue Fei's surviving family members were exiled to scattered areas on the periphery of the empire.

There is no doubt that Qin Gui instituted a reign of terror among both the military and civil officialdom of the Song court. Yet some have seen this as an overly simplistic explanation for the Song court's action in dividing up the realm with the Jurchens. Qin Gui's action, they assert, was consistent with early Song policy regarding the military. In this telling, when Jurchen forces were rampaging throughout central and even southern China, it was necessary to give a great deal of independent authority to the military commanders. Once this emergency situation was resolved, however, steps could be taken to ensure the continued safety of the dynasty from a military coup. The court had seen that Jurchen cavalry was greatly hobbled in its effectiveness in the varied topography of south China, and now that order had been restored to the south, it was safe to disarm the military generals, who were becoming, from the Song viewpoint, too independent and arrogant. After all, Yue Fei himself was sounding more and more like the founder of a new dynasty, though his claims never became explicit.

The humbling of the military could not be accomplished safely until the Jurchens were convinced that they could not take the south. By 1140, with their hold on north China increasingly precarious, the Jurchens decided to deal with the Song. Thus, according to this view, the Song were willing to give a major portion of China to barbarians in order to preserve not only the dynasty but the principle of civilian control over the military. This was not done solely at the instigation of Qin Gui, they point out, since he at all times had the confidence and support of the emperor and most of the high civil officials.

In recent years, some have analyzed the situation from a strictly military standpoint and note that, although Yue Fei had pushed the Jurchens back quite a distance, his recovery of the rest of north China was not at all a foregone conclusion. The Jurchens, though somewhat disorganized by their defeats, were by this point fighting in land much more suited to their nomadic cavalry tactics. Yue Fei's last offensives were repulsed by the Jurchens, and though he was determined to take the fight to the Jurchens, the records show that the other top military commanders did not share his confidence and advised securing their gains before continuing on the offensive. Also, the Jurchens were engaged in increasingly sucessful negotiations with the Mongols, their enemies to the north. With their rear secure, the Jurchens would have been able to focus an attack on the Song forces strung out in the north.

Of course, we cannot really know if Yue Fei would have succeeded in expelling the Jurchens from China, but failure could have had disastrous consequences. Shattered Song armies might have emboldened the Jurchen to mount new assaults on south China. Retreat by the Song to the Huai River at least allowed them to preserve the bulk of their armies to fight off any Jurchen incursions, even with the celebrated generals dead and many officers purged. We might say, then, that court intrigue, dynastic fear of strong and independent generals, and even military necessity played a role in the removal of Yue Fei on the eve of possibly his greatest triumph.

CONCLUSION

During the period of disunion (220–589), the mass of sedentary agriculturalists in north China was ruled by an elite military-political class of nomads and a rising class of Chinese who had to a considerable degree adopted the culture of the nomadic conquerors. It was this new class that led the wars of conquest in the late sixth century that resulted in the reunification of the Chinese world. The resulting Sui (581–618) and early Tang (618–907) dynasties reflected the combination of the two cultures, with their military forces composed of a mix of massed hereditary soldiers who were expected to be self-supporting and an elite cavalry force as their main offensive weapon.

The growing economic and cultural importance of the south, and the sheer mass of people there, led to the cavalry arm of the military becoming more and more foreign in nature and less and less integrated into the Tang sociopolitical system. By the late Tang, the nomadic cavalry was a fully hired force, but the succeeding Song dynasty, soon after its founding in the tenth century, lacked much of a cavalry force at all. This put the Song at a distinct disadvantage in its military encounters with its northern adversaries, particularly the Khitans and Jurchens.

The trend away from synthesis of Chinese and nomadic elements in Chinese armies also contributed to the decline of the great aristocratic families who had been in the forefront of that synthesis. When their power was destroyed in the chaos of the end of the Tang and the Five Dynasties period, the stage was set for a decisive civilianization of Chinese society under the Song, who were acutely conscious of the role of overpowerful military governors in the previous dynasty's fall. But the Song army proved incapable of holding northern China, and it would be a newly reconstructed Song army and state that would face Jurchen and Mongol threats after 1128.

SUGGESTED READINGS

Forage, Paul C. "The Sino-Tangut War of 1081–1085." *Journal of Asian History,* 25 (1991):1–28. An especially good article demonstrating the tremendous logistic abilities of the Song military.

Graff, David A. *Medieval Chinese Warfare, 300–900.* London and New York: Routledge, 2002. An excellent survey of the Sui and Tang military, utilizing a tremendous amount of research in the primary sources.

Graff, David A., and Robin Higham, eds. *A Military History of China.* Boulder: Westview Press, 2001. A narrative history focusing on military institutions and strategy.

Haeger, John, ed. *Crisis and Prosperity in Sung China.* Tucson: University of Arizona Press, 1975. Includes several chapters covering Song dealings with the nomadic kingdoms in north China.

Pulleyblank, E. G. *The Background to the Rebellion of An Lushan.* London: Oxford University Press, 1955. Although primarily focused on the politics behind the great rebellion of the Tang dynasty, also contains much information on the organization of the early Tang military.

Rossabi, Morris, ed. *China Among Equals.* Berkeley: University of California Press, 1983. While not concerned primarily with military matters, includes several chapters dealing with Tang and especially Song diplomatic and strategic concerns.

Van de Ven, Hans, ed. *Warfare in Chinese History.* Leiden: Brill, 2000. Includes several analytical chapters concerning China's military relations with its northern neighbors.

Wright, Arthur. *The Sui Dynasty.* New York: Knopf, 1978. Not only the best survey of the history of this dynasty, but a font of information on Sui campaigns against Korea.

Wright, Arthur, and Denis Twitchett, eds. *Cambridge History of China. Vol. 3: Sui and T'ang China 589–906.* Cambridge: Cambridge University Press, 1979. A good general survey of these two dynasties, with a great deal of specific information on Chinese military institutions and their evolution.

CHAPTER 10

Predators and Police: Naval Warfare, 400–1100

Naval warfare in the age of migration and invasion reflected the patterns of the age. While most of the threats to Afro-Eurasian civilizations came from the horsed nomads of the Asian steppes, some migratory peoples moved by sea. As a result, the scope of naval warfare spread beyond the confines of the Mediterranean world, whose comparatively benevolent seas had fostered the ancient world's only real arena of naval conflict. New patterns of trade in the more fragmented postclassical world also stimulated maritime activity. For both these reasons, naval warfare assumed greater importance globally than it had in the previous age.

Naval operations between 400 and 1100 may be analyzed in terms of two major types, or models: imperial defense and the activity of predatory sea peoples. Most of the naval powers of the age fell into one of the two categories, but the models represent poles on a continuum, and some naval forces were hybrids of the two.

Navies of imperial defense were parts of unified, centrally directed defensive strategies. They were supported by bureaucracies that saw to the recruitment of sailors and marines, the building and repair of ships, and logistical support for fleets. In other words, navies of imperial defense were under state direction. Naval defense in this model was thus linked to trade and general maritime activity through the government: Taxes on trade often funded the navy, and maritime resources of ships and experienced sailors moved from the merchant to the military sphere via government direction or appropriation. Technologically, navies of imperial defense tended to be sophisticated—in fact, they tended to be among the most technologically advanced products of their civilizations—and to be well adapted to the particular marine geography and climate in which they operated. The tactical aim of such navies was, broadly, to sink enemy ships, a task for which their technology was also well developed.

The Byzantine Empire is the dominant example of this model of naval activity. Near the end of the period, Song China also created such a navy.

The characteristics of predatory sea peoples contrast sharply in each case with imperial navies. Naval activity in this model was generated spontaneously from the socioeconomic structure, rather than being a creation of government policy. It was mainly economic and offensive in its goals—that is, it was aimed at predatory plunder. Rather than the fleet or formal squadron, the boatload was the basic unit of military, and indeed social, organization in this model: A leader and his followers used their own boat for their own purposes. Naval activity among predatory sea peoples is tied to state formation and political structure, but in the context of weak central authority. Thus, much of the activity of such naval powers was private or semiprivate, rather than being under state direction in support of a clear policy. Technologically, such naval forces were less sophisticated, and certainly much less specialized, than imperial navies. Though capable of impressive accomplishments, their ships did not press the limits of the age's technical know-how. The tactical aim of predatory naval forces, if it came to a fight at sea (which was less likely than for imperial navies, which sought such encounters), was not to sink but to capture enemy ships. Ships were valuable prizes, of significant economic worth in themselves, as tools for further raiding, and also likely to contain rich booty in goods and in people who could be sold as slaves. But the more common tactical (and strategic) aim of such forces was to raid unguarded shores. The key examples of this model were the Vikings of northwest Europe, the Cholas of southern India, and Srivijaya in the Straits of Malacca in Southeast Asia.

Two important naval powers in the Mediterranean—the Muslims and later the Italian city-states—were in varying ways hybrids of the two models. For them, naval activity was a combination of predation and imperial offensive (as well as defensive) strategy. For these powers, the state played a role closer to the imperial model, but often in a more fragmented and limited political context. That is, aside from the Caliphate at the height of its powers, these were strong but small states. Some, such as Venice, were, in effect, parasitic on an imperial power. Technologically, such powers proved to be skillful at adapting, adopting, and innovating technologically, though with less of a specialized military focus than the imperial powers. The Muslim world, especially, with one oar in the Mediterranean and one oar (or sail) in the Indian Ocean, would become a breeding ground for maritime technological advances. The tactical aim of these naval forces varied with circumstances but was likely to lean to capture rather than sinking, since for small states, even strong ones, a ship was likely to be a valuable resource.

These models provide us with a framework for examining the naval powers of the age in more detail. But for all the naval powers of this age, naval activity was still, as in the ancient Mediterranean, essentially amphibious. That is, a maritime technology limited fleets largely to coastal waters, and control of the seas was, in the modern sense, an impossibility.

IMPERIAL NAVIES

Byzantium and the Mediterranean World

The Byzantine naval forces from the fifth through the tenth centuries were, like the Byzantine army, the heirs of Roman military organization, tactics, and traditions (see Chapter 8 for the Byzantine army). In the case of Byzantium's navy, it inherited the main mission of the Roman fleet: to serve as an auxiliary arm to the army. The Byzantine navy would, however, be faced with new problems during the seventh and subsequent centuries that would force it to deal with a major maritime threat from Muslim naval forces, something the Romans had not really faced since the first century BCE.

The Roman Tradition From the end of the first century BCE, the naval forces that Rome had developed over the previous two and a half centuries found themselves in what might seem to be an enviable position. The naval victory over Ptolemaic Egypt (as Augustus liked to frame his victory in

Actium in 31 BCE) meant that, for the first time in her history, Rome had truly removed all of her major rivals from the Mediterranean Sea. For the next three centuries, the Roman fleet would be relegated to serving as an ancillary force to the army, used primarily for ferrying troops and providing logistical support or for protecting the grain supply that kept the city of Rome fed (see Chapter 5 for the role of the Roman fleet until the middle of the third century). Indeed, without a major threat, Rome was virtually able to abandon construction of large warships, instead concentrating on smaller craft and transports.

By the middle of the third century, however, the various political and military crises that beset Rome opened the way for Germanic and Celtic raiders to hit the coastal regions of the empire, sometimes even attacking major urban centers such as Athens. This led to an effort to re-create a fighting navy, although the Roman navy from the late third century onward would be not a fleet of major warships, but rather more of a coastal defense force. These forces often combined squadrons of small, fast warships with land forces quartered in coastal fortifications. One of the best-known examples of this scheme, the Saxon Shore, was detailed to defend the coasts of Britain and Gaul from various groups of raiders. The count of the Saxon Shore was a Roman military official who commanded both naval and land forces in an effort to combine preclusive security through the use of coastal fortifications with the more elastic defense provided by squadrons of warships.

The Age of Byzantine Supremacy By the end of the fifth century, the naval situation had changed dramatically. The Western Roman Empire had fallen to the depredations of the barbarians (who incidentally made their major inroads overland rather than by sea). The Byzantine Empire, the eastern remnant of the Roman Empire, survived and, with the possible exception of the Vandals, faced little in the way of a challenge to its control of the eastern Mediterranean. As a result, the Roman navy once again became of force of relatively few warships and a greater number of transports.

Consequently, many of the military operations that took place during the sixth and early seventh centuries saw the navy play only a supporting role. Most often, the fleet transported troops and provided logistical support to the army. Indeed, the Byzantines pioneered the role of amphibious warfare during this period. Specialized transports were developed to make the conveyance of horses easier than had been the case, as one of the major problems facing armies in the period before this was finding a manner in which animals could be transported easily and safely by sea. Byzantine naval skill was put to good use by Heraclius in his campaigns against the Persians: The fleet prevented the Persians and Avars from combining across the Bosporus to besiege Constantinople in 626 and then transported Heraclius's army to the coast of Cilicia behind the Persian invasion, compelling their withdrawal from Asia Minor.

Byzantium and the Arab Challenge

Byzantine naval superiority ended with the rise of the Caliphate (see below), even as the challenge posed by Arab raiding fleets reinforced the character of the Byzantine navy as an imperial defense force. The front line of defense rested with squadrons based along the coasts of western Asia Minor and southern Greece. By the 670s, these forces were organized as a theme (the divisions of the empire used to support the army; see Chapter 8) called the Karabisianoi, led by a *strategos,* just as army themes were. The theme provided rowers and marines instead of soldiers, but it otherwise mirrored the somewhat localized, defensive organization and structure of the provincial armies. Additions and administrative subdivision eventually created two more naval themes.

Just as a central professional army based in the capital backed up the provincial armies, a central imperial fleet in the capital remained a crucial element of Byzantine naval organization. The central fleet—which included the admiral in charge of the entire imperial navy, the *droungarios* of the *ploimon*—protected the capital, served ceremonial purposes (see the Sources box on page 183), provided the administrative heart of the navy, and controlled Byzantine shipbuilding, which was concentrated in Constantinople. It was especially with regard to such technical matters as construction and administration that the Roman heritage of the Byzantine navy proved valuable, since Mediterranean galley warfare was a difficult, technically sophisticated business that could not easily be started up from scratch.

Tactically, the Byzantine navy relied on relatively small, light galleys known as *dromons,* powered by two banks of oars. Their offensive weaponry included the ram at the prow of the ship, Greek Fire (see the Issues box "Greek Fire"), and marines who supplied both firepower with bows and the capability of boarding enemy ships. Strategically, the fleet benefited from the prevailing weather patterns of the eastern Mediterranean, which made raids from south to north more difficult to sustain, especially when the raiders lacked a secure base in the Aegean (Figure 10.1). But the strategic situation grew markedly worse around 827, when both Sicily and Crete fell to Arab seaborne invasions. Crete, especially, gave Muslim raiders a base within easy reach of the Greek mainland, the coasts of Asia Minor, and the main Aegean shipping lanes—and a century and a half of insecurity for those areas ensued.

Although acting mostly on the defensive between 650 and 900, the Byzantine fleet also launched occasional raids against the Syrian and even Egyptian coasts. Such raids may have been militarily insignificant, but they probably gave morale boosts to an empire whose land forces struggled simply to stay intact while on the defensive during this period.

Tenth-Century Naval Offensives

The shift in Byzantine military fortunes that followed the fragmentation of the Caliphate after 900 (see Chapter 8) was felt at sea as much as on the empire's land frontiers. The naval offensive focused on retaking Arab-held Crete. Invasions in 911 and 949 under Emperor Constantine VII Porphyrogenitus failed. However, in 960, a third expedition under Nicephoras Phocas succeeded in retaking the island for the Byzantines and, as a result, in making Aegean shipping and the Anatolian coastline much more secure from Arab raids, which lost their only effective base of operations.

The details of the first two operations are preserved in an official collection of documents known as the *De Ceremoniis,* compiled by Constantine VII, and provide a window on the size of such expeditions and the organizational problems that beset them. (See the Sources box "Constantine VII Porphyrogenitus" for extracts from *De Administrando Imperio.*) The sources testify to the organizational difficulty of launching such expeditions, as the documents resulted from imperial inquests into who actually went on them (as opposed to who was called out to go on them) so that numerous claims for back pay and rewards could be settled.

The 911 expedition consisted of several hundred ships of all types, *dromons* as well as supply ships. Sailors and oarsmen for the ships numbered about 34,000; another 13,000 soldiers served as part of the naval units, presumably as marines accustomed to naval combat. In addition, the fleet transported units

Greek Fire

The Chronicle of Theophanes reports that "at that time [673/4] Kallinikos, an artificer from Heliopolis [in Lebanon], fled to the Romans. He had devised a sea fire which ignited the Arab ships and burned them with all hands. Thus it was that the Romans returned with victory and discovered the sea fire." Later Byzantine historians and chroniclers elaborated on this account of the origins of what became known as

Greek Fire   This illustration from a Byzantine manuscript shows the flaming substance being shot through bronze tubes.

Greek Fire to build a long-accepted picture of a great secret weapon. According to this tradition, the formula for Greek Fire, a combustible substance made from some combination of petroleum, naphtha, and other ingredients that at the least could not be put out with water and perhaps was either spread or even ignited by contact with water, remained a closely guarded state secret. The substance itself, either pumped at high pressure out of bronze siphons mounted on the bows of galleys or lobbed, from on-board catapults, in earthenware pots that would shatter on impact, constituted a deadly weapon against wooden ships that the Byzantine navy used again and again to devastating effect, most decisively at the siege of Constantinople in 717. Only when the Turks discovered how to combat it in the late eleventh century (vinegar, rather than water, did the trick in dousing the flames) did Greek Fire lose importance as a Byzantine naval weapon; the

of the central professional army and the provincial army, which combined numbered around 4000 men; at least 1000 of these, the professionals, were cavalrymen, whose horses also had to be transported. Thus, over 50,000 men, at least 2000–3000 horses, and all their attendant equipment and supplies sailed from Constantinople in an expedition that ultimately failed. The numbers in 949 were similar—regular army units came to about 5400, but fewer marines are listed. We have no figures for the expedition of 960, but it must have been at least as large. In any case, the key to its success, where the earlier expeditions failed, seems to have been

not the size of the forces involved, but the effectiveness of the leadership exercised over the combined naval and land forces. Political infighting and incompetence plagued the earlier expeditions, but Nicephoras Phocas was an experienced general, a charismatic leader, and, perhaps most important, an excellent administrator. Even so, it took a hard siege of Chandax, the capital of Crete, over the winter of 960–961, ending with its storming in March, before the conquest could be completed. During the siege, the fleet played a vital role in keeping the besiegers supplied and preventing intervention by any relief forces. In many ways, the challenges facing Nicephoras were

formula was lost with the fall of the empire, never to be recovered.

Subsequent European historiography, until recently, has largely followed this account and it remains in popular circulation. This is perhaps not surprising, as the tale certainly has all the elements of a high-tech spy thriller. Furthermore, it suited a Byzantine self-image of a Chosen People specially favored by God, and it may have continued to suit a Western self-image that has contrasted inventive, technologically adept Westerners (with Byzantines in this instance counting as "Western") with tradition-bound, technologically backward non-Westerners.

The problem with this account is that investigation into Arab sources makes clear not only that Arab naval forces were familiar with Greek Fire—that is, it was not a very secret weapon—but that they used it themselves. Both Arab and Byzantine naval handbooks, as distinct from court-generated propaganda, portray Greek Fire as a standard part of the weaponry of eastern Mediterranean fleets in the period 700–1100. It was, to be sure, an important and useful weapon, especially against more lightly built ships and against enemies trapped in confined waters or unprepared for its use, such as a Viking-Rus fleet destroyed on the Black Sea by the Byzantines in 941. But it

was by no means surefire, so to speak, as siphons had limited range and catapulted pots had limited accuracy. This, as much as effective Turkish countermeasures and the Turkish conquest of Byzantium, accounts for the later disappearance of Greek Fire from Mediterranean naval arsenals. And its historical effect has been exaggerated. The fires that disrupted the Arab fleet at Constantinople in 717 seem, on closer reading of the sources, to have been set by fireships—entire ships loaded with combustible materials and launched into the midst of a closely confined fleet at anchor, a common trick used to good effect by the English against the Spanish Armada in 1588, for example (see Chapter 20).

The long emphasis on Greek Fire has also tended to obscure the real reasons for Byzantine naval survival in the face of the Caliphate's navies, which were probably larger and certainly better funded than Byzantine fleets. Inherited Roman traditions of organization, seamanship, and shipbuilding continued to sustain the Byzantine naval effort against the Arabs and would carry the Greeks back into the offensive at sea by the tenth century. As in other cases, Greek Fire is an example of flashy weaponry that has overshadowed the technological and tactical essentials of military success in the historical imagination.

the tenth-century equivalent of those Eisenhower faced on D-Day in 1944 and demonstrated the sophisticated combined-arms operations a well-led imperial navy was capable of.

Challenges to Byzantine Dominance

The Caliphate and Muslim Naval Forces   There was a long pre-Islamic tradition of Arab seafaring. But sailing was the occupation of those Arabs living on the southern and eastern coasts of Arabia, who conducted strictly merchant shipping—there was no Arab tradition of naval warfare—in the Indian Ocean,

not the Mediterranean. Their ships, small craft constructed from planks sewn together with coconut husks, reflected both the small-scale, private nature of Arab trading and the lack of cheap iron for nails and would have been unsuitable for warfare in any case. Thus, the Caliphate, created by Arabs from the northwestern interior of Arabia, really had no native resources of either men or material to draw on to create a combat navy in the Mediterranean.

Given their background, it is not surprising that the earliest caliphs in fact had no interest in naval forces. Umar, the second caliph, tried to prohibit naval raids on Byzantine islands (some took place

Figure 10.1 The Mediterranean Maritime World, 800–1000

The pattern of winds and currents in the Mediterranean made from west-to-east and north-to-south travel easier than east-to-west and south-to-north travel, benefiting naval powers on the north coast and making the major midsea islands strategically vital.

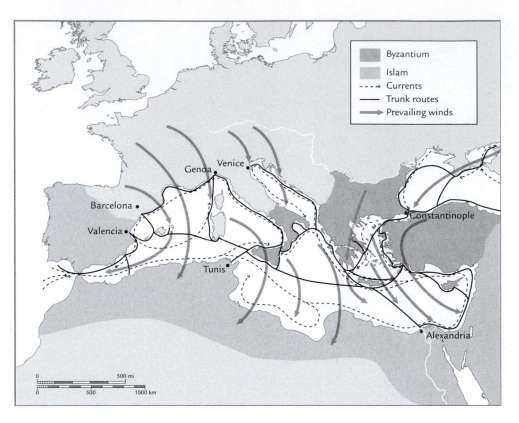

anyway, drawing his wrath). When the Muslim governor of Syria asked permission to raid Cyprus, Umar reflected on the advice that "man at sea is an insect on a splinter, now engulfed, now scared to death" and wrote back that "the safety of my people is dearer to me than all the treasures of Greece" and refused. Yet the necessity for naval forces became clear, first to local Muslim commanders, then to the caliphs, when the Byzantine navy threatened Muslim holdings with impunity. The great Egyptian port of Alexandria proved crucial in this process in several ways. Captured by the Muslims in 641, its vulnerability was exposed when a Byzantine fleet recaptured it in 645. Lack of support from Constantinople and the local Coptic population allowed the Arabs to recapture the city, but with any naval reinforcement, it could have been held against almost any land force. Yet the recapture of the city also provided the solution, for Alexandria was not only a port but a major naval base with facilities and skilled Coptic workmen. Supplied with Syrian timber, it could build a fleet for the Caliphate and supply Coptic oarsmen and navigators to serve under Arab admirals, who had no experience

of command at sea. The wholesale Muslim adoption of the Byzantine naval infrastructure in the African provinces they captured is reflected even in the administrative divisions of the Caliphate's navy, which retained their Roman names, and Copts continued to provide many of the sailors in Muslim naval forces for several centuries.

Arab armies thus took to the sea as marines aboard ships built and manned by recently conquered Egyptians. Success came remarkably quickly. In 655, a Muslim navy moved to invade Lycia, perhaps to secure supplies of timber for further shipbuilding. A major Byzantine fleet, said to have numbered 500 ships, moved to oppose the invasion, and a battle ensued off the coast of Lycia in Southwest Asia Minor. In what seems to have been a standard tactic for the times, the two fleets came together for what was essentially a land battle at sea, featuring hand-to-hand combat between each side's marines. The Byzantines probably counted on maintaining greater cohesion to give them the advantage, but the Copts apparently did well enough for their Muslim masters to allow Arab swordsmen to win the day.

SOURCES

Constantine VII Porphyrogenitus, De Administrando Imperio

As imposing and sophisticated pieces of technology, imperial warships were good not only for conducting naval campaigns but for conspicuously displaying imperial might and power. The following extracts from one of Emperor Constantine VII's treatises on imperial administration exemplify both the symbolic and the administrative sides of the imperial navy.

■   ■   ■

Until the reign of Leo [886–912, Constantine's father], the glorious and most wise emperor, there was no imperial galley (*dromon*) for the emperor to embark in, but he used to embark in a scarlet barge; except that, in the time of the Christ-loving sovereign Basil [867–886], when this same emperor visited the hot baths of Prousa, . . . he embarked in a galley and another galley followed behind. And the rowers who embarked in it were taken from the imperial barge and from the sailors of the Stenon. For of old the Stenon too had up to ten ships of war in the imperial navy. . . . But the glorious and most wise Leo, the emperor, who was rather more hospitably inclined towards magisters and patricians and familiars of senatorial rank, and who always wished them to share his pleasure in this, reckoned that the barge was inadequate for the reception of a larger number of nobles, and constructed a galley, and would invariably embark in it wherever he desired to go. And there would go with him whomsoever he might desire of the nobles, both of magisters and patricians. . . . For this reason, then, Leo, the glorious and most wise emperor, constructed the galley, and, some while after, he constructed another galley as well, which was known as the 'second' and christened 'Attache'. . . .

In the reign of Leo, the glorious and most wise emperor, when the new galleys were constructed by the imperial mandate, [the] protospatharius of the basin [a chief naval officer] had beneath his authority the oarsmen of these galleys also. Now, the aforesaid protospatharius of the basin would go down every day in the afternoon and take his seat in the basin (for which reason he was called protospatharius of the basin), and would judge cases arising between the oarsmen, both of the barges and of the galleys, over whom he had authority, and would give sentence and administer according to the law. And whenever he found anyone acting beyond his competence or wrongdoing another or remiss in his own work, he would punish him with a sound cudgelling. . . . The protospatharius Podaron and the protospatharius Leo Armenius had been chief oarsmen of the patrician Nasar, the lord admiral (*droungarios* of the *ploimon*), and in the time of Basil, the Christ-loving sovereign, were promoted from the navy and became the chief oarsmen of the barge of the emperor; and in the reign of Leo, the glorious and most wise emperor, when he constructed the galleys, he made them steersmen for their bravery and seamanship. And when a crisis arose, the emperor seconded the oarsmen of the two galleys, together with the two steersmen of the first galley, to ships of war in the navy, giving them much needful equipment, such as shields, leather targes, very fine coats of mail and everything else that naval personnel require to take with them; and the patrician Eustathius, the lord admiral, took them with the imperial fleet and went off against the enemy.

SOURCE: Constantine Porphyrogenitus, *De Administrando Imperio,* ed. G. Moravcsik, trans. R. J. H. Jenkins (Washington, DC; Dumbarton Oaks, 1993), pp. 247–251.

The battle of Dhat al-Sawari opened the way for further Arab offensives at sea, and by the 680s, Arab fleets were raiding Sicily and threatening Constantinople. Combined land and naval offensives against the Byzantine capital culminated in the unsuccessful siege of the city in 717–718. After that, major naval offensives tailed off, though 827 saw both Sicily and Crete fall to Arab invasions, as noted above. Coastal raiding, only nominally under the control of the Caliphate, came to dominate Muslim naval activity in the eastern Mediterranean.

Thus, although organizationally the naval forces of the Caliphate bore some resemblance to an imperial navy, their offensive doctrine and strategic aims more closely resembled those of predatory sea peoples. The tension, perhaps exacerbated by a continuing reluctance of many northern Arabs to take up seafaring, which was viewed as less than noble, resulted in a lack of full commitment on the part of the Caliphate to maintain a true navy of imperial defense. This is reflected in the decline of Alexandria as a naval base in the 700s (a decline that also reflected shifts in trade routes brought about by Muslim conquests, emphasizing again the close connection of trade to military naval activity). It is also reflected in the fact that much Muslim naval activity even at the height of the Caliphate involved small-scale raiding by privateers who had the spiritual but not the material backing of the imperial government.

Sea Ghazis

With the decline of the Caliphate and the fragmentation of the Muslim world politically, Muslim naval activity especially in the western Mediterranean moved even more toward the predatory model. But political fragmentation was not the only factor that encouraged this development. The Muslim world had early on established a pattern of somewhat marginalized frontier warriors, *ghazis,* who carried the holy war to the infidels on a daily basis (see Chapter 8). This pattern proved easily adaptable to maritime frontiers as well, and Muslim corsairs in individual ships and small squadrons began to fight the *jihad* as a *guerre de course* (war by commerce raiding) against Christian shipping and as raids for plunder against Christian coastal settlements from early in the Caliphate, as we have seen.

These raids intensified in the ninth century as Carolingian defenses crumbled in western Europe (see Chapter 7) and reached their height in the tenth century. Based ultimately on the North African coast west of Tunis, the raiders created and profited from Muslim control of the central islands of the western sea: Sicily, Sardinia, Corsica, and the Balearics, all of which put them athwart the major Christian shipping routes and within easy range of Christian ports. In fact, significant pirate forces established themselves for a time in bases in southern France, whence they raided well inland. Though nominally part of the larger struggle of Islam with Christianity, much of this activity was typical of predatory sea peoples: private, piratical sometimes even of Muslim shipping, and not centrally directed. It did, however, contribute to the economic disruption and political fragmentation of post-Carolingian Europe.

The raids were carried out in small, fast galleys that could slip into and out of sheltered coves to take on water and provisions. The crews doubled as rowers and marines and were all free men sharing in the spoils of the raids. Such corsairs were hard to contain once at sea because of their mobility. Byzantine defenses were more effective against the *ghazis* in the eastern Mediterranean, but the empire had neither the inclination nor the resources to deal with Muslim piracy in the west, far from the empire's main bases. Defense against this threat was left to be developed by the maritime cities of Italy in the later tenth and eleventh centuries.

The Emergence of the Italians

Venice, in fact, as an outpost of Byzantium, might have contributed to imperial defenses against Muslim corsairs, but Venice looked first to the Adriatic and then to the east. It was western Italian cities led by Genoa and Bari that spearheaded the Christian resurgence in western waters. Slowly reviving trade spurred in such cities a greater interest in maritime defenses while providing greater resources for naval activity.

The Italian response was of necessity a primarily active defense. Ports erected walls and fortifications, but the tide turned when Christian ships took the offensive against Muslim shipping and above all when the pirate bases became the object of attack not just from Italian naval forces but from armies raised in southern France. That coast having been cleared, Genoese as well as Spanish galley forces began to raid and then contest control of the islands crucial to Muslim access to shipping routes. Again, non-Italians played a significant role: The Norman conquest of Sicily in the mid-eleventh century seriously restricted Muslim shipping. The advantages that Mediterranean wind and current patterns gave to those on the northern shores in any contest for the central islands and sea-lanes magnified the success of the Christian revival. By 1050, Christian ships, led by the Italians, controlled the western Mediterranean well enough that they increasingly turned their attention to fighting each other for dominance (Genoa and Venice emerged as the crucial rivals) and to contesting the eastern Mediterranean with Muslims and Byzantines.

The Italian revival demonstrated the vital connection between trade and naval warfare, and the governments of the cities reflected this. Increasingly dominated by merchant oligarchies, they took an active part in fostering trade and maritime defense. True hybrids between the imperial and predatory models, they would in the next age help develop a new, more mercantile, model of naval force.

Song China

A Chinese imperial navy emerged as a result of the founding of the Song dynasty in 960; the Song had a very different character from the earlier Tang dynasty (618–907). The Tang had been land-based in a number of ways. Its political center of gravity was in the north, facing Central Asia. Its expansionist energies were directed westward toward the steppes, following the route of its most important trade contacts, which were overland via the Silk Road. A strong seaborne trade in porcelain also developed out of the southern ports but was carried out almost exclusively by Persian and Arab merchants. Foreign domination of overseas trade was partly a result of official policy. Tang government and society were dominated by a militaristic aristocracy, hostile by inclination and philosophy to merchant activity, especially maritime trade. Great landowners looked to land for wealth and power, and the government regulated trade tightly and at times arbitrarily. In such an environment, a navy was quite low on the government's priority list.

The Song found themselves in a very different situation from the Tang. Hemmed in to the north and west by resurgent Asian nomads, the Song adopted a defensive strategy and looked much more actively to the sea for foreign contact and trade. Ports were refurbished, lighthouses were built along the coast, and government assistance flowed to merchants willing to challenge the Arab and Persian monopoly at sea. Social change opened the door to the policy shift. Many of the great aristocratic families had killed each other off in the fighting that brought down the Tang. The gentry, still traditional but less hostile (if only because less militaristic) to economic development, emerged to take their place, and merchants assumed a new social importance as well.

The government therefore became more supportive of trade, including providing for an imperial navy to protect Chinese merchants and patrol the coasts. A more active Chinese merchant marine not only encouraged this move but provided the resources in money, ships, and skilled sailors to create the navy. Consistent with an imperial defensive force, the tactics of Chinese warships evolved toward ship killing. The creation of ships with heavy prows for ramming opponents complemented the development of gunpowder bombs launched from shipboard catapults.

All of these trends would be intensified, and the imperial navy would take on a new importance in guarding the rivers that shielded southern China, when the northern Song capital fell to barbarians in 1127 and the dynasty retreated south of the Yangzi. With the loss of the cavalry lands of the north, the navy became, in effect, the second arm of Chinese defense alongside the infantry, and special river-going paddle-wheel ships with rams joined the Song naval arsenal. These developments are considered further in Chapters 14 and 15.

PREDATORY SEA PEOPLES

The Vikings

In contrast and sometimes in direct opposition to the great defensive naval establishments of the Byzantine and Chinese empires stood the decentralized but devastating seaborne raiders of the age of migration. The Vikings are undoubtedly the prototypical popular image of a predatory seagoing folk.

Origins and Types The reasons for the sudden irruption of Viking raiders out of Scandinavia in the late 700s have long been a matter of scholarly dispute, complicated by arguments about how large an irruption it actually was. Given the limits of even the best Viking maritime technology, the total numbers of explorers and settlers was probably fairly small. This casts doubt on population pressure as a major factor in the rise of Viking activity.

Rather, two factors seem most important. First, Scandinavian naval technology improved in the mid-700s. Sail power now complemented the traditional oars, and hulls got larger and more seaworthy. Neither change was revolutionary and probably only brought Viking technology up to the prevailing Baltic–North Sea standard, but together they made possible longer, more profitable voyages over more open seas. Second, political developments in Scandinavia probably provided the most important motive for the raids. As kings began to attempt to assert greater control over their kingdoms, local aristocrats and their followers decided that foreign adventure was preferable to restricted opportunities at home. Plunder was an attractive source of income not subject to royal taxation, one that gave the raid leader the wealth and prestige to attract followers. Exile could also be an escape from legal trouble. Christianity was often supported by and favorable to centralizing monarchs; abroad, missionaries need not be respected, and churches, in fact, provided a rich source of booty. In other words, centralization and aristocratic competition at first pushed the most troublesome elements of Scandinavian society onto the outside world. (The word *Viking* was originally a verb: *To go viking* meant "to go raiding," so, like Muslim *ghazis*, Vikings were raiders whose bands were often composed of different Scandinavian ethnic groups.) Later, as kings gained greater power, they launched expeditions of plunder and conquest, which served to harness and direct the warlike energies of the aristocracy and, through the distribution of plunder, bind their loyalties to the monarchy.

Thus, Viking warfare fell into several different categories: small-scale fights and feuds, mostly internal to Viking society; small private raids with the boatload as the basic military unit; larger, more extended raids of a dozen to several hundred ships, sometimes under royal or pseudoroyal leadership (the leader of a major and successful excursion might claim the title "king"); and full royal expeditions of conquest. Generally, the smaller raids and larger but still nonroyal campaigns took place from the late 700s to the early 900s. Such forays were as likely to be defeated as not and resulted in little permanent conquest. Then, from about 900 to the mid-1000s, expeditions were increasingly royal—whether Norwegian, Swedish, or Danish—and saw greater success in conquest. We include all these different peoples under the loose heading of Vikings.

Viking Military Forces   Viking boats came in a variety of shapes and sizes, with a definite difference between the deep-draught, round merchant sailing ships and the famous longboats—narrow, shallow-draught ships with oars as well as sail—used for war. The difference is similar to, though not quite as pronounced or specialized as, the Mediterranean ships of the day, for similar reasons. The warships' chief advantage was tactical maneuverability and speed, and, for battle, they carried a large crew relative to their cargo capacity.

The Oseberg Ship   Recovered by naval archaeologists, this partial hull (note that the sides were originally built up higher) shows the long, lean lines and high stem and stern typical of Viking longships.

A typical warship might be 18–20 meters in length, with room for 24–30 oars. Loaded for battle it could conceivably carry as many as 100 men, but as few as 30 would be more common for sailing any distance, as a large crew was logistically difficult to sustain and made the boat far less seaworthy. A similar tradeoff applied to ship size. Some warships reached 29 meters in length, with room for 52 oars, and might carry up to 300 men in battle. The size of the crew and the size of the boat, especially the height of the gunwales, made such monsters formidable in a sea fight, but their strategic range was much more limited because of their crew size.

Despite a formidable modern reputation, Viking navigation was not terribly advanced. Longboats were shallow, open vessels with little cargo space, so almost all Viking voyages were coastal, or at best one- or two-day hops between known islands and landfalls. Only the trip to Iceland required significant sailing out of sight of land (even the Iceland-to-Greenland crossing is visible from both ends because of the height of the mountains on each); the Iceland voyage was not made by huge numbers of settlers, and the island remained fairly isolated once settled. But Europe's long coastline and many navigable rivers, for which Viking boats were also well suited, put nearly the whole continent from Russia to Spain and into the Mediterranean within reach.

Given the limits of ships' size and navigation, Viking armies never numbered more than a few thousand at their largest, and a typical raiding party might range from a few score to a couple hundred. Viking warriors were armed with spears, axes, swords, and bows, and they carried round shields. Some wore chain-mail shirts, but many did not, especially at sea. They were too expensive for many Vikings, and they made rowing difficult and swimming impossible. Thus, Viking armies ashore had no particular advantage over their enemies in armor or arms, and indeed were often at a disadvantage in the latter, as indicated by the Frankish origin of many Viking swords. Nor were Viking armies unusually formidable in terms of organization, tactics, or morale. It was their ships, and thus their strategic mobility, that made them terrifying. Overall, as engineers, the Vikings were capable but limited, inventing little. Good at creative ways of moving ships overland, they proved far less successful at building siege engines.

Viking Warfare   The aim of Viking warfare was economic gain, as well as enhancement of a warriors' prestige. If the warrior were a king, his success could help strengthen the state—certainly, the distribution of plunder bound the ruling class together more tightly. But that again comes back to economic gain. Vikings could therefore be traders, pirates, raiders, or conquerors interchangeably, depending on the opportunities and the capabilities and strength of any opposition. In any of these roles, it was their ships, and thus their mobility, as noted already, that was their key capability. Any place within reach of a beachable coastline or impression river was vulnerable to sudden attack.

Viking raiders recognized the need for mobility on land as well and so took to seizing herds of horses when they established a beachhead, so that they could then roam farther over the countryside in search of loot. The aim, whether by land or water, was to hit soft, rich targets and avoid a major fight. Monasteries were ideal targets, and the fact that monks wrote the only chronicles of the times accounts in part for the pagan Vikings' reputation for brutality and the perhaps exaggerated impression of the extent of their depredations.

Battles with local defense forces could not always be avoided, however, and major Viking armies sometimes even sought battle to further territorial conquest, or at least accepted it when defending armies moved to relieve a city or fort under Viking attack.

But success or failure in battle was a less important limitation on Viking strategies of conquest than was their weakness in siege warfare (see the Highlights box "The Siege of Paris, 885"). Siege engines could not be carried aboard ship and proved difficult to improvise on the spot, nor were Vikings enthusiastic miners. Viking forces most often resorted to sudden surprise attacks, treachery, or, failing all else, blockades to take fortified cities. Not surprisingly, then, the most successful Viking conquests came in areas where fortifications were either few in number (Anglo-Saxon England) or virtually nonexistent (Ireland, Russia).

Given Viking weakness in siege warfare, systematic programs of fortification were the best defenses against their raids. Charles the Bald of France ordered the construction of fortified bridges to restrict the mobility of Viking fleets. But none of the powers facing the Vikings managed to sustain such a campaign for long, save for England under Alfred, whose system of fortified burghs and field armies turned the tide in his wars with the Danes (see Chapter 7).

When it came to battle, Viking land tactics were unexceptional for their age. They fought in a shield-wall sometimes divided into one to three divisions or lines, with warriors grouped around their immediate chiefs—groupings probably carried over from shipboard to land. The formation in defense might offer refused flanks or even all-around defense, and, in attack, the Vikings at times used a sort of wedge formation, with the best-armed and most enthusiastic warriors leading the way. But Viking armies were capable of little in the way of tactical maneuver once a battle was under way. The only other tactic of note among Viking armies was *berserking*—a battle frenzy that could carry a warrior to seemingly superhuman feats of strength and endurance even with major wounds. Again, Viking berserkers have a fearsome modern reputation, but similar sorts of behavior are attested not just in other ancient and medieval armies from heroic societies (the *Iliad* offers fine examples) but in modern wars as well, where it is seen as a form of temporary insanity often associated with posttraumatic stress disorder, the symptoms of which can also be seen in Viking accounts of strange warrior behavior after battles. What seems most unusual about Viking berserking is not the behavior itself but the degree to which the culture celebrated and even encouraged it. But even berserking did not make Viking armies invincible. Viking forces lost battles more frequently than they won them.

The Siege of Paris, 885

Between 865 and 895, Viking forces in western Europe concentrated into a Great Army of several thousand men supported by several hundred ships. The Great Army operated initially in England, successfully pursuing a strategy of conquest and eliminating every Saxon kingdom save Alfred's Wessex. After a crisis in the mid-870s, Alfred defeated the Great Army and its king, Guthrum, at Eddington in 878. Contained by the Saxons, the Great Army received reinforcements and moved to the Continent, where growing political chaos after Charles the Bald's death in 876 beckoned. For several years after 879, the Vikings ravaged in the valleys of the Scheldt, Rhine, and Meuse rivers, seizing or establishing fortified bases each winter from which to plunder the surrounding territory on horseback. But, by 885, the area had been picked bare, and the army briefly split up in early 885, with part of the fleet going to Kent.

The West Frankish ruler Carloman had died without an heir in December 884, and the Great Army reunited in July on the Seine, whose valley had been untouched for nearly twenty years. Sailing upriver, the fleet forced a passage past the weakly held fortified bridge at Pont de l'Arche and arrived at Paris in the late fall. The city stood on an island in the middle of the river, connected to the banks by two bridges guarded by unfinished forts. Frankish forces were led by Count Odo of Paris and probably numbered several hundred. The Great Army was estimated at 40,000 men and 700 ships by Abbo, an eyewitness who memorialized the siege in a long poem, but was undoubtedly at least an order of magnitude smaller.

In late November, the Vikings attempted to storm the northern fort but were repulsed. With winter approaching, they established a fortified camp from which to blockade the city and ravage the surrounding territory. Active siege operations resumed in the spring, as rogue Frankish engineers helped the Vikings build siege towers and catapults. At one point, the Vikings sent a fireship against the bridge. But the attempt to burn the bridge was unsuccessful, and, through the summer, every assault on the forts failed. Furthermore, the Vikings were unable to maintain a complete blockade of the city. Several times, small relief forces and fresh provisions made it into the city either by river or by land. But larger relief efforts led by Henry of Saxony and Charles the Fat were both defeated by the Vikings, who remained secure in their fortified camp.

The Vikings kept the pressure on into the following fall. Charles the Fat, facing another winter of plundering in the heart of his kingdom, finally ended the stalemate by paying a huge bribe to the Great Army to move on, offering them passage past the fortified bridge at Paris. This opened up Burgundy, Champagne, and the upper Loire valley to the raiders. The fortifications at Paris thus saved the city but failed strategically to guard the territories upriver, which suffered several years of raiding that led to the deposition of Charles.

The Great Army operated until 892 in parts of Frankia. It met increasing resistance and more numerous fortifications but ultimately left only because of famine. Returning to England, it met further effective resistance from Alfred's reorganized kingdom and finally broke up in 896. The Siege of Paris was probably the high point of the first phase of Viking activity. The campaigns and the history of the Great Army show clearly both the strengths and the weaknesses of Viking warfare.

Viking tactics at sea are better documented than their land tactics, despite the fact that sea battles were far rarer than land battles. Like Mediterranean galleys, the longboats' striking power was centered in their bows; tapping the longboat's mobility, the Vikings could pick a vulnerable target and aim the ship at it. As a result, when faced with battle, the defenders (often the weaker or smaller fleet), if they were unable to avoid the fight, would try to lash their ships together in line abreast, bows to the attackers, presenting as solid a target as possible. Creating one large fighting platform out of a line of ships also allowed reinforcements to be moved most easily to threatened spots in the line. Where possible, one end of the line would be anchored to rocks, protecting that flank.

The attacking longboats, operating individually, rowed to the attack, attempting to pick off isolated defending ships, if any, or to concentrate their attack on the weakest point in the line and get around the flanks. As the ships came in range of each other, missile fire opened the battle, followed by attempts on the part of the attackers to grapple and board the defenders. When the battle reached this stage of hand-to-hand fighting, the architecture of the ships played a crucial role in the outcome. It was here that big ships had a definite advantage. For one thing, their larger crews could wear down the less numerous crew of a smaller ship. For another, their higher gunwales provided better protection against enemy arrows and an advantageous platform for firing and boarding. (Shields were hung over the sides of the ships only for ceremonial entrances and exits from harbor, and so would not have added to the defensive value of the gunwales.) Warriors on a small ship might have trouble boarding a large ship at all. Also, larger ships could stand rougher conditions at sea. As a result, the number of ships in a fleet or even the number of men in a fleet might not be an effective measure of its strength: at Roberry around 1044, thirty large ships defeated sixty smaller ships, for example. Especially large and strong boats might even be *barded*—sheathed in iron at the bow, increasing the strength of the ship at that vital spot. But, like larger crews, barding was a tactical device that entailed strategic penalties in terms of range and seaworthiness, as well as being quite costly.

Viking sea tactics were designed to capture ships, not to sink them. A ship was valuable in itself and was likely to be carrying valuable cargo. Viking tactics were effective in their home waters, mostly against other Vikings. But when Viking fleets, admittedly of smaller ships, reached the Black Sea in the tenth and eleventh centuries, the Byzantine navy was capable of dealing with them without much trouble (see above). Scandinavian warriors were useful enough to the Greeks to form the backbone of Basil II's Varangian Guard, which drew Vikings and Anglo-Saxons to imperial service for a century after the 980s, but their utility was as much in their lack of political connections as their fighting ability.

The Vikings' Impact   The Vikings certainly wreaked havoc through much of Europe for almost 200 years, but the extent of their depredations is easy to exaggerate. They conquered only in areas that were politically weak or disorganized, and they left only minor cultural imprints in areas they ruled or settled. Their lasting influence was much more in the creation and expansion of a vast maritime trade network stretching from Ireland through Russia to Byzantium. The Baltic Sea and North Sea ships that continued this trade past the Viking age would contribute significantly to later European naval development.

Srivijaya

The major maritime power in Southeast Asia for much of this period was Srivijaya. Centered on the east coast of Sumatra and the port of Palembang, the Srivijaya state flourished from the 600s into the 1000s (Figure 10.2). Its broad influence over the coasts of the region and the maritime trade that flowed through it, the profits of which were essential to Srivijaya's existence, have led historians to refer to it as a thalassocracy, that is, an imperial naval state like the classical Athenian empire. Unfortunately, the sources for Srivijayan history are scant and unclear, and projecting the image of Athens on these sources is probably unwarranted. Srivijaya was almost certainly not a centralized naval empire on the model of classical Athens. But as a looser polity, it did exercise naval power effectively for several centuries.

The rise of Chinese-centered maritime trade under the Tang dynasty stimulated the formation of port-states along the route from the Mediterranean, Arabia, and Persia to Canton, especially in the area of the Straits of Malacca (Melaka), an important layover and transshipment point because of the monsoon weather patterns. The ports also served to link their hinterlands to the international trade routes. Competition among such states resulted in the triumph of a center around Palembang, which then brought the other ports into a hierarchical confederation and focused trade on a few favored ports; the resulting polity became known as Srivijaya.

The military power of the Srivijayan ruler resulted from his ability to integrate forces from the hinterlands

Figure 10.2 Srivijaya and the Chola Kingdom, c. 1000.

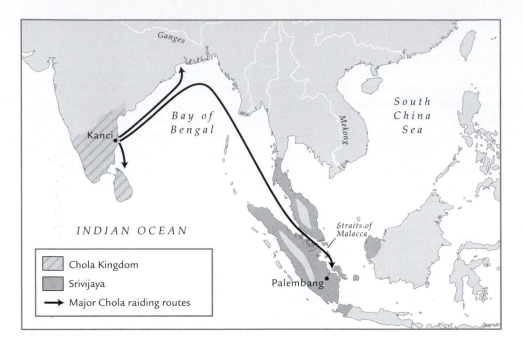

under the command of regional warlords and aristocrats with the naval resources of the nomadic sea peoples of the area. Careful alliance making backed by powerful religious sanctions helped create and maintain the system. Srivijaya's ability to suppress piracy and provide a safe haven for merchants allowed it to extend its influence over coastal entrepôts (trade cities) from Java to the Malay Peninsula. Once established, Chinese recognition and the resulting prestige of the Srivijaya name reinforced the ties binding the state together, as did the distribution of profits from the center to the component parts of the state.

Little can be said of the details of Srivijayan military methods. Southeast Asian and Indian Ocean ships were well but relatively lightly constructed, so that ship-to-ship action was unlikely to have played a major role in Srivijayan warfare. Amphibious operations were more the norm, especially as control of a port brought economic control, or at least influence, over the port's hinterlands, and so raids and military operations could be focused on concentrated targets.

As long as management of coastal competition and suppression of piracy were its chief military responsibilities, Srivijaya thrived. But from the middle of the tenth century, the spreading overseas trade brought increasing competition for its riches at the same time that it helped stimulate the growth of new land-based powers in the region. This exposed the weaknesses of

the Srivijaya polity. In the eleventh century, Srivijaya would prove incapable of containing the threats to its naval hegemony.

The Cholas

Origins and Structure The crucial challenge came from the Coromandel coast of south India, home of the expanding Chola Empire (see Figure 10.2). Initially, the focus of Chola activity was land-based, as it carved a place for itself between hostile established powers starting in the 700s. The state that emerged was not especially strong or centralized. Chola kingship had significant ritual elements: Influence over outlying provinces and regional elites was often fairly nominal and was exercised through religious symbolism. There was little in the way of a royal bureaucracy. As a result, the state was held together by its expansionism: Raiding expeditions brought plunder to the royal house, which distributed it to its followers as a demonstration of the kings' wealth and prestige. Permanent conquests provided not just plunder but lands. Thus, Chola warfare was politically motivated and primarily economic in its aims, even though it was mostly touted as religiously based. Raiding expeditions whose benefits were obscure to the larger population were justified as "quests for relics," the successful capture of which was broadcast as the result of such raids.

The economic aim of Chola warfare became important in maritime terms because of the nature of the empire's mercantile links with the wider world. Local production was tied to regional and overseas trade routes through temple centers where merchant associations operated. These merchant associations were virtually independent powers, maintaining operations around the Bay of Bengal. As Chola power expanded, both the royal government and the merchants saw benefits in an aggressive assertion of Chola might along the main trade routes.

Naval raiding increased the royal government's mobile wealth, already established as the source of their prestige; trade goods and centers were particularly suitable targets in this regard. Naval raids also provided, perhaps in even better form, the political advantages of land raids. By drawing local elites and their military forces into such activity, Chola kings both integrated the elites more tightly into their own power network and displaced their aggressive, predatory tendencies to areas outside the kingdom. Overseas expeditions had the additional benefit of creating concentrations of such forces far enough away to reduce the threat of internal discord or revolt. Finally, reasonable calculations of political advantage pointed to expeditions of plunder or conquest as an offensive defense: Carrying war to Sri Lanka, for example, forestalled Sri Lankan raids on Chola lands. To all of these push factors impelling Chola naval forces outward was added the pull factor of political instability or weakness in the main target areas, especially Sri Lanka.

Chola naval activity reached its peak between 985 and 1070, under the kings Rajaraja and his son Rajendra. Rajaraja was the innovator, initiating the naval strategy, forging the internal alliances, and amassing the forces necessary to carry out this new aggressive strategy. Rajendra reaped much of the glory from his spectacular exploitation of the system his father created, but he also inherited the growing problems the strategy created. It is an exaggeration of both Chola power and the naval technology of the time to say that during this time the Bay of Bengal was a Chola lake, but the sense in terms of prestige and impact is not far off the mark.

There were two major landmarks of Chola naval activity in this period. The conquest of northern Sri Lanka was the more conventional: Ships ferried troops to the island, where they waged a campaign of conquest. Of greater regional significance was a set of raids clear across the Bay of Bengal into the heart of the Srivijayan sphere of influence. In 1025, Rajendra launched a major expedition that ravaged the northeastern Sumatran coast, finally sacking the Srivijayan capital. Cholas inscriptions memorialize the "conquest" of Srivijaya; the Cholas did not actually take over and administer the Srivijayan state, but they did become significant political players in the straits for another fifty years. More important, the blow to Srivijayan prestige and their reputation for securing trade routes and centers was devastating, and trade patterns began to diffuse more widely through Southeast Asian waters as competition for the lucrative business intensified. A Chola raid in 1067 on the Srivijayan-influenced coast of the Malay Peninsula completed the work, and the Srivijaya thalassocracy collapsed. Political and economic patterns in the area would remain fragmented until the rise of Malacca in the fifteenth century with the assistance of the great Ming treasure fleets under Zheng He (see Chapter 15).

Despite the 1067 expedition, Chola activity decreased after Rajendra's death in 1044, and for the rest of the century, the Chola rulers attempted to shift from an exploitive raiding strategy to regular administration of their conquests, especially in Sri Lanka. However, continued guerrilla resistance by the islanders created a steady drain on Chola resources, exactly the sort of outflow of treasure the Chola polity was unable to sustain. By the 1070s, Chola forces were already withdrawing from Sri Lanka, and the empire thereafter went into decline.

Chola Warfare We have much less information about the details of Chola warfare than we do for the Vikings. The campaigns are well chronicled, though the sources are heavily biased, the "conquest" of Srivijaya being typical of the presentation of Chola feats of arms by official sources. But they provide few practical details of the basic military organization and technique. Nonetheless, some broad outlines are discernible.

The army consisted of a combination of forces. At the core was the body of royal troops maintained permanently by the king as an imperial guard, ceremonial corps, and personal warband. This small force was supplemented by mercenaries and by the warbands of powers subordinate to the king. The bulk of such forces came from the landed elites, but a significant number of soldiers were maintained as mercenary warbands by the merchant associations, and these, too, joined royal expeditions, emphasizing the economic aims of Chola warfare. Almost all the troops were infantry armed with spears and bows. South India was poor country for raising horses and mounting cavalry operations, and on overseas campaigns, horses would have been difficult and expensive to transport. Chola forces, like armies throughout the subcontinent in this period, included war elephants. But their use in naval or amphibious warfare was out of the question The army as a whole was thus a composite force assembled for particular campaigns, not a standing force except for a small core of royal household troops. Likewise, there was no royal navy, only ad hoc armadas drawn from the south Indian merchant community.

Chola strategy was straightforward: Pick a convenient or symbolically significant target, and make the raid. That there was little actual planning to the minimal strategy behind Chola naval activity is demonstrated by the difficulties the empire encountered in trying to manage the transition from raids to conquest to administration in Sri Lanka—the weakly centralized Chola state was not built for careful planning and systematic assimilation of new territory.

Tactically, the Cholas were similar to the Vikings in that there was nothing particularly innovative or effective about their methods of waging war. What made their raids effective was the seaborne mobility that gave them the element of surprise. As for naval tactics, ship-to-ship encounters were even rarer than for the Vikings—the navy was essentially an amphibious landing force. The hulls of the ships of the Indian Ocean were usually sewn together with coconut husks rather than nailed to frames, a lightweight but effective method for cargo carrying but one that made the ships unsuitable to be used as weapons themselves. The economic motive behind Chola warfare would in any case have tended toward the capture rather than the sinking of shipping, just as for the Vikings and the Srivijayans.

Like the Vikings and Srivijaya, Chola military techniques were conventional, and the political and military impact of their raids and conquests was transient. The limited naval technology at their disposal did not allow much more. The main impact of Chola naval operations was on patterns of trade, not on patterns of warfare. The decentralization and diffusion of southeast Asian trade stimulated by the Chola raids on Srivijaya had consequences as important and lasting as the Viking impact on trade in northern Europe. What the operations of all the predatory sea peoples show is the connection through maritime activity of world trade and state building. The wealth generated as goods flowed between the Mediterranean and China, and beyond in every direction, often proved decisive in bringing a higher level of political organization to areas that tapped into that wealth, whether through plunder, piracy, or commerce. This connection would continue to tie trade, piracy, and naval war closely together, and would help generate a new model of naval power in subsequent centuries.

CONCLUSION

Though the period 400–1100 saw significantly more global naval activity than the classical age, the scope and impact of naval warfare was still limited and acted essentially as an adjunct to land warfare in strictly military terms. This was because naval technology still placed severe constraints on the capabilities of seaborne military forces. Land-based powers remained far vaster and more influential than sea powers. Yet the globalization of naval warfare itself was important, as it reflected, followed, and drew on the growing world maritime trade, a trend that would continue in the following age and become decisive after 1500, creating in the process a new model of naval power.

SUGGESTED READINGS

Ahrweiler, Helene. *Byzance et la Mer.* Paris: Presses universitaires de France, 1966. The fundamental maritime history of the Byzantine Empire.

Fahmy, Aly Mohamed. *Muslim Naval Organization in the Eastern Mediterranean from the Seventh to the Tenth Century AD.* Cairo: National Publication and Print House, 1966. Focuses on the administrative, economic, and manpower issues of Muslim naval power.

Hall, Kenneth. *Maritime Trade and State Development in Early Asia.* Honolulu: University of Hawaii Press, 1985. Also *Trade and Statecraft in the Age of the Colas.* Delineates the close connections between economic activity, state building, and elite management, and Chola naval activity.

Hall, Kenneth, and John K. Whitmore, eds. *Explorations in Early Southeast Asian History: The Origins of Southeast Asian Statecraft.* Ann Arbor: Center for South and Southeast Asia Studies, University of Michigan, 1976. A collection of articles exploring Srivijayan naval power and its connection to state power and the network of Southeast Asian trade, 1000–1200.

Hourani, George. *Arab Seafaring,* Rev. and exp. ed. Princeton: Princeton University Press, 1995. A classic exploration of the Arab role in Indian Ocean trade networks from ancient times to about 1000.

Jesch, Judith. *Ships and Men in the Late Viking Age.* Woodbridge: Boydell, 2001. A significant recent work on Viking naval institutions; accessible despite being aimed at specialists.

Landstrom, Bjorn. *The Ship.* London: Allen & Unwin, 1961. A good introductory survey, lavishly illustrated, of the evolution of ship designs throughout the world, though focused on Europe.

Lewis, Archibald, and Timothy Runyon. *European Naval and Maritime History, 300–1500.* Bloomington: Indiana University Press, 1985. Fundamental survey of naval history that includes Byzantium and Islam in the Mediterranean.

Pryor, John H. *Geography, Technology, and War. Studies in the Maritime History of the Mediterranean 649–1571.* Cambridge: Cambridge University Press, 1988. A superb examination of the combined influence of geography, including weather patterns, and naval technology on naval conflict in the Mediterranean.

Sawyer, Peter. *Kings and Vikings.* New York: Methuen, 1982. A solid overview of the Viking impact on European society.

Shanmugam, P. *The Revenue System of the Cholas, 850–1279.* Madras: New Era Publications, 1987. Useful for the role of tribute and maritime exchange, including trade and plunder, in the Chola state system.

Spencer, George W. *The Politics of Expansion: The Chola Conquest of Sri Lanka and Srivijaya.* Madras: New Era Publications, 1983. A clear analysis of the internal dynamics of Chola expansionism, stressing the relationship of king and aristocracy.

Unger, Richard W. *The Ship in the Medieval Economy, 600–1600.* London: Croom Helm, 1980. Provides the important economic setting for naval warfare in an age before specialized navies, and traces in detail technological improvements of ship design.

Whittow, Mark. *The Making of Byzantium, 600–1025.* Berkeley: University of California Press, 1996. Contains brief but incisive sections on the Byzantine navy and its Roman heritage.

COMMENTARY: PART 2, 400–1100

We have called this section "The Age of Migration and Invasion," and the impact of nomads of various types is one of the key themes in this period. The end of the classical world witnessed significant movements of peoples across Eurasia and considerable flux in the boundaries and cultural content of the major civilized traditions. The instability of the age was one factor in the rise of the salvation religions, and the link between war and religion is the second major theme of this period. Both the impact of nomads and the rise of holy war highlight a central focus of this book as a whole: that warfare is one expression of the societies that wage it, an expression dominated in this age by landed warrior elites.

THE NOMADIC IMPACT

Horse-archers from the Asian steppes were the dominant nomadic military force at this time, but not the only one. Most of the seminomadic Germanic tribes facing the Roman Empire moved largely on foot, and their movements constituted migrations more than the rapid invasions and withdrawals of the horse peoples. Some, such as the Saxons, also moved by sea, putting them in the second major category of nomadic raiders, the sea peoples, of whom the Vikings are the most famous. The tribesmen of the Saudi Arabian peninsula constitute a special subclass of nomadic horse people. Their tactical traditions, having little emphasis on archery, differed from those of the steppe tribes. Their seventh-century explosion was unique in their history, in contrast to the steady waves of invasion and withdrawal on the steppes, as their homeland was too poor in resources to support the political hierarchies that powered the excursions of the Central Asian horsemen. But they shared many of the advantages, at least briefly, of nomads everywhere.

Mobility, strategic and tactical, was the military key to the success of all types of nomads. Horses or ships, tied to no particular base of operations, let nomadic forces strike from unexpected directions and at unexpected times, making planned responses to their raids difficult. To this advantage, the horsemen of the steppes added accurate firepower on a large scale from their composite bows and their unmatched soldierly skills bred from their lifestyle—the skills honed in constant competition with other nomadic groups, and the hardness that led them to hold settled peoples in contempt as "soft" and "effeminate." Used to a life on horseback with short rations, the horsemen added a ruthlessness such that massed infantry were viewed as just another slaughterable herd animal. Such conditions also trained effective leaders; unity among nomads was the major limitation on their offensive actions. Sea peoples were less formidable tactically, but fighting them was expensive. Only Byzantium and Song China, big empires with vital maritime interests, could afford the permanent combat navies that could check raiders at sea. Local responses tended toward systems of fortification that were only marginally effective.

The impact of nomadic invasions was felt throughout the Eurasian world in this period, from Rome to China—in the Arab regions, in Byzantium, in India, and again near the end of the period in southwest Asia. Nomadic activity and the movement of peoples created some links and cross-cultural fertilization, especially if the creation of the vast Islamic world is interpreted as resulting from an originally nomadic impulse. The trade networks that spread from the Straits of Gibraltar to the Straits of Malacca tied together a truly world civilization. But, in most cases, the migrations and invasions of 400–1100 probably disrupted existing patterns and links more than they added to them. The early waves certainly coincided with the breakdown of classical empires at both ends of the Silk Road and with the temporary decline of the road itself, and they advanced the political fragmentation that succeeded the Age of Empires everywhere. Nomadic horsemen thus contributed to an increase in the importance of cavalry in the warfare of this age both directly by their tactics and indirectly through the decline of the central authorities necessary to create effective infantry in settled polities.

Horse-archers had appeared on the scene early in the classical age, but their impact increased noticeably after 400. Why? Technological explanations based on the introduction and spread of the stirrup tend to bog down in the details of archaeological dating. The stirrup may have played a role in slowly increasing the military efficiency of nomadic horsemen, but it was not crucial to their increased impact after 400. Instead, larger social and economic trends stand out. Most important, the various civilizations surrounding the steppes had grown in size and wealth over the prior millennium. Not only did their greater wealth make them more attractive targets for nomadic raiders, but the export of some of that wealth to nomadic tribes in the form of trade and tribute stimulated and made possible the formation of the nomadic hierarchies and state structures that were a prerequisite to successful nomadic invasions. The geographic spread of areas under settled control put pressure on nomadic territories while at the same time making routes into settled lands more accessible. Such geographic expansion could also set up a domino effect, as, for example, when the Han expansion in the first century BCE contributed to the westward movement of tribes that eventually put pressure on Rome. Nomad populations, too, though more constrained by the economic limits of their homelands, had grown, as had the size of their herds. The combination of greater inputs of goods from settled areas and larger nomadic tribes resulted in larger confederations of Asiatic tribes that posed a greater threat to their neighbors. Whether the subsequent increase in nomadic activity was a cause or a result of the decline of the big classical empires (probably a combination of both), it certainly contributed to the disorders of the postclassical world. In the specific case of the Arab explosion, the exhaustion of the Byzantine and Persian empires after decades of war opened the door to Arab conquests, while the historically unusual unity of the Arabs flowed in small part from local economics and in large part from the leadership of Muhammad and his successors. The latter links the nomadic impact to the rise of the great salvation religions and their relationship to war.

WAR AND RELIGION

The rise of the great salvation religions—Buddhism, Christianity, and Islam (and perhaps parts of Hinduism)—was not fundamentally a military phenomenon, even in the case of Islam, whose early expansion was so closely tied to conquest. The religions responded to spiritual and political needs raised by the conditions of the classical and postclassical ages, meeting those needs across a broad spectrum of society. Indeed, all of them tended toward a democratization of classical cultures, helping create more peasant-friendly systems of belief in response to troubled times.

Inevitably, however, religion and war, two activities that along with agriculture dominated life in the traditional world, became intimately linked. The link was often forged early on: The rise of Buddhism and Christianity as mass religions is associated with the careers of converted conquerors, Asoka and Constantine, and Islam's founder,

Muhammad, also acted as early Islam's military leader. And with Christianity and Islam, the link developed into forms and theories of holy war, warfare conducted on behalf of religion and rewarded by the religion's god. *Jihad* motivated the early Arab explosion; militant religion proved a powerful weapon in the expansion of western Christianity into pagan lands and in the defense of eastern Christianity against pagans, Persians, and Muslims. "Holy war" cultures rose from a number of causes. The intolerance of the monotheistic religions meant that they could accommodate force (with more or less comfort) as a tool of converting or punishing unbelievers. The wide class appeal of the religions also meant that they could mobilize popular commitment, and so contributed to a deeper rootedness of the various civilized traditions that sometimes brought them into more lasting conflict. And the prospect of martyrdom and salvation tied the ultimate reward promised by these religions directly to heroic military effort. The end result of this link was the creation of an ideological dimension to war that had not existed before and that tended to emphasize the differences rather than the similarities between competing traditions.

War and Society: Land, Lordship, and Warriors

One job of the world historian, military or otherwise, is to recognize but see past differences to the underlying similarities and comparisons. It is true that different peoples have fought in different ways throughout history. In this period, nomads differed from settled peoples in styles of warfare; and, among the settled civilizations, there were a wide variety of tactical traditions and strategic patterns influenced by varying social, economic, religious, and cultural contexts. But fundamental economic constraints also imposed an underlying similarity on many of Eurasia's peoples in terms of social and therefore military organization, a similarity that stands out with particular clarity in this age.

All traditional, or preindustrial, civilizations drew the vast majority of their wealth from agriculture, making land (and control of land) the key to power and prestige. In this period, with the decline or contraction in many areas of the centralized monetary and administrative systems of the great classical empires, control of landed estates became even more directly a source of power as well as economic support. This was even more true where contractions or disruptions in trade damaged the economies of cities. Even temporary declines opened the door to a greater role for rural elites with lordship of some sort over peasantry. The need to protect their source of wealth, especially in the absence of a strong central authority, led such men naturally to the role of warrior strongman, while considerations of prestige and strategic mobility usually led them onto horseback wherever horses could be raised, though how they fought (mounted or on foot, with missile weapons or hand-to-hand) could vary widely.

This widespread tendency to the domination of society by a mounted, rural warrior elite manifested itself in a number of ways throughout Eurasia. In less centralized polities, arrangements for the landed support of warriors were formalized in one way or another, becoming central to the sociopolitical organization of such areas. The emergence of feudalism in western Europe, of the *iqta'*, in Islamic lands (especially under the Seljuk Turks), and of similar institutions in India exemplify this process. In areas that retained or recovered traditions of central control, accommodating the role and power of rural warrior elites proved a lasting challenge, for their very military usefulness made them a potential threat to state power. The Tang dynasty tried several ways to incorporate effective cavalry forces in their armies, and it was the dynasty most dominated by great warrior aristocrats. The Byzantine government's Farmer's Law institutionalized central protection of small farmers against the depredations of great landowners; when that balance broke down, the empire's defenses collapsed.

In military terms, the same factors that heightened the role of mounted rural warriors—weakened central authority and urban economies in decline or disruption—also made the creation of effective infantry forces more difficult. Thus, after the emphasis in the classical age on the emergence of trained massed infantry forces, this age appears, in contrast, to be an age of cavalry. The effectiveness of nomadic horsemen adds to this impression, and, in some cases, nomadic cavalry were the rural warrior elites of various civilizations: The Tang and many Islamic states drew heavily on the military skills of their nomadic neighbors and rewarded them with land.

Against this fundamental background, we may now turn to the developments of the next age of world history, developments that would affect social, economic, and political structures and, in turn, the military systems linked to them.

PART 3

THE AGE OF TRADITIONS IN CONFLICT, 1100–1500

CHAPTER 11

Cross and Crescent: The Middle East, 1100–1450

The period 1100–1500 was an age of increasing global contact through war and trade, dominated by the Mongol explosion of the thirteenth century. But it opened with the meeting of three civilizations and their military systems at the eastern end of the Mediterranean. The Crusades brought western Europe, Byzantium, and the Muslim world, with its connections to Central Asia's nomads, into an extended period of competition and exchange. As holy wars, the Crusades represented the culmination of trends connecting war and religion; as expressions of civilizational expansion, they pointed to a growing connection between war, commerce, and cultural contact. The eventual fall of Byzantium showed that such contact could be disastrous, but all three civilizations also demonstrate the creative potential of contact.

THE CRUSADES, 1095–1291

Conditions in each civilization contributed to the birth of the crusading era. Byzantium, rebuilding from fifty years of military atrophy that had culminated in the disaster of Manzikert in 1071 (see Chapter 8), looked to western Europe for aid against the Seljuk Turks in regaining Asia Minor. In the European context of aristocratic reconstruction, religious zeal, and economic revival (see Chapter 7), the Byzantine call for mercenaries became, with the preaching of an expedition by Pope Urban II at Claremont in 1095, a mass movement to liberate the Holy Land. Muslim disunity made the success of this First Crusade more likely, and so allowed the long-term development of the movement.

The First Crusade assembled in 1096; by August 1099, Jerusalem had fallen, and four Latin Crusader States had been carved out of Muslim Syria and Palestine (Figure 11.1). The rest of the twelfth century saw those states maintain a precarious existence against increasing Muslim pressure, punctuated by crises that called forth the Second Crusade in 1147–49 and the Third Crusade in 1189–92. The latter was a response to the disastrous Battle of Hattin and the subsequent fall of Jerusalem and most other crusader territory to the Muslim leader Saladin in 1187. Led by Richard the Lion-Hearted of England, the Third Crusade ensured the survival of a remnant of the Kingdom of Jerusalem (minus its namesake city) along the Mediterranean coast for another century (see Figure 11.1). The Fourth Crusade, diverted against Byzantium in 1204, sacked Constantinople and forms a tragic interlude between twelfth- and thirteenth-century crusading. The thirteenth century saw crusades directed mostly against Egypt. Success was increasingly hard to come by, and, in 1291, the last crusader stronghold in the Holy Land fell, though the broader crusading movement continued as part of western European expansion elsewhere (see Chapter 12). The history of the Crusades offers rich material for analysis across a range of themes, including the interaction of war, politics, and culture, and the conflict between different tactical systems.

War, Politics, and Culture

Holy War The Crusades were the ultimate expression of the connection between salvation religions and warfare that had been developing since the 300s (see the Issues box "Holy War"). While motives on all sides of the struggles in the eastern Mediterranean were mixed, religion was central to the ideology and practice of warfare.

On the Latin Christian side, crusading stimulated a sophisticated theology of war against infidels that

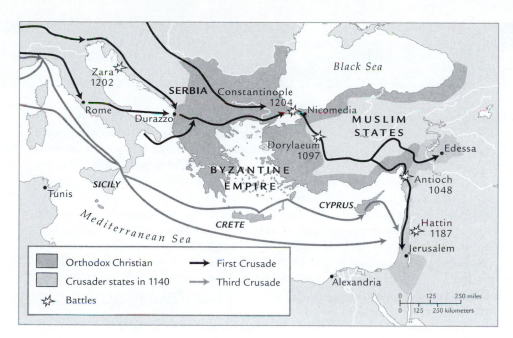

Figure 11.1 The First and Third Crusades

combined the Christian concept of *just war,* which dated back to Augustine, with the penitential nature of pilgrimage. The *legitimate authority* required by just-war theory was God: Crusading was a war for Christ himself. The hardships and eventual success of the First Crusade contributed to the idea that the enterprise was divinely inspired and directed. Death in such a cause was a martyrdom made possible by divine love.

As crusading developed, its theology became tied to the practical problem of recruiting. Those who took the cross received indulgences—remissions of sins granted by the papacy—as well as papal-sanctioned protection of the families and properties they left behind while crusading. Crusade theology thus fit into a larger papal conception of the right order of the Christian world that arose out of the Gregorian reform movement of the mid-eleventh century. The papacy saw itself as the ultimate power in Christendom, and it saw crusading as a vital part of the leadership it wished to exercise over secular powers. Thus, the theology of crusading was part of the church's effort to bring order to Christendom by directing the violence of the turbulent aristocracy against non-Christians.

Of course, many of the subtler distinctions of crusade theology (for example, that conversions to Christianity could not be achieved by force) were lost in the popular enthusiasm of the mass of crusaders.

Many saw the issues in contemporary terms of lordship: The crusade was a vendetta directed against those who had insulted the honor of the Lord, designed to recover his patrimony in the Holy Land. This popular conception was easily turned against any perceived enemies of Christ: Nearly every major crusade was accompanied by outbreaks of violent anti-Semitism and pogroms against the Jews of western Europe. The intolerance of popular crusading ideas later found expression against the Greek Orthodox Byzantines, as well as against heretics within Europe and pagans beyond the frontiers.

On the Muslim side, crusader zeal stimulated a revival of literal interpretations of the Koranic call to *jihad* (literally, "struggle") against the infidel. The urban, commercial, and largely nonmilitary society of the Islamic heartland had come to view *jihad* in terms of internal struggle, peaceful conversion, and personal purification. Faced with militant Christian holy warriors, however, and led by the more literalist and fundamentalist of the newly converted Turkish tribesmen who formed the bulk of Islamic *ghazis,* warriors for the faith, *jihad* as holy war against religious foes came again to the fore and became an important factor in Muslim recruiting for countercrusade wars. While the motivations of soldiers on both sides of the Crusades were mixed, with greed and lust for power lurking alongside piety, genuine religious conviction was prevalent on both sides.

Holy War

Many people in the modern world are made uncomfortable by the notion of "holy war": of wars fought in the name of religions whose central message (in the case of the major salvation religions) appears to be antiviolence. This discomfort leads some students and scholars to discount the genuineness of beliefs expressed in favor of holy war and to see religion as a mere rationalization or pretext for the real, usually material, motives they think more plausible. For example, some scholars have characterized the Crusades as western Europeans' device for hooking into the lucrative circuits of Asian trade that had theretofore largely passed them by.

Such a view imposes modern notions of believable motivation on a different world (almost as if the Crusades were the first Gulf War) and does violence to the evidence. Not only are religious motives as we see them in the sources clearly sincere, but the best economic evidence for the Crusades is that, at the individual level, crusading was almost always a losing bet. Only Italian merchants profited consistently from crusading, and they were neither crusaders themselves nor the motivating force behind crusading.

The discomfort may stem from the difficulty of reconciling modern notions of the role of religion with aggressive war. But religion's role as an all-encompassing worldview in the traditional world meant that it had to accommodate warfare in some way. How comfortably did it do so? A brief survey of the major salvation religions reveals a range of answers.

Buddhism conforms most closely to modern preconceptions: There is no Buddhist idea of holy war, and, although Buddhist polities have conducted warfare, the religion has legitimated war only in a limited range of cases, most notably medieval Tibet. Asoka, the first great Buddhist ruler, renounced wars of conquest on his conversion. Only in Japan, in this as in many things an exception, did a form of Buddhism, Zen, become central to the values of a warrior class. Japan and Korea also saw the rise of Buddhist warrior-monks, but in terms of the religion as a whole, they are an even greater aberration than the Zen beliefs of Japanese secular warriors, and they fought not in the name of religion but in defense of their landed estates.

Hinduism accommodated warfare early on: Warriors were one of the four major classes in the caste-bound Hindu conception of society and fulfilled their *dharma,* or class duty, through fighting. But the caste system that accommodated warfare also limited its legitimate scope to the warriors.

War and Political Authority   Despite the moral sanction that holy war gave to the use of military force, Christians and Muslims found that crusading did little for strong rulership. The Latin kings of Jerusalem experienced periodic inability to exert their authority over their kingdom despite their prestige and despite constant military crises that should have strengthened their leadership role. In part, their situation was unique: Pilgrims and the military orders (see below) were vital to the kingdom's defense but outside its legal structure. That legal and political structure, imported from Europe, with its mutual rights and obligations and limited conception of kingship, hamstrung the power of the kings even over their most powerful subjects. The problems involved in ruling a conquest society compli-

cated matters further. The Latin settlers could not carry out a permanent holy war against all Muslims, because the great mass of the population they ruled remained Muslim—European settlers were almost all knights and merchants, and not peasants. Local communities therefore retained their administrative structures, which the Latin rulers simply supervised from above. Muslims under Latin rule, though not always cooperative, were little threat militarily, but they further limited the legal reach of royal power. Overall, the cooperative nature of crusading meshed awkwardly with the centrally directed defense of the Crusader States.

After the First Crusade, led by nonroyal nobles, European royal leadership proved necessary for

A militant Hinduism did arise in response to Muslim raids and conquests, but not in any organized or centralized way, and not as a mass movement. Modern mass Hindu militancy is really a variant of nationalism, not holy war.

Islam apparently incorporated warfare into its theology from the beginning in the form of *jihad*, but this may be deceptive. The regular appearance of slave soldiers in a wide range of Islamic polities is a sign of discomfort at the heart of Islamic ideology with states wielding force (see the Issues box in Chapter 8). Islam maintains both military and spiritual interpretations of *jihad*, which in any case is supposed to be a defensive policy in terms of warfare. The history of Islamic holy war is further complicated by issues of conversion of nomadic peoples, fundamentalism, and, more recently, resistance to imperialism and western hegemony, in which nationalism and other modern ideologies play a large part.

Perhaps ironically, Christianity has historically made the easiest alliance with war. In contrast to Asoka's renunciation of conquest after his conversion, Constantine, the first great Christian ruler, converted after winning a battle under the sign of the cross. The tradition of *in hoc signo vinces*—"in this sign you shall conquer"—became a constant

part of the religion, expressed, among other ways, through the Crusades, through orders of warrior-monks unprecedented elsewhere (the Japanese monks being in truth incommensurable with the Templars and their like), and through the deep penetration into society of crusading ideals, as evidenced in events such as the Children's Crusade. Christianity's warlike zeal would later be turned inward in the Wars of Religion (though Islam too has had its Sunni–Shi'ite conflicts).

Two other religions are worthy of note in this context. Christianity's accommodation with war derived in part from the Jewish notion of holy war attested in numerous biblical stories and in the Jewish revolts against Roman rule. And Zoroastrianism, like Judaism the universal-seeming religion of a particular people and state, sanctioned the state's wars unproblematically. Indeed, Sassanid Persian warfare with the Byzantines rose to the level of a crusade on both sides at its climax around 600 (see Chapter 8).

Religion, of course, was not the only factor in traditional or modern motivations to war and patterns of the use of force. But especially in the traditional world, religion should not be discounted as a sincere motivation to violence as well as to nonviolence.

subsequent crusades due to the expense and control problems such expeditions raised. But because crusading removed them from their lands and often stretched their resources, kings found that it did little to enhance their power: Crusades served as an expression rather than a cause of growing royal control at home. Likewise, papal attempts to use crusading to enhance its leadership position had at best mixed results. Papal prestige reached its zenith under Innocent III, but the diversion of the Fourth Crusade and the failure of the Fifth, which Innocent called in 1215 but did not live to see, did nothing but harm during his tenure. In general, popes, like kings, overreached their resources in promoting crusading.

On the Muslim side, revived *jihad* failed to resolve the problems of political authority and legitimacy that had emerged under the Abbasid Caliphate (see Chapter 8). Caliphates in Baghdad and Egypt were dominated by sultans and *wazirs* (viziers or vasirs) whose military power continued to rest on elements essentially outside society: slave soldiers and tribesmen from the margins of the Islamic world. One slave group, the Mamluks in thirteenth-century Egypt, even came to power in their own right in the wake of crusading disruption. The existence of the crusader states did little to promote unity within the Muslim world or institutional strength within Muslim states.

On the Byzantine side, emperors found dealing with the Crusades to be fraught with dangers.

Crusaders in the empire often took to pillaging, damaging imperial prestige and resources. Managing crusader ambitions proved expensive, and the existence of the Crusader States complicated Byzantine diplomacy, which, being practical and aimed at territorial goals, made use of alliances with Muslim powers that irritated the Latins. Partly in that context, the involvement of crusaders in Byzantine succession politics brought disaster on the empire in 1204.

In short, crusading was consistently bad for strong rulership. It placed too heavy demands on the political and economic structures of the time, and, despite the religious sanction that crusading apparently gave to those wielding power, religion stimulated overambitious plans.

Cultural Exchange?   Did the military encounters of the Crusades promote cultural exchange between Christian and Muslim civilization? This is a much disputed topic. Certainly, there were diplomatic exchanges, as there were some attempts on the part of Christian leaders to exploit Muslim divisions and rivalries through diplomatic channels. Such contacts, however, were more common for the Byzantines, who already shared with their Muslim neighbors a degree of contempt for the barbarous Latin intruders. Despite some alliances, there are few real cases of Christian and Muslim armies working together, so opportunities for exchange in that way were limited. Diplomatic contact also created among Latin Christians an image of Saladin, the great Muslim leader of the later twelfth century, as an exemplar of chivalric values—perhaps a classic case of viewing a cultural other in one's own terms. What about more substantive exchanges?

At the military level, there was little adoption of military techniques or organization between any of the three civilizations. The organization of each society's armed forces was too much an outgrowth of each social structure to be borrowed easily, even if the idea had been conceived. Turkish cavalry tactics, for example, derived from an entire way of life, not just a tactical doctrine, and could be neither lightly discarded nor readily adopted by others. Traditions of arms use and the attitudes toward battle that accompanied them were also deeply embedded culturally. The Turkish willingness to retreat and return to the fight elsewhere, for instance, was incompatible with European notions of bravery and face-to-face combat. The Crusaders may have learned some of their responses to Turkish tactics from the Byzantines, who

had long experience with them, but the case is not proven. When borrowing did occur between armies, it was through the hiring of groups of foreign mercenaries who brought their whole practice, from life style to tactics, with them, and such cases were rare across religious boundaries. Even the evidence for Latin borrowing of Byzantine or Muslim fortification methods, once thought to be an important lesson learned by the Europeans from the Crusades, is thin. Western European castle building mostly followed its own trajectory; similarities among the three traditions are more likely the result of convergence on certain principles of good design than of direct borrowing in the Holy Land. Of course, all the armies of the Crusades adapted to each other's tactics as they learned each other's strengths and weaknesses. But leaders adapted within the traditions of their own armies, not by adopting the techniques of others.

Did the Crusades promote broader cultural exchanges? Again, the evidence is weak. European appropriation of Arab learning and science (often derived from classical Greek) took place more in Iberia and Sicily, where everyday contact was more the norm. The Crusader States were too tenuous a society to invest much in higher learning. Nor did crusading do much for overseas commerce. Italian trade was growing with or without the Crusades, which it predated, and war sometimes made trade more difficult. Perhaps crusading stimulated a taste for foreign luxury goods, but general economic revival did more to promote such trade (which was limited in any case), and many of the tastes in food and clothing picked up by Latin settlers in the Holy Land remained isolated there and did not spread to their stay-at-home cousins.

Basically, the Crusades created a sphere of military interaction. It is this we may now analyze in more detail.

The Armies of Crusading Warfare: Institutions and Manpower

Latin Christian Armies   Latin armies drew on four main sources of soldiers, all of which had serious limitations. At the beginning, all Latin soldiers were essentially armed pilgrims from Europe. Each major crusade directed a substantial army at the Holy Land. Between crusades, a small but steady flow of pilgrims to the holy sites visited the Crusader States. Many were knights along with their retainers. They were available for a campaigning season, as pilgrim ships arrived in the Holy Land in April and left in October, but they were available only sporadically and temporarily. In contrast, once the Crusader States were established, their defense needs were permanent and ongoing. Further, not all pilgrims were military personnel, and those who were, not being subjects of the local rulers, were only voluntarily obedient to their command.

Crusaders and pilgrims who did settle in the Holy Land became the backbone of the States' systems of defense as well as the core of their ruling class. The settlers imported the sociomilitary structure of their homelands to their new possessions. Thus, the ruler of each state granted lands to his followers to administer and draw income from, in return for which they owed military service roughly proportional to the land's value. Some grants were not of land, which was somewhat scarce, but of an annual fee in money derived from the active urban and maritime economy. The great nobles, in turn, granted parts of their estates to their followers to be used to maintain soldiers in their service. There were no limits on the service the ruler could demand, and the several Crusader States tended to support each other with their forces, but, as a system of property holding and administration, granting estates did limit the judicial powers of the ruler. Two problems plagued settler military forces. First, the districts most in need of defense forces were also those most liable to have their productivity damaged by Muslim raids. Maintaining forces at the frontiers without bankrupting the landholders was therefore a constant problem. Second, there were never enough landed settlers to provide an adequate defense.

The Latin rulers met some of the need for more troops by hiring mercenaries both from unlanded settlers and from Europe. Locals, especially the Turcopoles, who were the offspring of mixed unions, were often recruited in this way. But hiring a significant number of paid soldiers for any length of time always threatened the limited treasuries of the Latin states with bankruptcy, so while mercenaries were important on major campaigns, they could not be used to garrison castles on a permanent basis.

The problems of a standing defense force, especially in frontier regions, was alleviated in part by the rise of the Military Orders of the Knights of the Temple and of the Hospital. The Templars and the Hospitallers were, in effect, soldier-monks—knights who took vows of chastity, poverty, and obedience.

The Orders developed sophisticated administrative structures with locations throughout Europe that directed recruits and funds to the Holy Land. Donating lands and money to the Orders was popular in Europe as an indirect contribution to the cause of crusading, and it became popular in the Holy Land as well because the Orders could garrison exposed frontier castles. They were not dependent on the local estates of a castle for income, and their knights were full-time soldiers. Their standards of discipline and training made them an elite among Latin forces, and they earned the special enmity of their Muslim foes. But the numbers of the Orders' knights, while significant in the context of Latin armies as a whole, were never huge. More problematically, the Orders, as direct dependents of the pope, obeyed no secular ruler. They cooperated with the Latin rulers, especially in the Kingdom of Jerusalem where their lands were most numerous, but as independent allies, which complicated, and at times compromised, the Latin chain of command.

The sorts of soldiers, in terms of infantry and cavalry, raised from these four sources of manpower reflected the mix that had become typical in Europe in the eleventh century. The spearhead of Latin armies was the heavy cavalry of knights and sergeants, the latter (including the Turcopoles) armed like the knights but lower in social and legal rank. The cavalry wore chain-mail hauberks, often covered by a cloth surcoat, and iron helmets that became more complete and elaborate as the twelfth century progressed. They carried kite-shaped shields and fought with lance and sword. Horsemen formed a minority of the numbers in Latin armies—perhaps a fifth to a quarter at most. They were expensive to equip and maintain, and, at times, it was difficult to maintain an adequate supply of horses. But cavalry was the elite of armies both socially, as the legal status and privileges of knighthood became more defined in the twelfth century (though not all cavalry were knights or even landholders), and militarily, due to their greater economic resources, which gave them superior equipment and leisure for training in arms. The knights of the orders added religious prestige to their status as elite warriors.

The infantry consisted of landless adventurers, professional mercenary companies, the attendants of mounted men, and foot sergeants (men granted land for their service like knights and cavalry sergeants, but expected to serve only on foot)—in other words, a broad range of social types. On campaign, cavalry whose horses became unserviceable or died (not an unusual circumstance) became part of the infantry as well. Crossbowmen predominated, though spearmen were also common, and cavalry who fought on foot used their lances as infantry spears. Much of infantry must have been more transient from campaign to campaign than the cavalry of the landholders and Military Orders (yearly pilgrims were probably more likely to fight on foot, for instance). But regular campaigning would have produced an experienced core of foot soldiers in the Crusader States, and the infantry in crusader armies generally showed decent discipline and cohesion. Though less prestigious than the cavalry, the infantry were invaluable in defending and besieging fortifications and in providing a strong defensive base for the cavalry on the battlefield.

Muslim Armies   On the whole, then, the military establishment of the Crusader States could field good soldiers, but it always struggled to field enough of them. Given the flaws of Latin armies, part of what allowed the Crusader States to survive for as long as they did was that Muslim armies were equally if not more flawed.

First, with the political fragmentation of the Muslim world during most of crusading history, especially after the breakup of the Great Seljuk Empire around 1090, any large countercrusading army had to be a composite force, drawn from different areas under different *emirs,* the regional governors of the Islamic world. In the absence of a unified central authority, coalitions of emirs were highly unstable. Each was jealous of his independence, unwilling to see his rivals or the sultan profit overmuch from a campaign, and constantly concerned about threats to his control of his district in his absence. A strong ruler such as Saladin could overcome these divisions to some extent, but not completely. Part of the problem was that there was no equivalent in the Muslim world to the papal protection given to the lands and families of crusaders during their absence. As a result, the *jihad* against the infidel was rarely a top priority for regional Muslim rulers.

Second, Muslim armies were also composite forces in terms of the support systems used to raise soldiers. So, too, it could be said, were crusader armies. But the lines separating one sort of Latin soldier from another were not firm: A landholding, settler knight could serve as a mercenary in some circumstances or could join a Military Order; pilgrims and crusaders could become settlers. In other words, all Latin soldiers were products of a single social system, even if

from different strata within that system. Furthermore, all the Latin sources of manpower produced soldiers from the same tactical tradition, so that melding them into a unified force on campaign was not overly difficult. Neither condition was true of Muslim armies. The social origins of Muslim armies were not just diverse; two of the three main sources of manpower were essentially outside the mainstream of Muslim society, each in a different way. And the breadth and social diversity of the Muslim world encompassed a number of distinct tactical traditions, not to mention that Muslim military systems evolved over time. Creating a unified fighting force out of such material and keeping it in the field was a frequent challenge for Muslim leaders.

To take manpower first, Muslim armies were drawn from three main sources. At their core were the ʿaskar forces, or professional soldiers (including some slaves), of the major political leaders, the sultans and regional emirs (see Chapter 8). As standing units of full-time, well-trained warriors, ʿaskar could conduct small-scale raids on their own. But their numbers were too limited even at the top of the political ladder for independent campaigning aimed at conquest. They could provide infantry or cavalry forces and were supplemented at times by mercenaries (especially infantrymen) from among the poorer and more troublesome elements of the cities.

For greater numbers, leaders called on the holders of *iqtaʾ* to bring themselves and a contingent of followers based on the size of the *iqtaʾ* to the leader's army. *Iqtaʾ* were granted to individuals in exchange for service of many sorts (including ʿaskar forces) and could consist of revenue from a particular area, administrative control of a district, outright land grants, or some combination thereof. The service originally was mostly administrative, but, by the twelfth century, the Seljuks had made military service the major form of this institution. The extent of Muslim lands meant that considerable numbers could be raised this way, but the problem with *iqtaʾ* holders was the problem of emirs writ small. As they became attached to the district of their grant, they became more reluctant to leave it for extended campaigning, as personal supervision, especially at harvest time, could increase their income and protect the land from potential rivals. Most of the soldiers produced by this system, therefore, were part-timers who were hard to keep in the field beyond the end of the campaigning season. Large parts of Muslim armies regularly melted away as winter approached, a fact the Byzantines had regularly taken advantage of in their defensive operations.

The third source of manpower for Muslim armies was tribal auxiliaries, drawn from the warlike peoples who lived on the margins of the Islamic world. These included many of the Arab descendants of the founders of this world, but above all the seminomadic Turkmen who moved with their flocks between the summer hills and winter valley pastures throughout the Muslim world, maintaining the lifestyle of their Central Asian ancestors. While fierce fighters, as semi-independent groups they were usually hard to discipline and control. Plunder was their motivation for fighting: They often failed to pursue a beaten foe if booty beckoned, at times even took to plundering the baggage of their allies, and tended to abandon a campaign when plunder became scarce. Thus, they were of little use in sieges and, like *iqta'* forces, were nearly impossible to hold together past the end of the regular campaigning season.

Tactically, two main traditions competed. The Saljuk Turks were classic Central Asian horse-archers who depended on maneuvers and firepower to wear down their foes before coming to grips at close quarters. Ambushes, envelopments, and feigned retreats were standard elements of the Turkish tactical repertoire. There were infantry (probably in substantial numbers) in Turkish armies, but their tactics and weaponry is virtually ignored by the sources, so their role is difficult to assess. The armor of infantry and cavalry were relatively light. This facilitated mobility, but more heavily armored European soldiers created some problems for Turkish armies. Fatimid Egypt, however, relied on spear- and bow-bearing Ethiopian infantry and on Arab cavalry for whom the lance was the main weapon. Fatimid armies thus relied on infantry firepower and cavalry charges much as Latin armies did, but with lighter weapons, less armor, and smaller horses than the Latins deployed. The superiority of the Turkish tradition is reflected not just in contemporary crusader opinions of their two main foes (they respected the Turks but not the Egyptians), but also in the dominance in thirteenth-century Egypt of the Mamluks, slave soldiers in the Turkish tactical tradition (though with some more heavily armed lancers) who revolted in 1250 and came to rule Egypt themselves.

Byzantine Armies Byzantine armies of the crusader period are difficult to characterize, as they consisted in large part of groups of foreign mercenaries around a small core of Byzantine troops, a development initiated under Basil II and accelerated in the years between his death in 1025 and Manzikert. Thus, neither the natives nor the foreign elements had any strong tactical traditions (though the accumulated military wisdom of the military treatises survived) or sense of identity; they depended instead on strong and innovative leadership by the Comneni. The military institutions of Byzantium under the Comneni dynasty are examined further below. Byzantine armies played only a small role in some northern Syrian campaigns, being more occupied with the Turks in Asia Minor and with the empire's European possessions in the Balkans and Italy.

The Armies of Crusading Warfare in Action

Strategy and Campaigning Each of the civilizations that met in this area had grand strategic and political goals that affected the shape of crusading warfare, though for the Byzantines and the Muslim powers, the Crusader States themselves were often a secondary factor in strategic planning. They were central to western European policy, however, and raised two different strategic problems: the goals of offensive crusades and the defense of Latin lands.

The ultimate goal of crusading was possession of the Holy Land and the city of Jerusalem. Through the Fourth Crusade, the Latin approach to this goal was direct: Crusades were aimed at Jerusalem. Two routes to the Holy Land were possible. The overland path, through the Balkans to Constantinople, and then through Asia Minor, was at first the only possibility, but the conquest of the seacoast after the First Crusade made sailing to the Holy Land possible. The size of major crusades favored the land route, though sea transport as far as Constantinople was an option. But, especially in the disputed regions of Asia Minor, the land route was prone to supply shortages and Turkish opposition. With the development of Italian maritime power in the twelfth century, and particularly once Richard I captured Cyprus as a staging post in the course of the Third Crusade (see Chapter 15), naval transport came to dominate.

The development of naval transport also opened up another strategic option. The experience of the Crusader States in the twelfth century, read in the light of the disaster of Hattin and the loss of Jerusalem in 1187 (see the Highlights box "The Campaign and Battle of Hattin, 1187"), seemed to teach that the

The Campaign and Battle of Hattin, 1187

The long-brewing succession crisis that followed the death of king Baldwin IV, the Leper, in 1185 divided the leadership of the Kingdom of Jerusalem. Count Raymond of Tripoli was the most able crusader leader, but his enemy Guy of Lusignan became king by marrying the late king's sister. Crusader troubles gave Saladin plenty of room to complete his conquest of Syria, bringing all the lands around the Crusader States under his leadership, while regularly raiding the kingdom. The Muslim threat thus increased just as crusader unity faltered. In such circumstances, maintaining the truce Baldwin and Raymond had negotiated with Saladin was crucial. But the renegade marcher (border) lord Reynald of Chatillon twice broke the truce by pillaging Muslim trade caravans. After the second incident, in 1187, Saladin declared a *jihad*, gathered a substantial army, and in June moved to besiege the town of Tiberias (Figure 11.2).

Stripping all the castle garrisons of the kingdom to raise an army nearly the equal of Saladin's, King Guy gathered his forces at Saffuriya on July 2. A debate ensued among the crusader leaders about the proper course of action. Despite the fact that Tiberias was his town and his wife was threatened with capture there, Raymond urged not marching to the town's relief. He pointed out that Saladin could not hold Tiberias even if he took it; that the walls could be rebuilt if destroyed; and that prisoners, including his wife, could be ransomed. Beyond Tiberias, Saladin would have to traverse the fifteen waterless miles between Tiberias and

Saffuriya to confront Guy's army, leaving his soldiers tired and thirsty before an encounter. But if the Latin army marched to Tiberias, it would have to cross that same waterless track, exposing itself to destruction; and if the army were lost, so would be the entire kingdom.

This urge for caution apparently carried the day, but that night, the Master of the Temple persuaded Guy to change his mind. He claimed that Raymond was trying to undermine the king, pointing out that if Guy failed to go to the defense of his vassal's land, Raymond would be legally absolved from obedience to the king. The argument was the more persuasive because of Raymond and Guy's long enmity and because Guy had pursued a cautious strategy four years earlier as regent; the subsequent criticism of his inaction had ended his regency. The master also threatened to withdraw the support of the Templars if the king took no action. So the next morning, to the surprise of many, the army was ordered to march.

Everything now depended on the Latin army reaching Tiberias and water in one day. Saladin is said to have rejoiced when scouts brought news of the Latin advance, and the Muslim army immediately set out to harass and slow the Latins. A classic fight on the march ensued, with the Muslim attacks directed with particular ferocity at the rear of the Latin column, where the Templars were stationed. Eventually, the rear was so hard pressed that it could not proceed. The van pressed on for a time, becoming separated from

Holy Land on its own did not possess the resources to defend itself in the long run. Thirteenth-century crusades thus took an indirect approach and came to be directed against Egypt, control of which was seen as the key to control of the Holy Land. The riches of Egypt, including potential control of trade routes to India and China, made such an approach plausible; in fact, they had drawn to Egypt a major expedition by the Kingdom of Jerusalem in 1167. Its value had

been proven by Saladin, whose success at Hattin was founded in his control of Egypt. Unfortunately for the crusaders, every attempt at the conquest of Egypt failed.

With the creation of the Crusader States, defense became a strategic challenge for the Latin forces. Control of territory was based above all on possession of fortified castles and towns, which served as refuges for Latin field forces and from which administration

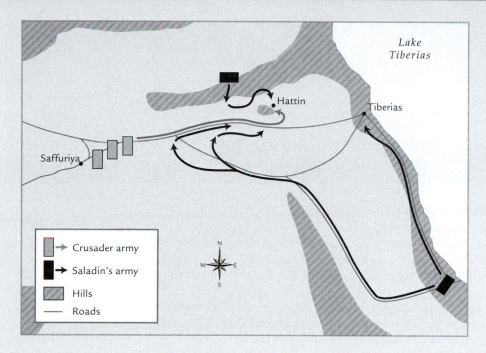

Figure 11.2 The Battle of Hattin

the rest of the army, which gathered around Guy on the double hill called the Horns of Hattin. Forced to halt for the night, the Latin army was now doomed. They spent the night harassed by Muslim archery, exhausted by a day's marching and fighting in midsummer heat, without water. The Muslims set fire to the brush around the hill, adding smoke to their misery. Morale collapsed, and the next day the slaughter was completed. Raymond escaped but died soon after from disease; Reynald was captured and executed by Saladin; and Guy was captured and released on oath not to fight again. All the captured Templars were slaughtered save the Master of the Temple, whom Saladin spared.

The result was disaster. Saladin faced an ungarrisoned kingdom and rapidly took all the major cities except Tyre, where the fortuitous arrival of Conrad of Montferrat and a small group of new crusaders provided a defense. On October 2, Jerusalem fell. The Crusader States would never be the same.

and intimidation of the native population emanated. The goal of controlling fortifications and the characteristics of the various armies shaped strategy and campaigning patterns decisively.

The key problem for the Latin defenders was the shortage of resources. There was never enough land secure from Muslim raids for economic prosperity to be established, and so never enough soldiers. As a result, the Latins could not garrison their strongpoints and raise a substantial field army at the same time. Raising an army involved stripping many forts of their defenders, which put a premium on preserving the army. Loss of the army in battle could leave the country defenseless, and battle was definitely a risk, more susceptible than most military activity to being decided by chance. Fortunately for the Latins, they could usually obtain their strategic goals without risking battle. The ideal Latin defense strategy was to

Krak des Chevaliers
Massive towers and concentric walls substituted for scarce manpower in crusader castles.

meet an invasion with their field army. Basing themselves near secure water supplies (a crucial consideration in the hot, dry desert climate), they would shadow the Muslim army closely enough to restrict its foraging and so prevent it from besieging major strongholds. Denied easy plunder or facing the end of the campaign season, the Muslim forces would disperse, leaving the Latins in control of their territory. Winning a battle could accomplish nothing more than this, since the Muslims were never short of troops and so could replace battle losses. But winning a battle could facilitate conquest of forts and territory, and Latin forces fought more battles down through the 1120s, when they were still expanding their lands. Having lost several of the battles they did fight, Latin offensives became difficult after the 1120s and, with the failure of the Second Crusade, aimed at Damascus in Syria, virtually ceased. Skillful maneuvering and access to food, water, and fodder were thus the keys to successful campaigning.

The problem with this strategy was that it sometimes conflicted with the ruler's legal obligation to defend the lands of his vassals from enemy attack and with popular sentiment in the army, both of which leaned toward a more active attack on Muslim invaders. When Latin leadership was divided or weak, this problem could lead to serious political difficulties and disciplinary or morale breakdown in the army.

Unity was the key problem for the Muslims. Their overall grand strategy was simple and was ordered explicitly by the Seljuk sultan as early as 1110: Reconquer the Christian-held lands. But the political division of the Muslim world, as we have already seen, was a major obstacle to achieving this goal. Competition between Muslim power centers and dynastic wars within them often took precedence over the effort at reconquest (and was exploited diplomatically by the Latins when possible), and other fronts demanded attention—notably, the Seljuk frontier with Byzantium. These divisions prevented the vast disparity of resources between the Muslim powers and the Crusader States from being brought to bear against the Christian occupiers.

Saladin was the major exception to this rule, but only by also proving it. He spent most of his military career campaigning against other Muslims, building on his father's achievements in uniting Syria by seizing control of Egypt and then gradually reducing a great many northern Mesopotamian emirates to his authority. Once he had built his empire, he could execute a consistent strategy against the Crusader States that took advantage of his greater resources. Frequent campaigning kept the pressure on the defenders, stretching their limited reserves of manpower. The ravaging that accompanied raids and incursions damaged the economic base of the Christian defenders. Saladin utilized his manpower advantage by invading with a major force in one area of the Kingdom of Jerusalem and sending secondary forces into areas whose defenses had been stripped to man the field army gathered to face his main force. He (like other Muslim commanders) adopted a battle-seeking strategy, knowing that the consequences of a loss were far worse for the Christians than for his forces. This often involved attempting to draw the Latin army away from its sources of food and water by threatening isolated castles or towns and harassing it on the march (see below). Yet, even with all his advantages, had the Latins avoided the disaster at Hattin, Saladin might not have conquered much Latin territory. The strength of crusader castles and the seasonal weakness of Muslim armies made sieges—and therefore conquest—difficult. The coastal cities of the kingdom, able to be resupplied by sea, survived for almost a century after Hattin.

Byzantine strategy aimed at recovering lost imperial territory, and the Byzantines viewed the crusaders in terms of their own request for mercenaries. They thus distrusted the First Crusade as an independent force—understandably, given that Normans were a substantial contingent in the crusade and Normans had been attacking imperial territory for forty years—and seem to have radically underestimated the religious motivations of the crusaders. They extracted promises that any territory the crusaders won would be turned over to the Byzantine Empire, used their supplies to try to control the crusaders, and abandoned the expedition at the first sign of trouble in Asia Minor. A legacy of distrust was thus created on both sides. The empire proved indifferent or hostile to the continued existence of the Crusader States, to the detriment of both sides: The Crusader States were not supported by the only major Christian power in the region, while the Byzantines found their relations with western Europe poisoned and lost influence they could have exercised in the Crusader States. The exception to this general pattern occurred under Emperor Manuel Comnenus (1143–80). Concerned with protecting imperial possessions in Italy and the Balkans and disputing the right to the imperial title with the German emperor, Manuel fostered better relations with the Crusader States to further his diplomacy in the west. As a result, Byzantine influence in and military cooperation with the Kingdom of Jerusalem peaked between 1150 and 1180. But an internal crisis after 1180 coincided with a return to an antiwestern policy in the empire, setting the stage for the disaster of the Fourth Crusade. Military operations reflected this strategy. The Byzantines focused their efforts elsewhere than Syria, campaigning only a handful of times around Antioch and Edessa.

Combat Tactical action in crusading warfare consisted of three types of conflict: sieges, fighting on the march, and pitched battles. But the lines between these types were not clear. Sorties and relief efforts could bring battle to a siege, and fighting on the march could easily escalate into a set-piece engagement.

The strength of fortifications in the Holy Land shaped the patterns of siege warfare. Byzantines, Latins, and Muslims all knew the main technologies for attacking walls: battering rams, mines, and projectile-hurling engines. The Latin forces may well have borrowed the technology of the traction trebuchet—an engine with which a team of men pulling down on a large lever arm launched stones at opposing forts—from the Muslims. The larger and more powerful counterweight trebuchet, in which a huge fixed weight pulled down the lever, appeared later in Europe, probably again a borrowed refinement of the technology. But none of the techniques for destroying walls were terribly quick or effective, especially against massive walls often set on inaccessible and rocky ground perfect for defeating mining efforts or hindering the approach of engines. Against a well-defended fort, an extended blockade designed to starve the garrison into submission was often the only option for either side. The outcome of such an operation depended on the ability of the besiegers to keep their army supplied and in existence—not an easy task, as the siege of Antioch shows (see the Sources box "The Siege of Antioch, 1098"). The service limitations of Muslim soldiers were particularly important in this respect. The other way to take such fortresses was a quick and massive direct assault on the walls using scaling ladders or mobile platforms; this was effective particularly against large forts with small garrisons. Latin castles and cities whose defenders had joined a field army were always vulnerable to such quick assaults, but Latin forces used the technique as well, as at Jerusalem in 1099. Treachery within the walls, again as at Antioch, could assist such attacks.

Fights on the march were a form of combat characteristic of crusading warfare, given the contrasting strategic goals, strengths, and weaknesses of Turkish and Latin armies. Latin armies, defending the strongholds through which they controlled the countryside, often had to march from one fortified post to another; crusading armies also had to march to their objectives. Stopping to fight a battle would only slow their progress toward their objective, and battle entailed major risks, so Latin armies usually tried to avoid set battles. The Turks wanted to impede the movement of Latin armies so as to isolate particular strongholds from relief or defend them from attack and aimed at destroying Latin armies in combat, so they sought battles. But the heavier defensive armor and dense

SOURCES

The Siege of Antioch, 1098

These selections from a Latin and a Byzantine source for the siege of Antioch, a crucial episode in the First Crusade, illustrate the key role of logistics in crusading warfare and the importance of religion in how Latin armies functioned. The brief note from Anna Comnena shows the role of division and treachery among their foes in facilitating Latin success, though the treachery for her extended to the Latins: Antioch, a former imperial city, was a key Byzantine goal, and the crusaders treacherously (in Anna's eyes) failed to hand it over to the empire after its capture.

■　■　■

[*Fulcher of Chartres.*]　However, when the Franks had for a time camped around the city, and by ravaging the nearby region for supplies necessary for themselves had devastated it everywhere, it was impossible to find bread to buy, and they faced a great famine. Everyone was therefore very desolate and many secretly thought to take themselves away from the siege by flight, either by land or by sea. For they had no rations on which to live: It became necessary to search for their food far away with great fear, going forty or fifty miles from the siege, where in the mountains it is clear to see that they were often killed by the Turks lying in ambush. Nevertheless, we believed that these misfortunes happened to the Franks because of their sins, and because of them were for so long unable to take the city: Excess as much as avarice or pride or rapaciousness corrupted them. Holding council about this, they expelled the women from the army, married as well as unmarried, lest they displease the Lord by their sordid wastefulness. . . . At that time, starving men ate bean sprouts growing in the fields, and various herbs unseasoned with salt; even thistles, which because of the shortage of firewood were not well cooked and pierced the tongues of those eating them; also horses, asses, and camels,

and even dogs and rats. The poorer even ate the skins of the beasts and seeds of grain they picked out of manure. They endured cold, heat, and pouring rains for God. Their tents became old and torn and rotten from the constant rains. Because of this, many of them were covered only by the sky.

[*Anna Comnena.*]　Now there happened to be an Armenian on the tower above guarding the portion of the wall assigned to Bohemund. As he often bent over from above Bohemund plied him with honeyed words, tempted him with many promises and thus persuaded him to betray the city to him. . . . And at dawn of day Bohemund at once made for the tower, and the Armenian according to agreement opened the gate to him; he immediately rushed up with his followers more quickly than can be told and was seen by the people within and without standing on the battlements of the tower and ordering the trumpeters to sound the call to battle.

SOURCE: Fulcheri Cartonensis, *Historia Hierosolymitana*, ed. Heinrich Haganmeyer (Heidelberg, 1913), pp. 222–226. Anna Comnena, *The Alexiad of Anna Comnena*, trans E. R. A. Sewter (New York: Penguin Classics, 1969), p. 344.

masses of infantry in Latin armies made a full direct assault by Turkish forces a poor option. Not only could Turkish attacks be repulsed, but they exposed the Turkish army to counterattack by the Latin cavalry, whose charge was their battle-winning tactic.

The Turks therefore made use of their superior mobility to harass Latin forces with arrows and hit-and-run tactics. The goal was to weaken the Latin army piecemeal, to separate contingents from each

other and pick them off separately, and to deny the marching Latins access to sources of water. The Turks also hoped to provoke rash attacks by parts of the Latin army, often using feigned retreats to draw ill-timed charges. The Turks thus played on the impetuous bravery and individualistic indiscipline that Latin knights tended toward. They launched such attacks with particular ferocity against the rear of the Latin column. This slowed the whole march most

Frank and Saracen in Combat   This manuscript illustration shows a western knight jousting with a Turkish cavalryman. Larger horses and heavier arms and weapons gave European soldiers the advantage in such hand-to-hand fighting.

effectively, as the head of the column had to wait to avoid becoming separated from those under assault. At times, when the Turks pressed the hardest, the Latin army had to stop and launch a limited attack with their cavalry to clear the lines.

The Latin response was to adopt a variation of an order of march common in this part of the world for centuries. The infantry formed a screen—either a hollow square or, if the march were along the coast, a column to the land side—that shielded the cavalry and the baggage. The density of the infantry screen prevented effective Turkish attacks, and the crossbowmen helped keep the Turkish horse-archers at a distance. Still, the soldiers of Latin armies found Turkish harassment infuriating, and they chafed under the restrictions imposed by their leaders on breaking formation and striking back. Because the key to Latin success in such an engagement was patience and discipline, Latin leaders imposed stiff penalties for breaking rank. They usually made provision for the wounded to be carried and the dead to be buried during the march, to disguise from the enemy any losses and to maintain morale. "Victory" for Latin armies in such circumstances meant reaching their goal intact, not necessarily defeating the enemy army. It was a frustrating sort of combat that went against the grain of the common soldier's impulse, and it thus had the potential to create tension, or even division, in the army. Strong Latin commanders usually overcame this problem, but the potential for disaster always lurked close beneath the surface.

Many of the same factors shaped the patterns of pitched battles between Latin and Turkish armies, with the key being mobility versus shock. The focus of each side's tactics was the Latin cavalry charge. The superior weight of Latin arms, armor, and horses meant that if such an attack could be driven home, it usually succeeded in breaking the lighter Turkish lines and winning the day. But the charge was a fragile weapon. It had to succeed in one attempt, for Latin cavalry proved difficult to rally and re-form after an initial charge, reflecting their limited levels of training in large groups and their tendency to indiscipline. The numbers of Latin cavalry were also often quite limited, and their very weight meant that even if they managed to re-form, men and horses were often too tired after a charge to deliver another effective blow. So Latin tactics consisted of extended infantry fighting designed to entangle the Turks so closely that they could be pinned down for the decisive charge. For their part, the Turks used feigned retreats, ruses, ambushes, and harassment to try to provoke a premature charge, one that they could avoid on their faster horses. They could then return to the attack against the scattered Latin forces.

Latins and Turks thus presented each other with a difficult tactical challenge. Neither side had a clear advantage over the other, casting luck and the quality of leadership into the decisive role on both sides in determining the outcome of battles. When the best commanders on both sides faced each other, as when Saladin faced Richard during the Third Crusade, the result was a tactical standoff, as neither general would be drawn into a fight on the other's terms. The strategic result of such tactical stalemate depended heavily on the logistical situation and favored maintenance of the status quo: Richard, for instance, secured the coastal cities but decided that Jerusalem was beyond the safe range of his grasp.

When Latin armies faced Fatimid forces from Egypt, however, two similar tactical traditions met. Both sides brought a defensive mass of infantry and a supporting force of shock cavalry to the field, but the Latin advantage in armor (and probably consistently better morale) quickly made the difference. One Latin attack against a stationary target would end such battles within an hour. But when first Saladin and then the Mamluks brought the Turkish tactical tradition to Egypt, the Latin advantage disappeared, and the thirteenth-century crusades in Egypt saw familiar tactical patterns reasserted.

BYZANTIUM, 1081–1453

Byzantine calls to the west for help against the Seljuks in the wake of Manzikert had contributed to the calling of the First Crusade. However, the crusading movement as a whole did little to advance the interests of Byzantium in the twelfth century, and relations between the two sets of Christian states were often unfriendly. Nevertheless, between 1081 and 1180, the Comneni emperors Alexius, John, and Manuel managed to rebuild a good deal of Byzantium's power and prestige. Alexius secured almost all the empire's European territory and some of the coast of Asia Minor; John and Manuel gradually took more of the coast, and Manuel, through friendly relations with Jerusalem, exerted influence in the Crusader States. Byzantine trade wealth remained substantial, and the agricultural base of the empire in the Balkans was strong. Byzantine success in this century was based on wealth, diplomacy and the prestige of the empire, backed by a military system rebuilt by the Comneni along very different lines from the old Byzantine army.

The disaster at Manzikert and the subsequent loss of Anatolia had been the death knell for the already declining thematic army, and almost all the tagmata units had also ceased to exist in the ten years of civil war after Manzikert (see Chapter 8). Thus, the Comnenian military system, while drawing on the strategic and tactical wisdom contained in the treatises of the earlier age, had almost no institutional continuity with the pre-1025 army. It depended on two main sources of manpower. First, there were the remaining military aristocrats and their followers. But this source was limited by the Comnenian policy, most clearly under Manuel, of concentrating land and power in the hands of the royal family—a reaction to the civil wars and dissension that had led to disaster in the first place. So, while this source provided a cadre of leadership, it could not supply the manpower for major armies. The second source of manpower, foreign mercenaries, made up the bulk of Byzantine forces in this period. Such soldiers ranged from western Latin knights to Petchenegs and other Asiatic horsemen. This heterogeneous force perhaps lacked the common tactical doctrine of the old Byzantine army, but it was capable of responding flexibly to a wide range of challenges and avoided the political dangers of the old system by remaining loyal to the emperor who hired it.

Both sources were supported increasingly not by direct payments from the treasury but by *pronoia*—a grant of the income (or a share of the income) from a piece of land. It was similar to the Muslim *iqta'*, though it carried less in the way of administrative duties; it also had few of the implications of lordship carried by Latin fiefs. It was thus more purely a fiscal measure, representing an adaptive response by the Comneni to the changing economic base of the empire. There was no connection between the soldiers and their *pronoia* lands, and the foreignness of most *pronoia* recipients slowly became a source of unrest among the population. A gulf opened between the Byzantine military system and the social structure on which it was based, a development that made the empire more closely resemble Muslim states, where socially marginal nomads and *iqta'* holders dominated a civilian population.

This Byzantine army, backed by the government's wealth and led energetically and creatively by the early Comneni emperors, performed well for almost a century. By 1176, Manuel was strong enough to contemplate the reconquest of Anatolia from the Seljuk sultanate. If Manuel had been successful—and there was no reason inherent in the situation at the time that he could not have been—the subsequent course of history in the region would have been very different. But chance intervened, and the attempt ended in disaster. On September 17, Kilij Arslan's Turkish army ambushed Manuel's huge invading force in a pass near Myriocephalum and annihilated it; the emperor himself barely escaped. This "second Manzikert" sealed the possession of Anatolia by the Turks, did severe damage to Byzantine strength, and so freed Saladin in Syria to focus on the Crusader States exclusively. Four years later, Manuel died, and the traditional Achilles heel of Byzantium, succession problems, prevented any recovery. Byzantium turned away from Manuel's policy of cooperation with the Crusader States. The Fourth Crusade in 1204 became entangled in Byzantine politics, opening an opportunity for western intervention and the venting of growing anti-Greek hostility in western Europe. The crusaders ended up taking and sacking Constantinople and dividing the empire.

The Fourth Crusade represented the end of Byzantium as a significant military power. The Greeks retook Constantinople in 1261, and the late Byzantine army retained some key administrative elements of the Comnenian period, including the *pronoia* system. But Turks and Mongols were the significant military players in the area, and in 1453, the Ottoman Turks extinguished the last territorial remnant of the empire by taking Constantinople. Byzantine culture lived on, though, and its influence spread, both to Russia and to Renaissance Italy, despite—or perhaps because of—the state's decline and eventual disappearance.

THE RISE OF THE OTTOMANS

The Seljuks in Anatolia, 1071–1300

The Turkish victory at Manzikert was part of the larger creation of the Great Seljuk Empire. When the empire fragmented in the 1090s, the area of Anatolia became the Seljuk Sultanate of Rum (that is, Rome—former Byzantine territory). Between Manzikert and Myriocephalum, a substantial part of the Byzantine population seems to have moved to the European provinces of the empire or to have otherwise declined in the unsettled conditions, and Anatolia received extensive Turkish settlement. The vast majority became farmers, but there were also numerous Turkish townsmen and merchants. Militarily, the most important facet of Turkish settlement was the Turkmen tribes who moved with their herds to the hills and valleys of the Anatolian plateau and maintained their seminomadic lifestyle. Anatolia thus became an important new source of Asian-style horse-archers.

Politically, the Anatolian sultanate began to fragment in the thirteenth century, for much the same reasons the Great Seljuk Empire had. The Turkish notion of collective sovereignty, in which every member of the ruling family had a stake in the state's

authority, and the practice of assigning semi-independent commands in marcher districts to such family members and other important supporters, tended toward the creation of virtually autonomous *beyliks* (the principality of a *bey*, or local chief) throughout the sultanate.

Any chance of the sultanate recovering its power and bringing the *beyliks* to obedience was smashed in the mid-thirteenth century by the Mongols (see Chapter 13). Their incursions and conquests in the Islamic world, starting in the 1230s, seriously altered the patterns of power throughout southwest Asia. Baghdad suffered tremendous damage as a political and cultural center, and the Mongols defeated the Seljuk Sultanate and reduced it to a protectorate. The political and military situation was further complicated by the rise of the Mamluk Sultanate in Egypt, which exerted pressure in Anatolia while disputing control of Syria with the Mongols. But by 1300, the Ilkhan Mongols based in Persia and the Mamluks in Egypt were at most indirect influences in Anatolia. In this political vacuum, the *beyliks* of the former Seljuk Sultanate began to assert themselves and expand their zones of control.

The Ottomans, 1300–1453

One of the local powers that began to create an independent polity for itself at the beginning of the fourteenth century was a small group of Turkmen under the leadership of Osman (1290–1326), who would give his name to an empire ("Ottoman," like "Seljuk," is a dynastic, not an ethnic, term). The Ottoman state was located in the northwest corner of Anatolia, on the borders with Byzantium. By expanding into Byzantine territory, Osman and his successors were able to attract to their service other nomadic tribesmen and *ghazi* warriors; principalities in the interior of Anatolia, surrounded by other Muslim powers, had faced earlier limits on their ability to sustain expansion by attracting such supporters. But even the Ottomans would have run out of room to expand in the fourteenth century had they not made the leap across the Dardenelles to Europe.

The Ottomans established a beachhead in Europe in 1345, and by 1360, large-scale Turkish settlement of Thrace was underway. It was this that would truly doom Constantinople by isolating the city completely. The Ottomans steadily extended their hold over the Balkans, defeating the Serbs in 1371 and again, decisively, at Kosovo in 1389. Between 1391 and 1399,

Figure 11.3 Early Ottoman Expansion By 1362, the Ottomans had a beachhead in Europe; their expansion thereafter was rapid, encompassing much of the Balkans and Asia Minor.

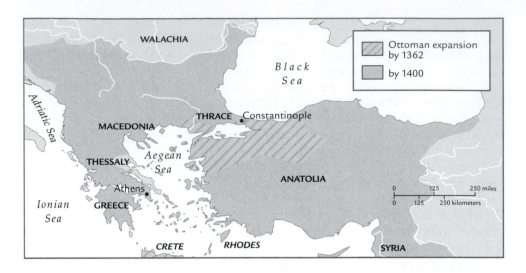

they besieged Constantinople for the first time, even as they were annexing more and more of the Turkish *beyliks* of Anatolia (Figure 11.3). But in 1402, Tamerlane invaded Anatolia and defeated the Ottoman sultan Bayazid at the battle of Angora. This proved a near-fatal setback, and the Ottoman state took several decades to recover fully. But by 1453, the Ottomans were back at the gates of Constantinople. Armed this time with cannon, they took the city and made it their new capital (see Chapter 17).

The Ottoman move into Europe was crucial in a number of ways, aside from making the capture of Constantinople possible. It opened up much more land for Turkish settlement and the support of Turkish cavalry forces. Conquests in the Balkans made available a substantial Christian population from which children could be taken and raised into the elite slave-soldier guards of the Sultan: The Janissaries were founded in 1370, though they would not be a central part of the Ottoman military establishment for another century. The move to Europe also stimulated the Ottoman expansion into maritime warfare and trade; their establishment on the northern shore of the eastern Mediterranean vastly increased their ability to disrupt Christian shipping and project their power westward (see Chapter 15). But this acquisition of sea power came only after the empire was well established on land—unlike the coastal *beyliks* in Anatolia, the landlocked early Ottomans faced no pressure from Latin naval forces. Ottoman European provinces, untouched by Tamerlane's depredations, speeded the empire's recovery from his invasion. Also, becoming a European power put the empire in

closer contact with the late medieval west, from which they profitably borrowed the use of cannon and infantry small arms.

The Ottoman military system was rooted in the military capabilities of the seminomadic tribesmen who flocked to their standards. As the state expanded, such warriors were granted *iqta'* (or *timar*, to use the Ottoman term) in the new lands, spreading Turkish influence, administration, and settlement and keeping forces available near the frontiers. This was an important consideration, since, like such forces in the Muslim armies of the Crusades, Ottoman tribal cavalry were essentially seasonal warriors. In the fifteenth century, the Janissary corps gained prominence as a permanent, trained infantry imperial guard, which would quite successfully adopt gunpowder weapons. But the bulk of Ottoman forces remained the cavalry. Tactically, this army was by no means invincible, as the decisive defeat inflicted by Tamerlane demonstrates. But especially once the Janissaries provided a solid defensive corps around which the cavalry could maneuver, the Ottoman army would prove tactically formidable. The development of an effective artillery train also proved decisive in sieges and against foes such as the Mamluks who resisted adopting gunpowder weapons. And the sheer size of the forces the empire could raise as it expanded rapidly made it into an important power. The capture of Constantinople only confirmed its world power status.

The Ottomans could raise substantial forces because as they expanded they drew on the Seljuk, Ilkhan, Byzantine, and Mamluk experiences to build a sophisticated administrative and financial system. In this, the spread of the Turkish urban and educated class went hand in hand with the spread of the rural cavalry class, and both depended on a substantial and prosperous farming population. Thus, the Ottomans may be seen to have successfully combined many of the best elements of the military striking power of nomadic warriors such as the Mongols with the staying power and administrative strength of settled civilizations. Nomadic conquerors of settled areas usually followed one (or both) of two paths: assimilation into the conquered population, and consequent loss of their nomadic military advantages (a common result in China, for example); or isolation and eventual expulsion as a foreign elite of tribute-extracting rulers (essentially, the fate of the Mamluks in Egypt). But a combination of luck, policy, and Turkish demographic expansion allowed the Ottomans a creative middle ground. The sultans certainly ruled a large, polyglot empire, but not as foreign overlords (save to the extent that almost all Muslim polities resembled conquest societies): Turkish was the language of a substantial portion of the population as well as of government and culture, and the sultans certainly created a stable, settled government system. But they also consciously retained a nomadic ethos as part of their identity. The sultans lived in tents on campaign every summer, decorated their palaces like tents, and celebrated their heritage in such oddities as jewel-encrusted water bottles—the riches of civilization attached to a symbol of a life lived on horseback. The security of a culture of nomadism may have allowed the Ottomans the flexibility to adopt gunpowder weapons, something the Mamluks, whose identity and institutional structure were tied more specifically to their style of fighting, never accomplished. But the Ottomans also ruled enough territory to maintain a part of their population in at least a seminomadic life, at some cost to the security of their villagers but to the benefit of their military power.

The other key to Ottoman success was good, stable leadership. The early Ottoman sultans—Osman, Orhan and Murad—were remarkable commanders, and their individual talents certainly helped establish Ottoman power. Greater stability came with an Ottoman reinterpretation of the Turkish concept of sovereignty. The Ottomans came to see legitimate power as unitary, residing only in the leader of the ruling family, not in all its members collectively. While this did not prevent succession disputes within the direct line—one of a set of Ottoman brothers would usually succeed to the throne by killing all his sibling rivals—it did prevent the division of the empire by the assignment of semi-autonomous regions to princes of the royal family, the problem that had plagued the Great Seljuk Empire. The Ottoman Empire thus not only grew large but stayed in one piece, drew on the military skills and heritages of its many and varied subjects, and so became one heir to the meeting of military traditions in the eastern Mediterranean initiated by the Crusades. By 1500, the empire was the greatest military power on earth.

CONCLUSION

The military history of the Middle East between 1100 and 1500 is rich and at times paradoxical. The regions along the Mediterranean coast focused on Jerusalem became the battleground of Latin Christians, Greek Christians, Arab Muslims, and Turkish Muslims. The two groups most native to the area, the Arabs and Greeks, ended up the losers: Arab influence continued to recede before the military superiority of the Turks within the Islamic world, while the Byzantine Empire had disappeared territorially by 1500. The expulsion of the Latin presence in the Middle East, however, made little difference to a western European trajectory of development that had been stimulated by contact with the east but was not dependent on it. The eventual winners for control of the area, the Ottomans, like the Latin Christians, benefited from the cultural cross-currents of the larger region. But they were latecomers for whom the Holy Lands in which so much blood had been shed were of peripheral concern at best. Indeed, after so much conflict, the Holy Lands would fall into military insignificance until the twentieth century.

The outcomes point to the role of contingency in military history, for the eventual result was not predetermined. Byzantium's decline followed an almost accidental disaster at Myriocephalum; the Greek Empire could well have continued as an increasingly major player in the region, foreclosing any opportunity for the rise of the Ottomans. And

Turkish ascendancy came despite the tendency to political fragmentation that Turkish polities suffered from and despite Tamerlane's nearly extinguishing the rising Ottoman power at Angora. Neither result was predictable.

The outcomes also point, however, to the creative and destructive potential of cross-cultural contact, of war connected to commerce and ideology. The remaining chapters of Part 3 will trace these influences elsewhere in the world.

Suggested Readings

Amitai-Preiss, Reuven. *Mongols and Mamluks*. See Chapter 13.

Bachrach, David. *Religion and the Conduct of War c. 300–c. 1215*. Woodbridge: Boydell, 2003. An analysis of the multifaceted roles religion played in the conduct of warfare in western Christendom.

Bartusis, Mark C. *The Late Byzantine Army, Arms and Society, 1204–1453*. Philadelphia: University of Pennsylvania Press, 1992. An excellent study of the evolution of military manpower, landholding and social structure in the declining days of Byzantine power.

France, John. *Victory in the East: A Military History of the First Crusade*. Cambridge: Cambridge University Press, 1994. A fine analysis of the First Crusade as a military enterprise, including strong chapters on leadership, numbers of combatants, logistics, and the clash of tactical styles.

Hillenbrand, Carol. *The Crusades: Islamic Perspectives*. London: Routledge, 2000. A valuable survey of contemporary Muslim attitudes toward the Crusades.

Holt, P. M. *The Age of the Crusades. The Near East from the Eleventh Century to 1517*. London: Routledge, 1986. A solid overview of the entire Near East, of which the Crusader States were only a part.

Housley, Norman. *Religious Warfare in Europe 1400–1536*. Oxford: Oxford University Press, 2002. An examination of the various forms religious warfare assumed and the cultural effects of religious motivation in war.

Irwin, Robert. *The Middle East in the Middle Ages: The Early Mamluk Sultanate, 1250–1382*. Carbondale: Southern Illinois University Press, 1986. A valuable survey of Mamluk institutions and the dynamics of crusade-era politics from the Egyptian perspective.

Kafesoglu, Ibrahim. *A History of the Seljuks*. Ed., trans., and intro. by Gary Leiser. Carbondale: Southern Illinois University Press, 1988. A classic Turkish account of the rise of the Seljuks, the major force in the area at the time of the First Crusade; an instructive non-European perspective.

Koprulu, M. Faud. *The Origins of the Ottoman Empire*. Ed. and trans. Gary Leiser. Albany: SUNY Press, 1992. Carefully traces the early history of the Ottomans, a field fraught with legendary overtones and historiographical controversy.

Lyons, Malcolm, and D.E.P. Jackson. *Saladin: The Politics of the Holy War*. Cambridge: Cambridge University Press, 1997. A reassessment of the great Muslim leader's career using hitherto neglected Arab sources.

Magdalino, Paul. *The Empire of Manuel I Komnenos, 1143–1180*. Cambridge: Cambridge University Press, 1993. A detailed analysis of the world of the most powerful twelfth-century Byzantine ruler, including his military campaigns and diplomacy.

Marshall, Christopher. *Warfare in the Latin East, 1192–1291*. Cambridge: Cambridge University Press, 1992. A worthy companion to Smail (see below); looks at patterns of warfare—battles, raids, and sieges—in conjunction with military organization.

Riley-Smith, Jonathan. *The Crusades: A Short History*. London: Routledge, 1987. A concise introduction to the entire crusading movement, including religious motivations and governance of the holy land, in all its variety.

Rogers, Randall. *Latin Siege Warfare in the Twelfth Century*. Oxford: Oxford University Press, 1993. A focused examination of siege techniques in the Mediterranean world, with assessment of intercultural influences.

Smail, R. C. *Crusading Warfare, 1097–1193*. Cambridge: Cambridge University Press, 1995. A seminal work of medieval military history, relating campaigning patterns to political and manpower structures and to logistics; a classic.

CHAPTER 12

Knights, Castles, and Kings: Western Europe, 1050–1500

The political instability and social transformations of the period 350–950 in western Europe gave rise, in the century between 950 and 1050, to a new aristocratic social order and a new sociomilitary system (see Chapter 7). This system was built around three major elements: the private castle, knights, and mostly urban nonknightly soldiers. Especially at first, the private castle was the key to the system. It stimulated the shift to patrilineal family structures among the aristocracy that lay at the heart of the period's social reconstruction; it housed the local lords and their followers, who formed the knightly class and dominated politics; and it formed the focus of warfare.

It would seem at first glance that the rise of the private castle reduced western European warfare to localized violence and political futility under incompetent leadership—this used to be a common assessment of feudal warfare among historians. It is a mistaken conclusion, however. Medieval generals were no better or worse than generals in any other age—meaning that some were blunderers, a few were geniuses, and most were competent but not outstanding. They may have had fewer resources to work with in terms of administration and finances, but they made intelligent use of the resources they did command. More fundamentally, however, such a conclusion misleads because the system of castles, knights, and infantry acted as a foundation for two long-term trends whose significance can hardly be overstated.

First, the rise of the system as an aspect of the aristocratic reconstruction began to fuel a steady expansion of the frontiers of this civilization. Second, the system functioned as a foundation for new state building as regional rulers and then kings slowly reasserted some element of control over the elements of the system. Both these developments took place within a particular culture of war that also emerged as an aspect of this sociomilitary system.

The system that had emerged by 1050 proved prone over the next seven centuries and beyond to continuous instability, to competition—both between distinct political units within Europe and among the various elements of the system within the separate polities—and thus to innovation. There would be steady development and elaboration of the military elements of the system, and of the expansionism, state building, and culture of war that the military system fostered. Such evolution—essentially uninterrupted, unlike in much of the rest of Eurasia, by the Mongol scourge—eventually produced results that were increasingly noticeable, in a global context, after 1500, and revolutionary after about 1720. But there was no short moment in those seven centuries between 1050 and 1750 that can be convincingly pinpointed as the revolutionary turning point. Rather, the Military Revolution of early modern Europe is a somewhat illusory aspect of a military evolution whose roots are firmly planted in the medieval world of 1050–1500.

A CULTURE OF WAR

A crucial consequence of the emergence of this sociomilitary system was the establishment of a European *culture of war* that would remain fairly consistent for centuries. A set of values and attitudes evolved by the early twelfth century in relation to killing in warfare, conquest and colonization, and the legitimacy of authority.

Medieval warfare has often been portrayed as a relatively bloodless, restrained affair. The wars of knights between 1000 and 1300 were supposedly almost ritualized. At the least, battles were a matter of capturing opponents for ransom rather than killing. This picture is often drawn to emphasize the dramatic changes that supposedly overtook European warfare in the fourteenth to sixteenth centuries. But this picture is inaccurate. Certainly, there were battles between largely knightly armies that resulted in casualty rates of under ten in an army of several hundred. But such battles make up only a fraction of medieval warfare. Much medieval warfare was vicious and bloody after 1050 (as it had been before), and especially so when conflict crossed cultural divisions.

Warfare that crossed lines of ethnicity, class, and culture as broadly conceived, especially linguistic boundaries and boundaries of socioeconomic structure, saw plenty of killing. Knights who fought urban infantry rarely gave or received quarter, for example, either in formal battles or in communal riots and rebellions. This was only partly because infantrymen weren't worth ransoming. A real class antagonism, rooted in differing and not always compatible worldviews, fueled this hostility.

Similarly, Anglo-Saxons, Danes, and Normans all fought bloody battles for control of England; English and Welsh did not capture but killed each other; and Germans and Slavs fought deadly wars. The claim that European warfare was relatively restrained would certainly have surprised the inhabitants of Jerusalem in the wake of the city's capture by the forces of the First Crusade; knee-deep rivers of blood (according to Christian chroniclers) testified to the contrary. Perhaps the only change after 1300 was that conflict across such lines (especially social class) became more frequent. The culture of killing was already well established.

As the above examples show, the culture of killing intersected strongly with the culture of conquest and colonization fostered by the expansionism of this era. Expansion brought Europeans of the castles, knights, and towns culture into increased contact with peoples who spoke alien languages, had unrecognizable political structures and religions, and often supported themselves in ways antithetical to their aggressive neighbors—pastoralism or seminomadic agriculture versus the intensive cereal farming and urban trade of the European core. Such differences fostered visions of an uncivilized Other beyond the borders of Christendom, a world of savages who did not play by the rules and who therefore merited death if they refused to submit to civilized authority and convert to Christianity. Like the culture of killing, these colonial attitudes would also have a long history: The inhabitants of Jerusalem would not have been surprised at the fate of the inhabitants of the Aztec capital of Tenochtitlan at the hands of the Spaniards centuries later.

Further, the focus of the sociomilitary system on warrior-aristocrats affected to some extent the broader culture of this civilization. The ideology of crusade, the end result of the gradual fusing of warrior and Christian ideologies that took place throughout the period 350–1050, is one example of this, especially considering that the crusading ethos came to be applied with increasing frequency to conflicts between Christian forces as well as to external wars. French kings, for instance, could draw on crusadelike imagery in suppressing rebellious Flemings in the fourteenth century. The Wars of Religion were as much children of the Crusades as the conquest of the Americas was; conflict over the Reformation showed the European culture of war at work at almost every social level.

Another example of the dominance of warrior values in this civilization was the cementing of military success as a conveyor of legitimacy to rulers. This too had a religious element in the notion that the outcome of battles reflected God's judgment. It is evident in the iconography rulers often used to portray themselves on their coins and seals: on horseback, in full armor, sword raised in triumph——all a sort of shorthand for "might makes right." It is even reflected in the symbolism the church used to explain the legitimacy of political powers. The Two Swords theory divided authority between the spiritual sword of the church and the temporal sword of kings. After 1050, the church would attempt to assert the superiority of the spiritual sword, but, in a sense, it had already lost the symbolic battle. This was a culture with warrior values at its heart. The contrast with Chinese civilization, for example, is instructive. Whereas Chinese conquerors took up the image of the scholar-king in a tradition that looked back to Confucius, European religious leaders called for conquering crusades in a tradition that looked back to Alexander the Great.

THE EXPANSION OF LATIN CHRISTENDOM: FRONTIER WARFARE, 900–1300

Foundations and Frontiers

The rise of the European sociomilitary system, as an aspect of the aristocratic reconstruction, began by 1050 to fuel a steady expansion of the frontiers of this civilization. Initially, in the absence of a strong central authority that could bestow riches and prestige on its

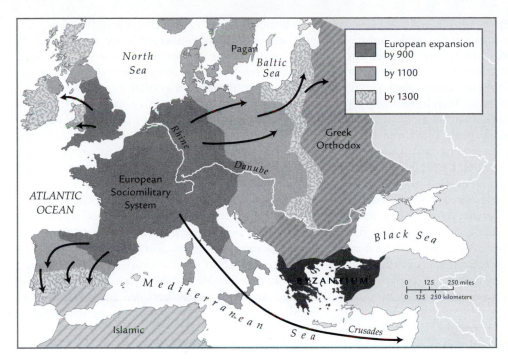

Figure 12.1 European Expansion, 900–1300 A combination of economic, military, and religious techniques and motives spread the core organizational features of western Europe.

followers, local lords who wanted to expand their resources were forced to turn to economic development. Many began to encourage the opening of new land for cultivation, the founding of new villages, and even the founding of towns with charters of liberty as potential market centers and tax revenue sources. While there was much land available on the internal frontiers of Europe—the tracts of wilderness between settlements in settled areas—abundant land beckoned even more invitingly on the external frontiers: the Baltic and Slavic lands to the east of Germany; the Muslim lands of the Iberian peninsula and Sicily; and the Celtic fringes of Europe: Ireland, Wales, and Scotland. The effect of the aristocratic reconstruction on this outward movement is still a matter of scholarly dispute, but it would seem that the need to find new lands for younger sons as primogeniture became more common probably played some role. What is more certain is that much of this expansion had the character of private enterprise at the level of local and regional lords. At least at first, kings played little role. The foundations for the expansion were laid in the century prior to 1050, when there arose both the social and economic conditions that would spur expansion and the military system that would spearhead it. The most prominent example of this expansionist movement was the Crusades (see Chapter 11),

but, in important ways, the expansion of civilization begun in this age continued uninterrupted for nine centuries.

Mechanisms of Expansion

The private castle, the heavily armed knight, and crossbow-bearing infantry drawn from the towns provided the military mechanisms that opened the way for expansion of western Europe's frontiers (Figure 12.1). Naval forces and technology also played a significant role (see Chapter 15).

The role of the castle in expansion shows that its tactical defensive strength also gave it an offensive role strategically. As secure bases of operations, castles allowed the soldiers housed within them to dominate the surrounding countryside, as well as standing as visual symbols of that domination. Especially once they were rebuilt in stone or brick, castles were difficult for the less technologically advanced peoples of eastern Europe and the Celtic fringe to take; Muslim foes in Iberia and the Mediterranean had sophisticated siege weapons, but the sheer number of castles erected by private lords along frontiers created a serious obstacle.

Armored knights were the offensive strike force in the field. Mounted for strategic mobility as much as for tactical reasons, knights were formidable less as cavalry than as elite warriors who could fight on horse or foot. Their social and economic dominance allowed them to be armed and armored with expensive iron and to be warriors on a full-time basis as a basic element of their lifestyle. Weight of armor and level of training were often knights' most significant advantages against external foes. Their social position also allowed them leadership over lower-status infantry forces, which provided the bulk of numbers in western European armies. For their part, the infantry not only had their own effective weapon system in the crossbow but drew on the demographic advantage that the intensive cereal farming of European culture provided over the less intensive pastoral and seminomadic agricultural economies of many neighboring cultures. Weight of numbers was particularly important in garrisoning numerous castles and besieging enemy forts.

Social cohesion under knightly leadership was supplemented by the cultural cohesion provided by Christianity, especially crusading ideology. Crusading fervor could be directed not just against pagans and Muslims but against nonstandard Christians, whose different social organization or lack of ties to the regular church structure centered on Rome put them on the wrong side of a cultural boundary. Social and cultural cohesion came together in the crusading orders that participated in frontier warfare in both eastern Europe and the Mediterranean. Orders such as the Teutonic Knights, who carved the state of Prussia from the pagan lands along the Baltic, were significant because their transregional organization allowed them to draw resources in wealth and manpower from more than just the local region. Their direct ties to the pope meant that crusades were often preached in support of critical campaigns, again drawing recruits from a broader demographic base.

But the western European advance should not be seen as irresistible in purely military terms. Military success was ultimately secured by colonization, not conquest, and life along the frontiers was characterized by much give-and-take technologically and culturally. The spread of western European systems of law and urban organization were crucial mechanisms in expansion and were closely tied to military organization and effort. New castles were often closely associated with new towns; castles both protected and controlled urban populations, while the economy of a town, especially if it had a successful market, helped support the lord of the castle. Security helped attract

new settlers, as did the legal privileges offered to peasants and townsmen alike as lords sought to populate their new lands with productive workers. The legal codes granted to new settlements or extended to older ones in frontier areas often regulated the military responsibilities and militia duties of the townsmen. The various legal codes of the Spanish marcher communities are probably the best-known and most militarily intensive examples. Militia arrangements were not just defensive but could encompass offensive action as well: Spanish urban militias could profit from aggressive cattle-raiding expeditions, for example. Such connections between legal codes and military service also extended the notion that legal rights and responsibilities were closely tied to the right to bear arms. Much of the success of western European expansion in the Middle Ages can be traced to the linkage on the frontiers between demographic and economic growth on one hand, and military aggression on the other.

Another reason for this success was the adaptability that Europeans showed to local conditions. Here the regional and semiprivate nature of much frontier expansion undoubtedly fostered the ability to respond to a wide range of challenges: There was no central imperial authority imposing doctrine or stifling initiatives. Adaptation was necessary in part because of terrain and climate. For example, heavily wooded or mountainous frontier regions such as Wales were unsuited to the charge of heavy cavalry. There, lighter, more mobile troops—cavalry and infantry—were more valuable, and English forces learned Welsh methods of raid and ambush to complement their castle building; knights were important as leaders rather than as heavy cavalry. Eventually, the Welsh longbow became an important part of the English tactical arsenal. In contrast, Spain was suited to cavalry action, but the hot climate meant that Spanish knights wore lighter armor and rode lighter horses than their northern counterparts. There were, however, cultural limits to such adaptability, as the refusal of western European forces to adopt massed horse-archery in the Holy Land or elsewhere shows. And in the end, Wales was conquered not by Welsh methods but by the massive application of demographic and economic force by Edward I, cemented by his construction of a network of formidable castles.

Adaptation went both ways as well. At times, peoples threatened by European expansion responded by adopting European methods of social and military organization. Creating a force of armored cavalry depended on creating a nobility who could provide such forces (or, as in the case of Scotland, importing a new nobility, at least in part). Rulers in loosely organized tribal areas were often eager to follow this path as a means of increasing their power within their society, and the more stratified hierarchies that emerged did allow some areas to defend themselves more effectively. However, this came with the cost of a decline in freedoms and standards of living for much of the population. Western Europe's sociomilitary structure was thus still readily exportable, and the civilization spread by assimilation as well as conquest and colonization. This too proved a two-way process, as western Europeans absorbed elements of pagan and, most important, Arab culture even as they settled pagan and Arab lands.

Missing the Mongols

Given the political fragmentation of western European civilization, the still rudimentary powers of even its most powerful kings, and the semiprivate nature of frontier warfare, much of the success of western European expansionism resulted from the fact that the cultures and polities it faced on its frontiers were usually at least as fragmented, if not more so, and often less technologically advanced. The major western European kingdoms did not face a strong, sophisticated, expansionist foe until late in the fifteenth century, at which point the Ottomans proved more than a match for European armies for several centuries. And there was one major piece of luck in this freedom from significant outside threat: western Europe avoided the Mongols.

Mongol armies, having subjugated Russia, advanced into eastern Europe in 1241, smashing Polish and Hungarian armies in the course of their campaigns. Mongol *Tumens* then approached Vienna and Venice (see Chapter 13). Western Europe was in a panic, and rightly so. Despite papal attempts to mount a unified response to the threat, European disunity and ignorance of their foes contrasted sharply with the Mongols' unity of command, clarity of purpose, and sophisticated intelligence. Their operational mobility and remarkable siege capabilities almost guaranteed success in campaigns farther west. Logistical difficulties might have slowed or limited their progress somewhat—western Europe was unsuited by climate and geography to support vast cavalry armies (the horsed aristocratic elites of medieval Europe were a minority in their own armies and tiny

in absolute terms). Mongol difficulties in Syria illustrate the possibility, but much of southern China was equally unsuitable, yet it fell under Mongol rule for nearly a century. The fate of Baghdad, sacked so brutally by the Mongols in 1258 that it did not recover fully for centuries, shows the potential for damage that western Europe faced.

But in 1241, the hordes turned back to elect a new Great Khan, and they never returned. As a result, western European political, economic, and cultural development was allowed to continue uninterrupted. This continuity enabled the civilization to weather a century of internal crises from 1350 to 1450 and then to resume the steady external expansion that had characterized it since 1050.

KINGS AND ARMIES, 1050–1350

State Building

In addition to fueling expansion, the sociomilitary system of castles, knights, and infantry functioned as a foundation for new state building. The effective political units that first emerged in this period were smaller than the Roman successor kingdoms and the overambitious empire of the Carolingians. In fact, Carolingian counties often provided sites of renewed central authority. The process was uneven: Where regional lords failed to control their castellans (governors or wardens of castles or forts), their power remained truncated. But the counts and dukes who did manage their own aristocrats, castellans, and kinsmen effectively built a solid base of regional power. The counts of Anjou and Flanders and the dukes of Normandy (descendants of Vikings settled in the Seine valley around Rouen) led the way in northern France; certain German duchies and the tiny Christian kingdoms of northern Spain followed the model elsewhere. Fulk Nerra, Count of Anjou from 980 to around 1030, virtually pioneered a power-building strategy based a network of castles, increasingly constructed in stone, held by loyal castellans. Despite its tenuous beginnings, Anjou was probably by 1050 the most powerful dynastic polity in Europe. Kings, including the dukes of Normandy who became kings of England, then followed in this path.

The almost independent military power of the aristocracy and their knights on the one hand and of towns and their nonknightly forces on the other meant that the leaders of these new-style states could not be all-powerful despots. Indeed, since most were not royal at first, they lacked even the aura of sanctity that attached to anointed Christian kings. Instead, they should be seen more as the leaders of cooperative enterprises. They could not "tame" their aristocracy without making the result profitable to those "tamed," because the bulk of knightly warriors were attached to the aristocracy. They could not afford to oppress or suppress towns and limit their legal liberties, because they needed urban military forces and economic resources, and townsmen were willing and able to defend their rights and privileges. Such leaders therefore needed to build up networks of loyal kinsmen in key castles and regions and to co-opt their most powerful followers, often through their joint participation in predatory expansion. The spoils of expansion were then parceled out among the participants in the enterprise. The most spectacularly successful of such enterprises was the conquest of England in 1066 by William, Duke of Normandy (see the Highlights box on page 136).

One result of this style of leadership was a political structure built around mutual rights and obligations and constant consultation. The focus of politics was the leader's court, where the magnates of the state met to bargain, advise, and settle disputes. The magnates were churchmen as well as lay aristocrats, in part because the church was a major landholder. But the moral and administrative resources of rulers were reinforced by their alliance with the church. The violence and constant local warfare that a turbulent aristocracy engaged in, in the absence of strong central authority, had led to the rise of the Peace Movement by about 1000. Initiated by peasants (who always suffered the worst of the violence) and soon backed by churchmen, the Peace of God attempted to put certain people (women, children, churchmen), places (monasteries, churches), and possessions (peasant livestock) beyond the scope of warfare. The Truce of God prohibited fighting on certain days. However, the Peace Movement met with little success, except where effective leaders took up the cause as a way of harnessing the violent energies of their vassals to their own ends. The Peace Movement gave moral force to the ruler who outlawed private warfare among his followers, forcing them to fight for him or not at all. And, in general, whatever increase in order the new leaders could bring to their lands benefited the church. In turn, the church backed the ruler and provided, as virtually the only source of literate men, the manpower of a rudimentary bureaucracy. When the foundations of state building laid down by counts

and dukes were taken up by kings, military force remained central to the process and to the shape that politics took.

Another result of this leadership was that European states became firmly rooted in particular localities. The tight relationship between leaders and their followers, aristocratic and urban, embedded in local legal traditions and defended by walls around both knights and urban infantry, made rapid conquest of such states increasingly difficult. In other words, the military system that arose in this period came to guarantee that Europe would remain politically divided, rather than being subject to the rise and fall of vast empires, such as the Carolingian, or such as remained common in other parts of the world. In turn, political division gave to European warfare a context of ongoing competition that would stimulate further evolution of armies and military systems.

The locally rooted and governmentally limited polities that emerged after 1050 took advantage of European-wide demographic and economic growth. Contributing to and fueled by expansion of both internal and external frontiers, the economy benefited from more stable conditions after the cessation of invasions by the Vikings and Magyars. And new technologies such as three-field rotation and the heavy plow contributed to increased agricultural productivity. More agricultural wealth, in turn, stimulated trade, manufacturing, and town growth, all operating on the basis of a growing money economy. And these provided the economic foundations for increasing lay literacy and a twelfth-century cultural flowering that included renewed traditions of Roman law (and the emerging Common Law in England). All these trends gave to rulers greater resources for better governance. The result, between 1100 and 1350, was a steady increase in most states' administrative and fiscal capabilities, driven by the increasing costs of war in the context of constant competition. In turn, military systems and the armies they produced were transformed as rulers brought increasing resources and control to bear on them.

Military Systems and Armies

Manpower and Administration   Increased security and prosperity affected military manpower in two ways. First, the period saw an increase in the legal definition of military obligations. Feudal service—the service owed by the knightly holders of fiefs—came to be defined as part of the land law of fief holding, and in restricted ways: Forty days of service a year was the primary wartime obligation. This was accompanied by the emergence of knighthood as a recognized social class with specific legal rights and privileges. Landed service below the knightly level was defined by sergeantry tenure, which often supported not just nonknightly horsemen but foot soldiers and specialists such as engineers. The limitations of feudal service led some rulers, particularly the kings of England from Henry II on, to experiment with mandatory and universal systems of obligation based on landed wealth: Henry's Assize of Arms of 1181 established the precedent. Under Edward I a century later, the legal obligation extended down to the level of yeoman farmers through a system of Commissioners of Array, who would muster a county's eligible men and select a proportion for service, allowing Edward to raise substantial infantry forces of fair quality. More commonly for nonknightly duty throughout most of Europe, town charters came to specify the military and financial duties the townsmen owed the ruler in exchange for the freedom to run their own affairs commercially. There was even some reinvigoration of the truly universal obligation for all free men to muster in defensive emergencies, though peasant levies remained rare and almost always worse than useless.

Second, increased resources led to even more crucial changes in how rulers actually created and maintained armies: There was a steady increase in the use of paid service as governments tapped the growing cash economy. Rulers hired mercenaries, sometimes maintained a small core of professional soldiers in their household establishments, and even came to pay soldiers who nominally owed feudal service, especially once their term of unpaid service was up. Despite steadily rising incomes, however, rulers were always short of money, so plunder, booty, and ransom remained essential attractions to military service for most soldiers, from infantry to knights. In their search for cash to meet the sudden short-term expenses of war, some rulers by the late thirteenth century were turning to loans from merchants and bankers, guaranteed against future tax revenue.

In administrative terms, the king's role as the war leader meant that administration started with the *familia regis,* the king's military household. The *familia* of the English kings became the central professional core of their military. But elsewhere, a variety of mechanisms prevailed for calling up troops and organizing them on campaign. Local units of

administration were not standardized in many areas, nor, as a result, were the small units of an army. Small units were built around aristocratic households (royal *familiae* in miniature) of varying size or around the administrative divisions in urban militias, while mercenary bands varied according to the ability and success of their leaders and to their employers' ability to pay.

The limitations of military systems in this period thus remained clear. While the armies grew slowly but steadily in size—from maximum forces of perhaps 5000 in 1050 to 20,000–30,000 around 1300—no state could afford a true standing army, and so there was no large-unit training. Such small-unit and individual training as there was resulted from social ties and culture rather than government; and, naturally, it favored the aristocracy, whose accepted role was fighting. These limitations affected the battlefield capabilities of medieval armies. And yet, the period 1050–1350 witnessed a steady assertion of greater royal control. Legal limits on private warfare were increasingly enforced, and the growing expense of war favored kings, whose incomes, despite their inadequacies, still greatly exceeded those of individual lords. The keys to success for kings in creating and controlling effective military forces were to gain a preponderance in fortifications and to bind together the potentially hostile elements of the system, especially infantry and cavalry forces often drawn from very different social classes.

The Elements of Military Force Social change and improvements in royal administration, finances, and control affected all three elements of the western European sociomilitary system: castles, knights, and urban nonknightly forces.

The increase in resources was evident in castle building as more and more construction was in stone and designs became more massive and elaborate, culminating in the magnificent and costly Edwardian castles that secured Wales. Concentric designs, in which an outer wall shielded an inner wall, which sometimes shielded a keep, added to the defensive strength of major castles. As on Europe's frontiers, such defensive strength not only provided a secure base—Henry II's extensive program of castle building in England proved its worth during two revolts by his eldest son—but could be part of an offensive strategy as well. For example, Henry's son Richard the Lionhearted made Chateau Gallaird on the Seine the linchpin of his defense of Normandy and his

Medieval Knights   This illustration of knights at the Battle of Bouvines shows the development of plate armor, initially to supplement chain mail over vulnerable areas.

reconquest of the border district between Normandy and the Ile de France. Royal control of castles was exercised by the garrisoning of key castles with royal troops and, much more widely, by royal licensing of private castles. Thus, royal dominance over castellation grew significantly but by 1350 was far from complete, while the increased strength of baronial castles meant rebellions were still difficult to crush quickly.

The social status of knights became more defined in this period, as noted above. At the same time, the armor of knights became more elaborate as plate armor increasingly replaced chain mail for both the warrior and his horse. (The lance and sword remained the main offensive weapons.) This was partly a reaction to the penetrating power of crossbows, partly a conspicuous display made possible by growing wealth and improved metallurgy, and partly related to the rise of tournaments as a road to fame and wealth—plate was better suited to tournament jousting and helped ensure that melee tournament foes could be captured for ransom rather than accidentally killed. The tactical result of heavier armor was the gradual slowing of cavalry, with direct shock favored at the expense of mobility. This and hardened class lines were not

necessarily beneficial in strictly tactical terms: The cavalry forces of 1150 may well have been more effective than those of 1300 in terms of both physical and cultural flexibility. But, in the general absence of strong central authority, imperatives of social status, individual protective advantages, and the lure of ransoms in restricted warfare among the knightly class outweighed tactical logic. Kings, also members of the knightly class, were slow to respond to this trend.

It should also be noted that an increasing percentage of mounted soldiers in medieval armies were not technically knights but sergeants, vavassors, and squires—either the retainers of or men of lower social status than knights proper. The closing of knighthood socially and the increasing costs of knightly service, which discouraged some who qualified from becoming knights, both contributed to this trend. But the arms and tactics of nonknightly cavalry were similar to those of knights, if not quite as elaborate.

Perhaps the most significant transformation in this period occurred among urban infantry forces. The revival of towns and the rise of politically independent communes to govern them led to a re-creation of a Greek-style effective infantry: neighbors bound together by common interests fighting side by side. The process was unevenly spread across the continent (as was urbanization). For example, the size and social dominance of the French knightly class stunted the emergence of confident French urban troops somewhat, though French communal infantry fought well at Bouvines (see the Highlights box). But mercenary service by urban infantry provided foot soldiers even where local forces remained less developed.

Spanish urban militias (which were, in fact, mixed cavalry and infantry) were effective early on because they campaigned often and as offensive forces. But the major Christian advances of the thirteenth century removed many towns from frontier zones, and their martial traditions faded somewhat. Northern Italy and Flanders, the two most urbanized and commercial zones in western Europe, were the most consistent producers of infantry forces. Italian crossbowmen served as mercenaries in many theaters, and the urban spearmen of the Lombard League played a crucial role in defeating Emperor Frederick Barbarossa at Legnano in 1176, making a solid defensive stand around the Milanese *carrocio*, an ox-drawn wagon that carried the city banner and served as a symbol of its communal solidarity, until the league's cavalry could rally and counterattack. Flemish and Brabançon mercenary infantry served English kings in the twelfth century: Henry II's force of several thousand Brabançons were fearsome castle crackers, though the king's success as a strategist and besieger meant that his infantry were never tested in battle. By 1300, Flemish urban forces were acting independently during revolts.

English infantry forces of the late thirteenth and early fourteenth centuries (see the section on the Hundred Years War for a tactical discussion) were a bit odder. An unusual level of royal direction of local communities, both urban and shire based, was established during the twelfth century—what constitutional historians have called "self-government at the king's command." Furthermore, a less rigid class structure meant that mounted and unmounted soldiers were less separated socially than on the continent. When royal power revived in the 1260s under Edward I after a period of baronial turbulence in the wake of the Magna Carta, Edward developed ways, such as the Commissioners of Array noted above, to tap the military potential of this governmental structure. This allowed the English kings to raise substantial infantry forces that came to include the famous longbowmen. Renewed royal control also enabled the kings to fuse the knightly and nonknightly elements of their armed forces more successfully than elsewhere. In addition, it enabled them to reimpose tactical flexibility on their knights, reflected in their willingness to dismount and fight as infantry—a technique lost during the period of baronial dominance but used regularly by Anglo-Norman knights in the twelfth century.

Infantry arms and armor tended not to become more elaborate as knights' did, as status was less an issue and economic constraints were tighter. Most infantry wore leather jerkins, and some wore mail shirts and steel helmets. The crossbow and the spear or pike were the main weapons, with the pike gaining in importance and the longbow being adopted by the English in the late thirteenth century.

Warfare

Campaigning The patterns of warfare in this period did not change radically from earlier ages. Since control of castles and the landed estates dominated by castles was now the key to power, distribution of booty lost some of its importance as a linchpin of political prestige. But plundering raids still served to damage an opponent's economic base, to feed and reward a leader's army, and to threaten fortified positions, so nearly every campaign began with episodes

of burning, looting, and pillaging. At times, as in many Scots raids into England, plundering constituted the sum total of a campaign's activity. But more often, it was part of a larger scheme of attack or defense. The spread of castles made sieges even more frequent than they had been in the early Middle Ages and further reduced the number of battles. Where castles were rare or absent, as in Anglo-Saxon England prior to 1066, battles were more common.

Despite poor roads and no maps to speak of, medieval commanders could show considerable strategic skill and insight in campaign maneuvers. Reconnaissance, scouting, and intelligence gathering were limited but by no means nonexistent. Some armies found each other by accident or by the smoke from burning villages, but, more often, mounted scouts provided at least some sense of where an opponent was. On the grand strategic level, however, the same limitations meant that conception often exceeded execution. For example, John of England planned his reconquest of Normandy in 1214 around a two-pronged pincer attack, with his forces moving northeast from Poitou and his imperial allies moving southwest into Flanders from the empire. But time and distance made close coordination of the two thrusts difficult; relying on interior lines, the French under Philip Augustus first stalled John at a siege in Anjou, then moved north and defeated the imperial forces at Bouvines—a rare pitched battle that cemented the prestige of the French monarchy (see the Highlights box "The Battle of Bouvines, 1214"). In short, no medieval European armies achieved the levels of strategic planning, mobility, and coordination displayed by the Mongols.

Sieges Again, most strategy centered on holding or capturing fortified positions, as their possession was the key to territorial domination and political power. As a result, sieges were by far the most common tactical action engaged in by medieval armies—one reason infantry forces usually predominated numerically, even if an army's spearhead was mounted elites. Siege techniques advanced somewhat but generally failed to keep up with advances in fortification, so that sieges in 1350 probably took longer on average, and were more often settled by starvation or negotiation, than in 1100.

Assault was the most direct method of taking a castle and was especially useful against large castles with small garrisons. Henry II of England's success as a castle taker was built on rapid marching that

The Battle of Bouvines, 1214

King John of England launched an ambitious campaign to reconquer Normandy in 1214. While he landed in Poitou and advanced into Anjou, an allied army financed by John and led by Emperor Otto IV, Count Ferdinand of Flanders, and Renaud de Dammartin moved southwest into Flanders. Having stalled John's advance in June, King Philip Augustus of France left his son Louis in Anjou to keep an eye on the English king and took the bulk of his army against the allies. By July 26, the two armies had actually marched past each other when they became aware of their proximity. The next day, Philip marched back west from Tournai toward Lille, reaching the bridge at Bouvines by late morning. The majority of his army, including all his infantry, was already over the bridge when messengers from the rear guard, which had been sent south to watch the allied army, reported that the allies were approaching rapidly, intent on fighting even though it was a Sunday. Louis reversed his march and began to deploy onto the plain to the east of Bouvines, where his heavy cavalry could be most effective.

The best estimates of the numbers in each army give Philip around 1200 knightly cavalry (and a few hundred more lightly armed sergeants) and perhaps 4000 infantry drawn from the communes of northern France, while the allies had about 1500 cavalry and 5000–6000 infantry, both mercenaries and urban pikemen from the Flemish towns. But the way the battle developed nullified the allied advantage in numbers.

The allies, when they learned how close Philip's army was, were apparently divided over whether to attack that day. Otto and Renaud urged patience, but more aggressive counsel—driven partly by pride and partly by the hope of catching Philip's army divided by the bridge—prevailed, and the army set off on a rapid march to the northwest. As they approached Bouvines, the leading allied cavalry, Flemings under Ferdinand, became engaged in a running skirmish with the crossbowmen, light cavalry, and a few knights of the French rear guard. The French resistance and the wooded terrain served to slow the Flemings enough that the rear guard reached Philip intact and deployed as part of what became the French right wing. The pursuit then turned into a running deployment from south to north as the allies brought up their long column and Philip matched them with troops returning

brought his crack Brabançon infantry up for a massive, overwhelming assault with scaling ladders before the defense had time to properly organize. Higher curtain walls, stronger keeps, and sites designed to restrict attacks to one path were responses to such tactics. Attacks on the walls themselves used stone-throwing machines—above all, the increasingly effective counterweight trebuchet developed in this period—battering rams, and mining, which was often the most effective method where it could be used. Fire was a deadly tool not just against wooden fortifications but against the interiors of walled towns and against the roofs and interior buildings of stone castles. Techniques associated with more methodical blockades included poisoning or diverting a castle's water supply and ravaging the surrounding countryside both to deny the supplies to the castle (and feed the besiegers) and to demoralize the garrison.

Battles   Battles were rare, not just because they advanced the strategic aims of armies only indirectly, but because they were recognized by medieval commanders to be risky affairs, far more likely to be decided by chance than campaigning and sieges were. The limited visual range of leaders, the lack of standard command structures, and the somewhat limited abilities of armies that did not drill or train in mass maneuvers—all these made medieval battles particularly difficult to direct, increasing the potential for accidents and chaotic unpredictability. The continuing view that battles' outcomes were decisions made by God, not men, reflected this. Paradoxically, the importance of leadership was heightened as a morale

over the bridge, extending his line to avoid being flanked. Philip and Otto faced each other in the center of each line, with Philip's communal infantry, the last of his troops to deploy, stationed in front of him. The French right then opened the battle with an attack on Ferdinand's Flemings, probably before the allied right was in position and certainly before substantial units of Flemish infantry from Ghent and Bruges were even on the battlefield.

As the largely cavalry action on the southern wing turned the battle slowly in favor of the French, Otto launched a combined infantry and cavalry attack in the center, aiming for Philip. The French infantry gave way to the better-trained German mercenary infantry, a group of which actually unhorsed Philip and briefly put him in danger of losing his life. But a cavalry counterattack rescued the king and then surged on to Otto's position. The emperor's horse was mortally wounded and carried him away from the line before collapsing; when Otto remounted, his retainers led him from the field. His retreat eventually led to a general collapse of the allied center. Meanwhile, on the allied right, Renaud de Dammartin with a strong mercenary force and an

English contingent under King John's half-brother William Longsword distinguished themselves in an attack begun perhaps after the center was already giving way. Renaud formed his 700 Brabançon pikemen into a two-rank circle and used this impregnable human fortress as a base from which to launch attacks with his cavalry. But, eventually, reduced to just six mounted retainers and heavily outnumbered as elements of the French right moved to reinforce the left, Renaud was captured during a sally; the French then surrounded the Brabançons with infantry forces, probably including archers, and overwhelmed the fierce mercenaries, who were slaughtered almost to a man.

The rest of the allied army fled; Philip's forces pursued only for a mile or so before he recalled them to protect the prisoners already taken. The allies lost several hundred knights killed or captured and many more infantry; French losses are unknown but certainly far fewer.

Bouvines, the first battle fought by a Capetian monarch in over a century, secured the conquest of Normandy and made the French monarchy the most prestigious in Europe. It stands as a decisive and tactically fascinating example of medieval combat.

factor in such circumstances: The army whose leader fell in battle or ran away nearly always collapsed. As a result, the leader was often the object of the most determined individual and group attacks, further reducing his ability to direct the battle as a whole while putting a premium on his personal skill and bravery.

This is not to say that generalship was impossible. Within the limits of the forces at their disposal, many medieval commanders did what they could to direct battles intelligently and learn from experience. Most generalship took place in dispositions for battle: Keeping back a force in reserve was common, and arrangements of cavalry protected behind a line of infantry or archers stationed before or on the flanks of a formation to provide covering fire were common. In 1106, Henry I of England won the battle of Tinchebrai by prearranged generalship. The knights

of his and his brother Robert's armies dismounted to fight on foot in the front lines of the substantial infantry forces on both sides, but Henry concealed a cavalry unit behind a hill. Its charge into the rear of Robert's line after the fight was joined caused the flight of Robert's second in command and the rout of Robert's army.

Their dispositions also indicate that medieval generals usually understood the relative strengths and weaknesses of the different types of troops under their command. Knights used as cavalry provided a mobile strike force best used for a single, decisive attack (as in the Holy Land). Once a charge failed, it was difficult for the cavalry to regroup and charge again. Infantry, especially spearmen, created a solid defensive base. Knights fighting as infantry stiffened a defensive formation with their superior arms, armor, and individual prowess; dismounting also made it harder to run away, stiffening a defense psychologically. Archers could assist in such defense or soften up a target for an attack and help neutralize opposing missile troops.

Some recent scholarship has purported to see an infantry revolution around 1300, in which blocks of pikemen (Flemish, Scottish, and English, mostly) suddenly rose to dominate battlefields. However, this picture is radically overdrawn and misleading. There was no sudden break around 1300: Solid masses of infantry had always been able to turn back cavalry charges if they maintained their cohesion and morale. The slow but steady recovery of the urban and communal bases of effective infantry made forces with such cohesion somewhat more common by 1300—in addition to which, knightly cavalry had become socially, and thus tactically, more rigid and stereotyped by that time. A small rash of widely noted battles in which infantry forces defeated knightly cavalry—notably, Courtrai, Bannockburn, and Crécy—brought this trend to prominence but created no major change in tactical fundamentals. Thus, the picture also overstates the effectiveness of infantry forces after 1300. Though the longbow gave English infantry added defensive range, early-fourteenth-century infantry remained effective almost only in defense. No infantry force was well trained enough to maintain its cohesion in attack, especially against opposing forces with mounted troops available. Only in the next century, when the Swiss reintroduced marching in time to music, did infantry regain a real offensive role on the battlefield, a role lost since Roman times in Europe. Nor was there any change in the culture of war after 1300. If intra-European warfare began to appear more bloody than it had previously, this was because the sources began to take more notice of nonknightly forces and because cultural lines (of class, in this case) perhaps began to be crossed more often than before, with the same results already evident in frontier and crusading warfare for centuries. As in most battles prior to the introduction of effective gunpowder small arms, casualties were always far greater in the losing army, as it was not killing but psychological collapse that decided battles: Men died when they stopped fighting or ran.

The picture also overstates the nature of knightly armies as cavalry forces. Knights dominated as a social class and as elites, not necessarily as cavalry, and commanders did generally recognize the advantages of combined-arms tactics. But using such tactics was also as much a social as a tactical problem, and their successful imposition on an army depended heavily on the power and prestige of the leader. Dismounting knights involved not just making them fight as infantry but making them fight alongside their social inferiors. Even their effective use as cavalry involved cooperation across class lines. That French knights rode down their own archers in the opening stages of the battle of Crécy had as much to do with the French defeat as did the tactical capabilities of the English army. Similarly, English knights blocked their own archers at Bannockburn under the weak Edward II, despite cooperating admirably with them under both his father and his son. Again, it was the ruler who could impose unity on the dynamic and potentially hostile elements of his military forces who stood the greatest chance of victory—and it was only a chance—in medieval battles. England's precociously effective and unusually cooperative political structure let its kings lead the way in creating socially mixed, tactically flexible and effective armies; France, dominated by a large and truculent knightly class, lagged.

Good generalship was thus, for medieval leaders, a complex problem of tactics, strategy, social policy, and cultural symbolism, learned mostly by experience. Vegetius remained a popular text through this period (see Chapters 4 and 7), but the practical usefulness of his *De Re Militari* is open to question. Its logistical and strategic advice consisted of common-sense principles. Much of the text is concerned with the systematic drill of infantry forces, a topic that the social structure and governmental limitations of the day rendered opaque to medieval generals. Not until Maurice of Nassau in the late sixteenth century would that crucial aspect of the text be read as a practical guide. Apprenticeship in the field, not book learning, educated medieval commanders in the Art of War.

Sowing the Seeds of Disaster

By the mid-fourteenth century, the developments of the previous three centuries had produced stronger states that could call on better administrative techniques and more-sophisticated financial mechanisms in pursuit of their aims. Their aims continued to be dominated by war. Armies therefore tended to get bigger, and there was a slow shift to more-effective infantry forces.

Yet, in another way, the intra-European wars of this period had been remarkably limited in their ambitions and conquests. Small armies, the defensive strength of castles, and theories of just war that favored the defense of rightful claims and kept rulers'

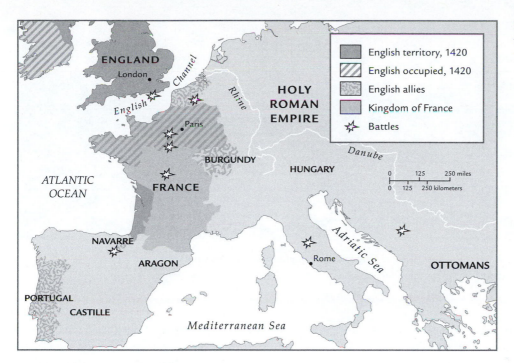

Figure 12.2 Europe and the Hundred Years War, 1337–1453

Legend:
- English territory, 1420
- English occupied, 1420
- English allies
- Kingdom of France
- Battles

ambitions limited combined to keep the damages of warfare relatively confined. This certainly contributed to the impressive growth of population, economic activity, and cultural output that also characterized the period 1050–1350.

But, by 1300, strains were beginning to show. Population growth slowed as the productive capacity of the land was pushed to its limits. Famine hit in 1315 as the long-term European weather pattern turned colder and wetter. Social tensions rose. And the bigger armies and better control over them that governments could exercise created a temptation to bigger, more destructive, wars. The Hundred Years War, medieval Europe's largest and longest armed conflict, bridged the traumatic transition from the high to the late Middle Ages and showcased both the advances and continuing weaknesses of Europe's military systems.

THE HUNDRED YEARS WAR, 1337–1453

Overview

The Hundred Years War was really a series of wars beginning in 1337 (related wars had been waged in the 1290s and 1320s). At issue was English rule in Gascony, the last remnant of the great Angevin Empire of the twelfth century, which the English king held as a fief from the French king, an unstable arrangement. The French aimed at taking Gascony; Edward III of England aimed at gaining sovereign title to it. Edward also exploited his claim to the French throne, created by the end of the Capetian line of kings. Territorial and dynastic ambitions remained entangled until the end of the war.

Although both England and France sustained remarkable levels of military effort for much of the war, with sophistication achieved especially by the English military administration, the history of the war also reveals the weaknesses of both sides. Both sides raised large armies, especially prior to the Black Death, yet neither side could maintain such forces for very long without serious financial problems for the government and serious opposition arising among their subjects. Furthermore, armed forces proved easier to raise than to disband—much of the expansion of the war after 1360 was spurred by the private initiative of the Free Companies, professional mercenary bands threatened with unemployment by the peace negotiated that year. The scale of military effort spread the normal ravages of war far and wide through France and elsewhere, adding to the economic and social damage of famine, plague, and other crises sweeping Europe after 1348. French peasants rose in a bloody revolt (responding to

Longbowmen Practicing   Use of the longbow required long practice, not just to gain accuracy but even more to develop the strength necessary to draw these powerful weapons.

the plundering of both sides' armies) in 1358, and English peasants did the same (responding to the burdens of war taxation) in 1381. The concentration of government effort on the war also contributed to breakdowns in internal order, judicial functions, and social cooperation in both countries.

The war falls broadly into four phases. Up until 1360, the English were unexpectedly successful, achieving their territorial goals in the Treaty of Bretigny. From 1360 to 1396, the French recovered during a period of weak English leadership, and the war spread to Spain and Portugal while mercenary companies spawned by the war found employment in Italy and farther east. After a period of exhausted peace, Henry V led a new wave of English triumphs between 1415 and the late 1420s. Stalemate in the 1430s and early 1440s gave way to the final phase in the late 1440s—the rapid French conquest of all English territory in France.

From a military perspective, the war may also be divided more simply into two phases: a long period of English tactical dominance (with two subphases based on differences in English strategy) and a brief period of French tactical innovation at the end of the war.

The English System, 1340–1435

Edward I had begun experimenting with the use of longbowmen (initially Welsh, then increasingly English as the weapon spread) in his wars against the Scots, and, by the 1320s, his grandson Edward III had developed the tactical methods that would

dominate the Hundred Years War. Faced with battle, English knights dismounted and formed blocks of heavy infantry, using their lances as short pikes. Lighter-armed Welsh spearmen sometimes added depth to this part of the infantry formation. Longbowmen formed up in solid masses on the wings of the heavy infantry, sometimes angled forward. Whenever possible, the defensive formation was arrayed at the top of a slope, maximizing the archers' field of fire and slowing attackers, with natural obstacles protecting the flanks and rear of the line. The archers also sometimes placed artificial obstacles like sharpened stakes in front of their positions as further protection against cavalry attacks. This arrangement proved devastatingly effective in defense against both infantry and cavalry attacks, even against much greater numbers, as Dupplin Moor (1332), Halidon Hill (1333), Crécy (1346), Poitiers (1356) (see the Sources box "The Battle of Poitiers, 1356"), Agincourt (1415), and numerous smaller engagements testify.

While the defensive strength of the armored men-at-arms anchored these tactics, the longbowmen were crucial to their consistent effectiveness. The longbow, with considerably greater rate of fire and range than and comparable penetrating power to the crossbow, extended the range of the defensive formation and allowed the archers to provoke enemy armies at a distance into attacking, often rashly or prematurely. When an attack came, the massed fire of thousands of longbowmen (crossbowmen had tended to operate in smaller groups) transformed the power of missile weapons: Their withering fire inflicted casualties on

The Battle of Poitiers, 1356

In the following excerpts from his Chroniques, *the herald, or semi-official battle chronicler, Jean Froissart describes the devastatingly effective English tactics.*

■ ■ ■

. . . the fighting became general. The Marshals' battalion had already advanced for action, headed by men who were to break through the ranks of the archers. All on horseback they entered the road which had the thick hedge on either side. No sooner were they engaged in it than the archers began to shoot murderously from both flanks, knocking down horses and piercing everything before them with their long barbed arrows. The injured and terrified horses refused to go on. They swerved or turned back, or else fell beneath their riders, who could neither use their weapons nor get up again, so that the battalion of the Marshals never got near the Prince's division. . . . Rarely have skilled fighting-men suffered such losses in so short a time as were inflicted on the battalion of the Marshals, for they became jammed against each other and could make no headway. Seeing the carnage and unable to advance themselves, those behind turned back and ran up against the Duke of Normandy's division, whose ranks were close and numerous in front. But the rear ranks soon began to melt away when they learnt that the Marshals had been defeated. Most of them took to their horses and rode off, for the English detachment which had ridden round the hill with their mounted archers in front of them charged in and took them on the flank. If the truth must be told, the English archers were a huge asset to their side and a terror to the French; their shooting was so heavy and accurate that the French did not know where to turn to avoid their arrows. So the English kept advancing and slowly gaining ground.

When the Prince's men-at-arms saw that the Marshals' battalion was routed and that the Duke of Normandy's division was wavering and beginning to break up, their strength flooded back to them and their spirits rose. They made for their horses which they had kept near them and scrambled on to them. . . . The English, now all mounted, made straight for the battalion of the Duke of Athens, Constable of France. There followed a great melee. . . . No one could face the heavy, rapid fire of the English archers, who in that encounter killed and wounded many who found no chance of offering ransoms or pleading for mercy. . . .

You read earlier in this chronicle about the Battle of Crécy, and heard how unfavorable fortune was there to the French. At Poitiers similarly it was unfavorable, fickle and treacherous, for the French were at least seven to one in trained fighting men. But it must be said that the Battle of Poitiers was fought much better than Crécy. Both armies had greater opportunities to observe and weigh up the enemy, for the Battle of Crécy began without proper preparation in the late afternoon, while Poitiers began in the early morning, and in good enough order, if only luck had been with the French. There were incomparably more fine feats of arms than at Crécy. . . .

SOURCE: Jean Froissart, *Chronicles*, ed. and trans. Geoffrey Brereton (New York: Penguin Books, 1968), pp. 134–138.

men and horses, disrupted the momentum of an attack, and tended to channel it into the spearmen so that the attackers became overcrowded. The effectiveness of the archers is indicated by their increase in proportion to the men-at-arms in English armies, from about 1 to 1 in early campaigns to 4 or 5 to 1 seventy years later. Finally, the knights occasionally remounted for a counterattack or pursuit, as at Poitiers.

The effectiveness of the whole system was also founded on close military (and thus social) cooperation between knights and yeoman archers, which, in turn, reflected the ability of the English government to harness and mold the military skills and energies of its population more effectively than any other large kingdom. This, in turn, was an aspect of the political cooperation and broad participation that characterized the English kingdom and made it effective beyond its ability to raise tax revenues as well as troops. Indeed, English armies throughout the war were raised by contracts of indenture, in which the government contracted with captains to provide specified numbers of men for specified periods (a form of contract that dated back to Anglo-Norman times as the money fief), a method that created paid, professional armies. In short, English infantry tactics were built in part on effective central government—perhaps not at the Roman level of achievement, but a significant pointer to the ongoing development of the European infantry tradition.

While fighting in battle as infantry, English knights and, increasingly, archers were mounted for campaigning and were thus capable of rapid strategic movement. Mounted English armies typically launched *chevauchees*. These were long, destructive raids through the French countryside that fed English armies, reduced the resources available to the French armies, and harnessed the essentially defensive tactical capabilities of English armies into a kind of passive-aggressive offensive strategy: *Chevauchees* drew French armies into attacks on the raiders, who could then choose a site for a defensive stand. The *chevauchee* strategy was the basic English approach until the 1390s. But the limitations of the *chevauchee* strategy were exposed after 1360 in two ways. First, it was less effective in defense of lands already won, which required instead less rewarding and more expensive garrison defenses; second, it could be countered. Bertrand du Guesclin developed the Fabian approach of shadowing an English army to limit its foraging and destruction, while refusing battle.

Henry V succeeded in 1415 in using the traditional *chevauchee* to create and win the battle of Agincourt. Already at the beginning of the campaign, however, when he took several months to besiege Harfleur as a base of operations in Normandy, he showed that he would link the tactical abilities of English soldiers to a new strategy: systematic conquest through castle taking. This was made possible in part by French civil war and confusion in the wake of Agincourt, which allowed Henry to spread his forces over several sieges at once, and in part by his use of small but effective siege guns. Henry also proved himself a master of the logistical arrangements, including shipping of supplies from England, and he possessed the dogged determination necessary to such a strategy. Henry conquered Normandy and much of the Ile de France in a mere five years and had made himself heir to the French throne by treaty when he died prematurely in 1422. Able captains carried on English conquests on behalf of the infant Henry VI for another ten years, but in the absence of Henry's leadership, the expense of maintaining a standing army of several thousand garrison and field troops eventually wore down the English people's support for the war. Renewed French efforts after 1435 would meet an increasingly enfeebled English defense.

The French System, 1435–1453

Charles VII, building on the recovery of French morale sparked by Joan of Arc, and on diplomatic successes that increasingly isolated English-held Normandy, and exploiting divided English command, began turning the tide of the war decisively after 1435. His gains were slow for ten years, but a truce in 1444 allowed him to reorganize his kingdom's finances and finally exert firm control over royal armies. Establishing the first permanent standing units in French history, Charles was able to impose discipline on his troops, and for the first time, French forces began to demonstrate the ability to coordinate infantry, cavalry, and the newly established artillery forces on campaign and in battle. It was the artillery that proved most decisive. Reopening the war in the summer of 1449, within a year, Charles had reconquered all of English-held Normandy, as his culverins (long cannons), battering fortresses held by depleted, demoralized garrisons, made quick work of the sieges that usually were so time-consuming. French artillery even proved useful in battle. An English relief force landed in April 1450 and met a French force of roughly equal size. Drawing up in their traditional defensive array, the English found their wings battered by the French guns from beyond longbow range. Forced to abandon their position, they were routed in the subsequent melee by a French force with better discipline and morale. By 1453, all English possessions in France except Calais had fallen, and the war was over.

A WORLD IN FLUX, 1350–1500

Social Crises

Though the effectiveness of the French armies in the last stages of the war can be exaggerated—English collapse played a large role—the establishment of a permanent core of cavalry companies and artillery units in the king's pay presaged developments in European warfare generally. These developments, in France and elsewhere, arose out of the effects of the widespread crises that afflicted most of Europe in the fourteenth and fifteenth centuries.

Demographic crisis was heralded by famines starting in 1315. The eruption of the Black Death into Europe in 1347 resulted in the loss of between a quarter and a third of the population of Europe within three years; periodic outbreaks of plague continued for centuries, and population levels did not begin to grow again for a century. The economic and social disruption caused by such a pandemic was exacerbated by the spreading violence of the Hundred Years War and other conflicts and by the breakdown of public order brought on by governmental overreach in conducting those wars. Meanwhile, the removal of the papacy to Avignon in 1305 and the subsequent schism between 1378 and 1415 eroded the solidarity of religious authority and compounded the church's inability to cope with the psychological effects of the plague. In short, life was bad, and with rival popes and anti-popes excommunicating each other's followers, the afterlife promised little better.

One consequence of this atmosphere of crisis and breakdown seems to have been some weakening of traditions and an increase in the questioning of established authority. A younger leadership class (one demographic result of the plague) seemed more willing to experiment. The results showed not just in culture, religion, and government but also in military matters. The tendency of the western European sociomilitary system to conflict, competition, and change was accelerated.

Military Developments

The military changes fostered in this period tended not to affect strategy, which remained grounded in time-tested principles and constrained by logistical limitations. Instead, there were changes in the culture of war and in tactics.

Increased social tensions and breakdowns in public order heightened the general levels of violence in this civilization. Cultural boundaries of class and religion stood out in greater relief, boundaries that when crossed in war led to more prominent examples of the sort of butchery Europeans had been capable of for centuries already. This was especially true as more effective infantry forces—generally drawn from classes antagonistic to the knightly aristocracy—served more widely as mercenaries. English archers, Flemish pikemen, and Italian infantry of all sorts were as likely to kill as to capture and ransom noble opponents. The Swiss above all developed a reputation for savagery, neither taking nor giving any quarter on the battlefield. New religious divisions had the same effect; the Hussite Wars, for example, saw massacres on both sides. There was even some breakdown of the codes of behavior between knightly opponents (see the Issues box "Chivalry").

Tactical flux and experimentation focused on a reassertion of true offensive capabilities by heavy infantry forces and on the beginnings of a steady rise in the importance of missile weapons. The bewildering variety of types of troops characteristic of fifteenth-century warfare led the most creative generals to try many ways of combining the strengths of heavy infantry, missile weapons, and cavalry, as well as the artillery that slowly came to play a small role on the battlefield and a large role in sieges.

The Swiss created the first heavy infantry forces with a consistent offensive capability, even in the face of good cavalry forces, since the heyday of the Roman legions. Organizationally, however, they harked back more to the phalanxes of the Greeks. The cantons of the Swiss valleys raised forces in which neighbor fought next to neighbor in defense of their lands and liberties. They carried halberds—fearsome ax-headed spears that could turn back a cavalry charge and then, in a melee, hook a man-at-arms from his saddle and smash through his plate armor—and pikes. (The proportion of the latter, better for frontal attacks, increased dramatically when the Swiss fought as mercenaries in combination with other types of troops who could cover the pikemen's more vulnerable flanks.) Above all, they learned to march in time, which gave them the ability to maintain the cohesion of their blocky formations while maneuvering on the battlefield. Swiss pike phalanxes were copied first by German mercenary *landsknechts* and later by the Spanish. Despite Spanish experiments with sword-and-buckler formations that were effective against pikemen, Swiss-style phalanxes would become the foundation of European infantry forces for several centuries, in combination with missile troops.

Chivalry

Chivalry was a knightly ethos or ideal of conduct that fused warrior, aristocratic, and religious values. It arose after 1100 in France and spread rapidly in conjunction with troubadours, romances, and courtly love as a central aspect of elite secular culture. It was an aspect of the emergence of knighthood as a defined social class. Chivalry stressed knighthood as a sacred order with its own rituals of initiation (dubbing), its own historical mythology (above all, the whole Arthurian cycle), and its own visual symbolism (heraldry). Christian values and symbols pervaded the chivalric ethos—it was certainly a part of the Christianizing of warrior culture—and the growth of chivalry was linked to crusading. But the knightly class's self-definition as a sacred order was resisted by the church, which viewed chivalry with ambivalence at best, given chivalry's glorification of war. But by 1300, chivalry was the dominant cultural theme of aristocratic and even royal courtly culture, and the fourteenth century saw the spread of secular Orders of Chivalry such as Edward III of England's Knights of the Garter.

Chivalry was linked to war in two related ways. First, it was intimately tied up with the rise and spread of tournaments and with the evolution of the tournament from a free-for-all melee into the individual jousting of modern popular imagery. Tourneying served as the practical initiation into knighthood that dubbing performed symbolically. It allowed knights to prove themselves in near-real combat and perhaps earn the favor of a powerful patron, to make (or lose) their fortune through ransoms, and simply to meet with members of the knightly class from all over Europe. The value of tournaments as training for actual warfare was mixed, however, and declined as individual jousting in the lists replaced the melee.

Second, the central values of chivalry epitomized the contradictions of medieval warfare. On the one hand, chivalry stressed courage expressed through heroic feats of arms, a value that could easily emphasize individual glory at the expense of group cohesion—indeed, this aspect of chivalry long influenced historians' views of medieval warfare as artless and undisciplined. And it is true that chivalry flourished in the period after 1300 when knights were challenged with increasing effectiveness on the battlefield by masses of disciplined foot soldiers.

On the other hand, the second central value of chivalry was loyalty to one's lord and companions, a value that did encourage group cohesion. Chivalry survived for as long as it did because it supplied some of the moral glue that held late-medieval armies together. It died out when more effective central governments could apply that glue with drill and regular pay instead.

Modern notions of chivalry can also seriously distort our understanding of its social effects. Chivalry was definitely a class-bound code. Chivalric knights may have shown honor and mercy to other knights of their class (encouraged by the financial rewards of capturing versus killing one's foes), but such behavior did not extend any further. Chivalric knights could pillage, plunder peasants, and kill infantrymen with the best of marauders. And, despite the modern connotations of the word, chivalry had little to do with behavior toward women except, perhaps, again in a class context. Peasant and merchant women were the victims of violence and rape by chivalrous warriors as often as by nonchivalrous ones. Even treatment of noblewomen was essentially beyond the bounds of chivalric codes, for chivalry was a code for and about knightly warriors. All other types of people—women, merchants, peasants—fell outside its purview and remained objects of contempt and potential violence.

The English longbowmen of the Hundred Years War demonstrated the battlefield potential of massed missile fire, and English archers served as mercenaries in Spanish, Italian, and Burgundian armies in the fourteenth and fifteenth centuries. But the longbow was a difficult weapon to learn to use, and English archers were always in short supply outside of English armies. (In the Wars of the Roses, longbowmen

Medieval Bombard
An example of an early gunpowder weapon, this piece, known as the Boxted Bombard, was used to fire cannon balls.

on both sides tended to cancel each other out, leaving the heavy infantry of dismounted men-at-arms to play the decisive role.) So generals turned to increased use of crossbowmen and then to handguns.

Gunpowder was a Chinese invention that made its way across Eurasia during Mongol rule. Europeans appear to have first harnessed the power of the explosive through cannon and handguns; the first pot guns appear in European manuscripts in the 1330s. Heavy, clumsy, slow to fire, quick to clog or misfire, and certainly at first less effective than bows, handguns were, however, no more expensive to make (counting ammunition) and easier to use. Thus, handgunners could eventually be raised in larger numbers than archers. Indeed, some historians have characterized guns as a labor-saving device encouraged—like the printing press and the full-rigged ship—by the high cost of labor in postplague Europe. Gradual improvements in design added to their novel psychological impact, but even by 1500, handgunners were far from a decisive element on any battlefield. Rather, handguns' effect on tactics was simply to reinforce trends toward better infantry and greater missile fire that had already developed for other reasons, not to initiate change by themselves.

Cannon had an earlier and greater impact on warfare. In the 1420s and 1430s, the Hussites used armored wagon-forts as bases for the battlefield use of small cannon and handguns. By the 1460s, Charles the Bold of Burgundy was bringing considerable numbers of cannon on wheeled carriages to battlefields, though their effect was limited and they were captured in large numbers in Charles's defeats.

Cannon were still too heavy to be maneuvered in battle, and their rate of fire was even slower than handguns, so their tactical significance remained largely unrealized in this period. In two other areas, however, cannon began to have a huge impact. Mounted on ships, they represented a revolutionary development in naval warfare (see Chapter 15), and in siege work, they created a brief but significant period of flux. The low trajectory of fire cannon could achieve, compared to traditional siege engines, allowed them to quickly collapse high medieval walls. For a time in the fifteenth century, sieges could be shortened dramatically, and extensive rapid conquests seemed possible. But new cannon-resistant fortification designs returned European warfare to its traditional siege-based patterns and political fragmentation in the sixteenth century (see Chapter 16).

With disciplined pikemen added to crossbowmen, longbowmen, handgunners, armored cavalry, and lighter-armed cavalry, a bewildering variety of tactical combinations presented themselves to European generals. The most creative experimented. Charles the Bold of Burgundy (1467–77) combined troops from his realm with mercenaries into a small standing army, training the various types of troops separately and together, and issuing codes of discipline and uniforms. His tactical aim was to combine the firepower of archers and handgunners with heavy infantry, cavalry, and field artillery. If his reach exceeded his grasp (strategically as well as tactically), his army pointed the way to later developments. By the end of the era, Spanish *tercios* had standardized an effective combination of shot and pike that would dominate European warfare for 150 years.

CONCLUSION

After about 1450, Europe began to recover from its century of crisis, and the trends established since 1050 resumed. By the close of the fifteenth century, the dynamics of the western European sociomilitary system had resulted in significant developments in European warfare and civilization. Steady gains by governments in administrative ability and fiscal resources, interrupted only temporarily by the ravages of the Black Death, had shifted the balance of power somewhat away from aristocrats and their military expression as heavy cavalry, though both remained important in politics and warfare. The shift in the balance of power was even more notable in fortification, where the increasing cost of building again favored kings over their aristocrats; siege cannon furthered the trend. Fostered by stronger central authority and thriving urban economies, infantry forces played a steadily greater role throughout the period 1050–1500. Originally built around essentially Greek-style, communally based infantry, by the end of the period, significant traces of Roman-style infantry—a heterogeneous mass raised and trained by strong central authorities—were again visible in European warfare.

But the essential elements of military force and their relationship to political structures and power, while significantly transformed in every case, remained recognizable, and the lines of development established since 1050 would continue after 1500. Even more, the sociocultural matrix of European military power was firmly established. Thus, a series of events in the last decade of the fifteenth century are Janus-faced, standing as both culminations of medieval trends and harbingers of new developments. In 1492, Columbus unwittingly opened the door to the conquistadors' conquest of the Americas. In 1494, Charles VIII of France invaded Italy as the first step in a planned crusade against the Ottoman Turks and set off an intense new period of innovative warfare. And, in 1498, Vasco da Gama sailed around Africa to India, opening a new route to lucrative Asian trade and empire. The already familiar pattern of European crusading mercantile expansion linked to governmental evolution and military competition was about to leap to a global stage.

SUGGESTED READINGS

Ayton, Andrew, and J. L. Price, eds. *The Medieval Military Revolution*. New York: I. B. Tauris, 1995. A good collection of articles examining critically the concept of a European Military Revolution (see Chapter 16) from a medieval perspective.

Bartlett, Robert. *The Making of Europe*. Princeton: Princeton University Press, 1993. An important study linking European social structure, law, and culture to conquest, colonization, and expansion.

Bradbury, Jim. *The Medieval Siege*. Woodbridge: Boydell, 1992. A wide-ranging introduction to the attack and defense of castles in medieval Europe.

Contamine, Philipe. *War in the Middle Ages*. See Chapter 7.

Curry, Anne, and M. Hughes, eds. *Arms, Armies and Fortifications in the Hundred Years War*. Woodbridge: Boydell, 1994. Brings together the latest research on the largest war in medieval Europe.

France, John. *Western Warfare in the Age of the Crusades*. Ithaca: Cornell University Press, 1999. A fine study taking a social and cultural approach to the patterns of European warfare between 1000 and 1300.

Gillingham, John. *Richard Coeur de Lion*. London: Routledge, 1994. A collection of articles by a master of the new medieval military history. See also his *Richard the Lionheart* (London: Routledge, 1989) and *The Wars of the Roses* (London: Weidenfeld & Nicolson, 1981).

Hooper, Nicholas, and Matthew Bennett. *The Cambridge Illustrated Atlas of Warfare: The Middle Ages, 768–1497*. See Chapter 7.

Kaeuper, Richard. *Chivalry and Violence in Medieval Europe*. Oxford: Oxford University Press, 2001. An excellent examination of the culture of violence built into the aristocratic structure of medieval Europe.

Keen, Maurice, ed. *Medieval Warfare. A History*. Oxford: Oxford University Press, 1999. A solid edited collection providing a chronological survey and focused studies on particular aspects of warfare. See also Keen's *Chivalry* (New Haven: Yale University Press, 1984), a nuanced cultural history.

Morillo, Stephen. *Warfare Under the Anglo-Norman Kings, 1066–1135*. Woodbridge: Boydell, 1994. A readable study examining the patterns of warfare in their administrative and political contexts.

Prestwich, Michael. *Armies and Warfare in the Middle Ages: The English Experience*. New Haven: Yale University Press, 1996. An excellent synthesis of much recent research; argues against a military revolution in the medieval or early modern periods.

Strickland, Matthew. *War and Chivalry*. Cambridge: Cambridge University Press, 1996. A superb study of the conduct and perception of warfare in England and Normandy from 1066 to 1216; examines the early influence of chivalry. See also his excellent edited collection, *Anglo-Norman Warfare*.

Vale, Malcolm. *War and Chivalry*. London: Routledge, 1981. An important examination of the culture and laws of war in the late Middle Ages.

Verbruggen, J. F. *The Art of Warfare in Western Europe During the Middle Ages*. Woodbridge: Boydell, 2002, reprint ed. Somewhat dated but still a valuable survey of strategy, tactics, and manpower in the central Middle Ages.

CHAPTER 13

Khans and Conquest: The Mongols, 1150–1400

In the thirteenth century, the Mongols fought in a variety of climates and environments and carved out a vast empire. Their defeated enemies often trembled as they talked of the vast numbers in the "Mongol Hordes." When the Mongols invaded Europe, they were said to have come with 500,000 warriors. In one battle in Persia, they were said to have attacked with over 700,000. These were great exaggerations, however, as defeated peoples tried to explain and justify their defeats. In fact, the largest army the Mongols put into the field, the army that completed the conquest of China, numbered at most 200,000 warriors, and it was composed mostly of Chinese and Koreans. On only a few occasions were the Mongols able to muster more than about 60,000 men for a battle. Rarely did they outnumber their enemies on the field of battle; in fact, they were almost always greatly outnumbered, both in battle and in a campaign. Yet, over the course of the thirteenth century, Mongol armies succeeded in establishing the largest continuous land empire in history.

This chapter traces the Mongol origins and conquests to show how they were able to subdue such a vast territory. The Mongols came out of the Central Asian steppes, and though there had been many steppe empires in the past (see especially Chapter 6), there had never been one as vast and efficient as that created by the Mongols. Within a few decades, the Mongol rulers could call on the resources of a far-flung realm that included several sedentary civilizations. The foundation for Mongol success was established by Chingiz Khan (Genghis Khan), who organized the Mongol military and tribal society. The Mongol military was hardly unique for a steppe army and almost never had technological superiority over its enemies; what was distinctive was its organization.

ORIGINS OF THE MONGOL EXPLOSION

Mongol Society

Geography provides a partial explanation for why the Mongols would explode into adjoining lands. The population of Mongolia lived at one end of the Eurasian steppes, practicing nomadic pastoralism as had their predecessors for many centuries (see Chapter 6). The Mongols, like their neighbors the Turks, depended on Chinese trade for many manufactured goods as well as grain. When China refused this trade, the Mongols resorted to plundering raids.

In the late twelfth century, Mongolia was divided into numerous patriarchal clans, each headed by a chieftain who gained his position usually, though not necessarily, through heredity. Mongol males in the clan spent most of their time hunting, tending their herds, and fighting. Raids on other clans were frequent, spurred in part by the need to acquire wives from outside the clan. Some clans united with others to form tribes of varying size, but these groupings were rarely very stable. The most common impetus to unity was the need to raid in China for plunder, and a tribal chieftain could maintain his position only through success in these endeavors.

Through most of his life, Temujin, who would become Chingiz Khan (or Great Khan), was bound by these rules and customs. Yet, when he eventually succeeded in uniting the various tribes into one confederation, he effected a great change in traditional Mongol society, allowing him to create a fierce instrument of conquest. His success in molding a lasting military institution can be seen in the continuation of his system after he died, for his successors led his armies to even greater conquests.

Chingiz Khan About age 60, near the end of his life of war and conquest

The Rise of Chingiz Khan

Temujin arose at a time when Mongolia was much divided. He came from an illustrious line of earlier Mongol leaders, but his father had a relatively small lineage and was leader of a relatively small clan. This was a problem for Temujin since Mongols did not simply join putative chieftains due to their ancestry; these leaders had to demonstrate their capabilities. As Temujin would learn, Mongols would flock to a successful leader and desert one who failed.

Temujin's unification of the Mongols was strewn with failures, but these failures actually served him well in the long run, as he learned that he could not trust the traditional Mongol social system based on family, clan, and tribe. He had to constantly fight to gain and maintain his position, and so the system that he eventually organized was one based on commanders whose loyalty was to him and him alone, not to their tribes or clans. In effect, he created a new supratribe, one loyal to him and his successors. However, in doing this, he depended on military victories to keep the loyalty of his commanders. This meant that he had to take risks, and take them often.

This organization along personal lines was very different from the traditional organization of the

steppe nomadic armies. Such armies typically had been coalitions or confederations of several tribes that based their organization on kinship. What Temujin offered was a system that ultimately provided for a much better and more efficient military force; but, until it had become firmly established, it constantly threatened to fly apart.

Temujin was born in 1167. Within a few years, his father had been killed, and he was left alone, as most of his clan members left to find other protection. Through military prowess on the field and great gifts of leadership, by 1190 he had become one of the three or four most powerful leaders in Mongolia, commanding about 30,000 warriors. On the verge of being named Great Khan, he was suddenly attacked and defeated, and many of his followers deserted him. By 1196, however, firm alliances and new victories in the field had restored him to a position of leadership. Once again, in 1198 in a major battle against the Naiman, a related tribe, he was deserted by many of his allies (they had arranged this with one of Temujin's rivals prior to the battle). Despite this desertion, he won the battle and retained his position, but he was weakened. In 1203, he was further weakened when a rival was able to convince many of the allied tribes to desert Temujin. At that low point, he commanded no more than 5000 men.

Nevertheless, within a year, he claimed a masterful victory by attacking his main enemies while they were celebrating—nearly all of them were drunk. This victory earned him the mastery of Mongolia, though it was not officially proclaimed until the famous Quriltai of 1206, a meeting of all the Mongol tribes.

Temujin, now Chingiz Khan, had learned an important lesson from all his struggles: Never give any power to others unless he could limit it and make them somehow dependent on him. He had seen men who swore loyalty desert him the next day; even several of his uncles and two brothers had deserted him when times were hard. He had found that the only men he could trust were those who had been appointed his personal bodyguards. This was not surprising—in Mongolia, bodyguards took a personal oath of loyalty that was considered almost sacred. Chingiz Khan enforced this loyalty by decreeing that any who violated this oath, even the bodyguards of others, were to be harshly punished. Those who remained loyal were rewarded. When he became master of Mongolia and reorganized the military, he placed these personal bodyguards in the highest positions of authority in the army. Chingiz Khan proved to be a good judge of ability. Not all of his body-guards were given high military positions, but those who were proved to be very able military commanders. Yet his suspicions always remained. Though he would eventually appoint his sons to high military positions, he never fully trusted them, and several members of his family were killed when he thought they were challenging him, including all but one of his father's brothers.

Chingiz Khan and the Yasa

An important aspect of Chingiz Khan's efforts to convert the Mongols from a confederation of tribes to one supratribe was his institution of a supreme law code, called the *Yasa* (Mongolian, "code"). The traditional story has it that Chingiz Khan promulgated this code at the great Quriltai of 1206, but scholars have cast doubt on this, claiming that the earliest it could have reached final form was 1225. Still, there is little doubt that some forms of the Yasa were known soon after Temujin was named Great Khan, for he ordered scribes to write down his orders and concerns regarding management of the new Mongol supratribe. Numerous sources refer to the Yasa, but only fragments have survived, and we are not even clear as to the order of the various ordinances in the Yasa.

What remains of the Yasa makes clear that it was considered a code for all Mongols. The Yasa covered such things as military duties, international relations, taxation, inheritance, and the division of spoils, but there is little concerning everyday customs on matters such as marriage and death rituals. All Mongols were considered to have a duty to the Great Khan, and so murder of another Mongol, for example, was considered a crime against the state and was punishable by death. Murder of a Chinese or Muslim (the only others specifically mentioned) was to be punished by payment of a fine. Other crimes for which a Mongol could be punished by execution included adultery, theft (from another Mongol), homosexuality, and failure to share a meal with another Mongol. Regarding plunder, the code stated that all Mongols were to get a share or keep what they had taken after payment of a portion to the khan. All beautiful women taken captive, however, had to be presented to the khan and his top officers for first selection.

The military regulations in the Yasa also pointed to Chingiz Kahn's desire to organize the Mongols as one people rather than as a confederation. The Mongols were given a uniform military organization (see below), and once a Mongol soldier had been placed in a unit, he could not shift to another unit without approval from the khan. Absolute obedience to officers was commanded, and officers were held strictly responsible for their units. The khan's orders were to be carried out without hesitation by all officers, no matter what their rank. Finally, all Mongols not on active campaign were to take part in the Great Hunts, which Chingiz Khan considered the best training for organized combat.

MONGOL MILITARY ORGANIZATION

Administration and Logistics

In general organization and tactics, the Mongol army was not unique for the Inner Asian steppes. What was atypical was the unity and discipline of the Mongols. The Mongols were also fortunate in having some excellent leadership, which continued through several generations. The army was organized into a decimal system: groups of 10, then 100, then 1000, and finally, a *Tumen* of 10,000. Except as part of a strategy to incorporate allied tribes, these units were usually not based on tribal identity. Chingiz Khan worked to break up all old tribal unities and forge new loyalty to himself, in effect creating one new supratribe.

There is evidence that, very early in the process of creating the unified Mongol army, Chingiz Khan laid down numerous military regulations. Separate from the Yasa, these regulations covered the order of march into battle, the organization of night camps, the maintenance of weaponry, and relations among the Mongol tribesmen. We do not know whether these regulations were truly disseminated to all Mongol units at the time of Chingiz Khan, but later rulers attempted to have them strictly enforced.

Of all the innovations of Chingiz Khan, the most radical for the steppe nomads was the *Keshig*. This began as an elite personal bodyguard, possibly based on the bodyguard units of the Khitans (see Chapter 9), but its numbers expanded greatly over time. By 1206, the *Keshig* numbered exactly 10,000 and included a hand-picked group of 1000 called *Baturs*. The members of the *Keshig* were drawn from the ranks, but the officers of the guard all came from leading Mongol families, and especially from the families of the Khan's subordinate commanders. *Keshig* officers were all younger brothers or sons of these leading commanders, meaning that besides being bodyguards for Chingiz Khan, they served as hostages for the good behavior of their relatives. Chingiz also apparently believed that their being younger sons and younger brothers would tie them to him personally. The *Keshig* did not go into battle except with Chingiz Khan himself, but it also served as a training ground for future Mongol leaders. This, not his birth family, was where the Great Khan went for leadership replacements, which was highly unusual in Mongolia. (See the Sources box "The Secret History of the Mongols" for more on his rules and regulations.)

Every able-bodied adult male Mongol was considered liable for military duty, making Mongolia truly a people in arms. In the first invasions, in addition to his kit, each Mongol had several ponies, but the army lived off the land, devouring the countryside to supply its needs. In later campaigns, more sophisticated logistics were called for as the Mongol armies at times included tens of thousands of non-Mongol auxiliaries, as well as siege engines and long baggage trains. These campaigns also were not always in lands that could be pillaged for supplies. Therefore, the Mongols established mechanisms for supplying armies on campaign through exploitation of the sedentary populations under their control.

The conquered lands and tributaries were required to provide the necessary foodstuffs, weapons, clothing, carts, draftsmen, and workers. On taking control of a region, the administrators of the land were ordered to create a thorough record of its population and resources. These reports were supervised by officials working directly for the Mongols. Usually, these officials were from distant lands, to prevent collusion with the locals. For example, Mongol officials in China were usually of Persian, Arab, Central Asian, or even European descent, while large numbers of Chinese were brought to Persia to administer that land. Once these reports had been confirmed, the Mongol court in Karakorum had a fairly good knowledge of the resources available throughout the empire. By the 1250s, some regions of the empire were being required to pay taxes in cash, with which the Mongols could purchase some of what they needed in regions closer to the planned invasion route. Thus, when launching the assaults on the Assassins, a fanatic Ismaeli sect that terrorized much of the Muslim Middle East, vast numbers of auxiliaries were raised from eastern Iran, the Caucasus, and Russia, and supplies were gathered from Armenia, Georgia, and Central Asia.

Mongol Horsemen Hunting   Hunting honed the skills of horsemanship and archery that the Mongols used effectively in combat.

The Mongol logistical achievement cannot be overstated. These steppe nomads imposed a uniform system of extraction on regions with widely varying traditions and administrative systems. They administered this system from their capital at Karakorum in the middle of the steppe lands, utilizing the services of vast numbers of officials with nothing in common other than their service to the Mongol Empire.

The Mongol Soldier

Like his steppe predecessor, the Mongol soldier was by any measure an incredible fighting man. His training really began at age 3, when he was taught to ride one of the excellent Mongol ponies. The young boy was tied to a horse by his mother until he could ride on his own. At age 5, the young Mongol was given his first bow and arrows; he was expected to spend a good deal of his time hunting on horseback. The boy practiced these skills until age 16, when he became a full-fledged Mongol warrior. During his training, he was also expected to learn how to ride for several days without stopping, sleeping in the saddle.

The Mongol bow was a common one in the steppe lands—a compound bow, with an effective range of 200–300 yards (see Chapter 6). The Mongol learned to use two types of arrows: those with small, sharp points for long range, and those tipped with heavier iron heads for short range. On campaign, the Mongol typically carried two bows and about thirty each of the two types of arrows with him. In his quiver were also a few specialized arrows, such as armor-piercing arrows and whistling arrows. Training in peacetime for adult Mongols consisted of great hunts in which a large area was cordoned off and beaters chased the animals

The Secret History of the Mongols

The following passages from The Secret History of the Mongols, *composed in the years immediately following his death, detail Chingiz Khan's rules regarding combat and leadership.*

■ ■ ■

[In the early years of Chingiz Khan's career, he set rules for his soldiers regarding combat.]

At the end of that winter in the autumn of the Year of the Dog, Chingiz Khan assembled his army at Seventy Felt Cloaks to go to war with the four Tatar clans. Before the battle began Chingiz Khan spoke with his soldiers and set down these rules: "If we overcome their soldiers no one will stop to gather their spoils. When they're beaten and the fighting is over then there'll be time for that. We'll divide their possessions equally among us. If we're forced to retreat by their charge every man will ride back to the place where we started our attack. Any man who doesn't return to his place for a counterattack will be killed."

[In Chingiz Khan's last years, he decided to announce his heir. He had delayed this decision until finally one of his favorite wives broached the subject.]

"When your body falls like an old tree who will rule your people, these fields of tangled grasses? When your body crumbles like an old pillar who will rule your people . . . ? Which of your four heroic sons will you name? What I've said everyone knows is true, your sons, your commanders, all the common people, even someone as low as myself. You should decide now who it will be." Chingiz Khan replied: . . . I've been forgetting it as if I won't follow my ancestors someday. I've been sleeping like I won't someday be taken by death. Jochi, you are my eldest son. What do you say?"

But before Jochi could speak, Chagadai spoke up: "When you tell Jochi to speak do you offer him the succession? How could we allow ourselves to be ruled by this bastard son of a Merkit?"

[This was in reference to the fact that Jochi had been born while his mother was a prisoner of the Merkits. There was always suspicion that his father was not Chingiz Khan, but Chingiz treated him as his son nonetheless.]

Jochi rose up and grabbed Chagadai by the collar saying: "I've never been set apart from my brothers by my father the Khan. What gives you the right to say that I'm different? What makes you any better than I am . . . ? If you can shoot an arrow farther than I can, I'll cut off my thumb and throw it away. If you can beat me at wrestling, I'll lay still on the ground where I fall. Let the word of our father the Khan decide."

[The two brothers began to fight but were interrupted when others pointed out that they shared the same mother and should not treat each other this way.]

Then Chingiz Khan spoke: "How can you say this about Jochi? Jochi is my eldest son, isn't he? Don't ever say that again."

Hearing this, Chagadai smiled and said: "I won't say anything about whether Jochi is stronger than I am, nor answer this boast that his ability is greater than mine. I'll only say that the meat you kill with words can't be carried home for your dinner. . . . Brother Ogedei is honest. Let's agree on Ogodei. If Ogodei stays at the side of our father, if our father instructs him in how to wear the hat of the Great Khan, that will be fine."

Hearing this, Chingiz Khan spoke: "Jochi, what do you say? Speak up!" And Jochi said: "Chagadai speaks for me."

So Chingiz Khan made a decree: "Don't forget what you've pledged today, Jochi and Chagadai. Don't do anything that will give men cause to insult you. Don't give men cause to laugh at your promises. In the past Altan and Khuchar gave their word like this and didn't keep it. *[They deserted Chingiz Khan and were later executed.]* You know what happened to them."

SOURCE: Paul Kahn, trans., *The Secret History of the Mongols: The Origin of Chingis Khan* (Boston: Cheng & Tsui, 1998).

toward a ring of Mongols. After all the animals had been killed, the commanders critiqued the hunt as if it had been a major military campaign.

When going into battle, the Mongol warrior took along at least three spare horses. These horses were trained to respond to voice commands and to maintain their speed and balance as the Mongol shot arrows toward both front and rear. Each Mongol also carried a short sword as well as a short lance with an attached hook, which he used to pull opponents out of the saddle. Other equipment included a hatchet, a file for sharpening arrowheads, a rope for pulling wagons, an iron cooking pot, leather bottles, and a leather bag that contained jerky, needles and thread, a fur helmet, a small tent, and other items that might be needed in the field. This leather bag was also waterproof, making it very handy when crossing bodies of water. As for armor, the Mongol was equipped with a steel helmet with a leather neckpiece and with body armor of layered hides lacquered to prevent damage from moisture or of overlapping scales of iron laced together. The hide armor was usually six layers sewn tightly together, boiled to soften, and molded to fit the body. Various types of shields were also available, though the Mongol usually carried only a small one when on the attack, used primarily to ward off enemy arrows.

Strategy and Tactics

Most Mongol strategy consisted of traditional forms of steppe warfare, especially the use of ambushes and feigned retreats. But the Mongols under Chingiz Khan also diverged from the traditional pattern in some notable respects. In particular, they relied on a significant amount of intelligence work and meticulous planning before launching a major attack on a region. For example, before invading the Khwarizmian Empire (see below), Mongol generals called in Muslim merchants the Mongols knew well and had them report all they knew about conditions in the region. Similarly, before attacking Jin China, they interviewed Chinese and other merchants and travelers. To aid in planning a campaign, Mongol scouts were also sent ahead to note roads, bridges, mountain passes, towns, fortifications, and anything else that might be militarily useful to know before attacking. The Mongols were not unique in this respect, but they were very systematic about it, not launching an expedition until they were fairly certain they knew what they were up against.

When the Mongols advanced on a target, they rode in several widely dispersed columns. These columns would time their advance so that all arrived at roughly the same time. This was an amazing feat, one not often replicated by premodern armies until the campaigns of Napoleon.

One other aspect that distinguishes the Mongols from just about any other premodern army was their willingness to improvise and utilize whatever might be helpful in achieving their aims. One tactic was to tie branches to their horses so that, when they rode, the dust kicked up would make it look like they had far more men than they really had. Or they would gather up thousands of local people while advancing and put these people in front of the army, making it appear that these thousands were part of the Mongol army; they would be the first to be hit when the enemy attacked. Another related tactic was to ally with the enemies of their targets. After such alliances had served their purpose, the Mongols often turned on their erstwhile allies. Possibly the most significant instance of this was their alliance with Southern Song China against Jin China, which diverted tens of thousands of Jin soldiers from the Mongol invasion. The only allies the Mongols themselves remained loyal to were those from the steppes, mainly other Turkic peoples. This willingness to innovate and to adopt the tactics of their opponents should not be underestimated. Militaries throughout premodern history were often reluctant to alter established patterns, strategies, and tactics because styles of warfare were so often expressions of deeper cultural patterns and social structures. Mongol military flexibility was one of their greatest weapons.

For example, the most serious problem the Mongols encountered in their early assaults was fortified cities. The fortifications around some Chinese cities were tremendously large and complex, and thus impossible for a cavalry force to take. For this task, they learned to employ those who could help, especially Chinese who were experienced in the art of siege craft. Thousands of Chinese were set to work building the siege engines and then traveling with the Mongol army to operate them. In the siege of Kaifeng, and again in Korea, the Mongols also used other Chinese inventions—namely, exploding bombs and flaming explosive devices. In later sieges, they employed Chinese rapid-fire explosive arrow launchers. In one siege in Persia, it is recorded that a heavily fortified city was assaulted by the Mongols with 3000 ballistas, 300 catapults, and 700 machines that hurled flaming naphtha over the walls. They also had 4000 scaling ladders, and literally tons of rocks were carried to the scene to be launched at the city walls. These duties were carried out by the large Chinese siege and artillery units in Mongol service.

After their conquests of Muslim lands, the Mongols began to utilize siege techniques from the Islamic world as well. When invading the Southern Song in the 1260s, they found that the Chinese siege devices they were using were not able to penetrate the extremely thick, high walls the Song Chinese had constructed there. Therefore, they imported thousands of Persians and Arabs with their specialized catapults and trebuchets, which were apparently the most effective in the world for launching projectiles at and over such walls. (See the Highlights box on page 260.)

In battle, the Mongols were experts at the feint, especially in weakening the center and having the flanks envelop the enemy. Signals were relayed by officers with flags or bugles or, at night, with lamps. The Mongols also perfected the arrow storm, a shock tactic designed to disorient the enemy while the heavy cavalry attacked. At times, this arrow storm would be directed at a central point or points of the enemy line.

Also, regarding strategy and tactics, a word must be said about terror and pursuit. Terror was a major instrument of Mongol military efforts, designed to demoralize the enemy and weaken its will to resist. The Mongols also emphasized from the time of Chingiz Khan that defeated enemies must be pursued and completely destroyed to prevent them from being able to regroup. Sometimes the Mongols would chase defeated enemies over 30 miles, and, in one recorded case, that of Salamiya in 1299, they pursued for over 200 miles. Only if they were too tired or it had been a marginal victory would they pass this up. The fear the Mongols inspired can be seen in this remark by a Chinese historian writing during the Mongol conquests: "People hide in vain among mountains and caves to escape the Mongol sword, hardly one or two in a hundred saving themselves, while the fields are strewn with the bones of human beings. Since the beginning of time no barbarians have been so powerful as the Mongols are today. They destroy kingdoms as one tears up grass. Why does Heaven permit it?" This was a sentiment expressed not only by Chinese but also by Muslims and Christians of the time.

THE MONGOL EMPIRE: THE CAMPAIGNS OF CONQUEST

The Invasion of Jin China

At the time of the unification of the Mongols under Chingiz Khan in the early thirteenth century, China was divided into two realms. Northern China was under the rule of the Jin dynasty, led by the Jurchen peoples of Manchuria (see Chapter 14). Southern China was under the Song dynasty and was by far the larger and wealthier land. But bordering Jin China and to the southwest of Mongolia was the sinicized state of Xi Xia, or "Western" Xia. Chingiz launched several campaigns against Xi Xia in 1207–1209, but each time he was faced with the fact that the Mongols at this time were not well equipped to conduct sieges of cities. The enormous destruction of the lands of Xi Xia convinced its rulers to at least accept nominal subordination to the Mongols, and Chingiz was able to acquire the large amounts of loot he needed to reward his followers. Without these rewards, the new Mongol unity would have proved just as fragile as all the previous nomadic confederations. The subjugation of Xi Xia also protected Chingiz's right flank as he prepared for the main assault against the wealthy lands of Jin China.

The Mongol assaults on Jin China began in 1211, and many scholars believe that at this time Chingiz Khan's goal was not the occupation of China, but the acquisition of loot with which to reward his followers. He was aided from the beginning by defections from within the Jin ranks. The Jurchens were actually a fairly small proportion of the Jin army, and the other tribal peoples, and especially the Chinese in their ranks, were little trusted. Yet the Jurchens were not so far removed from their steppe origins and usually were not taken in by the Mongol's use of feigned retreats and other typical steppe warfare tactics. Most Mongol victories over the Jurchens resulted from the mobility of the Mongol forces and Chingiz Khan's ability to get more men to the point of battle than his enemy could. The destruction of northern Chinese farmland was immense, and far more died from famine and disease than from Mongol weapons. Each year the Mongols would launch their raids against Jin China but at the end of the year would return to Mongolia.

Figure 13.1 The Mongol Empire

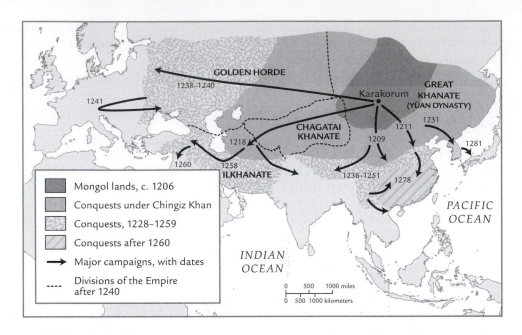

In 1215, the Mongols seemed to change their focus from raiding to invading and occupying. In the intervening years, Chingiz Khan had acquired large numbers of captured or defected Chinese troops, including units of siege specialists, which he used in the assault on Jin cities. That year Chingiz's forces took the city of Beijing and torched it; flames from the burning city reportedly were observed from afar for as long as a month. Jin forces were very weak by this time, especially since large numbers were posted along the frontier with Song China. By 1218, the once-mighty Jurchen Jin dynasty ruled over little more than a province, with the rest of northern China subject to Mongol whim. However, it was not until 1234 that north China was firmly within the Mongol Empire (Figure 13.1).

The Invasion of Khwarizm

To the west of Chingiz Khan's empire lay the Iranian empire of Khwarizm, with its capital at Samarkand. This empire, which included much of central Asia and Persia, was ruled in 1218 by Ala al-Din Muhammad, who had only recently taken control of the empire and was interested in its expansion. At this time, Chingiz Khan was not interested in war or expansion to the west, and so he sent envoys to Muhammad requesting normal trade relations. There are various stories of the contents of Chingiz's letter to Muhammad, but whatever he wrote, Muhammad took it as an insult and

ordered his governor at the city of Utrar to kill most of the envoys and send the rest back after shaving off their beards. Whatever Chingiz's plans had been regarding China, he then initiated a major military operation against Khwarizm.

In the summer of 1219, Chingiz Khan collected a large military force that included several Turkish and Central Asian allies, for a total force of probably about 100,000. This was sent into Khawarizm in three columns, with Chingiz leading the northernmost. Muhammad could count on an army many times the size of the Mongols, but it was scattered in garrisons throughout the region. Muhammad's failure to take advantage of his dominance in numbers was partly a strategic blunder; but it was partly calculated on Muhammad's part, as he could not count on the loyalty of many of his generals. Also, due to conflicts within the Muslim world, the caliph in Baghdad, Al-Nasir, refused to support Muhammad and even expressed hope for a Mongol victory.

The Mongols were tightly disciplined and took the Khwarizmian garrisons one by one. As usual, those fortresses or fortified cities that surrendered without contesting Mongol rule were mostly spared, while those that resisted were invested, taken, and destroyed, often with frightful slaughter. Chingiz Khan's column reached the city of Bukhara in February 1220 and so frightened the defenders that they fled without a fight. After looting and burning the city, Chingiz marched on to Samarkand, where he linked up with the other two Mongol columns. Samarkand held out a little longer, and, for its efforts, an enormous number of the population were slaughtered. Reportedly, each Mongol soldier was assigned a set number of people that he was expected to take out of the city and kill. Muhammad had managed to escape the destruction but was eventually tracked down and killed by a Mongol detachment.

In the spring of 1221, Chingiz led his army across the Amu Darya River into Afghanistan and Kurasan, the remaining lands of the Khwarizmian Empire. Within only a few weeks, many of the major cities of the region had been destroyed, including the city of Merv. Mongol terror tactics were particularly fierce in the taking of Kurasan, even more so than in the easternmost regions of Khwarizm. Many of the forces arrayed against the Mongols were Turkish or other steppe tribes, which were culturally and militarily similar to the Mongols. However, they lacked the numbers and discipline of the Mongol forces, and most of these tribesmen were killed in battle, fled further westward, or were incorporated into the Mongol military structure. One Oghuz Turkish tribe that fled the Mongols eventually settled in Anatolia, where it went on to form the Ottoman Empire.

Possibly because they faced armies with similar traditions, the Mongols wielded terror to a greater extent here than in most of their conquests. The hope—often realized—was that when word of the Mongol terror spread, enemy armies would become not so much demoralized as preoccupied with maintaining order among a panic-stricken population. Also, in most cases, the Mongols did not bring up their Chinese siege artillery, and so saw terror as a replacement tactic. In one recorded instance, the Mongol general Tolui—the youngest son of Chingiz Khan whose descendants would later become the longest-lasting Mongol dynasty—sat on a golden throne on a hill observing as his men systematically slaughtered the population of Merv. In addition to the many thousands of city-dwellers slaughtered, the Mongols destroyed the irrigation works of the region, leading to the death through starvation of possibly millions. In many ways, this region of Central Asia has still not recovered from the Mongol depredations.

The almost endless rounds of Mongol success and consequent destruction were marred only by a continuing resistance led by the son of Muhammad, Jalal al-Din. A very competent field commander, Jalal al-Din organized his resistance from a mountain fortress in Ghazni in Afghanistan. In late 1221, he defeated a Mongol force near Ghazni but abandoned that city on the arrival of another Mongol army under Chingiz Khan. Soon, Jalal al-Din's army was slaughtered or drowned in the Indus River, but legend has it that Jalal al-Din escaped by swimming across the Indus under a hail of Mongol arrows.

Apparently, Chingiz did not intend to incorporate the lands of Khwarizm into his empire. In 1223, after placing puppets in positions of authority and ordering that his name be invoked in the *kutba*, he led his main armies back into Mongolia. Jebe and Subodei were left in command of about 25,000 men and ordered to reconnoiter the lands of the Caspian Sea.

The Invasion of Russia

Moving swiftly, Jebe and Subodei left a swath of destruction that included such Iranian cities as Rai and Qum; Tabriz was spared only because its ruler bribed the Mongol generals with enormous loads of precious jewels. Without Chinese siege engines, the Mongols were forced to use various ruses in order to capture cities. One of their most successful strategies was to besiege a city for a certain period of time and then leave in ostentatious disgust. After spies had informed them that the defenders were sufficiently relaxed, the Mongol armies executed a rapid return, catching the city unprepared and usually taking it.

After ravaging the Azeri lands, the Mongols moved up through the Caucasus into Georgia, at the time defended by a well-regarded army centered on mounted knights more in the western European fashion than the Turkish or Iranian. A feigned retreat by Subodei led the Georgian knights into an ambush where they were destroyed by the Mongol horse-archers of Jebe's force. Several Georgian towns and cities were then razed, though the Mongols were forced to end the siege of Tiflis on meeting stubborn resistance.

The Mongols went on to achieve several more victories, most notably against a Kipchak army that saw many of its members defect to the Mongols. The remaining Kipchaks, a people who were cultural and linguistic cousins of the Mongols, fled into Russian territory and requested Russian assistance. Several Russian princes, not quite sure what to make of the Mongols, combined their forces and, in alliance with the Kipchaks, forced the Mongols to withdraw. The Russian and Kipchak force probably outnumbered the Mongols three or four to one, and the Mongol withdrawal may have been simply a modified feigned retreat, for after the Russian force had become somewhat strung out and its lead elements had wearied, the Mongols stopped their withdrawal. At a spot along the Kalka River, the Mongols turned and attacked the Russian-Kipchak force before they could establish their camp. The main fighting was between the Mongols and the Kipchaks, who were forced back on the Russians, causing a great deal of confusion. Many were killed, but one of the Russian princes, Mstislav of Kiev, was able to effect an orderly retreat and construct some sort of fortification on the other side of the Kalka River. After several days of fighting, Subodei allowed Mstislav and his men an honorable surrender. However, once the Mongols were in possession of the camp, Mstislav and all his men were slaughtered.

The remaining Russian princes were in disorganization, but, fortunately for them, the Mongols were not on a march of conquest at that time. Jebe and Subodei returned to Mongolia, and the true invasion of Russia occurred about twelve years later. Still, how had this relatively small Mongol force reaped so much battlefield success? The usual Mongol discipline, skill, and tactics such as the feigned retreat certainly account for much of the Mongol success. But, as in many of their other campaigns, they were assisted by the disunity of their enemy. And Russia was more divided than nearly anywhere else the Mongols advanced. The Russian force that confronted the Mongols at the Kalka River was actually four independent armies led by their respective princes. There was little coordination, as each sought to attain victory for himself and deny it to his fellow princes. Indeed, a fifth Russian army under Duke Yuri of Vladimir was expected to be part of the force, but Yuri was late, and the others pursued the Mongols without him. This turned out to be fortunate for Yuri, who returned to his lands with his army intact.

The Mongols were also assisted by good intelligence. According to some reports, whole units of Russians went over to the Mongols and provided them with information about the true situation in Russia. Other reports say that Venetian traders provided intelligence to the Mongols in return for their plundering Genoese trading posts along the Crimea. And still other reports insist that it was the Kipchaks who provided the intelligence. Whatever the source, the Mongols were clearly much better informed about the Russians than the Russians were about them.

Not until 1236 did the real invasion of Russia take place, and it was a meticulously planned assault. The total numbers in the Mongol invasion army are estimated to have been somewhat over 150,000, but this figure includes allies, guards on the supply train, and Chinese and Muslim siege and artillery units. The total number of Mongols and Turkish allies was probably not more than about 60,000. Spies preceded the main army, spreading rumors and tales of terror.

Leading the invasion force was Batu, Chingiz Khan's grandson, but the real organizer of the expedition was the redoubtable Subodei. In the usual Mongol manner, the invasion force was split into two columns, and its initial assault was not on Russia but against the Bulgars and some Kipchak tribes along the Volga River to the east of the main Russian principalities. Batu and Subodei led one column against the city of Bulgar, a wealthy trade city, while the Mongol general Mangu went farther south to attack the Kipchaks. Both assaults proved successful, and those Kipchaks not integrated into the Mongol army fled to Hungary where they were given sanctuary on converting to Christianity.

In 1237, Subodei determined to destroy the Russian principalities even though it was the dead of winter. The Mongols were once again immensely aided by the disunity of the Russian princes. Two main cities, Riazan and Kolumna, stood directly in their path, but the Russian princes remained in their respective cities and refused to aid each other. Some Russian units did meet the Mongols in battle but were swiftly defeated. Next, to take the city of Riazan, the Mongols first devastated the countryside and then constructed a wooden wall to encircle the city to prevent anyone from escaping or providing relief to the defenders. Then, the Mongols bombarded the walls of Riazan with Chinese siege missiles. After several days of this battering, flame projectiles were used against the wooden walls. Within a few days, the Mongols were inside the city, it was looted and burned, and the population was slaughtered. Soon after, the same fate was meted to Kolumna. The relief column sent by Duke Yuri of Vladimir failed to arrive in time to help but was in time to be destroyed by a large Mongol force. In the process, Yuri's son, Vladimir, was captured.

For the assault on Yuri's capital at Vladimir, the Mongols moved with their customary swiftness to block any relief forces from arriving. The rest of the army arrived a few days later with thousands of prisoners, who were set to work constructing a wooden wall to surround Vladimir as had been done at Riazan. After several days of bombardment by siege missiles, the Mongols launched a furious assault on February 14, 1238, taking the city by storm. The city was burned while many of the population remained inside. Reportedly, the stench of thousands of burning bodies was overpowering even to the hardened Mongol warriors.

With the main Russian armies destroyed, Mongol columns were sent against the remaining princes and into the Ukraine. After more death and destruction, the main Mongol armies returned to the steppes in late spring to regroup and plan the next phase of the invasion. This came a few months later, and the main object of attack was the Ukrainian city of Kiev. Once again, Mongol cavalry swiftly laid a cordon around the city to prevent reinforcements while the siege machines were moved up to weaken the walls and the will of the inhabitants. In November 1240, Kiev and several other Ukrainian cities fell to the Mongols, and Russia was now a part of the Mongol imperium. The next targets were Hungary and Poland.

The Invasion of Poland and Hungary

The invasion of Poland and Hungary was carefully planned as a campaign of conquest, not a raid for plunder. Mongol scouts and spies flooded the marked territory, apparently making no secret of their intentions. Fear gripped much of central and western Europe, and merchants and other travelers stayed away from the eastern lands. Reportedly, even fishermen feared to take their boats into the eastern Baltic Sea, preferring to have their livelihood ruined than to possibly confront the Mongols.

The Mongol army began its campaign in February 1241 and, as it left Russia, divided into two forces. The smaller one marched into Poland, and the larger into Hungary. We do not have a clear idea of the numbers involved, but the smaller force probably had no more than 25,000 while the larger force had 40,000 or so. Poland was not united at this time, but attempts had been made to organize a combined force to confront the Mongols. The leading Polish lord was Prince Henry of Silesia, who commanded at most 20,000 men. Several other Polish and German lords also contributed forces, but Henry's best soldiers were knights of various military orders, including units from the Knights Templar and the Teutonic Knights. Unfortunately for Henry, he had only a few hundred of these elite fighters.

Henry gathered his forces near the city of Liegnitz while the Mongols ravaged the countryside. After winning a couple of small battles, the Mongols took the city of Kracow, which had already been abandoned by its inhabitants. There they learned the location of Henry's forces and that he was waiting for reinforcements from Bohemia. Henry probably had by this time a force of at least 40,000 men, which helps explain why he chose to initiate an attack on the approaching Mongol forces. The battle was fought on April 9, 1241, with Henry sending his knights directly at the lead Mongol units. As they had done many times in the past, the Mongols used feigned flight to lure the enemy into an ambush. At one point during the battle, the Mongols released smoke on the battlefield between Henry's cavalry and infantry forces, further contributing to the confusion. Thousands were killed, including Henry and many of the Polish nobility. Several more towns and cities were destroyed before the Mongol force turned to assist the larger force that had invaded Hungary.

On April 9, 1241, ironically the same day Duke Henry was losing the battle of Liegnitz, King Bela of Hungary marched with about 80,000 men to meet the Mongols. Hungary's weaknesses were similar to Poland's: a lack of unity compounded by years of infighting among the Hungarian princes. Still, a semblance of unity had been forged in order to meet the Mongol threat, although Bela had stupidly chased away several of the tribes of Kipchaks who had offered to fight for him. Over several days, Bela's force followed the Mongols as they seemingly retreated. The Mongols had lured Bela to a carefully chosen field of battle near the River Sajo. The resulting battle was another major Mongol victory, this time involving the use of catapults to hurl flame and smoke pots to disrupt and divide the Hungarians. The slaughter went on for days, and Hungary was added to the Mongol territories.

The pope preached another crusade, and knights from throughout western Europe prepared for the expected Mongol onslaught. However, in December 1241, the Great Khan Ogodei died, and the *Tumen* in central Europe were ordered to pull back to more defensible positions in Russia while their leader, Batu, returned to Karakorum to join in the choice of the next Great Khan. There would be numerous Mongol raids of plunder into both Poland and Hungary over the next decades, but no occupation or campaigns further west.

The Invasion of Persia

Nothing illustrates the success of Chingiz Khan's new tribal system better than the fact that, after his death, the empire remained united and continued to expand,

and it did so under his sons, as he had intended. He had accomplished the task of transferring loyalty from tribe and family to the tribe of Chingiz Khan. Certainly, the extraordinary successes of the Mongols in the field had helped cement their loyalty to their Khan, as had the vast amounts of loot distributed to the Mongol warriors. That the conquests continued for several decades after the founder's death is further tribute to the organizational skills of Chingiz Khan.

The first few years after Chingiz Khan's death saw the Mongols first preoccupied with completing the conquest of Jin China and then the conquest of Russia and eastern Europe (see above). By the 1250s, however, they were ready to return to the lands of Islam. They had not exactly left, since much of Central Asia and Korasan was ruled by Mongol puppets. The only Muslim powers left were the Mamluks in Egypt and Syria; the Abbasid caliph, based in Baghdad but claiming the allegiance of several Turkish and Kurdish Muslim lords in Iraq and western Iran; and the Assassins, the Ismailis in their fortresses.

At a Quriltai in 1251, the Great Khan Mongke sent Qubilai to conquer Song China (see Chapter 14) and Qubilai's brother Hulegu to conquer western Asia. His instructions were to first destroy the Ismailis and their castles, destroy the independent Muslim lords, force the Abbasid caliph to submit, and then incorporate Syria and Egypt into the Mongol Empire. There is some speculation that the main reason for the desire to destroy the Ismailis was that they had sent 400 Assassins to Karakorum (the new Mongol capital) to kill Mongke.

Hulegu's expedition left for Persia in 1253 and didn't arrive until 1256. This was an exceptionally slow advance for a Mongol army, but it displays the Mongol ability to adapt and modify their tactics to fit the circumstances. The provisioning of the army was organized by Mongol parties riding in advance of the main army. Principalities along the way were encouraged to submit and supply the army. In addition to roughly 60,000 Mongol and other allied steppe warriors, Hulegu brought with him several tens of thousands of Chinese infantry as well as a large complement of Chinese siege artillery. These were to be used to batter down the stone castles of the Assassins.

Most of the Muslim rulers in the region quickly submitted to Hulegu, including the lords of the strategic Iranian province of Fars. Hulegu led his army to the castle of Rukn ad-Din Kunshah, the young grand master of the Ismailis. Hulegu immediately began a bombardment of the castle with his Chinese siege

missiles. Rukn ad-Din was reportedly terrified of the consequences of a Mongol victory and decided to surrender and hope for mercy. Hulegu was delighted to ensure the young master's safety in return for his surrender, and most of the remaining Assassin castles were taken without a struggle after Rukn ad-Din was marched in front of them to order their surrender. Thus, Hulegu was spared many years of siege warfare.

Hulegu next turned his attention to Baghdad and demanded that the reigning caliph, al-Mutasim, submit to the Mongols. The letter was apparently very insulting, so the caliph, despite not being in any position to make demands, refused to submit and instead demanded that Hulegu and his Mongol army submit. Hulegu responded by sending his army in two columns (the usual Mongol manner) to besiege Baghdad. One column arrived on the west bank of the Tigris side of Baghdad, and Hulegu led the main column, which arrived to the east of Baghdad. In January 1258, after swiftly scattering a small Abbasid force that had attempted to prevent the two Mongol armies from encircling the city, Hulegu tightened his noose around the city.

At this point, the caliph realized that resistance was futile and attempted to negotiate the departure of the Mongols. His Shi'ite vizier was sent out to parlay with the Mongols, but this man was probably already working with the Mongols against his master. In any case, the inhabitants of Baghdad began to panic as the Mongols closed in. By February 5, the Chinese siege artillery had battered down the outer walls along the eastern side of the city. People who tried to escape were caught and killed by the Mongols, the idea being to put more pressure on the caliph to surrender. This he did on February 10, arriving in person in front of Hulegu. The Mongols ordered the entire population to leave the city, carrying nothing with them. They then began another of their horrific slaughters of those who had not obeyed their order to leave. The city was burned, and reportedly over 90,000 were killed, though the Christian inhabitants were allegedly spared the Mongol sword. The caliph himself was rolled in a carpet and trampled by horses, though not before he had disclosed the hiding place of his vast fortune.

Hulegu moved on to the next step in his mission, which was to incorporate Syria and Egypt into the empire. The devastation thus far to the Muslim world was practically incalculable. In addition to the massive death and destruction, the Mongols had utterly

Siege of Baghdad
A Persian manuscript illustration shows Mongol forces besieging Baghdad with stone-throwing machines. The outnumbered defenders look out from behind the city walls.

destroyed the Caliphate, the symbol of the Dar al-Islam since the time of the Prophet. Muslims were psychologically as well as physically overwhelmed by this annihilation of their symbolic leader. To many at the time, it seemed that only the Mamluk kingdom in Egypt stood in the way of the Mongol elimination of the world of Islam. Mamluk victory at Ayn Jalut (see the Highlights box "The Battle of Ayn Jalut, 1260") thus not only stemmed the Mongol tide but was seen as the salvation of Islam.

Further Campaigns in the East

Even while at war in various other theaters, the Mongols in 1231 sent an army to subjugate Korea. After the Korean armies were swiftly swept from the field, their remnants took to the numerous hills and mountains of Korea, constructing stone fortresses both for defense and as bases of offensive operations. Meanwhile, the Korean royal court fled to the small island of Kanghwa, near Seoul. Korean resistance frustrated the Mongols, who were forced to bring in Chinese siege experts to reduce the Korean fortresses. In this campaign, we see one of the first recorded uses of gunpowder to create explosive flame pots, which were hurled into the Korean forts by catapults. By 1236, the Mongols had con-

trol over most of the country, but it was not until 1241 that the Korean court ordered its remaining forces to surrender and accept Mongol overlordship. Even then, the royal court remained on Kanghwa for nearly thirty more years.

At the same meeting at which Hulegu was sent to subdue Persia, it was also decided to complete the conquest of Southern Song China. Although the Mongols had firm control of northern China, they had great difficulty obtaining sufficient grain and other food supplies from the land. The destruction caused by the conquest had been extensive, and northern China was in any case relatively poor agricultural land. Adequate supplies could only be obtained through control of wealthy southern China. The Great Khan Mongke personally led the armies in this campaign, with Qubilai, one of Chingiz Khan's grandsons, as his chief lieutenant.

Fairly early in the campaign, Mongke died, and the assaults on Song China halted while Qubilai contested for the throne. After finally succeeding as Great Khan, Qubilai spent almost as much time combating rival claimants as he did subduing Song China. The latter task required incorporation into the Mongol military system of Chinese infantry and naval forces and still took nearly forty years to complete. Even before Qubilai had consolidated his rule, he turned

The Battle of Ayn Jalut, 1260

One of the key battles of history was fought in 1260 at Ayn Jalut in Syria between the Mongols and the Mamluks of Egypt. Many historians (then and now) believe that a Mongol victory in this battle would have threatened the very existence of Islam. The Mamluk kingdom was the last large organized outpost in the Islamic world, and their victory over the Mongols, then, was seen as having provided the Islamic world with time to recover after the devastating Mongol invasions. Other present-day historians feel that the stakes at Ayn Jalut were not nearly so dire, that even had the Mongols won this battle, there was little chance that they could have followed up with the conquest and occupation of Egypt. The land, so goes this argument, was not suitable as pasture for the herds of Mongol ponies.

Probably the key factor that helped determine the outcome of the Battle of Ayn Jalut was that the Mongol side was represented, not by one of the main Mongol armies, but by an advance guard of at most 12,000 men. By early 1260, the Mongol army under Hulegu had reaped consistent success in its campaigns in the Middle East, having taken not only Baghdad but a good portion of Syria as well. However, the Great Khan Mongke had died in 1259, and word of this reached Hulegu in early 1260. Since he was concerned about the possibility

of a hostile Great Khan being chosen, Hulegu moved his army closer to Mongolia to ensure that he had some say in the selection. He left about 12,000 men with his chief lieutenant, Kitbuka, but it is unclear why so few were left to manage such a large territory with a potentially hostile enemy close by.

Kitbuka led his reduced force deeper into Syria and sent an insulting letter to the Mamluk sultan, Qutuz, demanding that he submit. Qutuz responded by killing the Mongol envoys and displaying their heads outside the walls of his encampment. This action ensured that war with the Mongols would follow, and all of Qutuz's subordinate emirs were aware of how angry the Mongols became when their envoys were killed. Unlike many of the Mongols' opponents, however, the Mamluks were actually united in the face of the Mongol threat, and Qutuz was able to confront the Mongols without concern over treachery. Qutuz also decided not to wait for the Mongols to arrive in Egypt but to confront them farther north.

Kitbuka and his Mongol army, supplemented by units of Armenians and some Turks, arrived at a place called Ayn Jalut in early September 1260. The Mamluk force of probably over 20,000 arrived soon thereafter. Qutuz had arranged for safe passage through Crusader territory. The Crusader

---

his attention to extending Mongol rule to even more distant lands. For the invasions of Japan and Java, the Mongols were forced to take to the sea for the first time, a radical departure for the steppe nomads, although they had had some experience fighting in the rivers of China.

The invasion of Japan was to be launched from Korea. The preparations for the invasion were an onerous burden on the Koreans, for they were required to construct the ships and provide the sailors for the expedition. At first, the Koreans were also ordered to provide the supplies, but devastated Korea was unable to, and so supplies were brought from

China. The Mongols used the efficient Chinese transport systems to deliver massive quantities of foodstuffs and weapons.

The first invasion of Japan took place in November 1274 and was composed of roughly 20,000 Mongol soldiers (with some Jurchens) and several thousand very unhappy Korean soldiers. Landing first at Hakata Bay on Kyushu's west coast, the Mongols made a significant impression on the unprepared Japanese samurai (see Chapter 14 for the rise of the samurai in Japan and their response to the Mongol invasions). While the Japanese charged out to engage in individual combat, the Mongols fought in tight ranks and

nobility had decided that the Mongols were by far the bigger threat and, of course, hoped that they themselves would ultimately benefit from a Mongol–Mamluk confrontation. They not only granted safe passage but provided provisions for Qutuz's transiting force of Mamluks.

Skirmishing began between the advance guards of the two forces, but actual battle did not take place until dawn of September 3. It was long believed that the Mamluks had lured the Mongols into a trap, but recent examination of the evidence shows that this was not so. The Mongols charged first and threatened to break through and destroy the Mamluk left. But the Mamluk left wing held, supposedly due to the exhortations of Qutuz and his chief lieutenant and rival, Baybars. In any case, the Mamluks launched a counterattack that was, in turn, repulsed by the Mongols. Kitbuka then led his Mongols in a second attack that once again threatened to roll up the Mamluk army but was repulsed through the discipline of the Mamluks and the leadership of Qutuz. When it was once more the turn of the Mamluks to charge, they were helped by the sudden defection of Kitbuka's Turkish allies. This time, the Mongols broke, and Kitbuka himself was killed. Soon, the Mongol defeat turned into a rout, and the surviving Mongols fled the field.

The Mamluk victory was due partly to the fact that they outnumbered their Mongol opponents, and, of course, the Mamluks were helped by the timely defection of part of the Mongol force. Yet, the main reason for the Mamluk dominance at Ayn Jalut was that, although both sides were composed of military forces that were essentially horse-archers, the Mamluks were much better suited to the climate and terrain of the region. Mamluk armor was sturdier than that of the Mongols, providing more protection; but, also, Mamluk horses were much larger and sturdier than the Mongol ponies. Simply put, as the battle wore on, the Mongols became exhausted, and their ponies could not continue the extreme level of exertion in the heat of Syria. The larger, more plodding, Mamluk horses were much better adapted for this type of fighting. In effect, the Mamluks were able to outlast and wear out the Mongols.

Even if it was not the history-making victory that historians through the ages have made it out to be, the Battle of Ayn Jalut was certainly an important psychological victory. The myth of Mongol invincibility that had served the Mongols so well over the years was now broken. There were several more battles between the Mongols and the Mamluks, but the Battle of Ayn Jalut marked the end of Mongol expansion to the west.

overwhelmed the Japanese with arrow storms. In addition, the Mongols had brought Chinese siege engines and bombarded the Japanese with exploding projectiles. The stunned Japanese were forced to retreat behind fortifications, but their strong resistance had been unexpected, and, as night fell, the Mongols withdrew to their ships. A raging storm destroyed much of the Mongol fleet, and Qubilai was forced to wait several years before reinitiating hostilities.

The second Mongol invasion, in 1281, was not only much better prepared but included tens of thousands of Chinese and Korean troops in addition to the core force of Mongols. By this time, the Japanese samurai had learned the lesson of how inadequate their style of warfare was against this enemy, and they were far better prepared as well. The first waves of the Mongol assault in June and July were beaten back, and the Mongols were unable to get a firm beachhead. Nearly as many Mongols were felled by disease on the cramped ships as were killed by samurai, but they were heartened by the arrival in mid-August of several thousand shiploads of reinforcements. However, as this enormous armada prepared its assault, a typhoon arose and devastated the fleet. The Japanese believed the gods themselves had

The Mongol Legacy

How can we assess the Mongol legacy? Historians have argued over the relative impact of the Mongols, especially about whether the pan-Eurasian trade facilitated by their unified control of the steppe caravan routes outweighed the economic destruction they caused.

Certainly, one result of the Mongol Empire was the creation of one vast Eurasian trading market, such as had never been seen before (Figure 13.2). The Mongols encouraged trade and respected traders, probably because steppe nomads traditionally had depended on trade for many of the goods they could not produce or loot from nearby sedentary civilizations. Merchants from the Islamic world and even Europe traveled fairly securely throughout Mongol lands. Goods from China were brought to Europe in quantities not seen for centuries, and the loss of these products with the collapse of the Mongol Empire would help spark European attempts to find a sea route to Asia. In addition to trade, as we saw in an earlier section, merchants sometimes acquired the provisions that supplied the Mongol armies on campaign.

On the other hand, the facilitation of trade throughout the Eurasian world was of minor importance in comparison with the unprecedented death and destruction that attended the Mongol expansion and conquest. Cities were left in ruins, farmlands were made desolate, and untold millions died from Mongol slaughters or, more often, the diseases and famine that accompanied the invasions. The early decades of the Mongol onslaught saw the Mongols apparently confused as to what to do with cities. Chingiz Khan feared the consequences of his nomadic horsemen becoming influenced by urban civilization, and so he encouraged the destruction of cities and their inhabitants. Slaughter and devastation became the norm in such cities as Samarkand, Bukhara, Beijing, and Kiev. These massacres were often conducted in a deliberate manner: the population herded into nearby fields, forced into groups, divided among the Mongol units, and then methodically slaughtered. Yet it was not only cities that felt the Mongol wrath. Myriad towns and villages also suffered, frequently from Mongol destruction of essential irrigation works or deliberate burning of croplands to starve enemy populations. In one instance, millions perished in northern China from famine caused by the destruction of Yellow River dikes. Not until the campaigns against Song China would the Mongols revise this strategy; but, in the lands of the Golden Horde and Chagadai's Khanate, policies of willful destruction of lands and people continued. Also, Mongol taxation policies led many times to the starvation of hundreds of thousands and even millions.

Mongol devastation was often accompanied by epidemics of disease. For example, a large majority of the over 100,000 who died during the Mongol capture of Kaifeng in Jin China perished as a result of disease. In fact, far more people died as a result of disease than from direct Mongol actions. The most devastating of these epidemics was the Mongol facilitation of the spread of the

saved them, and the typhoon even at the time was called the "Kamikaze," or "Divine Wind." Qubilai made preliminary preparations for a third invasion, but this was never carried out.

The invasion of Java in 1293 met with only somewhat more success than had the invasions of Japan, even though, like the earlier campaign, it was very well prepared. The ships departed Quanzhou with about 30,000 Mongol and Chinese soldiers, and supplies of food, weapons, and ammunition to last at least a year. The expedition also left with a quantity of silver with which to purchase any additional supplies that might be needed. Unlike Japan, Java was not a united kingdom, and the Mongol expeditionary leaders were able

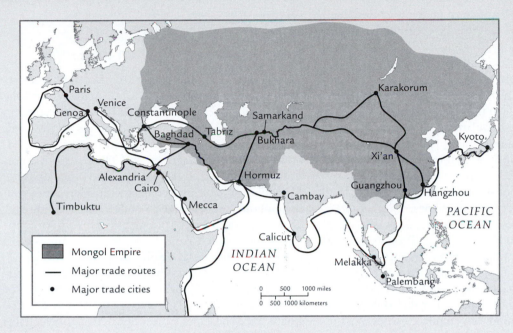

Figure 13.2
Mongol-Era Trade Links

Black Death throughout several regions of the world. In the 1330s, untold millions died in China from the Black Death, and soon the disease appeared in the Middle East with terrible consequences. By the late 1340s, the disease had reached Europe, resulting in the death of a third to a half of that population.

The world was a different place after its encounter with the Mongols. The expanded trade proved ephemeral, whereas the destruction proved long-lived. China lost its preeminent position as the major center of world trade and scientific development, even if in later centuries it recovered some of its prominence. The complete destruction of the Abbasid Caliphate meant that the Islamic world was no longer even technically a united civilization. Persia would take centuries to recover from the devastation of the Mongols, and the devastation of the civilization centers of Central Asia has been all but permanent. The Mongols themselves eventually either assimilated to the lands they had conquered or returned to Mongolia. They contributed little to the civilizations within their empire, and the unique military unity they provided the Inner Asia nomads was never again duplicated.

to follow one of their long-tested strategies and ally with one faction against another. The combined forces met with resounding victory, but before the Mongols could turn on their allies, the Javanese struck. An ambush destroyed much of the Mongol invasion force, and the remainder barely managed to withdraw to its ships. The fleet then sailed back to China.

While the Mongol campaigns against Japan and Java were generally unsuccessful, they do more than show us the limits of Mongol military success. These campaigns involved the dispatch of thousands of ships across the seas and displayed the capacity the Mongols had to distance themselves from their steppe origins and to use the resources of their vast empire.

THE MONGOLS AS RULERS

Administration of Conquered Territories

Administration of conquered lands was designed to serve the Mongol interest in continued military expansion. The Mongol logistic effort discussed above was absolutely dependent on efficient management of imperial territories. The Mongols had no experience in administering sedentary populations and so relied on those in their lands who did. Control over both subject populations and officials was ensured through the use of nonnatives as intermediaries. In general, Mongol overlords did little when these officials engaged in oppressive and confiscatory actions. Rebellious locals were forcibly repressed by Mongol forces or recruited auxiliaries.

Mongol rule throughout the empire was marked by heavy demands on both people and resources. The populations were required to perform sometimes onerous work duties, including the construction of bridges, roads, irrigation works, buildings, and walls. Vast numbers of artisans, engineers, and other skilled craftsmen were shifted throughout the empire to wherever the Mongols needed them. Mongol princes and military commanders were supplied with thousands of these craftsmen as slaves. There were also large numbers of Chinese boatmen whose only task was to see to the ferrying of men and supplies along the rivers of China and Central Asia. Locals throughout the empire were responsible for maintaining the immense postal relay system of the Mongols. In Persia and the Caucasian lands, whole villages typically were responsible for the supply and maintenance of one station.

To a significant extent, the Mongols achieved their goal of subordinating the resources of the whole empire to their personal and military needs. Mongol rulers were able to mobilize and transport men, material resources, and technological expertise in whatever quantities they required from one end of their enormous realm to another. Karakorum became the fabulously wealthy and busy capital of this empire, but when the empire collapsed, so did Karakorum. (See the Issues box "The Mongol Legacy.")

Success and Stress Within the Empire

The creation of this empire led to enormous amounts of wealth flowing into Karakorum. Actually, until the creation of the empire, there had been no capital in the steppe lands and few urban centers of any kind. The Mongol rulers still dwelled in tents, which had, however, become elaborate and filled with treasures from China, Persia, India, Europe, and other lands the Mongols had come into contact with. Merchants from throughout Eurasia came to trade at Karakorum.

As with all steppe societies, there was no established succession to the leadership. Chingiz Khan's decision to anoint Ogodei, his third son, as his immediate successor as Great Khan was only done after gaining the support of his other sons and high officials (see the Sources box on page 243). The next two Great Khans were chosen at a meeting of Mongol chieftains and princes. Until the new khan was chosen, administration was managed by the prior Great Khan's wife, giving these women a great deal of power to influence the selection. This method of choosing the next leader lasted until the death of Mongke (1251–59), at which point a violent struggle ensued among the claimants for the throne. The victor was Qubilai (1260–94), the last to hold real power as Great Khan. However, even Qubilai never commanded as much power over the far-flung empire as his predecessors had. In effect, the unified Mongol Empire broke into four independent realms, and each of these focused much of its attention on warring with the others. The age of Mongol expansion came to a halt with the death of Qubilai.

CONCLUSION

Though there would be later conquerors with roots in the steppes, including the Manchus, the Mughals, and the Ottoman Turks, the Mongols represent the last great irruption of steppe conquerors whose center of political and cultural gravity remained on the steppes. They therefore stand at the climax in Eurasia of a two-millennium-long cycle of interaction between nomadic and sedentary peoples outlined in Chapter 6. Armies of nomadic horse-archers would remain a substantial military threat for another three centuries after the breakup of the Mongol Empire, but never again would they dominate their sedentary neighbors the way the Mongols did.

The impact of the Mongol conquests was mixed and the balance sheet remains a matter of historical contention to this day (see the Issues box). But whether the Eurasian world benefited from or was harmed by the Mongols, there is no denying their tremendous impact. Recent genetic studies suggest that this impact extends to the level of modern demographics: It has been calculated that roughly 16 million people today are descended from Chingiz Khan and his immediate relatives. From this measure, at least, Chingiz Khan's career must be judged a success.

SUGGESTED READINGS

There are quite a few books on the Mongols, with much repetition in each. However, a few stand out as descriptions of the Mongols, Chingiz Khan, and the various military campaigns of the Mongol armies. The following are among the most useful of these books.

Amitai-Preiss, Reuven. *Mongols and Mamluks: The Mamluk-Ilkhanid War, 1260–1281*. Cambridge: Cambridge University Press, 1995. An incisive analysis of the Mamluk victory over the Mongols and of the ecological limits of steppe-based empires.

Chambers, James. *The Devil's Horsemen: The Mongol Invasion of Europe*. London: Routledge, 1979. A good narrative description of the Mongol conquests, particularly the Russian and European campaigns.

Grousset, Rene. *Empire of the Steppes: A History of Central Asia*. New Brunswick: Rutgers State University Press, 1997. Provides tremendous detail on the Mongols, especially their conquests.

Kahn, Paul. *The Secret History of the Mongols: The Origin of Chingis Khan; An Adaptation of the Yüan Chao Pi Shih*. San Francisco: Harper & Row, 1984. A description of the rise of Chingiz Khan from the "official" Mongol version.

Lococo, Paul Jr. *Genghis Khan: History's Greatest Empire Builder*. Washington, D.C.: Potomac Books, 2008. Succinct narrative account of the military talents and accomplishments of Chingiz Khan.

Morgan, David. *The Mongols*. Cambridge: Cambridge University Press, 1990. Probably the best introduction to the Mongols; a well-organized treatment of the people, their rise to power, and the administration of their empire.

Rossabi, Morris. *Khubilai Khan: His Life and Times*. Berkeley: University of California Press, 1988. More a political and cultural history; also contains much on the Mongols of Khubilai's reign.

Saunders, J. J. *The History of the Mongol Conquests*. Philadelphia: University of Pennsylvania Press, 2001. The most accessible overall narrative of the Mongol conquests.

Sinor, Denis. "The Mongols and Western Europe." In *A History of the Crusades*, vol. 3. Madison: University of Wisconsin Press, 1975. A more academic treatment of the Mongol contact with Europe.

CHAPTER 14

Scholars, Samurai, and Sultans: Asia, 1100–1500

The period 1100–1500 in east and south Asia was dominated by the Mongol conquests. China, the central civilization in the area, fell under direct Mongol rule for nearly a century and faced the challenge of nomadic peoples throughout this age. Japan successfully repelled two Mongol invasions, and India felt only indirect consequences of the Mongol conquests in the Islamic world. In both cases, however, Mongol activity had long-term consequences seemingly out of proportion to its direct influence.

The differing reactions of China, Japan, and India, to the Mongols in particular and to the generally increasing level of global contact through war and trade, reveal much about the different institutions and values of the three civilizations. The role and place of warriors in the larger social and political structures of each civilization, especially the relationship of military to civil power, is one key to understanding these differences.

CHINA

The Southern Song, 1127–1279

The Military System As noted in Chapter 9, the Jurchen invasions that forced the retreat of the Northern Song court in 1127 were devastating to China. The garrisons that the Song had established along its northern frontiers, led by military officers controlled by the civilian government, were quickly swept away. The Jurchens, seizing an opportunity for further looting and possibly conquest, launched their large cavalry armies into southern China. The Song armies were scattered and ineffective, and the remnants of the Song court were at one point forced to flee onto junks and take to the sea. Unable to acquire enough craft or experienced sailors, the small Jurchen navy was forced to abandon its attempts to destroy the Song leadership.

Southern China's topography, unfriendly to cavalry armies, combined with rebellions in Jurchen-occupied areas and the rise of an experienced officer corps, spearheaded a Song revival in the 1130s. Once they had pushed the Jurchens north of the Huai River, the Song armies found their roles reversed. Under the capable leadership of several generals leading now battle-tested soldiers, the Song army reached all the way to the Yellow River. Faced with a devastated north that was unable to supply these new armies, and unwilling to press their luck, the Song court signed a peace treaty with the Jurchens that divided China between them (see Chapter 9). The Song armies were brought back below the Huai River, and most of the powerful, almost independent generals who had commanded them were arrested and executed. Once the crisis with the Jurchen had been managed, the Song court was not willing to invest independent power in the hands of military leaders. Many in the Song court believed that it was better to be conquered by barbarians than to allow Chinese military commanders to threaten the basic Confucian system.

With northern China in the hands of the Jurchens, the Song could not revert to the military system of the recent past, which had proved completely unable to defend the dynasty and the Chinese people. But most of the elite in China were passionate about eventually retaking the north from the Jurchens. The Song court's goals were thus somewhat contradictory: to have a military too weak to threaten the dynasty, yet strong enough to both defend against further invasions and recover the north.

As the Jurchen threat subsided, the Song military was organized into four main armies and an Imperial Guard. The armies were stationed mainly along the northern and western frontier, with the Imperial Guard in the capital at Hangzhou. Unlike the Tang and Northern Song, the Imperial Guard was not the main army of the dynasty, but only a bodyguard for the emperor. Each of the frontier armies had its own internal administration and exercised a good deal of autonomy, very much unlike the Northern Song armies. The Southern Song armies also each had an attached riverine force, which sometimes numbered in the hundreds of craft. This water force patrolled the major rivers, on which enormous stone and wood fortresses controlled strategic points.

Civilian control was maintained, but in a much looser fashion than in the Northern Song. Officers usually gained their positions through inheritance, with a percentage also gaining rank through the famous Song examination system. Eunuchs could no longer be employed as military commanders, something that had become common in the last decades of the Northern Song. In fact, many of the eunuchs in command of Song armies at the time of the Jurchen invasions were beheaded.

All officers were expected to be conversant in the military classics of Chinese history, which had been collected and edited as the *Seven Military Classics*. Those gaining officer positions through the exam system were tested on these classics, as well as on their physical strength and ability at archery and horseback riding. The military exam system was a means to introduce fresh blood into the officer ranks and ensure that at least a certain percentage of the officer corps was familiar with Chinese literary traditions. By the late twelfth century, those who had obtained military degrees through the exam system were accorded a great deal of prestige. During times of crisis, which were frequent in the remaining years of the dynasty, local militias were also encouraged. Those that proved successful were often added to one of the four frontier armies, and their leaders given officer positions. And, yet, for all the increasing professionalism of the officer corps, in most instances, the highest commands in the armies were given to civilian officials, and promotion in the army was primarily based on seniority.

The most significant contributions of the Southern Song to the military arts were in the areas of siege warfare and technology. The Yangzi and Han rivers were dotted with fortresses and other fortifications to prevent an enemy from sailing down the rivers or crossing them. Catapults, ballistae, and other weapons were used to defend these fortresses. The fortresses were also equipped with a great number of incendiary devices, many of them launched by catapult. The various river craft included some that were equipped with paddle wheels, enabling them to move swiftly along the rivers. Southern China was very prosperous during the twelfth and thirteenth centuries, allowing the dynasty to equip its armies with vast quantities of iron and steel weapons. In addition, production centers manufactured such things as smoke and incendiary grenades, repeating crossbows, and a kind of flamethrower. (The sources are not entirely clear about Chinese use of gunpowder in guns. There are references to bamboo and iron cannons, or perhaps proto-cannons, but these seem to have been small, unreliable, handheld weapons in this period. The Chinese do seem to have invented guns independently of the Europeans, at least in principle; but, in terms of effective cannon, the edge goes to Europe.) To protect their soldiers from the arrows of the Jurchens, the Song manufactured carts that were sheathed in iron, somewhat like a crude premodern tank. The Song created a complex organization to produce and test new weapons before equipping the army with them. Certainly, the constant threat of Jurchen invasions, and the Song's determination to recover the north, played a role in encouraging innovation in the military realm.

Conflicts with the Jurchen Jin Dynasty   The century following the peace treaty between the Jurchen Jin and Southern Song was not one of peaceful coexistence. Periods of peace were often used to prepare for coming wars. But topography, manpower problems, and political complications limited the ability of either side to threaten the other seriously. The only war of conquest launched by the Jurchens after the peace treaty, in 1161, met with resounding failure. The Song defenses held the Jurchens to only minor gains and achieved a reduction of the Song tribute. But a major Song offensive in 1206, designed to take advantage of Khitan uprisings in and Mongol raids on Jin territory, was equally unsuccessful. The Chinese population under Jin rule failed to rise in support of the invasion, and, by 1208, the Song were again below the Huai River and paying increased tribute. The payments put only a minor dent in the Song treasury, but the defeat was humiliating. For the Jin, though they won the war, their military had been seriously weakened only a few years before they would have to face the newly unified Mongol armies of Chingiz Khan.

Destruction of the Jin and Defense Against the Mongols   The Mongol invasions of both Jin and Southern Song China are covered in Chapter 13. Here we will look briefly at the Song reaction to these

The Siege of Xiangyang, 1268–72

In 1266, the Mongol armies of Qubilai Khan resumed their attacks on the Song after completion of a series of civil wars. By early 1268, the armies under one of the greatest Mongol generals, Bayan, had reached the twin fortresses of Xiangyang and Fancheng. Constructed of sturdy stone and well armed with catapults, ballistae, and trebuchets, the two fortresses were connected by a floating bridge. Regular naval patrols ensured that the garrisons had an abundance of supplies and weapons. This complex had to be overcome if the Mongols wished to proceed to the Yangzi valley. The first assaults on Xiangyang were initiated with a massive bombardment by the Mongols' artillery. The Mongol artillery units were composed almost solely of Chinese from the north, many of whom were by now second- or even third-generation servants of the Mongols. However, the projectiles from the Mongol artillery were ineffective against the strong stone walls, and the attempts to scale the walls and mine underneath the fortress were easily turned back. The Song de-fenders rained down a steady stream of explosive and flame-producing projectiles, killing thousands of the attackers, most of whom were Chinese, Jurchens, or Turks in the Mongol employ.

When direct assault proved fruitless against the sturdy fortresses, the Mongols next attempted a two-part strategy of pressure and starvation. The surrounding countryside was stripped, counter–siege works were constructed to prevent relief forces from arriving by land, and the Mongols' naval force was brought down to attempt to cut off relief of the fortress by water. Thousands more artillery pieces were also added in order to effect a continuous bombardment on the fortresses. After nearly two years, the strategy appeared near to suc-cess when a large Song naval force was able to fight its way into Xiangyang and Fancheng and resupply the defenders. By 1271, the Mongol forces were almost as exhausted as the defenders.

The Uighur commander of the Mongol forces involved in the siege, Ali Haya, informed Bayan

---

invasions. The Song military continued to be unable to engage in successful offensive operations, in large part because it lacked a significant cavalry arm. Defen-sively, the Song continued to use its advantages of both topography and wealth to stave off defeat by the Mongols for over forty years.

The Mongol invasions of north China, beginning in 1211, severely weakened the Jin dynasty. In 1214, the Song stopped paying tribute, further undermin-ing a Jin army and administration whose support suf-fered from Mongol plundering. By 1221, the ultimate fate of the Jin was not in serious doubt. Internal uprisings and Mongol attacks, assisted and supplied by the Song, brought collapse and, in 1233, the extinction of the Jin state.

When the Song received word from northerners that the Mongols had removed most of their armies from China, the Song decided to recover the north. Once again, the Song underestimated its appeal in the north, and it also greatly underestimated the amount of damage that had been done during the Mongol–Jin wars. Enormous armies were sent north with inade-quate provisions. The Song commanders had believed that they could live off the land, but the lands of north China were in ruins and could not even feed the pop-ulation already there. The Song army that reached Luoyang, for example, began to disintegrate as thou-sands of soldiers starved to death. The Song armies had not even made plans for the transport of supplies overland, as in the south they were accustomed to using the rivers for transport. The returning Mongol armies had little trouble sweeping the Song armies out of the north, the Mongol ponies finding more than enough fodder in the depopulated lands.

In 1235, the Mongols decided to invade and con-quer Song China, but for decades confronted the same defensive obstacles that had prevented Jurchen success in the south. It was really not until Song armies defected to the Mongols and provided them with a naval force that the conquest of all of China could be completed. (See the Highlights box "The Siege of Xiangyang, 1268–72.")

and Qubilai that it would not be possible to take these fortresses with the forces present. He requested the construction of much larger siege engines, like those he was aware of in Persia. Engineers from western Asia were then brought to the site, where they constructed trebuchets capable of hurling projectiles weighing more than 200 pounds. The building of these additional siege engines occurred just as another Song relief force had fought its way into Xiangyang, bringing in a large amount of food, weapons, and gunpowder.

The final assault on Xiangyang began in late 1272 and lasted less than three months. While the large trebuchets unrelentingly bombarded the walls, a select force of waterborne Mongols charged toward the connecting bridge. The Song defenders, aware of the danger, used all the weapons at their disposal in an attempt to repulse the attacking force. The waterborne Mongols suffered horrendous casualties before finally destroying the connecting bridge. The fortress of Fancheng was breached and captured a short time later, but Xiangyang itself held out until March 1273. The commander of the garrison, Lu Wenhuan, realized that he could not hold out much longer, as the new trebuchets had laid waste to much of the interior of the fort. After surrendering his position, he was recruited to serve the Mongol cause.

Once Xiangyang had been taken, the rest of southern China was open to the Mongol armies. To be sure, there were still four more years of hard fighting left, but the Mongols now had a much larger navy, a means to adequately move supplies to their troops, and the assistance of one of the Song's best siege generals. What we can observe in the siege of Xiangyang is the excellent and complex nature of Chinese defensive works, using topography and the most advanced weapons available. We can also see the adaptability of the Mongols of Qubilai Khan, who handily used whatever men, weapons, and strategies they felt would accomplish their goals.

The Yüan Dynasty, 1270–1368

The Military System   Qubilai and the Mongol overlords faced a daunting problem if they hoped to maintain control of China. They were overwhelmingly outnumbered by the people of China, which basically precluded leaving administration in the hands of Chinese hired by the dynasty. The Mongols feared a drift toward assimilation and had many more military adventures they wished to pursue.

What Qubilai instituted was a military occupation of China, one that was to preserve the economic base of China but allow for tremendous levels of taxation to fund the continuing military campaigns of the Yüan. Qubilai believed that China could not be administered from the steppes for long, so he had a new capital city built near the ruins of the Jin capital at present-day Beijing. Large areas of tilled land in north China were turned into pastures for the Mongol ponies, though this was never enough to meet the needs of the Mongol armies occupying China. Vast numbers of horses were brought down from Mongolia as well. Nevertheless, in the last decades of the dynasty, lack of ponies had become a serious problem for Mongol soldiers.

As an army of occupation, the Yüan found it necessary to maintain large military garrisons in the interior of China, ready to put down rebellions. The administration and army were divided into four classes. At the top socially, politically, and militarily, were the Mongols. Next were "Semu," Western and Central Asians who were neither Mongol nor sinicized, who staffed many midlevel and some top government positions, including tax officials. Next, came the "Han-ren"—northern Chinese, Jurchens, Khitans, and Koreans—and finally the "Nan-ren," or southern Chinese.

The Mongol army itself was divided into several parts, including the emperor's personal army, his imperial guard, and the armies of various Mongol tribal nobles. These nobles were usually given sometimes-enormous tracts of land within China, worked by

Qubilai Khan Qubilai Khan, center, wearing the ermine robe, is depicted in a contemporary Chinese painting riding on the steppes with a hunting party.

thousands of enslaved Chinese. While technically still under the administrative control of the central government, even during Qubilai's time, these territories were effectively autonomous, becoming hereditary fiefs of the Mongol nobles who controlled them. In return, these nobles maintained internal security and provided troops for Qubilai's expeditions. The common Mongol soldier within China was also given lands and slaves to work them. The Yüan tried to enroll every adult male Mongol in the army.

There were some Semu military units in the Yüan army, but they were usually specialized in such things as logistics or siege craft. More common in the interior garrisons, especially in southern China, were units of northern and southern Chinese. The northerners were given lands from which they were expected to support themselves; the southerners, almost all of whom were from surrendered Song armies or their descendants, were paid from central government coffers. The soldiers in all the Yüan armies were a privileged, hereditary class.

Because the Yüan was in a state of almost constant civil war, especially with struggles to maintain its control of Mongolia and Chinese Turkestan (present-day Xinjiang), the dynasty kept enormous garrisons based in these lands. There were nearly 300,000 troops kept in a series of camps in Mongolia alone. The dynasty was able to rely on transport of the needed

provisions from the wealthy south. Qubilai and later Yüan rulers invested heavily in building and repairing China's system of canals and river transport facilities, especially the Grand Canal, which linked the wealthy areas of the southeast with the capital at Beijing. It is difficult to exaggerate the significance of the rebuilding of the Grand Canal in facilitating the Yüan dynasty's ability to utilize the vast agricultural and manufacturing productivity of the south for the defense of the north of China. Still, the logistical needs of the Yüan dynasty led to extortionate levels of taxation on some areas of China.

The Collapse of the Yüan The efforts of the Mongols to resist sinicization were only partially successful. Few of the Mongols adopted Chinese culture, but many of them fell into debt and corruption enjoying the good life afforded by their conquest. The increasing inability of the Mongol leaders to provide adequate horses for training also contributed to diminution of fighting skills. Not all of the Mongols were so affected, but many of the rest were involved in the seemingly constant civil wars. The polity decentralized: Like the contemporary Delhi sultan in India (see below), the Yüan emperor was actually merely the chief of a collection of semi-independent nobles. Rebellions, especially in the south, became larger and more persistent from the early 1330s, for reasons that

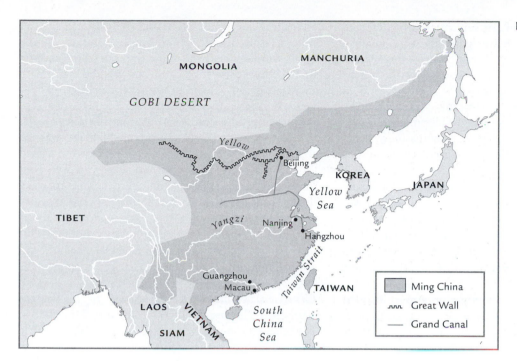

Figure 14.1 Ming China

are unclear. Natural disasters, bubonic plague, and increasing Mongol weakness probably all contributed. The 1350s saw south China freed of Mongol rule by competing Chinese warlords. In 1368, the whole of China came under the control of one of the southern warlords, a man named Zhu Yüanzhang, who founded the new Ming dynasty.

What is most surprising is not that the Mongols were eventually expelled from China but that Mongol rule endured such a relatively long time. This was the first time a nomadic people from Inner Asia had even succeeded in conquering south China, let alone ruling it. The sheer mass of people, strong cultural traditions, and inhospitable terrain worked against conquest and occupation by a people so unfamiliar with the traditions and topography of the south. In addition, unlike prior to the earlier Sui and Northern Song conquests, southern China in the thirteenth century was politically united, and its military defenses were strong and tested. That the Mongols ruled the vast population of China without being overwhelmed is testament to the system they established.

The Early Ming Dynasty, 1368–1449

With the founding of the Ming dynasty (1368–1644), China went from being a land occupied by a people dismissive of its culture and traditions to renewed glory abroad and economic and cultural reconstruction at home (Figure 14.1). The Ming military, initially organized in imitation of and reaction to Yüan insitutions, evolved under pressure from two factors. First, the struggle resumed to determine the proper mix of militarism and Confucian-based civilianism in the governing institutions. At the beginning of the Ming, the military element was clearly in command; but, by 1449, the civilian elements of Ming society had come to dominate the military, affecting the whole Ming attitude toward war, defense, and relations with its neighbors. Second, the ongoing struggle with the Mongols continued to influence Chinese policy.

Military Organization of the Empire   The military institutions established by the first Ming emperor, Hongwu, were well suited for an army of conquest but had limited usefulness during long periods of peace, when defense against nomadic incursions was required. In the early Ming army, the highest commands went to those who had been Hongwu's original subordinates, while scholar-gentry were used for local administration. In all cases, the top civil posts went to Hongwu's generals. The Ming forces acquired an impressive logistics capability, including thousands of various types of waterborne craft to transport men and supplies. During the struggle to unify China, the Ming army also obtained a cavalry arm, consisting primarily of surrendered or defected Mongol units. While many generals were given a great deal of autonomy, all soldiers were registered, regulated, and subject to inspections from a central military organ based in the new Ming capital at Nanjing. Officer positions and rank continued to be hereditary, but, to prevent the development of independent centers of military power, increasingly, commands were subject to the central government and its bureaucracy.

By the early 1370s, Hongwu believed that Ming control of China was secure. Thus, in 1373, he instituted a set of reforms to ensure the continuance of that security, strengthen his and his family's position as rulers of the Ming, and rationalize the system of funding his military to reduce its drain on the Chinese economy.

First, army administration was organized into the "Wei-Suo" system. In this system, nearly all families in the empire were categorized into one of three hereditary categories: farmer, soldier, or artisan. Each household classified as military was required to provide at least one soldier. If a particular military family had no sons, distant relatives would be conscripted and their families reclassified as military. These soldiers were then assigned to established units called Wei, each of roughly 5600 men, garrisoned in a designated military district that normally comprised two or more prefectures. Each Wei was divided into five Suo, each with a standard complement of 1120 men and normally assigned to a particular prefecture. The soldiers were trained locally but administratively controlled by a central government organization called the Five Army Commands. Officer positions, hereditary as well, also were administered by the Five Army Commands. When an expedition was organized, the units were detailed from the Wei, with officers usually not leading the men they commanded in garrison. Once in the field, the expeditionary units came under the operational control of the Ministry of War, not the Five Army Commands. Officers thus found it hard to form bonds with their men.

Second, to feed and supply this vast Ming army, Hongwu established the "Tun-Tian" system, which was seen as a means to both supply the armies and bring lands devastated by the Mongols back under cultivation. The various military families were given lands from which they provided their own food and surpluses were given as salaries to the officers or sent to areas of food deficit. The Tun-Tian system was an expansion of the military colony system used in the Han and Tang dynasties. Rather than being a frontier system, as in those earlier times, however, in the Ming, the Tun-Tian was applied to the whole empire. In its early years, the Tun-Tian worked well, with anywhere from 70–80 percent of classified military men working on the farms, providing a decent overall surplus of production. However, within a few years, the relatively unproductive north, which also was the area requiring the posting of the bulk of the armed forces, needed to be supported. The surpluses from the southern Tun-Tian lands were unable to meet these needs, and funds from the imperial treasury were required.

Third, Hongwu created a military nobility. But this Mongol-influenced reform failed to take hold and was insignificant by the end of Hongwu's reign.

Civilianization and the Shift to a Passive Defense

The last Yüan court fled into Mongolia in 1368, and Hongwu was determined to destroy the Mongol ability to threaten China, if not gain actual control of Mongolia. Also, there were still some Mongol armies within China proper that Hongwu determined to destroy. The third Ming emperor, Yongle (1402–24), was even more aggressive in attacking the Mongols, leading several expeditions personally. These efforts were expensive for the Ming and were marked by periodic disasters as well as major successes. Offensive operations provided security to China but ceased at the death of Yongle.

Yongle had been satisfied with gaining the Mongol tribes' assent to tributary status, realizing that direct control of Mongolia would probably have been much too expensive to maintain. He was successful, but continued success after Yongle's death depended on a Chinese willingness to send military expeditions into Mongolia whenever a potential Mongol threat developed. That willingness disappeared. The only offensive expeditions that saw success in later decades of the Ming were those against the camps of Mongols away on expeditions. The Ming army then scored some impressive victories—against the Mongol women and children left in the camps—a strategy that did usually succeed in pulling the Mongols back from their raids on China and, in at least one case, drew them into a trap as they returned to help their dependents and flocks.

Until the last decades of the sixteenth century, Ming policy along the frontier shifted to passive defense. Eventually, great walls would be constructed to keep the Mongols out of China. This defensive policy was necessitated by the increasingly debilitated state of the Ming armies and encouraged by a gradual shift in control of the armies from veteran generals to civil officials and eunuchs. By the 1440s, all Wei and other military commanders answered directly to several layers of civil officials, including the governors of the provinces, who were at times given operational control. The armies located near the capital, which Yongle had moved from Nanjing to Beijing, were usually under the command of eunuchs, who were seen as more loyal to the emperor than either the military or civil officials.

As a result, the Wei-Suo system, really only effective in its early years, had deteriorated almost to uselessness by the 1440s. Training became lax, and the best units, such as they were, tended to concentrate in the capital. The final blow to the Ming army's ability to project imperial power came with the battle of Tumu in 1449, where the Mongols annihilated a major Ming army, almost completely destroying the last even partially effective military force available to the dynasty. Not until the second half of the sixteenth century do we see a great revival in Ming military affairs.

The native Chinese dynasties of Song and early Ming could not for long resolve the problem of effectively securing their northern frontiers and maintaining a basic civilian orientation and domination in society. Only the Mongol Yüan dynasty had shown success in establishing, like contemporary Japan and India, a militarily dominant social system. Tremendous brutality and exploitation had been necessary to enable the Yüan to control both China and the steppe lands. While unsuccessful in eliminating the northern threats, both the Ming and Song had some success in providing an adequate defense against nomadic invasions. But, as we will see in Chapter 19, the later Ming eventually succumbed to conquest from the north, and it was the resulting Qing dynasty that finally solved the great Chinese dilemma.

KAMAKURA AND MUROMACHI JAPAN, 1150–1477

Japan: An Overview

Japan enters somewhat late onto the historical stage and therefore requires some introduction. Because China so dominates east Asia, the first thing to emphasize is that Japan is not China. Despite significant cultural borrowing from its more powerful and developed neighbor, Japan had from the start a different economy, social structure, governmental structure, and culture from China. And it followed a very different trajectory of development, one in which a warrior class played a significant role (see the Issues box on page 276). In some ways, Japan's history is more comparable to western Europe's, as both were somewhat marginal outliers from the mainstream of Eurasian civilizations.

Japan's isolation was important. It was far enough removed, over difficult seas, from the major mainland powers, civilized and nomadic, to ensure its military safety for the most part. During the entire period from the dawn of Japanese history in the 300s until the nineteenth century, Japan faced only two serious external invasions, by the Mongols in 1274 and 1281 (see below). In addition to being difficult for a major military expedition to reach, Japan was for some time not a particularly rich target, nor after the eleventh century was it an easy one, due to the rise of its own warrior class. This near immunity from invasion meant that Japan's cultural borrowing from the mainland took place selectively and on its own terms, and that Japan's political and military development were almost entirely internally driven—uniquely for a major Eurasian civilization.

Indeed, the lack of any consistent external threat raises an interesting question: Why did Japan develop such a rich and sophisticated military tradition? What the isolated military development of Japan highlights is a universal but often overlooked feature of warfare in traditional civilizations—namely, that a main (if not the main) function of a warrior class is self-preservation, especially against rivals from within that same class, and maintenance of that class's dominance over the primary producers of wealth, the peasantry. War was thus as much, if not more, a feature of factional politics and internal state building as of defense against external threats. This was true everywhere; the isolation of Japan from outside threat simply demonstrates it unambiguously. And the dominance of the warrior class in Japan then had a profound influence on Japanese culture as a whole, as warrior values colored many aspects of Japanese life.

Early and Heian Japan

The Birth of Imperial Japan   A nominally unified Japanese polity arose out of struggles for dominance among various clans in the fourth and fifth centuries.

Mythology about the divine origins of Japan and the imperial family reinforced the ruler's moral position, but the imperial family still found its ability to rule fairly limited. To reinforce both their moral and their actual power, Japan's rulers began borrowing selected aspects of imperial Chinese ideology and administrative techniques in the sixth and seventh centuries. Buddhism's introduction into Japan played a role similar to the spread of Hinduism and Buddhism in southeast Asia, legitimating the imperial position further and linking the ruling house to the religious establishment. The seventh century saw decisive steps toward the establishment of a centralized state on the model of the Tang in China. A series of reforms in midcentury created a graded imperial bureaucracy, though without the open civil service exams used to fill the Chinese administrative machine. Instead, the powerful clans were drawn into the imperial structure by providing the officials of state and so became a civil aristocracy monopolizing power under imperial leadership.

Along with a Tang-style administrative system, the Taika reforms, as they were called, created an army establishment also modeled on the Tang. This was a conscript army, drawn selectively from the peasant population. The entire country was divided for taxation and recruitment purposes into administrative districts; conscripts from each district were armed, trained, and deployed by the central government. The newly invigorated military machine was launched at Korea in 662, but the invasion proved disastrous. Thereafter, the army was turned mostly against the Ainu, the indigenous population of the Japanese islands, who were steadily pushed northward and subdued during the 700s. But, as the campaigns moved farther north, away from the centers of power, the peasant conscript army proved increasingly ill suited for prosecuting this war. At the same time, a general transformation of the Japanese government was taking place.

The Heian Transformation

From the mid-700s, there was a steady trend toward privatization of government functions in all spheres. The growing heritability of offices within particular families, one result of the lack of a competitive exam system, contributed to this trend. So did the growth of *shoen*, landed estates that were exempt from the supposedly universal burdens of taxation and conscription. These were granted to powerful families as favors by the imperial court. Such grants were useful in the short term for building coalitions and gaining support, but in the long run,

they undermined the viability of a centralized Chinese model of administration—a model always at odds with the power of the aristocratic families anyway. There was a marked increase in factional competition as a result of the trend toward privatization, and central authority declined at first. Emperor Kammu reasserted central control over the more privatized model of government in the last decades of the 700s. The imperial court remained the sole source of prestige and of the titles that legitimized the officeholders in the system, so competition was not against the center but for control of the center.

The Rise of the Warrior Class

Together, these two factors—distant campaigning and the privatization of government—worked a momentous transformation on the bases of Japanese military organization. The conscript army was allowed to decay. It was expensive to maintain in both financial and administrative terms, and had been from the start an overambitious vehicle for Japan's limited economic development. Distant campaigns worsened the problem at the same time that the growth of the *shoen* system reduced the land available to support the conscript army.

In its place arose a class of "hired swords": professional warriors drawn from increasingly powerful, rurally based families. Their numbers were far fewer than the theoretical maximum of the conscript army, but they could be employed full-time and in any location far more easily than could reluctant peasant soldiers, and with less disruption of agricultural production. Their use and place in the hierarchy was, like that of the civil aristocracy, formalized and legitimized by grants of offices and titles by the imperial court. Under Kammu, an army reorganized around such hired swords subdued the last Ainu holdouts in northern Honshu and also proved effective against increasingly powerful sects of Buddhist warrior-monks—an odd phenomenon combining several strands of the emerging Japanese cultural and political establishment.

At this point, hired swords demonstrated another advantage over a public force. Under this model, both aristocratic families and the central government maintained their personal military retainers. Indeed, the decentralization of the cost of maintaining armed forces was one of the attractions of the system for the court. In addition, the *shoen*, lost to the government as a means for supporting a public army, became the basis for the maintenance of private forces as aristocratic families granted income from their *shoen* to their personal warriors in exchange for their support.

Samurai Warriors   This thirteenth-century scroll painting shows a twelfth-century samurai battle. Note that the key weapon for both horsemen and foot soldiers is the bow. The Japanese bow was unusually long and had an asymmetrical grip about a third of the way up the bow.

Aristocratic families could then deploy their forces in their factional disputes. Two broad leagues of warrior groups, headed by the Taira and Minamoto families, coalesced around these disputes.

The End of the Heian Polity   Despite such disputes, the ninth and tenth centuries were generally peaceful, and the warriors were limited to fighting the court's and aristocracy's battles—perhaps most accurately described as police actions—for them. But competition intensified in the eleventh century, and the warrior leagues began to be more assertive in their own right for influence at court. A series of wars of increasing directness broke out between the Taira and Minamoto clans after 1150. The Minamoto suffered defeat and near annihilation in 1160, but Minamoto Yoritomo, a young member of the clan, survived and led a Minamoto revival. Between 1180 and 1184, his forces overcame the Taira, inflicting the decisive defeat at the naval battle of Dannoura in 1184. Eliminating all opposition among both his enemies and his most powerful relatives, Yoritomo created a new institution, the *bakufu* (tent government), a military government within the imperial

government, headquartered at Kamakura in eastern Japan. He took the title *shogun* (generalissimo). A new era of Japanese warfare and political evolution, dominated by the warrior class, had opened.

Japanese Warfare

The style of warfare practiced by the Minamoto and Taira clans in the twelfth century remained relatively unchanged until the late fifteenth century, as did the types of soldiers who engaged in war. One reason this was possible was the lack of outside influence on Japanese military practice. But styles of warfare also became part of a larger web of stable and respected cultural traditions expressed through heroic literature and war stories familiar to every member of the warrior class. Such traditions became self-perpetuating within the country's political structure, and styles of warfare would not change significantly until the political context was revolutionized after 1477 (see Chapter 19).

Manpower   In discussing the composition of Japanese armies, it is necessary to clarify the meaning of the Japanese terms for various types of soldiers, as they are a potential source of confusion. Three terms are crucial: *Bushi* was the warrior class, elite warriors from dominant families who followed an informal code of conduct, *bushido*, "the way of the warrior." *Samurai* is often used as a synonym for *bushi*, but the terms are not, in fact, strictly interchangeable. *Samurai* comes from the verb *saburu*, "to serve," and designates a military retainer. Not all *bushi* were samurai, and not all samurai were *bushi*, though in this period most were. Finally, *ashigaru* designates low-born soldiers, often peasant conscripts. *Ashigaru* were definitely not *bushi*, but they might be samurai of a sort. The important thing to note about these terms is that they are primarily class markers: They specify the soldier's place in a social hierarchy rather than his battlefield function. Thus, almost all *ashigaru* were foot soldiers because of their economic status, but *ashigaru* does not mean *foot soldier*. Even more important, samurai and *bushi* might or might not be mounted; and, even if a warrior owned a horse, he might well fight on foot. One should not assume *cavalry* for a force of samurai.

Still, elite soldiers were likely to have horses—here, as elsewhere in the world, riding was a sure sign of status—and they were well armed and armored. Japanese armor generally consisted of small plates or chain mail sewn with silk cords to silk and leather backings. Elaborate decorative helmets, sometimes topped with antlers, plumes, and so on, served as ready battlefield identifiers (much like European heraldry) and as protective gear. Japanese arms reflected the high quality of Japanese metallurgy, especially in sword making, which contained significant ritual and religious elements and produced swords unmatched in the world at this time. A well-armed warrior carried both a long sword and a short sword; some carried massive two-handed swords. An elite warrior's other weaponry would have included a bow and arrows, which he could fire either from horseback or on foot, and at times a spear or lance. Again, depending on terrain and the tactical situation, elite warriors were as likely to fight on foot as on horseback.

Ashigaru were much less well armed in this period. In fact, archaeological evidence from battlefield graves indicates that even helmets or other forms of head protection were rare. *Ashigaru* would have been peasant levies called out in emergencies, armed with little more than a simple spear and perhaps wearing a coarse silk or leather body garment but little else in the way of protective gear. *Ashigaru* were therefore not terribly useful except in defending walls, and they ended up being slaughtered by the elites when caught on the losing side of a battle.

Throughout this period, army sizes were quite small, usually in the hundreds. For major conflicts, the numbers may have risen into the thousands; probably only to meet the emergency of the Mongol invasions, however, did the strength of a Japanese army rise into the tens of thousands, and that effort, though successful, put intolerable strain on the political structure of the Kamakura *bakufu* (see below). Japan's administrative and economic resources were mostly insufficient for maintaining larger forces, while the concentration of armed power in a small elite and the limited cultural and political function of combat made larger forces generally unnecessary.

Armies at War   Geography and logistics also contributed to small army sizes. Japan is very mountainous, and much of it was heavily wooded in this period. Such conditions complicated the movement of large armies and made transport of supplies in wheeled carts problematic. Smaller forces could more easily traverse mountain roads and paths and forage for supplies. Furthermore, Japan's wet-field rice agriculture was concentrated in valleys favorable for such cultivation. The combination of natural and human geography tended to restrict the routes available to armies, and, as a result, certain key roads and districts became regular foci of campaigns. This in itself could create logistical problems, as the frequent passage of armies through a district was likely to do significant damage to the area's farms and rice fields. Even a rich district could become temporarily unsuitable for campaigning, and famine halted several campaigns in this period.

With conditions militating against long, sustained campaigns, strategy depended heavily on political and psychological factors. Alliance making was a key to strategy, because full conquest of enemy areas was logistically difficult. Even more, all conflict took place in the context of a unified polity and was thus in a way civil war. The traditional or hereditary claims of certain families to certain districts could not easily be eliminated through war; takeovers had to be legitimated from the center. Thus, strategy focused on seizing control of the center, often in terms of possession of the capital and a legitimate heir to the imperial throne. To do this required, again, a strong coalition of allied powers, held together by symbolic legitimacy and material success. The need for visible successes to hold coalitions together, in turn, favored battle-seeking strategies as opposed to extended campaigns.

In this context, fortifications played a secondary role in Japanese warfare in this period. Forts served as refuges and bases of operation, but they were not large, elaborate stone structures. Instead, wooden hilltop forts were common. Siege techniques were correspondingly simple, relying less on machines than on sudden assault, fire, and blockade in the rare last resort.

Battle tactics, too, reflected the political and cultural context. Many battles, including some substantial ones as at Kurikara in 1183, at least opened in a formalized, almost ritualized, style that imitated the art of heroic tales (and, in turn, generated further tales). With two armies facing each other, selected champions would advance individually or in small groups and issue challenges to the enemy. Such challenges loudly proclaimed the family, lineage, and connections of the challenger for all to hear. When an individual or group emerged to answer the challenge, an exchange of archery preceded sword fights on horse or on foot, depending on the terrain (see the Sources box "Japanese War Tales").

But such stylized fighting was only a part of Japanese battle. Ambushes and surprise attacks were frequent—indeed, at Kurikara, one side used the ritual phase of battle to cover a flanking maneuver by a contingent that then attacked suddenly from the rear. Deception, especially the use of banners (carried for group identification and as rallying points) to mislead the enemy as to an army's size or whereabouts, was common, and trickery involving birds and oxen are also recorded (see the Sources box). And beyond the ritual phase, battles were likely to be bloody: There was no intraclass ethic of sparing an enemy's life, nor any tradition of capture for ransom. A losing commander and the surviving remnants of a beaten army actually do seem to have been as likely to commit suicide as to surrender at the end of the day.

How do we account for the unusual combination of ritualized tactical display with high levels of killing within the confines of a warrior class? Factional politics again supplies the answer. As noted, conquest of land was neither practical nor politically possible when legitimate title to land and income was dispensed by a central authority. This reduced the importance of fortifications, as holding forts was not directly useful in such a context. But maintaining one's honor was useful. Advertising one's family in the challenge phase of a ritual battle and winning fame for oneself and one's family in individual combat could build or enhance a heroic reputation, which would then be useful in attracting followers or the notice of a powerful patron—that is, in building a powerful coalition. Even the honor earned through a heroic suicide might rescue for the family some of the advantage lost in a battle.

On the other hand, killing off one's rivals was also directly useful. Slaying all the battleworthy heirs of a house could eliminate it as a factional player and might even result in the reassignment of its lands to another family. Thus, ritual conflict and real killing reinforced each other in an unusual way, but the combination was logical and utilitarian given the political context and the culture that supported it.

But such warfare was not without consequences, as the results of the wars of the period drove the evolution of the Japanese political structure.

Political and Military Evolution

The Kamakura Shogunate, 1189–1333 Yoritomo placed the headquarters of his *bakufu* in Kamakura, a fishing village south of modern Tokyo and far from the imperial capital at Kyoto (Figure 14.2). This symbolized the division of authority that obtained at every level of government under the *bakufu*. The civil aristocrats and their bureaucratic offices continued to wield power within restricted spheres of authority, alongside the new military officials. While the balance of actual power lay somewhat with the military government, especially in terms of policing the population and administering justice among the warrior class, legitimacy flowed from the civil government, and income rights from the *shoen* were divided between civil and military officials. Inevitably, the disparity of force available to the *bakufu* meant that tensions were exploited steadily in favor of warriors and against the civil aristocracy. Such tensions increased after the retired emperor Go-Toba led an unsuccessful revolt in 1221 designed to restore direct imperial rule. But, until the civil war of 1331–33, the power-sharing arrangement continued to function.

The organization of the *bakufu* started with the shogun, though after Yoritomo's early death the shoguns themselves were figureheads under the control of the Hojo, the family of Yoritomo's widow. Under the shogun were the *shugo*, the military governors of the provinces of Japan. *Shugo* could be moved from province to province and removed from office. The *shugo*, in turn, supervised the warrior clans in their provinces, some of whom were linked more securely to the ruling family than others, depending on ties of kinship and loyalty.

Japanese War Tales

Although not always accurate with respect to the details of specific historical incidents (especially the number of combatants), medieval Japanese war tales paint a vivid picture of the battle practices, customs, and cultural conventions of the warrior elite. The following passages from Yoshitsune *and* The Taiheike *illustrate a number of these, including an early example of ritual suicide.*

■ ■ ■

[From *Yoshitsune.*] Suzuki Saburo sought to engage Terui Taro. "What are you called?" he shouted.

"Terui Taro Takaharu, a retainer of Lord Yasuhira."

"Then your master is one of Yoritomo's retainers. . . . I can't even count the number of my ancestors who have served the Genji, and I certainly have no business bothering with you, but a man ought to be ready to fight any enemy he meets on the field. All right! They tell me that you at least are one of Yasuhira's men who knows the meaning of shame. Will you show your back to another honorable man? Stop, coward!"

Shamed by these words, Terui returned to the fight, only to suffer a wound on his right shoulder and retreat again. Then Suzuki cut down five warriors, two on his left and three on his right, and wounded seven or eight more. In the fighting he himself was severely injured.

"Don't sell your life cheaply, Kamei Rokuro. I am finished." Those were Suzuki's last words before he ripped open his belly and fell dead.

[From *Taiheiki.*] Akamatsu led his three thousand horsemen toward the enemy camp. . . . [A]s these approached, they beheld two or three hundred family banners, fluttering in the breeze from the treetops eastward and westward of Segawa station, as though the enemy were indeed a great host of twenty or thirty thousand riders.

At the sight of these banners, seven of Akamatsu's warriors thought, "Not even one or two can we match against a hundred, if our force meets them in battle. Nonetheless, we must fall on this field, since there is no way of gaining a victory without fighting."

They moved up toward the southern mountains from the shelter of some bamboo. . . . Beholding them, the enemy moved the edges of their shields as though to attack; yet after all they but watched hesitantly while the seven flew down from off their horses to the shelter of a thick clump of bamboo, wherefrom they shot arrows furiously. By no means might the enemy escape those arrows, crowded together as close as tacks in a shoe, . . . but sorely stricken twenty-five of the closest men fell down headlong from off their horses. And the enemy warriors shielded themselves behind the foremost of their numbers, fearful lest their horses be wounded.

Then seven hundred of Akamatsu's riders struck their quivers and raised a victory shout, saying, "Aha! The enemy wavers!" They attacked with bridles aligned. . . .

When the foremost men of Rokuhara fell back, the rearmost failed to come forward in their stead, for it is ever thus when a mighty force wavers. Although the leaders commanded, "Withdraw in good order! The road is narrow!" heedlessly did sons desert their fathers and retainers forget their lords, and all fled thinking only of themselves. So they made their way back toward the capital, but more than half of their host were slain.

Akamatsu cut off the heads of three hundred wounded men and prisoners at Shuka-ga-wara, [and] hung them up. . . . That night they left Shuka-ga-wara without delay, pursuing the fleeing enemy in the direction of the capital and burning houses on their way to make a light.

SOURCE: Helen Craig McCullough, trans., *The Taiheike: A Chronicle of Medieval Japan* (New York: Columbia University Press, 1959) and *Yoshitsune: A Fifteenth Century Japanese Chronicle* (Stanford: Stanford University Press, 1966).

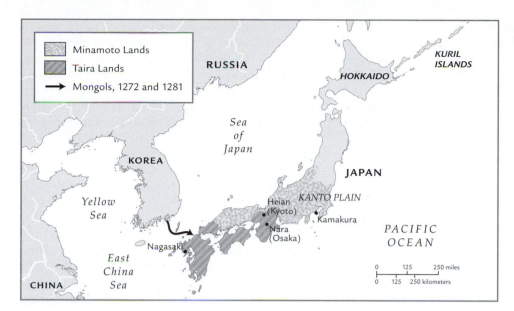

Figure 14.2 Kamakura and Muromachi Japan

The hierarchical system of warrior ties was held together in part by a system of grants and rewards. Income rights from the *shoen* were assigned for the maintenance of a warrior band and were usually augmented for meritorious service. Augmentation had to come from the incomes of losers in a struggle, as there was no external expansion possible to add to the *bakufu*'s landed resources. At the level of the *bakufu* and its major supporters and dependents among the warrior class, grants of landed income linked clan to clan rather than individual to individual, since the most important bond among the warrior class was kinship. Such ties were important both within extended families, with certain branches of a family recognized as senior, and between families, as some clans were traditionally dependents of others. Kinship ties could also be manufactured through adoption, as among the Roman ruling class. The importance of kinship as the primary bond of warrior society in this period also showed up at the highest level. The reason the Hojo family remained regents rather than assuming the shogunate themselves is that only descendants of the Minamoto could inherit that title, just as descendants of the imperial family had an exclusive claim to the throne, no matter how removed from actual power that title might be. Of course, this rule did not preclude civil war between different lines of the Minamoto clan (or the imperial family), as the civil war of 1331–33 would show. This demonstrates that the kinship bond held tremendous moral force, but practical sanctions for enforcing the claims of kin loyalty on uncooperative followers were often weak.

The potential flaws in the system holding together the *bakufu* were exposed in the aftermath of the Mongol invasions. The first of these, a large exploratory expedition, arrived from Korea in 1274, capturing the small islands of Tsushima and Iki before landing on northern Kyushu. Though caught somewhat by surprise by the invasion, the *bakufu* hastily assembled a force that attacked the Mongols near the beaches. This attack was defeated, in large part because the disciplined Mongols ignored the ritual elements of Japanese warfare and so caught the individualistic Japanese by surprise. But as more Japanese troops gathered, a storm wrecked part of the invasion fleet, and the remainder returned to Korea. A second, far larger, attack came in 1281, after the Japanese had refused to acknowledge Mongol suzerainty and killed the Mongol ambassadors. An army of perhaps 50,000 again landed on northern Kyushu, but this time met a prepared resistance. Though unable to drive the invaders back to their ships, the Japanese contained the landing force, limiting the space available for the Mongol cavalry to operate and restricting the invaders' ability to gather fresh supplies. Small Japanese ships also attacked the invading fleet at anchorage (see Chapter 15). When a typhoon wrecked the Mongol fleet, the stranded army, cut off from all supplies, was annihilated.

The invasions showed the Japanese warriors to be of high quality. Their weaponry and ability to fight equally well on horse or foot matched up well tactically against the Mongols, especially on a restricted battle-ground where Mongol unit cohesion could not be brought fully to bear. Japanese unity and morale in the face of the invasions was impressive. But once the threat had passed, the clans that had participated in the defense expected to be rewarded. The problem for the *bakufu* was that, again, there was no land from a defeated faction to distribute to meet these expectations. As a result, the bonds of loyalty between these clans and the Hojo weakened, and factional struggles within the *bakufu* increased.

In 1331, these simmering strains were brought to a boil by the revolt of Emperor Go Daigo, who aimed at restoring direct imperial rule. A number of important clans backed him, and the *bakufu* leadership responded less decisively than in 1221. Though defeated and captured in 1332, Go Daigo escaped and gained the backing of a number of top *bakufu* generals, including Ashikaga Takauji, a relative of the shogunal house. Kamakura fell to Go Daigo's forces in 1333 after a bitter battle in the streets of the city; the last Hojo defenders committed suicide.

The Muromachi Period, 1335–1467

Takauji then expected to be made shogun, but Go Daigo intended to rule directly. Takauji revolted in 1335, driving Go Daigo from Kyoto, placing a different member of the imperial house on the throne, and becoming shogun. But Go Daigo continued the struggle, and, until 1392, a bitter civil war ensued. It was settled only when Yoshimitsu, the third and strongest of the Ashikaga shoguns, negotiated a settlement with Go Daigo's successor, who abdicated, reuniting the throne.

The Ashikaga shoguns established their capital in the Muromachi section of Kyoto (hence historians' name for the period) alongside the imperial court (see Figure 14.2). This symbolized the complete eclipse of the civil aristocracy and the end of the divided, power-sharing arrangement of the Kamakura period. The warrior class was now dominant. But this dominance came at a cost: The legitimacy provided to warrior power by the civil government now ceased to exist. The problem was exacerbated by the divided throne prior to 1392 and by the more obvious puppet status of the emperor in Kyoto throughout the period. The justification for rule was increasingly "might makes right," a recipe for instability that proved to be one of a set of structural weaknesses that plagued Ashikaga government.

In addition to establishing themselves in Kyoto, the shoguns required the *shugo*, the military gover-nors of the provinces, to reside much of the year in the capital, so as to manage them and their ambitions more closely. This put the shoguns at the center of the nation's politics, as somewhat more than a first among equals with the *shugo* but somewhat less than in complete control. But removing the *shugo* from their provinces for long periods meant a divorce of central authority figures from their local subordinates and lieutenants, who increasingly turned to bolstering their positions in the local areas they administered. As another curb on potential *shugo* revolts and independence, the shoguns tended to appoint *shugo* to provinces where they had little or no land of their own. Since control of land and the income it represented was the ultimate basis of the power and cohesion of warrior groups, this step tended to divorce formal authority from actual power in the provinces. Both absentee leadership and divided authority and power at the local level fostered continued village independence. In all, the warrior class of the Muromachi period was dominant politically but very insecurely rooted in the soil of local power, with underdeveloped mechanisms of district governance.

But the period also saw significant developments, and the power of the central government was not as stunted as appears on first inspection. First, this was a period of economic growth, especially in terms of overseas trade. The shoguns largely controlled the duties and taxes accruing from trade, and the financial resources this provided contributed in large part to their dominant position among the *shugo*. Second, most trade was with China, and the period also saw a new and significant wave of cultural borrowing from the Ming. This indicates the growing cultural sophistication of the warrior class—literacy was widespread, and, as they moved to the capital, the warriors assumed some of the literary trappings of the old civil aristocracy. The shoguns, partly because of their control of trade, were at the center of cultural developments and derived significant prestige from their patronage of the arts.

Two other developments were important for the structure of the warrior class. First, the long civil war and the instability of a might-makes-right justification of power led to a decline in kinship as the key bond among warriors, as its weakening moral force proved unable to meet the stresses of the age. Second, the same instabilities, combined with the disappearance of the old civil aristocracy, gradually erased the remains of the old *shoen*, and assignment of income rights from them faded as the chief mechanism of material reward for armed retainers. Instead, in an attempt to tie their increasingly unruly subordinates to them more securely, local and regional warlords began granting control over actual pieces of land, called *chiggyo*, to their followers. *Chiggyo* began to form the bases of local power alliances, underneath the level of the *shugo*, and carried a potential new emphasis on territoriality since the grants came from areas under a local warlord's direct control. These two developments, clearly related, would take on added significance when the mechanisms of central government that contained local conflict disintegrated after 1467.

The Onin War, 1467–77   A succession dispute in 1467 in the Ashikaga family triggered an intense conflict in and around Kyoto. It lasted ten years and drew in most of the *shugo* and their immediate followers. Many of the most prominent *shugo* died in the struggle, and the *shugo* as a class virtually self-destructed. Though the succession to the shogunate was settled in 1477, the balance of *shugo* power on which the shogun's authority had rested was destroyed. From 1477 until the Ashikaga shogunate was ended by Oda Nobunaga in 1573, it was little more than a regional power around Kyoto.

In fact, the Onin War effectively destroyed central power in Japan, as the shogun and emperor were for the time being merely figureheads. The *daimyo*, the subordinates of the *shugo* who had been building their power bases in the provinces, now emerged as effectively independent powers ruling the more than 100 small states into which the Japanese archipelago was now divided. These independent states would become the breeding ground for a Japanese military revolution in the following century, a topic taken up in Chapter 19.

India, 1192–1565

Politics and Warfare

The classical roots of Indian political structures and warfare had developed by this era into a pattern with several important characteristics for military history. First, Indian warfare was conducted not by states but by a complex hierarchy of elites: There was little notion in the culture of firm borders and governments with monopolies on the use of violence, partly because the right, and duty, of bearing arms was class

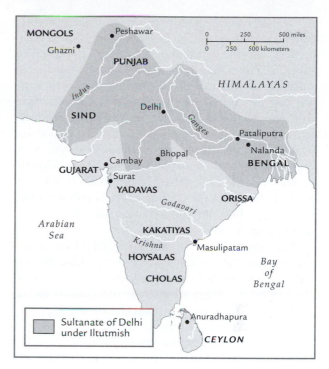

Figure 14.3 India in the Time of the Delhi Sultanate

and caste bound. This created a shifting political terrain for conflicts that were more about confirming a symbolic pecking order than about territorial conquest. This led to a second characteristic of Indian politics: Allegiances were almost always for sale at any time in a conflict. The geopolitics of the subcontinent were further complicated by the continued existence of a large inner frontier consisting of the jungle and arid areas unsuitable to settled agriculture. Such areas became pathways for pastoralists, merchants, and warrior bands, and they were therefore paradoxically sources of both instability and resources, monetary and military, for settled areas. It was into this complex landscape that Muslims began to raid in the 800s and to initiate conquests in the late 900s.

The Delhi Sultanate   Muslim armies were composed primarily of Turkish slave soldiers (see Chapters 8 and 11)—mounted archers supported by heavy lancers. They found easy pickings in the rich north Indian plains. Drawn by plunder and the divided resistance of the Hindu Rajput states, raiding became conquest. A major victory over a Rajput coalition in 1192 opened nearly all north India to occupation; in 1206, the Delhi Sultanate was founded (Figure 14.3).

The Muslim Turkish population of the Sultanate formed a military ruling class, but it was tiny in comparison with the vast numbers of their Hindu Indian subjects. The sultans in the early decades also limited rulership to Turks, meaning other Muslims and Muslim converts were excluded from the top positions. This also hindered administration of their territories and required that they receive constant infusions of fresh Turkish slave soldiers. In this, the sultans were both assisted and ultimately harmed by the Mongol invasions of the rest of the Muslim world (see Chapter 13): Early Mongol conquests drove refugee Turks into India, but the consolidation of Mongol rule dried up the supply.

The most successful and powerful of the Delhi sultans was Balban (ruled 1249–87), whose success lay not so much in conquest as in his steps to strengthen the sultan's power at the expense of the Turkish nobles who exercised much local power. Much like Qubilai Khan in Yüan China, Balban attempted to establish a true monarchy with centrally administered and directed armies. But his successors were unable to continue his progress, and the Delhi Sultanate reverted to the previous pattern whereby the sultan was more a Central Asian chieftain who directly controlled only his own forces and needed the approval of the nobility for any major actions or military expeditions. The Central Asian pattern was reinforced by the Indian pattern of shifting alliances, which continued to operate among Hindu princes within the context of the sultan's nominal overlordship. Muslim rule therefore failed to transform the Indian political structure.

Military Transformations

Militarily, however, the Islamic Turkish style of fighting had a significant impact on Indian warfare. In almost every encounter in northern India, and most of those in the south as well, the Muslim armies were smaller—sometimes considerably so—than their Rajput opponents. That they won most of these battles was not usually due to the inexperience of Rajput forces. Rajput armies were veterans of centuries of constant combat with each other. Defeat at the hands of Muslim armies was primarily due to two factors: Rajput disunity and inferior tactics, strategy, and weapons.

Rajput princes rarely saw the invasions as invaders versus Indians or Muslims versus Hindus. Some Rajput princes, in fact, were quite happy to see longtime local enemies destroyed by the Muslims, and some even helped the invaders against their traditional enemies—a logical extension of the practice of shifting alliances. Most of the few attempts at unity were acts of desperation in the face of an oncoming enemy force. Such unity as resulted was mainly formal, with little coordination of the allied units. In contrast, the Muslim armies, in the first couple of centuries of the invasions at least, were united, disciplined, and well led. The Muslims usually took care to see that their men were paid, they were supplied with adequate provisions, and they and their families were taken care of in case of injury or death.

In terms of experience, the centuries of Rajput warfare are misleading, since Rajput strategy and tactics were basically the same as those of the Guptas centuries earlier (see Chapter 4). The key to most of their battles was the use of elephants as instruments of shock. There was almost no cavalry, which formed the main military arm of the invading Muslims. Horses and camels gave the Muslims much greater mobility, and they learned not only how to evade the massive elephant charges but how to turn them against the Rajputs. Often, the elephants ended up killing and disrupting the Indians far more than they did the Muslims. The Muslim use of cavalry was also devastating to the large but untrained infantry formations of the Rajputs. Time and again, disciplined cavalry formations handily dispersed the Rajput infantry.

The use of cavalry in Indian warfare was not new, but it had been limited by the small number of Indian regions in which horses could be bred. The Muslim conquests radically increased the importance of the warhorse and mounted archer in Indian warfare, while opening wide the trade routes to central Asia that supplied horses. Horse-archers were able to campaign across the inner frontier and so make widespread conquests easier, but they could not occupy or tame the outer frontier regions, which remained a source of instability. The Delhi Sultanate's political disintegration therefore began soon after its expansion.

Also, Muslim weapons were generally superior to those possessed by the Rajput armies. For the most part, their advantage was simply in the quality of their individual weapons, especially swords and bows. This was due both to the relative isolation of the Indian states and to the deleterious effect of the caste system. By this period, the caste system had become much more rigid. During earlier periods, especially the time of the Mauryans and Guptas, weapons makers held high prestige, and many members of higher castes were engaged in weapons production. By the eleventh century, however, this was uncommon, as weapons makers had been relegated to some of the lowest castes. Military commanders, unlike many of the Muslim generals, paid little heed to weapons and their construction. But Muslim armies also brought improved siege weapons, especially the traction trebuchet, from the Near East. Combined with mobile armies of horse-archers, these siege weapons boosted offensive capabilities and aided conquests.

Such advantages proved decisive in north India. But the difficult terrain of south India and its distance from the centers of Muslim power and horse breeding in the north, made for a much more even contest. And, in the thirteenth and fourteenth centuries, Indian fortress building improved in response to the challenge of the trebuchet, renewing the advantage of the defense, which, in turn, reinforced shifting alliances and the tendency to end sieges by bribery. In addition, the rise of a major southern kingdom provided unity in the south for over two centuries.

Vijayanagara, 1336–1565

The Delhi Sultanate tried to but could never maintain a consistent presence in southern India. However, the military campaigns of the Sultanate to conquer the south stimulated the establishment of the kingdom of Vijayanagara. Much Indian political and military history of the late fourteenth and fifteenth centuries consists of war between various Muslim territories and Vijayanagara.

The kingdom became very wealthy through control of trade and tribute in the region, such tribute often being obtained through military force. Vijayanagara was named for its capital city, whose name means "City of Victory" and which was defended by an elaborate series of walls and trenches. This was necessary to defend against not only the Muslims but other Hindu enemies in the southeast, especially the kingdom of Orissa. Throughout its history, Vijayanagara was an armed state with an army that reportedly reached into the hundreds of thousands.

The army of Vijayanagara was primarily infantry, with a small but important cavalry arm. Harihara, the founder of the kingdom, had introduced cavalry after his experiences fighting with the Delhi sultans. Most of the early cavalrymen were Turks who had been persuaded to defect to Vijayanagara or who had been captured in battle and offered the choice of defection or execution. Vijayanagara's cavalry could never be large, especially because it was always difficult to acquire the necessary horses. Vijayanagara's greatest period of glory came with the arrival of Portuguese traders, for the main item purchased from the Portuguese was horses for its cavalry. After victories over neighbors, Vijayanagara usually required payment of tribute and provision of soldiers, but it did not impose direct administration.

The kingdom of Vijayanagara was utterly destroyed in the battle of Talikot in 1565. The collapse of the kingdom seriously weakened Portuguese power in the area, as Vijayanagara had been Portugal's main land-based ally in India, and left south India exposed to conquest by the newly established Mughal Empire (see Chapter 17).

CONCLUSION

While the pressures of this age, especially the direct and indirect consequences of the Mongol invasions, were similar for most of east and south Asia, the responses differed considerably, even in purely military terms. This reflected in part the very different place that warriors held in the social and political hierarchies of China, Japan, and India (see the Issues box "Warrior Elites"). In turn, the differing military responses of each area meant that each would face the new challenges of an age of even greater global contact after 1500 in different ways. The weight of China and India in global systems of trade would give worldwide significance to how they met those challenges.

ISSUES

Warrior Elites

Successive Chinese dynasties struggled with a serious problem: Too much civilian control of the army, and military effectiveness suffered; too little control, and overmighty generals could threaten the stability of the government. A similar struggle between military and civil aristocrats dominated Japanese politics for centuries. These two cases highlight what was, in fact, a general problem in traditional societies: the place of warriors among a civilization's elites. For the military historian, this is a rich theme whose outlines we can only sketch here.

Because of their ability to wield force directly, warriors formed at least a portion of the socio-political ruling class in nearly every traditional society, sedentary or nomadic. (*Warriors,* conceived here as elites whose lifestyle and values were military, are to be distinguished from *soldiers,* the mass of non-elite members of a military system. The distinction is one of individual status, not necessarily military function.) Warrior elites were often, though not always, rural-based landholders. This was in part because land was necessary for raising horses and horsemen, and warrior elites tended to be horsemen because of the status, prestige, and individual military advantage that ownership of horses (large, expensive, mobile commodities) conveyed. This rural bias set up one potential conflict with other elites, civil or religious, who tended to be city-based: the tension between rural warrior values and urban civilian values.

This tension often exacerbated a deeper structural problem. Warriors might have wielded power and influence, but they rarely wielded, strictly as warriors, legitimate authority. In other words, claiming "might makes right" was recognized as a limited and inadequate justification of social or state power, even if the might lay behind some other form of legitimation. The Chinese proverb that one could win but not govern an empire from horseback expresses this problem neatly. The ques-

tion, therefore, became this: What connected military force to the philosophical and religious justifications of social and state power? In practice, this was often expressed in terms of the relationship of warrior elites to civil and religious elites.

The answers to this problem proved manifold. In China, civilian control was generally dominant, while in Japan, the practical triumph of the warriors led to instability, military transformation, and a search for legitimacy (see this chapter and Chapter 19). Balance initially, but eventually destructive conflict, between military and civil aristocrats was central to Byzantium's history (see Chapter 8). A long but more creative conflict between states dominated by a warrior aristocracy and a separate church hierarchy defined crucial aspects of western Europe's development (see Chapter 12). Islam seemed to have the most difficulty with this issue, as the widespread use of slave soldiers (who at times came to rule, as in Mamluk Egypt) attests (see Chapters 8 and 11). The division of legitimacy in the Hindu tradition between religious and military leaders, at the other extreme, proved uncontentious within the culture but failed to provide either political stability or military effectiveness in the face of Muslim invasions (as we discussed in this chapter). Perhaps only in the societies of horsed nomads, where military authority, lifestyle, and social structure came together seamlessly and pervaded the entire society, not just its elites, was this issue not problematic—and, then, only until a successful nomad group conquered a sedentary area and set themselves up as a rural warrior elite. Then, as the Yüan emperors of China and the Ottoman emperors discovered, the same issues reappeared.

Clearly, the integration of warriors and military force into a stable and legitimate hierarchy was one of the enduring problems for traditional civilizations. There is plenty of room for further comparative exploration of the dynamics of this problem.

SUGGESTED READINGS

The Cambridge History of Japan, Vol. 3: Medieval Japan. Cambridge: Cambridge University Press, 1990. Not focused on military history, but the standard wide-ranging introduction to this period in Japan.

Chan, Albert. *The Glory and Fall of the Ming Dynasty.* Norman: University of Oklahoma Press, 1982. Includes several chapters dealing specifically with the organization and use of the armies of the Ming dynasty.

Dreyer, Edward L. *Early Ming China: A Political History, 1355–1435.* Stanford: Stanford University Press, 1982. An excellent discussion of the early Ming military system, including some information on the early campaigns.

Friday, Karl. *Samurai, Warfare and the State in Early Medieval Japan.* London: Routledge, 2004. An excellent reinterpretation of Japanese warfare up to 1400; stresses the intimate connection of war and politics. See also his *Hired Swords: The Rise of Private Warrior Power in Early Japan* (Stanford: Stanford University Press, 1992), which reassesses the growth of warrior power, emphasizing legitimate ties to civil government.

Hsiao, Ch'i Ch'ing. *The Military Establishment of the Yüan Dynasty.* Cambridge: Harvard University Press, 1978. Mostly a translation of the military sections of the official history of the Yüan dynasty, with some commentary.

Jackson, Peter. *The Delhi Sultanate: A Political and Military History.* Cambridge: Cambridge University Press, 1999. Contains an enormous amount of information on the political intrigue of this complicated era in India's history.

Mass, Jeffrey. *Warrior Government in Early Medieval Japan.* New Haven: Yale University Press, 1974. A detailed examination of the administrative and political structures of the Kamakura *bakufu.*

Rossabi, Morris. *Qubilai Khan: His Life and Times.* See Chapter 13.

Tillman, Hoyt T., and Stephen H. West, eds. *China Under Jurchen Rule.* Albany: SUNY Press, 1995. Discusses the reaction of Song Chinese to the Jurchen invasions, with some excellent sections on military responses.

Turnbull, Stephen. *The Samurai. A Military History.* London: Routledge, 1987. A straightforward narrative account of the wars of the period, based closely on primary sources.

Varley, Paul. *Warriors of Japan as Portrayed in the War Tales.* Honolulu: University of Hawaii Press, 1994. Analyzes the culture, values, and methods of warfare of the warrior class through their literature.

Wolpert, Stanley. *A New History of India,* 5th ed., Oxford: Oxford University Press, 1997. A generally good narrative overview of India, including the political, religious, and military problems associated with the Muslim invasions.

CHAPTER 15

Mariners and Merchants: Naval Warfare, 1100–1571

The centuries between 1100 and 1571 saw significant developments in maritime activity and naval warfare. Continued growth in the size and importance of global trade networks acted as the major stimulus for change, affecting the organization, goals, and technology of merchant and war fleets.

The two models of naval activity that dominated the previous period of naval warfare—navies of imperial defense and predatory sea peoples—continued to exist. Song China fit the former, while Japanese *wako,* pirates who roamed the China Sea, carried on the latter tradition. But both models declined in importance. Byzantium, the classic model of imperial defense, ceased to be a naval power; and, with the decline in Viking and Chola raids, predation generally gave way to more organized naval activity, peaceful and warlike. This was possible in part because the growing wealth generated by world trade made higher levels of political organization possible along the international trade routes.

In fact, both models tended to converge on a new model of naval activity that was government directed or sponsored, as in the imperial defense model, but in greater partnership with thriving merchant marines and with trade assuming a more central role. Thus, this new model also tended to be outward looking and even aggressive, as the predatory model had been, but, again, with a far greater measure of formal government organization and permanence. Imperial navies assumed a more offensive role, as under the Yüan in China and the Ottomans in the Mediterranean. In addition, increasing exploration of trade routes by naval forces combined mercantile, military, and even religious motivations, as under the Ming in China and the Portuguese in western Europe. While the balance between governmental and private interests varied widely among the many instances of this developing model, it is nevertheless reasonable to refer to this as the capitalist, or at least proto-capitalist, model of naval activity.

In large part because of the emergence of this new model, this was also a period of significant advances in maritime technology. The changes mostly affected the seaworthiness and navigability of sailing ships. Such changes made ships more efficient and profitable carriers of goods, and so created a self-reinforcing trend of rising trade and improving technology. They also presaged the eventual decline of oared ships as a significant factor in trade or warfare. But only late in the period would technology begin to affect tactics or significantly change the potential uses of naval force. For most of this period, naval tactics, including those of oared galleys, remained relatively stable, as traditions established in earlier ages in response to the particular environments of each area were developed and elaborated. And the basic character of naval warfare—as essentially an amphibious extension of land warfare—remained unchanged. *Control of the seas*—in terms of active, continual patrol and domination of sea-lanes by cruising fleets—was still a technological impossibility. "Control" therefore remained conceived of and practiced more as an adjunct of land-based power.

In the latter half of this period, two areas in particular, China and Europe, would lead the way in exploiting the technological advances of the age to extend the range and influence of seaborne military might. Comparison of these two areas, however, demonstrates the variations the new model of naval activity was subject to and shows that the context into which technology is introduced influences the effect of that technology significantly. There was no simple, deterministic path from better technology to domination of the seas. In the end, new models of naval organization and technological advances laid foundations for a new age of naval warfare as a much more independent branch of military endeavor—indeed, perhaps the most important branch in the following 250 years.

EXPERIMENTATION, 1050–1368

The Mediterranean

The Mediterranean remained dominated by fleets of oared fighting ships. Galleys, with their large crews of rowers (almost exclusively free men in this period) who doubled as fighting men, efficiently performed several military functions (see below). But the same large crews tied the galleys close to shore and friendly ports and bases, as did their limited sailing characteristics. Large crews also made galley fleets sensitive to fluctuations in their economic and governmental support systems. Geography, commerce, and politics all shaped the shifting fortunes of the Mediterranean's major naval powers.

Arab Decline   The south coast of the Mediterranean was at a disadvantage as a base for naval operations of any kind. It had fewer safe harbors than the north, and prevailing northwesterly wind patterns made it more dangerous and harder to get from there to the main trade routes. As the central islands of the sea, especially Crete and then Sicily and the Balearics of east Spain, fell to Christian powers, this geographic disadvantage became acute. As a result, up through the mid-fourteenth century, trade fell increasingly into Christian hands, and Muslim navies were more and more restricted in their size, scope, and effectiveness. A strong, centralized Arab state may have been able to hold the central islands and maintain a greater balance, but it was a fragmented Arab world that faced newly aggressive assaults by Normans, Italians, and Spaniards from the late eleventh century. Compounding Muslim problems, Arab lands began to suffer timber shortages. Higher prices for wood made Muslim shipbuilding less competitive commercially. Thus, though Muslim piracy and commerce raiding never disappeared, especially from the western basin while Muslims held on to parts of the Iberian Peninsula, Christian trade was fairly secure in most areas, and much Muslim trade ended up carried in Christian ships.

Byzantine Decline   As a Christian power with the advantage of the north shore, the decline of Byzantine naval power—once dominant in the eastern Mediterranean—after 1050 is more complex and essentially political.

In the first place, naval military forces suffered from the same internal power struggles that undermined the army in the half-century after Basil II's death in 1025 (see Chapter 8). Briefly, rivalry between civil bureaucrats in the capital at Constantinople and military aristocrats in the provinces wreaked havoc on the Byzantine military establishment. The bureaucrats, anxious to undermine the powers of the provincial military families, disbanded the forces of the themes (military districts)—forces that included rowers and marines in the coastal themes of Asia Minor and Greece. The central, professional units of the military, the tagmata, were also both weakened and increasingly manned by foreign mercenaries; this undermined the central squadrons of the imperial navy as well as the army. The results of this civil-military rivalry showed up for the army in 1071 at Manzikert. But, in the same year, the Normans took Bari, the last Byzantine outpost in Italy, restricting Byzantine naval options and exposing the decline in Byzantine amphibious capability.

A deeper political dynamic also affected the imperial navy. The empire's grand strategic posture had been essentially defensive for centuries, and even as it expanded in the tenth century, a "fortress Byzantium" outlook remained dominant. One consequence of this was that trade and commerce were viewed as part of imperial defense policy. Greek merchants were tightly regulated and prohibited from trading outside the empire, leaving long-distance commerce to be carried out by foreign merchants. With the loss of Byzantine possessions in Italy, this restriction increasingly undermined the Greek merchant marine. Given the close connection of all types of seafaring activity, this competitive disadvantage also undermined the financial and manpower bases of the Byzantine navy.

In the period of crisis after 1071, the Italians gained a decisive hold over Byzantine commerce. This proved profitable for Italy but damaging for Byzantium, as the tensions the arrangement created contributed directly to the redirection of the Fourth Crusade to Constantinople and the sack of the city in 1204.

The Rise of the Italians and Iberians   Though Norman military power played a significant role in taking ports from both Arabs and Byzantines, the major contributors to and beneficiaries of these declines were Italian city-states, followed later by Aragon in Spain. Venice, nominally a Byzantine outpost, rose in its former protector's place, while western Italian cities led by Genoa spearheaded the assault on Muslim power. A number of factors contributed to Italian success, including natural geography, political geography, and political structure.

First, Italian ports were well situated geographically. They lay at the center of the major trade arteries that followed the north shore of the Mediterranean, with easy access to the central islands and thence to all corners of the sea. At least prior to the mid-fourteenth century, supplies of timber and other raw materials were plentiful.

Second, they also benefited from their political geography. The north Italian cities that led the Latin Christian naval resurgence were effectively independent city-states. Venice was subject to a distant and weakening Byzantine emperor; much of the rest of north Italy was under a distant German emperor, whose attempts at closer rule were repulsed in the twelfth century. Lacking large hinterlands, these city-states depended on trade and piracy for their wealth and power, and so had a large stake in maintaining effective naval forces.

Indeed, given that much of their trade in eastern luxuries could profitably and safely be carried in galleys, there was often little distinction between each city-state's merchant and war fleets. Success in piracy and raids on rival Muslim ports was good for business; thriving business financed the ships that conducted raids. Mediterranean commerce was always at some level a *guerre de course,* a little war against commerce, of corsairs and merchants, which exploded periodically into larger fleet actions, both between Christian and Muslim fleets and, at times, between Christian fleets in contests for commercial dominance. Venice and Genoa became particularly heated rivals. The independent political position of these city-states served well in this environment and contributed to their third advantage, political structure. Limited hinterlands not only made the city-states dependent on trade but reduced the power of landed aristocrats in government. Instead, merchant oligarchs often dominated city-state governments, ensuring trade-friendly policies and support for maritime defense. In most cases, "private" commerce and "public" military action were so entwined as to be almost inseparable. Large land-based states, Muslim or Byzantine, could not easily develop such a symbiotic relationship with their merchants because traditional landed interests predominated. In short, Italian city-states pioneered the proto-capitalist organization of naval force.

The key weapon in Mediterranean maritime struggles was, as noted above, the galley. Long and narrow, it was powered by oars set on two levels, on the model of the Byzantine *dromon;* by the twelfth century, an arrangement of three men to a bench on one level, each with his own oar, was more common. Rowing provided the galley with tactical maneuverability, the capability of short bursts of speed, and the ability to get in and out of harbors and to make progress in calm winds. For cruising, galleys had one or two large lateen-rigged sails on masts that could be lowered for tactical action. Galleys were not great sailers and had limited seaworthiness, and so kept close to shore, but they were made for the Mediterranean's generally flat, tideless seas and predictable weather patterns between mid-March and mid-October.

Galleys by the eleventh century were no longer equipped with underwater beaks for ramming. Rather, the beak had moved above the waterline and become a combination grappling hook and boarding ramp, as the main galley battle tactic in this age was boarding. The primary reason for this was economic. Ships were expensive, not to mention the value of their cargo and the potential value of their crews as slaves. With the decline of Byzantium, no power in the Mediterranean was wealthy enough or sufficiently strategically focused on imperial defense to afford tactics based predominantly on sinking enemy ships. In addition, the Byzantines had given up ramming in favor of Greek Fire (see Chapter 10) as a more effective way of ship killing, but the formula for Greek Fire was gradually lost during this period. Boarding for capture was thus left as the dominant galley tactic. This tactic was also reflected in the rowers—skilled free men who added to a galley's fighting manpower and often shared in the financial rewards of its success. The semiprivate, proto-capitalist organization of Italian naval forces especially reinforced this trend, with the galley functioning as a communal enterprise. The galley's ability to reliably deliver large numbers of soldiers over and above its 120–150 oarsmen, as well as its tactical maneuverability, made it the perfect craft for amphibious raids and assaults on enemy coasts and ports, for commerce raiding and piracy, and for fleet actions.

The Crusades advanced the interests of the Italian maritime powers and showed the amphibious nature of sea power in this age. The capture of the ports of the Holy Land, after the First Crusade took Jerusalem, was facilitated by Italian fleets, which brought supplies to the Latin besiegers, prevented seaborne relief from getting into the ports, and carried new pilgrims and crusaders to the sieges. In exchange, the Italians received trading privileges in the new Crusader States. In addition, by pushing the nearest Muslim naval bases down into Egypt, the Latin conquest of the coast secured the safety of that trade, as the lack of watering stations between Egypt and Palestine put Muslim fleets at the end of their logistical rope by the time they reached Christian ports. This effect was magnified greatly when crusading forces carried on Italian fleets captured key islands: Richard the Lion-Hearted's conquest of Cyprus in the Third Crusade was probably the most significant of these actions. The establishment of the Crusader States then stimulated expansion of the pilgrim trade, much of which was carried (at a profit, of course) on Italian ships. Likewise, major crusades came increasingly to depend on naval transport, which was quicker and easier than the overland route through Turkish Asia Minor. Thus, while trade with the Near East was growing anyway, the Crusades (including the Fourth against Byzantium) helped seal Italian dominance in the eastern Mediterranean, at least until the rise of Ottoman power in the fifteenth century. Meanwhile, the same crusading impulse was advancing the Christian reconquest of Iberia (Lisbon fell to English and Norman forces on the way to the Second Crusade in 1147, for example), raising the fortunes of Spanish naval power in the western Mediterranean. By 1350, the whole sea was virtually one big Christian lake.

The North Sea–Baltic Sea World

The maritime world of the North Atlantic, the North Sea, and the Baltic Sea saw less armed conflict than the Mediterranean. In large part, this was because nature was more hostile there: The seas of the north are rougher, the tides significant, and the shores often treacherous with shallows and strong currents. Thus, the battle was not among ships, but between ships and the seas. Mediterranean-style galleys could not survive in such waters, and so there was much less differentiation of warships from merchant vessels—a condition that was, globally, the norm.

There was conflict involving ships, and, as in the Mediterranean (and as earlier in this world with the Vikings), it was essentially the amphibious warfare of coastal and river raids. Oared ships in the Scandinavian shipbuilding tradition continued to play a limited role in such warfare. Ships played a significant role in the Latin Christian advances into Baltic lands, acting as supply and troop transports. It was this capacity that

Medieval Cog   This drawing shows a cog—a deep, round merchant craft driven by a single square sail. Temporary wooden "castles" could be added at the bow and stern to convert it into a warship.

focused German colonization first along coasts and rivers, and it was this capacity also that helped make the new colonies economically viable by tying them to existing waterborne trade networks.

The apparent exception to this rule was the English Channel, which did see periodic battles between fleets. In 1088, King William Rufus's fleet (possibly of Anglo-Saxons) defeated an invasion fleet sent by his brother Robert of Normandy off Rochester, reportedly sinking many ships. In 1217, the followers of the late King John defeated a French fleet off Sandwich. And the Hundred Years War saw intensified conflict in the Channel, including the major battle of Sluys in 1340 (see the Sources box "The Battle of Sluys, 1340"). But all these actions were fought close to shore, and control of the sea was again not possible in a modern sense. Though northern ships, especially by the time of Sluys, theoretically had greater logistical range than Mediterranean galleys ever could, their still-limited sailing and navigational abilities prevented their staying at sea for any length of time. Even more, the limited administrative and financial resources of northern kingdoms meant that fleets were temporary creations made up largely of requisitioned merchant vessels. Neither their governments nor their economies could yet afford to maintain such fleets permanently.

The key advances in ship design were, in fact, driven by commerce, as it was during this period that

SOURCES

The Battle of Sluys, 1340

In these excerpts, the chronicler and poet Jean Froissart gives a vivid account of a contemporary sea battle.

■ ■ ■

On 22 June 1340, [King Edward III] set sail from the Thames Estuary with a large fleet of fine ships and steered straight towards Sluys. . . . [The French fleet] was made up of close on a hundred and fifty big ships, without counting the barges, and carried a good forty thousand men—Normans, light infantry, Genoese and Picards. This fleet was drawn up at anchor, on orders from the King of France, to await the English, who they knew must pass that way, and prevent them from reaching the coast.

The King [Edward] then redisposed his whole fleet, putting his most powerful ships in the van and placing vessels filled with archers on all the sides, and between every two shiploads of archers there was one of men-at-arms. In addition, he detached a flanking squadron made up entirely of archers, which was to give support wherever needed to the most heavily engaged. . . .

When King Edward and his Marshal had completed the disposition of their fleet, they had the sails hoisted to catch the wind on their starboard quarter, in order to avoid the glare of the sun, which was shining straight in their faces. Considering that this would be a disadvantage, they fell away a little and came around until they had all the wind they wanted. . . . [The French] put their ships in readiness, like the skilled seamen and good fighters they were, and set the big ship *Christopher,* which they had taken from the English that same year, in the van with a big company of Genoese crossbowmen on board to defend it and harass the English. Then they sounded scores of trumpets, horns and other instruments and bore down on their enemies to engage them.

Fierce fighting broke out on every side, archers and crossbowmen shooting arrows and bolts at each other pell-mell, and men-at-arms struggling and striking in hand-to-hand combat. In order to come to close quarters, they had great iron grappling-hooks fixed to chains, and these they hurled into each others' ships to draw them together and hold them fast while the men engaged. Many deadly blows were struck and gallant deeds performed, ships and men were battered, captured and recaptured. The great ship *Christopher* was recovered by the English at the beginning of the battle and all those on board were killed or taken prisoner. This capture took place in the midst of tremendous clamour and shouting, at which more English came to the scene and immediately re-manned her with a force made up entirely of archers, before sending her forward to confront the Genoese.

It was indeed a bloody and murderous battle. Sea-fights are always fiercer than fights on land, because retreat and flight are impossible. Every man is obliged to hazard his life and hope for success, relying on his own personal bravery and skill. . . . Thus the battle continued to rage furiously from the early morning until afternoon, during which time there were many notable feats of arms and the English were hard put to it to hold their own, since they were opposed by hardened soldiers and seamen, who outnumbered them four to one. . . .

But they performed with such courage that, thanks to a reinforcement from Bruges and the surrounding district that came to their support, they at last obtained the victory. The Normans and all who were with them were utterly defeated, killed or drowned, not a single one escaping in the general slaughter. . . . The next day the King entered the harbour and disembarked with all his men.

SOURCE: Jean Froissart, *Chronicles,* ed. and trans. Geoffrey Brereton (New York: Penguin Books, 1968).

the cog emerged as the workhorse of northern waters. The cog was an excellent cargo ship due to its large capacity, and with a single square sail and a sternpost rudder, a significant advance over sideboard rudders, it sailed well enough to be a very profitable vessel. It formed the backbone of the northern merchant fleets of the Hanseatic League, the Netherlands, and England.

The cog also proved to be readily and effectively adaptable to wartime use: Substantial cargo capacity meant that it could carry large numbers of armed men, horses, or military supplies as a transport ship. And loading a cog with soldiers also instantly made it a formidable warship, since boarding was the primary tactic in northern naval warfare. The cog offered a further advantage as a warship: a high freeboard. This feature contributed to the cog's improved sea-keeping ability and increased cargo space and also made it a superior fighting platform, especially when wooden "castles" were added fore and aft. Such structures could be added on temporarily but were increasingly incorporated into the hulls from the start. They gave archers and crossbowmen a height advantage in firing down at their opponents. Archers could be stationed in fighting tops on the mast for the same reason.

Naval battles, when they occurred, were thus mass melees fought ship to ship. A fleet might also be trapped in port and burnt. Such decisive actions were rare, however. The meeting of two relatively equal fleets seldom came about, and the limitations of maneuverability of vessels rigged with a single square sail meant that, if one fleet wished to avoid combat, it almost always could. Small coastal raids and amphibious actions were more common and, as in the Mediterranean, crossed the already blurry lines between piracy, commerce, and war.

China

The already active Song era of Chinese maritime history intensified in 1127, when the Song court abandoned its northern capital and retreated south of the Yangzi River. The river, the canal system to the west, and the sea to the east became the Song line of defense against the nomads and northern kingdoms. The government depended initially on requisitioned merchant vessels, much as kings raised fleets in northern Europe. But the centralized Song administrative machine, drawing increasingly on revenues from newly encouraged trade, rapidly established a standing navy that was a classic of the imperial defense model. This included fleets of flat-bottomed junks and paddle wheelers that guarded the rivers, lakes, and canals inland in conjunction with the Song army (see Chapters 9 and 14), and a seagoing fleet. Superior Chinese ships came to dominate the China seas and extend Chinese influence into the Indian Ocean. Chinese navigators borrowed knowledge from Persian, Arab, and Indian sources, creating detailed maps and charts of common trade routes, and added to their navigational technology by inventing the floating magnetic compass. Government support stimulated creativity; trade revenues and an active shipbuilding industry supported the navy. At its height, the Song navy deployed twenty squadrons of ships and over 50,000 conscripted sailors and marines, dwarfing any other navy of the time. The sea-keeping abilities of Chinese ships and the empire's wealth and defensive strategic orientation gave the Song navy a tactical emphasis on ship killing as opposed to capture, much like the Byzantine navy in its heyday.

In 1161, the Song navy defeated a major invading fleet launched by the Jin kingdom, making use of tactical mobility and gunpowder bombs to defeat the more numerous foe. But after 1200, a change in the navy's command structure and adverse court politics led to a decline in standards and efficiency. Though still large, the fleet was in poor condition when the Mongols renewed the threat from the north in the mid-thirteenth century. Showing the adaptability that made them so formidable, the Mongols met Song naval power by building their own fleet, making heavy use of captured or subverted Song merchants and ships. Mongol naval forces were instrumental in the conquest of the Southern Song under Qubilai Khan in the 1270s. The last Song emperor was actually captured at sea by Mongol ships in 1279.

The Yüan (Mongol) dynasty saw a shift in the basis of Chinese naval power. The aggressive, outward-looking foreign policy of the Mongols, their foreign contacts, and their vigorous promotion of commerce created an atmosphere in which Chinese merchant activity flourished. The Mongols also decreased the influence of the Confucian bureaucracy, traditionally hostile to merchant activity. The biggest oceangoing junks of the Mongol period were huge, with watertight bulkheads (not to be seen in Europe for centuries yet) and vast cargo space. They were driven by fore-and-aft-rigged sails stiffened with bamboo battens, often on multiple masts, and were steered with large sternpost rudders. Chinese merchants came to dominate the spice routes of the Indian Ocean, and Chinese goods regularly reached Africa, while coastal trade within China, especially the grain trade that supplied the new capital at Beijing, reached new heights.

On this commercial foundation—the Chinese version of the new model of naval power—the Mongols could build a vast fleet of specialized warships designed for transporting troops, horses, and supplies and equipped with catapults and increasingly sophisticated gunpowder bombs. Under the Song and Yüan, government support allowed experimentation with new designs and weapons. This navy projected Chinese power into Vietnam and Southeast Asia and dominated the seas between China, Korea, and Japan.

It was the latter that drew the largest Mongol naval effort, but the invasions were skillfully opposed and proved disastrous. In 1274 and again in 1281, Qubilai Khan launched massive invasion fleets at Japan. The first is reported to have had over 900 ships and 40,000 men, and the second—the largest war fleet launched in the world to that time—over 4,000 ships and 150,000 men. They faced no real opposition on water, as Japanese naval activity was of the piratical-predatory type. The small, swift Japanese boats were clearly no match for the big Chinese ships at sea. The Japanese therefore left open the passage into waters of southwest Japan, luring the Mongol fleet into an area of shoals, treacherous currents, and unpredictable weather, where Japanese soldiers in small skiffs made some successful guerrilla attacks on Mongol junks at anchor. The Kamakura government then opposed both landings on the beach, hitting Mongol forces as they came ashore—which, as any Mediterranean admiral knew, was the most vulnerable moment for both landing force and fleet. The Mongols did manage to get landing parties ashore, but both invasions were ultimately undone by sudden typhoons that caught the fleets in the shallows and destroyed them—the *kamikaze* (divine winds) the Japanese believed were sent from the gods.

The destruction of the invasion fleets in Japanese waters slowed down Mongol efforts at sea. By the mid-fourteenth century, the dynasty was far less vigorous, was preoccupied with internal revolts, and was no longer expansionist. In addition, Confucian scholars in the bureaucracy again began to assert control over trade policy, imposing new regulations

and making travel abroad by Chinese merchants more difficult. Even coastal shipping declined as the grain trade shifted to the safer inland routes of the rebuilt canal system. The navy again was allowed to decay. Naval power played little role in the overthrow of the Yüan dynasty by a peasant-born rebel leader who would become the first Ming emperor in 1368. But the first century of Ming rule would see the last great era of Chinese naval assertiveness, with the issues of the Mongol period intensified and concentrated at the Ming court.

The Indian Ocean

While the Mediterranean and Chinese waters saw major naval wars, the Indian Ocean, like the North Sea, was more peaceful and trade oriented. Three sets of powers shared south Asian waters: Arabs, Indians, and small kingdoms in the Indonesian archipelagos. In all cases, the use of naval power was closely connected with the protection of maritime trade, but this function was largely defensive and so was rarely a cause for conflict.

Arabs were the major traders from the Persian Gulf to western India and often beyond, to the spice islands and China. Their ships were lightly built dhows, fairly small ships with lateen-rigged sails that were efficient coastal traders. The major source of Muslim sea power in the area was Egypt, which could easily send its war fleets down the Red Sea to guard the western trade routes. But while Mediterranean galley fleets could dominate the Red Sea, they were again not seaworthy enough for, nor logistically capable of, long voyages into the ocean beyond.

The Indian kingdoms of the subcontinent had a thriving merchant marine tradition. Indian shipbuilding skills and techniques were excellent, and India benefited from being the source of many raw materials that were not only trade goods but also shipbuilding materials, especially timber and cotton, the latter for sails. Given the importance of trade, many Indian rulers especially in the south maintained small war fleets to protect their merchant interests, but after the decline of the Chola Empire, no Indian state made maritime power the basis of its military strategy. The Vijayanagara Empire, the major power in south India in this period, was firmly land based and looked north to the similarly land-based Delhi Sultanate for its biggest defense challenge. Only in Bengal around the mouth of the Ganges were major naval forces regularly necessary for transport of armies across the numerous branches of the river in the delta. In such conditions, oared vessels played as big a role as sailing ships, but the field of play was too small, and the game too infrequently played, for specialized fighting ships to emerge as they did in the Mediterranean or on the Yangzi.

In the islands and straits of Malaysia and Indonesia, a variety of small kingdoms rose and fell in the vacuum created by the decline of Srivijaya. The power of such kingdoms was limited, as they were at once dependent on not killing off the trade that enriched them and vulnerable to shifts in trade routes and to domination by a larger power. China, especially, asserted itself in these waters periodically on behalf of Chinese merchants and managed the political competition in the area to its benefit.

The Pacific and Polynesia

Like the Indian Ocean, the Pacific during this period was not the scene of true naval warfare. But it did witness the climax of a long period of amazing seamanship by Polynesian peoples. Originating in Taiwan sometime in the first millennium BCE, Polynesians settled the islands of the western Pacific in the first millennium CE and from there settled all the remaining islands of the central Pacific as far as Easter Island to the east and Hawaii, the most isolated piece of land on the planet, to the north by the middle of the period covered by this chapter.

These explorations represented stunning feats of navigation. The voyages took place in seagoing outrigger canoes, often double-hulled with a platform in between where passengers, water, food, and the plants and animals that supported Polynesian settlement were carried. Experienced Polynesian navigators not only used the sun and stars but were expert at reading wind, weather, currents, and waves—by dangling their feet off the front of the boats, they could feel echo waves bouncing back from unseen islands, against the prevailing swells.

In the areas of greatest island density, regular maritime contact was maintained between islands, ranging from trade and tribute to raiding and warfare. But the fighting seems to have been almost exclusively on land, with war canoes serving simply as transport, and we have few details. The same could be said of the maritime activity along the American coast of the Pacific, where trading and raiding played important but poorly documented roles in the development of coastal cultures from Alaska to Peru.

Winds of Change

The second half of the fourteenth century saw the developments that would significantly affect maritime trade and naval power. Perhaps most important but hardest to see clearly was the Eurasian epidemic of bubonic plague that killed off so many people between roughly 1330 and 1430. Population dislocation on this scale seriously disturbed traditional patterns of production and consumption, which, in turn, disrupted trade patterns and routes. Given the rising importance of world trade in the equation of naval power, this development had important consequences. Reductions in the scale of trade affected merchant and government revenues alike, which had lasting impacts on labor markets and technological developments that varied depending on the balance of political and economic factors in any given area.

The second change was the rise of the Ottoman Empire. Ottoman success in steadily extending their rule over the eastern end of the Mediterranean (see Chapter 11) had two effects. First, and most directly, it began to heighten the intensity of naval conflict in the Mediterranean, as Turkish fleets challenged the hegemony of Christian galleys at sea. Second, the increasing Ottoman monopoly over the western end of the great Eurasian trade routes connecting China with the eastern Mediterranean raised a problem for the Europeans dependent on those routes for eastern goods. The problem became acute when Mamluk Egypt fell to the Ottomans shortly after 1500, just as a potential solution appeared.

That solution derived from the third area of change, new technology. Developments in ship design, navigation, and naval weaponry—above all, gunpowder—began by 1400 to hold revolutionary potential for the shape and scope of naval power globally. But the actual trajectory of technological change and naval development, concentrated in two areas of the world, shows that technology, far from being an independent factor, responded sensitively to the social, political, and economic contexts into which it was introduced.

WHO WILL RULE THE SEAS? 1378–1571

The two areas of the most intense naval activity along the new pattern, and therefore of most intensive technological development, were China and

Zheng He's Treasure Ships This drawing shows the size and rigging plan of the largest Chinese ships. The smaller ship, for scale, is Columbus's *Santa Maria*.

western Europe. It is only with hindsight, oversimplification, and a large dose of anachronism that the two traditions can be said to have been engaged in a race for world naval dominance. Nevertheless, close comparison of their respective paths reveals much about naval warfare, maritime power more generally, and the structures of two very different civilizations.

China

The first Ming emperor had little interest in overseas commerce, but private trade and traditions of Chinese shipbuilding continued during his reign. Zhu Di, the third Ming emperor (1402–24), however, viewed such trade as a source of both wealth and prestige, and sponsored the last and most famous period of Chinese seafaring, the voyages of the treasure fleets under the Chinese Muslim eunuch admiral Zheng He.

Technology The unprecedented scale of the ships and fleets assembled by Zhu Di (who seems to have equated size with grandeur) required the assembly of a vast workforce of shipwrights from all of coastal China. As a result, shipbuilding traditions from the northern Yellow Sea coasts and the southern South China Sea coasts seem to have come together and cross-fertilized. Sailors in the Yellow Sea had to deal with shallows and shifting sandbanks; ships there,

called *shachuan* (sand boats), were maneuverable, with flat bottoms and shallow drafts. The South China Sea was rougher, and the danger was hidden reefs; pirates were also a more consistent problem. Southern ships, called *fuchuan*, had deep, V-shaped hulls on deep, strong keels. The prow was high and reinforced, which served both to protect the ship from reefs and to allow ramming of smaller, lower ships. A tall castle aft served as a fighting platform, as *fuchuan* were the standard design for Ming warships. The new ships of the treasure fleet combined features of both traditions, and the biggest of them did so on an unprecedented scale.

The best estimates of the size of the biggest treasure ships put them at almost 400 feet long and 160 feet wide, among the largest wooden ships ever built. They had up to seven or eight masts, fore-and-aft-rigged with efficient, bamboo-battened sails, and sternpost rudders. They had a massive cargo capacity and could carry many hundreds of sailors, soldiers, and officials; and they could be armed with siege engines throwing stones, bolts, and gunpowder bombs. (It is unclear how far the Chinese had progressed in designing gunpowder-powered projectile weapons— that is, guns.) The hulls featured numerous watertight bulkheads, massive internal beams, and multiple layers of external planking. While this created ships of tremendous strength and seaworthiness, it was also an expensive and labor-intensive process, especially on the largest ships.

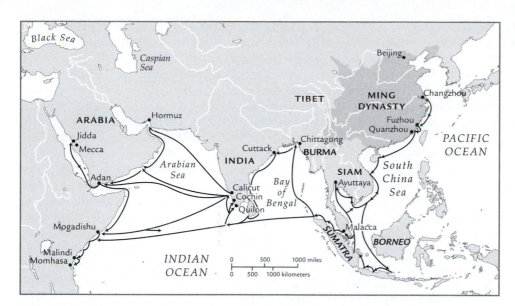

Figure 15.1 The Voyages of Zheng He, 1405–33

As noted above, the Chinese had invented the floating magnetic compass in the Song era. By the time of the treasure fleets, they had charts of the main trade routes with headings calibrated to compass readings and careful descriptions of landmarks and harbor entrances. Chinese mariners had also worked out fairly good methods for measuring speed and latitude. But, despite these charts, navigation had not become a fully written tradition yet.

The Treasure Fleets   Seven great treasure fleet expeditions sailed under Zheng He from Ming China, the first six sponsored by Zhu Di between 1405 and 1421, the last by his grandson Zhu Zhanji in 1431 (Figure 15.1). Each lasted almost two years. The main route extended from Longjiang near the mouth of the Yangzi to Champa (southern Vietnam), thence through the Straits of Malacca and past Ceylon to Calicut, and finally to Hormuz at the mouth of the Persian Gulf. Parts of various expeditions also explored routes to Taiwan, the Philippines, Borneo, Timor, Siam, Bengal, and the ports of Arabia on the Red Sea, as well as the east coast of Africa as far south as Madagascar.

The mission of the fleets was multifaceted, with perhaps the most important facet being political. The size and magnificence of the fleets and the value of the goods they carried both for trade and as gifts to the various rulers along the route advertised the wealth and prestige of the Dragon Throne, while the military might of the fleets—the many thousands of troops—backed that prestige with real power. This political function was not just for show. The early expeditions actively cleared the straits of pirates, and Zheng He acted as an ambassador, managing relations among the small kingdoms of the region to China's advantage. The fleets also supported an invasion and ongoing war in Annam (northern Vietnam).

But commerce was also an important aspect of the fleets' mission, which sought to stimulate China's trade with all the countries of south and southeast Asia. Sending out expensive gifts of Chinese manufactures, especially fine Ming porcelain, drew tribute gifts in return, including a number of giraffes sent from African kingdoms. It is difficult to arrive at a balance sheet for such political trade—that is, to decide whether the imperial treasury profited from such exchanges financially. They certainly added to the throne's prestige. But the fleets also engaged in straightforward trading, exchanging Chinese manufactures for spices and medicinal goods. In this they probably did turn a profit, at least on the exchanges themselves. Did such profits cover the cost of building and manning the fleets? Probably not directly, but the commercial contacts renewed by the fleets also stimulated private merchant activity as well as tribute missions, and the customs and import duties derived from expanded trade may well have put the entire enterprise in the black. Also, it is important to recognize that any trade coming into China was viewed, officially, as a form of tribute that acknowledged the suzerainty of the Dragon Throne and the centrality of the Middle Kingdom in the world.

It is also possible to detect an enthusiasm for exploration for its own sake among some of the fleets' supporters. Since interest in the world beyond China was not normally viewed favorably in official ideology, this interest was couched in terms of finding out what the emperor ruled and how the benefits of his policies could be extended to more of the world.

As military expeditions, the fleets were virtually unchallengeable at sea. The variety of ships in the fleets meant that they could deploy a range of tactics, from ramming, to the use of various missile weapons from bows to siege engines, to boarding. Given the number of soldiers the big ships carried, the latter threat would have presented no option to an enemy but flight. The fleets could not carry enough troops to be irresistible on land wherever they put into port. But they carried enough for defense against almost any threat, and since the fleets came in peace and not for conquest there was little problem with hostilities. In short, while the treasure fleets sailed, China dominated the waters of Asia from Persia to Korea. Had they stayed on the seas another seventy years after the last expedition returned home in 1433, they would surely have offered a virtually insurmountable obstacle to the Portuguese ships, small in both number and size, that then began to assert themselves in Indian waters.

Abdication   But the treasure fleets did not continue to sail. Zheng He died during the last expedition, and Zhu Zhanji died prematurely in 1435. No more treasure fleets sailed with Ming sponsorship. But the Chinese abandonment of the seas was far more complete than simply the ending of government-sponsored missions. Progressively, over the next century, private trade was more strictly regulated, and Chinese merchants were increasingly restricted in where they could sail. Foreign merchants coming to China also found themselves more restricted, and foreign populations living in Chinese cities faced growing xenophobia. Eventually, even the building of ocean-going junks by Chinese merchants was prohibited, and the once-thriving and technically superior Chinese shipbuilding industry contracted to local markets and lost many of the skills that had put it in the forefront of global maritime technology.

Why did this happen? This is a question scholars have debated for years—in part because of its relevance to the issue of the "rise of Europe." The deeper patterns of possible answers, involving the relationship of politics and culture to socioeconomic structure, will be discussed below. But a number of immediate factors are fairly clear.

Zhu Qizhen, the new emperor, had none of his father's or great-grandfather's interest in the fleets, and imperial sponsorship had to originate with the emperor himself. Zhu Qizhen thus also tended to side with the traditional Confucian bureaucrats in an emerging court battle. Confucians traditionally frowned on merchants and mercantile activity, though revisionism under the Song showed that, in the right circumstances, theory could be made friendlier to practice. Ming Confucian bureaucrats deployed tradition against their rivals for court power, the eunuchs. The eunuchs had, for obscure reasons, become the court patrons of trade and merchant activity; and, thus, whatever the bureaucracy could do to limit commerce undercut the eunuchs' source of wealth and power. But the eunuchs themselves contributed to the damage to commerce through corruption: Rather than fostering trade, they began to profiteer from customs and duties, further raising the cost of doing business. In short, structurally, the control the powerful central government of China could exercise over trade proved, in this climate, to be highly detrimental.

The complexities of measuring the balance sheets of the treasure fleets also contributed to their demise. The fleets were, in up-front costs, expensive to the government. A fiscal crisis or a shift in priorities for government spending could therefore make sending out a fleet an unaffordable luxury. Zhu Qizhen partly inherited such a shift: Zhu Di, who had sponsored the fleets, had also rebuilt an expensive new capital city in Beijing, which put a severe strain on government resources. Further, the fleets had sailed at a time when China's population was recovering from severe outbreaks of the plague in the 1330s. But new outbreaks in the mid-fifteenth century again reduced government income from the land tax, its main source of wealth. High expenses met shrinking resources, and the fleets suffered. Finally, Zhu Qizhen created a crisis by being captured by the Mongols in 1449. His eight-year captivity and the succession struggle that followed his release helped paralyze central policy, deepen the divisions at court, and damage imperial prestige. The latter had a direct effect on trade by discouraging tribute missions from abroad.

Consequently, Chinese seas were left to foreign merchants, Korean and Japanese pirates, and, from the 1530s, Europeans, with profound results for global commerce and naval warfare.

Western Europe

As in China, advances in European shipbuilding in this period resulted from the cross-breeding of northern and southern traditions. But whereas government policy encouraged the Chinese fusion, the European fusion evolved gradually. Europe's long coastlines, many peninsulas and islands, and lack of major canal systems (no European government having the ability to build one) made the European economy heavily dependent on seaborne trade. As ship technology improved, the European economy became steadily more integrated. One result was that ship technology became more integrated as well. In the fifteenth century, this integration reached a critical stage, and there was a rapid evolution of ship design with significant consequences for trade and warfare at sea.

Technology   Since Mediterranean galleys continued to follow their own developmental path (see below), the fusion mainly affected sailing ships. Northern hull shapes based on the cog had proved their worth as cargo carriers. These ships were deep and round, with high freeboards, sternpost rudders, and built-up fore and aft castles, so they both sailed well and were fairly defensible by the small crews that made them economical. But northern ships had been clinker-built— built up as a shell from the keel, with internal framing added later. Southern carvel-building—frame first with planks added on—spread north because it required less skilled labor and was thus cheaper, and it also allowed larger hulls to be built.

Larger ships rapidly reached the limit of what could be driven by the single square sail of the northern tradition. The southern tradition had long included multimasted ships; now, northern ships began to add a foremast, also square-rigged but smaller than the mainmast, and then a mizzenmast with a Mediterranean lateen sail that aided maneuverability. At the same time, the large, square sails began to be divided for greater ease of handling. By 1500, the result was the full-rigged ship, known at the time as a carrack, a far better sailer than its ancestors and thus a more economical cargo vessel.

What allowed the potential of the full-rigged ship for transoceanic sailing to be tapped was advances in navigational technology. By 1400, Europeans had the compass, either by indirect borrowing from the Chinese or by later independent invention (see the Issues box "Navies and Technology"). They also adopted the astrolabe, which allowed accurate calculation of latitude, from Arab sailors. In addition, there was rapid development of the use, first, of portolans— detailed descriptions of coasts and ports—in the Mediterranean and, then, of compass-influenced maps, all of which increasingly freed ships from having to hug the coastline. Navigation more than any other area of marine technology also profited from the European invention of the printing press in 1453. Maps, tables for calculating latitude, and other guides for literate ship captains rapidly became widely available.

The final piece in the naval technology puzzle was borrowed from land warfare. Ships became platforms for gunpowder weapons from the early fifteenth century. At first, these were small antipersonnel weapons mounted on the upper decks and castles. By later in the century, larger cannon were being mounted on the lower decks of sailing ships, with gun ports cut in the hulls. Galleys, too, began mounting guns, mostly in the bows pointing forward, adding to their offensive capability. As long as big cannon were scarce and expensive, gunpowder galleys could hold their own against gunpowder sailing ships. But by the 1570s, economic development, including wealth from the Americas, and cast-iron cannon, invented in England, were making big guns more affordable and plentiful, and sailing ships with broadside armament gained a decisive advantage.

The final product of this evolution in terms of warships came with the Iberian galleon in the early sixteenth century. Its name gives away one final southern influence on its design. It was a full-rigged ship, but with lines and hull shape influenced by the great galleys and galleasses of the Mediterranean: longer in proportion to its width and lower in profile. This made it a faster, more maneuverable sailer than the rounder carrack. But a narrower ship held less cargo and used more wood in relation to its cargo area than a rounder ship, and so was less economical. The galleon thus pointed to a differentiation between sail-driven warships and merchant vessels that would increase over time as cannon became cheaper and warships carried more and more of them.

By the second decade of the sixteenth century, the principal components of the new naval technology were in place. Full-rigged ships carrying large cannon would prove effective tools for exploration, commerce, and warfare. They would also prove technologically

ISSUES

Navies and Technology

Modern naval history, in which technological innovations from steam and steel to airplanes and radar play a crucial role in deciding warfare at sea, has tended to have a technological bias. Because of this, and perhaps because maritime enterprises are so clearly and obviously dependent on a whole set of technologies called *ships,* naval historians have long argued over the issues raised by the spread of technology.

This debate takes on added significance in the period after 1400 because of the connection of naval technology to a Big Question (or set of questions): how to account for the rise of Europe and the origins of the Industrial Revolution. Some older explanations for this phenomenon attributed to Europeans some special facility for technology that distinguished them from other, less inventive, peoples and focused on the naval and gunpowder technology that carried Europeans around the world after 1500.

Not surprisingly, attacks on this position stressed the non-European origins of many of the crucial inventions—gunpowder, the astrolabe, the compass—and the superiority of, say, Chinese ships over European ships. This line of attack may have undermined the European bias of the old position, but it sometimes simply replaced Eurocentric racist assumptions with other equally untenable centrisms in explaining the origins of technologies. And it kept technology at the center of the debate and so fostered a different form of Eurocentrism. In this formulation, since other people had, without revolutionary results, developed technologies that proved revolutionary in Europe, they must have been blocked somehow from being the birthplace of the modern world. There are two related problems with this argument: It assumes that Europe was the model for development, and it assumes that technology was the driving force in development.

More recent naval history has helped undermine many of these assumptions. Maritime history clearly shows the centrality of uncentered diffusion in the development of naval technology. Subtraditions within a region such as China crossbred, and the traditions of different regions and civilizations traded ideas and techniques along with goods. Thus, the pattern of maritime technology also applies to the spread and development of culture generally.

Just as important is that recent naval history emphasizes the crucial role of the economic, social, and political contexts of technology in determining its uses and effects. In some ways, this is not surprising since ships are not just technologies but also societies, as anyone who has seen *Master and Commander* knows. The close connection of naval warfare with piracy and commerce also leads naturally to such a view. Thus, for example, John Guilmartin's *Gunpowder and Galleys* explores the relationship between Mediterranean galley warfare and the climate, geography, economics, and politics of the region. He shows that the coming of gunpowder weapons and broadside tactics did not immediately spell the end of galley warfare. Rather, cannon enhanced the offensive and amphibious role of galleys in the attack and defense of fortified ports. The new technology did play a role in causing the galley system to collapse under its own weight, as logistical and manpower problems increasingly limited the strategic range of galley fleets, but it was the economics of the technology that was crucial. Thus, there was no straight line from a new technology (cannon) to a new and superior method of naval warfare (broadside tactics). Another example, the complex comparison of Chinese and European maritime exploration, is examined at length in this chapter.

Indeed, another Mediterranean naval technology demonstrates that there is no guarantee of continually improving technology—another expectation fostered by the modern world. Greek Fire (see Chapter 10) was an effective offensive weapon for Byzantine and Arab navies for centuries. But with changes in Byzantine culture and politics in the course of the twelfth century, the formula was lost, never to be recovered and destined to be argued about by naval historians ever since. There is no better example of the dependence of technology on its contexts.

Galleon With leaner, galley-influenced lines married to a large, coglike hull capable of carrying broadside-mounted cannon and powered by three full-rigged masts, the galleon was the prototype for 300 years of warship design.

capable of staying at sea for extended periods, making control of the sea possible in the modern sense for the first time. Given this capability, control of the sea-lanes along which traders traveled became far more valuable than any individual ship, and so the incentive for ship-killing tactics increased along with the gunpowder technology that made ship killing possible in a new way. Until the nineteenth century, changes in this technological package would consist of refinements in sail plans and hull shapes and, above all, the working out for warships of effective tactics for broadside batteries in the form of the line ahead (see Chapter 20). When European governments developed the financial and administrative resources to match the technological capabilities of their ships, the new capitalist model of naval power would also be fully in place.

Naval Warfare   The English Channel remained the site of the most intense naval warfare in northern waters. Henry V of England, concerned about his lines of communication as he set out to conquer Normandy, built a fleet to clear the French and their Genoese allies from the Channel. The fleet included ships armed with guns. Victory at Honfleur in 1417 achieved his goal. A small royal naval establishment continued in existence from that time forward, but it

would not assume a truly significant role in English defense until the reign of Edward VI in the early 1550s, when the Duke of Northumberland built it up in conjunction with encouraging overseas exploration and trade.

But northern naval warfare remained rudimentary compared to the sophisticated galley wars of the Mediterranean world. In the century after 1380, these wars tended to be localized: battles among Christian kingdoms in the western Mediterranean, Venetian battles against the rising Ottoman power in the east and against other Italian city-states in the central Mediterranean, and commerce and coastal raiding by North African Muslims against Spain and by the Knights of St. John on Rhodes against Muslim areas. The economics of naval power continued to tie warfare to piracy, with rowers predominantly skilled free men.

Northern round ships did begin to appear in the Mediterranean in increasing numbers, taking a larger share of the merchant trade. In some ways, a peculiar tactical standoff began to develop between round ships and galleys. The heavily built, high-sided round ships could often hold off single galleys and even small squadrons, especially if they carried a large-enough crew. This made commerce somewhat safer but had little effect on patterns of naval warfare because round ships had little offensive capability and could never force a galley into a fight. More important, the ability of galleys to deliver men and supplies directly to ports and beaches made them ideal for besieging the fortified ports on which naval power was based and for relieving ports under siege. Sailing ships could not perform such tasks reliably. And, as long as artillery remained expensive and scarce, galleys were also more effective gun platforms than sailing ships, able to row into position as mobile siege batteries and to hold their own in naval gunfights against undergunned broadside batteries. In terms of galley-versus-galley fights, the addition of forward-mounted, centerline cannon simply reinforced the concentration of a galley's offensive power in its bow. The guns were essentially antipersonnel weapons, discharged on impact as a prelude to boarding, though Venetian gunners in particular could aim to sink enemy ships from a distance. Thus, galley battles pitted lines of ships abreast meeting head-to-head (see the Highlights box).

In addition, the continuing spread of the Ottoman Empire and the rise of the Spanish kingdoms altered the political geography of Mediterranean warfare. Increasingly, the two major powers divided the sea between themselves, with Venice the only one of the lesser powers surviving as a significant player in the sixteenth century. Ottoman control of the coasts of the eastern Mediterranean also gave them control over the sea-lanes there, and when Mamluk Egypt fell to them, Venice was forced into avoiding war with the sultans as much as possible, since the Ottomans controlled the sources of Venetian trade wealth. Further, Christian outposts such as Rhodes became almost impossible to defend; in 1522, Rhodes fell and the Knights retreated to Malta.

The resources the great powers brought to galley warfare wrought changes of their own. The size of fleets grew steadily through the sixteenth century. The size of individual galleys and the numbers of soldiers each carried also grew as both sides looked to increase the tactical striking power of its ships: Bigger ships could carry more and heavier cannon as well as more soldiers. As marines, Spanish musketeers and Ottoman archers were evenly matched tactically. But the advantage of the musketeers was that a peasant could be turned into a good musketeer with a short period of training; a good archer was a lifetime product of a socioeconomic system that the Ottomans were struggling to maintain by the mid-sixteenth century.

But larger ships and fleets stretched the resources of skilled rowers, while labor costs were rising in the wake of the depopulation resulting from the plague. After 1450, there was an escalating shift toward the use of galley slaves placed five to an oar in place of three rowers on a bench, each with his own oar. This decreased the demand for skilled oarsmen but increased power only marginally while adding to the larger manpower complement of each ship. Since galleys had limited storage space, larger crews critically shortened the already restrictive logistical leash that tied fleets to friendly ports. Larger fleets added to the problem, as did ammunition for cannon. By midcentury, the strategic mobility and striking range of large galley fleets, within the restrictive parameters of the Mediterranean sailing season, had shrunk enough that strategic stalemate was setting in. The expense of raising large fleets, by 1550 almost unbearable even for the great powers, compounded the problem. The lengthy, costly, and ultimately unsuccessful Ottoman siege of Malta in 1565 signaled the end of large-scale amphibious offensives. Lepanto, six years later, was the swan song of big galley fleets (see the Highlights box "The Battle of Lepanto, 1571"). When English and Dutch privateers armed with plentiful cast-iron cannon entered the Mediterranean in the 1580s, even the *guerre de course* that was the lifeblood of the galley system became untenable, and the era of oared fighting ships that stretched back into antiquity finally came to an end.

Toward Expansion   Portugal led the way in the development of the full-rigged ship and broadside gunnery. Henry the Navigator sent such ships down the coast of Africa from the 1450s and was rewarded with gold and slaves, often obtained by trading guns. By 1488, a fleet under Vasco da Gama had reached the Cape and ten years after that reached Indian ports visited by the Chinese treasure fleets sixty-six years earlier. Unlike the treasure fleets, the European fleets were there to stay.

The Portuguese fleets were far smaller than those of the Chinese. But they were also, from the start, paying propositions of a government and merchant class with a large stake in their success. The Spanish too invested in exploration, with unexpectedly spectacular results in 1492. Soon the Dutch, English, and French would join the race. The merchant capitalists of Europe went looking for profits with the approval and support of their governments; those governments supported their merchants because they were involved in ongoing political and military competition among themselves. The kings of a divided Europe could not afford not to seek new sources of income. Merchants and kings looked beyond the traditional routes to the east through the Mediterranean out of a desire to bypass the Venetian monopoly over those routes and to avoid the growing power of the Ottomans. In fact, the Portuguese aimed to control trade in the Indian Ocean as a direct blow against the Ottomans, an ambitious and crusadelike strategy.

The cannon-bearing, full-rigged ship was the key tool of this expansion. The initial victories of the Portuguese captains da Gama, Almeida, and Albuquerque over larger Indian fleets, especially Almeida's victory over a combined Egyptian-Gujerati fleet off Diu in February 1509, demonstrated the potential of the Europeans' heavy-timbered ships, flexible sail plans, and superior heavy gunnery. But the socioeconomic system—the whole complex model of naval power—that produced these ships was, as much as the ships themselves, the sign of new directions in naval warfare, for the Chinese had demonstrated similar technological potential decades earlier. Ships were simply tools, a means to an end. It is to an examination of motives that we must turn in comparing the differing outcomes of Chinese and European maritime expansion.

Comparisons

A complex set of factors contributed to the different trajectories of Chinese and European naval history. No one factor was decisive by itself, and many were interrelated—each civilization was an organic whole, and its naval history a product of that whole. Counterfactual history—playing "what if" with single factors—is therefore an unproductive exercise. We should also avoid judging the Chinese trajectory by European standards, especially in terms of the outcome. Europe did not win, because there was no competition being waged between Europe and China. In each case, the results, though different, make sense, and if China had stayed active at sea (to use a counterfactual), the result is unlikely to have been a European-style industrial revolution in China.

The Role of Government China was ruled by a strong, centralized, and bureaucratic government. Though dynasties changed, the Ming rulers rightly considered themselves part of a ruling tradition that stretched back over 2000 years. The bureaucracy of scholar-gentry was recruited by examination based on the Confucian classics, which gave the government ideological coherence. That ideology saw the role of government as fostering the "good of the kingdom": the emperor and his ministers were responsible for the welfare of the empire. Thus, the imperial government had both the means and the motivation to control and regulate trade. Commerce was important to government finances through taxation, especially from the Song period on, but that importance was underacknowledged ideologically. Revenues from agricultural and land taxes were the most important source of government income, and the only true source of government wealth to most Confucians. Thus, in China, market forces were limited by and subordinate to political forces, a common situation in most preindustrial societies.

Europe, on the other hand, was fragmented politically. Further, individual governments were underdeveloped by Chinese standards. Their bureaucracies were rudimentary, and they exercised limited ability to control or regulate trade. In fact, most governments' limited authority to collect taxes meant that commerce was usually crucial to government finances, especially as kings looked for sources of revenue with which to wage war. They could not afford to risk killing off trade and, in fact, often looked to stimulate it. This also reflected long-standing attitudes to practical governance. Kings and princes ruled, in theory, for the good of the people, as in China, but in practice acted much more like business owners maximizing the returns on their private property, an attitude fostered by localism and weak powers of taxation. In such a political atmosphere, market forces were given much more leeway and influence over both public and private policy decisions.

The Role of Social Structure These government attitudes toward commerce were in some ways simply an outgrowth of deeper social structures and attitudes. In China, merchants were numerous and successful but had a subordinate role socially and in terms of influence. Confucian social theory assigned merchants to the lowest social strata, below peasants, and though rich merchants certainly had more influence and a better lifestyle than peasants, the ideology had an effect. Rich merchants aspired for their sons to become scholars and bureaucrats, reflecting both the monopoly of prestige that government service exercised in society and the openness of the meritocratic exam system to new entrants.

HIGHLIGHTS

The Battle of Lepanto, 1571

Having failed to take Malta in 1565, the Ottomans turned their attention to a closer target, Venetian-held Cyprus. Selim II dispatched a fleet of 116 galleys and 50,000 troops, which rapidly took the inland fortress of Nicosia in September. The port city of Famagusta was then blockaded for a spring assault.

Ably defended and reinforced by a small and daring relief contingent in January 1571, Famagusta held against bombardment, mining, and assault until August. The Venetians appealed to Spain for help, but divisions among the Christian powers and Spanish preoccupation with a Morisco revolt prevented relief from arriving in time. The Holy League of Spain, Venice, and the papacy was not formalized until May, and the fleet did not sail from Messina in Sicily until

Turkish Gunpowder Galley   This drawing shows a Turkish galley of the sort used at Lepanto. Small guns could fire in different directions, but the main firepower came from the bow.

after Famagusta surrendered. The Ottoman fleet had sailed west from Cyprus via Crete toward the Adriatic, rendezvousing with a North African flotilla, but on learning the position of the Christian fleet retreated slightly to the base at Lepanto.

European merchants, on the other hand, though less rich and numerous in absolute terms than their Chinese counterparts, were probably more numerous in relative terms, as well as more influential. To the extent that there was a social theory—the medieval Three Orders, consisting of those who worked, those who fought, and those who prayed—merchants fell outside it rather than at its base. Faced with a somewhat hostile church and a somewhat closed aristocracy, merchants had no choice but to use their wealth in pursuit of more wealth and, in some places, such as Renaissance Italy, to glorify the pursuit. As urban burgesses, merchants had a greater measure of self-rule than in China (another sign of weak central authority); indeed, some Italian city-states were ruled by merchant oligarchies.

A subtler aspect of social structure is that in China, social relationships were mediated by the idea of the Confucian hierarchy. Everyone had a place between superiors and inferiors, with the emperor at the top, tying social hierarchy to government hierarchy. In Europe, even outside the merchant class, social relationships had long been mediated by contract. Contracts, implicit or explicit, governed lord and vassal, landlord and peasant, and even king and consultative body (parliaments). Arguably, Europe's contract-mediated society was more open to merchant practices and influence than was China's Confucian hierarchy.

The Role of Economics   Economically, China was in a powerful position in the pre-1500 world system

There, on October 7, 1571, it met the advancing Christian fleet.

Both sides seem to have underestimated their opponent's strength and thus sought battle. The Christians had about 208 galleys and 6 large, heavily gunned Venetian galleasses. The Turks deployed about 230 galleys and perhaps 70 lighter galliots. The Turkish galleys were lighter and more maneuverable than the Christian (especially the Spanish) galleys but carried somewhat fewer cannon. Each fleet carried over 50,000 rowers and marines, and each fleet formed into three divisions and a reserve. Don Juan of Austria, the Christian commander, planned to use his heavier ships to crush the Muslim center; Muezzinzade Ali Pasha, the Ottoman commander, hoped to hold out in the center while his seaward left wing under Uluj Ali Pasha used superior numbers to flank the Christian line and bring about a general melee.

In effect, both plans worked. The heavily Venetian left wing of the Christian fleet used its skill to prevent a shoreward flank attack by the Muslim right and eventually crushed it against the shore. The center, preceded by two of the galleasses, which disordered the Muslim line, got into a long, hard fight that swung back and forth before bigger ships, more cannon, and the fighting qualities of the Spanish arquebusiers (matchlock gunners) slowly carried the day against the dogged Turkish Janissaries and archers. The seaward wings, with the farthest to sail to deploy, engaged last. In attempting to prevent a flanking move, the Christian right lost contact with the center, into which gap Uluj Ali Pasha attacked skillfully—but too late. By the time the Turkish left entered the battle, the right was lost and the center was losing, and Uluj was able to extricate only himself and under twenty galleys. The rest were either sunk or captured, with a massive loss of life—over 30,000 men, more than twice the Christian toll. At least half were skilled archers, sailors, and Janissaries, a loss especially among the archers that the Ottomans probably never made good.

It was this loss of life that made Lepanto decisive. They rebuilt a fleet the next year, but it was inexperienced, and the momentum of Ottoman naval conquest was halted for good. The divided and distracted Christian forces did not follow up the victory in any way; but, psychologically, it was a major victory. It was also the tactical apex and finale of Mediterranean galley warfare. The future belonged to sailing ships.

of trade. It was a central producer of valuable manufactured goods from laquerware and porcelain to jade jewelry and silks. It was a vast, rich consumer market for spices, medicines, and exotic foods. As a result, trade gravitated toward China whether Chinese merchants pursued it or not, and it usually produced a surplus balance of payments. Europe, on the other hand, lay at the far western end of the major Afro-Eurasian trade routes and had much less to offer in the way of raw or finished products for the world market: wool cloth and weapons (first swords, then guns) were its most valuable exports. European merchants thus had to pursue trade actively to meet the demand for Eastern luxury goods, and a negative balance of payments motivated a search for new sources of gold and silver. But in another way, Europe was in a fortuitous position geographically: closest of the Afro-Eurasian civilizations to the Americas and their potential for mineral extraction and slave-based agricultural wealth. Similar exploitation of the Americas from China was probably feasible technologically but would have proved at best marginally profitable given the greater distances and the proximity of the rich Southeast Asian trade.

Geography also shaped the methods of internal trade. For China, the seas were not crucial. China's was a large, land-based empire with decent rivers, canals, and roads. Europe's coasts and seas were relatively longer and far more significant as connectors of the regions whose differentiation was at the base of

European economic growth. Naval traditions were thus more widespread and intrinsic to European trade than in China.

Finally, the political structures outlined above shaped the economics of technology. Chinese technological innovation was significant and world leading but was often sponsored by and dependent on central investment and direction, or at least approval and fostering of private initiatives. Particular areas of technology such as warships were thus often subject to the whims of central policy. In Europe, governments had neither the influence nor the resources to direct technological innovation, except perhaps as purchasers of weapons. Technological innovation was thus more bottom up than top down and tended to follow market forces more closely.

These political, social, and economic differences show up in the effects of the plague on the two civilizations' naval activity. In China, plagues reduced agricultural output, causing a decline in government revenue and a consequent decline in investment in fleets and in the skilled labor that built them. The population decline in Europe affected levels of trade but also caused shifts in the type of trade and stimulated a search for efficiencies, including better ships, which, like the printing press and the arquebus, can be seen as savers of expensive labor. Labor was expensive because, in a contract society with weak powers of coercion, labor shortages meant expensive labor. The Chinese reaction was thus essentially politically governed, where the European reaction was market driven.

The Role of Culture   We have already outlined the social ideologies that differentiated the two civilizations in terms of merchant activity: Confucian hostility to merchant activity and the ability of the exam system to co-opt merchant success into the established system, in contrast to the corresponding benign neglect of merchants in European theory and the inability of the warrior and religious hierarchies to co-opt or control merchant activity. Another significant cultural difference concerns what might be called attitudes toward colonialism.

China's view of itself as the Middle Kingdom, the center of the world, encouraged an ideology of self-sufficiency that saw all trade as tribute honoring the emperor, not as a necessary activity. Similarly, a Middle Kingdom officially had little reason to conquer or directly control parts of the world that were nominally already subject to the Dragon Throne. Thus, especially during the voyages of the treasure fleets, the Chinese aimed to spread the benefits of Chinese civilization through indirect political management and encouragement of recognition of the emperor's prestige. Similarly, Chinese religion had little militant or missionary impulse. But in Europe, crusading ideals pervaded the culture, and militant missionary religion had long been entangled with a culture of conquest and colonization (see Chapter 12). This powerful mixture colored the European view of trade as a tool of dominance and aggression, and proved far more addictive than the benevolent Chinese attitude.

The Result   Thus, despite (or indeed, because of) European backwardness and an initial deficit in naval technology, European naval power—above all, its warships—emerged from the fabric of its socioeconomic structure, a potent genie barely controlled by the warring kingdoms that helped release it. European naval power was woven into the pattern of European commerce, expansion, and war. China's naval power and activity were much more at the whim of a central government for which such power and activity were at best a secondary concern for any number of reasons. The government firmly mediated naval warfare's connection to commerce and society as part of its overall management of Chinese civilization. It therefore had not only the ability to let the genie out of the bottle between 1405 and 1433 but the ability and motivation thereafter to stuff it back in.

CONCLUSION

By 1550, Europe had developed tools of global naval dominance. The same tools—the full-rigged ships heavily armed with large cannon—had the potential to transform war at sea from the amphibious adjunct of land power that it had always been into a new and much more independent sphere of military activity. It was European navies, far more than their armies, that would open a whole new world of global contact and conflict in subsequent centuries.

SUGGESTED READINGS

Abu-Lughod, Janet. *Before European Hegemony*. Oxford: Oxford University Press, 1989. An interesting application of world systems theory to world trade networks in this period, showing the commercial background of naval warfare.

Brooks, F. W. *The English Naval Forces, 1199–1272*. London: A. Brown & Sons, nd. A dated but useful examination of an early "royal" navy. See also the section on naval warfare in Stephen Morillo, *Warfare Under the Anglo-Norman Kings*. See Chapter 12.

Guilmartin, John. *Gunpowder and Galleys*. Cambridge: Cambridge University Press, 1974. An influential study of the impact of the introduction of gunpowder weapons on galley warfare, demonstrating how oared ships were not rendered immediately obsolete by cannon.

Landstrom, Bjorn. *The Ship*. See Chapter 10.

Levathes, Louise. *When China Ruled the Seas: The Treasure Fleet of the Dragon Throne 1405–1433*. New York: Simon & Shuster, 1994. A very readable examination of Zheng He's Treasure Fleets and the political, social, and economic factors behind their rise and demise.

Lewis, Archibald. *Nomads and Crusaders, AD 1000–1368*. Bloomington: Indiana University Press, 1988. A wide-ranging survey of Eurasian developments that includes substantial information on maritime activity.

Lewis, Archibald, and Timothy Runyon. *European Naval and Maritime History, 300–1500*. See Chapter 10.

Parry, J. H. *Discovery of the Sea*. Berkeley: University of California Press, 1974. A still useful examination of the origins of European maritime expansion.

Pryor, John H. *Geography, Technology, and War*. See Chapter 10.

Rose, Susan. *Medieval Naval Warfare 1000–1500*. London: Routledge, 2001. A solid survey of medieval naval warfare; especially good on infrastructure factors (ports and shipyards) and on fourteenth-century Mediterranean conflict.

Roy, Atul Chandra. *Mughal Navy and Naval Warfare*. Calcutta: World Press, 1972. One of the few examinations of Mughal naval power and its limits.

Unger, Richard W. *The Ship in the Medieval Economy 600–1600*. See Chapter 10.

COMMENTARY: PART 3, 1100–1500

The period 1100–1500 is characterized by two opposed trends. First, in the wake of the age of migration and invasion, stable cultural traditions emerged that, despite further disruptions, would influence the shape of the world's civilizations down to the present. Cultures specific to the warrior class would be a major aspect of that trend in many places. Second, even as distinct and stable traditions were emerging, they were also coming into increased contact and interaction, often militarily, with consequences of global significance. In several important respects, these trends were both the culmination of earlier developments and a prelude to later changes.

STABLE TRADITIONS AND WARRIOR CULTURES

The foundations of classical culture, the ending of the age of migration, and the rise of the salvation religions combined in this era to create a variety of cultural traditions that were either new or newly elaborated. The larger traditions were not necessarily military, but many of the world's civilizations contained warrior subcultures that exerted a strong pull on the culture as a whole.

Perhaps the best known and most formally worked out was western European chivalry, the code of conduct for the warrior aristocracy or knightly class. Treatises of a legal nature as well as philosophical tracts and popular literature all helped define proper modes of knightly behavior. Similarly, in Japan, a genre of war tales publicized the standards and ideals of warrior behavior there, creating the foundations of *bushido,* the "way of the warrior." A different context of philosophical and theological traditions meant that *bushido* was less precisely defined than chivalry (much as Buddhism largely lacked the theological hair-splitting of western Christianity), but its wider cultural influence through links to the tea ceremony and other art forms rivaled chivalry's influence on poetry and art. The Islamic world actually had widespread warrior cultures. The *ghazi* tradition of frontier warriors for the faith bore some resemblance to the crusading aspects of Christianity. Its appeal was strongest among newly converted peoples, especially of nomadic origin, and among other marginalized elements of the Islamic population, and it was adopted most widely among the Seljuk Turkish peoples of the Middle East. The peculiar slave soldier tradition also existed throughout Islam. These unfree but powerful groups often developed identities and traditions that, at times, as with the Mamluks in Egypt, became dominant at least in government. The caste system in India provided a framework for warrior conduct there, with philosophical foundations going back to the *Bhagavad Gītā,* while warfare continued to define the lifestyle of nomads such as the Mongols. Smaller warrior traditions existed throughout Southeast Asia, Africa, the Americas, and Polynesia. The two major civilizations without a distinct warrior tradition were Byzantium, where the transformations of the eleventh century had fostered reliance on groups of foreign mercenaries each with their own traditions, and China, where Confucian civilian domination of culture made soldiering a low-prestige way of life.

Despite their many differences in detail, all warrior cultures tended to share certain basic features. Foremost among these were an emphasis on individual honor expressed through fame, heroism, boasting, and fear of being shamed, and an emphasis on loyalty to the group and its leader—at times, as in Japan, to the point of death.

The potential contradiction between these two imperatives was often a source of creative tension in the traditions. Warrior traditions also leaned (as did most traditions among the elites of agrarian societies) toward conservatism. This expressed itself in the tendency of warrior classes, especially at the upper end, to become closed castes entered only by birth and in the attachment many warrior groups developed to particular weapons or tactics. Horse-archery was the pride of nomads, Mamluks, and Japanese warriors in the Kamakura period. Japanese samurai later developed a cult of the sword, moving them closer to the European chivalrous tradition of hand-to-hand combat with sword and lance, but trickery similar to the feigned flights of nomadic horsemen remained prized among samurai, whereas European knights disdained such tactics (at least in theory). Although in this age such conservatism was simply a characteristic of most warrior cultures, with no one tactical system being dominant, it would prove in some areas and in later centuries a barrier to meeting new challenges effectively.

TRADITIONS IN CONTACT AND CONFLICT

Such challenges were foreshadowed in this period by the increased interactions of Eurasia's traditions. These interactions came in three main forms. Crusaders from western Europe came into closer contact with the neighboring Byzantine and Islamic worlds. The creation of the Mongol Empire under Chingiz Khan and his successors brought more of Eurasia under one rule than ever before. And after the economic disruptions of the previous age, the eleventh and twelfth centuries saw a notable increase in the scope and scale of world trade, linking much of the Old World in a network of commercial routes that survived, even if in altered form, the Mongol conquests. All three paths of interaction had significant military consequences.

The Mongol conquests brought devastation to many areas and facilitated the spread of the Black Death to much of Eurasia in the mid-fourteenth century, as armies and travelers carried it from those areas of central Asia where it was endemic in the rodent population. Destruction was especially great in the Islamic heartlands, leading to a shift in the center of power in the Islamic world away from the Fertile Crescent and toward the westward-looking Ottomans. In this, the Mongol conquests reinforced the effect of the Crusades in heightening, at least for a time, the factionalism of the Islamic world. The combination of Mongol rule, Ming reaction, and Black Death mortality that was centered disproportionately in the cities dealt a setback to Chinese scientific culture, and the continuing Mongol threat played a major part in the cessation of Chinese interest in overseas exploration and the subsequent period of self-imposed withdrawal. Mongol rule isolated Russia from its European neighbors even more directly, turning the focus of Muscovite attention eastward for two centuries or more. The Mongols and later Tamerlane contributed to the fall of the Delhi Sultanate in India; the subsequent fragmentation of political power opened the door to the later Mughal invasions. The general stress and disruption of the Mongol conquests may have contributed to a conservative, traditionalist reaction in many parts of Eurasia, including a rise in mysticism. But in Japan and western Europe, where Mongol invasions reached only briefly and without leading to conquests, culture was dominated not by retrospection but by change in response to Mongol invasions and the Black Death, respectively.

In tactical terms, both the Crusades and the Mongol conquests brought into conflict many of the warrior cultures and their tactical systems that had evolved in this period. Of these, the Mongols easily proved the most widely successful, demonstrating again the effectiveness of nomadic horsemen when united and well led. Mongol armies defeated other nomadic cavalry, large Chinese infantry forces, Islamic horsemen and infantry levies, and European knights and townsmen. But part of their success rested on the flexibility of their tradition. They were willing to borrow foreign troops and techniques—most notably, Chinese siege engineers and their machines—and to adapt their methods to the opponent and the terrain. Although some terrains, especially areas with wet tropical climates where diseases killed horses or with insufficient fodder where horses starved, proved beyond the Mongol ability to penetrate effectively, they succeeded more widely than anyone else ever had and adapted more readily than any of their opponents were able to. Not only was their tradition flexible, but strong leadership and discipline subordinated the individualistic element in their warrior culture to the needs of the group, whereas individual interest and glory seeking may have hindered attempts at adaptation elsewhere. The discipline and massed tactics of the Mongols were a revelation to the Japanese in the first invasion there, for example.

There were limits even to Mongol adaptability. They remained essentially steppe horsemen, using foreign troops where their own style of fighting was inappropriate. Elsewhere, the clash of systems reveals the same limits to adaptation. Crusaders, Byzantines, and Turks adjusted their strategies and tactics to the nature of the opposing forces, for instance. But the adjustments worked within and played on the strengths of the troops each tradition had already produced, and they did not include adopting the tactics or weapons of the enemy in most cases, no matter how effective they were. The reason for this was the strength of the warrior cultural traditions each area had developed, reinforced by the close linkage between style of warfare and social system. That is, most tactical systems in this age were, not purely military inventions created for their battlefield effectiveness, but expressions of the ways of life and internal political and economic arrangements of each people. Thus, any significant change was likely to prove economically unfeasible and, more crucially, politically off limits because of the dishonor involved for individual warriors. Such change as did come to some areas reflected deeper social and economic transformations, and it was slow and evolutionary in character. Even responses to new technology took place within the social and cultural structures each tradition had already established and was likely to be most transformative where deeper changes were already under way.

Thus, the invention of gunpowder weapons took place in a Song China undergoing significant economic development and social realignment. Spread to other areas through the united Mongol realm, it was developed further in a western Europe in the process of its own long transformation, pushed by intra-European competition and the social and economic dislocations of the postplague period. It spread thence to the Ottomans, heirs to the mixed traditions of the Near East, and to others, a story for the next part of this book.

The spread of gunpowder along Mongol trade routes also highlights the growing importance of commerce as a path of interaction in these centuries. Important in its own right, the increase in trade also had significant effects on military history. It began to create a new source for the *sinews of war*—the economic and financial means rulers used to pay for armies. The wealth and produce of land was still fundamental to almost all military forces. But Song China relied heavily on revenues from foreign trade to finance its military establishment, whereas in England around 1300, kings leveraged the wealth of the wool trade through loans from Italian bankers, whose wealth also derived originally from commerce, to pay for expeditions to France. Such examples pointed toward future developments. The rise of commerce also directly affected modes of naval warfare, calling into being ships, sailors, financial incentives, and new forms of partnership between rulers and the merchant marines of their realms. The mercantile empires of Venice and Genoa were forerunners to the global trade empires of the centuries after 1500, again a story for the next part of this book.

CULMINATION AND PRELUDE

It is difficult not to see the period 1100–1500 as a prelude to a coming age of global contact and warfare after 1500. The rise of trade foreshadows the shift to ocean-centered trade routes, the creation of mercantile empires, and the development of new technologies and techniques of naval power. Similarly, the spread of gunpowder along Mongol routes is an ironic preface to the role of gunpowder in the subsequent decline of the nomadic threat.

However, it is equally possible to view this period as a culmination of trends begun centuries earlier. The Mongol conquests were the latest and largest of a longstanding pattern. Likewise, the Crusades and the Islamic *jihad* that responded to them arose easily from centuries of competition centered on the increasing role of religion in warfare.

Neither view is untrue, but both risk the error of thinking that what did happen had to happen, and both tend to lead away from understanding the period on its own terms. One reason for the emphasis in this commentary on warrior cultures is that those were the terms in which the fighting men of the time saw themselves. Warriors and their families were not faceless tools of large historical movements but men (and women) who constructed their own worlds around values that worked for them. The history of 1100–1500 with its separate traditions, none dominant, in increasing conflict highlights this fact especially well.

Credits

TEXT AND ILLUSTRATIONS

Page 9, Reprinted with the permission of The Free Press, a Division of Simon & Schuster Adult Publishing Group, from *Gilgamesh: A New English Version* by Stephen Mitchell. Copyright © 2004 by Stephen Mitchell. All rights reserved; **p. 27,** From *Sun-Tzu: The Art of Warfare* by Sun-Tzu, translated by Roger T. Ames, copyright © 1993 by Roger T. Ames. Used by permission of Ballantine Books, a division of Random House, Inc.; **pp. 154–155,** From George T. Dennis, *Three Byzantine Military Treatises* (Washington, DC: Dumbarton Oaks, 1985); **p. 163,** From *The Seven Military Classics of Ancient China,* translated by Ralph Sawyer (Boulder: Westview Press, 1993); **p. 183,** From Constantine Porphyrogenitus, *De Administrando Imperio,* edited by G. Moravcsik, translated by R. H. Jenkins (Washington, DC: Dumbarton Oaks, 1993); **p. 212,** Fulcher of Chartres from *Historia Hierosolymitana,* edited by Heinrich Haganmeyer (Heidelberg, 1913). Anna Comnena from *The Alexiad of Anna Comnena,* translated by E. R. A. Sewter (New York: Penguin Books, 1969); **p. 233,** From Jean Froissart, *Chronicles,* edited and translated by Geoffrey Brereton (New York: Penguin

Books, 1968); **p. 243,** From *The Secret History of the Mongols: The Origin of Chingis Khan,* translated by Paul Kahn (Boston: Cheng & Tsui, 1998); **p. 270,** *Taiheiki* excerpt from *The Taiheike: A Chronicle of Medieval Japan,* translated by Helen Craig McCullough (New York: Columbia University Press, 1959); **p. 282,** From Jean Froissart, *Chronicles,* edited and translated by Geoffrey Brereton (New York: Penguin Books, 1968), **p. 286,** Reprinted with the permission of Simon & Schuster Adult Publishing Group, from *When China Ruled the Seas* by Louise Levanthes, Copyright © 1994 by Prentice-Hall, Inc. All rights reserved.

PHOTOS

Page 8, © Visual Arts Library (London)/Alamy; **p. 9,** © Réunion des Musées Nationaux/Art Resource, NY; **p. 11,** Courtesy Michael F. Pavkovic; **p. 17,** Courtesy Michael F. Pavkovic; **p. 22,** © Gianni Dagli Orti/Corbis; **p. 28,** Getty Images; **p. 40,** © Scala/Art Resource, NY; **p. 44,** Courtesy Michael F. Pavkovic; **p. 65,** © Alinari Archives/The Image Works; **p. 67,** © Pixtal/age Fotostock; **p. 86,** © Susan Muhlhauser/Time Life Pictures/Getty Images; **p. 106,** © Topkapi Palace Museum, Istanbul, Turkey/The

Bridgeman Art Library; **p. 109,** © Mary Evans Picture Library/Alamy; **p. 137,** © Erich Lessing/Art Resource, NY; **p. 140,** © f1 online/Alamy; **p. 147,** © Archivo Iconografico, S.A./Corbis; **p. 152,** © The Print Collector/Alamy; **p. 162,** © The Art Archive/National Palace Museum Taiwan; **p. 165,** © Christie's Images/Corbis; **p. 180,** © The Granger Collection, New York; **p. 186,** © Werner Forman/Art Resource, NY; **p. 210,** © SOLTAN FREDERIC/Corbis SYGMA; **p. 213,** © The Art Archive/British Museum; **p. 226,** © The Art Archive/Bibliothèque Nationale Paris; **p. 232,** © British Library Board. All Rights Reserved/The Bridgeman Art Library; **p. 237,** © The Board of Trustees of the Armouries/HIP/The Image Works; **p. 240,** © National Palace Museum, Taipei, Taiwan, Republic of China; **p. 242,** © Bibliothèque Nationale de France, Paris (Ms. Persan Suppl. 1113f.49); **p. 251,** Bibliothèque Nationale de France, Paris (Ms. Persan Suppl. 1113f.180v); **p. 262,** © The Granger Collection, New York; **p. 267,** © Fenollosa-Weld collection, Museum of Fine Arts, Boston; **p. 281,** Seal of Stralsund; **p. 291,** © Bettmann/Corbis; **p. 294,** Courtesy The Anne S. K. Brown Military Collection

Index